Function prototype

D0908173

```
int     pthread_cancel(pthread_t tid);
void    pthread_cleanup_pop(int execute);
void    pthread_cleanup_push(void (*function)(void *), void *
```

UNIX Network Programming
Volume 2

Second Edition

Interprocess Communications

by W. Richard Stevens

Prentice Hall PTR
Upper Saddle River, NJ 07458
www.phptr.com

ISBN 0-13-081081-9

90000

9 780130 810816

Library of Congress Cataloging-in-Publication Data

Stevens, W. Richard.
    UNIX network programming / by W. Richard Stevens. -- 2nd ed.
    v. <1 > : ill. : 25 cm.
    Includes bibliographical references and index.
    Contents: v. 1. Networking APIs : sockets and XTI.
    ISBN 0-13-490012-X (v. 1)
    1. UNIX (Computer file)   2. Computer networks.   3. Internet
programming.   I. Title.
QA76.76.063S755   1998
005.7'12768--DC21   97-31761

Editorial/production supervision: *Patti Guerrieri*
Cover design director: *Jerry Votta*
Cover designer: *Scott Weiss*
Manufacturing manager: *Alexis R. Heydt*
Marketing manager: *Miles Williams*
Acquisitions editor: *Mary Franz*
Editorial assistant: *Noreen Regina*

©1999 by Prentice Hall PTR
Prentice-Hall, Inc.
A Simon & Schuster Company
Upper Saddle River, NJ 07458

Prentice Hall books are widely used by corporations and government agencies
for training, marketing, and resale.

The publisher offers discounts on this book when ordered in bulk quantities.
For more information, contact: Corporate Sales Department, Phone: 800-382-3419;
Fax: 201-236-7141; E-mail: corpsales@prenhall.com; or write: Prentice Hall PTR,
Corp. Sales Dept., One Lake Street, Upper Saddle River, NJ 07458.

Printed in the United States of America
10 9 8 7 6 5 4

ISBN   0-13-081081-9

Prentice-Hall International (UK) Limited, *London*
Prentice-Hall of Australia Pty. Limited, *Sydney*
Prentice-Hall Canada Inc., *Toronto*
Prentice-Hall Hispanoamericana, S.A., *Mexico*
Prentice-Hall of India Private Limited, *New Delhi*
Prentice-Hall of Japan, Inc., *Tokyo*
Simon & Schuster Asia Pte. Ltd., *Singapore*
Editora Prentice-Hall do Brasil, Ltda., *Rio de Janeiro*

To the Usenet community;
for many questions answered,
and many FAQs provided.

Abbreviated Table of Contents

Table of Contents

Preface

Introduction

Most nontrivial programs involve some form of *IPC* or *Interprocess Communication*. This is a natural effect of the design principle that the better approach is to design an application as a group of small pieces that communicate with each other, instead of designing one huge monolithic program. Historically, applications have been built in the following ways:

1. One huge monolithic program that does everything. The various pieces of the program can be implemented as functions that exchange information as function parameters, function return values, and global variables.

2. Multiple programs that communicate with each other using some form of IPC. Many of the standard Unix tools were designed in this fashion, using shell pipelines (a form of IPC) to pass information from one program to the next.

3. One program comprised of multiple threads that communicate with each other using some type of IPC. The term IPC describes this communication even though it is between threads and not between processes.

Combinations of the second two forms of design are also possible: multiple processes, each consisting of one or more threads, involving communication between the threads within a given process and between the different processes.

What I have described is distributing the work involved in performing a given application between multiple processes and perhaps among the threads within a process. On a system containing multiple processors (CPUs), multiple processes might be able to run at the same time (on different CPUs), or the multiple threads of a given process might be able to run at the same time. Therefore, distributing an application among multiple processes or threads might reduce the amount of time required for an application to perform a given task.

This book describes four different forms of IPC in detail:

1. message passing (pipes, FIFOs, and message queues),
2. synchronization (mutexes, condition variables, read–write locks, file and record locks, and semaphores),
3. shared memory (anonymous and named), and
4. remote procedure calls (Solaris doors and Sun RPC).

This book does not cover the writing of programs that communicate across a computer network. This form of communication normally involves what is called the *sockets API* (application program interface) using the TCP/IP protocol suite; these topics are covered in detail in Volume 1 of this series [Stevens 1998].

One could argue that single-host or nonnetworked IPC (the subject of this volume) should not be used and instead all applications should be written as distributed applications that run on various hosts across a network. Practically, however, single-host IPC is often much faster and sometimes simpler than communicating across a network. Techniques such as shared memory and synchronization are normally available only on a single host, and may not be used across a network. Experience and history have shown a need for both nonnetworked IPC (this volume) and IPC across a network (Volume 1 of this series).

This current volume builds on the foundation of Volume 1 and my other four books, which are abbreviated throughout this text as follows:

- UNPv1: *UNIX Network Programming, Volume 1* [Stevens 1998],
- APUE: *Advanced Programming in the UNIX Environment* [Stevens 1992],
- TCPv1: *TCP/IP Illustrated, Volume 1* [Stevens 1994],
- TCPv2: *TCP/IP Illustrated, Volume 2* [Wright and Stevens 1995], and
- TCPv3: *TCP/IP Illustrated, Volume 3* [Stevens 1996].

Although covering IPC in a text with "network programming" in the title might seem odd, IPC is often used in networked applications. As stated in the Preface of the 1990 edition of *UNIX Network Programming*, "A requisite for understanding how to develop software for a network is an understanding of interprocess communication (IPC)."

Changes from the First Edition

This volume is a complete rewrite and expansion of Chapters 3 and 18 from the 1990 edition of *UNIX Network Programming*. Based on a word count, the material has expanded by a factor of five. The following are the major changes with this new edition:

- In addition to the three forms of "System V IPC" (message queues, semaphores, and shared memory), the newer Posix functions that implement these three types of IPC are also covered. (I say more about the Posix family of standards in Section 1.7.) In the coming years, I expect a movement to the Posix IPC functions, which have several advantages over their System V counterparts.

- The Posix functions for synchronization are covered: mutex locks, condition variables, and read–write locks. These can be used to synchronize either threads or processes and are often used when accessing shared memory.

- This volume assumes a Posix threads environment (called "Pthreads"), and many of the examples are built using multiple threads instead of multiple processes.

- The coverage of pipes, FIFOs, and record locking focuses on their Posix definitions.

- In addition to describing the IPC facilities and showing how to use them, I also develop implementations of Posix message queues, read–write locks, and Posix semaphores (all of which can be implemented as user libraries). These implementations can tie together many different features (e.g., one implementation of Posix semaphores uses mutexes, condition variables, and memory-mapped I/O) and highlight conditions that must often be handled in our applications (such as race conditions, error handling, memory leaks, and variable-length argument lists). Understanding an implementation of a certain feature often leads to a greater knowledge of how to use that feature.

- The RPC coverage focuses on the Sun RPC package. I precede this with a description of the new Solaris doors API, which is similar to RPC but on a single host. This provides an introduction to many of the features that we need to worry about when calling procedures in another process, without having to worry about any networking details.

Readers

This text can be used either as a tutorial on IPC, or as a reference for experienced programmers. The book is divided into four main parts:

- message passing,
- synchronization,
- shared memory, and
- remote procedure calls

but many readers will probably be interested in specific subsets. Most chapters can be read independently of others, although Chapter 2 summarizes many features common to all the Posix IPC functions, Chapter 3 summarizes many features common to all the System V IPC functions, and Chapter 12 is an introduction to both Posix and System V shared memory. All readers should read Chapter 1, especially Section 1.6, which describes some wrapper functions used throughout the text. The Posix IPC chapters are independent of the System V IPC chapters, and the chapters on pipes, FIFOs, and record locking belong to neither camp. The two chapters on RPC are also independent of the other IPC techniques.

To aid in the use as a reference, a thorough index is provided, along with summaries on the end papers of where to find detailed descriptions of all the functions and structures. To help those reading topics in a random order, numerous references to related topics are provided throughout the text.

Source Code and Errata Availability

The source code for all the examples that appear in this book is available from the author's home page (listed at the end of this Preface). The best way to learn the IPC techniques described in this book is to take these programs, modify them, and enhance them. Actually writing code of this form is the *only* way to reinforce the concepts and techniques. Numerous exercises are also provided at the end of each chapter, and most answers are provided in Appendix D.

A current errata for this book is also available from the author's home page.

Acknowledgments

Although the author's name is the only one to appear on the cover, the combined effort of many people is required to produce a quality text book. First and foremost is the author's family, who put up with the long and weird hours that go into writing a book. Thank you once again, Sally, Bill, Ellen, and David.

My thanks to the technical reviewers who provided invaluable feedback (135 printed pages) catching lots of errors, pointing out areas that needed more explanation, and suggesting alternative presentations, wording, and coding: Gavin Bowe, Allen Briggs, Dave Butenhof, Wan-Teh Chang, Chris Cleeland, Bob Friesenhahn, Andrew Gierth, Scott Johnson, Marty Leisner, Larry McVoy, Craig Metz, Bob Nelson, Steve Rago, Jim Reid, Swamy K. Sitarama, Jon C. Snader, Ian Lance Taylor, Rich Teer, and Andy Tucker.

The following people answered email questions of mine, in some cases *many* questions, all of which improved the accuracy and presentation of the text: David Bausum, Dave Butenhof, Bill Gallmeister, Mukesh Kacker, Brian Kernighan, Larry McVoy, Steve Rago, Keith Skowran, Bart Smaalders, Andy Tucker, and John Wait.

A special thanks to Larry Rafsky at GSquared, for lots of things. My thanks as usual to the National Optical Astronomy Observatories (NOAO), Sidney Wolff, Richard Wolff, and Steve Grandi, for providing access to their networks and hosts. Jim Bound, Matt Thomas, Mary Clouter, and Barb Glover of Digital Equipment Corp. provided the Alpha system used for most of the examples in this text. A subset of the code in this book was tested on other Unix systems: my thanks to Michael Johnson of Red Hat Software for providing the latest releases of Red Hat Linux, and to Dave Marquardt and Jessie Haug of IBM Austin for an RS/6000 system and access to the latest releases of AIX.

My thanks to the wonderful staff at Prentice Hall—my editor Mary Franz, along with Noreen Regina, Sophie Papanikolaou, and Patti Guerrieri—for all their help, especially in bringing everything together on a tight schedule.

Colophon

I produced camera-ready copy of the book (PostScript), which was then typeset for the final book. The formatting system used was James Clark's wonderful `groff` package, on a SparcStation running Solaris 2.6. (Reports of troff's death are greatly exaggerated.) I typed in all 138,897 words using the `vi` editor, created the 72 illustrations using the `gpic` program (using many of Gary Wright's macros), produced the 35 tables using the `gtbl` program, performed all the indexing (using a set of `awk` scripts written by Jon Bentley and Brian Kernighan), and did the final page layout. Dave Hanson's `loom` program, the GNU `indent` program, and some scripts by Gary Wright were used to include the 8,046 lines of C source code in the book.

I welcome email from any readers with comments, suggestions, or bug fixes.

Tucson, Arizona   W. Richard Stevens
July 1998   `rstevens@kohala.com`
                                              `http://www.kohala.com/~rstevens`

Part 1

Introduction

1

Introduction

1.1 Introduction

IPC stands for *interprocess communication*. Traditionally the term describes different ways of *message passing* between different processes that are running on some operating system. This text also describes numerous forms of *synchronization*, because newer forms of communication, such as shared memory, require some form of synchronization to operate.

In the evolution of the Unix operating system over the past 30 years, message passing has evolved through the following stages:

- *Pipes* (Chapter 4) were the first widely used form of IPC, available both within programs and from the shell. The problem with pipes is that they are usable only between processes that have a common ancestor (i.e., a parent–child relationship), but this was fixed with the introduction of *named pipes* or *FIFOs* (Chapter 4).

- *System V message queues* (Chapter 6) were added to System V kernels in the early 1980s. These can be used between related or unrelated processes on a given host. Although these are still referred to with the "System V" prefix, most versions of Unix today support them, regardless of whether their heritage is System V or not.

> When describing Unix processes, the term *related* means the processes have some ancestor in common. This is another way of saying that these related processes were generated

from this ancestor by one or more `forks`. A common example is when a process calls `fork` twice, generating two child processes. We then say that these two children are related. Similarly, each child is related to the parent. With regard to IPC, the parent can establish some form of IPC before calling `fork` (a pipe or message queue, for example), knowing that the two children will inherit this IPC object across the `fork`. We talk more about the inheritance of the various IPC objects with Figure 1.6. We must also note that all Unix processes are theoretically related to the `init` process, which starts everything going when a system is bootstrapped. Practically speaking, however, process relationships start with a login shell (called a *session*) and all the processes generated by that shell. Chapter 9 of APUE talks about sessions and process relationships in more detail.

> Throughout the text, we use indented, parenthetical notes such as this one to describe implementation details, historical points, and minutiae.

- *Posix message queues* (Chapter 5) were added by the Posix realtime standard (1003.1b–1993, which we say more about in Section 1.7). These can be used between related or unrelated processes on a given host.

- *Remote Procedure Calls* (RPCs, which we cover in Part 5) appeared in the mid-1980s as a way of calling a function on one system (the server) from a program on another system (the client), and was developed as an alternative to explicit network programming. Since information is normally passed between the client and server (the arguments and return values of the function that is called), and since RPC can be used between a client and server on the same host, RPC can be considered as another form of message passing.

Looking at the evolution of the various forms of synchronization provided by Unix is also interesting.

- Early programs that needed some form of synchronization (often to prevent multiple processes from modifying the same file at the same time) used quirks of the filesystem, some of which we talk about in Section 9.8.

- *Record locking* (Chapter 9) was added to Unix kernels in the early 1980s and then standardized by Posix.1 in 1988.

- *System V semaphores* (Chapter 11) were added along with *System V shared memory* (Chapter 14) at the same time System V message queues were added (early 1980s). Most versions of Unix support these today.

- *Posix semaphores* (Chapter 10) and *Posix shared memory* (Chapter 13) were also added by the Posix realtime standard (1003.1b–1993, which we mentioned with regard to Posix message queues earlier).

- *Mutexes* and *condition variables* (Chapter 7) are two forms of synchronization defined by the Posix threads standard (1003.1c–1995). Although these are often used for synchronization between threads, they can also provide synchronization between different processes.

- *Read–write locks* (Chapter 8) are an additional form of synchronization. These have not yet been standardized by Posix, but probably will be soon.

1.2   Processes, Threads, and the Sharing of Information

In the traditional Unix programming model, we have multiple processes running on a system, with each process having its own address space. Information can be shared between Unix processes in various ways. We summarize these in Figure 1.1.

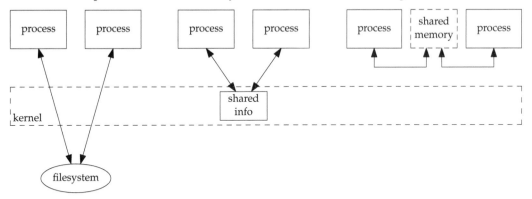

Figure 1.1 Three ways to share information between Unix processes.

1. The two processes on the left are sharing some information that resides in a file in the filesystem. To access this data, each process must go through the kernel (e.g., `read`, `write`, `lseek`, and the like). Some form of synchronization is required when a file is being updated, both to protect multiple writers from each other, and to protect one or more readers from a writer.

2. The two processes in the middle are sharing some information that resides within the kernel. A pipe is an example of this type of sharing, as are System V message queues and System V semaphores. Each operation to access the shared information now involves a system call into the kernel.

3. The two processes on the right have a region of shared memory that each process can reference. Once the shared memory is set up by each process, the processes can access the data in the shared memory without involving the kernel at all. Some form of synchronization is required by the processes that are sharing the memory.

Note that nothing restricts any of the IPC techniques that we describe to only two processes. Any of the techniques that we describe work with any number of processes. We show only two processes in Figure 1.1 for simplicity.

Threads

Although the concept of a process within the Unix system has been used for a long time, the concept of multiple *threads* within a given process is relatively new. The Posix.1 threads standard (called "Pthreads") was approved in 1995. From an IPC perspective, all the threads within a given process share the same global variables (e.g., the concept of shared memory is inherent to this model). What we must worry about, however, is *synchronizing* access to this global data among the various threads. Indeed, synchronization, though not explicitly a form of IPC, is used with many forms of IPC to control access to some shared data.

In this text, we describe IPC between processes and IPC between threads. We assume a threads environment and make statements of the form "if the pipe is empty, the calling thread is blocked in its call to `read` until some thread writes data to the pipe." If your system does not support threads, you can substitute "process" for "thread" in this sentence, providing the classic Unix definition of blocking in a `read` of an empty pipe. But on a system that supports threads, only the thread that calls `read` on an empty pipe is blocked, and the remaining threads in the process can continue to execute. Writing data to this empty pipe can be done by another thread in the same process or by some thread in another process.

Appendix B summarizes some of the characteristics of threads and the five basic Pthread functions that are used throughout this text.

1.3   Persistence of IPC Objects

We can define the *persistence* of any type of IPC as how long an object of that type remains in existence. Figure 1.2 shows three types of persistence.

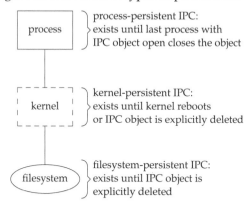

Figure 1.2   Persistence of IPC objects.

1. A *process-persistent* IPC object remains in existence until the last process that holds the object open closes the object. Examples are pipes and FIFOs.

2. A *kernel-persistent* IPC object remains in existence until the kernel reboots or until the object is explicitly deleted. Examples are System V message queues, semaphores, and shared memory. Posix message queues, semaphores, and shared memory must be at least kernel-persistent, but may be file-system-persistent, depending on the implementation.

3. A *filesystem-persistent* IPC object remains in existence until the object is explicitly deleted. The object retains its value even if the kernel reboots. Posix message queues, semaphores, and shared memory have this property, if they are implemented using mapped files (not a requirement).

We must be careful when defining the persistence of an IPC object because it is not always as it seems. For example, the data within a pipe is maintained within the kernel, but pipes have process persistence and not kernel persistence—after the last process that has the pipe open for reading closes the pipe, the kernel discards all the data and removes the pipe. Similarly, even though FIFOs have names within the filesystem, they also have process persistence because all the data in a FIFO is discarded after the last process that has the FIFO open closes the FIFO.

Figure 1.3 summarizes the persistence of the IPC objects that we describe in this text.

Type of IPC	Persistence
Pipe	process
FIFO	process
Posix mutex	process
Posix condition variable	process
Posix read–write lock	process
`fcntl` record locking	process
Posix message queue	kernel
Posix named semaphore	kernel
Posix memory-based semaphore	process
Posix shared memory	kernel
System V message queue	kernel
System V semaphore	kernel
System V shared memory	kernel
TCP socket	process
UDP socket	process
Unix domain socket	process

Figure 1.3 Persistence of various types of IPC objects.

Note that no type of IPC has filesystem persistence, but we have mentioned that the three types of Posix IPC may, depending on the implementation. Obviously, writing data to a file provides filesystem persistence, but this is normally not used as a form of IPC. Most forms of IPC are not intended to survive a system reboot, because the processes do not survive the reboot. Requiring filesystem persistence would probably degrade the performance for a given form of IPC, and a common design goal for IPC is high performance.

1.4 Name Spaces

When two unrelated processes use some type of IPC to exchange information between themselves, the IPC object must have a *name* or *identifier* of some form so that one process (often a server) can create the IPC object and other processes (often one or more clients) can specify that same IPC object.

Pipes do not have names (and therefore cannot be used between unrelated processes), but FIFOs have a Unix pathname in the filesystem as their identifier (and can therefore be used between unrelated processes). As we move to other forms of IPC in the following chapters, we use additional naming conventions. The set of possible names for a given type of IPC is called its *name space*. The name space is important, because with all forms of IPC other than plain pipes, the name is how the client and server connect with each other to exchange messages.

Figure 1.4 summarizes the naming conventions used by the different forms of IPC.

Type of IPC	Name space to open or create	Identification after IPC opened	Posix.1 1996	Unix 98
Pipe	(no name)	descriptor	•	•
FIFO	pathname	descriptor	•	•
Posix mutex	(no name)	`pthread_mutex_t` ptr	•	•
Posix condition variable	(no name)	`pthread_cond_t` ptr	•	•
Posix read–write lock	(no name)	`pthread_rwlock_t` ptr		•
`fcntl` record locking	pathname	descriptor	•	•
Posix message queue	Posix IPC name	`mqd_t` value	•	•
Posix named semaphore	Posix IPC name	`sem_t` pointer	•	•
Posix memory-based semaphore	(no name)	`sem_t` pointer	•	•
Posix shared memory	Posix IPC name	descriptor	•	•
System V message queue	`key_t` key	System V IPC identifier		•
System V semaphore	`key_t` key	System V IPC identifier		•
System V shared memory	`key_t` key	System V IPC identifier		•
Doors	pathname	descriptor		
Sun RPC	program/version	RPC handle		
TCP socket	IP addr & TCP port	descriptor	.1g	•
UDP socket	IP addr & UDP port	descriptor	.1g	•
Unix domain socket	pathname	descriptor	.1g	•

Figure 1.4 Name spaces for the various forms of IPC.

We also indicate which forms of IPC are standardized by the 1996 version of Posix.1 and Unix 98, both of which we say more about in Section 1.7. For comparison purposes, we include three types of sockets, which are described in detail in UNPv1. Note that the sockets API (application program interface) is being standardized by the Posix.1g working group and should eventually become part of a future Posix.1 standard.

Even though Posix.1 standardizes semaphores, they are an optional feature. Figure 1.5 summarizes which features are specified by Posix.1 and Unix 98. Each feature is mandatory, not defined, or optional. For the optional features, we specify the name of the constant (e.g., _POSIX_THREADS) that is defined (normally in the <unistd.h> header) if the feature is supported. Note that Unix 98 is a superset of Posix.1.

Type of IPC	Posix.1 1996	Unix 98
Pipe	mandatory	mandatory
FIFO	mandatory	mandatory
Posix mutex	`_POSIX_THREADS`	mandatory
Posix condition variable	`_POSIX_THREADS`	mandatory
process-shared mutex/CV	`_POSIX_THREAD_PROCESS_SHARED`	mandatory
Posix read–write lock	(not defined)	mandatory
`fcntl` record locking	mandatory	mandatory
Posix message queue	`_POSIX_MESSAGE_PASSING`	`_XOPEN_REALTIME`
Posix semaphores	`_POSIX_SEMAPHORES`	`_XOPEN_REALTIME`
Posix shared memory	`_POSIX_SHARED_MEMORY_OBJECTS`	`_XOPEN_REALTIME`
System V message queue	(not defined)	mandatory
System V semaphore	(not defined)	mandatory
System V shared memory	(not defined)	mandatory
Doors	(not defined)	(not defined)
Sun RPC	(not defined)	(not defined)
`mmap`	`_POSIX_MAPPED_FILES` or `_POSIX_SHARED_MEMORY_OBJECTS`	mandatory
Realtime signals	`_POSIX_REALTIME_SIGNALS`	`_XOPEN_REALTIME`

Figure 1.5 Availability of the various forms of IPC.

1.5 Effect of `fork`, `exec`, and `exit` on IPC Objects

We need to understand the effect of the `fork`, `exec`, and `_exit` functions on the various forms of IPC that we discuss. (The latter is called by the `exit` function.) We summarize this in Figure 1.6.

Most of these features are described later in the text, but we need to make a few points. First, the calling of `fork` from a multithreaded process becomes messy with regard to unnamed synchronization variables (mutexes, condition variables, read–write locks, and memory-based semaphores). Section 6.1 of [Butenhof 1997] provides the details. We simply note in the table that if these variables reside in shared memory and are created with the process-shared attribute, then they remain accessible to any thread of any process with access to that shared memory. Second, the three forms of System V IPC have no notion of being open or closed. We will see in Figure 6.8 and Exercises 11.1 and 14.1 that all we need to know to access these three forms of IPC is an identifier. So these three forms of IPC are available to any process that knows the identifier, although some special handling is indicated for semaphores and shared memory.

Type of IPC	`fork`	`exec`	`_exit`
Pipes and FIFOs	child gets copies of all parent's open descriptors	all open descriptors remain open unless descriptor's `FD_CLOEXEC` bit set	all open descriptors closed; all data removed from pipe or FIFO on last close
Posix message queues	child gets copies of all parent's open message queue descriptors	all open message queue descriptors are closed	all open message queue descriptors are closed
System V message queues	no effect	no effect	no effect
Posix mutexes and condition variables	shared if in shared memory and process-shared attribute	vanishes unless in shared memory that stays open and process-shared attribute	vanishes unless in shared memory that stays open and process-shared attribute
Posix read–write locks	shared if in shared memory and process-shared attribute	vanishes unless in shared memory that stays open and process-shared attribute	vanishes unless in shared memory that stays open and process-shared attribute
Posix memory-based semaphores	shared if in shared memory and process-shared attribute	vanishes unless in shared memory that stays open and process-shared attribute	vanishes unless in shared memory that stays open and process-shared attribute
Posix named semaphores	all open in parent remain open in child	any open are closed	any open are closed
System V semaphores	all `semadj` values in child are set to 0	all `semadj` values carried over to new program	all `semadj` values are added to corresponding semaphore value
`fcntl` record locking	locks held by parent are not inherited by child	locks are unchanged as long as descriptor remains open	all outstanding locks owned by process are unlocked
`mmap` memory mappings	memory mappings in parent are retained by child	memory mappings are unmapped	memory mappings are unmapped
Posix shared memory	memory mappings in parent are retained by child	memory mappings are unmapped	memory mappings are unmapped
System V shared memory	attached shared memory segments remain attached by child	attached shared memory segments are detached	attached shared memory segments are detached
Doors	child gets copies of all parent's open descriptors but only parent is a server for door invocations on door descriptors	all door descriptors should be closed because they are created with `FD_CLOEXEC` bit set	all open descriptors closed

Figure 1.6 Effect of calling `fork`, `exec`, and `_exit` on IPC.

1.6   Error Handling: Wrapper Functions

In any real-world program, we must check *every* function call for an error return. Since terminating on an error is the common case, we can shorten our programs by defining a *wrapper function* that performs the actual function call, tests the return value, and terminates on an error. The convention we use is to capitalize the name of the function, as in

```
Sem_post(ptr);
```

Our wrapper function is shown in Figure 1.7.

——— *lib/wrapunix.c*
```
387 void
388 Sem_post(sem_t *sem)
389 {
390     if (sem_post(sem) == -1)
391         err_sys("sem_post error");
392 }
```
——— *lib/wrapunix.c*

Figure 1.7 Our wrapper function for the sem_post function.

> *Whenever you encounter a function name in the text that begins with a capital letter, that is a wrapper function of our own. It calls a function whose name is the same but begins with the lowercase letter. The wrapper function always terminates with an error message if an error is encountered.*

> *When describing the source code that is presented in the text, we always refer to the lowest-level function being called (e.g.,* sem_post*) and not the wrapper function (e.g.,* Sem_post*). Similarly the index always refers to the lowest level function being called, and not the wrapper functions.*

> The format of the source code just shown is used throughout the text. Each nonblank line is numbered. The text describing portions of the code begins with the starting and ending line numbers in the left margin. Sometimes the paragraph is preceded by a short descriptive bold heading, providing a summary statement of the code being described.

> The horizontal rules at the beginning and end of the code fragment specify the source code filename: the file wrapunix.c in the directory lib for this example. Since the source code for all the examples in the text is freely available (see the Preface), you can locate the appropriate source file. Compiling, running, and especially modifying these programs while reading this text is an excellent way to learn the concepts of interprocess communications.

Although these wrapper functions might not seem like a big savings, when we discuss threads in Chapter 7, we will find that the thread functions do not set the standard Unix errno variable when an error occurs; instead the errno value is the return value of the function. This means that every time we call one of the pthread functions, we must allocate a variable, save the return value in that variable, and then set errno to this value before calling our err_sys function (Figure C.4). To avoid cluttering the code with braces, we can use C's comma operator to combine the assignment into errno and the call of err_sys into a single statement, as in the following:

```
int    n;

if ( (n = pthread_mutex_lock(&ndone_mutex)) != 0)
    errno = n, err_sys("pthread_mutex_lock error");
```

Alternately, we could define a new error function that takes the system's error number as an argument. But we can make this piece of code much easier to read as just

```
Pthread_mutex_lock(&ndone_mutex);
```

by defining our own wrapper function, shown in Figure 1.8.

―― *lib/wrappthread.c*
```
125 void
126 Pthread_mutex_lock(pthread_mutex_t *mptr)
127 {
128     int    n;

129     if ( (n = pthread_mutex_lock(mptr)) == 0)
130         return;
131     errno = n;
132     err_sys("pthread_mutex_lock error");
133 }
```
―― *lib/wrappthread.c*

Figure 1.8 Our wrapper function for pthread_mutex_lock.

> With careful C coding, we could use macros instead of functions, providing a little run-time efficiency, but these wrapper functions are rarely, if ever, the performance bottleneck of a program.
>
> Our choice of capitalizing the first character of the function name is a compromise. Many other styles were considered: prefixing the function name with an e (as done on p. 182 of [Kernighan and Pike 1984]), appending _e to the function name, and so on. Our style seems the least distracting while still providing a visual indication that some other function is really being called.
>
> This technique has the side benefit of checking for errors from functions whose error returns are often ignored: close and pthread_mutex_lock, for example.

Throughout the rest of this book, we use these wrapper functions unless we need to check for an explicit error and handle it in some form other than terminating the process. We do not show the source code for all our wrapper functions, but the code is freely available (see the Preface).

Unix errno Value

When an error occurs in a Unix function, the global variable errno is set to a positive value, indicating the type of error, and the function normally returns −1. Our err_sys function looks at the value of errno and prints the corresponding error message string (e.g., "Resource temporarily unavailable" if errno equals EAGAIN).

The value of errno is set by a function only if an error occurs. Its value is undefined if the function does not return an error. All the positive error values are constants with an all-uppercase name beginning with E and are normally defined in the

<sys/errno.h> header. No error has the value of 0.

   With multiple threads, each thread must have its own errno variable. Providing a per-thread errno is handled automatically, although this normally requires telling the compiler that the program being compiled must be reentrant. Specifying something like -D_REENTRANT or -D_POSIX_C_SOURCE=199506L to the compiler is typically required. Often the <errno.h> header defines errno as a macro that expands into a function call when _REENTRANT is defined, referencing a per-thread copy of the error variable.

   Throughout the text, we use phrases of the form "the mq_send function returns EMSGSIZE" as shorthand to mean that the function returns an error (typically a return value of −1) with errno set to the specified constant.

1.7   Unix Standards

Most activity these days with regard to Unix standardization is being done by Posix and The Open Group.

POSIX

Posix is an acronym for "Portable Operating System Interface." Posix is not a single standard, but a family of standards being developed by the Institute for Electrical and Electronics Engineers, Inc., normally called the *IEEE*. The Posix standards are also being adopted as international standards by ISO (the International Organization for Standardization) and IEC (the International Electrotechnical Commission), called ISO/IEC. The Posix standards have gone through the following iterations.

- IEEE Std 1003.1−1988 (317 pages) was the first of the Posix standards. It specified the C language interface into a Unix-like kernel covering the following areas: process primitives (fork, exec, signals, timers), the environment of a process (user IDs, process groups), files and directories (all the I/O functions), terminal I/O, the system databases (password file and group file), and the tar and cpio archive formats.

   > The first Posix standard was a trial use version in 1986 known as "IEEEIX." The name Posix was suggested by Richard Stallman.

- IEEE Std 1003.1−1990 (356 pages) was next and it was also International Standard ISO/IEC 9945−1: 1990. Minimal changes were made from the 1988 version to the 1990 version. Appended to the title was "Part 1: System Application Program Interface (API) [C Language]" indicating that this standard was the C language API.

- IEEE Std 1003.2−1992 was published in two volumes, totaling about 1300 pages, and its title contained "Part 2: Shell and Utilities." This part defines the shell (based on the System V Bourne shell) and about 100 utilities (programs normally executed from a shell, from awk and basename to vi and yacc). Throughout this text, we refer to this standard as *Posix.2*.

- IEEE Std 1003.1b–1993 (590 pages) was originally known as IEEE P1003.4. This was an update to the 1003.1–1990 standard to include the realtime extensions developed by the P1003.4 working group: file synchronization, asynchronous I/O, semaphores, memory management (`mmap` and shared memory), execution scheduling, clocks and timers, and message queues.

- IEEE Std 1003.1, 1996 Edition [IEEE 1996] (743 pages) includes 1003.1–1990 (the base API), 1003.1b–1993 (realtime extensions), 1003.1c–1995 (Pthreads), and 1003.1i–1995 (technical corrections to 1003.1b). This standard is also called ISO/IEC 9945–1: 1996. Three chapters on threads were added, along with additional sections on thread synchronization (mutexes and condition variables), thread scheduling, and synchronization scheduling. Throughout this text, we refer to this standard as *Posix.1*.

> Over one-quarter of the 743 pages are an appendix titled "Rationale and Notes." This rationale contains historical information and reasons why certain features were included or omitted. Often the rationale is as informative as the official standard.
>
> Unfortunately, the IEEE standards are not freely available on the Internet. Ordering information is given in the Bibliography entry for [IEEE 1996].
>
> Note that semaphores were defined in the realtime standard, separately from mutexes and condition variables (which were defined in the Pthreads standard), which accounts for some of the differences that we see in their APIs.
>
> Finally, note that read–write locks are not (yet) part of any Posix standard. We say more about this in Chapter 8.

Sometime in the future, a new version of IEEE Std 1003.1 should be printed to include the P1003.1g standard, the networking APIs (sockets and XTI), which are described in UNPv1.

The Foreword of the 1996 Posix.1 standard states that ISO/IEC 9945 consists of the following parts:

- Part 1: System application program interface (API) [C language],
- Part 2: Shell and utilities, and
- Part 3: System administration (under development).

Parts 1 and 2 are what we call Posix.1 and Posix.2.

Work on all of the Posix standards continues and it is a moving target for any book that attempts to cover it. The current status of the various Posix standards is available from `http://www.pasc.org/standing/sd11.html`.

The Open Group

The Open Group was formed in 1996 by the consolidation of the X/Open Company (founded in 1984) and the Open Software Foundation (OSF, founded in 1988). It is an international consortium of vendors and end-user customers from industry, government, and academia. Their standards have gone through the following iterations:

- X/Open published the *X/Open Portability Guide*, Issue 3 (XPG3) in 1989.

- Issue 4 was published in 1992 followed by Issue 4, Version 2 in 1994. This latest version was also known as "Spec 1170," with the magic number 1170 being the sum of the number of system interfaces (926), the number of headers (70), and the number of commands (174). The latest name for this set of specifications is the "X/Open Single Unix Specification," although it is also called "Unix 95."

- In March 1997, Version 2 of the Single Unix Specification was announced. Products conforming to this specification can be called "Unix 98," which is how we refer to this specification throughout this text. The number of interfaces required by Unix 98 increases from 1170 to 1434, although for a workstation, this jumps to 3030, because it includes the CDE (Common Desktop Environment), which in turn requires the X Window System and the Motif user interface. Details are available in [Josey 1997] and `http://www.UNIX-systems.org/version2`.

  Much of the Single Unix Specification is freely available on the Internet from this site.

Unix Versions and Portability

Most Unix systems today conform to some version of Posix.1 and Posix.2. We use the qualifier "some" because as updates to Posix occur (e.g., the realtime extensions in 1993 and the Pthreads addition in 1996), vendors take a year or two (sometimes more) to incorporate these latest changes.

Historically, most Unix systems show either a Berkeley heritage or a System V heritage, but these differences are slowly disappearing as most vendors adopt the Posix standards. The main differences still existing deal with system administration, one area that no Posix standard currently addresses.

Throughout this text, we use Solaris 2.6 and Digital Unix 4.0B for most examples. The reason is that at the time of this writing (late 1997 to early 1998), these were the only two Unix systems that supported System V IPC, Posix IPC, and Posix threads.

1.8   Road Map to IPC Examples in the Text

Three patterns of interaction are used predominantly throughout the text to illustrate various features:

1. File server: a client–server application in which the client sends the server a pathname and the server returns the contents of that file to the client.

2. Producer–consumer: one or more threads or processes (producers) place data into a shared buffer, and one or more threads or processes (consumers) operate on the data in the shared buffer.

3. Sequence-number-increment: one or more threads or processes increment a shared sequence number. Sometimes the sequence number is in a shared file, and sometimes it is in shared memory.

The first example illustrates the various forms of message passing, whereas the other two examples illustrate the various types of synchronization and shared memory.

To provide a road map for the different topics that are covered in this text, Figures 1.9, 1.10, and 1.11 summarize the programs that we develop, and the starting figure number and page number in which the source code appears.

1.9 Summary

IPC has traditionally been a messy area in Unix. Various solutions have been implemented, none of which are perfect. Our coverage is divided into four main areas:

1. message passing (pipes, FIFOs, message queues),
2. synchronization (mutexes, condition variables, read–write locks, semaphores),
3. shared memory (anonymous, named), and
4. procedure calls (Solaris doors, Sun RPC).

We consider IPC between multiple threads in a single process, and between multiple processes.

The persistence of each type of IPC can be process-persistent, kernel-persistent, or filesystem-persistent, based on how long the IPC object stays in existence. When choosing the type of IPC to use for a given application, we must be aware of the persistence of that IPC object.

Another feature of each type of IPC is its name space: how IPC objects are identified by the processes and threads that use the IPC object. Some have no name (pipes, mutexes, condition variables, read–write locks), some have names in the filesystem (FIFOs), some have what we describe in Chapter 2 as Posix IPC names, and some have other types of names (what we describe in Chapter 3 as System V IPC keys or identifiers). Typically, a server creates an IPC object with some name and the clients use that name to access the IPC object.

Throughout the source code in the text, we use the wrapper functions described in Section 1.6 to reduce the size of our code, yet still check every function call for an error return. Our wrapper functions all begin with a capital letter.

The IEEE Posix standards—Posix.1 defining the basic C interface to Unix and Posix.2 defining the standard commands—have been the standards that most vendors are moving toward. The Posix standards, however, are rapidly being absorbed and expanded by the commercial standards, notably The Open Group's Unix standards, such as Unix 98.

Figure	Page	Description
4.8	47	Uses two pipes, parent–child
4.15	53	Uses popen and cat
4.16	55	Uses two FIFOs, parent–child
4.18	57	Uses two FIFOs, stand-alone server, unrelated client
4.23	62	Uses FIFOs, stand-alone iterative server, multiple clients
4.25	68	Uses pipe or FIFO: builds records on top of byte stream
6.9	141	Uses two System V message queues
6.15	144	Uses one System V message queue, multiple clients
6.20	148	Uses one System V message queue per client, multiple clients
15.18	381	Uses descriptor passing across a door

Figure 1.9 Different versions of the file server client–server example.

Figure	Page	Description
7.2	162	Mutex only, multiple producers, one consumer
7.6	168	Mutex and condition variable, multiple producers, one consumer
10.17	236	Posix named semaphores, one producer, one consumer
10.20	242	Posix memory-based semaphores, one producer, one consumer
10.21	243	Posix memory-based semaphores, multiple producers, one consumer
10.24	246	Posix memory-based semaphores, multiple producers, multiple consumers
10.33	254	Posix memory-based semaphores, one producer, one consumer: multiple buffers

Figure 1.10 Different versions of the producer–consumer example.

Figure	Page	Description
9.1	194	Seq# in file, no locking
9.3	201	Seq# in file, fcntl locking
9.12	215	Seq# in file, filesystem locking using open
10.19	239	Seq# in file, Posix named semaphore locking
12.10	312	Seq# in mmap shared memory, Posix named semaphore locking
12.12	314	Seq# in mmap shared memory, Posix memory-based semaphore locking
12.14	316	Seq# in 4.4BSD anonymous shared memory, Posix named semaphore locking
12.15	316	Seq# in SVR4 /dev/zero shared memory, Posix named semaphore locking
13.7	334	Seq# in Posix shared memory, Posix memory-based semaphore locking
A.34	487	Performance measurement: mutex locking between threads
A.36	489	Performance measurement: read–write locking between threads
A.39	491	Performance measurement: Posix memory-based semaphore locking between threads
A.41	493	Performance measurement: Posix named semaphore locking between threads
A.42	494	Performance measurement: System V semaphore locking between threads
A.45	496	Performance measurement: fcntl record locking between threads
A.48	499	Performance measurement: mutex locking between processes

Figure 1.11 Different versions of the sequence-number-increment example.

Exercises

1.1   In Figure 1.1 we show two processes accessing a single file. If both processes are just appending new data to the end of the file (a log file perhaps), what kind of synchronization is required?

1.2   Look at your system's `<errno.h>` header and see how it defines errno.

1.3   Update Figure 1.5 by noting the features supported by the Unix systems that you use.

2

Posix IPC

2.1 Introduction

The three types of IPC,

- Posix message queues (Chapter 5),
- Posix semaphores (Chapter 10), and
- Posix shared memory (Chapter 13)

are collectively referred to as "Posix IPC." They share some similarities in the functions that access them, and in the information that describes them. This chapter describes all these common properties: the pathnames used for identification, the flags specified when opening or creating, and the access permissions.

A summary of their functions is shown in Figure 2.1.

2.2 IPC Names

In Figure 1.4, we noted that the three types of Posix IPC use "Posix IPC names" for their identification. The first argument to the three functions mq_open, sem_open, and shm_open is such a name, which may or may not be a real pathname in a filesystem. All that Posix.1 says about these names is:

- It must conform to existing rules for pathnames (must consist of at most PATH_MAX bytes, including a terminating null byte).

- If it begins with a slash, then different calls to these functions all reference the same queue. If it does not begin with a slash, the effect is implementation dependent.

	Message queues	Semaphores	Shared memory
Header	`<mqueue.h>`	`<semaphore.h>`	`<sys/mman.h>`

Functions to create, open, or delete	`mq_open`
	`mq_close`
	`mq_unlink`
		`sem_open`
		`sem_close`
		`sem_unlink`
			`shm_open`
			`shm_unlink`

		`sem_init` `sem_destroy`	
Functions for control operations	`mq_getattr` `mq_setattr`		`ftruncate` `fstat`

Functions for IPC operations	`mq_send`
	`mq_receive`
	`mq_notify`
		`sem_wait`
		`sem_trywait`
		`sem_post`
		`sem_getvalue`
			`mmap`
			`munmap`

Figure 2.1 Summary of Posix IPC functions.

- The interpretation of additional slashes in the name is implementation defined.

So, for portability, these names must begin with a slash and must not contain any other slashes. Unfortunately, these rules are inadequate and lead to portability problems.

Solaris 2.6 requires the initial slash but forbids any additional slashes. Assuming a message queue, it then creates three files in `/tmp` that begin with `.MQ`. For example, if the argument to `mq_open` is `/queue.1234`, then the three files are `/tmp/.MQDqueue.1234`, `/tmp/.MQLqueue.1234`, and `/tmp/.MQPqueue.1234`. Digital Unix 4.0B, on the other hand, creates the specified pathname in the filesystem.

The portability problem occurs if we specify a *name* with only one slash (as the first character): we must have write permission in that directory, the root directory. For example, `/tmp.1234` abides by the Posix rules and would be OK under Solaris, but Digital Unix would try to create this file, and unless we have write permission in the root directory, this attempt would fail. If we specify a *name* of `/tmp/test.1234`, this will succeed on all systems that create an actual file with that name (assuming that the `/tmp` directory exists and that we have write permission in that directory, which is normal for most Unix systems), but fails under Solaris.

To avoid these portability problems we should always `#define` the *name* in a header that is easy to change if we move our application to another system.

> This case is one in which the standard tries to be so general (in this case, the realtime standard was trying to allow message queue, semaphore, and shared memory implementations all within existing Unix kernels and as stand-alone diskless systems) that the standard's solution is nonportable. Within Posix, this is called "a standard way of being nonstandard."

Posix.1 defines the three macros

```
S_TYPEISMQ(buf)
S_TYPEISSEM(buf)
S_TYPEISSHM(buf)
```

that take a single argument, a pointer to a `stat` structure, whose contents are filled in by the `fstat`, `lstat`, or `stat` functions. These three macros evaluate to a nonzero value if the specified IPC object (message queue, semaphore, or shared memory object) is implemented as a distinct file type and the `stat` structure references such a file type. Otherwise, the macros evaluate to 0.

> Unfortunately, these macros are of little use, since there is no guarantee that these three types of IPC are implemented using a distinct file type. Under Solaris 2.6, for example, all three macros always evaluate to 0.

> All the other macros that test for a given file type have names beginning with `S_IS` and their single argument is the `st_mode` member of a `stat` structure. Since these three new macros have a different argument, their names were changed to begin with `S_TYPEIS`.

`px_ipc_name` Function

Another solution to this portability problem is to define our own function named `px_ipc_name` that prefixes the correct directory for the location of Posix IPC names.

```
#include "unpipc.h"

char *px_ipc_name(const char *name);
                                    Returns: nonnull pointer if OK, NULL on error
```

> This is the notation we use for functions of our own throughout this book that are not standard system functions: the box around the function prototype and return value is dashed. The header that is included at the beginning is usually our `unpipc.h` header (Figure C.1).

The *name* argument should not contain any slashes. For example, the call

```
px_ipc_name("test1")
```

returns a pointer to the string `/test1` under Solaris 2.6 or a pointer to the string `/tmp/test1` under Digital Unix 4.0B. The memory for the result string is dynamically allocated and is returned by calling `free`. Additionally, the environment variable `PX_IPC_NAME` can override the default directory.

Figure 2.2 shows our implementation of this function.

> This may be your first encounter with `snprintf`. Lots of existing code calls `sprintf` instead, but `sprintf` cannot check for overflow of the destination buffer. `snprintf`, on the other hand, requires that the second argument be the size of the destination buffer, and this buffer will not be overflowed. Providing input that intentionally overflows a program's `sprintf` buffer has been used for many years by hackers breaking into systems.

> `snprintf` is not yet part of the ANSI C standard but is being considered for a revision of the standard, currently called C9X. Nevertheless, many vendors are providing it as part of the standard C library. We use `snprintf` throughout the text, providing our own version that just calls `sprintf` when it is not provided.

lib/px_ipc_name.c

```
 1 #include    "unpipc.h"

 2 char *
 3 px_ipc_name(const char *name)
 4 {
 5     char   *dir, *dst, *slash;

 6     if ( (dst = malloc(PATH_MAX)) == NULL)
 7         return (NULL);

 8         /* can override default directory with environment variable */
 9     if ( (dir = getenv("PX_IPC_NAME")) == NULL) {
10 #ifdef  POSIX_IPC_PREFIX
11         dir = POSIX_IPC_PREFIX; /* from "config.h" */
12 #else
13         dir = "/tmp/";          /* default */
14 #endif
15     }
16         /* dir must end in a slash */
17     slash = (dir[strlen(dir) - 1] == '/') ? "" : "/";
18     snprintf(dst, PATH_MAX, "%s%s%s", dir, slash, name);

19     return (dst);                /* caller can free() this pointer */
20 }
```

lib/px_ipc_name.c

Figure 2.2 Our px_ipc_name function.

2.3 Creating and Opening IPC Channels

The three functions that create or open an IPC object, mq_open, sem_open, and shm_open, all take a second argument named *oflag* that specifies how to open the requested object. This is similar to the second argument to the standard open function. The various constants that can be combined to form this argument are shown in Figure 2.3.

Description	mq_open	sem_open	shm_open
read-only	O_RDONLY		O_RDONLY
write-only	O_WRONLY		
read–write	O_RDWR		O_RDWR
create if it does not already exist	O_CREAT	O_CREAT	O_CREAT
exclusive create	O_EXCL	O_EXCL	O_EXCL
nonblocking mode	O_NONBLOCK		
truncate if it already exists			O_TRUNC

Figure 2.3 Various constants when opening or creating a Posix IPC object.

The first three rows specify how the object is being opened: read-only, write-only, or read–write. A message queue can be opened in any of the three modes, whereas none of these three constants is specified for a semaphore (read and write access is required for any semaphore operation), and a shared memory object cannot be opened write-only.

The remaining O_*xxx* flags in Figure 2.3 are optional.

O_CREAT   Create the message queue, semaphore, or shared memory object if it does not already exist. (Also see the O_EXCL flag, which is described shortly.)

When creating a new message queue, semaphore, or shared memory object at least one additional argument is required, called *mode*. This argument specifies the permission bits and is formed as the bitwise-OR of the constants shown in Figure 2.4.

Constant	Description
S_IRUSR	user read
S_IWUSR	user write
S_IRGRP	group read
S_IWGRP	group write
S_IROTH	other read
S_IWOTH	other write

Figure 2.4 *mode* constants when a new IPC object is created.

These constants are defined in the <sys/stat.h> header. The specified permission bits are modified by the *file mode creation mask* of the process, which can be set by calling the umask function (pp. 83–85 of APUE) or by using the shell's umask command.

As with a newly created file, when a new message queue, semaphore, or shared memory object is created, the user ID is set to the effective user ID of the process. The group ID of a semaphore or shared memory object is set to the effective group ID of the process or to a system default group ID. The group ID of a new message queue is set to the effective group ID of the process. (Pages 77–78 of APUE talk more about the user and group IDs.)

> This difference in the setting of the group ID between the three types of Posix IPC is strange. The group ID of a new file created by open is either the effective group ID of the process or the group ID of the directory in which the file is created, but the IPC functions cannot assume that a pathname in the filesystem is created for an IPC object.

O_EXCL   If this flag and O_CREAT are both specified, then the function creates a new message queue, semaphore, or shared memory object only if it does not already exist. If it already exists, and if O_CREAT | O_EXCL is specified, an error of EEXIST is returned.

The check for the existence of the message queue, semaphore, or shared memory object and its creation (if it does not already exist) must be *atomic* with regard to other processes. We will see two similar flags for System V IPC in Section 3.4.

O_NONBLOCK   This flag makes a message queue nonblocking with regard to a read on an empty queue or a write to a full queue. We talk about this more with the mq_receive and mq_send functions in Section 5.4.

O_TRUNC   If an existing shared memory object is opened read–write, this flag specifies that the object be truncated to 0 length.

Figure 2.5 shows the actual logic flow for opening an IPC object. We describe what we mean by the test of the access permissions in Section 2.4. Another way of looking at Figure 2.5 is shown in Figure 2.6.

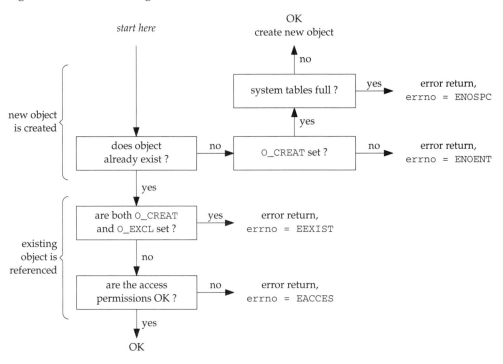

Figure 2.5 Logic for opening or creating an IPC object.

oflag argument	Object does not exist	Object already exists
no special flags	error, errno = ENOENT	OK, references existing object
O_CREAT	OK, creates new object	OK, references existing object
O_CREAT | O_EXCL	OK, creates new object	error, errno = EEXIST

Figure 2.6 Logic for creating or opening an IPC object.

Note that in the middle line of Figure 2.6, the O_CREAT flag without O_EXCL, we do not get an indication whether a new entry has been created or whether we are referencing an existing entry.

2.4 IPC Permissions

A new message queue, named semaphore, or shared memory object is created by mq_open, sem_open, or shm_open when the *oflag* argument contains the O_CREAT flag. As noted in Figure 2.4, permission bits are associated with each of these forms of IPC, similar to the permission bits associated with a Unix file.

When an existing message queue, semaphore, or shared memory object is opened by these same three functions (either O_CREAT is not specified, or O_CREAT is specified without O_EXCL and the object already exists), permission testing is performed based on

1. the permission bits assigned to the IPC object when it was created,

2. the type of access being requested (O_RDONLY, O_WRONLY, or O_RDWR), and

3. the effective user ID of the calling process, the effective group ID of the calling process, and the supplementary group IDs of the process (if supported).

The tests performed by most Unix kernels are as follows:

1. If the effective user ID of the process is 0 (the superuser), access is allowed.

2. If the effective user ID of the process equals the owner ID of the IPC object: if the appropriate user access permission bit is set, access is allowed, else access is denied.

    By *appropriate access permission bit*, we mean if the process is opening the IPC object for reading, the user-read bit must be on. If the process is opening the IPC object for writing, the user-write bit must be on.

3. If the effective group ID of the process or one of the supplementary group IDs of the process equals the group ID of the IPC object: if the appropriate group access permission bit is set, access is allowed, else permission is denied.

4. If the appropriate other access permission bit is set, access is allowed, else permission is denied.

These four steps are tried in sequence in the order listed. Therefore, if the process owns the IPC object (step 2), then access is granted or denied based only on the user access permissions—the group permissions are never considered. Similarly, if the process does not own the IPC object, but the process belongs to an appropriate group, then access is granted or denied based only on the group access permissions—the other permissions are not considered.

We note from Figure 2.3 that sem_open does not use the O_RDONLY, O_WRONLY, or O_RDWR flag. We note in Section 10.2, however, that some Unix implementations assume O_RDWR, since any use of a semaphore involves reading and writing the semaphore value.

2.5   Summary

The three types of Posix IPC—message queues, semaphores, and shared memory—are identified by pathnames. But these may or may not be real pathnames in the filesystem, and this discrepancy can be a portability problem. The solution that we employ throughout the text is to use our own px_ipc_name function.

When an IPC object is created or opened, we specify a set of flags that are similar to those for the open function. When a new IPC object is created, we must specify the permissions for the new object, using the same S_*xxx* constants that are used with open (Figure 2.4). When an existing IPC object is opened, the permission testing that is performed is the same as when an existing file is opened.

Exercises

2.1   In what way do the set-user-ID and set-group-ID bits (Section 4.4 of APUE) of a program that uses Posix IPC affect the permission testing described in Section 2.4?

2.2   When a program opens a Posix IPC object, how can it determine whether a new object was created or whether it is referencing an existing object?

3

System V IPC

3.1 Introduction

The three types of IPC,

- System V message queues (Chapter 6),
- System V semaphores (Chapter 11), and
- System V shared memory (Chapter 14)

are collectively referred to as "System V IPC." This term is commonly used for these three IPC facilities, acknowledging their heritage from System V Unix. They share many similarities in the functions that access them, and in the information that the kernel maintains on them. This chapter describes all these common properties.

A summary of their functions is shown in Figure 3.1.

	Message queues	Semaphores	Shared memory
Header	`<sys/msg.h>`	`<sys/sem.h>`	`<sys/shm.h>`
Function to create or open	`msgget`	`semget`	`shmget`
Function for control operations	`msgctl`	`semctl`	`shmctl`
Functions for IPC operations	`msgsnd` `msgrcv`	`semop`	`shmat` `shmdt`

Figure 3.1 Summary of System V IPC functions.

Information on the design and development of the System V IPC functions is hard to find. [Rochkind 1985] provides the following information: System V message queues, semaphores, and shared memory were developed in the late 1970s at a branch laboratory of Bell

Laboratories in Columbus, Ohio, for an internal version of Unix called (not surprisingly) "Columbus Unix" or just "CB Unix." This version of Unix was used for "Operation Support Systems," transaction processing systems that automated telephone company administration and recordkeeping. System V IPC was added to the commercial Unix system with System V around 1983.

3.2   `key_t` Keys and `ftok` Function

In Figure 1.4, the three types of System V IPC are noted as using `key_t` values for their names. The header `<sys/types.h>` defines the `key_t` datatype, as an integer, normally at least a 32-bit integer. These integer values are normally assigned by the `ftok` function.

The function `ftok` converts an existing pathname and an integer identifier into a `key_t` value (called an *IPC key*).

```
#include <sys/ipc.h>

key_t ftok(const char *pathname, int id);
```
                                                     Returns: IPC key if OK, −1 on error

This function takes information derived from the *pathname* and the low-order 8 bits of *id*, and combines them into an integer IPC key.

This function assumes that for a given application using System V IPC, the server and clients all agree on a single *pathname* that has some meaning to the application. It could be the pathname of the server daemon, the pathname of a common data file used by the server, or some other pathname on the system. If the client and server need only a single IPC channel between them, an *id* of one, say, can be used. If multiple IPC channels are needed, say one from the client to the server and another from the server to the client, then one channel can use an *id* of one, and the other an *id* of two, for example. Once the *pathname* and *id* are agreed on by the client and server, then both can call the `ftok` function to convert these into the same IPC key.

Typical implementations of `ftok` call the `stat` function and then combine

1. information about the filesystem on which *pathname* resides (the `st_dev` member of the `stat` structure),

2. the file's i-node number within the filesystem (the `st_ino` member of the `stat` structure), and

3. the low-order 8 bits of the *id* (which must not be 0).

The combination of these three values normally produces a 32-bit key. No guarantee exists that two different pathnames combined with the same *id* generate different keys, because the number of bits of information in the three items just listed (filesystem identifier, i-node, and *id*) can be greater than the number of bits in an integer. (See Exercise 3.5.)

The i-node number is never 0, so most implementations define IPC_PRIVATE (which we describe in Section 3.4) to be 0.

If the *pathname* does not exist, or is not accessible to the calling process, ftok returns –1. Be aware that the file whose *pathname* is used to generate the key must not be a file that is created and deleted by the server during its existence, since each time it is created, it can assume a new i-node number that can change the key returned by ftok to the next caller.

Example

The program in Figure 3.2 takes a pathname as a command-line argument, calls stat, calls ftok, and then prints the st_dev and st_ino members of the stat structure, and the resulting IPC key. These three values are printed in hexadecimal, so we can easily see how the IPC key is constructed from these two values and our *id* of 0x57.

—— *svipc/ftok.c*
```
 1 #include    "unpipc.h"

 2 int
 3 main(int argc, char **argv)
 4 {
 5      struct stat stat;

 6      if (argc != 2)
 7          err_quit("usage: ftok <pathname>");

 8      Stat(argv[1], &stat);
 9      printf("st_dev: %lx, st_ino: %lx, key: %x\n",
10              (u_long) stat.st_dev, (u_long) stat.st_ino,
11              Ftok(argv[1], 0x57));

12      exit(0);
13 }
```
—— *svipc/ftok.c*

Figure 3.2 Obtain and print filesystem information and resulting IPC key.

Executing this under Solaris 2.6 gives us the following:

```
solaris % ftok /etc/system
st_dev: 800018, st_ino: 4a1b, key: 57018a1b
solaris % ftok /usr/tmp
st_dev: 800015, st_ino: 10b78, key: 57015b78
solaris % ftok /home/rstevens/Mail.out
st_dev: 80001f, st_ino: 3b03, key: 5701fb03
```

Apparently, the *id* is in the upper 8 bits, the low-order 12 bits of st_dev in the next 12 bits, and the low-order 12 bits of st_ino in the low-order 12 bits.

Our purpose in showing this example is not to let us count on this combination of information to form the IPC key, but to let us see how one implementation combines the *pathname* and *id*. Other implementations may do this differently.

> FreeBSD uses the lower 8 bits of the *id*, the lower 8 bits of st_dev, and the lower 16 bits of st_ino.

Note that the mapping done by `ftok` is one-way, since some bits from `st_dev` and `st_ino` are not used. That is, given a key, we cannot determine the pathname that was used to create the key.

3.3   `ipc_perm` Structure

The kernel maintains a structure of information for each IPC object, similar to the information it maintains for files.

```
struct ipc_perm {
    uid_t    uid;      /* owner's user id */
    gid_t    gid;      /* owner's group id */
    uid_t    cuid;     /* creator's user id */
    gid_t    cgid;     /* creator's group id */
    mode_t   mode;     /* read-write permissions */
    ulong_t  seq;      /* slot usage sequence number */
    key_t    key;      /* IPC key */
};
```

This structure, and other manifest constants for the System V IPC functions, are defined in the `<sys/ipc.h>` header. We talk about all the members of this structure in this chapter.

3.4   Creating and Opening IPC Channels

The three get*XXX* functions that create or open an IPC object (Figure 3.1) all take an IPC *key* value, whose type is `key_t`, and return an integer *identifier*. This identifier is *not* the same as the *id* argument to the `ftok` function, as we see shortly. An application has two choices for the *key* value that is the first argument to the three get*XXX* functions:

1. call `ftok`, passing it a *pathname* and *id*, or

2. specify a *key* of `IPC_PRIVATE`, which guarantees that a new, unique IPC object is created.

The sequence of steps is shown in Figure 3.3.

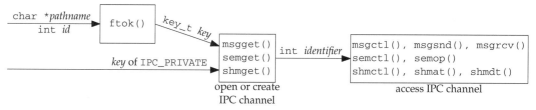

Figure 3.3 Generating IPC identifiers from IPC keys.

All three get*XXX* functions (Figure 3.1) also take an *oflag* argument that specifies the read–write permission bits (the `mode` member of the `ipc_perm` structure) for the IPC object, and whether a new IPC object is being created or an existing one is being referenced. The rules for whether a new IPC object is created or whether an existing one is referenced are as follows:

- Specifying a *key* of `IPC_PRIVATE` guarantees that a unique IPC object is created. No combinations of *pathname* and *id* exist that cause `ftok` to generate a *key* value of `IPC_PRIVATE`.

- Setting the `IPC_CREAT` bit of the *oflag* argument creates a new entry for the specified *key*, if it does not already exist. If an existing entry is found, that entry is returned.

- Setting both the `IPC_CREAT` and `IPC_EXCL` bits of the *oflag* argument creates a new entry for the specified *key*, only if the entry does not already exist. If an existing entry is found, an error of `EEXIST` is returned, since the IPC object already exists.

  The combination of `IPC_CREAT` and `IPC_EXCL` with regard to IPC objects is similar to the combination of `O_CREAT` and `O_EXCL` with regard to the `open` function.

  Setting the `IPC_EXCL` bit, without setting the `IPC_CREAT` bit, has no meaning.

The actual logic flow for opening an IPC object is shown in Figure 3.4. Figure 3.5 shows another way of looking at Figure 3.4.

Note that in the middle line of Figure 3.5, the `IPC_CREAT` flag without `IPC_EXCL`, we do not get an indication whether a new entry has been created or whether we are referencing an existing entry. In most applications, the server creates the IPC object and specifies either `IPC_CREAT` (if it does not care whether the object already exists) or `IPC_CREAT | IPC_EXCL` (if it needs to check whether the object already exists). The clients specify neither flag (assuming that the server has already created the object).

> The System V IPC functions define their own `IPC_xxx` constants, instead of using the `O_CREAT` and `O_EXCL` constants that are used by the standard `open` function along with the Posix IPC functions (Figure 2.3).

> Also note that the System V IPC functions combine their `IPC_xxx` constants with the permission bits (which we describe in the next section) into a single *oflag* argument. The `open` function along with the Posix IPC functions have one argument named *oflag* that specifies the various `O_xxx` flags, and another argument named *mode* that specifies the permission bits.

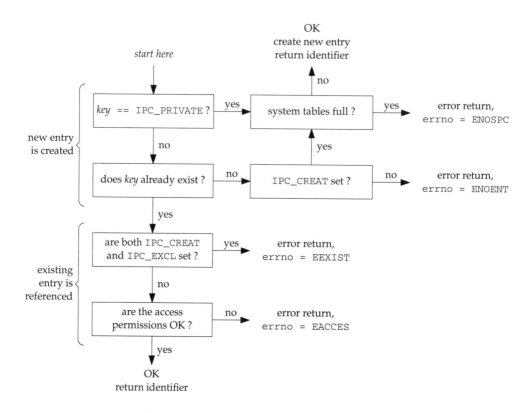

Figure 3.4 Logic for creating or opening an IPC object.

oflag argument	*key* does not exist	*key* already exists
no special flags	error, errno = ENOENT	OK, references existing object
IPC_CREAT	OK, creates new entry	OK, references existing object
IPC_CREAT | IPC_EXCL	OK, creates new entry	error, errno = EEXIST

Figure 3.5 Logic for creating or opening an IPC channel.

3.5   IPC Permissions

Whenever a new IPC object is created using one of the get*XXX* functions with the
IPC_CREAT flag, the following information is saved in the ipc_perm structure (Section 3.3):

1. Some of the bits in the *oflag* argument initialize the mode member of the
    ipc_perm structure. Figure 3.6 shows the permission bits for the three different
    IPC mechanisms. (The notation >> 3 means the value is right shifted 3 bits.)

Numeric (octal)	Symbolic values			Description
	Message queue	Semaphore	Shared memory	
0400	MSG_R	SEM_R	SHM_R	read by user
0200	MSG_W	SEM_A	SHM_W	write by user
0040	MSG_R >> 3	SEM_R >> 3	SHM_R >> 3	read by group
0020	MSG_W >> 3	SEM_A >> 3	SHM_W >> 3	write by group
0004	MSG_R >> 6	SEM_R >> 6	SHM_R >> 6	read by others
0002	MSG_W >> 6	SEM_A >> 6	SHM_W >> 6	write by others

Figure 3.6 *mode* values for IPC read–write permissions.

2. The two members cuid and cgid are set to the effective user ID and effective group ID of the calling process, respectively. These two members are called the *creator IDs*.

3. The two members uid and gid in the ipc_perm structure are also set to the effective user ID and effective group ID of the calling process. These two members are called the *owner IDs*.

The creator IDs never change, although a process can change the owner IDs by calling the ctl*XXX* function for the IPC mechanism with a command of IPC_SET. The three ctl*XXX* functions also allow a process to change the permission bits of the mode member for the IPC object.

> Most implementations define the six constants MSG_R, MSG_W, SEM_R, SEM_A, SHM_R, and SHM_W shown in Figure 3.6 in the <sys/msg.h>, <sys/sem.h>, and <sys/shm.h> headers. But these are not required by Unix 98. The suffix A in SEM_A stands for "alter."

> The three get*XXX* functions do not use the normal Unix *file mode creation mask*. The permissions of the message queue, semaphore, or shared memory segment are set to exactly what the function specifies.

> Posix IPC does not let the creator of an IPC object change the owner. Nothing is like the IPC_SET command with Posix IPC. But if the Posix IPC name is stored in the filesystem, then the superuser can change the owner using the chown command.

Two levels of checking are done whenever an IPC object is accessed by any process, once when the IPC object is opened (the get*XXX* function) and then each time the IPC object is used:

1. Whenever a process establishes access to an existing IPC object with one of the get*XXX* functions, an initial check is made that the caller's *oflag* argument does not specify any access bits that are not in the mode member of the ipc_perm structure. This is the bottom box in Figure 3.4. For example, a server process can set the mode member for its input message queue so that the group-read and other-read permission bits are off. Any process that tries to specify an *oflag* argument that includes these bits gets an error return from the msgget function. But this test that is done by the get*XXX* functions is of little use. It implies that

the caller knows which permission category it falls into—user, group, or other. If the creator specifically turns off certain permission bits, and if the caller specifies these bits, the error is detected by the get*XXX* function. Any process, however, can totally bypass this check by just specifying an *oflag* argument of 0 if it knows that the IPC object already exists.

2. Every IPC operation does a permission test for the process using the operation. For example, every time a process tries to put a message onto a message queue with the msgsnd function, the following tests are performed in the order listed. As soon as a test grants access, no further tests are performed.

    a. The superuser is always granted access.

    b. If the effective user ID equals either the uid value or the cuid value for the IPC object, and if the appropriate access bit is on in the mode member for the IPC object, permission is granted. By "appropriate access bit," we mean the read-bit must be set if the caller wants to do a read operation on the IPC object (receiving a message from a message queue, for example), or the write-bit must be set for a write operation.

    c. If the effective group ID equals either the gid value or the cgid value for the IPC object, and if the appropriate access bit is on in the mode member for the IPC object, permission is granted.

    d. If none of the above tests are true, the appropriate "other" access bit must be on in the mode member for the IPC object, for permission to be allowed.

3.6   Identifier Reuse

The ipc_perm structure (Section 3.3) also contains a variable named seq, which is a slot usage sequence number. This is a counter that is maintained by the kernel for every potential IPC object in the system. Every time an IPC object is removed, the kernel increments the slot number, cycling it back to zero when it overflows.

> What we are describing in this section is the common SVR4 implementation. This implementation technique is not mandated by Unix 98.

This counter is needed for two reasons. First, consider the file descriptors maintained by the kernel for open files. They are small integers, but have meaning only within a single process—they are process-specific values. If we try to read from file descriptor 4, say, in a process, this approach works only if that process has a file open on this descriptor. It has no meaning whatsoever for a file that might be open on file descriptor 4 in some other unrelated process. System V IPC identifiers, however, are *systemwide* and not process-specific.

We obtain an IPC identifier (similar to a file descriptor) from one of the get functions: msgget, semget, and shmget. These identifiers are also integers, but their meaning applies to *all* processes. If two unrelated processes, a client and server, for example, use a single message queue, the message queue identifier returned by the msgget function must be the same integer value in both processes in order to access the same message queue. This feature means that a rogue process could try to read a message from some other application's message queue by trying different small integer identifiers, hoping to find one that is currently in use that allows world read access. If the potential values for these identifiers were small integers (like file descriptors), then the probability of finding a valid identifier would be about 1 in 50 (assuming a maximum of about 50 descriptors per process).

To avoid this problem, the designers of these IPC facilities decided to increase the possible range of identifier values to include *all* integers, not just small integers. This increase is implemented by incrementing the identifier value that is returned to the calling process, by the number of IPC table entries, each time a table entry is reused. For example, if the system is configured for a maximum of 50 message queues, then the first time the first message queue table entry in the kernel is used, the identifier returned to the process is zero. After this message queue is removed and the first table entry is reused, the identifier returned is 50. The next time, the identifier is 100, and so on. Since seq is often implemented as an unsigned long integer (see the ipc_perm structure shown in Section 3.3), it cycles after the table entry has been used 85,899,346 times ($2^{32}/50$, assuming 32-bit long integers).

A second reason for incrementing the slot usage sequence number is to avoid short term reuse of the System V IPC identifiers. This helps ensure that a server that prematurely terminates and is then restarted, does not reuse an identifier.

As an example of this feature, the program in Figure 3.7 prints the first 10 identifier values returned by msgget.

svmsg/slot.c

```
 1 #include     "unpipc.h"

 2 int
 3 main(int argc, char **argv)
 4 {
 5     int     i, msqid;

 6     for (i = 0; i < 10; i++) {
 7         msqid = Msgget(IPC_PRIVATE, SVMSG_MODE | IPC_CREAT);
 8         printf("msqid = %d\n", msqid);

 9         Msgctl(msqid, IPC_RMID, NULL);
10     }
11     exit(0);
12 }
```

svmsg/slot.c

Figure 3.7 Print kernel assigned message queue identifier 10 times in a row.

Each time around the loop msgget creates a message queue, and then msgctl with a command of IPC_RMID deletes the queue. The constant SVMSG_MODE is defined in our unpipc.h header (Figure C.1) and specifies our default permission bits for a System V message queue. The program's output is

```
solaris % slot
msqid = 0
msqid = 50
```

```
msqid = 100
msqid = 150
msqid = 200
msqid = 250
msqid = 300
msqid = 350
msqid = 400
msqid = 450
```

If we run the program again, we see that this slot usage sequence number is a kernel variable that persists between processes.

```
solaris % slot
msqid = 500
msqid = 550
msqid = 600
msqid = 650
msqid = 700
msqid = 750
msqid = 800
msqid = 850
msqid = 900
msqid = 950
```

3.7   `ipcs` and `ipcrm` Programs

Since the three types of System V IPC are not identified by pathnames in the filesystem, we cannot look at them or remove them using the standard `ls` and `rm` programs. Instead, two special programs are provided by any system that implements these types of IPC: `ipcs`, which prints various pieces of information about the System V IPC features, and `ipcrm`, which removes a System V message queue, semaphore set, or shared memory segment. The former supports about a dozen command-line options, which affect which of the three types of IPC is reported and what information is output, and the latter supports six command-line options. Consult your manual pages for the details of all these options.

> Since System V IPC is not part of Posix, these two commands are not standardized by Posix.2. But these two commands are part of Unix 98.

3.8   Kernel Limits

Most implementations of System V IPC have inherent kernel limits, such as the maximum number of message queues and the maximum number of semaphores per semaphore set. We show some typical values for these limits in Figures 6.25, 11.9, and 14.5. These limits are often derived from the original System V implementation.

> Section 11.2 of [Bach 1986] and Chapter 8 of [Goodheart and Cox 1994] both describe the System V implementation of messages, semaphores, and shared memory. Some of these limits are described therein.

Unfortunately, these kernel limits are often too small, because many are derived from their original implementation on a small address system (the 16-bit PDP-11). Fortunately, most systems allow the administrator to change some or all of these default limits, but the required steps are different for each flavor of Unix. Most require rebooting the running kernel after changing the values. Unfortunately, some implementations still use 16-bit integers for some of the limits, providing a hard limit that cannot be exceeded.

Solaris 2.6, for example, has 20 of these limits. Their current values are printed by the sysdef command, although the values are printed as 0 if the corresponding kernel module has not been loaded (i.e., the facility has not yet been used). These may be changed by placing any of the following statements in the /etc/system file, which is read when the kernel bootstraps.

```
set msgsys:msginfo_msgseg = value
set msgsys:msginfo_msgssz = value
set msgsys:msginfo_msgtql = value
set msgsys:msginfo_msgmap = value
set msgsys:msginfo_msgmax = value
set msgsys:msginfo_msgmnb = value
set msgsys:msginfo_msgmni = value

set semsys:seminfo_semopm = value
set semsys:seminfo_semume = value
set semsys:seminfo_semaem = value
set semsys:seminfo_semmap = value
set semsys:seminfo_semvmx = value
set semsys:seminfo_semmsl = value
set semsys:seminfo_semmni = value
set semsys:seminfo_semmns = value
set semsys:seminfo_semmnu = value

set shmsys:shminfo_shmmin = value
set shmsys:shminfo_shmseg = value
set shmsys:shminfo_shmmax = value
set shmsys:shminfo_shmmni = value
```

The last six characters of the name on the left-hand side of the equals sign are the variables listed in Figures 6.25, 11.9, and 14.5.

With Digital Unix 4.0B, the sysconfig program can query or modify many kernel parameters and limits. Here is the output of this program with the -q option, which queries the kernel for the current limits, for the ipc subsystem. We have omitted some lines unrelated to the System V IPC facility.

```
alpha % /sbin/sysconfig -q ipc
ipc:
msg-max = 8192
msg-mnb = 16384
msg-mni = 64
msg-tql = 40

shm-max = 4194304
shm-min = 1
shm-mni = 128
shm-seg = 32
```

```
sem-mni = 16
sem-msl = 25
sem-opm = 10
sem-ume = 10
sem-vmx = 32767
sem-aem = 16384
num-of-sems = 60
```

Different defaults for these parameters can be specified in the /etc/sysconfigtab file, which should be maintained using the sysconfigdb program. This file is read when the system bootstraps.

3.9   Summary

The first argument to the three functions, msgget, semget, and shmget, is a System V IPC key. These keys are normally created from a pathname using the system's ftok function. The key can also be the special value of IPC_PRIVATE. These three functions create a new IPC object or open an existing IPC object and return a System V IPC identifier: an integer that is then used to identify the object to the remaining IPC functions. These integers are not per-process identifiers (like descriptors) but are systemwide identifiers. These identifiers are also reused by the kernel after some time.

Associated with every System V IPC object is an ipc_perm structure that contains information such as the owner's user ID, group ID, read–write permissions, and so on. One difference between Posix IPC and System V IPC is that this information is always available for a System V IPC object (by calling one of the three *XXXctl* functions with an argument of IPC_STAT), but access to this information for a Posix IPC object depends on the implementation. If the Posix IPC object is stored in the filesystem, and if we know its name in the filesystem, then we can access this same information using the existing filesystem tools.

When a new System V IPC object is created or an existing object is opened, two flags are specified to the get*XXX* function (IPC_CREAT and IPC_EXCL), combined with nine permission bits.

Undoubtedly, the biggest problem in using System V IPC is that most implementations have artificial kernel limits on the sizes of these objects, and these limits date back to their original implementation. These mean that most applications that make heavy use of System V IPC require that the system administrator modify these kernel limits, and accomplishing this change differs for each flavor of Unix.

Exercises

3.1   Read about the msgctl function in Section 6.5 and modify the program in Figure 3.7 to print the seq member of the ipc_perm structure in addition to the assigned identifier.

3.2   Immediately after running the program in Figure 3.7, we run a program that creates two message queues. Assuming no other message queues have been used by any other applications since the kernel was booted, what two values are returned by the kernel as the message queue identifiers?

3.3   We noted in Section 3.5 that the System V IPC get*XXX* functions do not use the file mode creation mask. Write a test program that creates a FIFO (using the mkfifo function described in Section 4.6) and a System V message queue, specifying a permission of (octal) 666 for both. Compare the permissions of the resulting FIFO and message queue. Make certain your shell umask value is nonzero before running this program.

3.4   A server wants to create a unique message queue for its clients. Which is preferable—using some constant pathname (say the server's executable file) as an argument to ftok, or using IPC_PRIVATE?

3.5   Modify Figure 3.2 to print just the IPC key and pathname. Run the find program to print all the pathnames on your system and run the output through the program just modified. How many pathnames map to the same key?

3.6   If your system supports the sar program ("system activity reporter"), run the command

```
sar -m 5 6
```

This prints the number of message queue operations per second and the number of semaphore operations per second, sampled every 5 seconds, 6 times.

Part 2

Message Passing

4

Pipes and FIFOs

4.1 Introduction

Pipes are the original form of Unix IPC, dating back to the Third Edition of Unix in 1973 [Salus 1994]. Although useful for many operations, their fundamental limitation is that they have no name, and can therefore be used only by related processes. This was corrected in System III Unix (1982) with the addition of FIFOs, sometimes called *named pipes*. Both pipes and FIFOs are accessed using the normal `read` and `write` functions.

> Technically, pipes can be used between unrelated processes, given the ability to pass descriptors between processes (which we describe in Section 15.8 of this text as well as Section 14.7 of UNPv1). But for practical purposes, pipes are normally used between processes that have a common ancestor.

This chapter describes the creation and use of pipes and FIFOs. We use a simple file server example and also look at some client–server design issues: how many IPC channels are needed, iterative versus concurrent servers, and byte streams versus message interfaces.

4.2 A Simple Client–Server Example

The client–server example shown in Figure 4.1 is used throughout this chapter and Chapter 6 to illustrate pipes, FIFOs, and System V message queues.

The client reads a pathname from the standard input and writes it to the IPC channel. The server reads this pathname from the IPC channel and tries to open the file for reading. If the server can open the file, the server responds by reading the file and writing it to the IPC channel; otherwise, the server responds with an error message. The

Figure 4.1 Client–server example.

client then reads from the IPC channel, writing what it receives to the standard output. If the file cannot be read by the server, the client reads an error message from the IPC channel. Otherwise, the client reads the contents of the file. The two dashed lines between the client and server in Figure 4.1 are the IPC channel.

4.3 Pipes

Pipes are provided with all flavors of Unix. A pipe is created by the `pipe` function and provides a one-way (unidirectional) flow of data.

```
#include <unistd.h>

int pipe(int fd[2]);
```
Returns: 0 if OK, −1 on error

Two file descriptors are returned: *fd[0]*, which is open for reading, and *fd[1]*, which is open for writing.

> Some versions of Unix, notably SVR4, provide full-duplex pipes, in which case, both ends are available for reading and writing. Another way to create a full-duplex IPC channel is with the `socketpair` function, described in Section 14.3 of UNPv1, and this works on most current Unix systems. The most common use of pipes, however, is with the various shells, in which case, a half-duplex pipe is adequate.
>
> Posix.1 and Unix 98 require only half-duplex pipes, and we assume so in this chapter.

The `S_ISFIFO` macro can be used to determine if a descriptor or file is either a pipe or a FIFO. Its single argument is the `st_mode` member of the `stat` structure and the macro evaluates to true (nonzero) or false (0). For a pipe, this structure is filled in by the `fstat` function. For a FIFO, this structure is filled in by the `fstat`, `lstat`, or `stat` functions.

Figure 4.2 shows how a pipe looks in a single process.

Although a pipe is created by one process, it is rarely used within a single process. (We show an example of a pipe within a single process in Figure 5.14.) Pipes are typically used to communicate between two different processes (a parent and child) in the following way. First, a process (which will be the parent) creates a pipe and then `forks` to create a copy of itself, as shown in Figure 4.3.

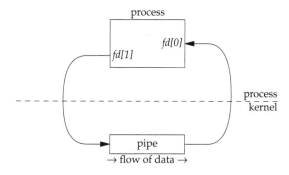

Figure 4.2   A pipe in a single process.

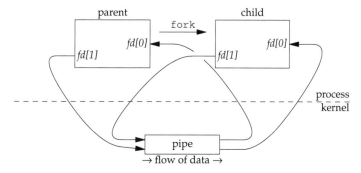

Figure 4.3   Pipe in a single process, immediately after `fork`.

Next, the parent process closes the read end of one pipe, and the child process closes the write end of that same pipe. This provides a one-way flow of data between the two processes, as shown in Figure 4.4.

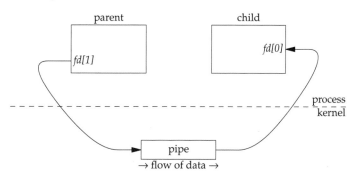

Figure 4.4   Pipe between two processes.

When we enter a command such as

```
who | sort | lp
```

to a Unix shell, the shell performs the steps described previously to create three

processes with two pipes between them. The shell also duplicates the read end of each
pipe to standard input and the write end of each pipe to standard output. We show this
pipeline in Figure 4.5.

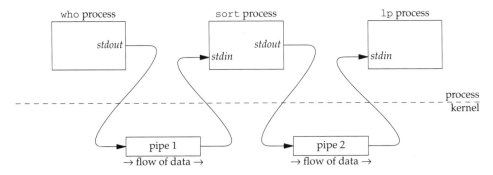

Figure 4.5 Pipes between three processes in a shell pipeline.

All the pipes shown so far have been half-duplex or unidirectional, providing a one-
way flow of data only. When a two-way flow of data is desired, we must create two
pipes and use one for each direction. The actual steps are as follows:

1. create pipe 1 (*fd1[0]* and *fd1[1]*), create pipe 2 (*fd2[0]* and *fd2[1]*),
2. `fork`,
3. parent closes read end of pipe 1 (*fd1[0]*),
4. parent closes write end of pipe 2 (*fd2[1]*),
5. child closes write end of pipe 1 (*fd1[1]*), and
6. child closes read end of pipe 2 (*fd2[0]*).

We show the code for these steps in Figure 4.8. This generates the pipe arrangement
shown in Figure 4.6.

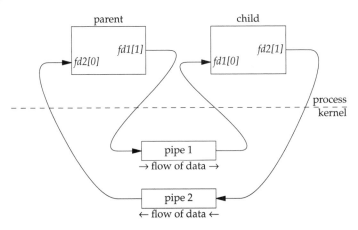

Figure 4.6 Two pipes to provide a bidirectional flow of data.

Example

Let us now implement the client–server example described in Section 4.2 using pipes. The `main` function creates two pipes and `forks` a child. The client then runs in the parent process and the server runs in the child process. The first pipe is used to send the pathname from the client to the server, and the second pipe is used to send the contents of that file (or an error message) from the server to the client. This setup gives us the arrangement shown in Figure 4.7.

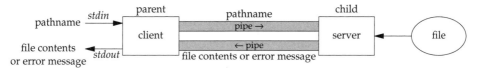

Figure 4.7 Implementation of Figure 4.1 using two pipes.

Realize that in this figure we show the two pipes connecting the two processes, but each pipe goes through the kernel, as shown previously in Figure 4.6. Therefore, each byte of data from the client to the server, and vice versa, crosses the user–kernel interface twice: once when written to the pipe, and again when read from the pipe.

Figure 4.8 shows our `main` function for this example.

pipe/mainpipe.c

```
 1 #include     "unpipc.h"

 2 void    client(int, int), server(int, int);

 3 int
 4 main(int argc, char **argv)
 5 {
 6      int     pipe1[2], pipe2[2];
 7      pid_t   childpid;

 8      Pipe(pipe1);                    /* create two pipes */
 9      Pipe(pipe2);

10      if ( (childpid = Fork()) == 0) {      /* child */
11          Close(pipe1[1]);
12          Close(pipe2[0]);

13          server(pipe1[0], pipe2[1]);
14          exit(0);
15      }
16          /* parent */
17      Close(pipe1[0]);
18      Close(pipe2[1]);

19      client(pipe2[0], pipe1[1]);

20      Waitpid(childpid, NULL, 0); /* wait for child to terminate */
21      exit(0);
22 }
```

pipe/mainpipe.c

Figure 4.8 `main` function for client–server using two pipes.

Create pipes, `fork`

8-19   Two pipes are created and the six steps that we listed with Figure 4.6 are performed. The parent calls the `client` function (Figure 4.9) and the child calls the `server` function (Figure 4.10).

`waitpid` for child

20   The server (the child) terminates first, when it calls `exit` after writing the final data to the pipe. It then becomes a *zombie*: a process that has terminated, but whose parent is still running but has not yet waited for the child. When the child terminates, the kernel also generates a `SIGCHLD` signal for the parent, but the parent does not catch this signal, and the default action of this signal is to be ignored. Shortly thereafter, the parent's `client` function returns after reading the final data from the pipe. The parent then calls `waitpid` to fetch the termination status of the terminated child (the zombie). If the parent did not call `waitpid`, but just terminated, the child would be inherited by the `init` process, and another `SIGCHLD` signal would be sent to the `init` process, which would then fetch the termination status of the zombie.

The `client` function is shown in Figure 4.9.

─── *pipe/client.c*

```
 1 #include    "unpipc.h"

 2 void
 3 client(int readfd, int writefd)
 4 {
 5     size_t  len;
 6     ssize_t n;
 7     char    buff[MAXLINE];

 8         /* read pathname */
 9     Fgets(buff, MAXLINE, stdin);
10     len = strlen(buff);          /* fgets() guarantees null byte at end */
11     if (buff[len - 1] == '\n')
12         len--;                   /* ignore newline from fgets() */

13         /* write pathname to IPC channel */
14     Write(writefd, buff, len);

15         /* read from IPC, write to standard output */
16     while ( (n = Read(readfd, buff, MAXLINE)) > 0)
17         Write(STDOUT_FILENO, buff, n);
18 }
```
─── *pipe/client.c*

Figure 4.9 `client` function for client–server using two pipes.

Read pathname from standard input

8-14   The pathname is read from standard input and written to the pipe, after deleting the newline that is stored by `fgets`.

Copy from pipe to standard output

15-17   The client then reads everything that the server writes to the pipe, writing it to standard output. Normally this is the contents of the file, but if the specified pathname cannot be opened, what the server returns is an error message.

Figure 4.10 shows the `server` function.

```
                                                                    pipe/server.c
1 #include     "unpipc.h"

2 void
3 server(int readfd, int writefd)
4 {
5     int     fd;
6     ssize_t n;
7     char    buff[MAXLINE + 1];

8         /* read pathname from IPC channel */
9     if ( (n = Read(readfd, buff, MAXLINE)) == 0)
10        err_quit("end-of-file while reading pathname");
11    buff[n] = '\0';               /* null terminate pathname */

12    if ( (fd = open(buff, O_RDONLY)) < 0) {
13            /* error: must tell client */
14        snprintf(buff + n, sizeof(buff) - n, ": can't open, %s\n",
15                strerror(errno));
16        n = strlen(buff);
17        Write(writefd, buff, n);

18    } else {
19            /* open succeeded: copy file to IPC channel */
20        while ( (n = Read(fd, buff, MAXLINE)) > 0)
21            Write(writefd, buff, n);
22        Close(fd);
23    }
24 }
                                                                    pipe/server.c
```

Figure 4.10 `server` function for client–server using two pipes.

Read pathname from pipe

8-11   The pathname written by the client is read from the pipe and null terminated. Note that a `read` on a pipe returns as soon as some data is present; it need not wait for the requested number of bytes (`MAXLINE` in this example).

Open file, handle error

12-17   The file is opened for reading, and if an error occurs, an error message string is returned to the client across the pipe. We call the `strerror` function to return the error message string corresponding to `errno`. (Pages 690–691 of UNPv1 talk more about the `strerror` function.)

Copy file to pipe

18-23   If the `open` succeeds, the contents of the file are copied to the pipe.

We can see the output from the program when the pathname is OK, and when an error occurs.

```
solaris % mainpipe
/etc/inet/ntp.conf                       a file consisting of two lines
multicastclient 224.0.1.1
driftfile /etc/inet/ntp.drift
solaris % mainpipe
/etc/shadow                              a file we cannot read
/etc/shadow: can't open, Permission denied
solaris % mainpipe
/no/such/file                            a nonexistent file
/no/such/file: can't open, No such file or directory
```

4.4 Full-Duplex Pipes

We mentioned in the previous section that some systems provide full-duplex pipes: SVR4's `pipe` function and the `socketpair` function provided by many kernels. But what exactly does a full-duplex pipe provide? First, we can think of a half-duplex pipe as shown in Figure 4.11, a modification of Figure 4.2, which omits the process.

Figure 4.11 Half-duplex pipe.

A full-duplex pipe could be implemented as shown in Figure 4.12. This implies that only one buffer exists for the pipe and everything written to the pipe (on either descriptor) gets appended to the buffer and any read from the pipe (on either descriptor) just takes data from the front of the buffer.

Figure 4.12 One possible (incorrect) implementation of a full-duplex pipe.

The problem with this implementation becomes apparent in a program such as Figure A.29. We want two-way communication but we need two independent data streams, one in each direction. Otherwise, when a process writes data to the full-duplex pipe and then turns around and issues a `read` on that pipe, it could read back what it just wrote.

Figure 4.13 shows the actual implementation of a full-duplex pipe.

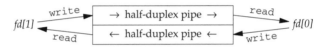

Figure 4.13 Actual implementation of a full-duplex pipe.

Here, the full-duplex pipe is constructed from two half-duplex pipes. Anything written to *fd[1]* will be available for reading by *fd[0]*, and anything written to *fd[0]* will be available for reading by *fd[1]*.

The program in Figure 4.14 demonstrates that we can use a single full-duplex pipe for two-way communication.

—————————————————————————————— pipe/fduplex.c

```
 1 #include      "unpipc.h"

 2 int
 3 main(int argc, char **argv)
 4 {
 5     int      fd[2], n;
 6     char     c;
 7     pid_t    childpid;

 8     Pipe(fd);                       /* assumes a full-duplex pipe (e.g., SVR4) */
 9     if ( (childpid = Fork()) == 0) {       /* child */
10         sleep(3);
11         if ( (n = Read(fd[0], &c, 1)) != 1)
12             err_quit("child: read returned %d", n);
13         printf("child read %c\n", c);
14         Write(fd[0], "c", 1);
15         exit(0);
16     }
17         /* parent */
18     Write(fd[1], "p", 1);
19     if ( (n = Read(fd[1], &c, 1)) != 1)
20         err_quit("parent: read returned %d", n);
21     printf("parent read %c\n", c);
22     exit(0);
23 }
```

—————————————————————————————— pipe/fduplex.c

Figure 4.14 Test a full-duplex pipe for two-way communication.

We create a full-duplex pipe and `fork`. The parent writes the character p to the pipe, and then reads a character from the pipe. The child sleeps for 3 seconds, reads a character from the pipe, and then writes the character c to the pipe. The purpose of the sleep in the child is to allow the parent to call `read` before the child can call `read`, to see whether the parent reads back what it wrote.

If we run this program under Solaris 2.6, which provides full-duplex pipes, we observe the desired behavior.

```
solaris % fduplex
child read p
parent read c
```

The character p goes across the half-duplex pipe shown in the top of Figure 4.13, and the character c goes across the half-duplex pipe shown in the bottom of Figure 4.13. The parent does not read back what it wrote (the character p).

If we run this program under Digital Unix 4.0B, which by default provides half-duplex pipes (it also provides full-duplex pipes like SVR4, if different options are specified at compile time), we see the expected behavior of a half-duplex pipe.

```
alpha % fduplex
read error: Bad file number
alpha % child read p
write error: Bad file number
```

The parent writes the character p, which the child reads, but then the parent aborts when it tries to read from *fd[1]*, and the child aborts when it tries to write to *fd[0]* (recall Figure 4.11). The error returned by read is EBADF, which means that the descriptor is not open for reading. Similarly, write returns the same error if its descriptor is not open for writing.

4.5   `popen` and `pclose` Functions

As another example of pipes, the standard I/O library provides the popen function that creates a pipe and initiates another process that either reads from the pipe or writes to the pipe.

```
#include <stdio.h>

FILE *popen(const char *command, const char *type);
```

Returns: file pointer if OK, NULL on error

```
int pclose(FILE *stream);
```

Returns: termination status of shell or −1 on error

command is a shell command line. It is processed by the sh program (normally a Bourne shell), so the PATH environment variable is used to locate the *command*. A pipe is created between the calling process and the specified command. The value returned by popen is a standard I/O FILE pointer that is used for either input or output, depending on the character string *type*.

- If *type* is r, the calling process reads the standard output of the *command*.
- If *type* is w, the calling process writes to the standard input of the *command*.

The pclose function closes a standard I/O *stream* that was created by popen, waits for the command to terminate, and then returns the termination status of the shell.

Section 14.3 of APUE provides an implementation of popen and pclose.

Example

Figure 4.15 shows another solution to our client–server example using the popen function and the Unix cat program.

pipe/mainpopen.c

```
 1 #include     "unpipc.h"

 2 int
 3 main(int argc, char **argv)
 4 {
 5     size_t  n;
 6     char    buff[MAXLINE], command[MAXLINE];
 7     FILE    *fp;

 8         /* read pathname */
 9     Fgets(buff, MAXLINE, stdin);
10     n = strlen(buff);           /* fgets() guarantees null byte at end */
11     if (buff[n - 1] == '\n')
12         buff[n - 1] = '\0';     /* delete newline from fgets() */

13     snprintf(command, sizeof(command), "cat %s", buff);
14     fp = Popen(command, "r");

15         /* copy from pipe to standard output */
16     while (Fgets(buff, MAXLINE, fp) != NULL)
17         Fputs(buff, stdout);

18     Pclose(fp);
19     exit(0);
20 }
```

pipe/mainpopen.c

Figure 4.15 Client–server using popen.

8–17   The pathname is read from standard input, as in Figure 4.9. A command is built
and passed to popen. The output from either the shell or the cat program is copied to
standard output.

One difference between this implementation and the implementation in Figure 4.8
is that now we are dependent on the error message generated by the system's cat program, which is often inadequate. For example, under Solaris 2.6, we get the following
error when trying to read a file that we do not have permission to read:

```
solaris % cat /etc/shadow
cat: cannot open /etc/shadow
```

But under BSD/OS 3.1, we get a more descriptive error when trying to read a similar
file:

```
bsdi % cat /etc/master.passwd
cat: /etc/master.passwd: cannot open [Permission denied]
```

Also realize that the call to popen succeeds in such a case, but fgets just returns an
end-of-file the first time it is called. The cat program writes its error message to standard error, and popen does nothing special with it—only standard output is redirected
to the pipe that it creates.

4.6   FIFOs

Pipes have no names, and their biggest disadvantage is that they can be used only between processes that have a parent process in common. Two unrelated processes cannot create a pipe between them and use it for IPC (ignoring descriptor passing).

FIFO stands for *first in, first out*, and a Unix FIFO is similar to a pipe. It is a one-way (half-duplex) flow of data. But unlike pipes, a FIFO has a pathname associated with it, allowing unrelated processes to access a single FIFO. FIFOs are also called *named pipes*.

A FIFO is created by the mkfifo function.

```
#include <sys/types.h>
#include <sys/stat.h>

int mkfifo(const char *pathname, mode_t mode);
```

Returns: 0 if OK, −1 on error

The *pathname* is a normal Unix pathname, and this is the name of the FIFO.

The *mode* argument specifies the file permission bits, similar to the second argument to open. Figure 2.4 shows the six constants from the <sys/stat.h> header used to specify these bits for a FIFO.

The mkfifo function implies O_CREAT | O_EXCL. That is, it creates a new FIFO or returns an error of EEXIST if the named FIFO already exists. If the creation of a new FIFO is not desired, call open instead of mkfifo. To open an existing FIFO or create a new FIFO if it does not already exist, call mkfifo, check for an error of EEXIST, and if this occurs, call open instead.

The mkfifo command also creates a FIFO. This can be used from shell scripts or from the command line.

Once a FIFO is created, it must be opened for reading or writing, using either the open function, or one of the standard I/O open functions such as fopen. A FIFO must be opened either read-only or write-only. It must not be opened for read–write, because a FIFO is half-duplex.

A write to a pipe or FIFO always appends the data, and a read always returns what is at the beginning of the pipe or FIFO. If lseek is called for a pipe or FIFO, the error ESPIPE is returned.

Example

We now redo our client–server from Figure 4.8 to use two FIFOs instead of two pipes. Our client and server functions remain the same; all that changes is the main function, which we show in Figure 4.16.

pipe/mainfifo.c

```
1 #include     "unpipc.h"

2 #define FIFO1    "/tmp/fifo.1"
3 #define FIFO2    "/tmp/fifo.2"

4 void    client(int, int), server(int, int);
```

```
 5 int
 6 main(int argc, char **argv)
 7 {
 8     int     readfd, writefd;
 9     pid_t   childpid;

10         /* create two FIFOs; OK if they already exist */
11     if ((mkfifo(FIFO1, FILE_MODE) < 0) && (errno != EEXIST))
12         err_sys("can't create %s", FIFO1);
13     if ((mkfifo(FIFO2, FILE_MODE) < 0) && (errno != EEXIST)) {
14         unlink(FIFO1);
15         err_sys("can't create %s", FIFO2);
16     }
17     if ( (childpid = Fork()) == 0) {        /* child */
18         readfd = Open(FIFO1, O_RDONLY, 0);
19         writefd = Open(FIFO2, O_WRONLY, 0);

20         server(readfd, writefd);
21         exit(0);
22     }
23         /* parent */
24     writefd = Open(FIFO1, O_WRONLY, 0);
25     readfd = Open(FIFO2, O_RDONLY, 0);

26     client(readfd, writefd);

27     Waitpid(childpid, NULL, 0); /* wait for child to terminate */

28     Close(readfd);
29     Close(writefd);

30     Unlink(FIFO1);
31     Unlink(FIFO2);
32     exit(0);
33 }
```
—— *pipe/mainfifo.c*

Figure 4.16 `main` function for our client–server that uses two FIFOs.

Create two FIFOs

10-16   Two FIFOs are created in the `/tmp` filesystem. If the FIFOs already exist, that is OK.
The FILE_MODE constant is defined in our `unpipc.h` header (Figure C.1) as

```
#define  FILE_MODE   (S_IRUSR | S_IWUSR | S_IRGRP | S_IROTH)
                    /* default permissions for new files */
```

This allows user-read, user-write, group-read, and other-read. These permission bits are
modified by the *file mode creation mask* of the process.

`fork`

17-27   We call `fork`, the child calls our `server` function (Figure 4.10), and the parent calls
our `client` function (Figure 4.9). Before executing these calls, the parent opens the first
FIFO for writing and the second FIFO for reading, and the child opens the first FIFO for
reading and the second FIFO for writing. This is similar to our pipe example, and Figure 4.17 shows this arrangement.

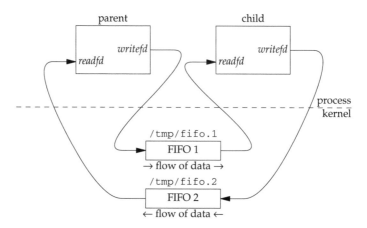

Figure 4.17 Client–server example using two FIFOs.

The changes from our pipe example to this FIFO example are as follows:

- To create and open a pipe requires one call to `pipe`. To create and open a FIFO requires one call to `mkfifo` followed by a call to `open`.

- A pipe automatically disappears on its last close. A FIFO's name is deleted from the filesystem only by calling `unlink`.

The benefit in the extra calls required for the FIFO is that a FIFO has a name in the filesystem allowing one process to create a FIFO and another unrelated process to open the FIFO. This is not possible with a pipe.

Subtle problems can occur with programs that do not use FIFOs correctly. Consider Figure 4.16: if we swap the order of the two calls to `open` in the parent, the program does not work. The reason is that the open of a FIFO for reading blocks if no process currently has the FIFO open for writing. If we swap the order of these two `open`s in the parent, both the parent and the child are opening a FIFO for reading when no process has the FIFO open for writing, so both block. This is called a *deadlock*. We discuss this scenario in the next section.

Example: Unrelated Client and Server

In Figure 4.16, the client and server are still related processes. But we can redo this example with the client and server unrelated. Figure 4.18 shows the server program. This program is nearly identical to the server portion of Figure 4.16.

The header `fifo.h` is shown in Figure 4.19 and provides the definitions of the two FIFO names, which both the client and server must know.

Figure 4.20 shows the client program, which is nearly identical to the client portion of Figure 4.16. Notice that the client, not the server, deletes the FIFOs when done, because the client performs the last operation on the FIFOs.

pipe/server_main.c

```
1 #include    "fifo.h"

2 void    server(int, int);

3 int
4 main(int argc, char **argv)
5 {
6     int    readfd, writefd;

7         /* create two FIFOs; OK if they already exist */
8     if ((mkfifo(FIFO1, FILE_MODE) < 0) && (errno != EEXIST))
9         err_sys("can't create %s", FIFO1);
10    if ((mkfifo(FIFO2, FILE_MODE) < 0) && (errno != EEXIST)) {
11        unlink(FIFO1);
12        err_sys("can't create %s", FIFO2);
13    }
14    readfd = Open(FIFO1, O_RDONLY, 0);
15    writefd = Open(FIFO2, O_WRONLY, 0);

16    server(readfd, writefd);
17    exit(0);
18 }
```

pipe/server_main.c

Figure 4.18 Stand-alone server `main` function.

pipe/fifo.h.c

```
1 #include    "unpipc.h"

2 #define FIFO1    "/tmp/fifo.1"
3 #define FIFO2    "/tmp/fifo.2"
```

pipe/fifo.h.c

Figure 4.19 `fifo.h` header that both the client and server include.

pipe/client_main.c

```
1 #include    "fifo.h"

2 void    client(int, int);

3 int
4 main(int argc, char **argv)
5 {
6     int    readfd, writefd;

7     writefd = Open(FIFO1, O_WRONLY, 0);
8     readfd = Open(FIFO2, O_RDONLY, 0);

9     client(readfd, writefd);

10    Close(readfd);
11    Close(writefd);

12    Unlink(FIFO1);
13    Unlink(FIFO2);
14    exit(0);
15 }
```

pipe/client_main.c

Figure 4.20 Stand-alone client `main` function.

In the case of a pipe or FIFO, where the kernel keeps a reference count of the number of open descriptors that refer to the pipe or FIFO, either the client or server could call `unlink` without a problem. Even though this function removes the pathname from the filesystem, this does not affect open descriptors that had previously opened the pathname. But for other forms of IPC, such as System V message queues, no counter exists and if the server were to delete the queue after writing its final message to the queue, the queue could be gone when the client tries to read the final message.

To run this client and server, start the server in the background

```
% server_fifo &
```

and then start the client. Alternately, we could start only the client and have it invoke the server by calling `fork` and then `exec`. The client could also pass the names of the two FIFOs to the server as command-line arguments through the `exec` function, instead of coding them into a header. But this scenario would make the server a child of the client, in which case, a pipe could just as easily be used.

4.7 Additional Properties of Pipes and FIFOs

We need to describe in more detail some properties of pipes and FIFOs with regard to their opening, reading, and writing. First, a descriptor can be set nonblocking in two ways.

1. The `O_NONBLOCK` flag can be specified when `open` is called. For example, the first call to `open` in Figure 4.20 could be

   ```
   writefd = Open(FIFO1, O_WRONLY | O_NONBLOCK, 0);
   ```

2. If a descriptor is already open, `fcntl` can be called to enable the `O_NONBLOCK` flag. This technique must be used with a pipe, since `open` is not called for a pipe, and no way exists to specify the `O_NONBLOCK` flag in the call to `pipe`. When using `fcntl`, we first fetch the current file status flags with the `F_GETFL` command, bitwise-OR the `O_NONBLOCK` flag, and then store the file status flags with the `F_SETFL` command:

   ```
   int     flags;

   if ( (flags = fcntl(fd, F_GETFL, 0)) < 0)
       err_sys("F_GETFL error");
   flags |= O_NONBLOCK;
   if (fcntl(fd, F_SETFL, flags) < 0)
       err_sys("F_SETFL error");
   ```

   Beware of code that you may encounter that simply sets the desired flag, because this also clears all the other possible file status flags:

   ```
       /* wrong way to set nonblocking */
   if (fcntl(fd, F_SETFL, O_NONBLOCK) < 0)
       err_sys("F_SETFL error");
   ```

Figure 4.21 shows the effect of the nonblocking flag for the opening of a FIFO and for the reading of data from an empty pipe or from an empty FIFO.

Current operation	Existing opens of pipe or FIFO	Return	
		Blocking (default)	O_NONBLOCK set
open FIFO read-only	FIFO open for writing	returns OK	returns OK
	FIFO not open for writing	blocks until FIFO is opened for writing	returns OK
open FIFO write-only	FIFO open for reading	returns OK	returns OK
	FIFO not open for reading	blocks until FIFO is opened for reading	returns an error of ENXIO
read empty pipe or empty FIFO	pipe or FIFO open for writing	blocks until data is in the pipe or FIFO, or until the pipe or FIFO is no longer open for writing	returns an error of EAGAIN
	pipe or FIFO not open for writing	read returns 0 (end-of-file)	read returns 0 (end-of-file)
write to pipe or FIFO	pipe or FIFO open for reading	(see text)	(see text)
	pipe or FIFO not open for reading	SIGPIPE generated for thread	SIGPIPE generated for thread

Figure 4.21   Effect of O_NONBLOCK flag on pipes and FIFOs.

Note a few additional rules regarding the reading and writing of a pipe or FIFO.

- If we ask to read more data than is currently available in the pipe or FIFO, only the available data is returned. We must be prepared to handle a return value from read that is less than the requested amount.

- If the number of bytes to write is less than or equal to PIPE_BUF (a Posix limit that we say more about in Section 4.11), the write is guaranteed to be *atomic*. This means that if two processes each write to the same pipe or FIFO at about the same time, either all the data from the first process is written, followed by all the data from the second process, or vice versa. The system does not intermix the data from the two processes. If, however, the number of bytes to write is greater than PIPE_BUF, there is no guarantee that the write operation is atomic.

  > Posix.1 requires that PIPE_BUF be at least 512 bytes. Commonly encountered values range from 1024 for BSD/OS 3.1 to 5120 for Solaris 2.6. We show a program in Section 4.11 that prints this value.

- The setting of the O_NONBLOCK flag has no effect on the atomicity of writes to a pipe or FIFO—atomicity is determined solely by whether the requested number of bytes is less than or equal to PIPE_BUF. But when a pipe or FIFO is set non-blocking, the return value from write depends on the number of bytes to write and the amount of space currently available in the pipe or FIFO. If the number of bytes to write is less than or equal to PIPE_BUF:

a. If there is room in the pipe or FIFO for the requested number of bytes, all the bytes are transferred.

b. If there is not enough room in the pipe or FIFO for the requested number of bytes, return is made immediately with an error of EAGAIN. Since the O_NONBLOCK flag is set, the process does not want to be put to sleep. But the kernel cannot accept part of the data and still guarantee an atomic write, so the kernel must return an error and tell the process to try again later.

If the number of bytes to write is greater than PIPE_BUF:

a. If there is room for at least 1 byte in the pipe or FIFO, the kernel transfers whatever the pipe or FIFO can hold, and that is the return value from write.

b. If the pipe or FIFO is full, return is made immediately with an error of EAGAIN.

• If we write to a pipe or FIFO that is not open for reading, the SIGPIPE signal is generated:

a. If the process does not catch or ignore SIGPIPE, the default action of terminating the process is taken.

b. If the process ignores the SIGPIPE signal, or if it catches the signal and returns from its signal handler, then write returns an error of EPIPE.

> SIGPIPE is considered a synchronous signal, that is, a signal attributable to one specific thread, the one that called write. But the easiest way to handle this signal is to ignore it (set its disposition to SIG_IGN) and let write return an error of EPIPE. An application should always detect an error return from write, but detecting the termination of a process by SIGPIPE is harder. If the signal is not caught, we must look at the termination status of the process from the shell to determine that the process was killed by a signal, and which signal. Section 5.13 of UNPv1 talks more about SIGPIPE.

4.8   One Server, Multiple Clients

The real advantage of a FIFO is when the server is a long-running process (e.g., a daemon, as described in Chapter 12 of UNPv1) that is unrelated to the client. The daemon creates a FIFO with a well-known pathname, opens the FIFO for reading, and the client then starts at some later time, opens the FIFO for writing, and sends its commands or whatever to the daemon through the FIFO. One-way communication of this form (client to server) is easy with a FIFO, but it becomes harder if the daemon needs to send something back to the client. Figure 4.22 shows the technique that we use with our example.

The server creates a FIFO with a well-known pathname, /tmp/fifo.serv in this example. The server will read client requests from this FIFO. Each client creates its own FIFO when it starts, with a pathname containing its process ID. Each client writes its

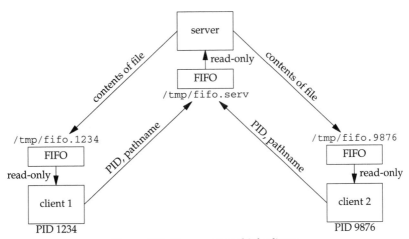

Figure 4.22 One server, multiple clients.

request to the server's well-known FIFO, and the request contains the client process ID along with the pathname of the file that the client wants the server to open and send to the client.

Figure 4.23 shows the server program.

Create well-known FIFO and open for read-only and write-only

10–15   The server's well-known FIFO is created, and it is OK if it already exists. We then open the FIFO twice, once read-only and once write-only. The `readfifo` descriptor is used to read each client request that arrives at the FIFO, but the `dummyfd` descriptor is never used. The reason for opening the FIFO for writing can be seen in Figure 4.21. If we do not open the FIFO for writing, then each time a client terminates, the FIFO becomes empty and the server's `read` returns 0 to indicate an end-of-file. We would then have to `close` the FIFO and call `open` again with the `O_RDONLY` flag, and this will block until the next client request arrives. But if we always have a descriptor for the FIFO that was opened for writing, `read` will never return 0 to indicate an end-of-file when no clients exist. Instead, our server will just block in the call to `read`, waiting for the next client request. This trick therefore simplifies our server code and reduces the number of calls to `open` for its well-known FIFO.

When the server starts, the first `open` (with the `O_RDONLY` flag) blocks until the first client opens the server's FIFO write-only (recall Figure 4.21). The second `open` (with the `O_WRONLY` flag) then returns immediately, because the FIFO is already open for reading.

Read client request

16   Each client request is a single line consisting of the process ID, one space, and then the pathname. We read this line with our `readline` function (which we show on p. 79 of UNPv1).

fifocliserv/mainserver.c

```
 1 #include    "fifo.h"

 2 void    server(int, int);

 3 int
 4 main(int argc, char **argv)
 5 {
 6     int     readfifo, writefifo, dummyfd, fd;
 7     char    *ptr, buff[MAXLINE + 1], fifoname[MAXLINE];
 8     pid_t   pid;
 9     ssize_t n;

10         /* create server's well-known FIFO; OK if already exists */
11     if ((mkfifo(SERV_FIFO, FILE_MODE) < 0) && (errno != EEXIST))
12         err_sys("can't create %s", SERV_FIFO);

13         /* open server's well-known FIFO for reading and writing */
14     readfifo = Open(SERV_FIFO, O_RDONLY, 0);
15     dummyfd = Open(SERV_FIFO, O_WRONLY, 0);     /* never used */

16     while ( (n = Readline(readfifo, buff, MAXLINE)) > 0) {
17         if (buff[n - 1] == '\n')
18             n--;                /* delete newline from readline() */
19         buff[n] = '\0';         /* null terminate pathname */

20         if ( (ptr = strchr(buff, ' ')) == NULL) {
21             err_msg("bogus request: %s", buff);
22             continue;
23         }
24         *ptr++ = 0;             /* null terminate PID, ptr = pathname */
25         pid = atol(buff);
26         snprintf(fifoname, sizeof(fifoname), "/tmp/fifo.%ld", (long) pid);
27         if ( (writefifo = open(fifoname, O_WRONLY, 0)) < 0) {
28             err_msg("cannot open: %s", fifoname);
29             continue;
30         }
31         if ( (fd = open(ptr, O_RDONLY)) < 0) {
32                 /* error: must tell client */
33             snprintf(buff + n, sizeof(buff) - n, ": can't open, %s\n",
34                     strerror(errno));
35             n = strlen(ptr);
36             Write(writefifo, ptr, n);
37             Close(writefifo);

38         } else {
39                 /* open succeeded: copy file to FIFO */
40             while ( (n = Read(fd, buff, MAXLINE)) > 0)
41                 Write(writefifo, buff, n);
42             Close(fd);
43             Close(writefifo);
44         }
45     }
46     exit(0);
47 }
```

fifocliserv/mainserver.c

Figure 4.23 FIFO server that handles multiple clients.

Parse client's request

17-26   The newline that is normally returned by readline is deleted. This newline is missing only if the buffer was filled before the newline was encountered, or if the final line of input was not terminated by a newline. The strchr function returns a pointer to the first blank in the line, and ptr is incremented to point to the first character of the pathname that follows. The pathname of the client's FIFO is constructed from the process ID, and the FIFO is opened for write-only by the server.

Open file for client, send file to client's FIFO

27-44   The remainder of the server is similar to our server function from Figure 4.10. The file is opened and if this fails, an error message is returned to the client across the FIFO. If the open succeeds, the file is copied to the client's FIFO. When done, we must close the server's end of the client's FIFO, which causes the client's read to return 0 (end-of-file). The server does not delete the client's FIFO; the client must do so after it reads the end-of-file from the server.

We show the client program in Figure 4.24.

Create FIFO

10-14   The client's FIFO is created with the process ID as the final part of the pathname.

Build client request line

15-21   The client's request consists of its process ID, one blank, the pathname for the server to send to the client, and a newline. This line is built in the array buff, reading the pathname from the standard input.

Open server's FIFO and write request

22-24   The server's FIFO is opened and the request is written to the FIFO. If this client is the first to open this FIFO since the server was started, then this open unblocks the server from its call to open (with the O_RDONLY flag).

Read file contents or error message from server

25-31   The server's reply is read from the FIFO and written to standard output. The client's FIFO is then closed and deleted.

We can start our server in one window and run the client in another window, and it works as expected. We show only the client interaction.

```
solaris % mainclient
/etc/shadow                          a file we cannot read
/etc/shadow: can't open, Permission denied
solaris % mainclient
/etc/inet/ntp.conf                   a 2-line file
multicastclient 224.0.1.1
driftfile /etc/inet/ntp.drift
```

We can also interact with the server from the shell, because FIFOs have names in the filesystem.

```
                                                                      ─── fifocliserv/mainclient.c
 1 #include    "fifo.h"

 2 int
 3 main(int argc, char **argv)
 4 {
 5     int     readfifo, writefifo;
 6     size_t  len;
 7     ssize_t n;
 8     char    *ptr, fifoname[MAXLINE], buff[MAXLINE];
 9     pid_t   pid;

10         /* create FIFO with our PID as part of name */
11     pid = getpid();
12     snprintf(fifoname, sizeof(fifoname), "/tmp/fifo.%ld", (long) pid);
13     if ((mkfifo(fifoname, FILE_MODE) < 0) && (errno != EEXIST))
14         err_sys("can't create %s", fifoname);

15         /* start buffer with pid and a blank */
16     snprintf(buff, sizeof(buff), "%ld ", (long) pid);
17     len = strlen(buff);
18     ptr = buff + len;

19         /* read pathname */
20     Fgets(ptr, MAXLINE - len, stdin);
21     len = strlen(buff);             /* fgets() guarantees null byte at end */

22         /* open FIFO to server and write PID and pathname to FIFO */
23     writefifo = Open(SERV_FIFO, O_WRONLY, 0);
24     Write(writefifo, buff, len);

25         /* now open our FIFO; blocks until server opens for writing */
26     readfifo = Open(fifoname, O_RDONLY, 0);

27         /* read from IPC, write to standard output */
28     while ( (n = Read(readfifo, buff, MAXLINE)) > 0)
29         Write(STDOUT_FILENO, buff, n);

30     Close(readfifo);
31     Unlink(fifoname);
32     exit(0);
33 }
                                                                      ─── fifocliserv/mainclient.c
```

Figure 4.24 FIFO client that works with the server in Figure 4.23.

```
solaris % Pid=$$                                        process ID of this shell
solaris % mkfifo /tmp/fifo.$Pid                         make the client's FIFO
solaris % echo "$Pid /etc/inet/ntp.conf" > /tmp/fifo.serv
solaris % cat < /tmp/fifo.$Pid                          and read server's reply
multicastclient 224.0.1.1
driftfile /etc/inet/ntp.drift
solaris % rm /tmp/fifo.$Pid
```

We send our process ID and pathname to the server with one shell command (echo)
and read the server's reply with another (cat). Any amount of time can occur between
these two commands. Therefore, the server appears to write the file to the FIFO, and
the client later executes cat to read the data from the FIFO, which might make us think

that the data remains in the FIFO somehow, even when no process has the FIFO open. This is not what is happening. Indeed, the rule is that when the final `close` of a pipe or FIFO occurs, any remaining data in the pipe or FIFO is discarded. What is happening in our shell example is that after the server reads the request line from the client, the server blocks in its call to `open` on the client's FIFO, because the client (our shell) has not yet opened the FIFO for reading (recall Figure 4.21). Only when we execute `cat` sometime later, which opens the client FIFO for reading, does the server's call to `open` for this FIFO return. This timing also leads to a *denial-of-service* attack, which we discuss in the next section.

Using the shell also allows simple testing of the server's error handling. We can easily send a line to the server without a process ID, and we can also send a line to the server specifying a process ID that does not correspond to a FIFO in the `/tmp` directory. For example, if we invoke the server and enter the following lines

```
solaris % cat > /tmp/fifo.serv
/no/process/id
999999 /invalid/process/id
```

then the server's output (in another window) is

```
solaris % server
bogus request: /no/process/id
cannot open: /tmp/fifo.999999
```

Atomicity of FIFO `writes`

Our simple client–server also lets us see why the atomicity property of `writes` to pipes and FIFOs is important. Assume that two clients send requests at about the same time to the server. The first client's request is the line

```
1234 /etc/inet/ntp.conf
```

and the second client's request is the line

```
9876 /etc/passwd
```

If we assume that each client issues one `write` function call for its request line, and that each line is less than or equal to `PIPE_BUF` (which is reasonable, since this limit is usually between 1024 and 5120 and since pathnames are often limited to 1024 bytes), then we are guaranteed that the data in the FIFO will be either

```
1234 /etc/inet/ntp.conf
9876 /etc/passwd
```

or

```
9876 /etc/passwd
1234 /etc/inet/ntp.conf
```

The data in the FIFO will *not* be something like

```
1234 /etc/inet9876 /etc/passwd
/ntp.conf
```

FIFOs and NFS

FIFOs are a form of IPC that can be used on a single host. Although FIFOs have names in the filesystem, they can be used only on local filesystems, and not on NFS-mounted filesystems.

```
solaris % mkfifo /nfs/bsdi/usr/rstevens/fifo.temp
mkfifo: I/O error
```

In this example, the filesystem /nfs/bsdi/usr is the /usr filesystem on the host bsdi.

Some systems (e.g., BSD/OS) do allow FIFOs to be created on an NFS-mounted filesystem, but data cannot be passed between the two systems through one of these FIFOs. In this scenario, the FIFO would be used only as a rendezvous point in the filesystem between clients and servers on the same host. A process on one host *cannot* send data to a process on another host through a FIFO, even though both processes may be able to open a FIFO that is accessible to both hosts through NFS.

4.9   Iterative versus Concurrent Servers

The server in our simple example from the preceding section is an *iterative server*. It iterates through the client requests, completely handling each client's request before proceeding to the next client. For example, if two clients each send a request to the server at about the same time—the first for a 10-megabyte file that takes 10 seconds (say) to send to the client, and the second for a 10-byte file—the second client must wait at least 10 seconds for the first client to be serviced.

The alternative is a *concurrent server*. The most common type of concurrent server under Unix is called a *one-child-per-client* server, and it has the server call fork to create a new child each time a client request arrives. The new child handles the client request to completion, and the multiprogramming features of Unix provide the concurrency of all the different processes. But there are other techniques that are discussed in detail in Chapter 27 of UNPv1:

- create a pool of children and service a new client with an idle child,
- create one thread per client, and
- create a pool of threads and service a new client with an idle thread.

Although the discussion in UNPv1 is for network servers, the same techniques apply to IPC servers whose clients are on the same host.

Denial-of-Service Attacks

We have already mentioned one problem with an iterative server—some clients must wait longer than expected because they are in line following other clients with longer requests—but another problem exists. Recall our shell example following Figure 4.24 and our discussion of how the server blocks in its call to open for the client FIFO if the client has not yet opened this FIFO (which did not happen until we executed our cat command). This means that a malicious client could tie up the server by sending it a request line, but never opening its FIFO for reading. This is called a *denial-of-service* (DoS) attack. To avoid this, we must be careful when coding the iterative portion of any server, to note where the server might block, and for how long it might block. One way to handle the problem is to place a timeout on certain operations, but it is usually simpler to code the server as a concurrent server, instead of as an iterative server, in which case, this type of denial-of-service attack affects only one child, and not the main server. Even with a concurrent server, denial-of-service attacks can still occur: a malicious client could send lots of independent requests, causing the server to reach its limit of child processes, causing subsequent `forks` to fail.

4.10 Streams and Messages

The examples shown so far, for pipes and FIFOs, have used the stream I/O model, which is natural for Unix. No record boundaries exist—reads and writes do not examine the data at all. A process that reads 100 bytes from a FIFO, for example, cannot tell whether the process that wrote the data into the FIFO did a single write of 100 bytes, five writes of 20 bytes, two writes of 50 bytes, or some other combination of writes that totals 100 bytes., One process could also write 55 bytes into the FIFO, followed by another process writing 45 bytes. The data is a *byte stream* with no interpretation done by the system. If any interpretation is desired, the writing process and the reading process must agree to it a priori and do it themselves.

Sometimes an application wants to impose some structure on the data being transferred. This can happen when the data consists of variable-length messages and the reader must know where the message boundaries are so that it knows when a single message has been read. The following three techniques are commonly used for this:

1. Special termination sequence in-band: many Unix applications use the newline character to delineate each message. The writing process appends a newline to each message, and the reading process reads one line at a time. This is what our client and server did in Figures 4.23 and 4.24 to separate the client requests. In general, this requires that any occurrence of the delimiter in the data must be escaped (that is, somehow flagged as data and not as a delimiter).

   Many Internet applications (FTP, SMTP, HTTP, NNTP) use the 2-character sequence of a carriage return followed by a linefeed (CR/LF) to delineate text records.

2. Explicit length: each record is preceded by its length. We will use this technique shortly. This technique is also used by Sun RPC when used with TCP. One advantage to this technique is that escaping a delimiter that appears in the data is unnecessary, because the receiver does not need to scan all the data, looking for the end of each record.

3. One record per connection: the application closes the connection to its peer (its TCP connection, in the case of a network application, or its IPC connection) to

indicate the end of a record. This requires a new connection for every record, but is used with HTTP 1.0.

The standard I/O library can also be used to read or write a pipe or FIFO. Since the only way to open a pipe is with the `pipe` function, which returns an open descriptor, the standard I/O function `fdopen` must be used to create a new standard I/O *stream* that is then associated with this open descriptor. Since a FIFO has a name, it can be opened using the standard I/O `fopen` function.

More structured messages can also be built, and this capability is provided by both Posix message queues and System V message queues. We will see that each message has a length and a priority (System V calls the latter a "type"). The length and priority are specified by the sender, and after the message is read, both are returned to the reader. Each message is a *record*, similar to UDP datagrams (UNPv1).

We can also add more structure to either a pipe or FIFO ourselves. We define a message in our `mesg.h` header, as shown in Figure 4.25.

pipemesg/mesg.h

```
 1 #include    "unpipc.h"

 2 /* Our own "messages" to use with pipes, FIFOs, and message queues. */

 3          /* want sizeof(struct mymesg) <= PIPE_BUF */
 4 #define MAXMESGDATA (PIPE_BUF - 2*sizeof(long))

 5          /* length of mesg_len and mesg_type */
 6 #define MESGHDRSIZE (sizeof(struct mymesg) - MAXMESGDATA)

 7 struct mymesg {
 8     long    mesg_len;           /* #bytes in mesg_data, can be 0 */
 9     long    mesg_type;          /* message type, must be > 0 */
10     char    mesg_data[MAXMESGDATA];
11 };

12 ssize_t mesg_send(int, struct mymesg *);
13 void    Mesg_send(int, struct mymesg *);
14 ssize_t mesg_recv(int, struct mymesg *);
15 ssize_t Mesg_recv(int, struct mymesg *);
```

pipemesg/mesg.h

Figure 4.25   Our `mymesg` structure and related definitions.

Each message has a *mesg_type*, which we define as an integer whose value must be greater than 0. We ignore the type field for now, but return to it in Chapter 6, when we describe System V message queues. Each message also has a length, and we allow the length to be zero. What we are doing with the `mymesg` structure is to precede each message with its length, instead of using newlines to separate the messages. Earlier, we mentioned two benefits of this design: the receiver need not scan each received byte looking for the end of the message, and there is no need to escape the delimiter (a newline) if it appears in the message.

Figure 4.26 shows a picture of the `mymesg` structure, and how we use it with pipes, FIFOs, and System V message queues.

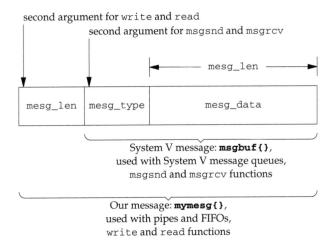

Figure 4.26 Our mymesg structure.

We define two functions to send and receive messages. Figure 4.27 shows our mesg_send function, and Figure 4.28 shows our mesg_recv function.

pipemesg/mesg_send.c
```
1 #include      "mesg.h"

2 ssize_t
3 mesg_send(int fd, struct mymesg *mptr)
4 {
5     return (write(fd, mptr, MESGHDRSIZE + mptr->mesg_len));
6 }
```
pipemesg/mesg_send.c

Figure 4.27 mesg_send function.

pipemesg/mesg_recv.c
```
1 #include      "mesg.h"

2 ssize_t
3 mesg_recv(int fd, struct mymesg *mptr)
4 {
5     size_t  len;
6     ssize_t n;

7         /* read message header first, to get len of data that follows */
8     if ( (n = Read(fd, mptr, MESGHDRSIZE)) == 0)
9         return (0);             /* end of file */
10    else if (n != MESGHDRSIZE)
11        err_quit("message header: expected %d, got %d", MESGHDRSIZE, n);

12    if ( (len = mptr->mesg_len) > 0)
13        if ( (n = Read(fd, mptr->mesg_data, len)) != len)
14            err_quit("message data: expected %d, got %d", len, n);
15    return (len);
16 }
```
pipemesg/mesg_recv.c

Figure 4.28 mesg_recv function.

It now takes two `reads` for each message, one to read the length, and another to read the actual message (if the length is greater than 0).

> Careful readers may note that `mesg_recv` checks for all possible errors and terminates if one occurs. Nevertheless, we still define a wrapper function named `Mesg_recv` and call it from our programs, for consistency.

We now change our client and server functions to use the `mesg_send` and `mesg_recv` functions. Figure 4.29 shows our client.

pipemesg/client.c
```
 1 #include     "mesg.h"

 2 void
 3 client(int readfd, int writefd)
 4 {
 5     size_t  len;
 6     ssize_t n;
 7     struct mymesg mesg;

 8         /* read pathname */
 9     Fgets(mesg.mesg_data, MAXMESGDATA, stdin);
10     len = strlen(mesg.mesg_data);
11     if (mesg.mesg_data[len - 1] == '\n')
12         len--;                  /* delete newline from fgets() */
13     mesg.mesg_len = len;
14     mesg.mesg_type = 1;

15         /* write pathname to IPC channel */
16     Mesg_send(writefd, &mesg);

17         /* read from IPC, write to standard output */
18     while ( (n = Mesg_recv(readfd, &mesg)) > 0)
19         Write(STDOUT_FILENO, mesg.mesg_data, n);
20 }
```
pipemesg/client.c

Figure 4.29 Our `client` function that uses messages.

Read pathname, send to server

8–16   The pathname is read from standard input and then sent to the server using `mesg_send`.

Read file's contents or error message from server

17–19   The client calls `mesg_recv` in a loop, reading everything that the server sends back. By convention, when `mesg_recv` returns a length of 0, this indicates the end of data from the server. We will see that the server includes the newline in each message that it sends to the client, so a blank line will have a message length of 1.

Figure 4.30 shows our server.

pipemesg/server.c

```
 1 #include    "mesg.h"

 2 void
 3 server(int readfd, int writefd)
 4 {
 5     FILE    *fp;
 6     ssize_t n;
 7     struct mymesg mesg;

 8         /* read pathname from IPC channel */
 9     mesg.mesg_type = 1;
10     if ( (n = Mesg_recv(readfd, &mesg)) == 0)
11         err_quit("pathname missing");
12     mesg.mesg_data[n] = '\0';   /* null terminate pathname */

13     if ( (fp = fopen(mesg.mesg_data, "r")) == NULL) {
14             /* error: must tell client */
15         snprintf(mesg.mesg_data + n, sizeof(mesg.mesg_data) - n,
16                 ": can't open, %s\n", strerror(errno));
17         mesg.mesg_len = strlen(mesg.mesg_data);
18         Mesg_send(writefd, &mesg);

19     } else {
20             /* fopen succeeded: copy file to IPC channel */
21         while (Fgets(mesg.mesg_data, MAXMESGDATA, fp) != NULL) {
22             mesg.mesg_len = strlen(mesg.mesg_data);
23             Mesg_send(writefd, &mesg);
24         }
25         Fclose(fp);
26     }

27         /* send a 0-length message to signify the end */
28     mesg.mesg_len = 0;
29     Mesg_send(writefd, &mesg);
30 }
```

pipemesg/server.c

Figure 4.30 Our server function that uses messages.

Read pathname from IPC channel, open file

8–18   The pathname is read from the client. Although the assignment of 1 to mesg_type appears useless (it is overwritten by mesg_recv in Figure 4.28), we call this same function when using System V message queues (Figure 6.10), in which case, this assignment is needed (e.g., Figure 6.13). The standard I/O function fopen opens the file, which differs from Figure 4.10, where we called the Unix I/O function open to obtain a descriptor for the file. The reason we call the standard I/O library here is to call fgets to read the file one line at a time, and then send each line to the client as a message.

Copy file to client

19–26   If the call to fopen succeeds, the file is read using fgets and sent to the client, one line per message. A message with a length of 0 indicates the end of the file.

When using either pipes or FIFOs, we could also close the IPC channel to notify the peer that the end of the input file was encountered. We send back a message with a length of 0, however, because we will encounter other types of IPC that do not have the concept of an end-of-file.

The `main` functions that call our `client` and `server` functions do not change at all. We can use either the pipe version (Figure 4.8) or the FIFO version (Figure 4.16).

4.11 Pipe and FIFO Limits

The only system-imposed limits on pipes and FIFOs are

OPEN_MAX   the maximum number of descriptors open at any time by a process (Posix requires that this be at least 16), and

PIPE_BUF   the maximum amount of data that can be written to a pipe or FIFO atomically (we described this in Section 4.7; Posix requires that this be at least 512).

The value of OPEN_MAX can be queried by calling the `sysconf` function, as we show shortly. It can normally be changed from the shell by executing the `ulimit` command (Bourne shell and KornShell, as we show shortly) or the `limit` command (C shell). It can also be changed from a process by calling the `setrlimit` function (described in detail in Section 7.11 of APUE).

The value of PIPE_BUF is often defined in the `<limits.h>` header, but it is considered a *pathname variable* by Posix. This means that its value can differ, depending on the pathname that is specified (for a FIFO, since pipes do not have names), because different pathnames can end up on different filesystems, and these filesystems might have different characteristics. The value can therefore be obtained at run time by calling either `pathconf` or `fpathconf`. Figure 4.31 shows an example that prints these two limits.

pipe/pipeconf.c

```
1 #include    "unpipc.h"

2 int
3 main(int argc, char **argv)
4 {
5     if (argc != 2)
6         err_quit("usage: pipeconf <pathname>");

7     printf("PIPE_BUF = %ld, OPEN_MAX = %ld\n",
8             Pathconf(argv[1], _PC_PIPE_BUF), Sysconf(_SC_OPEN_MAX));
9     exit(0);
10 }
```

pipe/pipeconf.c

Figure 4.31 Determine values of PIPE_BUF and OPEN_MAX at run time.

Here are some examples, specifying different filesystems:

```
solaris % pipeconf /                    Solaris 2.6 default values
PIPE_BUF = 5120, OPEN_MAX = 64
solaris % pipeconf /home
PIPE_BUF = 5120, OPEN_MAX = 64
solaris % pipeconf /tmp
PIPE_BUF = 5120, OPEN_MAX = 64

alpha % pipeconf /                      Digital Unix 4.0B default values
PIPE_BUF = 4096, OPEN_MAX = 4096
alpha % pipeconf /usr
PIPE_BUF = 4096, OPEN_MAX = 4096
```

We now show how to change the value of OPEN_MAX under Solaris, using the Korn-Shell.

```
solaris % ulimit -nS                    display max # descriptors, soft limit
64
solaris % ulimit -nH                    display max # descriptors, hard limit
1024
solaris % ulimit -nS 512                set soft limit to 512
solaris % pipeconf /                    verify that change has occurred
PIPE_BUF = 5120, OPEN_MAX = 512
```

Although the value of PIPE_BUF can change for a FIFO, depending on the underlying filesystem in which the pathname is stored, this should be extremely rare.

Chapter 2 of APUE describes the fpathconf, pathconf, and sysconf functions, which provide run-time information on certain kernel limits. Posix.1 defines 12 constants that begin with _PC_ and 52 that begin with _SC_. Digital Unix 4.0B and Solaris 2.6 both extend the latter, defining about 100 run-time constants that can be queried with sysconf.

The getconf command is defined by Posix.2, and it prints the value of most of these implementation limits. For example

```
alpha % getconf OPEN_MAX
4096
alpha % getconf PIPE_BUF /
4096
```

4.12 Summary

Pipes and FIFOs are fundamental building blocks for many applications. Pipes are commonly used with the shells, but also used from within programs, often to pass information from a child back to a parent. Some of the code involved in using a pipe (pipe, fork, close, exec, and waitpid) can be avoided by using popen and pclose, which handle all the details and invoke a shell.

FIFOs are similar to pipes, but are created by mkfifo and then opened by open. We must be careful when opening a FIFO, because numerous rules (Figure 4.21) govern whether an open blocks or not.

Using pipes and FIFOs, we looked at some client–server designs: one server with multiple clients, and iterative versus concurrent servers. An iterative server handles one client request at a time, in a serial fashion, and these types of servers are normally open to denial-of-service attacks. A concurrent server has another process or thread handle each client request.

One characteristic of pipes and FIFOs is that their data is a byte stream, similar to a TCP connection. Any delineation of this byte stream into records is left to the application. We will see in the next two chapters that message queues provide record boundaries, similar to UDP datagrams.

Exercises

4.1 In the transition from Figure 4.3 to Figure 4.4, what could happen if the child did not close(fd[1])?

4.2 In describing mkfifo in Section 4.6, we said that to open an existing FIFO or create a new FIFO if it does not already exist, call mkfifo, check for an error of EEXIST, and if this occurs, call open. What can happen if the logic is changed, calling open first and then mkfifo if the FIFO does not exist?

4.3 What happens in the call to popen in Figure 4.15 if the shell encounters an error?

4.4 Remove the open of the server's FIFO in Figure 4.23 and verify that this causes the server to terminate when no more clients exist.

4.5 In Figure 4.23, we noted that when the server starts, it blocks in its first call to open until the first client opens this FIFO for writing. How can we get around this, causing both opens to return immediately, and block instead in the first call to readline?

4.6 What happens to the client in Figure 4.24 if it swaps the order of its two calls to open?

4.7 Why is a signal generated for the writer of a pipe or FIFO after the reader disappears, but not for the reader of a pipe or FIFO after its writer disappears?

4.8 Write a small test program to determine whether fstat returns the number of bytes of data currently in a FIFO as the st_size member of the stat structure.

4.9 Write a small test program to determine what select returns when you select for writability on a pipe descriptor whose read end has been closed.

5

Posix Message Queues

5.1 Introduction

A message queue can be thought of as a linked list of messages. Threads with adequate permission can put messages onto the queue, and threads with adequate permission can remove messages from the queue. Each message is a *record* (recall our discussion of streams versus messages in Section 4.10), and each message is assigned a priority by the sender. No requirement exists that someone be waiting for a message to arrive on a queue before some process writes a message to that queue. This is in contrast to both pipes and FIFOs, for which having a writer makes no sense unless a reader also exists.

A process can write some messages to a queue, terminate, and have the messages read by another process at a later time. We say that message queues have *kernel persistence* (Section 1.3). This differs from pipes and FIFOs. We said in Chapter 4 that any data remaining in a pipe or FIFO when the last close of the pipe or FIFO takes place, is discarded.

This chapter looks at Posix message queues and Chapter 6 looks at System V message queues. Many similarities exist between the two sets of functions, with the main differences being:

- A read on a Posix message queue always returns the oldest message of the highest priority, whereas a read on a System V message queue can return a message of any desired priority.

- Posix message queues allow the generation of a signal or the initiation of a thread when a message is placed onto an empty queue, whereas nothing similar is provided by System V message queues.

Every message on a queue has the following attributes:

- an unsigned integer priority (Posix) or a long integer type (System V),
- the length of the data portion of the message (which can be 0), and
- the data itself (if the length is greater than 0).

Notice that these characteristics differ from pipes and FIFOs. The latter two are byte streams with no message boundaries, and no type associated with each message. We discussed this in Section 4.10 and added our own message interface to pipes and FIFOs.

Figure 5.1 shows one possible arrangement of a message queue.

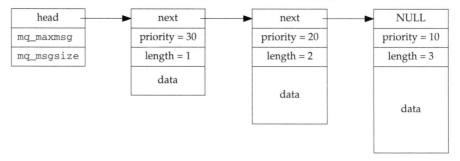

Figure 5.1 Possible arrangement of a Posix message queue containing three messages.

We are assuming a linked list, and the head of the list contains the two attributes of the queue: the maximum number of messages allowed on the queue, and the maximum size of a message. We say more about these attributes in Section 5.3.

In this chapter, we use a technique that we use in later chapters when looking at message queues, semaphores, and shared memory. Since all of these IPC objects have at least kernel persistence (recall Section 1.3), we can write small programs that use these techniques, to let us experiment with them and learn more about their operation. For example, we can write a program that creates a Posix message queue, write another program that adds a message to a Posix message queue, and write another that reads from one of these queues. By writing messages with different priorities, we can see how these messages are returned by the mq_receive function.

5.2 `mq_open`, `mq_close`, and `mq_unlink` Functions

The mq_open function creates a new message queue or opens an existing message queue.

```
#include <mqueue.h>

mqd_t mq_open(const char *name, int oflag, ...
                /* mode_t mode, struct mq_attr *attr */ );
```

                                Returns: message queue descriptor if OK, –1 on error

We describe the rules about the *name* argument in Section 2.2.

The *oflag* argument is one of O_RDONLY, O_WRONLY, or O_RDWR, and may be bit-wise-ORed with O_CREAT, O_EXCL, and O_NONBLOCK. We describe all these flags in Section 2.3.

When a new queue is created (O_CREAT is specified and the message queue does not already exist), the *mode* and *attr* arguments are required. We describe the *mode* values in Figure 2.4. The *attr* argument lets us specify some attributes for the queue. If this argument is a null pointer, the default attributes apply. We discuss these attributes in Section 5.3.

The return value from mq_open is called a *message queue descriptor*, but it need not be (and probably is not) a small integer like a file descriptor or a socket descriptor. This value is used as the first argument to the remaining seven message queue functions.

> Solaris 2.6 defines mqd_t as a void* whereas Digital Unix 4.0B defines it as an int. In our sample implementation in Section 5.8, these descriptors are pointers to a structure. Calling these datatypes a descriptor is an unfortunate mistake.

An open message queue is closed by mq_close.

```
#include <mqueue.h>

int mq_close(mqd_t mqdes);
```
                                                          Returns: 0 if OK, −1 on error

The functionality is similar to the close of an open file: the calling process can no longer use the descriptor, but the message queue is not removed from the system. If the process terminates, all open message queues are closed, as if mq_close were called.

To remove a *name* that was used as an argument to mq_open from the system, mq_unlink must be called.

```
#include <mqueue.h>

int mq_unlink(const char *name);
```
                                                          Returns: 0 if OK, −1 on error

Message queues have a reference count of how many times they are currently open (just like files), and this function is similar to the unlink function for a file: the *name* can be removed from the system while its reference count is greater than 0, but the destruction of the queue (versus removing its name from the system) does not take place until the last mq_close occurs.

Posix message queues have at least *kernel persistence* (recall Section 1.3). That is, they exist along with any messages written to the queue, even if no process currently has the queue open, until the queue is removed by calling mq_unlink and having the queue reference count reach 0.

We will see that if these message queues are implemented using memory-mapped files (Section 12.2), then they can have filesystem persistence, but this is not required and cannot be counted on.

Example: `mqcreate1` Program

Since Posix message queues have at least kernel persistence, we can write a set of small programs to manipulate these queues, providing an easy way to experiment with them. The program in Figure 5.2 creates a message queue whose name is specified as the command-line argument.

```
                                                            pxmsg/mqcreate1.c
 1 #include     "unpipc.h"

 2 int
 3 main(int argc, char **argv)
 4 {
 5     int     c, flags;
 6     mqd_t   mqd;

 7     flags = O_RDWR | O_CREAT;
 8     while ( (c = Getopt(argc, argv, "e")) != -1) {
 9         switch (c) {
10         case 'e':
11             flags |= O_EXCL;
12             break;
13         }
14     }
15     if (optind != argc - 1)
16         err_quit("usage: mqcreate [ -e ] <name>");

17     mqd = Mq_open(argv[optind], flags, FILE_MODE, NULL);

18     Mq_close(mqd);
19     exit(0);
20 }
                                                            pxmsg/mqcreate1.c
```

Figure 5.2 Create a message queue with the exclusive-create flags specified.

8-16   We allow a -e option that specifies an exclusive create. (We say more about the getopt function and our `Getopt` wrapper with Figure 5.5.) Upon return, getopt stores in `optind` the index of the next argument to be processed.

17   We call mq_open with the IPC name from the command-line, without calling our px_ipc_name function (Section 2.2). This lets us see exactly how the implementation handles these Posix IPC names. (We do this with all our simple test programs throughout this book.)

Here is the output under Solaris 2.6:

```
solaris % mqcreate1 /temp.1234                    first create works
solaris % ls -l /tmp/.*1234
-rw-rw-rw-   1 rstevens other1   132632 Oct 23 17:08 /tmp/.MQDtemp.1234
-rw-rw-rw-   1 rstevens other1        0 Oct 23 17:08 /tmp/.MQLtemp.1234
-rw-r--r--   1 rstevens other1        0 Oct 23 17:08 /tmp/.MQPtemp.1234
solaris % mqcreate1 -e /temp.1234                 second create with -e fails
mq_open error for /temp.1234: File exists
```

(We call this version of our program mqcreate1, because we enhance it in Figure 5.5 after describing attributes.) The third file has the permissions that we specify with our FILE_MODE constant (read–write for the user, read-only for the group and other), but the other two files have different permissions. We guess that the filename containing D contains the data, the filename containing L is some type of lock, and the filename containing P specifies the permissions.

Under Digital Unix 4.0B, we can see the actual pathname that is created.

```
alpha % mqcreate1 /tmp/myq.1234
alpha % ls -l  /tmp/myq.1234
-rw-r--r--   1 rstevens system   11976 Oct 23 17:04 /tmp/myq.1234
alpha % mqcreate1 -e /tmp/myq.1234
mq_open error for /tmp/myq.1234: File exists
```

Example: mqunlink Program

Figure 5.3 is our mqunlink program, which removes a message queue from the system.

pxmsg/mqunlink.c
```
1 #include    "unpipc.h"

2 int
3 main(int argc, char **argv)
4 {
5     if (argc != 2)
6         err_quit("usage: mqunlink <name>");

7     Mq_unlink(argv[1]);

8     exit(0);
9 }
```
pxmsg/mqunlink.c

Figure 5.3 mq_unlink a message queue.

We can remove the message queue that was created by our mqcreate program.

```
solaris % mqunlink /temp.1234
```

All three files in the /tmp directory that were shown earlier are removed.

5.3   mq_getattr and mq_setattr Functions

Each message queue has four attributes, all of which are returned by mq_getattr and one of which is set by mq_setattr.

```
#include <mqueue.h>

int mq_getattr(mqd_t mqdes, struct mq_attr *attr);

int mq_setattr(mqd_t mqdes, const struct mq_attr *attr, struct mq_attr *oattr);
```
Both return: 0 if OK, −1 on error

The mq_attr structure contains these attributes.

```
struct mq_attr {
  long  mq_flags;    /* message queue flag: 0, O_NONBLOCK */
  long  mq_maxmsg;   /* max number of messages allowed on queue */
  long  mq_msgsize;  /* max size of a message (in bytes) */
  long  mq_curmsgs;  /* number of messages currently on queue */
};
```

A pointer to one of these structures can be passed as the fourth argument to mq_open, allowing us to set both mq_maxmsg and mq_msgsize when the queue is created. The other two members of this structure are ignored by mq_open.

mq_getattr fills in the structure pointed to by *attr* with the current attributes for the queue.

mq_setattr sets the attributes for the queue, but only the mq_flags member of the mq_attr structure pointed to by *attr* is used, to set or clear the nonblocking flag. The other three members of the structure are ignored: the maximum number of messages per queue and the maximum number of bytes per message can be set only when the queue is created, and the number of messages currently on the queue can be fetched but not set.

Additionally, if the *oattr* pointer is nonnull, the previous attributes of the queue are returned (mq_flags, mq_maxmsg, and mq_msgsize), along with the current status of the queue (mq_curmsgs).

Example: mqgetattr Program

The program in Figure 5.4 opens a specified message queue and prints its attributes.

———————————————————————————————— *pxmsg/mqgetattr.c*
```
 1 #include    "unpipc.h"

 2 int
 3 main(int argc, char **argv)
 4 {
 5     mqd_t   mqd;
 6     struct mq_attr attr;

 7     if (argc != 2)
 8         err_quit("usage: mqgetattr <name>");

 9     mqd = Mq_open(argv[1], O_RDONLY);

10     Mq_getattr(mqd, &attr);
11     printf("max #msgs = %ld, max #bytes/msg = %ld, "
12            "#currently on queue = %ld\n",
13            attr.mq_maxmsg, attr.mq_msgsize, attr.mq_curmsgs);

14     Mq_close(mqd);
15     exit(0);
16 }
```
———————————————————————————————— *pxmsg/mqgetattr.c*

Figure 5.4 Fetch and print the attributes of a message queue.

We can create a message queue and print its default attributes.

```
solaris % mqcreate1 /hello.world
solaris % mqgetattr /hello.world
max #msgs = 128, max #bytes/msg = 1024, #currently on queue = 0
```

We can now see that the file size listed by `ls` when we created a queue with the default attributes following Figure 5.2 was $128 \times 1024 + 1560 = 132,632$. The 1560 extra bytes are probably overhead information: 8 bytes per message plus an additional 536 bytes.

Example: `mqcreate` Program

We can modify our program from Figure 5.2, allowing us to specify the maximum number of messages for the queue and the maximum size of each message. We cannot specify one and not the other; both must be specified (but see Exercise 5.1). Figure 5.5 is the new program.

pxmsg/mqcreate.c

```
 1 #include     "unpipc.h"

 2 struct mq_attr attr;              /* mq_maxmsg and mq_msgsize both init to 0 */

 3 int
 4 main(int argc, char **argv)
 5 {
 6     int     c, flags;
 7     mqd_t   mqd;

 8     flags = O_RDWR | O_CREAT;
 9     while ( (c = Getopt(argc, argv, "em:z:")) != -1) {
10         switch (c) {
11         case 'e':
12             flags |= O_EXCL;
13             break;

14         case 'm':
15             attr.mq_maxmsg = atol(optarg);
16             break;

17         case 'z':
18             attr.mq_msgsize = atol(optarg);
19             break;
20         }
21     }
22     if (optind != argc - 1)
23         err_quit("usage: mqcreate [ -e ] [ -m maxmsg -z msgsize ] <name>");

24     if ((attr.mq_maxmsg != 0 && attr.mq_msgsize == 0) ||
25         (attr.mq_maxmsg == 0 && attr.mq_msgsize != 0))
26         err_quit("must specify both -m maxmsg and -z msgsize");

27     mqd = Mq_open(argv[optind], flags, FILE_MODE,
28                   (attr.mq_maxmsg != 0) ? &attr : NULL);

29     Mq_close(mqd);
30     exit(0);
31 }
```

pxmsg/mqcreate.c

Figure 5.5 Modification of Figure 5.2 allowing attributes to be specified.

To specify that a command-line option requires an argument, we specify a colon following the option character for the m and z options in the call to getopt. When processing the option character, optarg points to the argument.

> Our Getopt wrapper function calls the standard library's getopt function and terminates the process if getopt detects an error: encountering an option letter not included in the third argument, or an option letter without a required argument (indicated by a colon following the option letter in the third argument). In either case, getopt writes an error message to standard error and returns an error, which causes our Getopt wrapper to terminate. For example, the following two errors are detected by getopt:
>
> ```
> solaris % mqcreate -z
> mqcreate: option requires an argument -- z
> solaris % mqcreate -q
> mqcreate: illegal option -- q
> ```
>
> The following error (not specifying the required name argument) is detected by our program:
>
> ```
> solaris % mqcreate
> usage: mqcreate [ -e ] [ -m maxmsg -z msgsize ] <name>
> ```

If neither of the two new options are specified, we must pass a null pointer as the final argument to mq_open, else we pass a pointer to our attr structure.

We now run this new version of our program, specifying a maximum of 1024 messages, each message containing up to 8192 bytes.

```
solaris % mqcreate -e -m 1024 -z 8192 /foobar
solaris % ls -al /tmp/.*foobar
-rw-rw-rw-   1 rstevens other1 8397336 Oct 25 11:29 /tmp/.MQDfoobar
-rw-rw-rw-   1 rstevens other1       0 Oct 25 11:29 /tmp/.MQLfoobar
-rw-r--r--   1 rstevens other1       0 Oct 25 11:29 /tmp/.MQPfoobar
```

The size of the file containing the data for this queue accounts for the maximum number of maximum-sized messages ($1024 \times 8192 = 8,388,608$), and the remaining 8728 bytes of overhead allows room for 8 bytes per message (8×1024) plus an additional 536 bytes.

If we execute the same program under Digital Unix 4.0B, we have

```
alpha % mqcreate -m 256 -z 2048 /tmp/bigq
alpha % ls -l /tmp/bigq
-rw-r--r--   1 rstevens system  537288 Oct 25 15:38 /tmp/bigq
```

This implementation appears to allow room for the maximum number of maximum-sized messages ($256 \times 2048 = 524,288$) and the remaining 13000 bytes of overhead allows room for 48 bytes per message (48×256) plus an additional 712 bytes.

5.4   mq_send and mq_receive Functions

These two functions place a message onto a queue and take a message off a queue. Every message has a *priority*, which is an unsigned integer less than MQ_PRIO_MAX. Posix requires that this upper limit be at least 32.

> Solaris 2.6 has an upper limit of 32, but this limit is 256 with Digital Unix 4.0B. We show how to obtain these values with Figure 5.8.

mq_receive always returns the oldest message of the highest priority from the specified queue, and the priority can be returned in addition to the actual contents of the message and its length.

> This operation of mq_receive differs from that of the System V msgrcv (Section 6.4). System V messages have a type field, which is similar to the priority, but with msgrcv, we can specify three different scenarios as to which message is returned: the oldest message on the queue, the oldest message with a specific type, or the oldest message whose type is less than or equal to some value.

```
#include <mqueue.h>

int mq_send(mqd_t mqdes, const char *ptr, size_t len, unsigned int prio);
```
                                                          Returns: 0 if OK, −1 on error

```
ssize_t mq_receive(mqd_t mqdes, char *ptr, size_t len, unsigned int *priop);
```
                                          Returns: number of bytes in message if OK, −1 on error

---

The first three arguments to both functions are similar to the first three arguments for write and read, respectively.

> Declaring the pointer argument to the buffer as a char* looks like a mistake. void* would be more consistent with other Posix.1 functions.

The value of the *len* argument for mq_receive must be at least as big as the maximum size of any message that can be added to this queue, the mq_msgsize member of the mq_attr structure for this queue. If *len* is smaller than this value, EMSGSIZE is returned immediately.

> This means that most applications that use Posix message queues must call mq_getattr after opening the queue, to determine the maximum message size, and then allocate one or more read buffers of that size. By requiring that the buffer always be large enough for any message on the queue, mq_receive does not need to return a notification if the message is larger than the buffer. Compare, for example, the MSG_NOERROR flag and the E2BIG error possible with System V message queues (Section 6.4) and the MSG_TRUNC flag with the recvmsg function that is used with UDP datagrams (Section 13.5 of UNPv1).

prio is the priority of the message for mq_send, and its value must be less than MQ_PRIO_MAX. If *priop* is a nonnull pointer for mq_receive, the priority of the returned message is stored through this pointer. If the application does not need messages of differing priorities, then the priority can always be specified as 0 for mq_send, and the final argument for mq_receive can be a null pointer.

> A 0-byte message *is* allowed. This instance is one in which what is important is not what is said in the standard (i.e., Posix.1), but what is *not* said: nowhere is a 0-byte message forbidden. The return value from mq_receive is the number of bytes in the message (if OK) or −1 (if an error), so a return value of 0 indicates a 0-length message.

> One feature is missing from both Posix message queues and System V message queues: accurately identifying the sender of each message to the receiver. This information could be useful

in many applications. Unfortunately, most IPC messaging mechanisms do not identify the sender. In Section 15.5, we describe how doors provide this identity. Section 14.8 of UNPv1 describes how BSD/OS provides this identity when a Unix domain socket is used. Section 15.3.1 of APUE describes how SVR4 passes the sender's identity across a pipe when a descriptor is passed across the pipe. The BSD/OS technique is not widely implemented, and although the SVR4 technique is part of Unix 98, it requires passing a descriptor across the pipe, which is normally more expensive than just passing data across a pipe. We cannot have the sender include its identity (e.g., its effective user ID) with the message, as we cannot trust the sender to tell the truth. Although the access permissions on a message queue determine whether the sender is allowed to place a message onto the queue, this still does not identify the sender. The possibility exists to create one queue per sender (which we talk about with regard to System V message queues in Section 6.8), but this does not scale well for large applications. Lastly, realize that if the message queue functions are implemented entirely as user functions (as we show in Section 5.8), and not within the kernel, then we could not trust any sender identity that accompanied the message, as it would be easy to forge.

Example: `mqsend` Program

Figure 5.6 shows our program that adds a message to a queue.

pxmsg/mqsend.c
```
 1 #include    "unpipc.h"

 2 int
 3 main(int argc, char **argv)
 4 {
 5     mqd_t    mqd;
 6     void    *ptr;
 7     size_t   len;
 8     uint_t   prio;

 9     if (argc != 4)
10         err_quit("usage: mqsend <name> <#bytes> <priority>");
11     len = atoi(argv[2]);
12     prio = atoi(argv[3]);

13     mqd = Mq_open(argv[1], O_WRONLY);

14     ptr = Calloc(len, sizeof(char));
15     Mq_send(mqd, ptr, len, prio);

16     exit(0);
17 }
```
pxmsg/mqsend.c

Figure 5.6 mqsend program.

Both the size of the message and its priority must be specified as command-line arguments. The buffer is allocated by `calloc`, which initializes it to 0.

Example: `mqreceive` Program

The program in Figure 5.7 reads the next message from a queue.

pxmsg/mqreceive.c

```
 1 #include      "unpipc.h"

 2 int
 3 main(int argc, char **argv)
 4 {
 5     int      c, flags;
 6     mqd_t    mqd;
 7     ssize_t  n;
 8     uint_t   prio;
 9     void     *buff;
10     struct mq_attr attr;

11     flags = O_RDONLY;
12     while ( (c = Getopt(argc, argv, "n")) != -1) {
13         switch (c) {
14         case 'n':
15             flags |= O_NONBLOCK;
16             break;
17         }
18     }
19     if (optind != argc - 1)
20         err_quit("usage: mqreceive [ -n ] <name>");

21     mqd = Mq_open(argv[optind], flags);
22     Mq_getattr(mqd, &attr);

23     buff = Malloc(attr.mq_msgsize);

24     n = Mq_receive(mqd, buff, attr.mq_msgsize, &prio);
25     printf("read %ld bytes, priority = %u\n", (long) n, prio);

26     exit(0);
27 }
```

pxmsg/mqreceive.c

Figure 5.7 mqreceive program.

Allow -n option to specify nonblocking

14-17   A command-line option of −n specifies nonblocking, which causes our program to return an error if no messages are in the queue.

Open queue and get attributes

21-25   We open the queue and then get its attributes by calling mq_getattr. We need to determine the maximum message size, because we must allocate a buffer of this size for the call to mq_receive. We print the size of the message that is read and its priority.

> Since n is a size_t datatype and we do not know whether this is an int or a long, we cast the value to be a long integer and use the %ld format string. On a 64-bit implementation, int will be a 32-bit integer, but long and size_t will both be 64-bit integers.

We can use these two programs to see how the priority field is used.

```
solaris % mqcreate /test1                        create and get attributes
solaris % mqgetattr /test1
max #msgs = 128, max #bytes/msg = 1024, #currently on queue = 0

solaris % mqsend /test1 100 99999                send with invalid priority
mq_send error: Invalid argument

solaris % mqsend /test1 100 6                     100 bytes, priority of 6
solaris % mqsend /test1 50 18                     50 bytes, priority of 18
solaris % mqsend /test1 33 18                     33 bytes, priority of 18

solaris % mqreceive /test1
read 50 bytes, priority = 18                      oldest, highest priority message is returned
solaris % mqreceive /test1
read 33 bytes, priority = 18
solaris % mqreceive /test1
read 100 bytes, priority = 6
solaris % mqreceive -n /test1                     specify nonblocking; queue is empty
mq_receive error: Resource temporarily unavailable
```

We can see that mq_receive returns the oldest message of the highest priority.

5.5   Message Queue Limits

We have already encountered two limits for any given queue, both of which are established when the queue is created:

mq_maxmsg   the maximum number of messages on the queue, and

mq_msgsize the maximum size of a given message.

No inherent limits exist on either value, although for the two implementations that we have looked at, room in the filesystem must exist for a file whose size is the product of these two numbers, plus some small amount of overhead. Virtual memory requirements may also exist based on the size of the queue (see Exercise 5.5).

Two other limits are defined by the implementation:

MQ_OPEN_MAX   the maximum number of message queues that a process can have open at once (Posix requires that this be at least 8), and

MQ_PRIO_MAX   the maximum value plus one for the priority of any message (Posix requires that this be at least 32).

These two constants are often defined in the <unistd.h> header and can also be obtained at run time by calling the sysconf function, as we show next.

Example: mqsysconf Program

The program in Figure 5.8 calls sysconf and prints the two implementation-defined limits for message queues.

pxmsg/mqsysconf.c
```
1 #include    "unpipc.h"

2 int
3 main(int argc, char **argv)
4 {
5     printf("MQ_OPEN_MAX = %ld, MQ_PRIO_MAX = %ld\n",
6             Sysconf(_SC_MQ_OPEN_MAX), Sysconf(_SC_MQ_PRIO_MAX));
7     exit(0);
8 }
```
pxmsg/mqsysconf.c

Figure 5.8 Call sysconf to obtain message queue limits.

If we execute this on our two systems, we obtain

```
solaris % mqsysconf
MQ_OPEN_MAX = 32, MQ_PRIO_MAX = 32

alpha % mqsysconf
MQ_OPEN_MAX = 64, MQ_PRIO_MAX = 256
```

5.6   mq_notify Function

One problem that we will see with System V message queues in Chapter 6 is their inability to notify a process when a message is placed onto a queue. We can block in a call to msgrcv, but that prevents us from doing anything else while we are waiting. If we specify the nonblocking flag for msgrcv (IPC_NOWAIT), we do not block, but we must continually call this function to determine when a message arrives. We said this is called *polling* and is a waste of CPU time. We want a way for the system to tell us when a message is placed onto a queue that was previously empty.

> This section and the remaining sections of this chapter contain advanced topics that you may want to skip on a first reading.

Posix message queues allow for an *asynchronous event notification* when a message is placed onto an empty message queue. This notification can be either

- the generation of a signal, or
- the creation of a thread to execute a specified function.

We establish this notification by calling mq_notify.

```
#include <mqueue.h>

int mq_notify(mqd_t mqdes, const struct sigevent *notification);
```
                                                              Returns: 0 if OK, −1 on error

This function establishes or removes the asynchronous event notification for the specified queue. The sigevent structure is new with the Posix.1 realtime signals, which we say more about in the next section. This structure and all of the new signal-related constants introduced in this chapter are defined by <signal.h>.

```
union sigval {
  int    sival_int;              /* integer value */
  void  *sival_ptr;              /* pointer value */
};

struct sigevent {
  int              sigev_notify; /* SIGEV_{NONE,SIGNAL,THREAD} */
  int              sigev_signo;  /* signal number if SIGEV_SIGNAL */
  union sigval     sigev_value;  /* passed to signal handler or thread */
                                 /* following two if SIGEV_THREAD */
  void             (*sigev_notify_function)(union sigval);
  pthread_attr_t  *sigev_notify_attributes;
};
```

We will show some examples shortly of the different ways to use this notification, but a few rules apply in general for this function.

1. If the *notification* argument is nonnull, then the process wants to be notified when a message arrives for the specified queue and the queue is empty. We say that "the process is registered for notification for the queue."

2. If the *notification* argument is a null pointer and if the process is currently registered for notification for the queue, the existing registration is removed.

3. Only one process at any given time can be registered for notification for a given queue.

4. When a message arrives for a queue that was previously empty and a process is registered for notification for the queue, the notification is sent only if no thread is blocked in a call to mq_receive for that queue. That is, blocking in a call to mq_receive takes precedence over any registration for notification.

5. When the notification is sent to the registered process, the registration is removed. The process must reregister (if desired) by calling mq_notify again.

> One of the original problems with Unix signals was that a signal's action was reset to its default each time the signal was generated (Section 10.4 of APUE). Usually the first function called by a signal handler was signal, to reestablish the handler. This provided a small window of time, between the signal's generation and the process reestablishing its signal handler, during which another occurrence of that signal could terminate the process. At first glance, we seem to have a similar problem with mq_notify, since the process must reregister each time the notification occurs. But message queues are different from signals, because the notification cannot occur again until the queue is empty. Therefore, we must be careful to reregister *before* reading the message from the queue.

Example: Simple Signal Notification

Before getting into the details of Posix realtime signals or threads, we can write a simple program that causes SIGUSR1 to be generated when a message is placed onto an empty queue. We show this program in Figure 5.9 and note that this program contains an error that we talk about in detail shortly.

─── *pxmsg/mqnotifysig1.c*

```
 1 #include    "unpipc.h"

 2 mqd_t    mqd;
 3 void     *buff;
 4 struct mq_attr attr;
 5 struct sigevent sigev;

 6 static void sig_usr1(int);

 7 int
 8 main(int argc, char **argv)
 9 {
10     if (argc != 2)
11         err_quit("usage: mqnotifysig1 <name>");

12         /* open queue, get attributes, allocate read buffer */
13     mqd = Mq_open(argv[1], O_RDONLY);
14     Mq_getattr(mqd, &attr);
15     buff = Malloc(attr.mq_msgsize);

16         /* establish signal handler, enable notification */
17     Signal(SIGUSR1, sig_usr1);
18     sigev.sigev_notify = SIGEV_SIGNAL;
19     sigev.sigev_signo = SIGUSR1;
20     Mq_notify(mqd, &sigev);

21     for ( ; ; )
22         pause();                 /* signal handler does everything */
23     exit(0);
24 }

25 static void
26 sig_usr1(int signo)
27 {
28     ssize_t n;

29     Mq_notify(mqd, &sigev);      /* reregister first */
30     n = Mq_receive(mqd, buff, attr.mq_msgsize, NULL);
31     printf("SIGUSR1 received, read %ld bytes\n", (long) n);
32     return;
33 }
```

─── *pxmsg/mqnotifysig1.c*

Figure 5.9 Generate SIGUSR1 when message placed onto an empty queue (incorrect version).

Declare globals

2–6   We declare some globals that are used by both the main function and our signal handler (sig_usr1).

Open queue, get attributes, allocate read buffer

12–15   We open the message queue, obtain its attributes, and allocate a read buffer.

Establish signal handler, enable notification

16–20   We first establish our signal handler for SIGUSR1. We fill in the sigev_notify member of the sigevent structure with the SIGEV_SIGNAL constant, which says that

we want a signal generated when the queue goes from empty to not-empty. We set the
`sigev_signo` member to the signal that we want generated and call `mq_notify`.

Infinite loop

21–22   Our `main` function is then an infinite loop that goes to sleep in the `pause` function,
which returns −1 each time a signal is caught.

Catch signal, read message

25–33   Our signal handler calls `mq_notify`, to reregister for the next event, reads the message, and prints its length. In this program, we ignore the received message's priority.

> The `return` statement at the end of `sig_usr1` is not needed, since there is no return value
> and falling off the end of the function is an implicit return to the caller. Nevertheless, the
> author always codes an explicit `return` at the end of a signal handler to reiterate that the
> return from this function is special. It might cause the premature return (with an error of
> `EINTR`) of a function call in the thread that handles the signal.

We now run this program from one window

```
solaris % mqcreate /test1            create queue
solaris % mqnotifysig1 /test1        start program from Figure 5.9
```

and then execute the following commands from another window:

```
solaris % mqsend /test1 50 16        send 50-byte message with priority of 16
```

As expected, our `mqnotifysig1` program outputs `SIGUSR1 received, read 50`
`bytes`.

We can verify that only one process at a time can be registered for the notification,
by starting another copy of our program from another window:

```
solaris % mqnotifysig1 /test1
mq_notify error: Device busy
```

This error message corresponds to `EBUSY`.

Posix Signals: Async-Signal-Safe Functions

The problem with Figure 5.9 is that it calls `mq_notify`, `mq_receive`, and `printf`
from the signal handler. None of these functions may be called from a signal handler.

Posix uses the term *async-signal-safe* to describe the functions that may be called
from a signal handler. Figure 5.10 lists these Posix functions, along with a few that are
added by Unix 98.

Functions not listed may not be called from a signal handler. Note that none of the
standard I/O functions are listed and none of the `pthread_XXX` functions are listed.
Of all the IPC functions covered in this text, only `sem_post`, `read`, and `write` are
listed (we are assuming the latter two would be used with pipes and FIFOs).

> ANSI C lists four functions that may be called from a signal handler: `abort`, `exit`, `longjmp`,
> and `signal`. The first three are not listed as async-signal-safe by Unix 98.

access	fpathconf	rename	sysconf
aio_return	fstat	rmdir	tcdrain
aio_suspend	fsync	sem_post	tcflow
alarm	getegid	setgid	tcflush
cfgetispeed	geteuid	setpgid	tcgetattr
cfgetospeed	getgid	setsid	tcgetpgrp
cfsetispeed	getgroups	setuid	tcsendbreak
cfsetospeed	getpgrp	sigaction	tcsetattr
chdir	getpid	sigaddset	tcsetpgrp
chmod	getppid	sigdelset	time
chown	getuid	sigemptyset	timer_getoverrun
clock_gettime	kill	sigfillset	timer_gettime
close	link	sigismember	timer_settime
creat	lseek	signal	times
dup	mkdir	sigpause	umask
dup2	mkfifo	sigpending	uname
execle	open	sigprocmask	unlink
execve	pathconf	sigqueue	utime
_exit	pause	sigset	wait
fcntl	pipe	sigsuspend	waitpid
fdatasync	raise	sleep	write
fork	read	stat	

Figure 5.10 Functions that are async-signal-safe.

Example: Signal Notification

One way to avoid calling *any* function from a signal handler is to have the handler just set a global flag that some thread examines to determine when a message has been received. Figure 5.11 shows this technique, although it contains a different error, which we describe shortly.

Global variable

2   Since the only operation performed by our signal handler is to set mqflag nonzero, the global variables from Figure 5.9 need not be global. Reducing the number of global variables is always a good technique, especially when threads are being used.

Open message queue

15–18   We open the message queue, obtain its attributes, and allocate a receive buffer.

Initialize signal sets

19–22   We initialize three signal sets and turn on the bit for SIGUSR1 in the set newmask.

Establish signal handler, enable notification

23–27   We establish a signal handler for SIGUSR1, fill in our sigevent structure, and call mq_notify.

pxmsg/mqnotifysig2.c

```
 1 #include    "unpipc.h"

 2 volatile sig_atomic_t mqflag;    /* set nonzero by signal handler */
 3 static void sig_usr1(int);

 4 int
 5 main(int argc, char **argv)
 6 {
 7     mqd_t    mqd;
 8     void    *buff;
 9     ssize_t n;
10     sigset_t zeromask, newmask, oldmask;
11     struct mq_attr attr;
12     struct sigevent sigev;

13     if (argc != 2)
14         err_quit("usage: mqnotifysig2 <name>");

15         /* open queue, get attributes, allocate read buffer */
16     mqd = Mq_open(argv[1], O_RDONLY);
17     Mq_getattr(mqd, &attr);
18     buff = Malloc(attr.mq_msgsize);

19     Sigemptyset(&zeromask);      /* no signals blocked */
20     Sigemptyset(&newmask);
21     Sigemptyset(&oldmask);
22     Sigaddset(&newmask, SIGUSR1);

23         /* establish signal handler, enable notification */
24     Signal(SIGUSR1, sig_usr1);
25     sigev.sigev_notify = SIGEV_SIGNAL;
26     sigev.sigev_signo = SIGUSR1;
27     Mq_notify(mqd, &sigev);

28     for ( ; ; ) {
29         Sigprocmask(SIG_BLOCK, &newmask, &oldmask);     /* block SIGUSR1 */
30         while (mqflag == 0)
31             sigsuspend(&zeromask);
32         mqflag = 0;                /* reset flag */

33         Mq_notify(mqd, &sigev); /* reregister first */
34         n = Mq_receive(mqd, buff, attr.mq_msgsize, NULL);
35         printf("read %ld bytes\n", (long) n);
36         Sigprocmask(SIG_UNBLOCK, &newmask, NULL);    /* unblock SIGUSR1 */
37     }
38     exit(0);
39 }

40 static void
41 sig_usr1(int signo)
42 {
43     mqflag = 1;
44     return;
45 }
```

pxmsg/mqnotifysig2.c

Figure 5.11 Signal handler just sets a flag for main thread (incorrect version).

Wait for signal handler to set flag

28-32   We call sigprocmask to block SIGUSR1, saving the current signal mask in oldmask. We then test the global mqflag in a loop, waiting for the signal handler to set it nonzero. As long as it is 0, we call sigsuspend, which atomically puts the calling thread to sleep and resets its signal mask to zeromask (no signals are blocked). Section 10.16 of APUE talks more about sigsuspend and why we must test the mqflag variable only when SIGUSR1 is blocked. Each time sigsuspend returns, SIGUSR1 is blocked.

Reregister and read message

33-36   When mqflag is nonzero, we reregister and then read the message from the queue. We then unblock SIGUSR1 and go back to the top of the for loop.

We mentioned that a problem still exists with this solution. Consider what happens if two messages arrive for the queue before the first message is read. We can simulate this by adding a sleep before the call to mq_notify. The fundamental problem is that the notification is sent *only* when a message is placed onto an empty queue. If two messages arrive for a queue before we can read the first, only one notification is sent: we read the first message and then call sigsuspend waiting for another message, which may never be sent. In the meantime, another message is already sitting on the queue waiting to be read that we are ignoring.

Example: Signal Notification with Nonblocking mq_receive

The correction to the problem just noted is to *always* read a message queue in a nonblocking mode when mq_notify is being used to generate a signal. Figure 5.12 shows a modification to Figure 5.11 that reads the message queue in a nonblocking mode.

Open message queue nonblocking

15-18   The first change is to specify O_NONBLOCK when the message queue is opened.

Read all messages from queue

34-38   The other change is to call mq_receive in a loop, processing each message on the queue. An error return of EAGAIN is OK and just means that no more messages exist.

Example: Signal Notification Using sigwait instead of a Signal Handler

Although the previous example is correct, it could be more efficient. Our program blocks, waiting for a message to arrive, by calling sigsuspend. When a message is placed onto an empty queue, the signal is generated, the main thread is stopped, the signal handler executes and sets the mqflag variable, the main thread executes again, finds mq_flag nonzero, and reads the message. An easier approach (and probably more efficient) would be to block in a function just waiting for the signal to be delivered, without having the kernel execute a signal handler just to set a flag. This capability is provided by sigwait.

pxmsg/mqnotifysig3.c

```c
 1 #include     "unpipc.h"
 2 volatile sig_atomic_t mqflag;    /* set nonzero by signal handler */
 3 static void sig_usr1(int);
 4 int
 5 main(int argc, char **argv)
 6 {
 7     mqd_t    mqd;
 8     void    *buff;
 9     ssize_t n;
10     sigset_t zeromask, newmask, oldmask;
11     struct mq_attr attr;
12     struct sigevent sigev;
13     if (argc != 2)
14         err_quit("usage: mqnotifysig3 <name>");
15         /* open queue, get attributes, allocate read buffer */
16     mqd = Mq_open(argv[1], O_RDONLY | O_NONBLOCK);
17     Mq_getattr(mqd, &attr);
18     buff = Malloc(attr.mq_msgsize);
19     Sigemptyset(&zeromask);      /* no signals blocked */
20     Sigemptyset(&newmask);
21     Sigemptyset(&oldmask);
22     Sigaddset(&newmask, SIGUSR1);
23         /* establish signal handler, enable notification */
24     Signal(SIGUSR1, sig_usr1);
25     sigev.sigev_notify = SIGEV_SIGNAL;
26     sigev.sigev_signo = SIGUSR1;
27     Mq_notify(mqd, &sigev);
28     for ( ; ; ) {
29         Sigprocmask(SIG_BLOCK, &newmask, &oldmask);      /* block SIGUSR1 */
30         while (mqflag == 0)
31             sigsuspend(&zeromask);
32         mqflag = 0;                /* reset flag */
33         Mq_notify(mqd, &sigev); /* reregister first */
34         while ( (n = mq_receive(mqd, buff, attr.mq_msgsize, NULL)) >= 0) {
35             printf("read %ld bytes\n", (long) n);
36         }
37         if (errno != EAGAIN)
38             err_sys("mq_receive error");
39         Sigprocmask(SIG_UNBLOCK, &newmask, NULL);    /* unblock SIGUSR1 */
40     }
41     exit(0);
42 }
43 static void
44 sig_usr1(int signo)
45 {
46     mqflag = 1;
47     return;
48 }
```

pxmsg/mqnotifysig3.c

Figure 5.12 Using a signal notification to read a Posix message queue.

```
#include <signal.h>

int sigwait(const sigset_t *set, int *sig);
```
Returns: 0 if OK, positive Exxx value on error

Before calling `sigwait`, we block some set of signals. We specify this set of signals as the *set* argument. `sigwait` then blocks until one or more of these signals is pending, at which time it returns one of the signals. That signal value is stored through the pointer *sig*, and the return value of the function is 0. This is called "synchronously waiting for an asynchronous event": we are using a signal but without an asynchronous signal handler.

Figure 5.13 shows the use of `mq_notify` with `sigwait`.

Initialize signal set and block SIGUSR1

18–20   One signal set is initialized to contain just SIGUSR1, and this signal is then blocked by sigprocmask.

Wait for signal

26–34   We now block, waiting for the signal, in a call to `sigwait`. When SIGUSR1 is delivered, we reregister the notification and read all available messages.

> `sigwait` is often used with a multithreaded process. Indeed, looking at its function proto-type, we see that its return value is 0 or one of the E*xxx* errors, which is the same as most of the Pthread functions. But `sigprocmask` cannot be used with a multithreaded process; instead, `pthread_sigmask` must be called, and it changes the signal mask of just the calling thread. The arguments for `pthread_sigmask` are identical to those for `sigprocmask`.

> Two variants of `sigwait` exist: `sigwaitinfo` also returns a `siginfo_t` structure (which we define in the next section) and is intended for use with reliable signals. `sigtimedwait` also returns a `siginfo_t` structure and allows the caller to specify a time limit.

> Most threads books, such as [Butenhof 1997], recommend using `sigwait` to handle all signals in a multithreaded process and never using asynchronous signal handlers.

Example: Posix Message Queues with `select`

A message queue descriptor (an `mqd_t` variable) is not a "normal" descriptor and cannot be used with either `select` or `poll` (Chapter 6 of UNPv1). Nevertheless, we can use them along with a pipe and the `mq_notify` function. (We show a similar technique in Section 6.9 with System V message queues, which involves a child process and a pipe.) First, notice from Figure 5.10 that the `write` function is async-signal-safe, so we can call it from a signal handler. Figure 5.14 shows our program.

```
                                                                  ───── pxmsg/mqnotifysig4.c
 1 #include    "unpipc.h"

 2 int
 3 main(int argc, char **argv)
 4 {
 5     int     signo;
 6     mqd_t   mqd;
 7     void    *buff;
 8     ssize_t n;
 9     sigset_t newmask;
10     struct mq_attr attr;
11     struct sigevent sigev;

12     if (argc != 2)
13         err_quit("usage: mqnotifysig4 <name>");

14         /* open queue, get attributes, allocate read buffer */
15     mqd = Mq_open(argv[1], O_RDONLY | O_NONBLOCK);
16     Mq_getattr(mqd, &attr);
17     buff = Malloc(attr.mq_msgsize);

18     Sigemptyset(&newmask);
19     Sigaddset(&newmask, SIGUSR1);
20     Sigprocmask(SIG_BLOCK, &newmask, NULL);      /* block SIGUSR1 */

21         /* establish signal handler, enable notification */
22     sigev.sigev_notify = SIGEV_SIGNAL;
23     sigev.sigev_signo = SIGUSR1;
24     Mq_notify(mqd, &sigev);

25     for ( ; ; ) {
26         Sigwait(&newmask, &signo);
27         if (signo == SIGUSR1) {
28             Mq_notify(mqd, &sigev);      /* reregister first */
29             while ( (n = mq_receive(mqd, buff, attr.mq_msgsize, NULL)) >= 0) {
30                 printf("read %ld bytes\n", (long) n);
31             }
32             if (errno != EAGAIN)
33                 err_sys("mq_receive error");
34         }
35     }
36     exit(0);
37 }
                                                                  ───── pxmsg/mqnotifysig4.c
```

Figure 5.13 Using mq_notify with sigwait.

```
                                                                  ───── pxmsg/mqnotifysig5.c
 1 #include    "unpipc.h"

 2 int     pipefd[2];
 3 static void sig_usr1(int);
```

```
 4 int
 5 main(int argc, char **argv)
 6 {
 7     int     nfds;
 8     char    c;
 9     fd_set  rset;
10     mqd_t   mqd;
11     void    *buff;
12     ssize_t n;
13     struct mq_attr attr;
14     struct sigevent sigev;

15     if (argc != 2)
16         err_quit("usage: mqnotifysig5 <name>");

17         /* open queue, get attributes, allocate read buffer */
18     mqd = Mq_open(argv[1], O_RDONLY | O_NONBLOCK);
19     Mq_getattr(mqd, &attr);
20     buff = Malloc(attr.mq_msgsize);

21     Pipe(pipefd);

22         /* establish signal handler, enable notification */
23     Signal(SIGUSR1, sig_usr1);
24     sigev.sigev_notify = SIGEV_SIGNAL;
25     sigev.sigev_signo = SIGUSR1;
26     Mq_notify(mqd, &sigev);

27     FD_ZERO(&rset);
28     for ( ; ; ) {
29         FD_SET(pipefd[0], &rset);
30         nfds = Select(pipefd[0] + 1, &rset, NULL, NULL, NULL);

31         if (FD_ISSET(pipefd[0], &rset)) {
32             Read(pipefd[0], &c, 1);
33             Mq_notify(mqd, &sigev);       /* reregister first */
34             while ( (n = mq_receive(mqd, buff, attr.mq_msgsize, NULL)) >= 0) {
35                 printf("read %ld bytes\n", (long) n);
36             }
37             if (errno != EAGAIN)
38                 err_sys("mq_receive error");
39         }
40     }
41     exit(0);
42 }

43 static void
44 sig_usr1(int signo)
45 {
46     Write(pipefd[1], "", 1);    /* one byte of 0 */
47     return;
48 }
```
                                                          pxmsg/mqnotifysig5.c

Figure 5.14 Using a signal notification with a pipe.

Create a pipe

21   We create a pipe that the signal handler will write to when a notification is received for the message queue. This is an example of a pipe being used within a single process.

Call `select`

27–40   We initialize the descriptor set `rset` and each time around the loop turn on the bit corresponding to `pipefd[0]` (the read end of the pipe). We then call `select` waiting for only this descriptor, although in a typical application, this is where input or output on multiple descriptors would be multiplexed. When the read end of the pipe is readable, we reregister the message queue notification and read all available messages.

Signal handler

43–48   Our signal handler just `writes` 1 byte to the pipe. As we mentioned, this is an async-signal-safe operation.

Example: Initiate Thread

Another alternative is to set `sigev_notify` to `SIGEV_THREAD`, which causes a new thread to be created. The function specified by the `sigev_notify_function` is called with the parameter of `sigev_value`. The thread attributes for the new thread are specified by `sigev_notify_attributes`, which can be a null pointer if the default attributes are OK. Figure 5.15 shows an example of this technique.

We specify a null pointer for the new thread's argument (`sigev_value`), so nothing is passed to the thread start function. We could pass a pointer to the message queue descriptor as the argument, instead of declaring it as a global, but the new thread still needs the message queue attributes and the `sigev` structure (to reregister). We specify a null pointer for the new thread's attributes, so system defaults are used. These new threads are created as detached threads.

> Unfortunately, neither of the systems being used for these examples, Solaris 2.6 and Digital Unix 4.0B, support `SIGEV_THREAD`. Both require that `sigev_notify` be either `SIGEV_NONE` or `SIGEV_SIGNAL`.

5.7   Posix Realtime Signals

Unix signals have gone through numerous evolutionary changes over the past years.

1. The signal model provided by Version 7 Unix (1978) was unreliable. Signals could get lost, and it was hard for a process to turn off selected signals while executing critical sections of code.

2. 4.3BSD (1986) added reliable signals.

3. System V Release 3.0 (1986) also added reliable signals, albeit differently from the BSD model.

4. Posix.1 (1990) standardized the BSD reliable signal model, and Chapter 10 of APUE describes this model in detail.

————————————————————— pxmsg/mqnotifythread1.c

```
 1 #include     "unpipc.h"

 2 mqd_t   mqd;
 3 struct mq_attr attr;
 4 struct sigevent sigev;

 5 static void notify_thread(union sigval);     /* our thread function */

 6 int
 7 main(int argc, char **argv)
 8 {
 9     if (argc != 2)
10         err_quit("usage: mqnotifythread1 <name>");

11     mqd = Mq_open(argv[1], O_RDONLY | O_NONBLOCK);
12     Mq_getattr(mqd, &attr);

13     sigev.sigev_notify = SIGEV_THREAD;
14     sigev.sigev_value.sival_ptr = NULL;
15     sigev.sigev_notify_function = notify_thread;
16     sigev.sigev_notify_attributes = NULL;
17     Mq_notify(mqd, &sigev);

18     for ( ; ; )
19         pause();                  /* each new thread does everything */

20     exit(0);
21 }

22 static void
23 notify_thread(union sigval arg)
24 {
25     ssize_t n;
26     void   *buff;

27     printf("notify_thread started\n");
28     buff = Malloc(attr.mq_msgsize);
29     Mq_notify(mqd, &sigev);      /* reregister */

30     while ( (n = mq_receive(mqd, buff, attr.mq_msgsize, NULL)) >= 0) {
31         printf("read %ld bytes\n", (long) n);
32     }
33     if (errno != EAGAIN)
34         err_sys("mq_receive error");

35     free(buff);
36     pthread_exit(NULL);
37 }
```

————————————————————— pxmsg/mqnotifythread1.c

Figure 5.15 mq_notify that initiates a new thread.

5. Posix.1 (1996) added realtime signals to the Posix model. This work originated
    from the Posix.1b realtime extensions (which was called Posix.4).

Almost every Unix system today provides Posix reliable signals, and newer systems are
providing the Posix realtime signals. (Be careful to differentiate between reliable and

realtime when describing signals.) We need to say more about the realtime signals, as we have already encountered some of the structures defined by this extension in the previous section (the `sigval` and `sigevent` structures).

Signals can be divided into two groups:

1. The realtime signals whose values are between `SIGRTMIN` and `SIGRTMAX`, inclusive. Posix requires that at least `RTSIG_MAX` of these realtime signals be provided, and the minimum value for this constant is 8.

2. All other signals: `SIGALRM`, `SIGINT`, `SIGKILL`, and so on.

> On Solaris 2.6, the normal Unix signals are numbered 1 through 37, and 8 realtime signals are defined with values from 38 through 45. On Digital Unix 4.0B, the normal Unix signals are numbered 1 through 32, and 16 realtime signals are defined with values from 33 through 48. Both implementations define `SIGRTMIN` and `SIGRTMAX` as macros that call `sysconf`, to allow their values to change in the future.

Next we note whether or not the new `SA_SIGINFO` flag is specified in the call to `sigaction` by the process that receives the signal. These differences lead to the four possible scenarios shown in Figure 5.16.

Signal	Call to `sigaction`	
	`SA_SIGINFO` specified	`SA_SIGINFO` not specified
`SIGRTMIN` through `SIGRTMAX`	realtime behavior guaranteed	realtime behavior unspecified
all other signals	realtime behavior unspecified	realtime behavior unspecified

Figure 5.16   Realtime behavior of Posix signals, depending on `SA_SIGINFO`.

What we mean in the three boxes labeled "realtime behavior unspecified" is that some implementations may provide realtime behavior and some may not. If we want realtime behavior, we *must* use the new realtime signals between `SIGRTMIN` and `SIGRTMAX`, and we *must* specify the `SA_SIGINFO` flag to `sigaction` when the signal handler is installed.

The term *realtime behavior* implies the following characteristics:

- Signals are queued. That is, if the signal is generated three times, it is delivered three times. Furthermore, multiple occurrences of a given signal are queued in a first-in, first-out (FIFO) order. We show an example of signal queueing shortly. For signals that are not queued, a signal that is generated three times can be delivered only once.

- When multiple, unblocked signals in the range `SIGRTMIN` through `SIGRTMAX` are queued, lower-numbered signals are delivered before higher-numbered signals. That is, `SIGRTMIN` is a "higher priority" than the signal numbered `SIGRTMIN+1`, which is a "higher priority" than the signal numbered `SIGRTMIN+2`, and so on.

- When a nonrealtime signal is delivered, the only argument to the signal handler is the signal number. Realtime signals carry more information than other signals. The signal handler for a realtime signal that is installed with the SA_SIGINFO flag set is declared as

  ```
  void func(int signo, siginfo_t *info, void *context);
  ```

  signo is the signal number, and the siginfo_t structure is defined as

  ```
  typedef struct {
    int          si_signo; /* same value as signo argument */
    int          si_code;  /* SI_{USER,QUEUE,TIMER,ASYNCIO,MESGQ} */
    union sigval si_value; /* integer or pointer value from sender */
  } siginfo_t;
  ```

  What the *context* argument points to is implementation dependent.

  > Technically a nonrealtime Posix signal handler is called with just one argument. Many Unix systems have an older, three-argument convention for signal handlers that predates the Posix realtime standard.
  >
  > siginfo_t is the only Posix structure defined as a typedef of a name ending in _t. In Figure 5.17 we declare pointers to these structures as siginfo_t * without the word struct.

- Some new functions are defined to work with the realtime signals. For example, the sigqueue function is used instead of the kill function, to send a signal to some process, and the new function allows the sender to pass a sigval union with the signal.

The realtime signals are generated by the following Posix.1 features, identified by the si_code value contained in the siginfo_t structure that is passed to the signal handler.

SI_ASYNCIO   The signal was generated by the completion of an asynchronous I/O request: the Posix aio_*XXX* functions, which we do not describe.

SI_MESGQ   The signal was generated when a message was placed onto an empty message queue, as we described in Section 5.6.

SI_QUEUE   The signal was sent by the sigqueue function. We show an example of this shortly.

SI_TIMER   The signal was generated by the expiration of a timer that was set by the timer_settime function, which we do not describe.

SI_USER   The signal was sent by the kill function.

If the signal was generated by some other event, si_code will be set to some value other than the ones just shown. The contents of the si_value member of the siginfo_t structure are valid only when si_code is SI_ASYNCIO, SI_MESGQ, SI_QUEUE, or SI_TIMER.

Example

Figure 5.17 is a simple program that demonstrates realtime signals. The program calls fork, the child blocks three realtime signals, the parent then sends nine signals (three occurrences each of three realtime signals), and the child then unblocks the signals and we see how many occurrences of each signal are delivered and the order in which the signals are delivered.

Print realtime signal numbers

10   We print the minimum and maximum realtime signal numbers, to see how many realtime signals the implementation supports. We cast the two constants to an integer, because some implementations define these two constants to be macros that call sysconf, as in

```
#define  SIGRTMAX  (sysconf(_SC_RTSIG_MAX))
```

and sysconf returns a long integer (see Exercise 5.4).

fork: child blocks three realtime signals

11-17   A child is spawned, and the child calls sigprocmask to block the three realtime signals that we are using: SIGRTMAX, SIGRTMAX-1, and SIGRTMAX-2.

Establish signal handler

18-21   We call our signal_rt function (which we show in Figure 5.18) to establish our function sig_rt as the handler for the three realtime signals. This function sets the SA_SIGINFO flag, and since these three signals are realtime signals, we expect realtime behavior. This function also sets the mask of signals to block while the signal handler is executing.

Wait for parent to generate the signals, then unblock the signals

22-25   We wait 6 seconds to allow the parent to generate the nine signals. We then call sigprocmask to unblock the three realtime signals. This should allow all the queued signals to be delivered. We pause for another 3 seconds, to let the signal handler call printf nine times, and then the child terminates.

Parent sends the nine signals

27-36   The parent pauses for 3 seconds to let the child block all signals. The parent then generates three occurrences of each of the three realtime signals: i assumes three values, and j takes on the values 0, 1, and 2 for each value of i. We purposely generate the signals starting with the highest signal number, because we expect them to be delivered starting with the lowest signal number. We also send a different integer value (sival_int) with each signal, to verify that the three occurrences of a given signal are generated in FIFO order.

Signal handler

38-43   Our signal handler just prints the information about the signal that is delivered.

> We noted with Figure 5.10 that printf is not async-signal-safe and should not be called from a signal handler. We call it here as a simple diagnostic tool in this little test program.

———————————————————————— rtsignals/test1.c

```
 1 #include    "unpipc.h"

 2 static void sig_rt(int, siginfo_t *, void *);

 3 int
 4 main(int argc, char **argv)
 5 {
 6     int      i, j;
 7     pid_t    pid;
 8     sigset_t newset;
 9     union sigval val;

10     printf("SIGRTMIN = %d, SIGRTMAX = %d\n", (int) SIGRTMIN, (int) SIGRTMAX);

11     if ( (pid = Fork()) == 0) {
12             /* child: block three realtime signals */
13         Sigemptyset(&newset);
14         Sigaddset(&newset, SIGRTMAX);
15         Sigaddset(&newset, SIGRTMAX - 1);
16         Sigaddset(&newset, SIGRTMAX - 2);
17         Sigprocmask(SIG_BLOCK, &newset, NULL);

18             /* establish signal handler with SA_SIGINFO set */
19         Signal_rt(SIGRTMAX, sig_rt, &newset);
20         Signal_rt(SIGRTMAX - 1, sig_rt, &newset);
21         Signal_rt(SIGRTMAX - 2, sig_rt, &newset);

22         sleep(6);                 /* let parent send all the signals */

23         Sigprocmask(SIG_UNBLOCK, &newset, NULL);    /* unblock */
24         sleep(3);                 /* let all queued signals be delivered */
25         exit(0);
26     }
27         /* parent sends nine signals to child */
28     sleep(3);                     /* let child block all signals */
29     for (i = SIGRTMAX; i >= SIGRTMAX - 2; i--) {
30         for (j = 0; j <= 2; j++) {
31             val.sival_int = j;
32             Sigqueue(pid, i, val);
33             printf("sent signal %d, val = %d\n", i, j);
34         }
35     }
36     exit(0);
37 }

38 static void
39 sig_rt(int signo, siginfo_t *info, void *context)
40 {
41     printf("received signal #%d, code = %d, ival = %d\n",
42             signo, info->si_code, info->si_value.sival_int);
43 }
```

———————————————————————— rtsignals/test1.c

Figure 5.17 Simple test program to demonstrate realtime signals.

We first run the program under Solaris 2.6, but the output is not what is expected.

```
solaris % test1
SIGRTMIN = 38, SIGRTMAX = 45          8 realtime signals provided
                                      3-second pause in here
sent signal 45, val = 0               parent now sends the nine signals
sent signal 45, val = 1
sent signal 45, val = 2
sent signal 44, val = 0
sent signal 44, val = 1
sent signal 44, val = 2
sent signal 43, val = 0
sent signal 43, val = 1
sent signal 43, val = 2
solaris %                             parent terminates, shell prompt printed
                                      3-second pause before child unblocks the signals
received signal #45, code = -2, ival = 2   child catches the signals
received signal #45, code = -2, ival = 1
received signal #45, code = -2, ival = 0
received signal #44, code = -2, ival = 2
received signal #44, code = -2, ival = 1
received signal #44, code = -2, ival = 0
received signal #43, code = -2, ival = 2
received signal #43, code = -2, ival = 1
received signal #43, code = -2, ival = 0
```

The nine signals are queued, but the three signals are generated starting with the highest signal number (we expect the lowest signal number to be generated first). Then for a given signal, the queued signals appear to be delivered in LIFO, not FIFO, order. The si_code of −2 corresponds to SI_QUEUE.

We now run the program under Digital Unix 4.0B and see the expected results.

```
alpha % test1
SIGRTMIN = 33, SIGRTMAX = 48          16 realtime signals provided
                                      3-second pause in here
sent signal 48, val = 0               parent now sends the nine signals
sent signal 48, val = 1
sent signal 48, val = 2
sent signal 47, val = 0
sent signal 47, val = 1
sent signal 47, val = 2
sent signal 46, val = 0
sent signal 46, val = 1
sent signal 46, val = 2
alpha %                               parent terminates, shell prompt printed
                                      3-second pause before child unblocks the signals
received signal #46, code = -1, ival = 0   child catches the signals
received signal #46, code = -1, ival = 1
received signal #46, code = -1, ival = 2
received signal #47, code = -1, ival = 0
received signal #47, code = -1, ival = 1
received signal #47, code = -1, ival = 2
received signal #48, code = -1, ival = 0
received signal #48, code = -1, ival = 1
received signal #48, code = -1, ival = 2
```

The nine signals are queued and then delivered in the order that we expect: the lowest-numbered-signal first, and for a given signal, the three occurrences are delivered in FIFO order.

> The Solaris 2.6 implementation appears to have a bug.

`signal_rt` Function

On p. 120 of UNPv1, we show our `signal` function, which calls the Posix `sigaction` function to establish a signal handler that provides reliable Posix semantics. We now modify that function to provide realtime behavior. We call this new function `signal_rt` and show it in Figure 5.18.

```
                                                                ──── lib/signal_rt.c
 1 #include    "unpipc.h"

 2 Sigfunc_rt *
 3 signal_rt(int signo, Sigfunc_rt *func, sigset_t *mask)
 4 {
 5     struct sigaction act, oact;

 6     act.sa_sigaction = func;      /* must store function addr here */
 7     act.sa_mask = *mask;          /* signals to block */
 8     act.sa_flags = SA_SIGINFO;    /* must specify this for realtime */
 9     if (signo == SIGALRM) {
10 #ifdef  SA_INTERRUPT
11         act.sa_flags |= SA_INTERRUPT;    /* SunOS 4.x */
12 #endif
13     } else {
14 #ifdef  SA_RESTART
15         act.sa_flags |= SA_RESTART;      /* SVR4, 4.4BSD */
16 #endif
17     }
18     if (sigaction(signo, &act, &oact) < 0)
19         return ((Sigfunc_rt *) SIG_ERR);
20     return (oact.sa_sigaction);
21 }
                                                                ──── lib/signal_rt.c
```

Figure 5.18   `signal_rt` function to provide realtime behavior.

Simplify function prototype using `typedef`

1-3   In our `unpipc.h` header (Figure C.1), we define `Sigfunc_rt` as

```
typedef  void  Sigfunc_rt(int, siginfo_t *, void *);
```

We said earlier in this section that this is the function prototype for a signal handler installed with the `SA_SIGINFO` flag set.

Specify handler function

5-7   The `sigaction` structure changed when realtime signal support was added, with the addition of the new `sa_sigaction` member.

```
struct sigaction {
  void      (*sa_handler)(); /* SIG_DFL, SIG_IGN, or addr of signal handler */
  sigset_t  sa_mask;          /* additional signals to block */
  int       sa_flags;         /* signal options: SA_xxx */
  void      (*sa_sigaction)(int, siginfo_t, void *);
                              /* addr of signal handler if SA_SIGINFO set */
};
```

The rules are:

- If the SA_SIGINFO flag is set in the sa_flags member, then the sa_sigaction member specifies the address of the signal-handling function.

- If the SA_SIGINFO flag is not set in the sa_flags member, then the sa_handler member specifies the address of the signal-handling function.

- To specify the default action for a signal or to ignore a signal, set sa_handler to either SIG_DFL or SIG_IGN, and do not set SA_SIGINFO.

Set SA_SIGINFO

8-17   We always set the SA_SIGINFO flag, and also specify the SA_RESTART flag if the signal is not SIGALRM.

5.8   Implementation Using Memory-Mapped I/O

We now provide an implementation of Posix message queues using memory-mapped I/O, along with Posix mutexes and condition variables.

> We cover mutexes and condition variables in Chapter 7 and memory-mapped I/O in Chapters 12 and 13. You may wish to skip this section until you have read those chapters.

Figure 5.19 shows a layout of the data structures that we use to implement Posix message queues. In this figure, we assume that the message queue was created to hold up to four messages of 7 bytes each.

Figure 5.20 shows our mqueue.h header, which defines the fundamental structures for this implementation.

mqd_t datatype

1   Our message queue descriptor is just a pointer to an mq_info structure. Each call to mq_open allocates one of these structures, and the pointer to this structure is what gets returned to the caller. This reiterates that a message queue descriptor need not be a small integer, like a file descriptor—the only Posix requirement is that this datatype cannot be an array type.

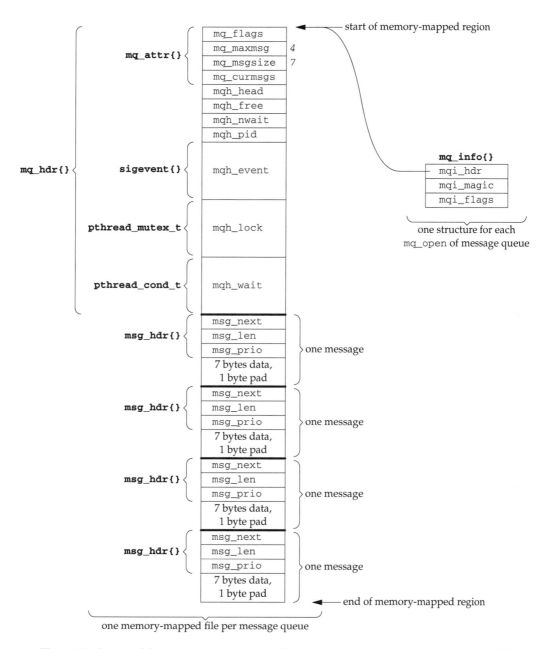

Figure 5.19 Layout of data structures to implement Posix message queues using a memory-mapped file.

―――――――――――――――――――――――――――――――――― *my_pxmsg_mmap/mqueue.h*
```
 1 typedef struct mq_info *mqd_t;   /* opaque datatype */

 2 struct mq_attr {
 3     long    mq_flags;             /* message queue flag: O_NONBLOCK */
 4     long    mq_maxmsg;            /* max number of messages allowed on queue */
 5     long    mq_msgsize;           /* max size of a message (in bytes) */
 6     long    mq_curmsgs;           /* number of messages currently on queue */
 7 };

 8          /* one mq_hdr{} per queue, at beginning of mapped file */
 9 struct mq_hdr {
10     struct mq_attr mqh_attr;   /* the queue's attributes */
11     long    mqh_head;           /* index of first message */
12     long    mqh_free;           /* index of first free message */
13     long    mqh_nwait;          /* #threads blocked in mq_receive() */
14     pid_t   mqh_pid;            /* nonzero PID if mqh_event set */
15     struct sigevent mqh_event;  /* for mq_notify() */
16     pthread_mutex_t mqh_lock;   /* mutex lock */
17     pthread_cond_t mqh_wait;    /* and condition variable */
18 };

19          /* one msg_hdr{} at the front of each message in the mapped file */
20 struct msg_hdr {
21     long    msg_next;           /* index of next on linked list */
22          /* msg_next must be first member in struct */
23     ssize_t msg_len;            /* actual length */
24     unsigned int msg_prio;      /* priority */
25 };

26          /* one mq_info{} malloc'ed per process per mq_open() */
27 struct mq_info {
28     struct mq_hdr *mqi_hdr;   /* start of mmap'ed region */
29     long    mqi_magic;          /* magic number if open */
30     int     mqi_flags;          /* flags for this process */
31 };
32 #define MQI_MAGIC    0x98765432

33          /* size of message in file is rounded up for alignment */
34 #define MSGSIZE(i)   ((((i) + sizeof(long)-1) / sizeof(long)) * sizeof(long))
```
―――――――――――――――――――――――――――――――――― *my_pxmsg_mmap/mqueue.h*

Figure 5.20 mqueue.h header.

mq_hdr structure

8–18   This structure appears at the beginning of the mapped file and contains all the per-queue information. The mq_flags member of the mqh_attr structure is not used, because the flags (the nonblocking flag is the only one defined) must be maintained on a per-open basis, not on a per-queue basis. The flags are maintained in the mq_info structure. We describe the remaining members of this structure as we use them in the various functions.

Note now that everything that we refer to as an *index* (the mqh_head and mqh_free members of this structure, and the msg_next member of the next structure) contains byte indexes from the beginning of the mapped file. For example, the size of the mq_hdr structure under Solaris 2.6 is 96 bytes, so the index of the first message following this header is 96. Each message in Figure 5.19 occupies 20 bytes (12 bytes for the msg_hdr structure and 8 bytes for the message data), so the indexes of the remaining three messages are 116, 136, and 156, and the size of this mapped file is 176 bytes. These indexes are used to maintain two linked lists in the mapped file: one list (mqh_head) contains all the messages currently on the queue, and the other (mqh_free) contains all the free messages on the queue. We cannot use actual memory pointers (addresses) for these list pointers, because the mapped file can start at different memory addresses in each process that maps the file (as we show in Figure 13.6).

msg_hdr structure

19-25   This structure appears at the beginning of each message in the mapped file. All messages are either on the message list or on the free list, and the msg_next member contains the index of the next message on the list (or 0 if this message is the end of the list). msg_len is the actual length of the message data, which for our example in Figure 5.19 can be between 0 and 7 bytes, inclusive. msg_prio is the priority assigned to the message by the caller of mq_send.

mq_info structure

26-32   One of these structures is dynamically allocated by mq_open when a queue is opened, and freed by mq_close. mqi_hdr points to the mapped file (the starting address returned by mmap). A pointer to this structure is the fundamental mqd_t datatype of our implementation, and this pointer is the return value from mq_open.

The mqi_magic member contains MQI_MAGIC, once this structure has been initialized, and is checked by each function that is passed an mqd_t pointer, to make certain that the pointer really points to an mq_info structure. mqi_flags contains the nonblocking flag for this open instance of the queue.

MSGSIZE macro

33-34   For alignment purposes, we want each message in the mapped file to start on a long integer boundary. Therefore, if the maximum size of each message is not so aligned, we add between 1 and 3 bytes of padding to the data portion of each message, as shown in Figure 5.19. This assumes that the size of a long integer is 4 bytes (which is true for Solaris 2.6), but if the size of a long integer is 8 bytes (as on Digital Unix 4.0), then the amount of padding will be between 1 and 7 bytes.

mq_open Function

Figure 5.21 shows the first part of our mq_open function, which creates a new message queue or opens an existing message queue.

my_pxmsg_mmap/mq_open.c

```
1 #include    "unpipc.h"
2 #include    "mqueue.h"

3 #include    <stdarg.h>
4 #define     MAX_TRIES    10      /* for waiting for initialization */

5 struct mq_attr defattr =
6 {0, 128, 1024, 0};
```

```
 7 mqd_t
 8 mq_open(const char *pathname, int oflag,...)
 9 {
10     int     i, fd, nonblock, created, save_errno;
11     long    msgsize, filesize, index;
12     va_list ap;
13     mode_t  mode;
14     int8_t *mptr;
15     struct stat statbuff;
16     struct mq_hdr *mqhdr;
17     struct msg_hdr *msghdr;
18     struct mq_attr *attr;
19     struct mq_info *mqinfo;
20     pthread_mutexattr_t mattr;
21     pthread_condattr_t cattr;

22     created = 0;
23     nonblock = oflag & O_NONBLOCK;
24     oflag &= ~O_NONBLOCK;
25     mptr = (int8_t *) MAP_FAILED;
26     mqinfo = NULL;
27 again:
28     if (oflag & O_CREAT) {
29         va_start(ap, oflag);     /* init ap to final named argument */
30         mode = va_arg(ap, va_mode_t) & ~S_IXUSR;
31         attr = va_arg(ap, struct mq_attr *);
32         va_end(ap);

33             /* open and specify O_EXCL and user-execute */
34         fd = open(pathname, oflag | O_EXCL | O_RDWR, mode | S_IXUSR);
35         if (fd < 0) {
36             if (errno == EEXIST && (oflag & O_EXCL) == 0)
37                 goto exists;     /* already exists, OK */
38             else
39                 return ((mqd_t) -1);
40         }
41         created = 1;
42             /* first one to create the file initializes it */
43         if (attr == NULL)
44             attr = &defattr;
45         else {
46             if (attr->mq_maxmsg <= 0 || attr->mq_msgsize <= 0) {
47                 errno = EINVAL;
48                 goto err;
49             }
50         }
```

my_pxmsg_mmap/mq_open.c

Figure 5.21 mq_open function: first part.

Handle variable argument list

29-32   This function can be called with either two or four arguments, depending on whether or not the O_CREAT flag is specified. When this flag is specified, the third argument is of type `mode_t`, but this is a primitive system datatype that can be any type of integer. The problem we encounter is on BSD/OS, which defines this datatype as an `unsigned short` integer (occupying 16 bits). Since an integer on this implementation occupies 32 bits, the C compiler expands an argument of this type from 16 to 32 bits, since all short integers are expanded to integers in the argument list. But if we specify `mode_t` in the call to `va_arg`, it will step past 16 bits of argument on the stack, when the argument has been expanded to occupy 32 bits. Therefore, we must define our own datatype, `va_mode_t`, that is an integer under BSD/OS, or of type `mode_t` under other systems. The following lines in our `unpipc.h` header (Figure C.1) handle this portability problem:

```
#ifdef   __bsdi__
#define  va_mode_t   int
#else
#define  va_mode_t   mode_t
#endif
```

30   We turn off the user-execute bit in the `mode` variable (`S_IXUSR`) for reasons that we describe shortly.

Create a new message queue

33-34   A regular file is created with the name specified by the caller, and the user-execute bit is turned on.

Handle potential race condition

35-40   If we were to just open the file, memory map its contents, and initialize the mapped file (as described shortly) when the `O_CREAT` flag is specified by the caller, we would have a race condition. A message queue is initialized by `mq_open` only if `O_CREAT` is specified by the caller *and* the message queue does not already exist. That means we need some method of detecting whether the message queue already exists. To do so, we always specify `O_EXCL` when we `open` the file that will be memory-mapped. But an error return of `EEXIST` from `open` becomes an error from `mq_open`, only if the caller specified `O_EXCL`. Otherwise, if `open` returns an error of `EEXIST`, the file already exists and we just skip ahead to Figure 5.23 as if the `O_CREAT` flag was not specified.

The possible race condition is because our use of a memory-mapped file to represent a message queue requires two steps to initialize a new message queue: first, the file must be created by `open`, and second, the contents of the file (described shortly) must be initialized. The problem occurs if two threads (in the same or different processes) call `mq_open` at about the same time. One thread can create the file, and then the system switches to the second thread before the first thread completes the initialization. This second thread detects that the file already exists (using the `O_EXCL` flag to `open`) and immediately tries to use the message queue. But the message queue cannot be used until the first thread initializes the message queue. We use the user-execute bit of the file to indicate that the message queue has been initialized. This bit is enabled only by the thread that actually creates the file (using the `O_EXCL` flag to detect which thread creates the file), and that thread initializes the message queue and then turns off the user-execute bit. We encounter similar race conditions in Figures 10.43 and 10.52.

Check attributes

42–50   If the caller specifies a null pointer for the final argument, we use the default attributes shown at the beginning of this figure: 128 messages and 1024 bytes per message. If the caller specifies the attributes, we verify that mq_maxmsg and mq_msgsize are positive.

The second part of our mq_open function is shown in Figure 5.22; it completes the initialization of a new queue.

my_pxmsg_mmap/mq_open.c
```
51              /* calculate and set the file size */
52          msgsize = MSGSIZE(attr->mq_msgsize);
53          filesize = sizeof(struct mq_hdr) + (attr->mq_maxmsg *
54                                  (sizeof(struct msg_hdr) + msgsize));
55          if (lseek(fd, filesize - 1, SEEK_SET) == -1)
56              goto err;
57          if (write(fd, "", 1) == -1)
58              goto err;

59              /* memory map the file */
60          mptr = mmap(NULL, filesize, PROT_READ | PROT_WRITE,
61                      MAP_SHARED, fd, 0);
62          if (mptr == MAP_FAILED)
63              goto err;

64              /* allocate one mq_info{} for the queue */
65          if ( (mqinfo = malloc(sizeof(struct mq_info))) == NULL)
66              goto err;

67          mqinfo->mqi_hdr = mqhdr = (struct mq_hdr *) mptr;
68          mqinfo->mqi_magic = MQI_MAGIC;
69          mqinfo->mqi_flags = nonblock;

70              /* initialize header at beginning of file */
71              /* create free list with all messages on it */
72          mqhdr->mqh_attr.mq_flags = 0;
73          mqhdr->mqh_attr.mq_maxmsg = attr->mq_maxmsg;
74          mqhdr->mqh_attr.mq_msgsize = attr->mq_msgsize;
75          mqhdr->mqh_attr.mq_curmsgs = 0;
76          mqhdr->mqh_nwait = 0;
77          mqhdr->mqh_pid = 0;
78          mqhdr->mqh_head = 0;
79          index = sizeof(struct mq_hdr);
80          mqhdr->mqh_free = index;
81          for (i = 0; i < attr->mq_maxmsg - 1; i++) {
82              msghdr = (struct msg_hdr *) &mptr[index];
83              index += sizeof(struct msg_hdr) + msgsize;
84              msghdr->msg_next = index;
85          }
86          msghdr = (struct msg_hdr *) &mptr[index];
87          msghdr->msg_next = 0;   /* end of free list */

88              /* initialize mutex & condition variable */
89          if ( (i = pthread_mutexattr_init(&mattr)) != 0)
90              goto pthreaderr;
```

```
 91            pthread_mutexattr_setpshared(&mattr, PTHREAD_PROCESS_SHARED);
 92            i = pthread_mutex_init(&mqhdr->mqh_lock, &mattr);
 93            pthread_mutexattr_destroy(&mattr);   /* be sure to destroy */
 94            if (i != 0)
 95                goto pthreaderr;

 96            if ( (i = pthread_condattr_init(&cattr)) != 0)
 97                goto pthreaderr;
 98            pthread_condattr_setpshared(&cattr, PTHREAD_PROCESS_SHARED);
 99            i = pthread_cond_init(&mqhdr->mqh_wait, &cattr);
100            pthread_condattr_destroy(&cattr);     /* be sure to destroy */
101            if (i != 0)
102                goto pthreaderr;

103                /* initialization complete, turn off user-execute bit */
104            if (fchmod(fd, mode) == -1)
105                goto err;
106            close(fd);
107            return ((mqd_t) mqinfo);
108        }
```
my_pxmsg_mmap/mq_open.c

Figure 5.22 Second part of mq_open function: complete initialization of new queue.

Set the file size

51–58   We calculate the size of each message, rounding up to the next multiple of the size of a long integer. To calculate the file size, we also allocate room for the mq_hdr structure at the beginning of the file and the msg_hdr structure at the beginning of each message (Figure 5.19). We set the size of the newly created file using lseek and then writing one byte of 0. Just calling ftruncate (Section 13.3) would be easier, but we are not guaranteed that this works to increase the size of a file.

Memory map the file

59–63   The file is memory mapped by mmap.

Allocate mq_info structure

64–66   We allocate one mq_info structure for each call to mq_open. This structure is initialized.

Initialize mq_hdr structure

67–87   We initialize the mq_hdr structure. The head of the linked list of messages (mqh_head) is set to 0, and all the messages in the queue are added to the free list (mqh_free).

Initialize mutex and condition variable

88–102   Since Posix message queues can be shared by any process that knows the message queue's name and has adequate permission, we must initialize the mutex and condition variable with the PTHREAD_PROCESS_SHARED attribute. To do so for the message queue, we first initialize the attributes by calling pthread_mutexattr_init, then call pthread_mutexattr_setpshared to set the process-shared attribute in this structure, and then initialize the mutex by calling pthread_mutex_init. Nearly identical steps are done for the condition variable. We are careful to destroy the mutex or condition variable attributes that are initialized, even if an error occurs, because the calls to `pthread_mutexattr_init` or `pthread_condattr_init` might allocate memory (Exercise 7.3).

Turn off user-execute bit

103-107   Once the message queue is initialized, we turn off the user-execute bit. This indicates that the message queue has been initialized. We also `close` the file, since it has been memory mapped and there is no need to keep it open (taking up a descriptor).

Figure 5.23 shows the final part of our `mq_open` function, which opens an existing queue.

```
                                                            my_pxmsg_mmap/mq_open.c
109    exists:
110        /* open the file then memory map */
111        if ( (fd = open(pathname, O_RDWR)) < 0) {
112            if (errno == ENOENT && (oflag & O_CREAT))
113                goto again;
114            goto err;
115        }
116        /* make certain initialization is complete */
117        for (i = 0; i < MAX_TRIES; i++) {
118            if (stat(pathname, &statbuff) == -1) {
119                if (errno == ENOENT && (oflag & O_CREAT)) {
120                    close(fd);
121                    goto again;
122                }
123                goto err;
124            }
125            if ((statbuff.st_mode & S_IXUSR) == 0)
126                break;
127            sleep(1);
128        }
129        if (i == MAX_TRIES) {
130            errno = ETIMEDOUT;
131            goto err;
132        }
133        filesize = statbuff.st_size;
134        mptr = mmap(NULL, filesize, PROT_READ | PROT_WRITE, MAP_SHARED, fd, 0);
135        if (mptr == MAP_FAILED)
136            goto err;
137        close(fd);

138        /* allocate one mq_info{} for each open */
139        if ( (mqinfo = malloc(sizeof(struct mq_info))) == NULL)
140            goto err;

141        mqinfo->mqi_hdr = (struct mq_hdr *) mptr;
142        mqinfo->mqi_magic = MQI_MAGIC;
143        mqinfo->mqi_flags = nonblock;
144        return ((mqd_t) mqinfo);
```

```
145   pthreaderr:
146     errno = i;
147   err:
148         /* don't let following function calls change errno */
149     save_errno = errno;
150     if (created)
151         unlink(pathname);
152     if (mptr != MAP_FAILED)
153         munmap(mptr, filesize);
154     if (mqinfo != NULL)
155         free(mqinfo);
156     close(fd);
157     errno = save_errno;
158     return ((mqd_t) -1);
159 }
```
——————————————————————————————————— *my_pxmsg_mmap/mq_open.c*

Figure 5.23 Third part of mq_open function: open an existing queue.

Open existing message queue

109–115   We end up here if either the O_CREAT flag is not specified or if O_CREAT is specified but the message queue already exists. In either case, we are opening an existing message queue. We open the file containing the message queue for reading and writing and memory map the file into the address space of the process (mmap).

> Our implementation is simplistic with regard to the open mode. Even if the caller specifies O_RDONLY, we must specify read–write access to both open and mmap, because we cannot read a message from a queue without changing the file. Similarly, we cannot write a message to a queue without reading the file. One way around this problem is to save the open mode (O_RDONLY, O_WRONLY, or O_RDWR) in the mq_info structure and then check this mode in the individual functions. For example, mq_receive should fail if the open mode was O_WRONLY.

Make certain that message queue is initialized

116–132   We must wait for the message queue to be initialized (in case multiple threads try to create the same message queue at about the same time). To do so, we call stat and look at the file's permissions (the st_mode member of the stat structure). If the user-execute bit is off, the message queue has been initialized.

This piece of code handles another possible race condition. Assume that two threads in different processes open the same message queue at about the same time. The first thread creates the file and then blocks in its call to lseek in Figure 5.22. The second thread finds that the file already exists and branches to exists where it opens the file again, and then blocks. The first thread runs again, but its call to mmap in Figure 5.22 fails (perhaps it has exceeded its virtual memory limit), so it branches to err and unlinks the file that it created. The second thread continues, but if we called fstat instead of stat, the second thread could time out in the for loop waiting for the file to be initialized. Instead, we call stat, and if it returns an error that the file does not exist and if the O_CREAT flag was specified, we branch to again (Figure 5.21) to create the file again. This possible race condition is why we also check for an error of ENOENT in the call to open.

Memory map file; allocate and initialize `mq_info` structure

133–144   The file is memory mapped, and the descriptor can then be closed. We allocate an `mq_info` structure and initialize it. The return value is a pointer to the `mq_info` structure that was allocated.

Handle errors

145–158   When an error is detected earlier in the function, the label `err` is branched to, with `errno` set to the value to be returned by `mq_open`. We are careful that the functions called to clean up after the error is detected do not affect the `errno` returned by this function.

`mq_close` Function

Figure 5.24 shows our `mq_close` function.

```
                                                      ── my_pxmsg_mmap/mq_close.c
 1 #include    "unpipc.h"
 2 #include    "mqueue.h"

 3 int
 4 mq_close(mqd_t mqd)
 5 {
 6     long    msgsize, filesize;
 7     struct mq_hdr *mqhdr;
 8     struct mq_attr *attr;
 9     struct mq_info *mqinfo;

10     mqinfo = mqd;
11     if (mqinfo->mqi_magic != MQI_MAGIC) {
12         errno = EBADF;
13         return (-1);
14     }
15     mqhdr = mqinfo->mqi_hdr;
16     attr = &mqhdr->mqh_attr;

17     if (mq_notify(mqd, NULL) != 0)     /* unregister calling process */
18         return (-1);

19     msgsize = MSGSIZE(attr->mq_msgsize);
20     filesize = sizeof(struct mq_hdr) + (attr->mq_maxmsg *
21                             (sizeof(struct msg_hdr) + msgsize));
22     if (munmap(mqinfo->mqi_hdr, filesize) == -1)
23         return (-1);

24     mqinfo->mqi_magic = 0;      /* just in case */
25     free(mqinfo);
26     return (0);
27 }
                                                      ── my_pxmsg_mmap/mq_close.c
```

Figure 5.24 `mq_close` function.

Get pointers to structures

10-16   The argument is validated, and pointers are then obtained to the memory-mapped region (mqhdr) and the attributes (in the mq_hdr structure).

Unregister calling process

17-18   We call mq_notify to unregister the calling process for this queue. If the process is registered, it will be unregistered, but if it is not registered, no error is returned.

Unmap region and free memory

19-25   We calculate the size of the file for munmap and then free the memory used by the mq_info structure. Just in case the caller continues to use the message queue descriptor before that region of memory is reused by malloc, we set the magic number to 0, so that our message queue functions will detect the error.

Note that if the process terminates without calling mq_close, the same operations take place on process termination: the memory-mapped file is unmapped and the memory is freed.

mq_unlink Function

Our mq_unlink function shown in Figure 5.25 removes the name associated with our message queue. It just calls the Unix unlink function.

my_pxmsg_mmap/mq_unlink.c

```
1 #include     "unpipc.h"
2 #include     "mqueue.h"

3 int
4 mq_unlink(const char *pathname)
5 {
6     if (unlink(pathname) == -1)
7         return (-1);
8     return (0);
9 }
```

my_pxmsg_mmap/mq_unlink.c

Figure 5.25 mq_unlink function.

mq_getattr Function

Figure 5.26 shows our mq_getattr function, which returns the current attributes of the specified queue.

Acquire queue's mutex lock

17-20   We must acquire the message queue's mutex lock before fetching the attributes, in case some other thread is in the middle of changing them.

my_pxmsg_mmap/mq_getattr.c

```
 1 #include     "unpipc.h"
 2 #include     "mqueue.h"

 3 int
 4 mq_getattr(mqd_t mqd, struct mq_attr *mqstat)
 5 {
 6     int     n;
 7     struct mq_hdr *mqhdr;
 8     struct mq_attr *attr;
 9     struct mq_info *mqinfo;

10     mqinfo = mqd;
11     if (mqinfo->mqi_magic != MQI_MAGIC) {
12         errno = EBADF;
13         return (-1);
14     }
15     mqhdr = mqinfo->mqi_hdr;
16     attr = &mqhdr->mqh_attr;
17     if ( (n = pthread_mutex_lock(&mqhdr->mqh_lock)) != 0) {
18         errno = n;
19         return (-1);
20     }
21     mqstat->mq_flags = mqinfo->mqi_flags;    /* per-open */
22     mqstat->mq_maxmsg = attr->mq_maxmsg;     /* remaining three per-queue */
23     mqstat->mq_msgsize = attr->mq_msgsize;
24     mqstat->mq_curmsgs = attr->mq_curmsgs;

25     pthread_mutex_unlock(&mqhdr->mqh_lock);
26     return (0);
27 }
```

my_pxmsg_mmap/mq_getattr.c

Figure 5.26 mq_getattr function.

mq_setattr Function

Figure 5.27 shows our mq_setattr function, which sets the current attributes of the specified queue.

Return current attributes

22-27   If the third argument is a nonnull pointer, we return the previous attributes and current status before changing anything.

Change mq_flags

28-31   The only attribute that can be changed with this function is mq_flags, which we store in the mq_info structure.

—————————————————————————————————— *my_pxmsg_mmap/mq_setattr.c*

```
 1 #include      "unpipc.h"
 2 #include      "mqueue.h"

 3 int
 4 mq_setattr(mqd_t mqd, const struct mq_attr *mqstat,
 5              struct mq_attr *omqstat)
 6 {
 7     int      n;
 8     struct mq_hdr *mqhdr;
 9     struct mq_attr *attr;
10     struct mq_info *mqinfo;

11     mqinfo = mqd;
12     if (mqinfo->mqi_magic != MQI_MAGIC) {
13         errno = EBADF;
14         return (-1);
15     }
16     mqhdr = mqinfo->mqi_hdr;
17     attr = &mqhdr->mqh_attr;
18     if ( (n = pthread_mutex_lock(&mqhdr->mqh_lock)) != 0) {
19         errno = n;
20         return (-1);
21     }
22     if (omqstat != NULL) {
23         omqstat->mq_flags = mqinfo->mqi_flags;  /* previous attributes */
24         omqstat->mq_maxmsg = attr->mq_maxmsg;
25         omqstat->mq_msgsize = attr->mq_msgsize;
26         omqstat->mq_curmsgs = attr->mq_curmsgs;    /* and current status */
27     }
28     if (mqstat->mq_flags & O_NONBLOCK)
29         mqinfo->mqi_flags |= O_NONBLOCK;
30     else
31         mqinfo->mqi_flags &= ~O_NONBLOCK;

32     pthread_mutex_unlock(&mqhdr->mqh_lock);
33     return (0);
34 }
```

—————————————————————————————————— *my_pxmsg_mmap/mq_setattr.c*

Figure 5.27 mq_setattr function.

mq_notify Function

The mq_notify function shown in Figure 5.28 registers or unregisters the calling process for the queue. We keep track of the process currently registered for a queue by storing its process ID in the mqh_pid member of the mq_hdr structure. Only one process at a time can be registered for a given queue. When a process registers itself, we also save its specified sigevent structure in the mqh_event structure.

```
                                                              ───── my_pxmsg_mmap/mq_notify.c
 1 #include    "unpipc.h"
 2 #include    "mqueue.h"

 3 int
 4 mq_notify(mqd_t mqd, const struct sigevent *notification)
 5 {
 6     int     n;
 7     pid_t   pid;
 8     struct mq_hdr *mqhdr;
 9     struct mq_info *mqinfo;

10     mqinfo = mqd;
11     if (mqinfo->mqi_magic != MQI_MAGIC) {
12         errno = EBADF;
13         return (-1);
14     }
15     mqhdr = mqinfo->mqi_hdr;
16     if ( (n = pthread_mutex_lock(&mqhdr->mqh_lock)) != 0) {
17         errno = n;
18         return (-1);
19     }
20     pid = getpid();
21     if (notification == NULL) {
22         if (mqhdr->mqh_pid == pid) {
23             mqhdr->mqh_pid = 0; /* unregister calling process */
24         }                       /* no error if caller not registered */
25     } else {
26         if (mqhdr->mqh_pid != 0) {
27             if (kill(mqhdr->mqh_pid, 0) != -1 || errno != ESRCH) {
28                 errno = EBUSY;
29                 goto err;
30             }
31         }
32         mqhdr->mqh_pid = pid;
33         mqhdr->mqh_event = *notification;
34     }
35     pthread_mutex_unlock(&mqhdr->mqh_lock);
36     return (0);

37  err:
38     pthread_mutex_unlock(&mqhdr->mqh_lock);
39     return (-1);
40 }
                                                              ───── my_pxmsg_mmap/mq_notify.c
```

Figure 5.28 mq_notify function.

Unregister calling process

20–24   If the second argument is a null pointer, the calling process is unregistered for this queue. Strangely, no error is specified if the calling process is not registered for this queue.

Register calling process

25-34   If some process is already registered, we check whether it still exists by sending it signal 0 (called the *null signal*). This performs the normal error checking, but does not send a signal and returns an error of ESRCH if the process does not exist. An error of EBUSY is returned if the previously registered process still exists. Otherwise, the process ID is saved, along with the caller's sigevent structure.

> Our test for whether the previously registered process exists is not perfect. This process can terminate and then have its process ID reused at some later time.

mq_send Function

Figure 5.29 shows the first half of our mq_send function.

Initialize

14-29   Pointers are obtained to the structures that we will use, and the mutex lock for the queue is obtained. A check is made that the size of the message does not exceed the maximum message size for this queue.

Check for empty queue and send notification if applicable

30-38   If we are placing a message onto an empty queue, we check whether any process is registered for this queue *and* whether any thread is blocked in a call to mq_receive. For the latter check, we will see that our mq_receive function keeps a count (mqh_nwait) of the number of threads blocked on the empty queue. If this counter is nonzero, we do not send any notification to the registered process. We handle a notification of SIGEV_SIGNAL and call sigqueue to send the signal. The registered process is then unregistered.

> Calling sigqueue to send the signal results in an si_code of SI_QUEUE being passed to the signal handler in the siginfo_t structure (Section 5.7), which is incorrect. Generating the correct si_code of SI_MESGQ from a user process is implementation dependent. Page 433 of [IEEE 1996] mentions that a hidden interface into the signal generation mechanism is required to generate this signal from a user library.

Check for full queue

39-48   If the queue is full but the O_NONBLOCK flag has been set, we return an error of EAGAIN. Otherwise, we wait on the condition variable mqh_wait, which we will see is signaled by our mq_receive function when a message is read from a full queue.

> Our implementation is simplistic with regard to returning an error of EINTR if this call to mq_send is interrupted by a signal that is caught by the calling process. The problem is that pthread_cond_wait does not return an error when the signal handler returns: it can either return a value of 0 (which appears as a spurious wakeup) or it need not return at all. Ways around this exist, all nontrivial.

Figure 5.30 shows the second half of our mq_send function. At this point, we know the queue has room for the new message.

―――――――――――――――――――――――――― *my_pxmsg_mmap/mq_send.c*

```
 1 #include     "unpipc.h"
 2 #include     "mqueue.h"

 3 int
 4 mq_send(mqd_t mqd, const char *ptr, size_t len, unsigned int prio)
 5 {
 6     int     n;
 7     long    index, freeindex;
 8     int8_t *mptr;
 9     struct sigevent *sigev;
10     struct mq_hdr *mqhdr;
11     struct mq_attr *attr;
12     struct msg_hdr *msghdr, *nmsghdr, *pmsghdr;
13     struct mq_info *mqinfo;

14     mqinfo = mqd;
15     if (mqinfo->mqi_magic != MQI_MAGIC) {
16         errno = EBADF;
17         return (-1);
18     }
19     mqhdr = mqinfo->mqi_hdr;    /* struct pointer */
20     mptr = (int8_t *) mqhdr;    /* byte pointer */
21     attr = &mqhdr->mqh_attr;
22     if ( (n = pthread_mutex_lock(&mqhdr->mqh_lock)) != 0) {
23         errno = n;
24         return (-1);
25     }
26     if (len > attr->mq_msgsize) {
27         errno = EMSGSIZE;
28         goto err;
29     }
30     if (attr->mq_curmsgs == 0) {
31         if (mqhdr->mqh_pid != 0 && mqhdr->mqh_nwait == 0) {
32             sigev = &mqhdr->mqh_event;
33             if (sigev->sigev_notify == SIGEV_SIGNAL) {
34                 sigqueue(mqhdr->mqh_pid, sigev->sigev_signo,
35                         sigev->sigev_value);
36             }
37             mqhdr->mqh_pid = 0; /* unregister */
38         }
39     } else if (attr->mq_curmsgs >= attr->mq_maxmsg) {
40             /* queue is full */
41         if (mqinfo->mqi_flags & O_NONBLOCK) {
42             errno = EAGAIN;
43             goto err;
44         }
45             /* wait for room for one message on the queue */
46         while (attr->mq_curmsgs >= attr->mq_maxmsg)
47             pthread_cond_wait(&mqhdr->mqh_wait, &mqhdr->mqh_lock);
48     }
```

―――――――――――――――――――――――――― *my_pxmsg_mmap/mq_send.c*

Figure 5.29 mq_send function: first half.

```
                                                         ──── my_pxmsg_mmap/mq_send.c
49              /* nmsghdr will point to new message */
50      if ( (freeindex = mqhdr->mqh_free) == 0)
51          err_dump("mq_send: curmsgs = %ld; free = 0", attr->mq_curmsgs);
52      nmsghdr = (struct msg_hdr *) &mptr[freeindex];
53      nmsghdr->msg_prio = prio;
54      nmsghdr->msg_len = len;
55      memcpy(nmsghdr + 1, ptr, len);   /* copy message from caller */
56      mqhdr->mqh_free = nmsghdr->msg_next;     /* new freelist head */

57          /* find right place for message in linked list */
58      index = mqhdr->mqh_head;
59      pmsghdr = (struct msg_hdr *) &(mqhdr->mqh_head);
60      while (index != 0) {
61          msghdr = (struct msg_hdr *) &mptr[index];
62          if (prio > msghdr->msg_prio) {
63              nmsghdr->msg_next = index;
64              pmsghdr->msg_next = freeindex;
65              break;
66          }
67          index = msghdr->msg_next;
68          pmsghdr = msghdr;
69      }
70      if (index == 0) {
71              /* queue was empty or new goes at end of list */
72          pmsghdr->msg_next = freeindex;
73          nmsghdr->msg_next = 0;
74      }
75          /* wake up anyone blocked in mq_receive waiting for a message */
76      if (attr->mq_curmsgs == 0)
77          pthread_cond_signal(&mqhdr->mqh_wait);
78      attr->mq_curmsgs++;

79      pthread_mutex_unlock(&mqhdr->mqh_lock);
80      return (0);

81  err:
82      pthread_mutex_unlock(&mqhdr->mqh_lock);
83      return (-1);
84 }
                                                         ──── my_pxmsg_mmap/mq_send.c
```

Figure 5.30 mq_send function: second half.

Get index of free block to use

50–52   Since the number of free messages created when the queue was initialized equals
mq_maxmsg, we should never have a situation where mq_curmsgs is less than
mq_maxmsg with an empty free list.

Copy message

53–56   nmsghdr contains the address in the mapped memory of where the message is
stored. The priority and length are stored in its msg_hdr structure, and then the contents of the message are copied from the caller.

Place new message onto linked list in correct location

57–74   The order of messages on our linked list is from highest priority at the front (mqh_head) to lowest priority at the end. When a new message is added to the queue and one or more messages of the same priority are already on the queue, the new message is added after the last message with its priority. Using this ordering, mq_receive always returns the first message on the linked list (which is the oldest message of the highest priority on the queue). As we step through the linked list, pmsghdr contains the address of the previous message in the list, because its msg_next value will contain the index of the new message.

> Our design can be slow when lots of messages are on the queue, forcing a traversal of a large number of list entries each time a message is written to the queue. A separate index could be maintained that remembers the location of the last message for each possible priority.

Wake up anyone blocked in mq_receive

75–77   If the queue was empty before we placed the message onto the queue, we call pthread_cond_signal to wake up any thread that might be blocked in mq_receive.

78   The number of messages currently on the queue, mq_curmsgs, is incremented.

mq_receive Function

Figure 5.31 shows the first half of our mq_receive function, which sets up the pointers that it needs, obtains the mutex lock, and verifies that the caller's buffer is large enough for the largest possible message.

Check for empty queue

30–40   If the queue is empty and the O_NONBLOCK flag is set, an error of EAGAIN is returned. Otherwise, we increment the queue's mqh_nwait counter, which was examined by our mq_send function in Figure 5.29, if the queue was empty and someone was registered for notification. We then wait on the condition variable, which is signaled by mq_send in Figure 5.29.

> As with our implementation of mq_send, our implementation of mq_receive is simplistic with regard to returning an error of EINTR if this call is interrupted by a signal that is caught by the calling process.

Figure 5.32 shows the second half of our mq_receive function. At this point, we know that a message is on the queue to return to the caller.

———— *my_pxmsg_mmap/mq_receive.c*

```
 1 #include    "unpipc.h"
 2 #include    "mqueue.h"

 3 ssize_t
 4 mq_receive(mqd_t mqd, char *ptr, size_t maxlen, unsigned int *priop)
 5 {
 6     int    n;
 7     long   index;
 8     int8_t *mptr;
 9     ssize_t len;
10     struct mq_hdr *mqhdr;
11     struct mq_attr *attr;
12     struct msg_hdr *msghdr;
13     struct mq_info *mqinfo;

14     mqinfo = mqd;
15     if (mqinfo->mqi_magic != MQI_MAGIC) {
16         errno = EBADF;
17         return (-1);
18     }
19     mqhdr = mqinfo->mqi_hdr;     /* struct pointer */
20     mptr = (int8_t *) mqhdr;     /* byte pointer */
21     attr = &mqhdr->mqh_attr;
22     if ( (n = pthread_mutex_lock(&mqhdr->mqh_lock)) != 0) {
23         errno = n;
24         return (-1);
25     }
26     if (maxlen < attr->mq_msgsize) {
27         errno = EMSGSIZE;
28         goto err;
29     }
30     if (attr->mq_curmsgs == 0) {     /* queue is empty */
31         if (mqinfo->mqi_flags & O_NONBLOCK) {
32             errno = EAGAIN;
33             goto err;
34         }
35             /* wait for a message to be placed onto queue */
36         mqhdr->mqh_nwait++;
37         while (attr->mq_curmsgs == 0)
38             pthread_cond_wait(&mqhdr->mqh_wait, &mqhdr->mqh_lock);
39         mqhdr->mqh_nwait--;
40     }
```

———— *my_pxmsg_mmap/mq_receive.c*

Figure 5.31 mq_receive function: first half.

my_pxmsg_mmap/mq_receive.c

```
41      if ( (index = mqhdr->mqh_head) == 0)
42          err_dump("mq_receive: curmsgs = %ld; head = 0", attr->mq_curmsgs);

43      msghdr = (struct msg_hdr *) &mptr[index];
44      mqhdr->mqh_head = msghdr->msg_next;      /* new head of list */
45      len = msghdr->msg_len;
46      memcpy(ptr, msghdr + 1, len);    /* copy the message itself */
47      if (priop != NULL)
48          *priop = msghdr->msg_prio;

49          /* just-read message goes to front of free list */
50      msghdr->msg_next = mqhdr->mqh_free;
51      mqhdr->mqh_free = index;

52          /* wake up anyone blocked in mq_send waiting for room */
53      if (attr->mq_curmsgs == attr->mq_maxmsg)
54          pthread_cond_signal(&mqhdr->mqh_wait);
55      attr->mq_curmsgs--;

56      pthread_mutex_unlock(&mqhdr->mqh_lock);
57      return (len);

58   err:
59      pthread_mutex_unlock(&mqhdr->mqh_lock);
60      return (-1);
61  }
```

my_pxmsg_mmap/mq_receive.c

Figure 5.32 mq_receive function: second half.

Return message to caller

43–51   msghdr points to the msg_hdr of the first message on the queue, which is what we return. The space occupied by this message becomes the new head of the free list.

Wake up anyone blocked in mq_send

52–54   If the queue was full before we took the message off the queue, we call pthread_cond_signal, in case anyone is blocked in mq_send waiting for room for a message.

5.9   Summary

Posix message queues are simple: a new queue is created or an existing queue is opened by mq_open; queues are closed by mq_close, and the queue names are removed by mq_unlink. Messages are placed onto a queue with mq_send and read with mq_receive. Attributes of the queue can be queried and set with mq_getattr and mq_setattr, and the function mq_notify lets us register a signal to be sent, or a thread to be invoked, when a message is placed onto an empty queue. Small integer priorities are assigned to each message on the queue, and mq_receive always returns the oldest message of the highest priority each time it is called.

Using `mq_notify` introduced us to the Posix realtime signals, named SIGRTMIN through SIGRTMAX. When the signal handler for these signals is installed with the SA_SIGINFO flag set, (1) these signals are queued, (2) the queued signals are delivered in a FIFO order, and (3) two additional arguments are passed to the signal handler.

Finally, we implemented most of the Posix message queue features in about 500 lines of C code, using memory-mapped I/O, along with a Posix mutex and a Posix condition variable. This implementation showed a race condition dealing with the creation of a new queue; we will encounter this same race condition in Chapter 10 when implementing Posix semaphores.

Exercises

5.1   With Figure 5.5, we said that if the *attr* argument to `mq_open` is nonnull when a new queue is created, both of the members `mq_maxmsg` and `mq_msgsize` must be specified. How could we allow either of these to be specified, instead of requiring both, with the one not specified assuming the system's default value?

5.2   Modify Figure 5.9 so that it does not call `mq_notify` when the signal is delivered. Then send two messages to the queue and verify that the signal is not generated for the second message. Why?

5.3   Modify Figure 5.9 so that it does not read the message from the queue when the signal is delivered. Instead, just call `mq_notify` and print that the signal was received. Then send two messages to the queue and verify that the signal is not generated for the second message. Why?

5.4   What happens if we remove the cast to an integer for the two constants in the first `printf` in Figure 5.17?

5.5   Modify Figure 5.5 as follows: before calling `mq_open`, print a message and `sleep` for 30 seconds. After `mq_open` returns, print another message, `sleep` for 30 seconds, and then call `mq_close`. Compile and run the program, specifying a large number of messages (a few hundred thousand) and a maximum message size of (say) 10 bytes. The goal is to create a large message queue (megabytes) and then see whether the implementation uses memory-mapped files. During the first 30-second pause, run a program such as `ps` and look at the memory size of the program. Do this again, after `mq_open` has returned. Can you explain what happens?

5.6   What happens in the call to `memcpy` in Figure 5.30 when the caller of `mq_send` specifies a length of 0?

5.7   Compare a message queue to the full-duplex pipes that we described in Section 4.4. How many message queues are needed for two-way communication between a parent and child?

5.8   In Figure 5.24, why don't we destroy the mutex and condition variable?

5.9   Posix says that a message queue descriptor cannot be an array type. Why?

5.10 Where does the `main` function in Figure 5.14 spend most of its time? What happens every time a signal is delivered? How do we handle this scenario?

5.11 Not all implementations support the PTHREAD_PROCESS_SHARED attributes for mutexes and condition variables. Redo the implementation of Posix message queues in Section 5.8 to use Posix semaphores (Chapter 10) instead of mutexes and condition variables.

5.12 Extend the implementation of Posix message queues in Section 5.8 to support SIGEV_THREAD.

6

System V Message Queues

6.1 Introduction

System V message queues are identified by a *message queue identifier*. Any process with adequate privileges (Section 3.5) can place a message onto a given queue, and any process with adequate privileges can read a message from a given queue. As with Posix message queues, there is no requirement that some process be waiting for a message to arrive on a queue before some process writes a message to that queue.

For every message queue in the system, the kernel maintains the following structure of information, defined by including <sys/msg.h>:

```
struct msqid_ds {
  struct ipc_perm  msg_perm;    /* read-write perms: Section 3.3 */
  struct msg       *msg_first;  /* ptr to first message on queue */
  struct msg       *msg_last;   /* ptr to last message on queue */
  msglen_t         msg_cbytes;  /* current # bytes on queue */
  msgqnum_t        msg_qnum;    /* current # of messages on queue */
  msglen_t         msg_qbytes;  /* max # of bytes allowed on queue */
  pid_t            msg_lspid;   /* pid of last msgsnd() */
  pid_t            msg_lrpid;   /* pid of last msgrcv() */
  time_t           msg_stime;   /* time of last msgsnd() */
  time_t           msg_rtime;   /* time of last msgrcv() */
  time_t           msg_ctime;   /* time of last msgctl()
                                   (that changed the above) */
};
```

Unix 98 does not require the msg_first, msg_last, or msg_cbytes members. Nevertheless, these three members are found in the common System V derived implementations. Naturally, no requirement exists that the messages on a queue be maintained as a linked list, as implied by the msg_first and msg_last members. If these two pointers are present, they point to kernel memory and are largely useless to an application.

129

We can picture a particular message queue in the kernel as a linked list of messages, as shown in Figure 6.1. Assume that three messages are on a queue, with lengths of 1 byte, 2 bytes, and 3 bytes, and that the messages were written in that order. Also assume that these three messages were written with *type*s of 100, 200, and 300, respectively.

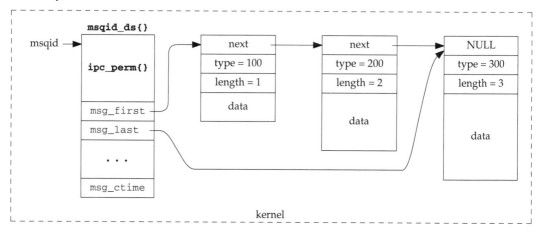

Figure 6.1 System V message queue structures in kernel.

In this chapter, we look at the functions for manipulating System V message queues and implement our file server example from Section 4.2 using message queues.

6.2 `msgget` Function

A new message queue is created, or an existing message queue is accessed with the `msgget` function.

```
#include    <sys/msg.h>

int msgget(key_t key, int oflag);
```
                                              Returns: nonnegative identifier if OK, −1 on error

The return value is an integer identifier that is used in the other three `msg` functions to refer to this queue, based on the specified *key*, which can be a value returned by `ftok` or the constant `IPC_PRIVATE`, as shown in Figure 3.3.

oflag is a combination of the read–write permission values shown in Figure 3.6. This can be bitwise-ORed with either `IPC_CREAT` or `IPC_CREAT | IPC_EXCL`, as discussed with Figure 3.4.

When a new message queue is created, the following members of the `msqid_ds` structure are initialized:

- The uid and cuid members of the msg_perm structure are set to the effective user ID of the process, and the gid and cgid members are set to the effective group ID of the process.

- The read–write permission bits in *oflag* are stored in msg_perm.mode.

- msg_qnum, msg_lspid, msg_lrpid, msg_stime, and msg_rtime are set to 0.

- msg_ctime is set to the current time.

- msg_qbytes is set to the system limit.

6.3   msgsnd Function

Once a message queue is opened by msgget, we put a message onto the queue using msgsnd.

```
#include  <sys/msg.h>

int msgsnd(int msqid, const void *ptr, size_t length, int flag);
```

                                                                       Returns: 0 if OK, −1 on error

msqid is an identifier returned by msgget. *ptr* is a pointer to a structure with the following template, which is defined in <sys/msg.h>.

```
struct msgbuf {
  long  mtype;      /* message type, must be > 0 */
  char  mtext[1];   /* message data */
};
```

The message type must be greater than 0, since nonpositive message types are used as a special indicator to the msgrcv function, which we describe in the next section.

The name mtext in the msgbuf structure definition is a misnomer; the data portion of the message is not restricted to text. Any form of data is allowed, binary data or text. The kernel does not interpret the contents of the message data at all.

We use the term "template" to describe this structure, because what *ptr* points to is just a long integer containing the message type, immediately followed by the message itself (if the length of the message is greater than 0 bytes). But most applications do not use this definition of the msgbuf structure, since the amount of data (1 byte) is normally inadequate. No compile-time limit exists to the amount of data in a message (this limit can often be changed by the system administrator), so rather than declare a structure with a huge amount of data (more data than a given implementation may support), this template is defined instead. Most applications then define their own message structure, with the data portion defined by the needs of the application.

For example, if some application wanted to exchange messages consisting of a 16-bit integer followed by an 8-byte character array, it could define its own structure as:

```
#define MY_DATA   8

typedef struct my_msgbuf {
  long      mtype;      /* message type */
  int16_t   mshort;     /* start of message data */
  char      mchar[MY_DATA];
} Message;
```

The *length* argument to msgsnd specifies the length of the message in bytes. This is the length of the user-defined data that follows the long integer message type. The length can be 0. In the example just shown, the length could be passed as sizeof(Message) - sizeof(long).

The *flag* argument can be either 0 or IPC_NOWAIT. This flag makes the call to msgsnd *nonblocking*: the function returns immediately if no room is available for the new message. This condition can occur if

- too many bytes are already on the specified queue (the msg_qbytes value in the msqid_ds structure), or
- too many messages exist systemwide.

If one of these two conditions exists and if IPC_NOWAIT is specified, msgsnd returns an error of EAGAIN. If one of these two conditions exists and if IPC_NOWAIT is not specified, then the thread is put to sleep until

- room exists for the message,
- the message queue identified by *msqid* is removed from the system (in which case, an error of EIDRM is returned), or
- the calling thread is interrupted by a caught signal (in which case, an error of EINTR is returned).

6.4   msgrcv Function

A message is read from a message queue using the msgrcv function.

```
#include  <sys/msg.h>

ssize_t msgrcv(int msqid, void *ptr, size_t length, long type, int flag);
                           Returns: number of bytes of data read into buffer if OK, −1 on error
```

The *ptr* argument specifies where the received message is to be stored. As with msgsnd, this pointer points to the long integer type field (Figure 4.26) that is returned immediately before the actual message data.

length specifies the size of the data portion of the buffer pointed to by *ptr*. This is the maximum amount of data that is returned by the function. This length excludes the long integer type field.

type specifies which message on the queue is desired:

- If *type* is 0, the first message on the queue is returned. Since each message queue is maintained as a FIFO list (first-in, first-out), a *type* of 0 specifies that the oldest message on the queue is to be returned.
- If *type* is greater than 0, the first message whose type equals *type* is returned.
- If *type* is less than 0, the first message with the *lowest* type that is less than or equal to the absolute value of the *type* argument is returned.

Consider the message queue example shown in Figure 6.1, which contains three messages:

- the first message has a type of 100 and a length of 1,
- the second has a type of 200 and a length of 2, and
- the last message has a type of 300 and a length of 3.

Figure 6.2 shows the message returned for different values of *type*.

type	Type of message returned
0	100
100	100
200	200
300	300
-100	100
-200	100
-300	100

Figure 6.2 Messages returned by msgrcv for different values of *type*.

The *flag* argument specifies what to do if a message of the requested type is not on the queue. If the IPC_NOWAIT bit is set and no message is available, the msgrcv function returns immediately with an error of ENOMSG. Otherwise, the caller is blocked until one of the following occurs:

1. a message of the requested type is available,
2. the message queue identified by *msqid* is removed from the system (in which case, an error of EIDRM is returned), or
3. the calling thread is interrupted by a caught signal (in which case, an error of EINTR is returned).

An additional bit in the *flag* argument can be specified: MSG_NOERROR. When set, this specifies that if the actual data portion of the received message is greater than the *length* argument, just truncate the data portion and return without an error. Not specifying the MSG_NOERROR flag causes an error return of E2BIG if *length* is not large enough to receive the entire message.

On successful return, `msgrcv` returns the number of bytes of data in the received message. This does not include the bytes needed for the long integer message type that is also returned through the *ptr* argument.

6.5   `msgctl` Function

The `msgctl` function provides a variety of control operations on a message queue.

```
#include  <sys/msg.h>

int msgctl(int msqid, int cmd, struct msqid_ds *buff);
```
Returns: 0 if OK, −1 on error

Three commands are provided:

IPC_RMID   Remove the message queue specified by *msqid* from the system. Any messages currently on the queue are discarded. We have already seen an example of this operation in Figure 3.7. The third argument to the function is ignored for this command.

IPC_SET   Set the following four members of the `msqid_ds` structure for the message queue from the corresponding members in the structure pointed to by the *buff* argument: `msg_perm.uid`, `msg_perm.gid`, `msg_perm.mode`, and `msg_qbytes`.

IPC_STAT   Return to the caller (through the *buff* argument) the current `msqid_ds` structure for the specified message queue.

Example

The program in Figure 6.3 creates a message queue, puts a message containing 1 byte of data onto the queue, issues the IPC_STAT command to `msgctl`, executes the `ipcs` command using the `system` function, and then removes the queue using the IPC_RMID command to `msgctl`.

We write a 1-byte message to the queue, so we just use the standard `msgbuf` structure defined in `<sys/msg.h>`.

Executing this program gives us

```
solaris % ctl
read-write: 664, cbytes = 1, qnum = 1, qbytes = 4096
IPC status from <running system> as of Mon Oct 20 15:36:40 1997
T         ID      KEY        MODE         OWNER     GROUP
Message Queues:
q        1150    00000000 --rw-rw-r-- rstevens   other1
```

The values are as expected. The key value of 0 is the common value for IPC_PRIVATE, as we mentioned in Section 3.2. On this system there is a limit of 4096 bytes per message queue. Since we wrote a message with 1 byte of data, and since msg_cbytes is 1,

svmsg/ctl.c

```
 1 #include    "unpipc.h"

 2 int
 3 main(int argc, char **argv)
 4 {
 5     int     msqid;
 6     struct msqid_ds info;
 7     struct msgbuf buf;

 8     msqid = Msgget(IPC_PRIVATE, SVMSG_MODE | IPC_CREAT);

 9     buf.mtype = 1;
10     buf.mtext[0] = 1;
11     Msgsnd(msqid, &buf, 1, 0);

12     Msgctl(msqid, IPC_STAT, &info);
13     printf("read-write: %03o, cbytes = %lu, qnum = %lu, qbytes = %lu\n",
14             info.msg_perm.mode & 0777, (ulong_t) info.msg_cbytes,
15             (ulong_t) info.msg_qnum, (ulong_t) info.msg_qbytes);

16     system("ipcs -q");

17     Msgctl(msqid, IPC_RMID, NULL);
18     exit(0);
19 }
```

svmsg/ctl.c

Figure 6.3 Example of `msgctl` function with `IPC_STAT` command.

this limit is apparently just for the data portion of the messages, and does not include the long integer message type associated with each message.

6.6   Simple Programs

Since System V message queues are kernel-persistent, we can write a small set of programs to manipulate these queues, and see what happens.

`msgcreate` Program

Figure 6.4 shows our `msgcreate` program, which creates a message queue.

9–12   We allow a command-line option of `-e` to specify the `IPC_EXCL` flag.

16   The pathname that is required as a command-line argument is passed as an argument to `ftok`. The resulting key is converted into an identifier by `msgget`. (See Exercise 6.1.)

`msgsnd` Program

Our `msgsnd` program is shown in Figure 6.5, and it places one message of a specified length and type onto a queue.

—————————————————————————————— svmsg/msgcreate.c

```
 1 #include    "unpipc.h"

 2 int
 3 main(int argc, char **argv)
 4 {
 5     int    c, oflag, mqid;

 6     oflag = SVMSG_MODE | IPC_CREAT;
 7     while ( (c = Getopt(argc, argv, "e")) != -1) {
 8         switch (c) {
 9         case 'e':
10             oflag |= IPC_EXCL;
11             break;
12         }
13     }
14     if (optind != argc - 1)
15         err_quit("usage: msgcreate [ -e ] <pathname>");

16     mqid = Msgget(Ftok(argv[optind], 1), oflag);
17     exit(0);
18 }
```

—————————————————————————————— svmsg/msgcreate.c

Figure 6.4 Create a System V message queue.

—————————————————————————————— svmsg/msgsnd.c

```
 1 #include    "unpipc.h"

 2 int
 3 main(int argc, char **argv)
 4 {
 5     int     mqid;
 6     size_t  len;
 7     long    type;
 8     struct msgbuf *ptr;

 9     if (argc != 4)
10         err_quit("usage: msgsnd <pathname> <#bytes> <type>");
11     len = atoi(argv[2]);
12     type = atoi(argv[3]);

13     mqid = Msgget(Ftok(argv[1], 1), MSG_W);

14     ptr = Calloc(sizeof(long) + len, sizeof(char));
15     ptr->mtype = type;

16     Msgsnd(mqid, ptr, len, 0);

17     exit(0);
18 }
```

—————————————————————————————— svmsg/msgsnd.c

Figure 6.5 Add a message to a System V message queue.

We allocate a pointer to a generic `msgbuf` structure but then allocate the actual structure (e.g., the output buffer) by calling `calloc`, based on the size of the message. This function initializes the buffer to 0.

`msgrcv` Program

Figure 6.6 shows our `msgrcv` function, which reads a message from a queue. An optional -n argument specifies nonblocking, and an optional -t argument specifies the *type* argument for `msgrcv`.

————————————————————————————— svmsg/msgrcv.c

```
 1 #include     "unpipc.h"

 2 #define MAXMSG  (8192 + sizeof(long))

 3 int
 4 main(int argc, char **argv)
 5 {
 6     int     c, flag, mqid;
 7     long    type;
 8     ssize_t n;
 9     struct msgbuf *buff;

10     type = flag = 0;
11     while ( (c = Getopt(argc, argv, "nt:")) != -1) {
12         switch (c) {
13         case 'n':
14             flag |= IPC_NOWAIT;
15             break;

16         case 't':
17             type = atol(optarg);
18             break;
19         }
20     }
21     if (optind != argc - 1)
22         err_quit("usage: msgrcv [ -n ] [ -t type ] <pathname>");

23     mqid = Msgget(Ftok(argv[optind], 1), MSG_R);

24     buff = Malloc(MAXMSG);

25     n = Msgrcv(mqid, buff, MAXMSG, type, flag);
26     printf("read %d bytes, type = %ld\n", n, buff->mtype);

27     exit(0);
28 }
```

————————————————————————————— svmsg/msgrcv.c

Figure 6.6   Read a message from a System V message queue.

2   No simple way exists to determine the maximum size of a message (we talk about this and other limits in Section 6.10), so we define our own constant for this limit.

`msgrmid` Program

To remove a message queue, we call `msgctl` with a command of `IPC_RMID`, as shown in Figure 6.7.

—————————————————————————— svmsg/msgrmid.c

```
1 #include     "unpipc.h"

2 int
3 main(int argc, char **argv)
4 {
5     int     mqid;

6     if (argc != 2)
7         err_quit("usage: msgrmid <pathname>");

8     mqid = Msgget(Ftok(argv[1], 1), 0);
9     Msgctl(mqid, IPC_RMID, NULL);

10     exit(0);
11 }
```
—————————————————————————— svmsg/msgrmid.c

Figure 6.7   Remove a System V message queue.

Examples

We now use the four programs that we have just shown. We first create a message
queue and write three messages to the queue.

```
solaris % msgcreate /tmp/no/such/file
ftok error for pathname "/tmp/no/such/file" and id 0: No such file or directory
solaris % touch /tmp/test1
solaris % msgcreate /tmp/test1
solaris % msgsnd /tmp/test1 1 100
solaris % msgsnd /tmp/test1 2 200
solaris % msgsnd /tmp/test1 3 300
solaris % ipcs -qo
IPC status from <running system> as of Sat Jan 10 11:25:45 1998
T      ID       KEY        MODE       OWNER     GROUP CBYTES  QNUM
Message Queues:
q      100      0x0000113e --rw-r--r-- rstevens   other1      6      3
```

We first try to create a message queue using a pathname that does not exist. This
demonstrates that the pathname argument for ftok must exist. We then create the file
/tmp/test1 and create a message queue using this pathname. Three messages are
placed onto the queue: the three lengths are 1, 2, and 3 bytes, and the three types are
respectively 100, 200, and 300 (recall Figure 6.1). The ipcs program shows 3 messages
comprising a total of 6 bytes on the queue.

We next demonstrate the use of the *type* argument to msgrcv in reading the messages in an order other than FIFO.

```
solaris % msgrcv -t 200 /tmp/test1
read 2 bytes, type = 200
solaris % msgrcv -t -300 /tmp/test1
read 1 bytes, type = 100
solaris % msgrcv /tmp/test1
read 3 bytes, type = 300
solaris % msgrcv -n /tmp/test1
msgrcv error: No message of desired type
```

The first example requests the message with a type field of 200, the second example requests the message with the lowest type field less than or equal to 300, and the third example requests the first message on the queue. The last execution of our msgrcv program shows the IPC_NOWAIT flag.

What happens if we specify a positive *type* argument to msgrcv but no message with that type exists on the queue?

```
solaris % ipcs -qo
IPC status from <running system> as of Sat Jan 10 11:37:01 1998
T      ID     KEY         MODE        OWNER      GROUP CBYTES  QNUM
Message Queues:
q       100   0x0000113e --rw-r--r-- rstevens   other1     0     0
solaris % msgsnd /tmp/test1 1 100
solaris % msgrcv -t 999 /tmp/test1
^?                                         type our interrupt key to terminate
solaris % msgrcv -n -t 999 /tmp/test1
msgrcv error: No message of desired type
solaris % grep desired /usr/include/sys/errno.h
#define ENOMSG  35      /* No message of desired type */
solaris % msgrmid /tmp/test1
```

We first execute ipcs to verify that the queue is empty, and then place a message of length 1 with a type of 100 onto the queue. When we ask for a message of type 999, the program blocks (in the call to msgrcv), waiting for a message of that type to be placed onto the queue. We interrupt this by terminating the program with our interrupt key. We then specify the -n flag to prevent blocking, and see that the error ENOMSG is returned in this scenario. We then remove the queue from the system with our msgrmid program. We could have removed the queue using the system-provided command

```
solaris % ipcrm -q 100
```

which specifies the message queue identifier, or using

```
solaris % ipcrm -Q 0x113e
```

which specifies the message queue key.

msgrcvid Program

We now demonstrate that to access a System V message queue, we need not call msgget: all we need to know is the message queue identifier (easily obtained with ipcs) and read permission for the queue. Figure 6.8 shows a simplification of our msgrcv program from Figure 6.6.

We do not call msgget. Instead, the caller specifies the message queue identifier on the command line.

svmsg/msgrcvid.c

```
 1 #include    "unpipc.h"

 2 #define MAXMSG  (8192 + sizeof(long))

 3 int
 4 main(int argc, char **argv)
 5 {
 6     int     mqid;
 7     ssize_t n;
 8     struct msgbuf *buff;

 9     if (argc != 2)
10         err_quit("usage: msgrcvid <mqid>");
11     mqid = atoi(argv[1]);

12     buff = Malloc(MAXMSG);

13     n = Msgrcv(mqid, buff, MAXMSG, 0, 0);
14     printf("read %d bytes, type = %ld\n", n, buff->mtype);

15     exit(0);
16 }
```

svmsg/msgrcvid.c

Figure 6.8 Read from a System V message queue knowing only the identifier.

Here is an example of this technique:

```
solaris % touch /tmp/testid
solaris % msgcreate /tmp/testid
solaris % msgsnd /tmp/testid 4 400
solaris % ipcs -qo
IPC status from <running system> as of Wed Mar 25 09:48:28 1998
T       ID      KEY        MODE       OWNER    GROUP CBYTES  QNUM
Message Queues:
q       150     0x0000118a --rw-r--r-- rstevens  other1    4     1
solaris % msgrcvid 150
read 4 bytes, type = 400
```

We obtain the identifier of 150 from `ipcs`, and this is the command-line argument to our `msgrcvid` program.

This same feature applies to System V semaphores (Exercise 11.1) and System V shared memory (Exercise 14.1).

6.7   Client–Server Example

We now code our client–server example from Section 4.2 to use two message queues. One queue is for messages from the client to the server, and the other queue is for messages in the other direction.

Our header `svmsg.h` is shown in Figure 6.9. We include our standard header and define the keys for each message queue.

svmsgcliserv/svmsg.h
```
1 #include      "unpipc.h"

2 #define MQ_KEY1 1234L
3 #define MQ_KEY2 2345L
```
svmsgcliserv/svmsg.h

Figure 6.9 svmsg.h header for client–server using message queues.

The main function for the server is shown in Figure 6.10. Both message queues are created and if either already exists, it is OK, because we do not specify the IPC_EXCL flag. The server function is the one shown in Figure 4.30 that calls our mesg_send and mesg_recv functions, versions of which we show shortly.

svmsgcliserv/server_main.c
```
 1 #include      "svmsg.h"

 2 void     server(int, int);

 3 int
 4 main(int argc, char **argv)
 5 {
 6      int     readid, writeid;

 7      readid = Msgget(MQ_KEY1, SVMSG_MODE | IPC_CREAT);
 8      writeid = Msgget(MQ_KEY2, SVMSG_MODE | IPC_CREAT);

 9      server(readid, writeid);

10      exit(0);
11 }
```
svmsgcliserv/server_main.c

Figure 6.10 Server main function using message queues.

svmsgcliserv/client_main.c
```
 1 #include      "svmsg.h"

 2 void     client(int, int);

 3 int
 4 main(int argc, char **argv)
 5 {
 6      int     readid, writeid;

 7          /* assumes server has created the queues */
 8      writeid = Msgget(MQ_KEY1, 0);
 9      readid = Msgget(MQ_KEY2, 0);

10      client(readid, writeid);

11          /* now we can delete the queues */
12      Msgctl(readid, IPC_RMID, NULL);
13      Msgctl(writeid, IPC_RMID, NULL);

14      exit(0);
15 }
```
svmsgcliserv/client_main.c

Figure 6.11 Client main function using message queues.

Figure 6.11 shows the `main` function for the client. The two message queues are opened and our `client` function from Figure 4.29 is called. This function calls our `mesg_send` and `mesg_recv` functions, which we show next.

Both the `client` and `server` functions use the message format shown in Figure 4.25. These two functions also call our `mesg_send` and `mesg_recv` functions. The versions of these functions that we showed in Figures 4.27 and 4.28 called `write` and `read`, which worked with pipes and FIFOs, but we need to recode these two functions to work with message queues. Figures 6.12 and 6.13 show these new versions. Notice that the arguments to these two functions do not change from the versions that called `write` and `read`, because the first integer argument can contain either an integer descriptor (for a pipe or FIFO) or an integer message queue identifier.

——— *svmsgcliserv/mesg_send.c*
```
1 #include    "mesg.h"

2 ssize_t
3 mesg_send(int id, struct mymesg *mptr)
4 {
5     return (msgsnd(id, &(mptr->mesg_type), mptr->mesg_len, 0));
6 }
```
——— *svmsgcliserv/mesg_send.c*

Figure 6.12 `mesg_send` function that works with message queues.

——— *svmsgcliserv/mesg_recv.c*
```
1 #include    "mesg.h"

2 ssize_t
3 mesg_recv(int id, struct mymesg *mptr)
4 {
5     ssize_t n;

6     n = msgrcv(id, &(mptr->mesg_type), MAXMESGDATA, mptr->mesg_type, 0);
7     mptr->mesg_len = n;        /* return #bytes of data */

8     return (n);                /* -1 on error, 0 at EOF, else >0 */
9 }
```
——— *svmsgcliserv/mesg_recv.c*

Figure 6.13 `mesg_recv` function that works with message queues.

6.8 Multiplexing Messages

Two features are provided by the type field that is associated with each message on a queue:

1. The type field can be used to identify the messages, allowing multiple processes to *multiplex* messages onto a single queue. One value of the type field is used for messages from the clients to the server, and a different value that is unique for each client is used for messages from the server to the clients. Naturally, the process ID of the client can be used as the type field that is unique for each client.

2. The type field can be used as a priority field. This lets the receiver read the messages in an order other than first-in, first-out (FIFO). With pipes and FIFOs, the data must be read in the order in which it was written. With System V message queues, we can read the messages in any order that is consistent with the values we associate with the message types. Furthermore, we can call `msgrcv` with the `IPC_NOWAIT` flag to read any messages of a given type from the queue, but return immediately if no messages of the specified type exist.

Example: One Queue per Application

Recall our simple example of a server process and a single client process. With either pipes or FIFOs, two IPC channels are required to exchange data in both directions, since these types of IPC are unidirectional. With a message queue, a single queue can be used, having the type of each message signify whether the message is from the client to the server, or vice versa.

Consider the next complication, a server with multiple clients. Here we can use a type of 1, say, to indicate a message from any client to the server. If the client passes its process ID as part of the message, the server can send its messages to the client processes, using the client's process ID as the message type. Each client then specifies its process ID as the *type* argument to `msgrcv`. Figure 6.14 shows how a single message queue can be used to multiplex these messages between multiple clients and one server.

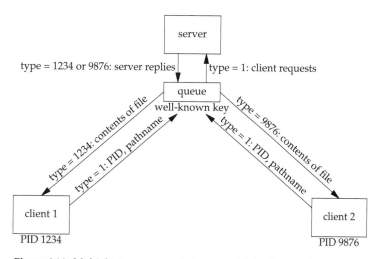

Figure 6.14 Multiplexing messages between multiple clients and one server.

A potential for deadlock always exists when one IPC channel is used by both the clients and the server. Clients can fill up the message queue (in this example), preventing the server from sending a reply. The clients are then blocked in msgsnd, as is the server. One convention that can detect this deadlock is for the server to always use a nonblocking write to the message queue.

We now redo our client–server example using a single message queue with different message types for messages in each direction. These programs use the convention that messages with a type of 1 are from the client to the server, and all other messages have a type equal to the process ID of the client. This client–server requires that the client request contain the client's process ID along with the pathname, similar to what we did in Section 4.8.

Figure 6.15 shows the server `main` function. The `svmsg.h` header was shown in Figure 6.9. Only one message queue is created, and if it already exists, it is OK. The same message queue identifier is used for both arguments to the `server` function.

——————————————————————————————————————— svmsgmpx1q/server_main.c

```
 1 #include     "svmsg.h"

 2 void     server(int, int);

 3 int
 4 main(int argc, char **argv)
 5 {
 6     int     msqid;

 7     msqid = Msgget(MQ_KEY1, SVMSG_MODE | IPC_CREAT);

 8     server(msqid, msqid);        /* same queue for both directions */

 9     exit(0);
10 }
```

——————————————————————————————————————— svmsgmpx1q/server_main.c

Figure 6.15 Server `main` function.

The `server` function does all the server processing, and is shown in Figure 6.16. This function is a combination of Figure 4.23, our FIFO server that read commands consisting of a process ID and a pathname, and Figure 4.30, which used our `mesg_send` and `mesg_recv` functions. Notice that the process ID sent by the client is used as the message type for all messages sent by the server to the client. Also, this `server` is an infinite loop that is called once and never returns, reading each client request and sending back the replies. Our server is an iterative server, as we discussed in Section 4.9.

Figure 6.17 shows the client `main` function. The client opens the message queue, which the server must have already created.

The `client` function shown in Figure 6.18 does all of the processing for our client. This function is a combination of Figure 4.24, which sent a process ID followed by a pathname, and Figure 4.29, which used our `mesg_send` and `mesg_recv` functions. Note that the type of messages requested from `mesg_recv` equals the process ID of the client.

Our `client` and `server` functions both use the `mesg_send` and `mesg_recv` functions from Figures 6.12 and 6.13.

——————————————————————— svmsgmpx1q/server.c

```
1 #include    "mesg.h"

2 void
3 server(int readfd, int writefd)
4 {
5      FILE    *fp;
6      char    *ptr;
7      pid_t   pid;
8      ssize_t n;
9      struct mymesg mesg;

10     for ( ; ; ) {
11             /* read pathname from IPC channel */
12         mesg.mesg_type = 1;
13         if ( (n = Mesg_recv(readfd, &mesg)) == 0) {
14             err_msg("pathname missing");
15             continue;
16         }
17         mesg.mesg_data[n] = '\0';   /* null terminate pathname */

18         if ( (ptr = strchr(mesg.mesg_data, ' ')) == NULL) {
19             err_msg("bogus request: %s", mesg.mesg_data);
20             continue;
21         }
22         *ptr++ = 0;                /* null terminate PID, ptr = pathname */
23         pid = atol(mesg.mesg_data);
24         mesg.mesg_type = pid;   /* for messages back to client */

25         if ( (fp = fopen(ptr, "r")) == NULL) {
26                 /* error: must tell client */
27             snprintf(mesg.mesg_data + n, sizeof(mesg.mesg_data) - n,
28                     ": can't open, %s\n", strerror(errno));
29             mesg.mesg_len = strlen(ptr);
30             memmove(mesg.mesg_data, ptr, mesg.mesg_len);
31             Mesg_send(writefd, &mesg);

32         } else {
33                 /* fopen succeeded: copy file to IPC channel */
34             while (Fgets(mesg.mesg_data, MAXMESGDATA, fp) != NULL) {
35                 mesg.mesg_len = strlen(mesg.mesg_data);
36                 Mesg_send(writefd, &mesg);
37             }
38             Fclose(fp);
39         }

40             /* send a 0-length message to signify the end */
41         mesg.mesg_len = 0;
42         Mesg_send(writefd, &mesg);
43     }
44 }
```

——————————————————————— svmsgmpx1q/server.c

Figure 6.16 server function.

—————————————————————— svmsgmpx1q/client_main.c

```
 1 #include     "svmsg.h"

 2 void    client(int, int);

 3 int
 4 main(int argc, char **argv)
 5 {
 6     int     msqid;

 7         /* server must create the queue */
 8     msqid = Msgget(MQ_KEY1, 0);

 9     client(msqid, msqid);        /* same queue for both directions */

10     exit(0);
11 }
```

—————————————————————— svmsgmpx1q/client_main.c

Figure 6.17 Client main function.

—————————————————————————— svmsgmpx1q/client.c

```
 1 #include     "mesg.h"

 2 void
 3 client(int readfd, int writefd)
 4 {
 5     size_t  len;
 6     ssize_t n;
 7     char    *ptr;
 8     struct mymesg mesg;

 9         /* start buffer with pid and a blank */
10     snprintf(mesg.mesg_data, MAXMESGDATA, "%ld ", (long) getpid());
11     len = strlen(mesg.mesg_data);
12     ptr = mesg.mesg_data + len;

13         /* read pathname */
14     Fgets(ptr, MAXMESGDATA - len, stdin);
15     len = strlen(mesg.mesg_data);
16     if (mesg.mesg_data[len - 1] == '\n')
17         len--;                   /* delete newline from fgets() */
18     mesg.mesg_len = len;
19     mesg.mesg_type = 1;

20         /* write PID and pathname to IPC channel */
21     Mesg_send(writefd, &mesg);

22         /* read from IPC, write to standard output */
23     mesg.mesg_type = getpid();
24     while ( (n = Mesg_recv(readfd, &mesg)) > 0)
25         Write(STDOUT_FILENO, mesg.mesg_data, n);
26 }
```

—————————————————————————— svmsgmpx1q/client.c

Figure 6.18 client function.

Example: One Queue per Client

We now modify the previous example to use one queue for all the client requests to the server and one queue per client for that client's responses. Figure 6.19 shows the design.

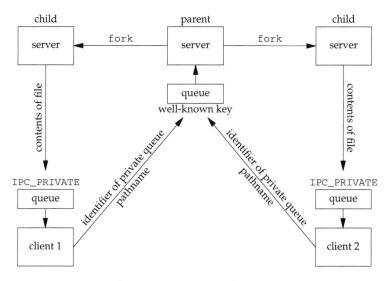

Figure 6.19 One queue per server and one queue per client.

The server's queue has a key that is well-known to the clients, but each client creates its own queue with a key of IPC_PRIVATE. Instead of passing its process ID with the request, each client passes the identifier of its private queue to the server, and the server sends its reply to the client's queue. We also write this server as a concurrent server, with one fork per client.

> One potential problem with this design occurs if a client dies, in which case, messages may be left in its private queue forever (or at least until the kernel reboots or someone explicitly deletes the queue).

The following headers and functions do not change from previous versions:

- mesg.h header (Figure 4.25),
- svmsg.h header (Figure 6.9),
- server main function (Figure 6.15), and
- mesg_send function (Figure 4.27).

Our client main function is shown in Figure 6.20; it has changed slightly from Figure 6.17. We open the server's well-known queue (MQ_KEY1) and then create our own queue with a key of IPC_PRIVATE. The two queue identifiers become the arguments to the client function (Figure 6.21). When the client is done, its private queue is removed.

svmsgmpxnq/client_main.c

```
 1 #include     "svmsg.h"

 2 void    client(int, int);

 3 int
 4 main(int argc, char **argv)
 5 {
 6     int     readid, writeid;

 7         /* server must create its well-known queue */
 8     writeid = Msgget(MQ_KEY1, 0);
 9         /* we create our own private queue */
10     readid = Msgget(IPC_PRIVATE, SVMSG_MODE | IPC_CREAT);

11     client(readid, writeid);

12         /* and delete our private queue */
13     Msgctl(readid, IPC_RMID, NULL);

14     exit(0);
15 }
```

svmsgmpxnq/client_main.c

Figure 6.20 Client main function.

svmsgmpxnq/client.c

```
 1 #include     "mesg.h"

 2 void
 3 client(int readid, int writeid)
 4 {
 5     size_t  len;
 6     ssize_t n;
 7     char    *ptr;
 8     struct mymesg mesg;

 9         /* start buffer with msqid and a blank */
10     snprintf(mesg.mesg_data, MAXMESGDATA, "%d ", readid);
11     len = strlen(mesg.mesg_data);
12     ptr = mesg.mesg_data + len;

13         /* read pathname */
14     Fgets(ptr, MAXMESGDATA - len, stdin);
15     len = strlen(mesg.mesg_data);
16     if (mesg.mesg_data[len - 1] == '\n')
17         len--;                     /* delete newline from fgets() */
18     mesg.mesg_len = len;
19     mesg.mesg_type = 1;

20         /* write msqid and pathname to server's well-known queue */
21     Mesg_send(writeid, &mesg);

22         /* read from our queue, write to standard output */
23     while ( (n = Mesg_recv(readid, &mesg)) > 0)
24         Write(STDOUT_FILENO, mesg.mesg_data, n);
25 }
```

svmsgmpxnq/client.c

Figure 6.21 client function.

Figure 6.21 is the `client` function. This function is nearly identical to Figure 6.18, but instead of passing the client's process ID as part of the request, the identifier of the client's private queue is passed instead. The message type in the `mesg` structure is also left as 1, because that is the type used for messages in both directions.

Figure 6.23 is the `server` function. The main change from Figure 6.16 is writing this function as an infinite loop that calls `fork` for each client request.

Establish signal handler for `SIGCHLD`

10   Since we are spawning a child for each client, we must worry about zombie processes. Sections 5.9 and 5.10 of UNPv1 talk about this in detail. Here we establish a signal handler for the SIGCHLD signal, and our function `sig_chld` (Figure 6.22) is called when a child terminates.

12-18   The server parent blocks in the call to `mesg_recv` waiting for the next client message to arrive.

25-45   A child is created with `fork`, and the child tries to open the requested file, sending back either an error message or the contents of the file. We purposely put the call to `fopen` in the child, instead of the parent, just in case the file is on a remote filesystem, in which case, the opening of the file could take some time if any network problems occur.

Our handler for the SIGCHLD function is shown in Figure 6.22. This is copied from Figure 5.11 of UNPv1.

```
                                                            ── svmsgmpxnq/sigchldwaitpid.c
1 #include    "unpipc.h"

2 void
3 sig_chld(int signo)
4 {
5     pid_t  pid;
6     int    stat;

7     while ( (pid = waitpid(-1, &stat, WNOHANG)) > 0) ;
8     return;
9 }
                                                            ── svmsgmpxnq/sigchldwaitpid.c
```

Figure 6.22 SIGCHLD signal handler that calls `waitpid`.

Each time our signal handler is called, it calls `waitpid` in a loop, fetching the termination status of any children that have terminated. Our signal handler then returns. This can create a problem, because the parent process spends most of its time blocked in a call to `msgrcv` in the function `mesg_recv` (Figure 6.13). When our signal handler returns, this call to `msgrcv` is *interrupted*. That is, the function returns an error of EINTR, as described in Section 5.9 of UNPv1.

We must handle this interrupted system call, and Figure 6.24 shows the new version of our `Mesg_recv` wrapper function. We allow an error of EINTR from `mesg_recv` (which just calls `msgrcv`), and when this happens, we just call `mesg_recv` again.

—————————————————————————— svmsgmpxnq/server.c

```
1 #include    "mesg.h"

2 void
3 server(int readid, int writeid)
4 {
5     FILE    *fp;
6     char    *ptr;
7     ssize_t n;
8     struct mymesg mesg;
9     void    sig_chld(int);

10    Signal(SIGCHLD, sig_chld);

11    for ( ; ; ) {
12            /* read pathname from our well-known queue */
13        mesg.mesg_type = 1;
14        if ( (n = Mesg_recv(readid, &mesg)) == 0) {
15            err_msg("pathname missing");
16            continue;
17        }
18        mesg.mesg_data[n] = '\0';   /* null terminate pathname */

19        if ( (ptr = strchr(mesg.mesg_data, ' ')) == NULL) {
20            err_msg("bogus request: %s", mesg.mesg_data);
21            continue;
22        }
23        *ptr++ = 0;              /* null terminate msgid, ptr = pathname */
24        writeid = atoi(mesg.mesg_data);

25        if (Fork() == 0) {       /* child */
26            if ( (fp = fopen(ptr, "r")) == NULL) {
27                    /* error: must tell client */
28                snprintf(mesg.mesg_data + n, sizeof(mesg.mesg_data) - n,
29                        ": can't open, %s\n", strerror(errno));
30                mesg.mesg_len = strlen(ptr);
31                memmove(mesg.mesg_data, ptr, mesg.mesg_len);
32                Mesg_send(writeid, &mesg);

33            } else {
34                    /* fopen succeeded: copy file to client's queue */
35                while (Fgets(mesg.mesg_data, MAXMESGDATA, fp) != NULL) {
36                    mesg.mesg_len = strlen(mesg.mesg_data);
37                    Mesg_send(writeid, &mesg);
38                }
39                Fclose(fp);
40            }

41                /* send a 0-length message to signify the end */
42            mesg.mesg_len = 0;
43            Mesg_send(writeid, &mesg);
44            exit(0);            /* child terminates */
45        }
46        /* parent just loops around */
47    }
48 }
```

—————————————————————————— svmsgmpxnq/server.c

Figure 6.23 server function.

————————————————————————————————— *svmsgmpxnq/mesg_recv.c*
```
10 ssize_t
11 Mesg_recv(int id, struct mymesg *mptr)
12 {
13     ssize_t n;

14     do {
15         n = mesg_recv(id, mptr);
16     } while (n == -1 && errno == EINTR);

17     if (n == -1)
18         err_sys("mesg_recv error");

19     return (n);
20 }
```
————————————————————————————————— *svmsgmpxnq/mesg_recv.c*

Figure 6.24 `Mesg_recv` wrapper function that handles an interrupted system call.

6.9 Message Queues with `select` and `poll`

One problem with System V message queues is that they are known by their own identifiers, and not by descriptors. This means that we cannot use either `select` or `poll`
(Chapter 6 of UNPv1) with these message queues.

> Actually, one version of Unix, IBM's AIX, extends `select` to handle System V message queues
> in addition to descriptors. But this is nonportable and works only with AIX.

This missing feature is often uncovered when someone wants to write a server that
handles both network connections and IPC connections. Network communications
using either the sockets API or the XTI API (UNPv1) use descriptors, allowing either
`select` or `poll` to be used. Pipes and FIFOs also work with these two functions,
because they too are identified by descriptors.

   One solution to this problem is for the server to create a pipe and then spawn a
child, with the child blocking in a call to `msgrcv`. When a message is ready to be processed, `msgrcv` returns, and the child reads the message from the queue and writes the
message to the pipe. The server parent can then `select` on the pipe, in addition to
some network connections. The downside is that these messages are then processed
three times: once when read by the child using `msgrcv`, again when written to the pipe
by the child, and again when read from the pipe by the parent. To avoid this extra processing, the parent could create a shared memory segment that is shared between itself
and the child, and then use the pipe as a flag between the parent and child (Exercise 12.5).

> In Figure 5.14 we showed a solution using Posix message queues that did not require a `fork`.
> We can use a single process with Posix message queues, because they provide a notification
> capability that generates a signal when a message arrives for an empty queue. System V mes-
> sage queues do not provide this capability, so we must `fork` a child and have the child block
> in a call to `msgrcv`.

Another missing feature from System V message queues, when compared to network programming, is the inability to peek at a message, something provided with the MSG_PEEK flag to the recv, recvfrom, and recvmsg functions (p. 356 of UNPv1). If such a facility were provided, then the parent–child scenario just described (to get around the select problem) could be made more efficient by having the child specify the peek flag to msgrcv and just write 1 byte to the pipe when a message was ready, and let the parent read the message.

6.10 Message Queue Limits

As we noted in Section 3.8, certain system limits often exist on message queues. Figure 6.25 shows the values for some different implementations. The first column is the traditional System V name for the kernel variable that contains this limit.

Name	Description	DUnix 4.0B	Solaris 2.6
msgmax	max #bytes per message	8192	2048
msgmnb	max #bytes on any one message queue	16384	4096
msgmni	max #message queues, systemwide	64	50
msgtql	max #messages, systemwide	40	40

Figure 6.25 Typical system limits for System V message queues.

Many SVR4-derived implementations have additional limits, inherited from their original implementation: msgssz is often 8, and this is the "segment" size (in bytes) in which the message data is stored. A message with 21 bytes of data would be stored in 3 of these segments, with the final 3 bytes of the last segment unused. msgseg is the number of these segments that are allocated, often 1024. Historically, this has been stored in a short integer and must therefore be less than 32768. The total number of bytes available for all message data is the product of these two variables, often 8×1024 bytes.

The intent of this section is to show some typical values, to aid in planning for portability. When a system runs applications that make heavy use of message queues, kernel tuning of these (or similar) parameters is normally required (which we described in Section 3.8).

Example

Figure 6.26 is a program that determines the four limits shown in Figure 6.25.

svmsg/limits.c

```
1 #include     "unpipc.h"

2 #define MAX_DATA    64*1024
3 #define MAX_NMESG   4096
4 #define MAX_NIDS    4096
5 int      max_mesg;

6 struct mymesg {
```

```
 7      long    type;
 8      char    data[MAX_DATA];
 9  } mesg;
10  int
11  main(int argc, char **argv)
12  {
13      int     i, j, msqid, qid[MAX_NIDS];
14          /* first try and determine maximum amount of data we can send */
15      msqid = Msgget(IPC_PRIVATE, SVMSG_MODE | IPC_CREAT);
16      mesg.type = 1;
17      for (i = MAX_DATA; i > 0; i -= 128) {
18          if (msgsnd(msqid, &mesg, i, 0) == 0) {
19              printf("maximum amount of data per message = %d\n", i);
20              max_mesg = i;
21              break;
22          }
23          if (errno != EINVAL)
24              err_sys("msgsnd error for length %d", i);
25      }
26      if (i == 0)
27          err_quit("i == 0");
28      Msgctl(msqid, IPC_RMID, NULL);

29          /* see how many messages of varying size can be put onto a queue */
30      mesg.type = 1;
31      for (i = 8; i <= max_mesg; i *= 2) {
32          msqid = Msgget(IPC_PRIVATE, SVMSG_MODE | IPC_CREAT);
33          for (j = 0; j < MAX_NMESG; j++) {
34              if (msgsnd(msqid, &mesg, i, IPC_NOWAIT) != 0) {
35                  if (errno == EAGAIN)
36                      break;
37                  err_sys("msgsnd error, i = %d, j = %d", i, j);
38                  break;
39              }
40          }
41          printf("%d %d-byte messages were placed onto queue,", j, i);
42          printf(" %d bytes total\n", i * j);
43          Msgctl(msqid, IPC_RMID, NULL);
44      }
45          /* see how many identifiers we can "open" */
46      mesg.type = 1;
47      for (i = 0; i <= MAX_NIDS; i++) {
48          if ( (qid[i] = msgget(IPC_PRIVATE, SVMSG_MODE | IPC_CREAT)) == -1) {
49              printf("%d identifiers open at once\n", i);
50              break;
51          }
52      }
53      for (j = 0; j < i; j++)
54          Msgctl(qid[j], IPC_RMID, NULL);

55      exit(0);
56  }
```
————————————————————————————————— svmsg/limits.c

Figure 6.26 Determine the system limits on System V message queues.

Determine maximum message size

14–28 To determine the maximum message size, we try to send a message containing 65536 bytes of data, and if this fails, we try a message containing 65408 bytes of data, and so on, until the call to `msgsnd` succeeds.

How many messages of varying size can be put onto a queue?

29–44 Next we start with 8-byte messages and see how many can be placed onto a given queue. Once we determine this limit, we delete the queue (discarding all these messages) and try again with 16-byte messages. We keep doing so until we pass the maximum message size that was determined in the first step. We expect smaller messages to encounter a limit on the total number of messages per queue and larger messages to encounter a limit on the total number of bytes per queue.

How many identifiers can be open at once?

45–54 Normally a system limit exists on the maximum number of message queue identifiers that can be open at any time. We determine this by just creating queues until `msgget` fails.

We first run this program under Solaris 2.6 and then Digital Unix 4.0B, and the results confirm the values shown in Figure 6.25.

```
solaris % limits
maximum amount of data per message = 2048
40 8-byte messages were placed onto queue, 320 bytes total
40 16-byte messages were placed onto queue, 640 bytes total
40 32-byte messages were placed onto queue, 1280 bytes total
40 64-byte messages were placed onto queue, 2560 bytes total
32 128-byte messages were placed onto queue, 4096 bytes total
16 256-byte messages were placed onto queue, 4096 bytes total
8 512-byte messages were placed onto queue, 4096 bytes total
4 1024-byte messages were placed onto queue, 4096 bytes total
2 2048-byte messages were placed onto queue, 4096 bytes total
50 identifiers open at once

alpha % limits
maximum amount of data per message = 8192
40 8-byte messages were placed onto queue, 320 bytes total
40 16-byte messages were placed onto queue, 640 bytes total
40 32-byte messages were placed onto queue, 1280 bytes total
40 64-byte messages were placed onto queue, 2560 bytes total
40 128-byte messages were placed onto queue, 5120 bytes total
40 256-byte messages were placed onto queue, 10240 bytes total
32 512-byte messages were placed onto queue, 16384 bytes total
16 1024-byte messages were placed onto queue, 16384 bytes total
8 2048-byte messages were placed onto queue, 16384 bytes total
4 4096-byte messages were placed onto queue, 16384 bytes total
2 8192-byte messages were placed onto queue, 16384 bytes total
63 identifiers open at once
```

The reason for the limit of 63 identifiers under Digital Unix, and not the 64 shown in Figure 6.25, is that one identifier is already being used by a system daemon.

6.11 Summary

System V message queues are similar to Posix message queues. New applications should consider using Posix message queues, but lots of existing code uses System V message queues. Nevertheless, recoding an application to use Posix message queues, instead of System V message queues, should not be hard. The main feature missing from Posix message queues is the ability to read messages of a specified priority from the queue. Neither form of message queue uses real descriptors, making it hard to use either `select` or `poll` with a message queue.

Exercises

6.1 Modify Figure 6.4 to accept a pathname argument of `IPC_PRIVATE` and create a message queue with a private key if this is specified. What changes must then be made to the remaining programs in Section 6.6?

6.2 Why did we use a type of 1 in Figure 6.14 for messages to the server?

6.3 What happens in Figure 6.14 if a malicious client sends many messages to the server but never reads any of the server's replies? What changes with Figure 6.19 for this type of client?

6.4 Redo the implementation of Posix message queues from Section 5.8 to use System V message queues instead of memory-mapped I/O.

Part 3

Synchronization

7

Mutexes and Condition Variables

7.1 Introduction

This chapter begins our discussion of synchronization: how to synchronize the actions of multiple threads or multiple processes. Synchronization is normally needed to allow the sharing of data between threads or processes. Mutexes and condition variables are the building blocks of synchronization.

Mutexes and condition variables are from the Posix.1 threads standard, and can always be used to synchronize the various threads within a process. Posix also allows a mutex or condition variable to be used for synchronization between multiple processes, if the mutex or condition variable is stored in memory that is shared between the processes.

> This is an option for Posix but required by Unix 98 (e.g., the "process shared mutex/CV" line in Figure 1.5).

In this chapter, we introduce the classic producer–consumer problem and use mutexes and condition variables in our solution of this problem. We use multiple threads for this example, instead of multiple processes, because having multiple threads share the common data buffer that is assumed in this problem is trivial, whereas sharing a common data buffer between multiple processes requires some form of shared memory (which we do not describe until Part 4). We provide additional solutions to this problem in Chapter 10 using semaphores.

7.2 Mutexes: Locking and Unlocking

A mutex, which stands for *mutual exclusion*, is the most basic form of synchronization. A mutex is used to protect a *critical region*, to make certain that only one thread at a time executes the code within the region (assuming a mutex that is being shared by the threads) or that only one process at a time executes the code within the region (assuming a mutex is being shared by the processes). The normal outline of code to protect a critical region looks like

```
lock_the_mutex(...);
critical region
unlock_the_mutex(...);
```

Since only one thread at a time can lock a given mutex, this guarantees that only one thread at a time can be executing the instructions within the critical region.

Posix mutexes are declared as variables with a datatype of pthread_mutex_t. If the mutex variable is statically allocated, we can initialize it to the constant PTHREAD_MUTEX_INITIALIZER, as in

```
static pthread_mutex_t  lock = PTHREAD_MUTEX_INITIALIZER;
```

If we dynamically allocate a mutex (e.g., by calling malloc) or if we allocate a mutex in shared memory, we must initialize it at run time by calling the pthread_mutex_init function, as we show in Section 7.7.

> You may encounter code that omits the initializer because that implementation defines the initializer to be 0 (and statically allocated variables are automatically initialized to 0). But this is incorrect code.

The following three functions lock and unlock a mutex:

```
#include <pthread.h>

int pthread_mutex_lock(pthread_mutex_t *mptr);

int pthread_mutex_trylock(pthread_mutex_t *mptr);

int pthread_mutex_unlock(pthread_mutex_t *mptr);
```
All three return: 0 if OK, positive Exxx value on error

If we try to lock a mutex that is already locked by some other thread, pthread_mutex_lock blocks until the mutex is unlocked. pthread_mutex_trylock is a nonblocking function that returns EBUSY if the mutex is already locked.

> If multiple threads are blocked waiting for a mutex, which thread runs when the mutex is unlocked? One of the features added by the 1003.1b–1993 standard is an option for priority scheduling. We do not cover this area, but suffice it to say that different threads can be assigned different priorities, and the synchronization functions (mutexes, read–write locks, and semaphores) will wake up the highest priority thread that is blocked. Section 5.5 of [Butenhof 1997] provides more details on the Posix.1 realtime scheduling feature.

Although we talk of a critical region being protected by a mutex, what is really protected is the *data* being manipulated within the critical region. That is, a mutex is normally used to protect *shared data* that is being shared between multiple threads or between multiple processes.

Mutex locks are *cooperative* locks. That is, if the shared data is a linked list (for example), then all the threads that manipulate the linked list must obtain the mutex lock before manipulating the list. Nothing can prevent one thread from manipulating the linked list without first obtaining the mutex.

7.3   Producer–Consumer Problem

One of the classic problems in synchronization is called the *producer–consumer* problem, also known as the *bounded buffer* problem. One or more producers (threads or processes) are creating data items that are then processed by one or more consumers (threads or processes). The data items are passed between the producers and consumers using some type of IPC.

We deal with this problem all the time with Unix pipes. That is, the shell pipeline

```
grep pattern chapters.* | wc -l
```

is such a problem. `grep` is the single producer and `wc` is the single consumer. A Unix pipe is used as the form of IPC. The required synchronization between the producer and consumer is handled by the kernel in the way in which it handles the `write`s by the producer and the `read`s by the consumer. If the producer gets ahead of the consumer (i.e., the pipe fills up), the kernel puts the producer to sleep when it calls `write`, until more room is in the pipe. If the consumer gets ahead of the producer (i.e., the pipe is empty), the kernel puts the consumer to sleep when it calls `read`, until some data is in the pipe.

This type of synchronization is *implicit*; that is, the producer and consumer are not even aware that it is being performed by the kernel. If we were to use a Posix or System V message queue as the form of IPC between the producer and consumer, the kernel would again handle the synchronization.

When shared memory is being used as the form of IPC between the producer and the consumer, however, some type of *explicit* synchronization must be performed by the producers and consumers. We will demonstrate this using a mutex. The example that we use is shown in Figure 7.1.

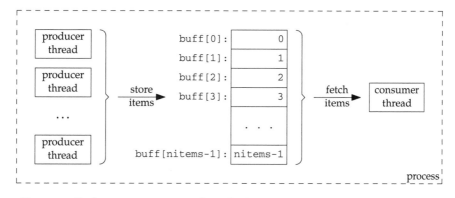

Figure 7.1   Producer–consumer example: multiple producer threads, one consumer thread.

We have multiple producer threads and a single consumer thread, in a single process. The integer array `buff` contains the items being produced and consumed (i.e., the shared data). For simplicity, the producers just set `buff[0]` to 0, `buff[1]` to 1, and so on. The consumer just goes through this array and verifies that each entry is correct.

In this first example, we concern ourselves only with synchronization between the multiple producer threads. We do not start the consumer thread until all the producers are done. Figure 7.2 is the `main` function for our example.

── mutex/prodcons2.c

```
 1 #include    "unpipc.h"

 2 #define MAXNITEMS        1000000
 3 #define MAXNTHREADS          100

 4 int     nitems;                    /* read-only by producer and consumer */
 5 struct {
 6     pthread_mutex_t mutex;
 7     int     buff[MAXNITEMS];
 8     int     nput;
 9     int     nval;
10 } shared = {
11     PTHREAD_MUTEX_INITIALIZER
12 };

13 void    *produce(void *), *consume(void *);

14 int
15 main(int argc, char **argv)
16 {
17     int     i, nthreads, count[MAXNTHREADS];
18     pthread_t tid_produce[MAXNTHREADS], tid_consume;

19     if (argc != 3)
20         err_quit("usage: prodcons2 <#items> <#threads>");
21     nitems = min(atoi(argv[1]), MAXNITEMS);
22     nthreads = min(atoi(argv[2]), MAXNTHREADS);

23     Set_concurrency(nthreads);
24         /* start all the producer threads */
25     for (i = 0; i < nthreads; i++) {
26         count[i] = 0;
27         Pthread_create(&tid_produce[i], NULL, produce, &count[i]);
28     }

29         /* wait for all the producer threads */
30     for (i = 0; i < nthreads; i++) {
31         Pthread_join(tid_produce[i], NULL);
32         printf("count[%d] = %d\n", i, count[i]);
33     }

34         /* start, then wait for the consumer thread */
35     Pthread_create(&tid_consume, NULL, consume, NULL);
36     Pthread_join(tid_consume, NULL);

37     exit(0);
38 }
```

── mutex/prodcons2.c

Figure 7.2 main function.

Globals shared between the threads

4–12   These variables are shared between the threads. We collect them into a structure named `shared`, along with the mutex, to reinforce that these variables should be accessed only when the mutex is held. `nput` is the next index to store in the `buff` array, and `nval` is the next value to store (0, 1, 2, and so on). We allocate this structure and initialize the mutex that is used for synchronization between the producer threads.

> We will always try to collect shared data with their synchronization variables (mutex, condition variable, or semaphore) into a structure as we have done here, as a good programming technique. In many cases, however, the shared data is dynamically allocated, say as a linked list. We might be able to store the head of the linked list in a structure with the synchronization variables (as we did with our mq_hdr structure in Figure 5.20), but other shared data (the rest of the list) is not in the structure. Therefore, this solution is often not perfect.

Command-line arguments

19–22   The first command-line argument specifies the number of items for the producers to store, and the next argument is the number of producer threads to create.

Set concurrency level

23   `set_concurrency` is a function of ours that tells the threads system how many threads we would like to run concurrently. Under Solaris 2.6, this is just a call to `thr_setconcurrency` and is required if we want the multiple producer threads to each have a chance to execute. If we omit this call under Solaris, only the first producer thread runs. Under Digital Unix 4.0B, our `set_concurrency` function does nothing (because all the threads within a process compete for the processor by default).

> Unix 98 requires a function named pthread_setconcurrency that performs the same function. This function is needed with threads implementations that multiplex user threads (what we create with pthread_create) onto a smaller set of kernel execution entities (e.g., kernel threads). These are commonly referred to as many-to-few, two-level, or M-to-N implementations. Section 5.6 of [Butenhof 1997] discusses the relationship between user threads and kernel entities in more detail.

Create producer threads

24–28   The producer threads are created, and each executes the function `produce`. We save the thread ID of each in the `tid_produce` array. The argument to each producer thread is a pointer to an element of the `count` array. We first initialize the counter to 0, and each thread then increments this counter each time it stores an item in the buffer. We print this array of counters when we are done, to see how many items were stored by each producer thread.

Wait for producer threads, then start consumer thread

29–36   We wait for all the producer threads to terminate, also printing each thread's counter, and only then start a single consumer thread. This is how (for the time being) we avoid any synchronization issues between the producers and consumer. We wait for the consumer to finish and then terminate the process.

Figure 7.3 shows the `produce` and `consume` functions for our example.

―― mutex/prodcons2.c
```
39 void *
40 produce(void *arg)
41 {
42     for ( ; ; ) {
43         Pthread_mutex_lock(&shared.mutex);
44         if (shared.nput >= nitems) {
45             Pthread_mutex_unlock(&shared.mutex);
46             return (NULL);      /* array is full, we're done */
47         }
48         shared.buff[shared.nput] = shared.nval;
49         shared.nput++;
50         shared.nval++;
51         Pthread_mutex_unlock(&shared.mutex);
52         *((int *) arg) += 1;
53     }
54 }

55 void *
56 consume(void *arg)
57 {
58     int     i;

59     for (i = 0; i < nitems; i++) {
60         if (shared.buff[i] != i)
61             printf("buff[%d] = %d\n", i, shared.buff[i]);
62     }
63     return (NULL);
64 }
```
―― mutex/prodcons2.c

Figure 7.3 produce and consume functions.

Generate the data items

42–53   The critical region for the producer consists of the test for whether we are done

```
if (shared.nput >= nitems)
```

followed by the three lines

```
shared.buff[shared.nput] = shared.nval;
shared.nput++;
shared.nval++;
```

We protect this region with a mutex lock, being certain to unlock the mutex when we are done. Notice that the increment of the count element (through the pointer arg) is not part of the critical region because each thread has its own counter (the count array in the main function). Therefore, we do not include this line of code within the region locked by the mutex, because as a general programming principle, we should always strive to minimize the amount of code that is locked by a mutex.

Consumer verifies contents of array

59–62   The consumer just verifies that each item in the array is correct and prints a message if an error is found. As we said earlier, only one instance of this function is run and only after all the producer threads have finished, so no need exists for any synchronization.

If we run the program just described, specifying one million items and five producer threads, we have

```
solaris % prodcons2 1000000 5
count[0] = 167165
count[1] = 249891
count[2] = 194221
count[3] = 191815
count[4] = 196908
```

As we mentioned, if we remove the call to set_concurrency under Solaris 2.6, count[0] then becomes 1000000 and the remaining counts are all 0.

If we remove the mutex locking from this example, it fails, as expected. That is, the consumer detects many instances of buff[i] not equal to i. We can also verify that the removal of the mutex locking has no effect if only one producer thread is run.

7.4 Locking versus Waiting

We now demonstrate that mutexes are for *locking* and cannot be used for *waiting*. We modify our producer–consumer example from the previous section to start the consumer thread right after all the producer threads have been started. This lets the consumer thread process the data as it is being generated by the producer threads, unlike Figure 7.2, in which we did not start the consumer until all the producer threads were finished. But we must now synchronize the consumer with the producers to make certain that the consumer processes only data items that have already been stored by the producers.

Figure 7.4 shows the main function. All the lines prior to the declaration of main have not changed from Figure 7.2.

mutex/prodcons3.c

```
14 int
15 main(int argc, char **argv)
16 {
17     int     i, nthreads, count[MAXNTHREADS];
18     pthread_t tid_produce[MAXNTHREADS], tid_consume;

19     if (argc != 3)
20         err_quit("usage: prodcons3 <#items> <#threads>");
21     nitems = min(atoi(argv[1]), MAXNITEMS);
22     nthreads = min(atoi(argv[2]), MAXNTHREADS);

23         /* create all producers and one consumer */
24     Set_concurrency(nthreads + 1);
25     for (i = 0; i < nthreads; i++) {
26         count[i] = 0;
27         Pthread_create(&tid_produce[i], NULL, produce, &count[i]);
28     }
29     Pthread_create(&tid_consume, NULL, consume, NULL);
```

```
30              /* wait for all producers and the consumer */
31          for (i = 0; i < nthreads; i++) {
32              Pthread_join(tid_produce[i], NULL);
33              printf("count[%d] = %d\n", i, count[i]);
34          }
35          Pthread_join(tid_consume, NULL);

36          exit(0);
37      }
```
——— *mutex/prodcons3.c*

Figure 7.4 main function: start consumer immediately after starting producers.

24   We increase the concurrency level by one, to account for the additional consumer thread.

25–29   We create the consumer thread immediately after creating the producer threads.

The produce function does not change from Figure 7.3.

We show in Figure 7.5 the consume function, which calls our new consume_wait function.

——— *mutex/prodcons3.c*
```
54 void
55 consume_wait(int i)
56 {
57      for ( ; ; ) {
58          Pthread_mutex_lock(&shared.mutex);
59          if (i < shared.nput) {
60              Pthread_mutex_unlock(&shared.mutex);
61              return;                 /* an item is ready */
62          }
63          Pthread_mutex_unlock(&shared.mutex);
64      }
65 }

66 void *
67 consume(void *arg)
68 {
69      int     i;

70      for (i = 0; i < nitems; i++) {
71          consume_wait(i);
72          if (shared.buff[i] != i)
73              printf("buff[%d] = %d\n", i, shared.buff[i]);
74      }
75      return (NULL);
76 }
```
——— *mutex/prodcons3.c*

Figure 7.5 consume_wait and consume functions.

Consumer must wait

71   The only change to the consume function is to call consume_wait before fetching the next item from the array.

Wait for producers

57-64   Our `consume_wait` function must wait until the producers have generated the `i`th item. To check this condition, the producer's mutex is locked and `i` is compared to the producer's `nput` index. We must acquire the mutex lock before looking at `nput`, since this variable may be in the process of being updated by one of the producer threads.

The fundamental problem is: what can we do when the desired item is *not* ready? All we do in Figure 7.5 is loop around again, unlocking and locking the mutex each time. This is calling *spinning* or *polling* and is a waste of CPU time.

We could also sleep for a short amount of time, but we do not know how long to sleep. What is needed is another type of synchronization that lets a thread (or process) sleep until some event occurs.

7.5   Condition Variables: Waiting and Signaling

A mutex is for *locking* and a condition variable is for *waiting*. These are two different types of synchronization and both are needed.

A condition variable is a variable of type `pthread_cond_t`, and the following two functions are used with these variables.

```
#include <pthread.h>

int pthread_cond_wait(pthread_cond_t *cptr, pthread_mutex_t *mptr);

int pthread_cond_signal(pthread_cond_t *cptr);

                                        Both return: 0 if OK, positive Exxx value on error
```

The term "signal" in the second function's name does not refer to a Unix SIG*xxx* signal.

We choose what defines the "condition" to wait for and be notified of: we test this in our code.

A mutex is always associated with a condition variable. When we call `pthread_cond_wait` to wait for some condition to be true, we specify the address of the condition variable and the address of the associated mutex.

We explain the use of condition variables by recoding the example from the previous section. Figure 7.6 shows the global declarations.

Collect producer variables and mutex into a structure

7-13   The two variables `nput` and `nval` are associated with the `mutex`, and we put all three variables into a structure named `put`. This structure is used by the producers.

Collect counter, condition variable, and mutex into a structure

14-20   The next structure, `nready`, contains a counter, a condition variable, and a mutex. We initialize the condition variable to `PTHREAD_COND_INITIALIZER`.

The `main` function does not change from Figure 7.4.

——————————————————————— mutex/prodcons6.c
```
 1 #include     "unpipc.h"

 2 #define MAXNITEMS        1000000
 3 #define MAXNTHREADS         100

 4         /* globals shared by threads */
 5 int     nitems;                    /* read-only by producer and consumer */
 6 int     buff[MAXNITEMS];
 7 struct {
 8     pthread_mutex_t mutex;
 9     int     nput;                  /* next index to store */
10     int     nval;                  /* next value to store */
11 } put = {
12     PTHREAD_MUTEX_INITIALIZER
13 };

14 struct {
15     pthread_mutex_t mutex;
16     pthread_cond_t cond;
17     int     nready;                /* number ready for consumer */
18 } nready = {
19     PTHREAD_MUTEX_INITIALIZER, PTHREAD_COND_INITIALIZER
20 };
```
——————————————————————— mutex/prodcons6.c

Figure 7.6 Globals for our producer–consumer, using a condition variable.

The produce and consume functions do change, and we show them in Figure 7.7.

Place next item into array

50-58   We now use the mutex put.mutex to lock the critical section when the producer places a new item into the array.

Notify consumer

59-64   We increment the counter nready.nready, which counts the number of items ready for the consumer to process. Before doing this increment, if the value of the counter was 0, we call pthread_cond_signal to wake up any threads (e.g., the consumer) that may be waiting for this value to become nonzero. We can now see the interaction of the mutex and condition variable associated with this counter. The counter is shared between the producers and the consumer, so access to it must be when the associated mutex (nready.mutex) is locked. The condition variable is used for waiting and signaling.

Consumer waits for nready.nready to be nonzero

72-76   The consumer just waits for the counter nready.nready to be nonzero. Since this counter is shared among all the producers and the consumer, we can test its value only while we have its associated mutex locked. If, while we have the mutex locked, the value is 0, we call pthread_cond_wait to go to sleep. This does two actions atomically:

```
                                                              ———————— mutex/prodcons6.c
46 void *
47 produce(void *arg)
48 {
49     for ( ; ; ) {
50         Pthread_mutex_lock(&put.mutex);
51         if (put.nput >= nitems) {
52             Pthread_mutex_unlock(&put.mutex);
53             return (NULL);        /* array is full, we're done */
54         }
55         buff[put.nput] = put.nval;
56         put.nput++;
57         put.nval++;
58         Pthread_mutex_unlock(&put.mutex);

59         Pthread_mutex_lock(&nready.mutex);
60         if (nready.nready == 0)
61             Pthread_cond_signal(&nready.cond);
62         nready.nready++;
63         Pthread_mutex_unlock(&nready.mutex);

64         *((int *) arg) += 1;
65     }
66 }

67 void *
68 consume(void *arg)
69 {
70     int     i;

71     for (i = 0; i < nitems; i++) {
72         Pthread_mutex_lock(&nready.mutex);
73         while (nready.nready == 0)
74             Pthread_cond_wait(&nready.cond, &nready.mutex);
75         nready.nready--;
76         Pthread_mutex_unlock(&nready.mutex);

77         if (buff[i] != i)
78             printf("buff[%d] = %d\n", i, buff[i]);
79     }
80     return (NULL);
81 }
                                                              ———————— mutex/prodcons6.c
```

Figure 7.7 produce and consume functions.

1. the mutex nready.mutex is unlocked, and

2. the thread is put to sleep until some other thread calls pthread_cond_signal for this condition variable.

Before returning, pthread_cond_wait locks the mutex nready.mutex. Therefore, when it returns, and we find the counter nonzero, we decrement the counter (knowing

that we have the mutex locked) and then unlock the mutex. Notice that when
`pthread_cond_wait` returns, we *always* test the condition again, because *spurious*
wakeups can occur: a wakeup when the desired condition is still not true. Implementations try to minimize the number of these spurious wakeups, but they can still occur.

In general, the code that signals a condition variable looks like the following:

```
struct {
    pthread_mutex_t    mutex;
    pthread_cond_t     cond;
    whatever variables maintain the condition
} var = { PTHREAD_MUTEX_INITIALIZER, PTHREAD_COND_INITIALIZER, ... };

Pthread_mutex_lock(&var.mutex);
set condition true
Pthread_cond_signal(&var.cond);
Pthread_mutex_unlock(&var.mutex);
```

In our example, the variable that maintains the condition was an integer counter, and
setting the condition was just incrementing the counter. We added the optimization that
the signal occurred only when the counter went from 0 to 1.

The code that tests the condition and goes to sleep waiting for the condition to be
true normally looks like the following:

```
Pthread_mutex_lock(&var.mutex);
while (condition is false)
    Pthread_cond_wait(&var.cond, &var.mutex);
modify condition
Pthread_mutex_unlock(&var.mutex);
```

Avoiding Lock Conflicts

In the code fragment just shown, as well as in Figure 7.7, `pthread_cond_signal` is
called by the thread that currently holds the mutex lock that is associated with the condition variable being signaled. In a worst-case scenario, we could imagine the system
immediately scheduling the thread that is signaled; that thread runs and then immediately stops, because it cannot acquire the mutex. An alternative to our code in Figure 7.7 would be

```
int  dosignal;

Pthread_mutex_lock(&nready.mutex);
dosignal = (nready.nready == 0);
nready.nready++;
Pthread_mutex_unlock(&nready.mutex);

if (dosignal)
    Pthread_cond_signal(&nready.cond);
```

Here we do not signal the condition variable until we release the mutex. This is explicitly allowed by Posix: the thread calling `pthread_cond_signal` need not be the current owner of the mutex associated with the condition variable. But Posix goes on to

say that if predictable scheduling behavior is required, then the mutex must be locked
by the thread calling `pthread_cond_signal`.

7.6   Condition Variables: Timed Waits and Broadcasts

Normally, `pthread_cond_signal` awakens one thread that is waiting on the condition variable. In some instances, a thread knows that multiple threads should be awak-
ened, in which case, `pthread_cond_broadcast` will wake up *all* threads that are
blocked on the condition variable.

> An example of a scenario in which multiple threads should be awakened occurs with the read-
> ers and writers problem that we describe in Chapter 8. When a writer is finished with a lock, it
> wants to awaken *all* queued readers, because multiple readers are allowed at the same time.
>
> An alternate (and safer) way of thinking about a signal versus a broadcast is that you can
> always use a broadcast. A signal is an optimization for the cases in which you know that all
> the waiters are properly coded, only one waiter needs to be awakened, and which waiter is
> awakened does not matter. In all other situations, you must use a broadcast.

```
#include <pthread.h>

int pthread_cond_broadcast(pthread_cond_t *cptr);

int pthread_cond_timedwait(pthread_cond_t *cptr, pthread_mutex_t *mptr,
                           const struct timespec *abstime);
```

                                   Both return: 0 if OK, positive E*xx* value on error

`pthread_cond_timedwait` lets a thread place a limit on how long it will block.
abstime is a `timespec` structure:

```
struct timespec {
  time_t tv_sec;      /* seconds */
  long   tv_nsec;     /* nanoseconds */
};
```

This structure specifies the system time when the function must return, even if the condition variable has not been signaled yet. If this timeout occurs, `ETIMEDOUT` is
returned.

  This time value is an *absolute time*; it is not a *time delta*. That is, *abstime* is the system
time—the number of seconds and nanoseconds past January 1, 1970, UTC—when the
function should return. This differs from `select`, `pselect`, and `poll` (Chapter 6 of
UNPv1), which all specify some number of fractional seconds in the future when the
function should return. (`select` specifies microseconds in the future, `pselect` specifies nanoseconds in the future, and `poll` specifies milliseconds in the future.) The
advantage in using an absolute time, instead of a delta time, is if the function prematurely returns (perhaps because of a caught signal): the function can be called again,
without having to change the contents of the `timespec` structure.

7.7   Mutexes and Condition Variable Attributes

Our examples in this chapter of mutexes and condition variables have stored them as globals in a process in which they are used for synchronization between the threads within that process. We have initialized them with the two constants PTHREAD_MUTEX_INITIALIZER and PTHREAD_COND_INITIALIZER. Mutexes and condition variables initialized in this fashion assume the default attributes, but we can initialize these with other than the default attributes.

First, a mutex or condition variable is initialized or destroyed with the following functions:

```
#include <pthread.h>

int pthread_mutex_init(pthread_mutex_t *mptr, const pthread_mutexattr_t *attr);

int pthread_mutex_destroy(pthread_mutex_t *mptr);

int pthread_cond_init(pthread_cond_t *cptr, const pthread_condattr_t *attr);

int pthread_cond_destroy(pthread_cond_t *cptr);
```
All four return: 0 if OK, positive Exxx value on error

Considering a mutex, *mptr* must point to a pthread_mutex_t variable that has been allocated, and pthread_mutex_init initializes that mutex. The pthread_mutexattr_t value, pointed to by the second argument to pthread_mutex_init (*attr*), specifies the attributes. If this argument is a null pointer, the default attributes are used.

Mutex attributes, a pthread_mutexattr_t datatype, and condition variable attributes, a pthread_condattr_t datatype, are initialized or destroyed with the following functions:

```
#include <pthread.h>

int pthread_mutexattr_init(pthread_mutexattr_t *attr);

int pthread_mutexattr_destroy(pthread_mutexattr_t *attr);

int pthread_condattr_init(pthread_condattr_t *attr);

int pthread_condattr_destroy(pthread_condattr_t *attr);
```
All four return: 0 if OK, positive Exxx value on error

Once a mutex attribute or a condition variable attribute has been initialized, separate functions are called to enable or disable certain attributes. For example, one attribute that we will use in later chapters specifies that the mutex or condition variable is to be shared between different processes, not just between different threads within a single process. This attribute is fetched or stored with the following functions.

```
#include <pthread.h>

int pthread_mutexattr_getpshared(const pthread_mutexattr_t *attr, int *valptr);

int pthread_mutexattr_setpshared(pthread_mutexattr_t *attr, int value);

int pthread_condattr_getpshared(const pthread_condattr_t *attr, int *valptr);

int pthread_condattr_setpshared(pthread_condattr_t *attr, int value);
```

All four return: 0 if OK, positive E*xxx* value on error

The two get functions return the current value of this attribute in the integer pointed to by *valptr* and the two set functions set the current value of this attribute, depending on *value*. The *value* is either PTHREAD_PROCESS_PRIVATE or PTHREAD_PROCESS_SHARED. The latter is also referred to as the process-shared attribute.

> This feature is supported only if the constant _POSIX_THREAD_PROCESS_SHARED is defined by including <unistd.h>. It is an optional feature with Posix.1 but required by Unix 98 (Figure 1.5).

The following code fragment shows how to initialize a mutex so that it can be shared between processes:

```
pthread_mutex_t      *mptr;  /* pointer to the mutex in shared memory */
pthread_mutexattr_t  mattr; /* mutex attribute datatype */

    . . .

    mptr = /* some value that points to shared memory */ ;
    Pthread_mutexattr_init(&mattr);
#ifdef _POSIX_THREAD_PROCESS_SHARED
    Pthread_mutexattr_setpshared(&mattr, PTHREAD_PROCESS_SHARED);
#else
# error this implementation does not support _POSIX_THREAD_PROCESS_SHARED
#endif
    Pthread_mutex_init(mptr, &mattr);
```

We declare a pthread_mutexattr_t datatype named mattr, initialize it to the default attributes for a mutex, and then set the PTHREAD_PROCESS_SHARED attribute, which says that the mutex is to be shared between processes. pthread_mutex_init then initializes the mutex accordingly. The amount of shared memory that must be allocated for the mutex is sizeof(pthread_mutex_t).

A nearly identical set of statements (replacing the five characters mutex with cond) is used to set the PTHREAD_PROCESS_SHARED attribute for a condition variable that is stored in shared memory for use by multiple processes.

We showed examples of these process-shared mutexes and condition variables in Figure 5.22.

Process Termination While Holding a Lock

When a mutex is shared between processes, there is always a chance that the process can terminate (perhaps involuntarily) while holding the mutex lock. There is no way to have the system automatically release held locks upon process termination. We will see that read–write locks and Posix semaphores share this property. The only type of synchronization locks that the kernel always cleans up automatically upon process termination is `fcntl` record locks (Chapter 9). When using System V semaphores, the application chooses whether a semaphore lock is automatically cleaned up or not by the kernel upon process termination (the `SEM_UNDO` feature that we talk about in Section 11.3).

A thread can also terminate while holding a mutex lock, by being canceled by another thread, or by calling `pthread_exit`. The latter should be of no concern, because the thread should know that it holds a mutex lock if it voluntarily terminates by calling `pthread_exit`. In the case of cancellation, the thread can install cleanup handlers that are called upon cancellation, which we demonstrate in Section 8.5. Fatal conditions for a thread normally result in termination of the entire process. For example, if a thread makes an invalid pointer reference, generating `SIGSEGV`, this terminates the entire process if the signal is not caught, and we are back to the previous condition dealing with the termination of the process.

Even if the system were to release a lock automatically when a process terminates, this may not solve the problem. The lock was protecting a critical region probably while some data was being updated. If the process terminates while it is in the middle of this critical region, what is the state of the data? A good chance exists that the data has some inconsistencies: for example, a new item may have been only partially entered into a linked list. If the kernel were to just unlock the mutex when the process terminates, the next process to use the linked list could find it corrupted.

In some examples, however, having the kernel clean up a lock (or a counter in the case of a semaphore) when the process terminates is OK. For example, a server might use a System V semaphore (with the `SEM_UNDO` feature) to count the number of clients currently being serviced. Each time a child is `forked`, it increments this semaphore, and when the child terminates, it decrements this semaphore. If the child terminates abnormally, the kernel will still decrement the semaphore. An example of when it is OK for the kernel to release a lock (not a counter as we just described) is shown in Section 9.7. The daemon obtains a write lock on one of its data files and holds this lock as long as it is running. Should someone try to start another copy of the daemon, the new copy will terminate when it cannot get the write lock, guaranteeing that only one copy of the daemon is ever running. But should the daemon terminate abnormally, the kernel releases the write lock, allowing another copy to be started.

7.8   Summary

Mutexes are used to protect critical regions of code, so that only one thread at a time is executing within the critical region. Sometimes a thread obtains a mutex lock and then discovers that it needs to wait for some condition to be true. When this happens, the thread waits on a condition variable. A condition variable is always associated with a mutex. The `pthread_cond_wait` function that puts the thread to sleep unlocks the mutex before putting the thread to sleep and relocks the mutex before waking up the thread at some later time. The condition variable is signaled by some other thread, and that signaling thread has the option of waking up one thread (`pthread_cond_signal`) or all threads that are waiting for the condition to be true (`pthread_cond_broadcast`).

Mutexes and condition variables can be statically allocated and statically initialized. They can also be dynamically allocated, which requires that they be dynamically initialized. Dynamic initialization allows us to specify the process-shared attribute, allowing the mutex or condition variable to be shared between different processes, assuming that the mutex or condition variable is stored in memory that is shared between the different processes.

Exercises

7.1   Remove the mutex locking from Figure 7.3 and verify that the example fails if more than one producer thread is run.

7.2   What happens in Figure 7.2 if the call to `Pthread_join` for the consumer thread is removed?

7.3   Write a program that just calls `pthread_mutexattr_init` and `pthread_condattr_init` in an infinite loop. Watch the memory usage of the process, using a program such as `ps`. What happens? Now add the appropriate calls to `pthread_mutexattr_destroy` and `pthread_condattr_destroy` and verify that no memory leak occurs.

7.4   In Figure 7.7, the producer calls `pthread_cond_signal` only when the counter `nready.nready` goes from 0 to 1. To see what this optimization does, add a counter each time `pthread_cond_signal` is called, and print this counter in the main thread when the consumer is done.

8

Read–Write Locks

8.1   Introduction

A mutex lock blocks all other threads from entering what we call a *critical region*. This critical region usually involves accessing or updating one or more pieces of data that are shared between the threads. But sometimes, we can distinguish between *reading* a piece of data and *modifying* a piece of data.

We now describe a *read–write lock* and distinguish between obtaining the read–write lock for reading and obtaining the read–write lock for writing. The rules for allocating these read–write locks are:

1. Any number of threads can hold a given read–write lock for reading as long as no thread holds the read–write lock for writing.

2. A read–write lock can be allocated for writing only if no thread holds the read–write lock for reading or writing.

Stated another way, any number of threads can have read access to a given piece of data as long as no thread is modifying that piece of data. A piece of data can be modified only if no other thread is reading or modifying the data.

In some applications, the data is read more often than the data is modified, and these applications can benefit from using read–write locks instead of mutex locks. Allowing multiple readers at any given time can provide more concurrency, while still protecting the data while it is modified from any other readers or writers.

This sharing of access to a given resource is also known as *shared–exclusive* locking, because obtaining a read–write lock for reading is called a *shared lock*, and obtaining a read–write lock for writing is called an *exclusive lock*. Other terms for this type of problem (multiple readers and one writer) are the *readers and writers* problem and *readers–writer* locks. (In the last term, "readers" is intentionally plural, and "writer" is intentionally singular, emphasizing the multiple-readers but single-writer nature of the problem.)

A common analogy for a read–write lock is accessing bank accounts. Multiple threads can be reading the balance of an account at the same time, but as soon as one thread wants to update a given balance, that thread must wait for all readers to finish reading that balance, and then only the updating thread should be allowed to modify the balance. No readers should be allowed to read the balance until the update is complete.

The functions that we describe in this chapter are defined by Unix 98 because read–write locks were not part of the 1996 Posix.1 standard. These functions were developed by a collection of Unix vendors in 1995 known as the Aspen Group, along with other extensions that were not defined by Posix.1. A Posix working group (1003.1j) is currently developing a set of Pthreads extensions that includes read–write locks, which will hopefully be the same as described in this chapter.

8.2 Obtaining and Releasing Read–Write Locks

A read–write lock has a datatype of `pthread_rwlock_t`. If a variable of this type is statically allocated, it can be initialized by assigning to it the constant `PTHREAD_RWLOCK_INITIALIZER`.

`pthread_rwlock_rdlock` obtains a read-lock, blocking the calling thread if the read–write lock is currently held by a writer. `pthread_rwlock_wrlock` obtains a write-lock, blocking the calling thread if the read–write lock is currently held by either another writer or by one or more readers. `pthread_rwlock_unlock` releases either a read lock or a write lock.

```
#include <pthread.h>

int pthread_rwlock_rdlock(pthread_rwlock_t *rwptr);

int pthread_rwlock_wrlock(pthread_rwlock_t *rwptr);

int pthread_rwlock_unlock(pthread_rwlock_t *rwptr);
```
All return: 0 if OK, positive Exxx value on error

The following two functions try to obtain either a read lock or a write lock, but if the lock cannot be granted, an error of `EBUSY` is returned instead of putting the calling thread to sleep.

```
#include <pthread.h>

int pthread_rwlock_tryrdlock(pthread_rwlock_t *rwptr);

int pthread_rwlock_trywrlock(pthread_rwlock_t *rwptr);
```
Both return: 0 if OK, positive Exxx value on error

8.3   Read–Write Lock Attributes

We mentioned that a statically allocated read–write lock can be initialized by assigning it the value `PTHREAD_RWLOCK_INITIALIZER`. These variables can also be dynamically initialized by calling `pthread_rwlock_init`. When a thread no longer needs a read–write lock, it can call the function `pthread_rwlock_destroy`.

```
#include <pthread.h>

int pthread_rwlock_init(pthread_rwlock_t *rwptr,
                        const pthread_rwlockattr_t *attr);

int pthread_rwlock_destroy(pthread_rwlock_t *rwptr);
```
> Both return: 0 if OK, positive E*xxx* value on error

When initializing a read–write lock, if *attr* is a null pointer, the default attributes are used. To assign other than these defaults, the following two functions are provided:

```
#include <pthread.h>

int pthread_rwlockattr_init(pthread_rwlockattr_t *attr);

int pthread_rwlockattr_destroy(pthread_rwlockattr_t *attr);
```
> Both return: 0 if OK, positive E*xxx* value on error

Once an attribute object of datatype `pthread_rwlockattr_t` has been initialized, separate functions are called to enable or disable certain attributes. The only attribute currently defined is `PTHREAD_PROCESS_SHARED`, which specifies that the read–write lock is to be shared between different processes, not just between different threads within a single process. The following two functions fetch and set this attribute:

```
#include <pthread.h>

int pthread_rwlockattr_getpshared(const pthread_rwlockattr_t *attr, int *valptr);

int pthread_rwlockattr_setpshared(pthread_rwlockattr_t *attr, int value);
```
> Both return: 0 if OK, positive E*xxx* value on error

The first function returns the current value of this attribute in the integer pointed to by *valptr*. The second function sets the current value of this attribute to *value*, which is either `PTHREAD_PROCESS_PRIVATE` or `PTHREAD_PROCESS_SHARED`.

8.4   Implementation Using Mutexes and Condition Variables

Read–write locks can be implemented using just mutexes and condition variables. In this section, we examine one possible implementation. Our implementation gives preference to waiting writers. This is not required and there are other alternatives.

> This section and the remaining sections of this chapter contain advanced topics that you may want to skip on a first reading.

> Other implementations of read–write locks merit study. Section 7.1.2 of [Butenhof 1997] provides an implementation that gives priority to waiting readers and includes cancellation handling (which we say more about shortly). Section B.18.2.3.1 of [IEEE 1996] provides another implementation that gives priority to waiting writers and also includes cancellation handling. Chapter 14 of [Kleiman, Shah, and Smaalders 1996] provides an implementation that gives priority to waiting writers. The implementation shown in this section is from Doug Schmidt's ACE package, http://www.cs.wustl.edu/~schmidt/ACE.html (Adaptive Communications Environment). All four implementations use mutexes and condition variables.

`pthread_rwlock_t` Datatype

Figure 8.1 shows our `pthread_rwlock.h` header, which defines the basic `pthread_rwlock_t` datatype and the function prototypes for the functions that operate on read–write locks. Normally, these are found in the `<pthread.h>` header.

—————————————————————————————————— my_rwlock/pthread_rwlock.h

```
 1 #ifndef __pthread_rwlock_h
 2 #define __pthread_rwlock_h

 3 typedef struct {
 4     pthread_mutex_t rw_mutex;    /* basic lock on this struct */
 5     pthread_cond_t rw_condreaders;  /* for reader threads waiting */
 6     pthread_cond_t rw_condwriters;  /* for writer threads waiting */
 7     int      rw_magic;           /* for error checking */
 8     int      rw_nwaitreaders;    /* the number waiting */
 9     int      rw_nwaitwriters;    /* the number waiting */
10     int      rw_refcount;
11          /* -1 if writer has the lock, else # readers holding the lock */
12 } pthread_rwlock_t;

13 #define RW_MAGIC    0x19283746

14          /* following must have same order as elements in struct above */
15 #define PTHREAD_RWLOCK_INITIALIZER  { PTHREAD_MUTEX_INITIALIZER, \
16             PTHREAD_COND_INITIALIZER, PTHREAD_COND_INITIALIZER, \
17             RW_MAGIC, 0, 0, 0 }

18 typedef int pthread_rwlockattr_t;   /* dummy; not supported */

19          /* function prototypes */
20 int    pthread_rwlock_destroy(pthread_rwlock_t *);
21 int    pthread_rwlock_init(pthread_rwlock_t *, pthread_rwlockattr_t *);
22 int    pthread_rwlock_rdlock(pthread_rwlock_t *);
23 int    pthread_rwlock_tryrdlock(pthread_rwlock_t *);
24 int    pthread_rwlock_trywrlock(pthread_rwlock_t *);
25 int    pthread_rwlock_unlock(pthread_rwlock_t *);
26 int    pthread_rwlock_wrlock(pthread_rwlock_t *);
```

```
27          /* and our wrapper functions */
28 void     Pthread_rwlock_destroy(pthread_rwlock_t *);
29 void     Pthread_rwlock_init(pthread_rwlock_t *, pthread_rwlockattr_t *);
30 void     Pthread_rwlock_rdlock(pthread_rwlock_t *);
31 int      Pthread_rwlock_tryrdlock(pthread_rwlock_t *);
32 int      Pthread_rwlock_trywrlock(pthread_rwlock_t *);
33 void     Pthread_rwlock_unlock(pthread_rwlock_t *);
34 void     Pthread_rwlock_wrlock(pthread_rwlock_t *);

35 #endif   /* __pthread_rwlock_h */
```
———————————————————————————————— *my_rwlock/pthread_rwlock.h*

Figure 8.1 Definition of `pthread_rwlock_t` datatype.

3–13   Our `pthread_rwlock_t` datatype contains one mutex, two condition variables, one flag, and three counters. We will see the use of all these in the functions that follow. Whenever we examine or manipulate this structure, we must hold the `rw_mutex`. When the structure is successfully initialized, the `rw_magic` member is set to `RW_MAGIC`. This member is then tested by all the functions to check that the caller is passing a pointer to an initialized lock, and then set to 0 when the lock is destroyed.

Note that `rw_refcount` always indicates the current status of the read–write lock: −1 indicates a write lock (and only one of these can exist at a time), 0 indicates the lock is available, and a value greater than 0 means that many read locks are currently held.

14–17   We also define the static initializer for this datatype.

`pthread_rwlock_init` Function

Our first function, `pthread_rwlock_init`, dynamically initializes a read–write lock and is shown in Figure 8.2.

7–8   We do not support assigning attributes with this function, so we check that the `attr` argument is a null pointer.

9–19   We initialize the mutex and two condition variables that are in our structure. All three counters are set to 0 and `rw_magic` is set to the value that indicates that the structure is initialized.

20–25   If the initialization of the mutex or condition variables fails, we are careful to destroy the initialized objects and return an error.

`pthread_rwlock_destroy` Function

Figure 8.3 shows our `pthread_rwlock_destroy` function, which destroys a read–write lock when the caller is finished with it.

8–13   We first check that the lock is not in use and then call the appropriate destroy functions for the mutex and two condition variables.

——————————————————————————— my_rwlock/pthread_rwlock_init.c

```
1 #include    "unpipc.h"
2 #include    "pthread_rwlock.h"

3 int
4 pthread_rwlock_init(pthread_rwlock_t *rw, pthread_rwlockattr_t *attr)
5 {
6     int     result;

7     if (attr != NULL)
8         return (EINVAL);          /* not supported */

9     if ( (result = pthread_mutex_init(&rw->rw_mutex, NULL)) != 0)
10        goto err1;
11    if ( (result = pthread_cond_init(&rw->rw_condreaders, NULL)) != 0)
12        goto err2;
13    if ( (result = pthread_cond_init(&rw->rw_condwriters, NULL)) != 0)
14        goto err3;
15    rw->rw_nwaitreaders = 0;
16    rw->rw_nwaitwriters = 0;
17    rw->rw_refcount = 0;
18    rw->rw_magic = RW_MAGIC;

19    return (0);

20 err3:
21    pthread_cond_destroy(&rw->rw_condreaders);
22 err2:
23    pthread_mutex_destroy(&rw->rw_mutex);
24 err1:
25    return (result);              /* an errno value */
26 }
```

——————————————————————————— my_rwlock/pthread_rwlock_init.c

Figure 8.2 `pthread_rwlock_init` function: initialize a read–write lock.

——————————————————————————— my_rwlock/pthread_rwlock_destroy.c

```
1 #include    "unpipc.h"
2 #include    "pthread_rwlock.h"

3 int
4 pthread_rwlock_destroy(pthread_rwlock_t *rw)
5 {
6     if (rw->rw_magic != RW_MAGIC)
7         return (EINVAL);
8     if (rw->rw_refcount != 0 ||
9         rw->rw_nwaitreaders != 0 || rw->rw_nwaitwriters != 0)
10        return (EBUSY);

11    pthread_mutex_destroy(&rw->rw_mutex);
12    pthread_cond_destroy(&rw->rw_condreaders);
13    pthread_cond_destroy(&rw->rw_condwriters);
14    rw->rw_magic = 0;

15    return (0);
16 }
```

——————————————————————————— my_rwlock/pthread_rwlock_destroy.c

Figure 8.3 `pthread_rwlock_destroy` function: destroy a read–write lock.

pthread_rwlock_rdlock Function

Our pthread_rwlock_rdlock function is shown in Figure 8.4.

my_rwlock/pthread_rwlock_rdlock.c

```
 1 #include    "unpipc.h"
 2 #include    "pthread_rwlock.h"

 3 int
 4 pthread_rwlock_rdlock(pthread_rwlock_t *rw)
 5 {
 6     int     result;

 7     if (rw->rw_magic != RW_MAGIC)
 8         return (EINVAL);

 9     if ( (result = pthread_mutex_lock(&rw->rw_mutex)) != 0)
10         return (result);

11         /* give preference to waiting writers */
12     while (rw->rw_refcount < 0 || rw->rw_nwaitwriters > 0) {
13         rw->rw_nwaitreaders++;
14         result = pthread_cond_wait(&rw->rw_condreaders, &rw->rw_mutex);
15         rw->rw_nwaitreaders--;
16         if (result != 0)
17             break;
18     }
19     if (result == 0)
20         rw->rw_refcount++;        /* another reader has a read lock */

21     pthread_mutex_unlock(&rw->rw_mutex);
22     return (result);
23 }
```

my_rwlock/pthread_rwlock_rdlock.c

Figure 8.4 pthread_rwlock_rdlock function: obtain a read lock.

9-10   Whenever we manipulate the pthread_rwlock_t structure, we must lock the rw_mutex member.

11-18   We cannot obtain a read lock if (a) the rw_refcount is less than 0 (meaning a writer currently holds the lock), or (b) if threads are waiting to obtain a write lock (rw_nwaitwriters is greater than 0). If either of these conditions is true, we increment rw_nwaitreaders and call pthread_cond_wait on the rw_condreaders condition variable. We will see shortly that when a read–write lock is unlocked, a check is first made for any waiting writers, and if none exist, then a check is made for any waiting readers. If readers are waiting, the rw_condreaders condition variable is broadcast.

19-20   When we get the read lock, we increment rw_refcount. The mutex is released.

> A problem exists in this function: if the calling thread blocks in the call to pthread_cond_wait and the thread is then canceled, the thread terminates while it holds the mutex lock, and the counter rw_nwaitreaders is wrong. The same problem exists in our implementation of pthread_rwlock_wrlock in Figure 8.6. We correct these problems in Section 8.5.

`pthread_rwlock_tryrdlock` Function

Figure 8.5 shows our implementation of `pthread_rwlock_tryrdlock`, the non-blocking attempt to obtain a read lock.

─── *my_rwlock/pthread_rwlock_tryrdlock.c*

```
 1 #include     "unpipc.h"
 2 #include     "pthread_rwlock.h"

 3 int
 4 pthread_rwlock_tryrdlock(pthread_rwlock_t *rw)
 5 {
 6     int     result;

 7     if (rw->rw_magic != RW_MAGIC)
 8         return (EINVAL);

 9     if ( (result = pthread_mutex_lock(&rw->rw_mutex)) != 0)
10         return (result);

11     if (rw->rw_refcount < 0 || rw->rw_nwaitwriters > 0)
12         result = EBUSY;          /* held by a writer or waiting writers */
13     else
14         rw->rw_refcount++;       /* increment count of reader locks */

15     pthread_mutex_unlock(&rw->rw_mutex);
16     return (result);
17 }
```

─── *my_rwlock/pthread_rwlock_tryrdlock.c*

Figure 8.5 `pthread_rwlock_tryrdlock` function: try to obtain a read lock.

11-14   If a writer currently holds the lock, or if threads are waiting for a write lock, EBUSY is returned. Otherwise, we obtain the lock by incrementing `rw_refcount`.

`pthread_rwlock_wrlock` Function

Our `pthread_rwlock_wrlock` function is shown in Figure 8.6.

11-17   As long as readers are holding read locks or a writer is holding a write lock (`rw_refcount` is not equal to 0), we must block. To do so, we increment `rw_nwaitwriters` and call `pthread_cond_wait` on the `rw_condwriters` condition variable. We will see that this condition variable is signaled when the read–write lock is unlocked and writers are waiting.

18-19   When we obtain the write lock, we set `rw_refcount` to –1.

`pthread_rwlock_trywrlock` Function

The nonblocking function `pthread_rwlock_trywrlock` is shown in Figure 8.7.

11-14   If `rw_refcount` is nonzero, the lock is currently held by either a writer or one or more readers (which one does not matter) and EBUSY is returned. Otherwise, we obtain the write lock and `rw_refcount` is set to –1.

—————————————————————————————— *my_rwlock/pthread_rwlock_wrlock.c*

```
 1 #include      "unpipc.h"
 2 #include      "pthread_rwlock.h"

 3 int
 4 pthread_rwlock_wrlock(pthread_rwlock_t *rw)
 5 {
 6     int     result;

 7     if (rw->rw_magic != RW_MAGIC)
 8         return (EINVAL);

 9     if ( (result = pthread_mutex_lock(&rw->rw_mutex)) != 0)
10         return (result);

11     while (rw->rw_refcount != 0) {
12         rw->rw_nwaitwriters++;
13         result = pthread_cond_wait(&rw->rw_condwriters, &rw->rw_mutex);
14         rw->rw_nwaitwriters--;
15         if (result != 0)
16             break;
17     }
18     if (result == 0)
19         rw->rw_refcount = -1;

20     pthread_mutex_unlock(&rw->rw_mutex);
21     return (result);
22 }
```
—————————————————————————————— *my_rwlock/pthread_rwlock_wrlock.c*

Figure 8.6 `pthread_rwlock_wrlock` function: obtain a write lock.

—————————————————————————————— *my_rwlock/pthread_rwlock_trywrlock.c*

```
 1 #include      "unpipc.h"
 2 #include      "pthread_rwlock.h"

 3 int
 4 pthread_rwlock_trywrlock(pthread_rwlock_t *rw)
 5 {
 6     int     result;

 7     if (rw->rw_magic != RW_MAGIC)
 8         return (EINVAL);

 9     if ( (result = pthread_mutex_lock(&rw->rw_mutex)) != 0)
10         return (result);

11     if (rw->rw_refcount != 0)
12         result = EBUSY;            /* held by either writer or reader(s) */
13     else
14         rw->rw_refcount = -1;    /* available, indicate a writer has it */

15     pthread_mutex_unlock(&rw->rw_mutex);
16     return (result);
17 }
```
—————————————————————————————— *my_rwlock/pthread_rwlock_trywrlock.c*

Figure 8.7 `pthread_rwlock_trywrlock` function: try to obtain a write lock.

pthread_rwlock_unlock Function

Our final function, pthread_rwlock_unlock, is shown in Figure 8.8.

```
                                                    ── my_rwlock/pthread_rwlock_unlock.c
 1 #include    "unpipc.h"
 2 #include    "pthread_rwlock.h"

 3 int
 4 pthread_rwlock_unlock(pthread_rwlock_t *rw)
 5 {
 6     int     result;

 7     if (rw->rw_magic != RW_MAGIC)
 8         return (EINVAL);
 9     if ( (result = pthread_mutex_lock(&rw->rw_mutex)) != 0)
10         return (result);

11     if (rw->rw_refcount > 0)
12         rw->rw_refcount--;         /* releasing a reader */
13     else if (rw->rw_refcount == -1)
14         rw->rw_refcount = 0;       /* releasing a writer */
15     else
16         err_dump("rw_refcount = %d", rw->rw_refcount);

17     /* give preference to waiting writers over waiting readers */
18     if (rw->rw_nwaitwriters > 0) {
19         if (rw->rw_refcount == 0)
20             result = pthread_cond_signal(&rw->rw_condwriters);
21     } else if (rw->rw_nwaitreaders > 0)
22         result = pthread_cond_broadcast(&rw->rw_condreaders);

23     pthread_mutex_unlock(&rw->rw_mutex);
24     return (result);
25 }
                                                    ── my_rwlock/pthread_rwlock_unlock.c
```

Figure 8.8 pthread_rwlock_unlock function: release a read lock or a write lock.

11-16   If rw_refcount is currently greater than 0, then a reader is releasing a read lock. If rw_refcount is currently −1, then a writer is releasing a write lock.

17-22   If a writer is waiting, the rw_condwriters condition variable is signaled if the lock is available (i.e., if the reference count is 0). We know that only one writer can obtain the lock, so pthread_cond_signal is called to wake up one thread. If no writers are waiting but one or more readers are waiting, we call pthread_cond_broadcast on the rw_condreaders condition variable, because all the waiting readers can obtain a read lock. Notice that we do not grant any additional read locks as soon as a writer is waiting; otherwise, a stream of continual read requests could block a waiting writer forever. For this reason, we need two separate if tests, and cannot write

```
    /* give preference to waiting writers over waiting readers */
if (rw->rw_nwaitwriters > 0 && rw->rw_refcount == 0)
    result = pthread_cond_signal(&rw->rw_condwriters);
} else if (rw->rw_nwaitreaders > 0)
    result = pthread_cond_broadcast(&rw->rw_condreaders);
```

We could also omit the test of rw->rw_refcount, but that can result in calls to pthread_cond_signal when read locks are still allocated, which is less efficient.

8.5   Thread Cancellation

We alluded to a problem with Figure 8.4 if the calling thread gets blocked in the call to pthread_cond_wait and the thread is then canceled. A thread may be *canceled* by any other thread in the same process when the other thread calls pthread_cancel, a function whose only argument is the thread ID to cancel.

```
#include <pthread.h>

int pthread_cancel(pthread_t tid);
```
                                              Returns: 0 if OK, positive E*xxx* value on error

Cancellation can be used, for example, if multiple threads are started to work on a given task (say finding a record in a database) and the first thread that completes the task then cancels the other tasks. Another example is when multiple threads start on a task and one thread finds an error, necessitating that it and the other threads stop.

To handle the possibility of being canceled, any thread can install (push) and remove (pop) cleanup handlers.

```
#include <pthread.h>

void pthread_cleanup_push(void (*function)(void *), void *arg);

void pthread_cleanup_pop(int execute);
```

These handlers are just functions that are called

- when the thread is canceled (by some thread calling pthread_cancel), or
- when the thread voluntarily terminates (either by calling pthread_exit or returning from its thread start function).

The cleanup handlers can restore any state that needs to be restored, such as unlocking any mutexes or semaphores that the thread currently holds.

The *function* argument to pthread_cleanup_push is the address of the function that is called, and *arg* is its single argument. pthread_cleanup_pop always removes the function at the top of the cancellation cleanup stack of the calling threads and calls the function if *execute* is nonzero.

> We encounter thread cancellation again with Figure 15.31 when we see that a doors server is canceled if the client terminates while a procedure call is in progress.

Example

An example is the easiest way to demonstrate the problem with our implementation in the previous section. Figure 8.9 shows a time line of our test program, and Figure 8.10 shows the program.

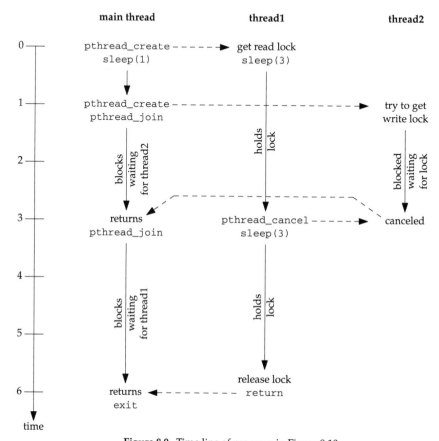

Figure 8.9 Time line of program in Figure 8.10.

Create two threads

10–13   Two threads are created, the first thread executing the function thread1 and the second executing the function thread2. We sleep for a second after creating the first thread, to allow it to obtain a read lock.

Wait for threads to terminate

14–23   We wait for the second thread first, and verify that its status is PTHREAD_CANCEL. We then wait for the first thread to terminate and verify that its status is a null pointer. We then print the three counters in the pthread_rwlock_t structure and destroy the lock.

—————————————————————————————— *my_rwlock_cancel/testcancel.c*

```
 1 #include     "unpipc.h"
 2 #include     "pthread_rwlock.h"

 3 pthread_rwlock_t rwlock = PTHREAD_RWLOCK_INITIALIZER;
 4 pthread_t tid1, tid2;
 5 void   *thread1(void *), *thread2(void *);

 6 int
 7 main(int argc, char **argv)
 8 {
 9     void   *status;

10     Set_concurrency(2);
11     Pthread_create(&tid1, NULL, thread1, NULL);
12     sleep(1);                    /* let thread1() get the lock */
13     Pthread_create(&tid2, NULL, thread2, NULL);

14     Pthread_join(tid2, &status);
15     if (status != PTHREAD_CANCELED)
16         printf("thread2 status = %p\n", status);
17     Pthread_join(tid1, &status);
18     if (status != NULL)
19         printf("thread1 status = %p\n", status);

20     printf("rw_refcount = %d, rw_nwaitreaders = %d, rw_nwaitwriters = %d\n",
21             rwlock.rw_refcount, rwlock.rw_nwaitreaders,
22             rwlock.rw_nwaitwriters);
23     Pthread_rwlock_destroy(&rwlock);

24     exit(0);
25 }

26 void *
27 thread1(void *arg)
28 {
29     Pthread_rwlock_rdlock(&rwlock);
30     printf("thread1() got a read lock\n");
31     sleep(3);                    /* let thread2 block in pthread_rwlock_wrlock() */
32     pthread_cancel(tid2);
33     sleep(3);
34     Pthread_rwlock_unlock(&rwlock);
35     return (NULL);
36 }

37 void *
38 thread2(void *arg)
39 {
40     printf("thread2() trying to obtain a write lock\n");
41     Pthread_rwlock_wrlock(&rwlock);
42     printf("thread2() got a write lock\n");     /* should not get here */
43     sleep(1);
44     Pthread_rwlock_unlock(&rwlock);
45     return (NULL);
46 }
```

—————————————————————————————— *my_rwlock_cancel/testcancel.c*

Figure 8.10 Test program to show thread cancellation.

thread1 function

26–36   This thread obtains a read lock and then sleeps for 3 seconds. This pause allows the other thread to call `pthread_rwlock_wrlock` and block in its call to `pthread_cond_wait`, because a write lock cannot be granted while a read lock is active. The first thread then calls `pthread_cancel` to cancel the second thread, sleeps another 3 seconds, releases its read lock, and terminates.

thread2 function

37–46   The second thread tries to obtain a write lock (which it cannot get, since the first thread has already obtained a read lock). The remainder of this function should never be executed.

If we run this program using the functions from the previous section, we get

```
solaris % testcancel
thread1() got a read lock
thread2() trying to obtain a write lock
```

and we never get back a shell prompt. The program is hung. The following steps have occurred:

1. The second thread calls `pthread_rwlock_wrlock` (Figure 8.6), which blocks in its call to `pthread_cond_wait`.

2. The `sleep(3)` in the first thread returns, and `pthread_cancel` is called.

3. The second thread is canceled (it is terminated). When a thread is canceled while it is blocked in a condition variable wait, the mutex is reacquired before calling the first cancellation cleanup handler. (We have not installed any cancellation cleanup handlers yet, but the mutex is still reacquired before the thread is canceled.) Therefore, when the second thread is canceled, it holds the mutex lock for the read–write lock, and the value of `rw_nwaitwriters` in Figure 8.6 has been incremented.

4. The first thread calls `pthread_rwlock_unlock`, but it blocks forever in its call to `pthread_mutex_lock` (Figure 8.8), because the mutex is still locked by the thread that was canceled.

If we remove the call to `pthread_rwlock_unlock` in our `thread1` function, the main thread will print

```
rw_refcount = 1, rw_nwaitreaders = 0, rw_nwaitwriters = 1
pthread_rwlock_destroy error: Device busy
```

The first counter is 1 because we removed the call to `pthread_rwlock_unlock`, but the final counter is 1 because that is the counter that was incremented by the second thread before it was canceled.

The correction for this problem is simple. First we add two lines of code (preceded by a plus sign) to our `pthread_rwlock_rdlock` function in Figure 8.4 that bracket the call to `pthread_cond_wait`:

```
            rw->rw_nwaitreaders++;
    +       pthread_cleanup_push(rwlock_cancelrdwait, (void *) rw);
            result = pthread_cond_wait(&rw->rw_condreaders, &rw->rw_mutex);
    +       pthread_cleanup_pop(0);
            rw->rw_nwaitreaders--;
```

The first new line of code establishes a cleanup handler (our `rwlock_cancelrdwait` function), and its single argument will be the pointer `rw`. If `pthread_cond_wait` returns, our second new line of code removes the cleanup handler. The single argument of 0 to `pthread_cleanup_pop` specifies that the handler is not called. If this argument is nonzero, the cleanup handler is first called and then removed.

If the thread is canceled while it is blocked in its call to `pthread_cond_wait`, no return is made from this function. Instead, the cleanup handlers are called (after reacquiring the associated mutex, which we mentioned in step 3 earlier).

Figure 8.11 shows our `rwlock_cancelrdwait` function, which is our cleanup handler for `pthread_rwlock_rdlock`.

——— my_rwlock_cancel/pthread_rwlock_rdlock.c
```
 3  static void
 4  rwlock_cancelrdwait(void *arg)
 5  {
 6      pthread_rwlock_t *rw;
 7      rw = arg;
 8      rw->rw_nwaitreaders--;
 9      pthread_mutex_unlock(&rw->rw_mutex);
10  }
```
——— my_rwlock_cancel/pthread_rwlock_rdlock.c

Figure 8.11 `rwlock_cancelrdwait` function: cleanup handler for read lock.

8–9   The counter `rw_nwaitreaders` is decremented and the mutex is unlocked. This is the "state" that was established before the call to `pthread_cond_wait` that must be restored after the thread is canceled.

Our fix to our `pthread_rwlock_wrlock` function in Figure 8.6 is similar. First we add two new lines around the call to `pthread_cond_wait`:

```
            rw->rw_nwaitwriters++;
    +       pthread_cleanup_push(rwlock_cancelwrwait, (void *) rw);
            result = pthread_cond_wait(&rw->rw_condwriters, &rw->rw_mutex);
    +       pthread_cleanup_pop(0);
            rw->rw_nwaitwriters--;
```

Figure 8.12 shows our `rwlock_cancelwrwait` function, the cleanup handler for a write lock request.

8–9   The counter `rw_nwaitwriters` is decremented and the mutex is unlocked.

```
                                                        ——— my_rwlock_cancel/pthread_rwlock_wrlock.c
 3 static void
 4 rwlock_cancelwrwait(void *arg)
 5 {
 6     pthread_rwlock_t *rw;

 7     rw = arg;
 8     rw->rw_nwaitwriters--;
 9     pthread_mutex_unlock(&rw->rw_mutex);
10 }
                                                        ——— my_rwlock_cancel/pthread_rwlock_wrlock.c
```

Figure 8.12 `rwlock_cancelwrwait` function: cleanup handler for write lock.

If we run our test program from Figure 8.10 with these new functions, the results are now correct.

```
solaris % testcancel
thread1() got a read lock
thread2() trying to obtain a write lock
rw_refcount = 0, rw_nwaitreaders = 0, rw_nwaitwriters = 0
```

The three counts are correct, `thread1` returns from its call to `pthread_rwlock_unlock`, and `pthread_rwlock_destroy` does not return EBUSY.

> This section has been an overview of thread cancellation. There are more details; see, for example, Section 5.3 of [Butenhof 1997].

8.6 Summary

Read–write locks can provide more concurrency than a plain mutex lock when the data being protected is read more often than it is written. The read–write lock functions defined by Unix 98, which is what we have described in this chapter, or something similar, should appear in a future Posix standard. These functions are similar to the mutex functions from Chapter 7.

Read–write locks can be implemented easily using just mutexes and condition variables, and we have shown a sample implementation. Our implementation gives priority to waiting writers, but some implementations give priority to waiting readers.

Threads may be canceled while they are blocked in a call to `pthread_cond_wait`, and our implementation allowed us to see this occur. We provided a fix for this problem, using cancellation cleanup handlers.

Exercises

8.1   Modify our implementation in Section 8.4 to give preference to readers instead of writers.

8.2   Measure the performance of our implementation in Section 8.4 versus a vendor-provided implementation.

9

Record Locking

9.1 Introduction

The read–write locks described in the previous chapter are allocated in memory as variables of datatype `pthread_rwlock_t`. These variables can be within a single process when the read–write locks are shared among the threads within that process (the default), or within shared memory when the read–write locks are shared among the processes that share that memory (and assuming that the `PTHREAD_PROCESS_SHARED` attribute is specified when the read–write lock is initialized).

This chapter describes an extended type of read–write lock that can be used by related or unrelated processes to share the reading and writing of a file. The file that is being locked is referenced through its descriptor, and the function that performs the locking is `fcntl`. These types of locks are normally maintained within the kernel, and the owner of a lock is identified by its process ID. This means that these locks are for locking between different processes and not for locking between the different threads within one process.

In this chapter, we introduce our sequence-number-increment example. Consider the following scenario, which comes from the Unix print spoolers (the BSD `lpr` command and the System V `lp` command). The process that adds a job to the print queue (to be printed at a later time by another process) must assign a unique sequence number to each print job. The process ID, which is unique while the process is running, cannot be used as the sequence number, because a print job can exist long enough for a given process ID to be reused. A given process can also add multiple print jobs to a queue, and each job needs a unique number. The technique used by the print spoolers is to have a file for each printer that contains the next sequence number to be used. The file is just a single line containing the sequence number in ASCII. Each process that needs to assign a sequence number goes through three steps:

1. it reads the sequence number file,
2. it uses the number, and
3. it increments the number and writes it back.

The problem is that in the time a single process takes to execute these three steps, another process can perform the same three steps. Chaos can result, as we will see in some examples that follow.

> What we have just described is a mutual exclusion problem. It could be solved using mutexes from Chapter 7 or with the read–write locks from Chapter 8. What differs with this problem, however, is that we assume the processes are unrelated, which makes using these techniques harder. We could have the unrelated processes share memory (as we describe in Part 4) and then use some type of synchronization variable in that shared memory, but for unrelated processes, fcntl record locking is often easier to use. Another factor is that the problem we described with the line printer spoolers predates the availability of mutexes, condition variables, and read–write locks by many years. Record locking was added to Unix in the early 1980s, before shared memory and threads.

What is needed is for a process to be able to set a *lock* to say that no other process can access the file until the first process is done. Figure 9.2 shows a simple program that does these three steps. The functions my_lock and my_unlock are called to lock the file at the beginning and unlock the file when the process is done with the sequence number. We will show numerous implementations of these two functions.

20   We print the name by which the program is being run (argv[0]) each time around the loop when we print the sequence number, because we use this main function with various versions of our locking functions, and we want to see which version is printing the sequence number.

> Printing a process ID requires that we cast the variable of type pid_t to a long and then print it with the %ld format string. The problem is that the pid_t type is an integer type, but we do not know its size (int or long), so we must assume the largest. If we assumed an int and used a format string of %d, but the type was actually a long, the code would be wrong.

To show the results when locking is not used, the functions shown in Figure 9.1 provide no locking at all.

─── *lock/locknone.c*

```
1 void
2 my_lock(int fd)
3 {
4     return;
5 }

6 void
7 my_unlock(int fd)
8 {
9     return;
10 }
```
─── *lock/locknone.c*

Figure 9.1 Functions that do no locking.

```
                                                                          lock/lockmain.c
 1 #include    "unpipc.h"

 2 #define SEQFILE "seqno"          /* filename */

 3 void    my_lock(int), my_unlock(int);

 4 int
 5 main(int argc, char **argv)
 6 {
 7     int     fd;
 8     long    i, seqno;
 9     pid_t   pid;
10     ssize_t n;
11     char    line[MAXLINE + 1];

12     pid = getpid();
13     fd = Open(SEQFILE, O_RDWR, FILE_MODE);

14     for (i = 0; i < 20; i++) {
15         my_lock(fd);                /* lock the file */

16         Lseek(fd, 0L, SEEK_SET);    /* rewind before read */
17         n = Read(fd, line, MAXLINE);
18         line[n] = '\0';             /* null terminate for sscanf */

19         n = sscanf(line, "%ld\n", &seqno);
20         printf("%s: pid = %ld, seq# = %ld\n", argv[0], (long) pid, seqno);

21         seqno++;                    /* increment sequence number */

22         snprintf(line, sizeof(line), "%ld\n", seqno);
23         Lseek(fd, 0L, SEEK_SET);    /* rewind before write */
24         Write(fd, line, strlen(line));

25         my_unlock(fd);              /* unlock the file */
26     }
27     exit(0);
28 }
                                                                          lock/lockmain.c
```

Figure 9.2 main function for file locking example.

If the sequence number in the file is initialized to one, and a single copy of the program is run, we get the following output:

```
solaris % locknone
locknone: pid = 15491, seq# = 1
locknone: pid = 15491, seq# = 2
locknone: pid = 15491, seq# = 3
locknone: pid = 15491, seq# = 4
locknone: pid = 15491, seq# = 5
locknone: pid = 15491, seq# = 6
locknone: pid = 15491, seq# = 7
locknone: pid = 15491, seq# = 8
locknone: pid = 15491, seq# = 9
locknone: pid = 15491, seq# = 10
locknone: pid = 15491, seq# = 11
```

```
locknone: pid = 15491, seq# = 12
locknone: pid = 15491, seq# = 13
locknone: pid = 15491, seq# = 14
locknone: pid = 15491, seq# = 15
locknone: pid = 15491, seq# = 16
locknone: pid = 15491, seq# = 17
locknone: pid = 15491, seq# = 18
locknone: pid = 15491, seq# = 19
locknone: pid = 15491, seq# = 20
```

Notice that the main function (Figure 9.2) is in a file named lockmain.c, but when we compile and link edit this with the functions that perform no locking (Figure 9.1), we call the executable locknone. This is because we will provide other implementations of the two functions my_lock and my_unlock that use other locking techniques, so we name the executable based on the type of locking that we use.

When the sequence number is again initialized to one, and the program is run twice in the background, we have the following output:

```
solaris % locknone & locknone &
solaris % locknone: pid = 15498, seq# = 1
locknone: pid = 15498, seq# = 2
locknone: pid = 15498, seq# = 3
locknone: pid = 15498, seq# = 4
locknone: pid = 15498, seq# = 5
locknone: pid = 15498, seq# = 6
locknone: pid = 15498, seq# = 7
locknone: pid = 15498, seq# = 8
locknone: pid = 15498, seq# = 9
locknone: pid = 15498, seq# = 10
locknone: pid = 15498, seq# = 11
locknone: pid = 15498, seq# = 12
locknone: pid = 15498, seq# = 13
locknone: pid = 15498, seq# = 14
locknone: pid = 15498, seq# = 15
locknone: pid = 15498, seq# = 16
locknone: pid = 15498, seq# = 17
locknone: pid = 15498, seq# = 18
locknone: pid = 15498, seq# = 19
locknone: pid = 15498, seq# = 20          everything through this line is OK
locknone: pid = 15499, seq# = 1           this is wrong when kernel switches processes
locknone: pid = 15499, seq# = 2
locknone: pid = 15499, seq# = 3
locknone: pid = 15499, seq# = 4
locknone: pid = 15499, seq# = 5
locknone: pid = 15499, seq# = 6
locknone: pid = 15499, seq# = 7
locknone: pid = 15499, seq# = 8
locknone: pid = 15499, seq# = 9
locknone: pid = 15499, seq# = 10
locknone: pid = 15499, seq# = 11
locknone: pid = 15499, seq# = 12
locknone: pid = 15499, seq# = 13
locknone: pid = 15499, seq# = 14
```

```
locknone: pid = 15499, seq# = 15
locknone: pid = 15499, seq# = 16
locknone: pid = 15499, seq# = 17
locknone: pid = 15499, seq# = 18
locknone: pid = 15499, seq# = 19
locknone: pid = 15499, seq# = 20
```

The first thing we notice is that the shell's prompt is output before the first line of output from the program. This is OK and is common when running programs in the background.

The first 20 lines of output are OK and are generated by the first instance of the program (process ID 15498). But a problem occurs with the first line of output from the other instance of the program (process ID 15499): it prints a sequence number of 1, indicating that it probably was started first by the kernel, it read the sequence number file (with a value of 1), and the kernel then switched to the other process. This process only ran again when the other process terminated, and it continued executing with the value of 1 that it had read before the kernel switched processes. This is not what we want. Each process reads, increments, and writes the sequence number file 20 times (there are exactly 40 lines of output), so the ending value of the sequence number should be 40.

What we need is some way to allow a process to prevent other processes from accessing the sequence number file while the three steps are being performed. That is, we need these three steps to be performed as an *atomic operation* with regard to other processes. Another way to look at this problem is that the lines of code between the calls to my_lock and my_unlock in Figure 9.2 form a *critical region*, as we described in Chapter 7.

When we run two instances of the program in the background as just shown, the output is *nondeterministic*. There is no guarantee that each time we run the two programs we get the same output. This is OK if the three steps listed earlier are handled atomically with regard to other processes, generating an ending value of 40. But this is not OK if the three steps are not handled atomically, often generating an ending value less than 40, which is an error. For example, we do not care whether the first process increments the sequence number from 1 to 20, followed by the second process incrementing it from 21 to 40, or whether each process runs just long enough to increment the sequence number by two (the first process would print 1 and 2, then the next process would print 3 and 4, and so on).

Being nondeterministic does not make it incorrect. Whether the three steps are performed atomically is what makes the program correct or incorrect. Being nondeterministic, however, usually makes debugging these types of programs harder.

9.2 Record Locking versus File Locking

The Unix kernel has no notion whatsoever of records within a file. Any interpretation of records is up to the applications that read and write the file. Nevertheless, the term *record locking* is used to describe the locking features that are provided. But the application specifies a *byte range* within the file to lock or unlock. Whether this byte range has any relationship to one or more logical records within the file is left to the application.

Posix record locking defines one special byte range—a starting offset of 0 (the beginning of the file) and a length of 0—to specify the entire file. Our remaining discussion concerns record locking, with file locking just one special case.

The term *granularity* is used to denote the size of the object that can be locked. With Posix record locking, this granularity is a single byte. Normally the smaller the granularity, the greater the number of simultaneous users allowed. For example, assume five processes access a given file at about the same time, three readers and two writers. Also assume that all five are accessing different records in the file and that each of the five requests takes about the same amount of time, say 1 second. If the locking is done at the file level (the coarsest granularity possible), then all three readers can access their records at the same time, but both writers must wait until the readers are done. Then one writer can modify its record, followed by the other writer. The total time will be about 3 seconds. (We are ignoring lots of details in these timing assumptions, of course.) But if the locking granularity is the record (the finest granularity possible), then all five accesses can proceed simultaneously, since all five are working on different records. The total time would then be only 1 second.

> Berkeley-derived implementations of Unix support *file locking* to lock or unlock an entire file, with no capabilities to lock or unlock a range of bytes within the file. This is provided by the `flock` function.

History

Various techniques have been employed for file and record locking under Unix over the years. Early programs such as UUCP and line printer daemons used various tricks that exploited characteristics of the filesystem implementation. (We describe three of these filesystem techniques in Section 9.8.) These are slow, however, and better techniques were needed for the database systems that were being implemented in the early 1980s.

The first true file and record locking was added to Version 7 by John Bass in 1980, adding a new system call named `locking`. This provided mandatory record locking and was picked up by many versions of System III and Xenix. (We describe the differences between mandatory and advisory locking, and between record locking and file locking later in this chapter.)

4.2BSD provided file locking (not record locking) with its `flock` function in 1983. The 1984 `/usr/group` Standard (one of the predecessors to X/Open) defined the `lockf` function, which provided only exclusive locks (write locks), not shared locks (read locks).

In 1984, System V Release 2 (SVR2) provided advisory record locking through the `fcntl` function. The `lockf` function was also provided, but it was just a library function that called `fcntl`. (Many current systems still provide this implementation of `lockf` using `fcntl`.) In 1986, System V Release 3 (SVR3) added mandatory record locking to `fcntl` using the set-group-ID bit, as we describe in Section 9.5.

The 1988 Posix.1 standard standardized advisory file and record locking with the `fcntl` function, and that is what we describe in this chapter. The X/Open Portability Guide Issue 3 (XPG3, dated 1988) also specifies that record locking is to be provided through the `fcntl` function.

9.3   Posix **fcntl** Record Locking

The Posix interface for record locking is the fcntl function.

```
#include <fcntl.h>

int fcntl(int fd, int cmd, ... /* struct flock *arg */ );
```

Returns: depends on *cmd* if OK, −1 on error

Three values of the *cmd* argument are used with record locking. These three commands require that the third argument, *arg*, be a pointer to an flock structure:

```
struct flock {
  short  l_type;   /* F_RDLCK, F_WRLCK, F_UNLCK */
  short  l_whence; /* SEEK_SET, SEEK_CUR, SEEK_END */
  off_t  l_start;  /* relative starting offset in bytes */
  off_t  l_len;    /* #bytes; 0 means until end-of-file */
  pid_t  l_pid;    /* PID returned by F_GETLK */
};
```

The three commands are:

F_SETLK   Obtain (an l_type of either F_RDLCK or F_WRLCK) or release (an l_type of F_UNLCK) the lock described by the flock structure pointed to by *arg*.

  If the lock cannot be granted to the process, the function returns immediately (it does not block) with an error of EACCES or EAGAIN.

F_SETLKW This command is similar to the previous command; however, if the lock cannot be granted to the process, the thread blocks until the lock can be granted. (The W at the end of this command name means "wait.")

F_GETLK   Examine the lock pointed to by *arg* to see whether an existing lock would prevent this new lock from being granted. If no lock currently exists that would prevent the new lock from being granted, the l_type member of the flock structure pointed to by *arg* is set to F_UNLCK. Otherwise, information about the existing lock, including the process ID of the process holding the lock, is returned in the flock structure pointed to by *arg* (i.e., the contents of the structure are overwritten by this function).

  Realize that issuing an F_GETLK followed by an F_SETLK is not an atomic operation. That is, if we call F_GETLK and it sets the l_type member to F_UNLCK on return, this does not guarantee that an immediate issue of the F_SETLK will return success. Another process could run between these two calls and obtain the lock that we want.

  The reason that the F_GETLK command is provided is to return information about a lock when F_SETLK returns an error, allowing us to determine who has the region locked, and how (a read lock or a write lock). But even in this scenario, we must be prepared for the F_GETLK command to return that the region is unlocked, because the region can be unlocked between the F_SETLK and F_GETLK commands.

The flock structure describes the type of lock (a read lock or a write lock) and the byte range of the file to lock. As with lseek, the starting byte offset is specified as a relative offset (the l_start member) and how to interpret that relative offset (the l_whence member) as

- SEEK_SET: l_start relative to the beginning of the file,
- SEEK_CUR: l_start relative to the current byte offset of the file, and
- SEEK_END: l_start relative to the end of the file.

The l_len member specifies the number of consecutive bytes starting at that offset. A length of 0 means "from the starting offset to the largest possible value of the file offset." Therefore, two ways to lock the entire file are

1. specify an l_whence of SEEK_SET, an l_start of 0, and an l_len of 0; or

2. position the file to the beginning using lseek and then specify an l_whence of SEEK_CUR, an l_start of 0, and an l_len of 0.

The first of these two ways is most common, since it requires a single function call (fcntl) instead of two function calls. (See Exercise 9.10 also.)

A lock can be for reading or writing, and at most, one type of lock (read or write) can exist for any byte of a file. Furthermore, a given byte can have multiple read locks but only a single write lock. This corresponds to the read–write locks that we described in the previous chapter. Naturally, an error occurs if we request a read lock when the descriptor was not opened for reading, or request a write lock when the descriptor was not opened for writing.

All locks associated with a file for a given process are removed when a descriptor for that file is closed by that process, or when the process holding the descriptor terminates. Locks are not inherited by a child across a fork.

> This cleanup of existing locks by the kernel when the process terminates is provided only by fcntl record locking and as an option with System V semaphores. The other synchronization techniques that we describe (mutexes, condition variables, read–write locks, and Posix semaphores) do not perform this cleanup on process termination. We talked about this at the end of Section 7.7.

Record locking should not be used with the standard I/O library, because of the internal buffering performed by the library. When a file is being locked, read and write should be used with the file to avoid problems.

Example

We now return to our example from Figure 9.2 and recode the two functions my_lock and my_unlock from Figure 9.1 to use Posix record locking. We show these functions in Figure 9.3.

―― *lock/lockfcntl.c*

```
 1 #include      "unpipc.h"

 2 void
 3 my_lock(int fd)
 4 {
 5     struct flock lock;

 6     lock.l_type = F_WRLCK;
 7     lock.l_whence = SEEK_SET;
 8     lock.l_start = 0;
 9     lock.l_len = 0;                  /* write lock entire file */

10     Fcntl(fd, F_SETLKW, &lock);
11 }

12 void
13 my_unlock(int fd)
14 {
15     struct flock lock;

16     lock.l_type = F_UNLCK;
17     lock.l_whence = SEEK_SET;
18     lock.l_start = 0;
19     lock.l_len = 0;                  /* unlock entire file */

20     Fcntl(fd, F_SETLK, &lock);
21 }
```
―― *lock/lockfcntl.c*

Figure 9.3 Posix fcntl locking.

Notice that we must specify a write lock, to guarantee only one process at a time updates the sequence number. (See Exercise 9.4.) We also specify a command of F_SETLKW when obtaining the lock, because if the lock is not available, we want to block until it is available.

> Given the definition of the flock structure shown earlier, we might think we could initialize our structure in my_lock as
>
> ```
> static struct flock lock = { F_WRLCK, SEEK_SET, 0, 0, 0 };
> ```
>
> but this is wrong. Posix defines only the required members that must be in a structure, such as flock. Implementations can arrange these members in any order, and can also add implementation-specific members.

We do not show the output, but it appears correct. Realize that running our simple program from Figure 9.2 does not let us state that our program works. If the output is wrong, as we have seen, we can say that our program is *not* correct, but running two copies of the program, each looping 20 times is not an adequate test. The kernel could run one program that updates the sequence number 20 times, and then run the other program that updates the sequence number another 20 times. If no switch occurs between the two processes, we might never see the error. A better test is to run the functions from Figure 9.3 with a main function that increments the sequence number say, ten thousand times, without printing the value each time through the loop. If we initialize the sequence number to 1 and run 20 copies of this program at the same time, then we expect the ending value of the sequence number file to be 200,001.

Example: Simpler Macros

In Figure 9.3, to request or release a lock takes six lines of code. We must allocate a structure, fill in the structure, and then call `fcntl`. We can simplify our programs by defining the following seven macros, which are from Section 12.3 of APUE:

```
#define read_lock(fd, offset, whence, len) \
            lock_reg(fd, F_SETLK, F_RDLCK, offset, whence, len)
#define readw_lock(fd, offset, whence, len) \
            lock_reg(fd, F_SETLKW, F_RDLCK, offset, whence, len)
#define write_lock(fd, offset, whence, len) \
            lock_reg(fd, F_SETLK, F_WRLCK, offset, whence, len)
#define writew_lock(fd, offset, whence, len) \
            lock_reg(fd, F_SETLKW, F_WRLCK, offset, whence, len)
#define un_lock(fd, offset, whence, len) \
            lock_reg(fd, F_SETLK, F_UNLCK, offset, whence, len)

#define is_read_lockable(fd, offset, whence, len) \
            lock_test(fd, F_RDLCK, offset, whence, len)
#define is_write_lockable(fd, offset, whence, len) \
            lock_test(fd, F_WRLCK, offset, whence, len)
```

These macros use our `lock_reg` and `lock_test` functions, which are shown in Figures 9.4 and 9.5. When using these macros, we need not worry about the structure or the function that is actually called. The first three arguments to these macros are purposely the same as the first three arguments to the `lseek` function.

We also define two wrapper functions, `Lock_reg` and `Lock_test`, which terminate with an error upon an `fcntl` error, along with seven macros whose names also begin with a capital letter that call these two wrapper functions.

Using these macros, our `my_lock` and `my_unlock` functions from Figure 9.3 become

```
#define my_lock(fd)   (Writew_lock(fd, 0, SEEK_SET, 0))
#define my_unlock(fd) (Un_lock(fd, 0, SEEK_SET, 0))
```

―― *lib/lock_reg.c*
```
 1 #include    "unpipc.h"

 2 int
 3 lock_reg(int fd, int cmd, int type, off_t offset, int whence, off_t len)
 4 {
 5     struct flock lock;

 6     lock.l_type = type;         /* F_RDLCK, F_WRLCK, F_UNLCK */
 7     lock.l_start = offset;      /* byte offset, relative to l_whence */
 8     lock.l_whence = whence;     /* SEEK_SET, SEEK_CUR, SEEK_END */
 9     lock.l_len = len;           /* #bytes (0 means to EOF) */

10     return (fcntl(fd, cmd, &lock));    /* -1 upon error */
11 }
```
―― *lib/lock_reg.c*

Figure 9.4 Call `fcntl` to obtain or release a lock.

————————————————————————————————— lib/lock_test.c

```
 1 #include    "unpipc.h"

 2 pid_t
 3 lock_test(int fd, int type, off_t offset, int whence, off_t len)
 4 {
 5     struct flock lock;

 6     lock.l_type = type;         /* F_RDLCK or F_WRLCK */
 7     lock.l_start = offset;      /* byte offset, relative to l_whence */
 8     lock.l_whence = whence;     /* SEEK_SET, SEEK_CUR, SEEK_END */
 9     lock.l_len = len;           /* #bytes (0 means to EOF) */

10     if (fcntl(fd, F_GETLK, &lock) == -1)
11         return (-1);            /* unexpected error */

12     if (lock.l_type == F_UNLCK)
13         return (0);             /* false, region not locked by another proc */
14     return (lock.l_pid);        /* true, return positive PID of lock owner */
15 }
```
————————————————————————————————— lib/lock_test.c

Figure 9.5 Call `fcntl` to test a lock.

9.4   Advisory Locking

Posix record locking is called *advisory locking*. This means the kernel maintains correct
knowledge of all files that have been locked by each process, but it does not prevent a
process from writing to a file that is read-locked by another process. Similarly, the kernel does not prevent a process from reading from a file that is write-locked by another
process. A process can ignore an advisory lock and write to a file that is read-locked, or
read from a file that is write-locked, assuming the process has adequate permissions to
read or write the file.

Advisory locks are fine for *cooperating processes*. The programming of daemons used
by network programming is an example of cooperative processes—the programs that
access a shared resource, such as the sequence number file, are all under control of the
system administrator. As long as the actual file containing the sequence number is not
writable by any process, some random process cannot write to the file while it is locked.

Example: Noncooperating Processes

We can demonstrate that Posix record locking is advisory by running two instances of
our sequence number program: one instance (`lockfcntl`) uses the functions from Figure 9.3 and locks the file before incrementing the sequence number, and the other
(`locknone`) uses the functions from Figure 9.1 that perform no locking.

```
solaris % lockfcntl & locknone &
lockfcntl: pid = 18816, seq# = 1
lockfcntl: pid = 18816, seq# = 2
lockfcntl: pid = 18816, seq# = 3
```

```
lockfcntl: pid = 18816, seq# = 4
lockfcntl: pid = 18816, seq# = 5
lockfcntl: pid = 18816, seq# = 6
lockfcntl: pid = 18816, seq# = 7
lockfcntl: pid = 18816, seq# = 8
lockfcntl: pid = 18816, seq# = 9
lockfcntl: pid = 18816, seq# = 10
lockfcntl: pid = 18816, seq# = 11
locknone: pid = 18817, seq# = 11      switch processes; error
locknone: pid = 18817, seq# = 12
locknone: pid = 18817, seq# = 13
locknone: pid = 18817, seq# = 14
locknone: pid = 18817, seq# = 15
locknone: pid = 18817, seq# = 16
locknone: pid = 18817, seq# = 17
locknone: pid = 18817, seq# = 18
lockfcntl: pid = 18816, seq# = 12      switch processes; error
lockfcntl: pid = 18816, seq# = 13
lockfcntl: pid = 18816, seq# = 14
lockfcntl: pid = 18816, seq# = 15
lockfcntl: pid = 18816, seq# = 16
lockfcntl: pid = 18816, seq# = 17
lockfcntl: pid = 18816, seq# = 18
lockfcntl: pid = 18816, seq# = 19
lockfcntl: pid = 18816, seq# = 20
locknone: pid = 18817, seq# = 19      switch processes; error
locknone: pid = 18817, seq# = 20
locknone: pid = 18817, seq# = 21
locknone: pid = 18817, seq# = 22
locknone: pid = 18817, seq# = 23
locknone: pid = 18817, seq# = 24
locknone: pid = 18817, seq# = 25
locknone: pid = 18817, seq# = 26
locknone: pid = 18817, seq# = 27
locknone: pid = 18817, seq# = 28
locknone: pid = 18817, seq# = 29
locknone: pid = 18817, seq# = 30
```

Our lockfcntl program runs first, but while it is performing the three steps to increment the sequence number from 11 to 12 (and while it holds the lock on the entire file), the kernel switches processes and our locknone program runs. This new program reads the sequence number value of 11 before our lockfcntl program writes it back to the file. The advisory record lock held by the lockfcntl program has no effect on our locknone program.

9.5   Mandatory Locking

Some systems provide another type of record locking, called *mandatory locking*. With a mandatory lock, the kernel checks every read and write request to verify that the operation does not interfere with a lock held by a process. For a normal blocking descriptor, the read or write that conflicts with a mandatory lock puts the process to sleep until the lock is released. With a nonblocking descriptor, issuing a `read` or `write` that conflicts with a mandatory lock causes an error return of `EAGAIN`.

> Posix.1 and Unix 98 define only advisory locking. Many implementations derived from System V, however, provide both advisory and mandatory locking. Mandatory record locking was introduced with System V Release 3.

To enable mandatory locking for a particular file,

- the group-execute bit must be *off*, and
- the set-group-ID bit must be *on*.

Note that having the set-user-ID bit on for a file without having the user-execute bit on also makes no sense, and similarly for the set-group-ID bit and the group-execute bit. Therefore, mandatory locking was added in this way, without affecting any existing user software. New system calls were not required.

On systems that support mandatory record locking, the `ls` command looks for this special combination of bits and prints an `l` or `L` to indicate that mandatory locking is enabled for that file. Similarly, the `chmod` command accepts a specification of `l` to enable mandatory locking for a file.

Example

On a first glance, using mandatory locking should solve the problem of an uncooperating process, since any `reads` or `writes` by the uncooperating process on the locked file will block that process until the lock is released. Unfortunately, the timing problems are more complex, as we can easily demonstrate.

To change our example using `fcntl` to use mandatory locking, all we do is change the permission bits of the `seqno` file. We also run a different version of the `main` function that takes the `for` loop limit from the first command-line argument (instead of using the constant 20) and does not call `printf` each time around the loop.

```
solaris % cat > seqno                       first initialize value to 1
1
^D                                          Control-D is our terminal end-of-file character
solaris % ls -l seqno
-rw-r--r--   1 rstevens other1        2 Oct  7 11:24 seqno
solaris % chmod +l seqno                    enable mandatory locking
solaris % ls -l seqno
-rw-r-lr--   1 rstevens other1        2 Oct  7 11:24 seqno
```

We now start two programs in the background: `loopfcntl` uses `fcntl` locking, and `loopnone` does no locking. We specify a command-line argument of 10,000, which is the number of times that each program reads, increments, and writes the sequence number.

```
solaris % loopfcntl 10000 & loopnone 10000 &   start both programs in the background
solaris % wait                                 wait for both background jobs to finish
solaris % cat seqno                            and look at the sequence number
14378                                          error: should be 20,001
```

Each time we run these two programs, the ending sequence number is normally between 14,000 and 16,000. If the locking worked as desired, the ending value would always be 20,001. To see where the error occurs, we need to draw a time line of the individual steps, which we show in Figure 9.6.

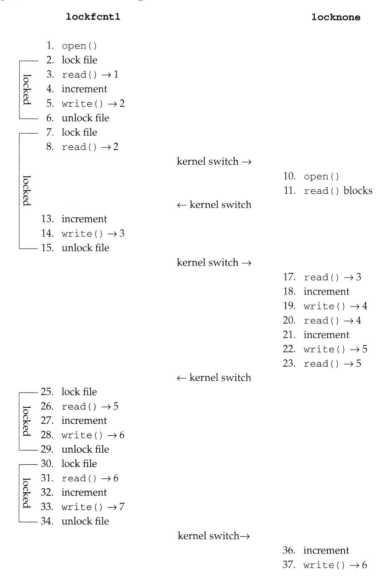

    lockfcntl   **locknone**

```
              1.  open()
              2.  lock file
              3.  read() → 1
   locked     4.  increment
              5.  write() → 2
              6.  unlock file
              7.  lock file
              8.  read() → 2
                                    kernel switch →
                                                          10.  open()
                                                          11.  read() blocks
   locked                          ← kernel switch
             13.  increment
             14.  write() → 3
             15.  unlock file
                                    kernel switch →
                                                          17.  read() → 3
                                                          18.  increment
                                                          19.  write() → 4
                                                          20.  read() → 4
                                                          21.  increment
                                                          22.  write() → 5
                                                          23.  read() → 5
                                    ← kernel switch
             25.  lock file
             26.  read() → 5
   locked    27.  increment
             28.  write() → 6
             29.  unlock file
             30.  lock file
             31.  read() → 6
   locked    32.  increment
             33.  write() → 7
             34.  unlock file
                                    kernel switch →
                                                          36.  increment
                                                          37.  write() → 6
```

Figure 9.6 Time line of `loopfcntl` and `loopnone` programs.

We assume that the `loopfcntl` program starts first and executes the first eight steps shown in the figure. The kernel then switches processes while `loopfcntl` has a record lock on the sequence number file. `loopnone` is then started, but its first `read` blocks, because the file from which it is reading has an outstanding mandatory lock owned by another process. We assume that the kernel switches back to the first program and it executes steps 13, 14, and 15. This behavior is the type that we expect: the kernel blocks the read from the uncooperating process, because the file it is trying to read is locked by another process.

The kernel then switches to the locknone program and it executes steps 17 through 23. The reads and writes are allowed, because the first program unlocked the file in step 15. The problem, however, appears when the program reads the value of 5 in step 23 and the kernel then switches to the other process. It obtains the lock and also reads the value of 5. This process increments the value twice, storing a value of 7, before the next process runs in step 36. But the second process writes a value of 6 to the file, which is wrong.

What we see in this example is that mandatory locking prevents a process from reading a file that is locked (step 11), but this does not solve the problem. The problem is that the process on the left is allowed to update the file (steps 25 through 34) while the process on the right is in the middle of its three steps to update the sequence number (steps 23, 36, and 37). If multiple processes are updating a file, *all* the processes must cooperate using some form of locking. One rogue process can create havoc.

9.6 Priorities of Readers and Writers

In our implementation of read–write locks in Section 8.4, we gave priority to waiting writers over waiting readers. We now look at some details of the solution to the readers and writer problem provided by fcntl record locking. What we want to look at is how pending lock requests are handled when a region is already locked, something that is not specified by Posix.

Example: Additional Read Locks While a Write Lock Is Pending

The first question we ask is: if a resource is read-locked with a write lock queued, is another read lock allowed? Some solutions to the readers and writers problem do not allow another reader if a writer is already waiting, because if new read requests are continually allowed, a possibility exists that the already pending write request will never be allowed.

To test how fcntl record locking handles this scenario, we write a test program that obtains a read lock on an entire file and then forks two children. The first child tries to obtain a write lock (and will block, since the parent holds a read lock on the entire file), followed in time by the second child, which tries to obtain a read lock. Figure 9.7 shows a time line of these requests, and Figure 9.8 is our test program.

Parent opens file and obtains read lock

6–8   The parent opens the file and obtains a read lock on the entire file. Notice that we call read_lock (which does not block but returns an error if the lock cannot be granted) and not readw_lock (which can wait), because we expect this lock to be granted immediately. We also print a message with the current time (our gf_time function from p. 404 of UNPv1) when the lock is granted.

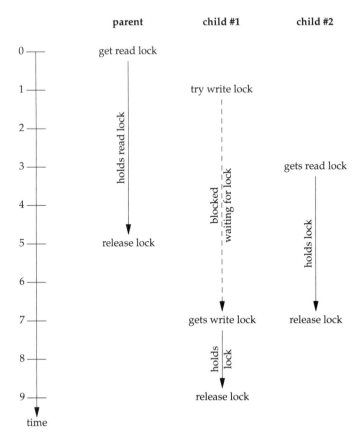

Figure 9.7 Determine whether another read lock is allowed while a write lock is pending.

`fork` first child

9–19   The first child is created and it sleeps for 1 second and then blocks while waiting for a write lock of the entire file. When the write lock is granted, this first child holds the lock for 2 seconds, releases the lock, and terminates.

`fork` second child

20–30   The second child is created, and it sleeps for 3 seconds to allow the first child's write lock to be pending, and then tries to obtain a read lock of the entire file. We can tell by the time on the message printed when `readw_lock` returns whether this read lock is queued or granted immediately. The lock is held for 4 seconds and released.

Parent holds read lock for 5 seconds

31–35   The parent holds the read lock for 5 seconds, releases the lock, and terminates.

―――――――――――――――――――――――――――――――――― *lock/test2.c*

```
 1 #include     "unpipc.h"

 2 int
 3 main(int argc, char **argv)
 4 {
 5     int     fd;

 6     fd = Open("test1.data", O_RDWR | O_CREAT, FILE_MODE);

 7     Read_lock(fd, 0, SEEK_SET, 0);  /* parent read locks entire file */
 8     printf("%s: parent has read lock\n", Gf_time());

 9     if (Fork() == 0) {
10             /* first child */
11         sleep(1);
12         printf("%s: first child tries to obtain write lock\n", Gf_time());
13         Writew_lock(fd, 0, SEEK_SET, 0);    /* this should block */
14         printf("%s: first child obtains write lock\n", Gf_time());
15         sleep(2);
16         Un_lock(fd, 0, SEEK_SET, 0);
17         printf("%s: first child releases write lock\n", Gf_time());
18         exit(0);
19     }
20     if (Fork() == 0) {
21             /* second child */
22         sleep(3);
23         printf("%s: second child tries to obtain read lock\n", Gf_time());
24         Readw_lock(fd, 0, SEEK_SET, 0);
25         printf("%s: second child obtains read lock\n", Gf_time());
26         sleep(4);
27         Un_lock(fd, 0, SEEK_SET, 0);
28         printf("%s: second child releases read lock\n", Gf_time());
29         exit(0);
30     }
31         /* parent */
32     sleep(5);
33     Un_lock(fd, 0, SEEK_SET, 0);
34     printf("%s: parent releases read lock\n", Gf_time());
35     exit(0);
36 }
```
―――――――――――――――――――――――――――――――――― *lock/test2.c*

Figure 9.8 Determine whether another read lock is allowed while a write lock is pending.

The time line shown in Figure 9.7 is what we see under Solaris 2.6, Digital Unix 4.0B, and BSD/OS 3.1. That is, the read lock requested by the second child is granted even though a write lock is already pending from the first child. This allows for potential starvation of write locks as long as read locks are continually issued. Here is the output with some blank lines added between the major time events for readability:

```
alpha % test2
16:32:29.674453: parent has read lock

16:32:30.709197: first child tries to obtain write lock

16:32:32.725810: second child tries to obtain read lock
16:32:32.728739: second child obtains read lock

16:32:34.722282: parent releases read lock

16:32:36.729738: second child releases read lock
16:32:36.735597: first child obtains write lock

16:32:38.736938: first child releases write lock
```

Example: Do Pending Writers Have a Priority Over Pending Readers?

The next question we ask is: do pending writers have a priority over pending readers? Some solutions to the readers and writers problem build in this priority.

Figure 9.9 is our test program and Figure 9.10 is a time line of our test program.

Parent creates file and obtains write lock

6–8   The parent creates the file and obtains a write lock on the entire file.

fork and create first child

9–19   The first child is created, and it sleeps for 1 second and then requests a write lock on the entire file. We know this will block, since the parent has a write lock on the entire file and holds this lock for 5 seconds, but we want this request queued when the parent's lock is released.

fork and create second child

20–30   The second child is created, and it sleeps for 3 seconds and then requests a read lock on the entire file. This too will be queued when the parent releases its write lock.

Under both Solaris 2.6 and Digital Unix 4.0B, we see that the first child's write lock is granted before the second child's read lock, as we show in Figure 9.10. But this doesn't tell us that write locks have a priority over read locks, because the reason could be that the kernel grants the lock requests in FIFO order, regardless whether they are read locks or write locks. To verify this, we create another test program nearly identical to Figure 9.9, but with the read lock request occurring at time 1 and the write lock request occurring at time 3. These two programs show that Solaris and Digital Unix handle lock requests in a FIFO order, regardless of the type of lock request. These two programs also show that BSD/OS 3.1 gives priority to read requests.

———————————————————————————————— lock/test3.c
```
 1 #include     "unpipc.h"

 2 int
 3 main(int argc, char **argv)
 4 {
 5     int     fd;

 6     fd = Open("test1.data", O_RDWR | O_CREAT, FILE_MODE);

 7     Write_lock(fd, 0, SEEK_SET, 0);      /* parent write locks entire file */
 8     printf("%s: parent has write lock\n", Gf_time());

 9     if (Fork() == 0) {
10             /* first child */
11         sleep(1);
12         printf("%s: first child tries to obtain write lock\n", Gf_time());
13         Writew_lock(fd, 0, SEEK_SET, 0);    /* this should block */
14         printf("%s: first child obtains write lock\n", Gf_time());
15         sleep(2);
16         Un_lock(fd, 0, SEEK_SET, 0);
17         printf("%s: first child releases write lock\n", Gf_time());
18         exit(0);
19     }
20     if (Fork() == 0) {
21             /* second child */
22         sleep(3);
23         printf("%s: second child tries to obtain read lock\n", Gf_time());
24         Readw_lock(fd, 0, SEEK_SET, 0);
25         printf("%s: second child obtains read lock\n", Gf_time());
26         sleep(4);
27         Un_lock(fd, 0, SEEK_SET, 0);
28         printf("%s: second child releases read lock\n", Gf_time());
29         exit(0);
30     }
31     /* parent */
32     sleep(5);
33     Un_lock(fd, 0, SEEK_SET, 0);
34     printf("%s: parent releases write lock\n", Gf_time());
35     exit(0);
36 }
```
———————————————————————————————— lock/test3.c

Figure 9.9 Test whether writers have a priority over readers.

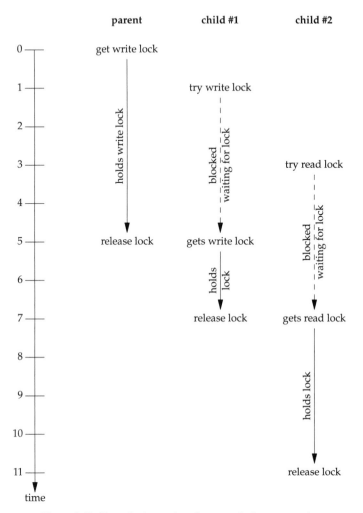

Figure 9.10 Test whether writers have a priority over readers.

Here is the output from Figure 9.9, from which we constructed the time line in Figure 9.10:

```
alpha % test3
16:34:02.810285: parent has write lock
16:34:03.848166: first child tries to obtain write lock
16:34:05.861082: second child tries to obtain read lock
16:34:07.858393: parent releases write lock
16:34:07.865222: first child obtains write lock
16:34:09.865987: first child releases write lock
16:34:09.872823: second child obtains read lock
16:34:13.873822: second child releases read lock    .
```

9.7 Starting Only One Copy of a Daemon

A common use for record locking is to make certain that only one copy of a program (such as a daemon) is running at a time. The code fragment shown in Figure 9.11 would be executed when a daemon starts.

————————————————————————— lock/onedaemon.c
```
 1 #include    "unpipc.h"

 2 #define PATH_PIDFILE    "pidfile"

 3 int
 4 main(int argc, char **argv)
 5 {
 6     int     pidfd;
 7     char    line[MAXLINE];

 8         /* open the PID file, create if nonexistent */
 9     pidfd = Open(PATH_PIDFILE, O_RDWR | O_CREAT, FILE_MODE);

10         /* try to write lock the entire file */
11     if (write_lock(pidfd, 0, SEEK_SET, 0) < 0) {
12         if (errno == EACCES || errno == EAGAIN)
13             err_quit("unable to lock %s, is %s already running?",
14                     PATH_PIDFILE, argv[0]);
15         else
16             err_sys("unable to lock %s", PATH_PIDFILE);
17     }
18         /* write my PID, leave file open to hold the write lock */
19     snprintf(line, sizeof(line), "%ld\n", (long) getpid());
20     Ftruncate(pidfd, 0);
21     Write(pidfd, line, strlen(line));

22     /* then do whatever the daemon does ... */

23     pause();
24 }
```
————————————————————————— lock/onedaemon.c

Figure 9.11 Make certain only one copy of a program is running.

Open and lock a file

8–17   The daemon maintains a 1-line file that contains its process ID. This file is opened, being created if necessary, and then a write lock is requested on the entire file. If the lock is not granted, then we know that another copy of the program is running, and we print an error and terminate.

> Many Unix systems have their daemons write their process ID to a file. Solaris 2.6 stores some of these files in the /etc directory. Digital Unix and BSD/OS both store these files in the /var/run directory.

Write our PID to file

18–21   We truncate the file to 0 bytes and then write a line containing our PID. The reason for truncating the file is that the previous copy of the program (say before the system was rebooted) might have had a process ID of 23456, whereas this instance of the program has a process ID of 123. If we just wrote the line, without truncating the file, the contents would be 123\n6\n. While the first line would still contain the process ID, it is cleaner and less confusing to avoid the possibility of a second line in the file.

Here is a test of the program in Figure 9.11:

```
solaris % onedaemon &          start first copy
[1]     22388
solaris % cat pidfile          check PID written to file
22388
solaris % onedaemon            and try to start a second copy
unable to lock pidfile, is onedaemon already running?
```

Other ways exist for a daemon to prevent another copy of itself from being started. A semaphore could also be used. The advantages in the method shown in this section are that many daemons already write their process ID to a file, and should the daemon prematurely crash, the record lock is automatically released by the kernel.

9.8   Lock Files

Posix.1 guarantees that if the open function is called with the O_CREAT (create the file if it does not already exist) and O_EXCL flags (exclusive open), the function returns an error if the file already exists. Furthermore, the check for the existence of the file and the creation of the file (if it does not already exist) must be *atomic* with regard to other processes. We can therefore use the file created with this technique as a lock. We are guaranteed that only one process at a time can create the file (i.e., obtain the lock), and to release the lock, we just unlink the file.

Figure 9.12 shows a version of our locking functions using this technique. If the open succeeds, we have the lock, and the my_lock function returns. We close the file because we do not need its descriptor: the lock is the existence of the file, regardless of whether the file is open or not. If open returns an error of EEXIST, then the file exists and we try the open again.

There are three problems with this technique.

1. If the process that currently holds the lock terminates without releasing the lock, the filename is not removed. There are ad hoc techniques to deal with this—check the last-access time of the file and assume it has been orphaned if it is older than some amount of time—but none are perfect. Another technique is to write the process ID of the process holding the lock into the lock file, so that other processes can read this process ID and check whether that process is still running. This is imperfect because process IDs are reused after some time.

    This scenario is not a problem with fcntl record locking, because when a process terminates, any record locks held by that process are automatically released.

2. If some other process currently has the file open, we just call open again, in an infinite loop. This is called *polling* and is a waste of CPU time. An alternate

---

lock/lockopen.c

```
 1 #include     "unpipc.h"

 2 #define LOCKFILE    "/tmp/seqno.lock"

 3 void
 4 my_lock(int fd)
 5 {
 6     int     tempfd;

 7     while ( (tempfd = open(LOCKFILE, O_RDWR | O_CREAT | O_EXCL, FILE_MODE)) < 0) {
 8         if (errno != EEXIST)
 9             err_sys("open error for lock file");
10         /* someone else has the lock, loop around and try again */
11     }
12     Close(tempfd);              /* opened the file, we have the lock */
13 }

14 void
15 my_unlock(int fd)
16 {
17     Unlink(LOCKFILE);           /* release lock by removing file */
18 }
```

lock/lockopen.c

Figure 9.12 Lock functions using open with O_CREAT and O_EXCL flags.

technique would be to `sleep` for 1 second, and then try the `open` again. (We saw this same problem in Figure 7.5.)

This is not a problem with `fcntl` record locking, assuming that the process that wants the lock specifies the FSETLKW command. The kernel puts the process to sleep until the lock is available and then awakens the process.

3. Creating and deleting a second file by calling `open` and `unlink` involves the filesystem and normally takes much longer than calling `fcntl` twice (once to obtain the lock and once to release the lock). When the time was measured to execute 1000 loops within our program that increments the sequence number, `fcntl` record locking was faster than calling `open` and `unlink` by a factor of 75.

Two other quirks of the Unix filesystem have also been used to provide ad hoc locking. The first is that the `link` function fails if the name of the new link already exists. To obtain a lock, a unique temporary file is first created whose pathname contains the process ID (or some combination of the process ID and thread ID, if locking is needed between threads in different processes and between threads within the same process). The `link` function is then called to create a link to this file under the well-known pathname of the lock file. If this succeeds, then the temporary pathname can be `unlink`ed. When the thread is finished with the lock, it just `unlink`s the well-known pathname. If the `link` fails with an error of EEXIST, the thread must try again (similar to what we did in Figure 9.12). One requirement of this technique is that the temporary file and the well-known pathname must both reside on the same filesystem, because most versions of Unix do not allow hard links (the result of the `link` function) across different filesystems.

The second quirk is based on `open` returning an error if the file exists, if O_TRUNC is specified, and if write permission is denied. To obtain a lock, we call `open`, specifying O_CREAT | O_WRONLY | O_TRUNC and a *mode* of 0 (i.e., the new file has no permission bits enabled). If this succeeds, we have the lock and we just `unlink` the pathname when we are done. If `open` fails with an error of EACCES, the thread must try again (similar to what we did in Figure 9.12). One caveat is that this trick does not work if the calling thread has superuser privileges.

The lesson from these examples is to use `fcntl` record locking. Nevertheless, you may encounter code that uses these older types of locking, often in programs written before the widespread implementation of `fcntl` locking.

9.9   NFS Locking

NFS is the Network File System and is discussed in Chapter 29 of TCPv1. `fcntl` record locking is an extension to NFS that is supported by most implementations of NFS. Unix systems normally support NFS record locking with two additional daemons: `lockd` and `statd`. When a process calls `fcntl` to obtain a lock, and the kernel detects that the descriptor refers to a file that is on an NFS-mounted filesystem, the local `lockd` sends the request to the server's `lockd`. The `statd` daemon keeps track of the clients holding locks and interacts with `lockd` to provide crash and recovery functions for NFS locking.

We should expect record locking for an NFS file to take longer than record locking for a local file, since network communication is required to obtain and release each lock. To test NFS record locking, all we need to change is the filename specified by SEQFILE in Figure 9.2. If we measure the time required for our program to execute 10,000 loops using `fcntl` record locking, it is about 80 times faster for a local file than for an NFS file. Also realize that when the sequence number file is on an NFS-mounted filesystem, network communication is involved for both the record locking and for the reading and writing of the sequence number.

> *Caveat emptor*: NFS record locking has been a problem for many years, and most of the problems have been caused by poor implementations. Despite the fact that the major Unix vendors have finally cleaned up their implementations, using `fcntl` record locking over NFS is still a religious issue for many. We will not take sides on this issue but will just note that `fcntl` record locking is supposed to work over NFS, but your success depends on the quality of the implementations, both client and server.

9.10   Summary

`fcntl` record locking provides advisory or mandatory locking of a file that is referenced through its open descriptor. These locks are for locking between different processes and not for locking between the different threads within one process. The term "record" is a misnomer because the Unix kernel has no concept of records within a file. A better term is "range locking," because we specify a range of bytes within the file to lock or unlock. Almost all uses of this type of record locking are advisory between cooperating processes, because even mandatory locking can lead to inconsistent data, as we showed.

With `fcntl` record locking, there is no guarantee as to the priority of pending readers versus pending writers, which is what we saw in Chapter 8 with read–write locks. If this is important to an application, tests similar to the ones we developed in Section 9.6 should be coded and run, or the application should provide its own read–write locks (as we did in Section 8.4), providing whatever priority is desired.

Exercises

9.1 Build the `locknone` program from Figures 9.2 and 9.1 and run it multiple times on your system. Verify that the program does not work without any locking, and that the results are nondeterministic.

9.2 Modify Figure 9.2 so that the standard output is unbuffered. What effect does this have?

9.3 Continue the previous exercise by also calling `putchar` for every character that is output to standard output, instead of calling `printf`. What effect does this have?

9.4 Change the lock in the `my_lock` function in Figure 9.3 to be a read lock instead of a write lock. What happens?

9.5 Change the call to `open` in the `loopmain.c` program to specify the O_NONBLOCK flag also. Build the `loopfcntlnonb` program and run two instances of it at the same time. Does anything change? Why?

9.6 Continue the previous exercise by using the nonblocking version of `loopmain.c` to build the `loopnonenonb` program (using the `locknone.c` file, which performs no locking). Enable the `seqno` file for mandatory locking. Run one instance of this program and another instance of the `loopfcntlnonb` program from the previous exercise at the same time. What happens?

9.7 Build the `loopfcntl` program and run it 10 times in the background from a shell script. Each of the 10 instances should specify a command-line argument of 10,000. First, time the shell script when advisory locking is used, and then change the permissions of the `seqno` file to enable mandatory locking. What effect does mandatory locking have on performance?

9.8 In Figures 9.8 and 9.9, why did we call `fork` to create child processes instead of calling `pthread_create` to create threads?

9.9 In Figure 9.11, we call `ftruncate` to set the size of the file to 0 bytes. Why don't we just specify the O_TRUNC flag for `open` instead?

9.10 If we are writing a threaded application that uses `fcntl` record locking, should we use SEEK_SET, SEEK_CUR, or SEEK_END when specifying the starting byte offset to lock, and why?

10

Posix Semaphores

10.1 Introduction

A *semaphore* is a primitive used to provide synchronization between various processes or between the various threads in a given process. We look at three types of semaphores in this text.

- Posix named semaphores are identified by Posix IPC names (Section 2.2) and can be used to synchronize processes or threads.
- Posix memory-based semaphores are stored in shared memory and can be used to synchronize processes or threads.
- System V semaphores (Chapter 11) are maintained in the kernel and can be used to synchronize processes or threads.

For now, we concern ourselves with synchronization between different processes. We first consider a *binary semaphore*: a semaphore that can assume only the values 0 or 1. We show this in Figure 10.1.

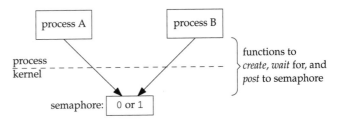

Figure 10.1 A binary semaphore being used by two processes.

We show that the semaphore is maintained by the kernel (which is true for System V semaphores) and that its value can be 0 or 1.

Posix semaphores need not be maintained in the kernel. Also, Posix semaphores are identified by names that might correspond to pathnames in the filesystem. Therefore, Figure 10.2 is a more realistic picture of what is termed a *Posix named semaphore*.

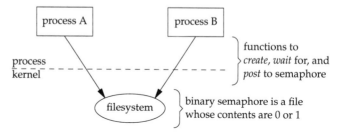

Figure 10.2   A Posix named binary semaphore being used by two processes.

> We must make one qualification with regard to Figure 10.2: although Posix named semaphores are identified by names that might correspond to pathnames in the filesystem, nothing requires that they actually be stored in a file in the filesystem. An embedded realtime system, for example, could use the name to identify the semaphore, but keep the actual semaphore value somewhere in the kernel. But if mapped files are used for the implementation (and we show such an implementation in Section 10.15), then the actual value does appear in a file and that file is mapped into the address space of all the processes that have the semaphore open.

In Figures 10.1 and 10.2, we note three operations that a process can perform on a semaphore:

1. *Create* a semaphore. This also requires the caller to specify the initial value, which for a binary semaphore is often 1, but can be 0.

2. *Wait* for a semaphore. This tests the value of the semaphore, waits (blocks) if the value is less than or equal to 0, and then decrements the semaphore value once it is greater than 0. This can be summarized by the pseudocode

```
while (semaphore_value <= 0)
    ;    /* wait; i.e., block the thread or process */
semaphore_value--;
/* we have the semaphore */
```

The fundamental requirement here is that the test of the value in the `while` statement, and its subsequent decrement (if its value was greater than 0), must be done as an *atomic* operation with respect to other threads or processes accessing this semaphore. (That is one reason System V semaphores were implemented in the mid-1980s within the kernel. Since the semaphore operations were system calls within the kernel, guaranteeing this atomicity with regard to other processes was easy.)

There are other common names for this operation: originally it was called *P* by Edsger Dijkstra, for the Dutch word *proberen* (meaning to try). It is also known as *down* (since the value of the semaphore is being decremented) and *lock*, but we will use the Posix term of *wait*.

3. *Post* to a semaphore. This increments the value of the semaphore and can be summarized by the pseudocode

```
semaphore_value++;
```

If any processes are blocked, waiting for this semaphore's value to be greater than 0, one of those processes can now be awoken. As with the wait code just shown, this post operation must also be atomic with regard to other processes accessing the semaphore.

There are other common names for this operation: originally it was called *V* for the Dutch word *verhogen* (meaning to increment). It is also known as *up* (since the value of the semaphore is being incremented), *unlock*, and *signal*. We will use the Posix term of *post*.

Obviously, the actual semaphore code has more details than we show in the pseudocode for the wait and post operations: namely how to queue all the processes that are waiting for a given semaphore and then how to wake up one (of the possibly many processes) that is waiting for a given semaphore to be posted to. Fortunately, these details are handled by the implementation.

Notice that the pseudocode shown does not assume a binary semaphore with the values 0 and 1. The code works with semaphores that are initialized to any nonnegative value. These are called *counting semaphores*. These are normally initialized to some value N, which indicates the number of resources (say buffers) available. We show examples of both binary semaphores and counting semaphores throughout the chapter.

> We often differentiate between a binary semaphore and a counting semaphore, and we do so for our own edification. No difference exists between the two in the system code that implements a semaphore.

A binary semaphore can be used for mutual exclusion, just like a mutex. Figure 10.3 shows an example.

```
initialize mutex;                           initialize semaphore to 1;

pthread_mutex_lock(&mutex);                 sem_wait(&sem);
critical region                             critical region
pthread_mutex_unlock(&mutex);               sem_post(&sem);
```

Figure 10.3 Comparison of mutex and semaphore to solve mutual exclusion problem.

We initialize the semaphore to 1. The call to sem_wait waits for the value to be greater than 0 and then decrements the value. The call to sem_post increments the value (from 0 to 1) and wakes up any threads blocked in a call to sem_wait for this semaphore.

Although semaphores can be used like a mutex, semaphores have a feature not provided by mutexes: a mutex must always be unlocked by the thread that locked the mutex, while a semaphore post need not be performed by the same thread that did the semaphore wait. We can show an example of this feature using two binary semaphores and a simplified version of the producer–consumer problem from Chapter 7. Figure 10.4 shows a producer that places an item into a shared buffer and a consumer that removes the item. For simplicity, assume that the buffer holds one item.

Figure 10.4 Simple producer–consumer problem with a shared buffer.

Figure 10.5 shows the pseudocode for the producer and consumer.

Producer	**Consumer**

```
       Producer                                   Consumer

  initialize semaphore get to 0;
  initialize semaphore put to 1;

  for ( ; ; ) {                          for ( ; ; ) {
      sem_wait(&put);                         sem_wait(&get);
      put data into buffer                    process data in buffer
      sem_post(&get);                         sem_post(&put);
  }                                      }
```

Figure 10.5 Pseudocode for simple producer–consumer.

The semaphore `put` controls whether the producer can place an item into the shared buffer, and the semaphore `get` controls whether the consumer can remove an item from the shared buffer. The steps that occur over time are as follows:

1. The producer initializes the buffer and the two semaphores.

2. Assume that the consumer then runs. It blocks in its call to `sem_wait` because the value of `get` is 0.

3. Sometime later, the producer starts. When it calls `sem_wait`, the value of `put` is decremented from 1 to 0, and the producer places an item into the buffer. It then calls `sem_post` to increment the value of `get` from 0 to 1. Since a thread is blocked on this semaphore (the consumer), waiting for its value to become positive, that thread is marked as ready-to-run. But assume that the producer continues to run. The producer then blocks in its call to `sem_wait` at the top of the `for` loop, because the value of `put` is 0. The producer must wait until the consumer empties the buffer.

4. The consumer returns from its call to `sem_wait`, which decrements the value of the `get` semaphore from 1 to 0. It processes the data in the buffer, and calls `sem_post`, which increments the value of `put` from 0 to 1. Since a thread is blocked on this semaphore (the producer), waiting for its value to become positive, that thread is marked as ready-to-run. But assume that the consumer continues to run. The consumer then blocks in its call to `sem_wait`, at the top of the `for` loop, because the value of `get` is 0.

5. The producer returns from its call to sem_wait, places data into the buffer, and this scenario just continues.

We assumed that each time sem_post was called, even though a process was waiting and was then marked as ready-to-run, the caller continued. Whether the caller continues or whether the thread that just became ready runs does not matter (you should assume the other scenario and convince yourself of this fact).

We can list three differences among semaphores and mutexes and condition variables.

1. A mutex must always be unlocked by the thread that locked the mutex, whereas a semaphore post need not be performed by the same thread that did the semaphore wait. This is what we just showed in our example.

2. A mutex is either locked or unlocked (a binary state, similar to a binary semaphore).

3. Since a semaphore has state associated with it (its count), a semaphore post is always remembered. When a condition variable is signaled, if no thread is waiting for this condition variable, the signal is lost. As an example of this feature, consider Figure 10.5 but assume that the first time through the producer loop, the consumer has not yet called sem_wait. The producer can still put the data item into the buffer, call sem_post on the get semaphore (incrementing its value from 0 to 1), and then block in its call to sem_wait on the put semaphore. Some time later, the consumer can enter its for loop and call sem_wait on the get variable, which will decrement the semaphore's value from 1 to 0, and the consumer then processes the buffer.

> The Posix.1 Rationale states the following reason for providing semaphores along with mutexes and condition variables: "Semaphores are provided in this standard primarily to provide a means of synchronization for processes; these processes may or may not share memory. Mutexes and condition variables are specified as synchronization mechanisms between threads; these threads always share (some) memory. Both are synchronization paradigms that have been in widespread use for a number of years. Each set of primitives is particularly well matched to certain problems." We will see in Section 10.15 that it takes about 300 lines of C to implement counting semaphores with kernel persistence, using mutexes and condition variables—applications should not have to reinvent these 300 lines of C themselves. Even though semaphores are intended for interprocess synchronization and mutexes and condition variables are intended for interthread synchronization, semaphores can be used between threads and mutexes and condition variables can be used between processes. We should use whichever set of primitives fits the application.

We mentioned that Posix provides two types of semaphores: *named* semaphores and *memory-based* (also called *unnamed*) semaphores. Figure 10.6 compares the functions used for both types of semaphores.

Figure 10.2 illustrated a Posix named semaphore. Figure 10.7 shows a Posix memory-based semaphore within a process that is shared by two threads.

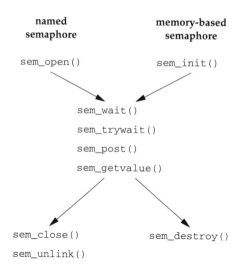

Figure 10.6 Function calls for Posix semaphores.

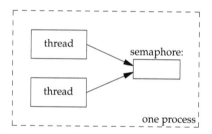

Figure 10.7 Memory-based semaphore shared between two threads within a process.

Figure 10.8 shows a Posix memory-based semaphore in shared memory (Part 4) that is shared by two processes. We show that the shared memory belongs to the address space of both processes.

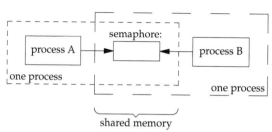

Figure 10.8 Memory-based semaphore in shared memory, shared by two processes.

In this chapter, we first describe Posix named semaphores and then Posix memory-based semaphores. We return to the producer–consumer problem from Section 7.3 and expand it to allow multiple producers with one consumer and finally multiple producers and multiple consumers. We then show that the common I/O technique of multiple buffers is just a special case of the producer–consumer problem.

We show three implementations of Posix named semaphores: the first using FIFOs, the next using memory-mapped I/O with mutexes and condition variables, and the last using System V semaphores.

10.2 sem_open, sem_close, and sem_unlink Functions

The function sem_open creates a new named semaphore or opens an existing named semaphore. A named semaphore can always be used to synchronize either threads or processes.

```
#include <semaphore.h>

sem_t *sem_open(const char *name, int oflag, ...
                    /* mode_t mode, unsigned int value */ );
```
Returns: pointer to semaphore if OK, SEM_FAILED on error

We described the rules about the *name* argument in Section 2.2.

The *oflag* argument is either 0, O_CREAT, or O_CREAT | O_EXCL, as described in Section 2.3. If O_CREAT is specified, then the third and fourth arguments are required: *mode* specifies the permission bits (Figure 2.4), and *value* specifies the initial value of the semaphore. This initial value cannot exceed SEM_VALUE_MAX, which must be at least 32767. Binary semaphores usually have an initial value of 1, whereas counting semaphores often have an initial value greater than 1.

If O_CREAT is specified (without specifying O_EXCL), the semaphore is initialized only if it does not already exist. Specifying O_CREAT if the semaphore already exists is not an error. This flag just means "create and initialize the semaphore if it does not already exist." But specifying O_CREAT | O_EXCL is an error if the semaphore already exists.

The return value is a pointer to a sem_t datatype. This pointer is then used as the argument to sem_close, sem_wait, sem_trywait, sem_post, and sem_getvalue.

> The return value of SEM_FAILED to indicate an error is strange. A null pointer would make more sense. Earlier drafts that led to the Posix standard specified a return value of −1 to indicate an error, and many implementations define
>
> ```
> #define  SEM_FAILED  ((sem_t *)(-1))
> ```
>
> Posix.1 says little about the permission bits associated with a semaphore when it is created or opened by sem_open. Indeed, notice from Figure 2.3 and our discussion above that we do not even specify O_RDONLY, O_WRONLY, or O_RDWR in the *oflag* argument when opening a named semaphore. The two systems used for the examples in this book, Digital Unix 4.0B and Solaris 2.6, both require read access and write access to an existing semaphore for sem_open to succeed. The reason is probably that the two semaphore operations—post and wait—both read and change the value of the semaphore. Not having either read access or write access for an existing semaphore on these two implementations causes the sem_open function to return an error of EACCES ("Permission denied").

A named semaphore that was opened by sem_open is closed by sem_close.

```
#include <semaphore.h>

int sem_close(sem_t *sem);
```

                                                          Returns: 0 if OK, −1 on error

This semaphore close operation also occurs *automatically* on process termination for any named semaphore that is still open. This happens whether the process terminates voluntarily (by calling exit or _exit), or involuntarily (by being killed by a signal).

Closing a semaphore does not remove the semaphore from the system. That is, Posix named semaphores are at least *kernel-persistent*: they retain their value even if no process currently has the semaphore open.

A named semaphore is removed from the system by sem_unlink.

```
#include <semaphore.h>

int sem_unlink(const char *name);
```

                                                          Returns: 0 if OK, −1 on error

Semaphores have a reference count of how many times they are currently open (just like files), and this function is similar to the unlink function for a file: the *name* can be removed from the filesystem while its reference count is greater than 0, but the destruction of the semaphore (versus removing its name from the filesystem) does not take place until the last sem_close occurs.

10.3 `sem_wait` and `sem_trywait` Functions

The sem_wait function tests the value of the specified semaphore, and if the value is greater than 0, the value is decremented and the function returns immediately. If the value is 0 when the function is called, the calling thread is put to sleep until the semaphore value is greater than 0, at which time it will be decremented, and the function then returns. We mentioned earlier that the "test and decrement" operation must be atomic with regard to other threads accessing this semaphore.

```
#include <semaphore.h>

int sem_wait(sem_t *sem);

int sem_trywait(sem_t *sem);
```

                                                          Both return: 0 if OK, −1 on error

The difference between sem_wait and sem_trywait is that the latter does not put the calling thread to sleep if the current value of the semaphore is already 0. Instead, an error of EAGAIN is returned.

sem_wait can return prematurely if it is interrupted by a signal, returning an error of EINTR.

10.4 sem_post and sem_getvalue Functions

When a thread is finished with a semaphore, it calls sem_post. As discussed in Section 10.1, this increments the value of the semaphore by 1 and wakes up any threads that are waiting for the semaphore value to become positive.

```
#include <semaphore.h>

int sem_post(sem_t *sem);

int sem_getvalue(sem_t *sem, int *valp);
```
Both return: 0 if OK, −1 on error

sem_getvalue returns the current value of the semaphore in the integer pointed to by *valp*. If the semaphore is currently locked, then the value returned is either 0 or a negative number whose absolute value is the number of threads waiting for the semaphore to be unlocked.

We now see more differences among mutexes, condition variables, and semaphores. First, a mutex must always be unlocked by the thread that locked the mutex. Semaphores do not have this restriction: one thread can wait for a given semaphore (say, decrementing the semaphore's value from 1 to 0, which is the same as locking the semaphore), and another thread can post to the semaphore (say, incrementing the semaphore's value from 0 to 1, which is the same as unlocking the semaphore).

Second, since a semaphore has an associated value that is incremented by a post and decremented by a wait, a thread can post to a semaphore (say, incrementing its value from 0 to 1), even though no threads are waiting for the semaphore value to become positive. But if a thread calls pthread_cond_signal and no thread is currently blocked in a call to pthread_cond_wait, the signal is lost.

Lastly, of the various synchronization techniques—mutexes, condition variables, read–write locks, and semaphores—the only function that can be called from a signal handler is sem_post.

> These three points should not be interpreted as a bias by the author towards semaphores. All the synchronization primitives that we have looked at—mutexes, condition variables, read–write locks, semaphores, and record locking—have their place. We have many choices for a given application and need to be aware of the differences between the various primitives. Also realize in the comparison just listed that mutexes are optimized for locking, condition variables are optimized for waiting, and a semaphore can do both, which may bring with it more overhead and complication.

10.5 Simple Programs

We now provide some simple programs that operate on Posix named semaphores, to learn more about their functionality and implementation. Since Posix named semaphores have at least kernel persistence, we can manipulate them across multiple programs.

semcreate Program

Figure 10.9 creates a named semaphore, allowing a -e option to specify an exclusive-create, and a -i option to specify an initial value (other than the default of 1).

pxsem/semcreate.c

```
 1 #include     "unpipc.h"

 2 int
 3 main(int argc, char **argv)
 4 {
 5     int     c, flags;
 6     sem_t   *sem;
 7     unsigned int value;

 8     flags = O_RDWR | O_CREAT;
 9     value = 1;
10     while ( (c = Getopt(argc, argv, "ei:")) != -1) {
11         switch (c) {
12         case 'e':
13             flags |= O_EXCL;
14             break;

15         case 'i':
16             value = atoi(optarg);
17             break;
18         }
19     }
20     if (optind != argc - 1)
21         err_quit("usage: semcreate [ -e ] [ -i initalvalue ] <name>");

22     sem = Sem_open(argv[optind], flags, FILE_MODE, value);

23     Sem_close(sem);
24     exit(0);
25 }
```

pxsem/semcreate.c

Figure 10.9 Create a named semaphore.

Create semaphore

22   Since we always specify the O_CREAT flag, we must call sem_open with four arguments. The final two arguments, however, are used by sem_open only if the semaphore does not already exist.

Close semaphore

23   We call sem_close, although if this call were omitted, the semaphore is still closed (and the system resources released) when the process terminates.

`semunlink` Program

The program in Figure 10.10 unlinks a named semaphore.

————————————————————————— pxsem/semunlink.c
```
1 #include      "unpipc.h"

2 int
3 main(int argc, char **argv)
4 {
5     if (argc != 2)
6         err_quit("usage: semunlink <name>");

7     Sem_unlink(argv[1]);

8     exit(0);
9 }
```
————————————————————————— pxsem/semunlink.c

Figure 10.10 Unlink a named semaphore.

`semgetvalue` Program

Figure 10.11 is a simple program that opens a named semaphore, fetches its current value, and prints that value.

——————————————————————— pxsem/semgetvalue.c
```
1 #include      "unpipc.h"

2 int
3 main(int argc, char **argv)
4 {
5     sem_t   *sem;
6     int      val;

7     if (argc != 2)
8         err_quit("usage: semgetvalue <name>");

9     sem = Sem_open(argv[1], 0);
10    Sem_getvalue(sem, &val);
11    printf("value = %d\n", val);

12    exit(0);
13 }
```
——————————————————————— pxsem/semgetvalue.c

Figure 10.11 Get and print a semaphore's value.

Open semaphore

9   When we are opening a semaphore that must already exist, the second argument to sem_open is 0: we do not specify O_CREAT and there are no other O_*xxx* constants to specify.

`semwait` Program

The program in Figure 10.12 opens a named semaphore, calls `sem_wait` (which will block if the semaphore's value is currently less than or equal to 0, and then decrements the semaphore value), fetches and prints the semaphore's value, and then blocks forever in a call to `pause`.

pxsem/semwait.c
```
 1 #include     "unpipc.h"

 2 int
 3 main(int argc, char **argv)
 4 {
 5     sem_t  *sem;
 6     int    val;

 7     if (argc != 2)
 8         err_quit("usage: semwait <name>");

 9     sem = Sem_open(argv[1], 0);
10     Sem_wait(sem);
11     Sem_getvalue(sem, &val);
12     printf("pid %ld has semaphore, value = %d\n", (long) getpid(), val);

13     pause();                       /* blocks until killed */
14     exit(0);
15 }
```
pxsem/semwait.c

Figure 10.12 Wait for a semaphore and print its value.

`sempost` Program

Figure 10.13 is a program that posts to a named semaphore (i.e., increments its value by one) and then fetches and prints the semaphore's value.

pxsem/sempost.c
```
 1 #include     "unpipc.h"

 2 int
 3 main(int argc, char **argv)
 4 {
 5     sem_t  *sem;
 6     int    val;

 7     if (argc != 2)
 8         err_quit("usage: sempost <name>");

 9     sem = Sem_open(argv[1], 0);
10     Sem_post(sem);
11     Sem_getvalue(sem, &val);
12     printf("value = %d\n", val);

13     exit(0);
14 }
```
pxsem/sempost.c

Figure 10.13 Post to a semaphore.

Examples

We first create a named semaphore under Digital Unix 4.0B and print its (default) value.

```
alpha % semcreate /tmp/test1
alpha % ls -l /tmp/test1
-rw-r--r--   1 rstevens system        264 Nov 13 08:51 /tmp/test1
alpha % semgetvalue /tmp/test1
value = 1
```

As with Posix message queues, the system creates a file in the filesystem corresponding to the name that we specify for the named semaphore.

We now wait for the semaphore and then abort the program that holds the semaphore lock.

```
alpha % semwait /tmp/test1
pid 9702 has semaphore, value = 0        the value after sem_wait returns
^?                                        type our interrupt key to abort program
alpha % semgetvalue /tmp/test1
value = 0                                 and value remains 0
```

This example shows two features that we mentioned earlier. First, the value of a semaphore is kernel-persistent. That is, the semaphore's value of 1 is maintained by the kernel from when the semaphore was created in our previous example, even though no program had the semaphore open during this time. Second, when we abort our `semwait` program that holds the semaphore lock, the value of the semaphore does not change. That is, the semaphore is not unlocked by the kernel when a process holding the lock terminates without releasing the lock. This differs from record locks, which we said in Chapter 9 are automatically released when the process holding the lock terminates without releasing the lock.

We now show that this implementation uses a negative semaphore value to indicate the number of processes waiting for the semaphore to be unlocked.

```
alpha % semgetvalue /tmp/test1
value = 0                                 value is still 0 from previous example

alpha % semwait /tmp/test1 &              start in the background
[1]     9718                              it blocks, waiting for semaphore

alpha % semgetvalue /tmp/test1
value = -1                                one process waiting for semaphore

alpha % semwait /tmp/test1 &              start another in the background
[2]     9727                              it also blocks, waiting for semaphore

alpha % semgetvalue /tmp/test1
value = -2                                two processes waiting for semaphore

alpha % sempost /tmp/test1                now post to semaphore
value = -1                                value after sem_post returns
pid 9718 has semaphore, value = -1        output from semwait program

alpha % sempost /tmp/test1                post again to semaphore
value = 0
pid 9727 has semaphore, value = 0         output from other semwait program
```

When the value is −2 and we execute our `sempost` program, the value is incremented to −1 and one of the processes blocked in the call to `sem_wait` returns.

We now execute the same example under Solaris 2.6 to see the differences in the implementation.

```
solaris % semcreate /test2
solaris % ls -l /tmp/.*test2*
-rw-r--r--   1 rstevens other1      48 Nov 13 09:11 /tmp/.SEMDtest2
-rw-rw-rw-   1 rstevens other1       0 Nov 13 09:11 /tmp/.SEMLtest2
solaris % semgetvalue /test2
value = 1
```

As with Posix message queues, files are created in the /tmp directory containing the specified name as the filename suffixes. We see that the permissions on the first file correspond to the permissions specified in our call to `sem_open`, and we guess that the second file is used for locking.

We now verify that the kernel does not automatically post to a semaphore when the process holding the semaphore lock terminates without releasing the lock.

```
solaris % semwait /test2
pid 4133 has semaphore, value = 0
^?                                           type our interrupt key
solaris % semgetvalue /test2
value = 0                                    value remains 0
```

Next we see how this implementation handles the semaphore value when processes are waiting for the semaphore.

```
solaris % semgetvalue /test2
value = 0                                    value is still 0 from previous example

solaris % semwait /test2 &                   start in the background
[1]     4257                                 it blocks, waiting for semaphore

solaris % semgetvalue /test2
value = 0                                    this implementation does not use negative values

solaris % semwait /test2 &                   start another in the background
[2]     4263

solaris % semgetvalue /test2
value = 0                                    value remains 0 with two processes waiting

solaris % sempost /test2                      now post to semaphore
pid 4257 has semaphore, value = 0            output from semwait program
value = 0

solaris % sempost /test2                      output from other semwait program
pid 4263 has semaphore, value = 0            output from other semwait program
value = 0
```

One difference in this output, compared to the previous output under Digital Unix, is when the semaphore is posted to: it appears that the waiting process runs before the process that posted to the semaphore.

10.6 Producer–Consumer Problem

In Section 7.3, we described the *producer–consumer* problem and showed some solutions in which multiple producer threads filled an array that was processed by one consumer thread.

1. In our first solution (Section 7.2), the consumer started only after the producers were finished, and we were able to solve this synchronization problem using a single mutex (to synchronize the producers).

2. In our next solution (Section 7.5), the consumer started before the producers were finished, and this required a mutex (to synchronize the producers) along with a condition variable and its mutex (to synchronize the consumer with the producers).

We now extend the producer–consumer problem by using the shared buffer as a circular buffer: after the producer fills the final entry (buff[NBUFF-1]), it goes back and fills the first entry (buff[0]), and the consumer does the same. This adds another synchronization problem in that the producer must not get ahead of the consumer. We still assume that the producer and consumer are threads, but they could also be processes, assuming that some way existed to share the buffer between the processes (e.g., shared memory, which we describe in Part 4).

Three conditions must be maintained by the code when the shared buffer is considered as a circular buffer:

1. The consumer cannot try to remove an item from the buffer when the buffer is empty.

2. The producer cannot try to place an item into the buffer when the buffer is full.

3. Shared variables may describe the current state of the buffer (indexes, counts, linked list pointers, etc.), so all buffer manipulations by the producer and consumer must be protected to avoid any race conditions.

Our solution using semaphores demonstrates three different types of semaphores:

1. A binary semaphore named mutex protects the critical regions: inserting a data item into the buffer (for the producer) and removing a data item from the buffer (for the consumer). A binary semaphore that is used as a mutex is initialized to 1. (Obviously, we could use a real mutex for this, instead of a binary semaphore. See Exercise 10.10.)

2. A counting semaphore named nempty counts the number of empty slots in the buffer. This semaphore is initialized to the number of slots in the buffer (NBUFF).

3. A counting semaphore named nstored counts the number of filled slots in the buffer. This semaphore is initialized to 0, since the buffer is initially empty.

Figure 10.14 shows the status of our buffer and the two counting semaphores when the program has finished its initialization. We have shaded the array elements that are unused.

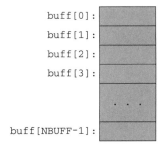

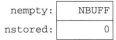

Figure 10.14 Buffer and the two counting semaphores after initialization.

In our example, the producer just stores the integers 0 through NLOOP-1 into the buffer (buff[0] = 0, buff[1] = 1, and so on), using the buffer as a circular buffer. The consumer takes these integers from the buffer and verifies that they are correct, printing any errors to standard output.

Figure 10.15 shows the buffer and the counting semaphores after the producer has placed three items into the buffer, but before the consumer has taken any of these items from the buffer.

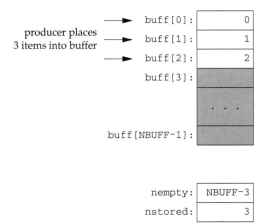

Figure 10.15 Buffer and semaphores after three items placed into buffer by producer.

We next assume that the consumer removes one item from the buffer, and we show this in Figure 10.16.

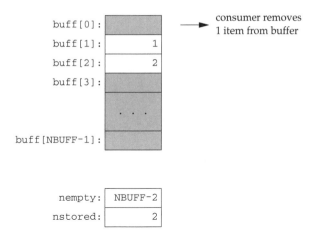

Figure 10.16 Buffer and semaphores after consumer removes first item from buffer.

Figure 10.17 is the `main` function that creates the three semaphores, creates two threads, waits for both threads to complete, and then removes the semaphores.

Globals

6–10   The buffer containing `NBUFF` items is shared between the two threads, as are the three semaphore pointers. As described in Chapter 7, we collect these into a structure to reiterate that the semaphores are used to synchronize access to the buffer.

Create semaphores

19–25   Three semaphores are created and their names are passed to our `px_ipc_name` function. We specify the `O_EXCL` flag because we need to initialize each semaphore to the correct value. If any of the three semaphores are still lying around from a previous run of this program that aborted, we could handle that by calling `sem_unlink` for each semaphore, ignoring any errors, before creating the semaphores. Alternately, we could check for an error of `EEXIST` from `sem_open` with the `O_EXCL` flag, and call `sem_unlink` followed by another call to `sem_open`, but this is more complicated. If we need to verify that only one copy of this program is running (which we could do before trying to create any of the semaphores), we would do so as described in Section 9.7.

Create two threads

26–29   The two threads are created, one as the producer and one as the consumer. No arguments are passed to the two threads.

30–36   The main thread then waits for both threads to terminate, and removes the three semaphores.

> We could also call `sem_close` for each semaphore, but this happens automatically when the process terminates. Removing the name of a named semaphore, however, must be done explicitly.

Figure 10.18 shows the `produce` and `consume` functions.

pxsem/prodcons1.c

```
 1 #include    "unpipc.h"

 2 #define NBUFF     10
 3 #define SEM_MUTEX   "mutex"      /* these are args to px_ipc_name() */
 4 #define SEM_NEMPTY  "nempty"
 5 #define SEM_NSTORED "nstored"

 6 int    nitems;                   /* read-only by producer and consumer */
 7 struct {                         /* data shared by producer and consumer */
 8     int     buff[NBUFF];
 9     sem_t  *mutex, *nempty, *nstored;
10 } shared;

11 void    *produce(void *), *consume(void *);

12 int
13 main(int argc, char **argv)
14 {
15     pthread_t tid_produce, tid_consume;

16     if (argc != 2)
17         err_quit("usage: prodcons1 <#items>");
18     nitems = atoi(argv[1]);

19         /* create three semaphores */
20     shared.mutex = Sem_open(Px_ipc_name(SEM_MUTEX), O_CREAT | O_EXCL,
21                         FILE_MODE, 1);
22     shared.nempty = Sem_open(Px_ipc_name(SEM_NEMPTY), O_CREAT | O_EXCL,
23                         FILE_MODE, NBUFF);
24     shared.nstored = Sem_open(Px_ipc_name(SEM_NSTORED), O_CREAT | O_EXCL,
25                         FILE_MODE, 0);

26         /* create one producer thread and one consumer thread */
27     Set_concurrency(2);
28     Pthread_create(&tid_produce, NULL, produce, NULL);
29     Pthread_create(&tid_consume, NULL, consume, NULL);

30         /* wait for the two threads */
31     Pthread_join(tid_produce, NULL);
32     Pthread_join(tid_consume, NULL);

33         /* remove the semaphores */
34     Sem_unlink(Px_ipc_name(SEM_MUTEX));
35     Sem_unlink(Px_ipc_name(SEM_NEMPTY));
36     Sem_unlink(Px_ipc_name(SEM_NSTORED));
37     exit(0);
38 }
```

pxsem/prodcons1.c

Figure 10.17 main function for semaphore solution to producer–consumer problem.

Producer waits until room for one item in buffer

44   The producer calls sem_wait on the nempty semaphore, to wait until room is available for another item in the buffer. The first time this statement is executed, the value of the semaphore will go from NBUFF to NBUFF-1.

―――――――――――――――――――――――――――――――――――――― *pxsem/prodcons1.c*
```
39 void *
40 produce(void *arg)
41 {
42     int    i;

43     for (i = 0; i < nitems; i++) {
44         Sem_wait(shared.nempty);    /* wait for at least 1 empty slot */
45         Sem_wait(shared.mutex);
46         shared.buff[i % NBUFF] = i;    /* store i into circular buffer */
47         Sem_post(shared.mutex);
48         Sem_post(shared.nstored);   /* 1 more stored item */
49     }
50     return (NULL);
51 }

52 void *
53 consume(void *arg)
54 {
55     int    i;

56     for (i = 0; i < nitems; i++) {
57         Sem_wait(shared.nstored);    /* wait for at least 1 stored item */
58         Sem_wait(shared.mutex);
59         if (shared.buff[i % NBUFF] != i)
60             printf("buff[%d] = %d\n", i, shared.buff[i % NBUFF]);
61         Sem_post(shared.mutex);
62         Sem_post(shared.nempty);     /* 1 more empty slot */
63     }
64     return (NULL);
65 }
```
―――――――――――――――――――――――――――――――――――――― *pxsem/prodcons1.c*

Figure 10.18 produce and consume functions.

Producer stores item in buffer

45–48   Before storing the new item into the buffer, the producer must obtain the mutex semaphore. In our example, where the producer just stores a value into the array element indexed by i % NBUFF, no shared variables describe the status of the buffer (i.e., we do not use a linked list that we need to update each time we place an item into the buffer). Therefore, obtaining and releasing the mutex semaphore is not actually required. Nevertheless, we show it, because in general it is required for this type of problem (updating a buffer that is shared by multiple threads).

   After the item is stored in the buffer, the mutex semaphore is released (its value goes from 0 to 1), and the nstored semaphore is posted to. The first time this statement is executed, the value of nstored will go from its initial value of 0 to 1.

Consumer waits for nstored semaphore

57–62   When the nstored semaphore's value is greater than 0, that many items are in the buffer to process. The consumer takes one item from the buffer and verifies that its value is correct, protecting this buffer access with the mutex semaphore. The consumer then posts to the nempty semaphore, telling the producer that another slot is empty.

Deadlock

What happens if we mistakenly swap the order of the two calls to Sem_wait in the consumer function (Figure 10.18)? If we assume the producer starts first (as in the solution shown for Exercise 10.1), it stores NBUFF items into the buffer, decrementing the value of the nempty semaphore from NBUFF to 0 and incrementing the value of the nstored semaphore from 0 to NBUFF. At that point, the producer blocks in the call Sem_wait(shared.nempty), since the buffer is full and no empty slots are available for another item.

The consumer starts and verifies the first NBUFF items from the buffer. This decrements the value of the nstored semaphore from NBUFF to 0 and increments the value of the nempty semaphore from 0 to NBUFF. The consumer then blocks in the call Sem_wait(shared.nstored) after calling Sem_wait(shared.mutex). The producer can resume, because the value of nempty is now greater than 0, but the producer then calls Sem_wait(shared.mutex) and blocks.

This is called a *deadlock*. The producer is waiting for the mutex semaphore, but the consumer is holding this semaphore and waiting for the nstored semaphore. But the producer cannot post to the nstored semaphore until it obtains the mutex semaphore. This is one of the problems with semaphores: if we make an error in our coding, our program does not work correctly.

> Posix allows sem_wait to detect a deadlock and return an error of EDEADLK, but neither of the systems being used (Solaris 2.6 and Digital Unix 4.0B) detected this error with this example.

10.7 File Locking

We now return to our sequence number problem from Chapter 9 and provide versions of our my_lock and my_unlock functions that use Posix named semaphores. Figure 10.19 shows the two functions.

One semaphore is used for an advisory file lock, and the first time this function is called, the semaphore value is initialized to 1. To obtain the file lock, we call sem_wait, and to release the lock, we call sem_post.

10.8 `sem_init` and `sem_destroy` Functions

Everything so far in this chapter has dealt with the Posix *named* semaphores. These semaphores are identified by a *name* argument that normally references a file in the filesystem. But Posix also provides *memory-based* semaphores in which the application allocates the memory for the semaphore (that is, for a sem_t datatype, whatever that happens to be) and then has the system initialize this semaphore.

———————————————————————— lock/lockpxsem.c
```
 1 #include    "unpipc.h"

 2 #define LOCK_PATH    "pxsemlock"

 3 sem_t  *locksem;
 4 int      initflag;

 5 void
 6 my_lock(int fd)
 7 {
 8     if (initflag == 0) {
 9         locksem = Sem_open(Px_ipc_name(LOCK_PATH), O_CREAT, FILE_MODE, 1);
10         initflag = 1;
11     }
12     Sem_wait(locksem);
13 }

14 void
15 my_unlock(int fd)
16 {
17     Sem_post(locksem);
18 }
```
———————————————————————— lock/lockpxsem.c

Figure 10.19 File locking using Posix named semaphores.

```
#include <semaphore.h>

int sem_init(sem_t *sem, int shared, unsigned int value);
```

Returns: −1 on error

```
int sem_destroy(sem_t *sem);
```

Returns: 0 if OK, −1 on error

A memory-based semaphore is initialized by sem_init. The *sem* argument points to the sem_t variable that the application must allocate. If *shared* is 0, then the semaphore is shared between the threads of a process, else the semaphore is shared between processes. When *shared* is nonzero, then the semaphore must be stored in some type of shared memory that is accessible to all the processes that will be using the semaphore. As with sem_open, the *value* argument is the initial value of the semaphore.

When we are done with a memory-based semaphore, sem_destroy destroys it.

> sem_open does not need a parameter similar to *shared* or an attribute similar to PTHREAD_PROCESS_SHARED (which we saw with mutexes and condition variables in Chapter 7), because a named semaphore is *always* sharable between different processes.

> Notice that there is nothing similar to O_CREAT for a memory-based semaphore: sem_init always initializes the semaphore value. Therefore, we must be careful to call sem_init only once for a given semaphore. (Exercise 10.2 shows the difference for a named semaphore.) The results are undefined if sem_init is called for a semaphore that has already been initialized.

> Make certain you understand a fundamental difference between sem_open and sem_init. The former returns a pointer to a sem_t variable that the *function* has allocated and initialized. The first argument to sem_init, on the other hand, is a pointer to a sem_t variable that the *caller* must allocate and that the function then initializes.
>
> Posix.1 warns that for a memory-based semaphore, only the location pointed to by the *sem* argument to sem_init can be used to refer to the semaphore, and using copies of this sem_t datatype is undefined.
>
> sem_init returns −1 on an error, but does *not* return 0 on success. This is indeed strange, and a note in the Posix.1 Rationale says that a future update may specify a return of 0 on success.

A memory-based semaphore can be used when the name associated with a named semaphore is not needed. Named semaphores are normally used when different, unrelated processes are using the semaphore. The name is how each process identifies the semaphore.

In Figure 1.3, we say that memory-based semaphores have process persistence, but their persistence really depends on the type of memory in which the semaphore is stored. A memory-based semaphore remains in existence as long as the memory in which the semaphore is contained is valid.

- If a memory-based semaphore is being shared between the threads of a single process (the *shared* argument to sem_init is 0), then the semaphore has process persistence and disappears when the process terminates.

- If a memory-based semaphore is being shared between different processes (the *shared* argument to sem_init is 1), then the semaphore must be stored in shared memory and the semaphore remains in existence as long as the shared memory remains in existence. Recall from Figure 1.3 that Posix shared memory and System V shared memory both have kernel persistence. This means that a server can create a region of shared memory, initialize a Posix memory-based semaphore in that shared memory, and then terminate. Sometime later, one or more clients can open the region of shared memory and access the memory-based semaphore stored therein.

Be warned that the following code does *not* work as planned:

```
sem_t    mysem;

    Sem_init(&mysem, 1, 0);   /* 2nd arg of 1 -> shared between processes */

    if (Fork() == 0) {        /* child */
        . . .
        Sem_post(&mysem);
    }

    Sem_wait(&mysem);         /* parent; wait for child */
```

The problem here is that the semaphore mysem is not in shared memory—see Section 10.12. Memory is normally not shared between a parent and child across a fork. The child starts with a *copy* of the parent's memory, but this is not the same as shared memory. We talk more about shared memory in Part 4 of this book.

Example

As an example, we convert our producer–consumer example from Figures 10.17 and 10.18 to use memory-based semaphores. Figure 10.20 shows the program.

———————————————————————————— pxsem/prodcons2.c

```
 1 #include    "unpipc.h"

 2 #define NBUFF    10

 3 int     nitems;                    /* read-only by producer and consumer */
 4 struct {                           /* data shared by producer and consumer */
 5     int     buff[NBUFF];
 6     sem_t   mutex, nempty, nstored;    /* semaphores, not pointers */
 7 } shared;

 8 void    *produce(void *), *consume(void *);

 9 int
10 main(int argc, char **argv)
11 {
12     pthread_t tid_produce, tid_consume;

13     if (argc != 2)
14         err_quit("usage: prodcons2 <#items>");
15     nitems = atoi(argv[1]);

16         /* initialize three semaphores */
17     Sem_init(&shared.mutex, 0, 1);
18     Sem_init(&shared.nempty, 0, NBUFF);
19     Sem_init(&shared.nstored, 0, 0);

20     Set_concurrency(2);
21     Pthread_create(&tid_produce, NULL, produce, NULL);
22     Pthread_create(&tid_consume, NULL, consume, NULL);

23     Pthread_join(tid_produce, NULL);
24     Pthread_join(tid_consume, NULL);

25     Sem_destroy(&shared.mutex);
26     Sem_destroy(&shared.nempty);
27     Sem_destroy(&shared.nstored);
28     exit(0);
29 }

30 void *
31 produce(void *arg)
32 {
33     int     i;

34     for (i = 0; i < nitems; i++) {
35         Sem_wait(&shared.nempty);   /* wait for at least 1 empty slot */
36         Sem_wait(&shared.mutex);
37         shared.buff[i % NBUFF] = i;    /* store i into circular buffer */
38         Sem_post(&shared.mutex);
39         Sem_post(&shared.nstored);  /* 1 more stored item */
40     }
41     return (NULL);
42 }
```

```
43 void *
44 consume(void *arg)
45 {
46     int     i;

47     for (i = 0; i < nitems; i++) {
48         Sem_wait(&shared.nstored);   /* wait for at least 1 stored item */
49         Sem_wait(&shared.mutex);
50         if (shared.buff[i % NBUFF] != i)
51             printf("buff[%d] = %d\n", i, shared.buff[i % NBUFF]);
52         Sem_post(&shared.mutex);
53         Sem_post(&shared.nempty);    /* 1 more empty slot */
54     }
55     return (NULL);
56 }
```
——— *pxsem/prodcons2.c*

Figure 10.20 Producer–consumer using memory-based semaphores.

Allocate semaphores

6   Our declarations for the three semaphores are now for three sem_t datatypes themselves, not for pointers to three of these datatypes.

Call sem_init

16–27   We call sem_init instead of sem_open, and then sem_destroy instead of sem_unlink. These calls to sem_destroy are really not needed, since the program is about to terminate.

Â Â Â Â Â The remaining changes are to pass pointers to the three semaphores in all the calls to sem_wait and sem_post.

10.9 Multiple Producers, One Consumer

The producer–consumer solution in Section 10.6 solves the classic one-producer, one-consumer problem. An interesting modification is to allow multiple producers with one consumer. We will start with the solution from Figure 10.20, which used memory-based semaphores. Figure 10.21 shows the global variables and main function.

Globals

4   The global nitems is the total number of items for all the producers to produce, and nproducers is the number of producer threads. Both are set from command-line arguments.

Shared structure

5–10   Two new variables are declared in the shared structure: nput, the index of the next buffer entry to store into (modulo NBUFF), and nputval, the next value to store in the buffer. These two variables are taken from our solution in Figures 7.2 and 7.3. These two variables are needed to synchronize the multiple producer threads.

pxsem/prodcons3.c

```
 1 #include    "unpipc.h"

 2 #define NBUFF        10
 3 #define MAXNTHREADS 100

 4 int    nitems, nproducers;      /* read-only by producer and consumer */

 5 struct {                             /* data shared by producers and consumer */
 6     int    buff[NBUFF];
 7     int    nput;
 8     int    nputval;
 9     sem_t  mutex, nempty, nstored;    /* semaphores, not pointers */
10 } shared;

11 void   *produce(void *), *consume(void *);

12 int
13 main(int argc, char **argv)
14 {
15     int    i, count[MAXNTHREADS];
16     pthread_t tid_produce[MAXNTHREADS], tid_consume;

17     if (argc != 3)
18         err_quit("usage: prodcons3 <#items> <#producers>");
19     nitems = atoi(argv[1]);
20     nproducers = min(atoi(argv[2]), MAXNTHREADS);

21         /* initialize three semaphores */
22     Sem_init(&shared.mutex, 0, 1);
23     Sem_init(&shared.nempty, 0, NBUFF);
24     Sem_init(&shared.nstored, 0, 0);

25         /* create all producers and one consumer */
26     Set_concurrency(nproducers + 1);
27     for (i = 0; i < nproducers; i++) {
28         count[i] = 0;
29         Pthread_create(&tid_produce[i], NULL, produce, &count[i]);
30     }
31     Pthread_create(&tid_consume, NULL, consume, NULL);

32         /* wait for all producers and the consumer */
33     for (i = 0; i < nproducers; i++) {
34         Pthread_join(tid_produce[i], NULL);
35         printf("count[%d] = %d\n", i, count[i]);
36     }
37     Pthread_join(tid_consume, NULL);

38     Sem_destroy(&shared.mutex);
39     Sem_destroy(&shared.nempty);
40     Sem_destroy(&shared.nstored);
41     exit(0);
42 }
```

pxsem/prodcons3.c

Figure 10.21 main function that creates multiple producer threads.

New command-line arguments

17-20   Two new command-line arguments specify the total number of items to be stored into the buffer and the number of producer threads to create.

Create all the threads

21-41   The semaphores are initialized, and all the producer threads and one consumer thread are created. We then wait for all the threads to terminate. This code is nearly identical to Figure 7.2.

Figure 10.22 shows the `produce` function that is executed by each producer thread.

─── *pxsem/prodcons3.c*
```
43 void *
44 produce(void *arg)
45 {
46     for ( ; ; ) {
47         Sem_wait(&shared.nempty);   /* wait for at least 1 empty slot */
48         Sem_wait(&shared.mutex);

49         if (shared.nput >= nitems) {
50             Sem_post(&shared.nempty);
51             Sem_post(&shared.mutex);
52             return (NULL);      /* all done */
53         }
54         shared.buff[shared.nput % NBUFF] = shared.nputval;
55         shared.nput++;
56         shared.nputval++;

57         Sem_post(&shared.mutex);
58         Sem_post(&shared.nstored);   /* 1 more stored item */
59         *((int *) arg) += 1;
60     }
61 }
```
─── *pxsem/prodcons3.c*

Figure 10.22 Function executed by all the producer threads.

Mutual exclusion among producer threads

49-53   The change from Figure 10.18 is that the loop terminates when `nitems` of the values have been placed into the buffer by all the threads. Notice that multiple producer threads can acquire the `nempty` semaphore at the same time, but only one producer thread at a time can acquire the `mutex` semaphore. This protects the variables `nput` and `nputval` from being modified by more than one producer thread at a time.

Termination of producers

50-51   We must carefully handle the termination of the producer threads. After the last item is produced, each producer thread executes

```
Sem_wait(&shared.nempty);   /* wait for at least 1 empty slot */
```

at the top of the loop, which decrements the `nempty` semaphore. But before the thread terminates, it must increment this semaphore, because the thread does not store an item in the buffer during its last time around the loop. The terminating thread must also release the `mutex` semaphore, to allow the other producer threads to continue. If we did not increment `nempty` on thread termination and if we had more producer threads than buffer slots (say 14 threads and 10 buffer slots), the excess threads (4) would be blocked forever, waiting for the `nempty` semaphore, and would never terminate.

The `consume` function in Figure 10.23 just verifies that each entry in the buffer is correct, printing a message if an error is detected.

———————————————————————————————————— *pxsem/prodcons3.c*
```
62 void *
63 consume(void *arg)
64 {
65     int    i;

66     for (i = 0; i < nitems; i++) {
67         Sem_wait(&shared.nstored);   /* wait for at least 1 stored item */
68         Sem_wait(&shared.mutex);

69         if (shared.buff[i % NBUFF] != i)
70             printf("error: buff[%d] = %d\n", i, shared.buff[i % NBUFF]);

71         Sem_post(&shared.mutex);
72         Sem_post(&shared.nempty);    /* 1 more empty slot */
73     }
74     return (NULL);
75 }
```
———————————————————————————————————— *pxsem/prodcons3.c*

Figure 10.23 Function executed by the one consumer thread.

Termination of the single consumer thread is simple—it just counts the number of items consumed.

10.10 Multiple Producers, Multiple Consumers

The next modification to our producer–consumer problem is to allow multiple producers and multiple consumers. Whether it makes sense to have multiple consumers depends on the application. The author has seen two applications that use this technique.

1. A program that converts IP addresses to their corresponding hostnames. Each consumer takes an IP address, calls `gethostbyaddr` (Section 9.6 of UNPv1), and appends the hostname to a file. Since each call to `gethostbyaddr` can take a variable amount of time, the order of the IP addresses in the buffer will normally not be the same as the order of the hostnames in the file appended by the consumer threads. The advantage in this scenario is that multiple calls to `gethostbyaddr` (each of which can take seconds) occur in parallel: one per consumer thread.

> This assumes a reentrant version of `gethostbyaddr`, and not all implementations have this property. If a reentrant version is not available, an alternative is to store the buffer in shared memory and use multiple processes instead of multiple threads.

2. A program that reads UDP datagrams, operates on the datagrams, and then writes the result to a database. One consumer thread processes each datagram, and multiple consumer threads are needed to overlap the potentially long processing of each datagram. Even though the datagrams are normally written to the database by the consumer threads in an order that differs from the original datagram order, the ordering of the records in the database handles this.

Figure 10.24 shows the global variables.

pxsem/prodcons4.c

```
 1 #include     "unpipc.h"

 2 #define NBUFF        10
 3 #define MAXNTHREADS 100

 4 int     nitems, nproducers, nconsumers;     /* read-only */

 5 struct {                         /* data shared by producers and consumers */
 6     int     buff[NBUFF];
 7     int     nput;              /* item number: 0, 1, 2, ... */
 8     int     nputval;           /* value to store in buff[] */
 9     int     nget;              /* item number: 0, 1, 2, ... */
10     int     ngetval;           /* value fetched from buff[] */
11     sem_t   mutex, nempty, nstored;     /* semaphores, not pointers */
12 } shared;

13 void    *produce(void *), *consume(void *);
```

pxsem/prodcons4.c

Figure 10.24 Global variables.

Globals and shared structure

4–12   The number of consumer threads is now a global variable and is set from a command-line argument. We have added two more variables to our `shared` structure: `nget`, the next item number for any one of the consumer threads to fetch, and `ngetval`, the corresponding value.

The `main` function, shown in Figure 10.25, is changed to create multiple consumer threads.

19–23   A new command-line argument specifies the number of consumer threads to create. We must also allocate an array (`tid_consume`) to hold all the consumer thread IDs, and an array (`conscount`) to hold our diagnostic count of how many items each consumer thread processes.

24–50   Multiple producer threads and multiple consumer threads are created and then waited for.

pxsem/prodcons4.c

```
14 int
15 main(int argc, char **argv)
16 {
17     int     i, prodcount[MAXNTHREADS], conscount[MAXNTHREADS];
18     pthread_t tid_produce[MAXNTHREADS], tid_consume[MAXNTHREADS];

19     if (argc != 4)
20         err_quit("usage: prodcons4 <#items> <#producers> <#consumers>");
21     nitems = atoi(argv[1]);
22     nproducers = min(atoi(argv[2]), MAXNTHREADS);
23     nconsumers = min(atoi(argv[3]), MAXNTHREADS);

24         /* initialize three semaphores */
25     Sem_init(&shared.mutex, 0, 1);
26     Sem_init(&shared.nempty, 0, NBUFF);
27     Sem_init(&shared.nstored, 0, 0);

28         /* create all producers and all consumers */
29     Set_concurrency(nproducers + nconsumers);
30     for (i = 0; i < nproducers; i++) {
31         prodcount[i] = 0;
32         Pthread_create(&tid_produce[i], NULL, produce, &prodcount[i]);
33     }
34     for (i = 0; i < nconsumers; i++) {
35         conscount[i] = 0;
36         Pthread_create(&tid_consume[i], NULL, consume, &conscount[i]);
37     }

38         /* wait for all producers and all consumers */
39     for (i = 0; i < nproducers; i++) {
40         Pthread_join(tid_produce[i], NULL);
41         printf("producer count[%d] = %d\n", i, prodcount[i]);
42     }
43     for (i = 0; i < nconsumers; i++) {
44         Pthread_join(tid_consume[i], NULL);
45         printf("consumer count[%d] = %d\n", i, conscount[i]);
46     }

47     Sem_destroy(&shared.mutex);
48     Sem_destroy(&shared.nempty);
49     Sem_destroy(&shared.nstored);
50     exit(0);
51 }
```

pxsem/prodcons4.c

Figure 10.25 `main` function that creates multiple producers and multiple consumers.

Our producer function contains one new line from Figure 10.22. When the producer threads terminate, the line preceded with the plus sign is new:

```
      if (shared.nput >= nitems) {
+         Sem_post(&shared.nstored);   /* let consumers terminate */
          Sem_post(&shared.nempty);
          Sem_post(&shared.mutex);
          return(NULL);               /* all done */
      }
```

We again must be careful when handling the termination of the producer threads and the consumer threads. After all the items in the buffer have been consumed, each consumer thread blocks in the call

```
      Sem_wait(&shared.nstored);   /* wait for at least 1 stored item */
```

We have the producer threads increment the `nstored` semaphore to unblock the consumer threads, letting them see that they are done.

Our consumer function is shown in Figure 10.26.

```
                                                          ——————— pxsem/prodcons4.c
72 void *
73 consume(void *arg)
74 {
75     int     i;

76     for ( ; ; ) {
77         Sem_wait(&shared.nstored);   /* wait for at least 1 stored item */
78         Sem_wait(&shared.mutex);

79         if (shared.nget >= nitems) {
80             Sem_post(&shared.nstored);
81             Sem_post(&shared.mutex);
82             return (NULL);       /* all done */
83         }
84         i = shared.nget % NBUFF;
85         if (shared.buff[i] != shared.ngetval)
86             printf("error: buff[%d] = %d\n", i, shared.buff[i]);
87         shared.nget++;
88         shared.ngetval++;

89         Sem_post(&shared.mutex);
90         Sem_post(&shared.nempty);   /* 1 more empty slot */
91         *((int *) arg) += 1;
92     }
93 }
                                                          ——————— pxsem/prodcons4.c
```

Figure 10.26 Function executed by all consumer threads.

Termination of consumer threads

79–83   Our consumer function must now compare `nget` to `nitems`, to determine when it is done (similar to the producer function). After the last item has been consumed from the buffer, the consumer threads block, waiting for the `nstored` semaphore to be greater than 0. Therefore, as each consumer thread terminates, it increments `nstored` to let another consumer thread terminate.

10.11 Multiple Buffers

In a typical program that processes some data, we find a loop of the form

```
while ( (n = read(fdin, buff, BUFFSIZE)) > 0) {
    /* process the data */
    write(fdout, buff, n);
}
```

Many programs that process a text file, for example, read a line of input, process that line, and write a line of output. For text files, the calls to `read` and `write` are often replaced with calls to the standard I/O functions `fgets` and `fputs`.

Figure 10.27 shows one way to depict this operation, in which we identify a function named `reader` that reads the data from the input file and a function named `writer` that writes the data to the output file. One buffer is used.

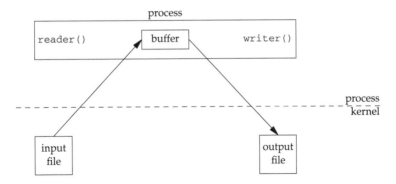

Figure 10.27   One process that reads data into a buffer and then writes the buffer out.

Figure 10.28 shows a time line of this operation. We have labeled the time line with numbers on the left, designating some arbitrary units of time. Time increases downward. We assume that a read operation takes 5 units of time, a write takes 7 units of time, and the processing time between the read and write consumes 2 units of time.

We can modify this application by dividing the processing into two threads, as shown in Figure 10.29. Here we use two threads, since a global buffer is automatically shared by the threads. We could also divide the copying into two processes, but that would require shared memory, which we have not yet covered.

Dividing the operation into two threads (or two processes) also requires some form of notification between the threads (or processes). The reader thread must notify the writer thread when the buffer is ready to be written, and the writer thread must notify the reader thread when the buffer is ready to be filled again. Figure 10.30 shows a time line for this operation.

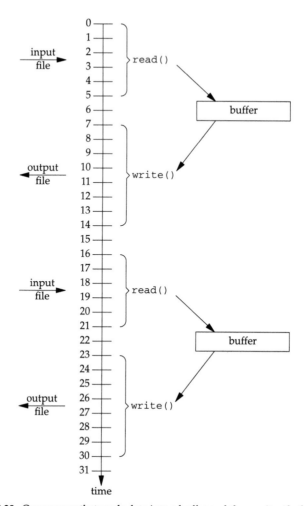

Figure 10.28 One process that reads data into a buffer and then writes the buffer out.

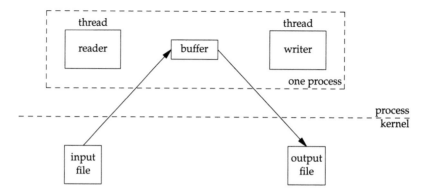

Figure 10.29 File copying divided into two threads.

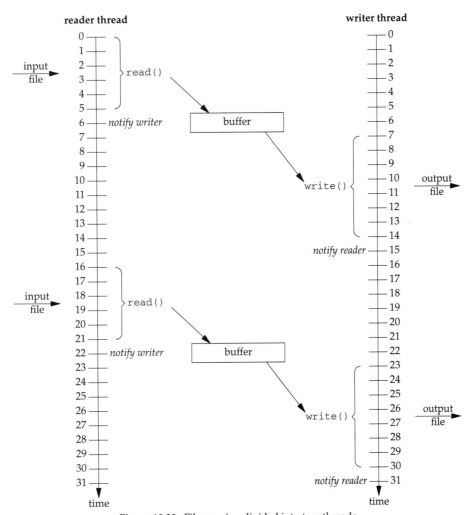

Figure 10.30 File copying divided into two threads.

We assume that the time to process the data in the buffer, along with the notification of the other thread, takes 2 units of time. The important thing to note is that dividing the reading and writing into two threads does not affect the total amount of time required to do the operation. We have not gained any speed advantage; we have only distributed the operation into two threads (or processes).

We are ignoring many fine points in these time lines. For example, most Unix kernels detect sequential reading of a file and do asynchronous *read ahead* of the next disk block for the reading process. This can improve the actual amount of time, called "clock time," that it takes to perform this type of operation. We are also ignoring the effect of other processes on our reading and writing threads, and the effects of the kernel's scheduling algorithms.

The next step in our example is to use two threads (or processes) and two buffers. This is the classic *double buffering* solution, and we show it in Figure 10.31.

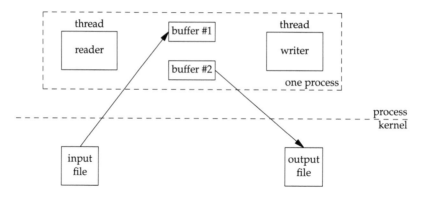

Figure 10.31   File copying divided into two threads using two buffers.

We show the reader thread reading into the first buffer while the writer thread is writing from the second buffer. The two buffers are then switched between the two threads.

Figure 10.32 shows a time line of double buffering. The reader first reads into buffer #1, and then notifies the writer that buffer #1 is ready for processing. The reader then starts reading into buffer #2, while the writer is writing buffer #1.

Note that we cannot go any faster than the slowest operation, which in our example is the write. Once the server has completed the first two reads, it has to wait the additional 2 units of time: the time difference between the write (7) and the read (5). The total clock time, however, will be almost halved for the double buffered case, compared to the single buffered case, for our hypothetical example.

Also note that the writes are now occurring as fast as they can: each write separated by only 2 units of time, compared to a separation of 9 units of time in Figures 10.28 and 10.30. This can help with some devices, such as tape drives, that operate faster if the data is written to the device as quickly as possible (this is called a *streaming* mode).

The interesting thing to note about the double buffering problem is that it is just a special case of the producer–consumer problem.

We now modify our producer–consumer to handle multiple buffers. We start with our solution from Figure 10.20 that used memory-based semaphores. Instead of just a double buffering solution, this solution handles any number of buffers (the NBUFF definition). Figure 10.33 shows the global variables and the `main` function.

Declare NBUFF buffers

2-9   Our `shared` structure now contains an array of another structure named `buff`, and this new structure contains a buffer and its count.

Open input file

18   The command-line argument is the pathname of a file that we will copy to standard output.

Figure 10.34 shows the `produce` and `consume` functions.

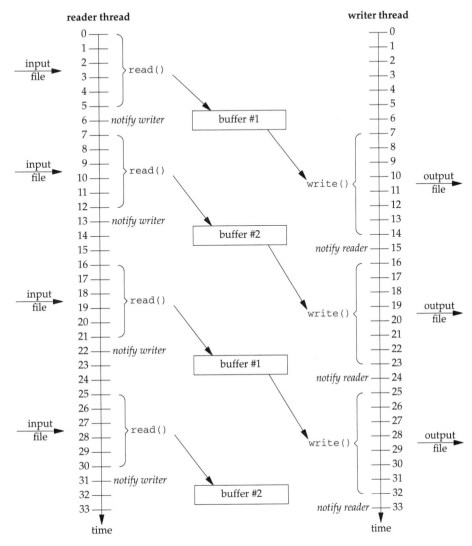

Figure 10.32 Time line for double buffering.

Empty critical region

40-42   The critical region that is locked by the mutex is empty for this example. If the data buffers were kept on a linked list, this would be where we could remove the buffer from the list, avoiding any conflict with the consumer's manipulation of this list. But in our example in which we just use the next buffer, with just one producer thread, nothing needs protection from the consumer. We still show the locking and unlocking of the mutex, to emphasize that this may be needed in other modifications to this code.

```
                                                                    ──── pxsem/mycat2.c
 1 #include    "unpipc.h"

 2 #define NBUFF    8

 3 struct {                              /* data shared by producer and consumer */
 4     struct {
 5         char    data[BUFFSIZE]; /* a buffer */
 6         ssize_t n;                    /* count of #bytes in the buffer */
 7     } buff[NBUFF];                    /* NBUFF of these buffers/counts */
 8     sem_t   mutex, nempty, nstored;   /* semaphores, not pointers */
 9 } shared;

10 int     fd;                           /* input file to copy to stdout */
11 void    *produce(void *), *consume(void *);

12 int
13 main(int argc, char **argv)
14 {
15     pthread_t tid_produce, tid_consume;

16     if (argc != 2)
17         err_quit("usage: mycat2 <pathname>");

18     fd = Open(argv[1], O_RDONLY);

19         /* initialize three semaphores */
20     Sem_init(&shared.mutex, 0, 1);
21     Sem_init(&shared.nempty, 0, NBUFF);
22     Sem_init(&shared.nstored, 0, 0);

23         /* one producer thread, one consumer thread */
24     Set_concurrency(2);
25     Pthread_create(&tid_produce, NULL, produce, NULL);  /* reader thread */
26     Pthread_create(&tid_consume, NULL, consume, NULL);  /* writer thread */

27     Pthread_join(tid_produce, NULL);
28     Pthread_join(tid_consume, NULL);

29     Sem_destroy(&shared.mutex);
30     Sem_destroy(&shared.nempty);
31     Sem_destroy(&shared.nstored);
32     exit(0);
33 }
```
                                                                    ──── pxsem/mycat2.c

Figure 10.33 Global variable and main function.

Read data and increment nstored semaphore

43–49   Each time the producer obtains an empty buffer, it calls read. When read returns,
the nstored semaphore is incremented, telling the consumer that the buffer is ready.
When read returns 0 (end-of-file), the semaphore is incremented and the producer
returns.

pxsem/mycat2.c

```
34 void *
35 produce(void *arg)
36 {
37     int     i;

38     for (i = 0;;) {
39         Sem_wait(&shared.nempty);    /* wait for at least 1 empty slot */

40         Sem_wait(&shared.mutex);
41             /* critical region */
42         Sem_post(&shared.mutex);

43         shared.buff[i].n = Read(fd, shared.buff[i].data, BUFFSIZE);
44         if (shared.buff[i].n == 0) {
45             Sem_post(&shared.nstored);   /* 1 more stored item */
46             return (NULL);
47         }
48         if (++i >= NBUFF)
49             i = 0;                      /* circular buffer */

50         Sem_post(&shared.nstored);   /* 1 more stored item */
51     }
52 }

53 void *
54 consume(void *arg)
55 {
56     int     i;

57     for (i = 0;;) {
58         Sem_wait(&shared.nstored);   /* wait for at least 1 stored item */

59         Sem_wait(&shared.mutex);
60             /* critical region */
61         Sem_post(&shared.mutex);

62         if (shared.buff[i].n == 0)
63             return (NULL);
64         Write(STDOUT_FILENO, shared.buff[i].data, shared.buff[i].n);
65         if (++i >= NBUFF)
66             i = 0;                      /* circular buffer */

67         Sem_post(&shared.nempty);    /* 1 more empty slot */
68     }
69 }
```

pxsem/mycat2.c

Figure 10.34 produce and consume functions.

Consumer thread

57–68   The consumer thread takes the buffers and writes them to standard output. A buffer containing a length of 0 indicates the end-of-file. As with the producer, the critical region protected by the mutex is empty.

In Section 22.3 of UNPv1, we developed an example using multiple buffers. In that example, the producer was the SIGIO signal handler, and the consumer was the main processing loop (the dg_echo function). The variable shared between the producer and consumer was the nqueue counter. The consumer blocked the SIGIO signal from being generated whenever it examined or modified this counter.

10.12 Sharing Semaphores between Processes

The rules for sharing memory-based semaphores between processes are simple: the semaphore itself (the sem_t datatype whose address is the first argument to sem_init) must reside in memory that is shared among all the processes that want to share the semaphore, and the second argument to sem_init must be 1.

> These rules are similar to those for sharing a mutex, condition variable, or read–write lock between processes: the synchronization object itself (the pthread_mutex_t variable, or the pthread_cond_t variable, or the pthread_rwlock_t variable) must reside in memory that is shared among all the processes that want to share the object, and the object must be initialized with the PTHREAD_PROCESS_SHARED attribute.

With regard to named semaphores, different processes (related or unrelated) can always reference the same named semaphore by having each process call sem_open specifying the same name. Even though the pointers returned by sem_open might be different in each process that calls sem_open for a given name, the semaphore functions that use this pointer (e.g., sem_post and sem_wait) will all reference the same named semaphore.

But what if we call sem_open, which returns a pointer to a sem_t datatype, and then call fork? The description of the fork function in Posix.1 says "any semaphores that are open in the parent process shall also be open in the child process." This means that code of the following form is OK:

```
sem_t    *mutex;        /* global pointer that is copied across the fork() */

    ...
        /* parent creates named semaphore */
mutex = Sem_open(Px_ipc_name(NAME), O_CREAT | O_EXCL, FILE_MODE, 0);

if ( (childpid = Fork()) == 0) {
        /* child */
    ...
    Sem_wait(mutex);
    ...
}
    /* parent */
...
Sem_post(mutex);
...
```

> The reason that we must be careful about knowing when we can and cannot share a semaphore between different processes is that the state of a semaphore might be contained in the sem_t datatype itself but it might also use other information (e.g., file descriptors). We will see in the next chapter that the only handle that a process has to describe a System V

semaphore is its integer identifier that is returned by semget. Any process that knows that identifier can then access the semaphore. All the state information for a System V semaphore is contained in the kernel, and the integer identifier just tells the kernel which semaphore is being referenced.

10.13 Semaphore Limits

Two semaphore limits are defined by Posix:

SEM_NSEMS_MAX the maximum number of semaphores that a process can have open at once (Posix requires that this be at least 256), and

SEM_VALUE_MAX the maximum value of a semaphore (Posix requires that this be at least 32767).

These two constants are often defined in the `<unistd.h>` header and can also be obtained at run time by calling the sysconf function, as we show next.

Example: `semsysconf` Program

The program in Figure 10.35 calls sysconf and prints the two implementation-defined limits for semaphores.

pxsem/semsysconf.c

```
1 #include    "unpipc.h"

2 int
3 main(int argc, char **argv)
4 {
5     printf("SEM_NSEMS_MAX = %ld, SEM_VALUE_MAX = %ld\n",
6             Sysconf(_SC_SEM_NSEMS_MAX), Sysconf(_SC_SEM_VALUE_MAX));
7     exit(0);
8 }
```

pxsem/semsysconf.c

Figure 10.35 Call sysconf to obtain semaphore limits.

If we execute this on our two systems, we obtain

```
solaris % semsysconf
SEM_NSEMS_MAX = 2147483647, SEM_VALUE_MAX = 2147483647

alpha % semsysconf
SEM_NSEMS_MAX = 256, SEM_VALUE_MAX = 32767
```

10.14 Implementation Using FIFOs

We now provide an implementation of Posix named semaphores using FIFOs. Each named semaphore is implemented as a FIFO using the same name. The nonnegative number of bytes in the FIFO is the current value of the semaphore. The sem_post function writes 1 byte to the FIFO, and the `sem_wait` function reads 1 byte from the FIFO (blocking if the FIFO is empty, which is what we want). The `sem_open` function creates the FIFO if the `O_CREAT` flag is specified, opens it twice (once read-only, once write-only), and if a new FIFO has been created, writes the number of bytes specified by the initial value to the FIFO.

> This section and the remaining sections of this chapter contain advanced topics that you may want to skip on a first reading.

We first show our `semaphore.h` header in Figure 10.36, which defines the fundamental `sem_t` datatype.

```
                                                              ─── my_pxsem_fifo/semaphore.h
1            /* the fundamental datatype */
2 typedef struct {
3     int     sem_fd[2];            /* two fds: [0] for reading, [1] for writing */
4     int     sem_magic;           /* magic number if open */
5 } sem_t;

6 #define SEM_MAGIC    0x89674523

7 #ifdef  SEM_FAILED
8 #undef  SEM_FAILED
9 #define SEM_FAILED  ((sem_t *)(-1))   /* avoid compiler warnings */
10 #endif
                                                              ─── my_pxsem_fifo/semaphore.h
```

Figure 10.36 `semaphore.h` header.

sem_t datatype

1-5   Our semaphore data structure contains two descriptors, one for reading the FIFO and one for writing the FIFO. For similarity with pipes, we store both descriptors in a two-element array, with the first descriptor for reading and the second descriptor for writing.

The `sem_magic` member contains `SEM_MAGIC` once this structure has been initialized. This value is checked by each function that is passed a `sem_t` pointer, to make certain that the pointer really points to an initialized semaphore structure. This member is set to 0 when the semaphore is closed. This technique, although not perfect, can help detect some programming errors.

sem_open Function

Figure 10.37 shows our `sem_open` function, which creates a new semaphore or opens an existing semaphore.

```
                                                              ─── my_pxsem_fifo/sem_open.c
1 #include     "unpipc.h"
2 #include     "semaphore.h"

3 #include     <stdarg.h>              /* for variable arg lists */

4 sem_t *
5 sem_open(const char *pathname, int oflag,...)
```

```
 6  {
 7      int     i, flags, save_errno;
 8      char    c;
 9      mode_t  mode;
10      va_list ap;
11      sem_t *sem;
12      unsigned int value;
13      if (oflag & O_CREAT) {
14          va_start(ap, oflag);     /* init ap to final named argument */
15          mode = va_arg(ap, va_mode_t);
16          value = va_arg(ap, unsigned int);
17          va_end(ap);
18          if (mkfifo(pathname, mode) < 0) {
19              if (errno == EEXIST && (oflag & O_EXCL) == 0)
20                  oflag &= ~O_CREAT;  /* already exists, OK */
21              else
22                  return (SEM_FAILED);
23          }
24      }
25      if ( (sem = malloc(sizeof(sem_t))) == NULL)
26          return(SEM_FAILED);
27      sem->sem_fd[0] = sem->sem_fd[1] = -1;
28      if ( (sem->sem_fd[0] = open(pathname, O_RDONLY | O_NONBLOCK)) < 0)
29          goto error;
30      if ( (sem->sem_fd[1] = open(pathname, O_WRONLY | O_NONBLOCK)) < 0)
31          goto error;
32          /* turn off nonblocking for sem_fd[0] */
33      if ( (flags = fcntl(sem->sem_fd[0], F_GETFL, 0)) < 0)
34          goto error;
35      flags &= ~O_NONBLOCK;
36      if (fcntl(sem->sem_fd[0], F_SETFL, flags) < 0)
37          goto error;
38      if (oflag & O_CREAT) {        /* initialize semaphore */
39          for (i = 0; i < value; i++)
40              if (write(sem->sem_fd[1], &c, 1) != 1)
41                  goto error;
42      }
43      sem->sem_magic = SEM_MAGIC;
44      return (sem);
45  error:
46      save_errno = errno;
47      if (oflag & O_CREAT)
48          unlink(pathname);         /* if we created FIFO */
49      close(sem->sem_fd[0]);        /* ignore error */
50      close(sem->sem_fd[1]);        /* ignore error */
51      free(sem);
52      errno = save_errno;
53      return (SEM_FAILED);
54  }
```
                                                        ————— *my_pxsem_fifo/sem_open.c*

Figure 10.37 sem_open function.

Create a new semaphore

13–17   If the caller specifies the O_CREAT flag, then we know that four arguments are required, not two. We call va_start to initialize the variable ap to point to the last named argument (oflag). We then use ap and the implementation's va_arg function to obtain the values for the third and fourth arguments. We described the handling of the variable argument list and our va_mode_t datatype with Figure 5.21.

Create new FIFO

18–23   A new FIFO is created with the name specified by the caller. As we discussed in Section 4.6, this function returns an error of EEXIST if the FIFO already exists. If the caller of sem_open does not specify the O_EXCL flag, then this error is OK, but we do not want to initialize the FIFO later in the function, so we turn off the O_CREAT flag.

Allocate sem_t datatype and open FIFO for reading and writing

25–37   We allocate space for a sem_t datatype, which will contain two descriptors. We open the FIFO twice, once read-only and once write-only. We do not want to block in either call to open, so we specify the O_NONBLOCK flag when we open the FIFO read-only (recall Figure 4.21). We also specify the O_NONBLOCK flag when we open the FIFO write-only, but this is to detect overflow (e.g., if we try to write more than PIPE_BUF bytes to the FIFO). After the FIFO has been opened twice, we turn off the nonblocking flag on the read-only descriptor.

Initialize value of newly create semaphore

38–42   If a new semaphore has been created, we initialize its value by writing value number of bytes to the FIFO. If the initial value exceeds the implementation's PIPE_BUF limit, the call to write after the FIFO is full will return an error of EAGAIN.

sem_close Function

Figure 10.38 shows our sem_close function.

11–15   We close both descriptors and free the memory that was allocated for the sem_t datatype.

sem_unlink Function

Our sem_unlink function, shown in Figure 10.39, removes the name associated with our semaphore. It just calls the Unix unlink function.

sem_post Function

Figure 10.40 shows our sem_post function, which increments the value of a semaphore.

11–12   We write an arbitrary byte to the FIFO. If the FIFO was empty, this will wake up any processes that are blocked in a call to read on this FIFO, waiting for a byte of data.

——————————————————————— my_pxsem_fifo/sem_close.c

```
 1 #include    "unpipc.h"
 2 #include    "semaphore.h"

 3 int
 4 sem_close(sem_t *sem)
 5 {
 6     if (sem->sem_magic != SEM_MAGIC) {
 7         errno = EINVAL;
 8         return (-1);
 9     }
10     sem->sem_magic = 0;          /* in case caller tries to use it later */
11     if (close(sem->sem_fd[0]) == -1 || close(sem->sem_fd[1]) == -1) {
12         free(sem);
13         return (-1);
14     }
15     free(sem);
16     return (0);
17 }
```

——————————————————————— my_pxsem_fifo/sem_close.c

Figure 10.38 sem_close function.

——————————————————————— my_pxsem_fifo/sem_unlink.c

```
 1 #include    "unpipc.h"
 2 #include    "semaphore.h"

 3 int
 4 sem_unlink(const char *pathname)
 5 {
 6     return (unlink(pathname));
 7 }
```

——————————————————————— my_pxsem_fifo/sem_unlink.c

Figure 10.39 sem_unlink function.

——————————————————————— my_pxsem_fifo/sem_post.c

```
 1 #include    "unpipc.h"
 2 #include    "semaphore.h"

 3 int
 4 sem_post(sem_t *sem)
 5 {
 6     char    c;

 7     if (sem->sem_magic != SEM_MAGIC) {
 8         errno = EINVAL;
 9         return (-1);
10     }
11     if (write(sem->sem_fd[1], &c, 1) == 1)
12         return (0);
13     return (-1);
14 }
```

——————————————————————— my_pxsem_fifo/sem_post.c

Figure 10.40 sem_post function.

`sem_wait` Function

The final function is shown in Figure 10.41, `sem_wait`.

—————————————————————————————— my_pxsem_fifo/sem_wait.c
```
 1 #include     "unpipc.h"
 2 #include     "semaphore.h"

 3 int
 4 sem_wait(sem_t *sem)
 5 {
 6     char    c;

 7     if (sem->sem_magic != SEM_MAGIC) {
 8         errno = EINVAL;
 9         return (-1);
10     }
11     if (read(sem->sem_fd[0], &c, 1) == 1)
12         return (0);
13     return (-1);
14 }
```
—————————————————————————————— my_pxsem_fifo/sem_wait.c

Figure 10.41 `sem_wait` function.

11-12   We `read` 1 byte from the FIFO, blocking if the FIFO is empty.

We have not implemented the `sem_trywait` function, but that could be done by enabling the nonblocking flag for the FIFO and calling `read`. We have also not implemented the `sem_getvalue` function. Some implementations return the number of bytes currently in a pipe or FIFO when the `stat` or `fstat` function is called, as the `st_size` member of the `stat` structure. But this is not guaranteed by Posix and is therefore nonportable. Implementations of these two Posix semaphore functions are shown in the next section.

10.15 Implementation Using Memory-Mapped I/O

We now provide an implementation of Posix named semaphores using memory-mapped I/O along with Posix mutexes and condition variables. An implementation similar to this is provided in Section B.11.3 (the Rationale) of [IEEE 1996].

> We cover memory-mapped I/O in Chapters 12 and 13. You may wish to skip this section until you have read those chapters.

We first show our `semaphore.h` header in Figure 10.42, which defines the fundamental `sem_t` datatype.

`sem_t` datatype

1-7   Our semaphore data structure contains a mutex, a condition variable, and an unsigned integer containing the current value of the semaphore. As discussed with Figure 10.36, the `sem_magic` member contains `SEM_MAGIC` once this structure has been initialized.

```
                                                              ── my_pxsem_mmap/semaphore.h
 1           /* the fundamental datatype */
 2 typedef struct {
 3     pthread_mutex_t sem_mutex;   /* lock to test and set semaphore value */
 4     pthread_cond_t  sem_cond;    /* for transition from 0 to nonzero */
 5     unsigned int sem_count;      /* the actual semaphore value */
 6     int      sem_magic;          /* magic number if open */
 7 } sem_t;

 8 #define SEM_MAGIC    0x67458923

 9 #ifdef  SEM_FAILED
10 #undef  SEM_FAILED
11 #define SEM_FAILED  ((sem_t *)(-1))   /* avoid compiler warnings */
12 #endif
                                                              ── my_pxsem_mmap/semaphore.h
```

Figure 10.42 semaphore.h header.

sem_open Function

Figure 10.43 shows the first half of our sem_open function, which creates a new semaphore or opens an existing semaphore.

Handle variable argument list

19–23   If the caller specifies the O_CREAT flag, then we know that four arguments are required, not two. We described the handling of the variable argument list and our va_mode_t datatype with Figure 5.21. We turn off the user-execute bit in the mode variable (S_IXUSR) for reasons that we describe shortly. A file is created with the name specified by the caller, and the user-execute bit is turned on.

Create a new semaphore and handle potential race condition

24–32   If, when the O_CREAT flag is specified by the caller, we were to just open the file, memory map its contents, and initialize the three members of the sem_t structure, we would have a race condition. We described this race condition with Figure 5.21, and the technique that we use is the same as shown there. We encounter a similar race condition in Figure 10.52.

Set the file size

33–37   We set the size of the newly created file by writing a zero-filled structure to the file. Since we know that the file has just been created with a size of 0, we call write to set the file size, and not ftruncate, because, as we note in Section 13.3, Posix does not guarantee that ftruncate works when the size of a regular file is being increased.

Memory map the file

38–42   The file is memory mapped by mmap. This file will contain the current value of the sem_t data structure, although since we have memory mapped the file, we just reference it through the pointer returned by mmap: we never call read or write.

—————————————————————————— my_pxsem_mmap/sem_open.c

```
 1 #include    "unpipc.h"
 2 #include    "semaphore.h"

 3 #include    <stdarg.h>          /* for variable arg lists */
 4 #define     MAX_TRIES   10      /* for waiting for initialization */

 5 sem_t *
 6 sem_open(const char *pathname, int oflag,...)
 7 {
 8     int     fd, i, created, save_errno;
 9     mode_t  mode;
10     va_list ap;
11     sem_t *sem, seminit;
12     struct stat statbuff;
13     unsigned int value;
14     pthread_mutexattr_t mattr;
15     pthread_condattr_t cattr;

16     created = 0;
17     sem = MAP_FAILED;            /* [sic] */
18 again:
19     if (oflag & O_CREAT) {
20         va_start(ap, oflag);     /* init ap to final named argument */
21         mode = va_arg(ap, va_mode_t) & ~S_IXUSR;
22         value = va_arg(ap, unsigned int);
23         va_end(ap);

24             /* open and specify O_EXCL and user-execute */
25         fd = open(pathname, oflag | O_EXCL | O_RDWR, mode | S_IXUSR);
26         if (fd < 0) {
27             if (errno == EEXIST && (oflag & O_EXCL) == 0)
28                 goto exists;     /* already exists, OK */
29             else
30                 return (SEM_FAILED);
31         }
32         created = 1;
33             /* first one to create the file initializes it */
34             /* set the file size */
35         bzero(&seminit, sizeof(seminit));
36         if (write(fd, &seminit, sizeof(seminit)) != sizeof(seminit))
37             goto err;

38             /* memory map the file */
39         sem = mmap(NULL, sizeof(sem_t), PROT_READ | PROT_WRITE,
40                 MAP_SHARED, fd, 0);
41         if (sem == MAP_FAILED)
42             goto err;

43             /* initialize mutex, condition variable, and value */
44         if ( (i = pthread_mutexattr_init(&mattr)) != 0)
45             goto pthreaderr;
46         pthread_mutexattr_setpshared(&mattr, PTHREAD_PROCESS_SHARED);
47         i = pthread_mutex_init(&sem->sem_mutex, &mattr);
48         pthread_mutexattr_destroy(&mattr);  /* be sure to destroy */
49         if (i != 0)
50             goto pthreaderr;
```

```
51          if ( (i = pthread_condattr_init(&cattr)) != 0)
52              goto pthreaderr;
53          pthread_condattr_setpshared(&cattr, PTHREAD_PROCESS_SHARED);
54          i = pthread_cond_init(&sem->sem_cond, &cattr);
55          pthread_condattr_destroy(&cattr);   /* be sure to destroy */
56          if (i != 0)
57              goto pthreaderr;

58          if ( (sem->sem_count = value) > sysconf(_SC_SEM_VALUE_MAX)) {
59              errno = EINVAL;
60              goto err;
61          }
62              /* initialization complete, turn off user-execute bit */
63          if (fchmod(fd, mode) == -1)
64              goto err;
65          close(fd);
66          sem->sem_magic = SEM_MAGIC;
67          return (sem);
68      }
```
——————————————————————————————————— *my_pxsem_mmap/sem_open.c*

Figure 10.43 sem_open function: first half.

Initialize `sem_t` data structure

43–57   We initialize the three members of the sem_t data structure: the mutex, the condition variable, and the value of the semaphore. Since Posix named semaphores can be
shared by any process that knows the semaphore's name and has adequate permission,
we must specify the PTHREAD_PROCESS_SHARED attribute when initializing the mutex
and condition variable. To do so for the semaphore, we first initialize the attributes by
calling pthread_mutexattr_init, then set the process-shared attribute in this structure by calling pthread_mutexattr_setpshared, and then initialize the mutex by
calling pthread_mutex_init. Three nearly identical steps are done for the condition
variable. We are careful to destroy the attributes in the case of an error.

Initialize semaphore value

58–61   Finally, the initial value of the semaphore is stored. We compare this value to the
maximum value allowed, which we obtain by calling sysconf (Section 10.13).

Turn off user-execute bit

62–67   Once the semaphore is initialized, we turn off the user-execute bit. This indicates
that the semaphore has been initialized. We close the file, since it has been memory
mapped and we do not need to keep it open.

Figure 10.44 shows the second half of our sem_open function. In Figure 5.23, we
described a race condition that we handle here using the same technique.

Open existing semaphore

69–78   We end up here if either the O_CREAT flag is not specified or if O_CREAT is specified
but the semaphore already exists. In either case, we are opening an existing semaphore.
We open the file containing the sem_t datatype for reading and writing, and memory
map the file into the address space of the process (mmap).

```
                                                                ─── my_pxsem_mmap/sem_open.c
 69    exists:
 70      if ( (fd = open(pathname, O_RDWR)) < 0) {
 71          if (errno == ENOENT && (oflag & O_CREAT))
 72              goto again;
 73          goto err;
 74      }
 75      sem = mmap(NULL, sizeof(sem_t), PROT_READ | PROT_WRITE,
 76                  MAP_SHARED, fd, 0);
 77      if (sem == MAP_FAILED)
 78          goto err;

 79          /* make certain initialization is complete */
 80      for (i = 0; i < MAX_TRIES; i++) {
 81          if (stat(pathname, &statbuff) == -1) {
 82              if (errno == ENOENT && (oflag & O_CREAT)) {
 83                  close(fd);
 84                  goto again;
 85              }
 86              goto err;
 87          }
 88          if ((statbuff.st_mode & S_IXUSR) == 0) {
 89              close(fd);
 90              sem->sem_magic = SEM_MAGIC;
 91              return (sem);
 92          }
 93          sleep(1);
 94      }
 95      errno = ETIMEDOUT;
 96      goto err;

 97    pthreaderr:
 98      errno = i;
 99    err:
100          /* don't let munmap() or close() change errno */
101      save_errno = errno;
102      if (created)
103          unlink(pathname);
104      if (sem != MAP_FAILED)
105          munmap(sem, sizeof(sem_t));
106      close(fd);
107      errno = save_errno;
108      return (SEM_FAILED);
109  }
                                                                ─── my_pxsem_mmap/sem_open.c
```

Figure 10.44   sem_open function: second half.

We can now see why Posix.1 states that "references to copies of the semaphore produce undefined results." When named semaphores are implemented using memory-mapped I/O, the semaphore (the sem_t datatype) is memory mapped into the address space of *all* processes that have the semaphore open. This is performed by sem_open in each process that opens the named semaphore. Changes made by one process (e.g., to the semaphore's count) are seen by all the other processes through the memory mapping. If we were to make our own copy of a sem_t data structure, this copy would no longer be shared by all the processes. Even though we might think it was working (the semaphore functions might not give any errors, at least until we call sem_close, which will unmap the memory, which would fail on the copy), no synchronization would occur with the other processes. Note from Figure 1.6, however, that memory-mapped regions in a parent are retained in the child across a fork, so a copy of a semaphore that is made by the kernel from a parent to a child across a fork is OK.

Make certain that semaphore is initialized

79-96   We must wait for the semaphore to be initialized (in case multiple threads try to create the same semaphore at about the same time). To do so, we call stat and look at the file's permissions (the st_mode member of the stat structure). If the user-execute bit is off, the semaphore has been initialized.

Error returns

97-108   When an error occurs, we are careful not to change errno.

sem_close Function

Figure 10.45 shows our sem_close function, which just calls munmap for the region that was memory mapped. Should the caller continue to use the pointer that was returned by sem_open, it should receive a SIGSEGV signal.

—————————————————————————— my_pxsem_mmap/sem_close.c

```
1 #include    "unpipc.h"
2 #include    "semaphore.h"

3 int
4 sem_close(sem_t *sem)
5 {
6     if (sem->sem_magic != SEM_MAGIC) {
7         errno = EINVAL;
8         return (-1);
9     }
10    if (munmap(sem, sizeof(sem_t)) == -1)
11        return(-1);

12    return (0);
13 }
```
—————————————————————————— my_pxsem_mmap/sem_close.c

Figure 10.45 sem_close function.

sem_unlink Function

Our sem_unlink function shown in Figure 10.46 removes the name associated with our semaphore. It just calls the Unix unlink function.

sem_post Function

Figure 10.47 shows our sem_post function, which increments the value of a semaphore, awaking any threads waiting for the semaphore if the semaphore value has just become greater than 0.

my_pxsem_mmap/sem_unlink.c

```
1 #include     "unpipc.h"
2 #include     "semaphore.h"

3 int
4 sem_unlink(const char *pathname)
5 {
6     if (unlink(pathname) == -1)
7         return (-1);
8     return (0);
9 }
```

my_pxsem_mmap/sem_unlink.c

Figure 10.46 sem_unlink function.

my_pxsem_mmap/sem_post.c

```
1 #include     "unpipc.h"
2 #include     "semaphore.h"

3 int
4 sem_post(sem_t *sem)
5 {
6     int     n;

7     if (sem->sem_magic != SEM_MAGIC) {
8         errno = EINVAL;
9         return (-1);
10     }
11     if ( (n = pthread_mutex_lock(&sem->sem_mutex)) != 0) {
12         errno = n;
13         return (-1);
14     }
15     if (sem->sem_count == 0)
16         pthread_cond_signal(&sem->sem_cond);
17     sem->sem_count++;
18     pthread_mutex_unlock(&sem->sem_mutex);
19     return (0);
20 }
```

my_pxsem_mmap/sem_post.c

Figure 10.47 sem_post function.

11-18   We must acquire the semaphore's mutex lock before manipulating its value. If the semaphore's value will be going from 0 to 1, we call pthread_cond_signal to wake up anyone waiting for this semaphore.

sem_wait **Function**

The sem_wait function shown in Figure 10.48 waits for the value of the semaphore to exceed 0.

—————————————————————————————— *my_pxsem_mmap/sem_wait.c*
```
 1 #include    "unpipc.h"
 2 #include    "semaphore.h"

 3 int
 4 sem_wait(sem_t *sem)
 5 {
 6     int     n;

 7     if (sem->sem_magic != SEM_MAGIC) {
 8         errno = EINVAL;
 9         return (-1);
10     }
11     if ( (n = pthread_mutex_lock(&sem->sem_mutex)) != 0) {
12         errno = n;
13         return (-1);
14     }
15     while (sem->sem_count == 0)
16         pthread_cond_wait(&sem->sem_cond, &sem->sem_mutex);
17     sem->sem_count--;
18     pthread_mutex_unlock(&sem->sem_mutex);
19     return (0);
20 }
```
—————————————————————————————— *my_pxsem_mmap/sem_wait.c*

Figure 10.48 sem_wait function.

11-18   We must acquire the semaphore's mutex lock before manipulating its value. If the value is 0, we go to sleep in a call to pthread_cond_wait, waiting for someone to call pthread_cond_signal for this semaphore, when its value goes from 0 to 1. Once the value is greater than 0, we decrement the value and release the mutex.

sem_trywait Function

Figure 10.49 shows the sem_trywait function, the nonblocking version of sem_wait.
11-22   We acquire the semaphore's mutex lock and then check its value. If the value is greater than 0, it is decremented and the return value is 0. Otherwise, the return value is –1 with errno set to EAGAIN.

sem_getvalue Function

Figure 10.50 shows our final function, sem_getvalue, which returns the current value of the semaphore.
11-16   We acquire the semaphore's mutex lock and return its value.

We can see from this implementation that semaphores are simpler to use than mutexes and condition variables.

my_pxsem_mmap/sem_trywait.c

```
 1 #include    "unpipc.h"
 2 #include    "semaphore.h"

 3 int
 4 sem_trywait(sem_t *sem)
 5 {
 6     int     n, rc;

 7     if (sem->sem_magic != SEM_MAGIC) {
 8         errno = EINVAL;
 9         return (-1);
10     }
11     if ( (n = pthread_mutex_lock(&sem->sem_mutex)) != 0) {
12         errno = n;
13         return (-1);
14     }
15     if (sem->sem_count > 0) {
16         sem->sem_count--;
17         rc = 0;
18     } else {
19         rc = -1;
20         errno = EAGAIN;
21     }
22     pthread_mutex_unlock(&sem->sem_mutex);
23     return (rc);
24 }
```

my_pxsem_mmap/sem_trywait.c

Figure 10.49 sem_trywait function.

my_pxsem_mmap/sem_getvalue.c

```
 1 #include    "unpipc.h"
 2 #include    "semaphore.h"

 3 int
 4 sem_getvalue(sem_t *sem, int *pvalue)
 5 {
 6     int     n;

 7     if (sem->sem_magic != SEM_MAGIC) {
 8         errno = EINVAL;
 9         return (-1);
10     }
11     if ( (n = pthread_mutex_lock(&sem->sem_mutex)) != 0) {
12         errno = n;
13         return (-1);
14     }
15     *pvalue = sem->sem_count;
16     pthread_mutex_unlock(&sem->sem_mutex);
17     return (0);
18 }
```

my_pxsem_mmap/sem_getvalue.c

Figure 10.50 sem_getvalue function.

10.16 Implementation Using System V Semaphores

We now provide one more implementation of Posix named semaphores using System V semaphores. Since implementations of the older System V semaphores are more common than the newer Posix semaphores, this implementation can allow applications to start using Posix semaphores, even if not supported by the operating system.

> We cover System V semaphores in Chapter 11. You may wish to skip this section until you have read that chapter.

We first show our `semaphore.h` header in Figure 10.51, which defines the fundamental `sem_t` datatype.

―― *my_pxsem_svsem/semaphore.h*
```
 1          /* the fundamental datatype */
 2 typedef struct {
 3    int     sem_semid;          /* the System V semaphore ID */
 4    int     sem_magic;          /* magic number if open */
 5 } sem_t;

 6 #define SEM_MAGIC    0x45678923

 7 #ifdef   SEM_FAILED
 8 #undef   SEM_FAILED
 9 #define SEM_FAILED  ((sem_t *)(-1))   /* avoid compiler warnings */
10 #endif

11 #ifndef SEMVMX
12 #define SEMVMX  32767               /* historical System V max value for sem */
13 #endif
```
―― *my_pxsem_svsem/semaphore.h*

Figure 10.51 `semaphore.h` header.

sem_t datatype

1–5   We implement a Posix named semaphore using a System V semaphore set consisting of one member. Our semaphore data structure contains the System V semaphore ID and a magic number (which we discussed with Figure 10.36).

sem_open Function

Figure 10.52 shows the first half of our `sem_open` function, which creates a new semaphore or opens an existing semaphore.

―― *my_pxsem_svsem/sem_open.c*
```
 1 #include     "unpipc.h"
 2 #include     "semaphore.h"

 3 #include     <stdarg.h>           /* for variable arg lists */
 4 #define      MAX_TRIES   10       /* for waiting for initialization */

 5 sem_t *
 6 sem_open(const char *pathname, int oflag,...)
```

```
 7  {
 8      int     i, fd, semflag, semid, save_errno;
 9      key_t   key;
10      mode_t  mode;
11      va_list ap;
12      sem_t *sem;
13      union semun arg;
14      unsigned int value;
15      struct semid_ds seminfo;
16      struct sembuf initop;

17          /* no mode for sem_open() w/out O_CREAT; guess */
18      semflag = SVSEM_MODE;
19      semid = -1;

20      if (oflag & O_CREAT) {
21          va_start(ap, oflag);    /* init ap to final named argument */
22          mode = va_arg(ap, va_mode_t);
23          value = va_arg(ap, unsigned int);
24          va_end(ap);

25              /* convert to key that will identify System V semaphore */
26          if ( (fd = open(pathname, oflag, mode)) == -1)
27              return (SEM_FAILED);
28          close(fd);
29          if ( (key = ftok(pathname, 1)) == (key_t) - 1)
30              return (SEM_FAILED);

31          semflag = IPC_CREAT | (mode & 0777);
32          if (oflag & O_EXCL)
33              semflag |= IPC_EXCL;

34              /* create the System V semaphore with IPC_EXCL */
35          if ( (semid = semget(key, 1, semflag | IPC_EXCL)) >= 0) {
36                  /* success, we're the first so initialize to 0 */
37              arg.val = 0;
38              if (semctl(semid, 0, SETVAL, arg) == -1)
39                  goto err;
40                  /* then increment by value to set sem_otime nonzero */
41              if (value > SEMVMX) {
42                  errno = EINVAL;
43                  goto err;
44              }
45              initop.sem_num = 0;
46              initop.sem_op = value;
47              initop.sem_flg = 0;
48              if (semop(semid, &initop, 1) == -1)
49                  goto err;
50              goto finish;

51          } else if (errno != EEXIST || (semflag & IPC_EXCL) != 0)
52              goto err;
53          /* else fall through */
54      }
```

my_pxsem_svsem/sem_open.c

Figure 10.52 sem_open function: first half.

Create a new semaphore and handle variable argument list

20–24   If the caller specifies the O_CREAT flag, then we know that four arguments are required, not two. We described the handling of the variable argument list and our va_mode_t datatype with Figure 5.21.

Create ancillary file and map pathname into System V IPC key

25–30   A regular file is created with the pathname specified by the caller. We do so just to have a pathname for ftok to identify the semaphore. The caller's *oflag* argument for the semaphore, which can be either O_CREAT or O_CREAT | O_EXCL, is used in the call to open. This creates the file if it does not already exist and will cause an error return if the file already exists and O_EXCL is specified. The descriptor is closed, because the only use of this file is with ftok, which converts the pathname into a System V IPC key (Section 3.2).

Create System V semaphore set with one member

31–33   We convert the O_CREAT and O_EXCL constants into their corresponding System V IPC_*xxx* constants and call semget to create a System V semaphore set consisting of one member. We always specify IPC_EXCL to determine whether the semaphore exists or not.

Initialize semaphore

34–50   Section 11.2 describes a fundamental problem with initializing System V semaphores, and Section 11.6 shows the code that avoids the potential race condition. We use a similar technique here. The first thread to create the semaphore (recall that we always specify IPC_EXCL) initializes it to 0 with a command of SETVAL to semctl, and then sets its value to the caller's specified initial value with semop. We are guaranteed that the semaphore's sem_otime value is initialized to 0 by semget and will be set nonzero by the creator's call to semop. Therefore, any other thread that finds that the semaphore already exists knows that the semaphore has been initialized once the sem_otime value is nonzero.

Check initial value

40–44   We check the initial value specified by the caller because System V semaphores are normally stored as unsigned shorts (the sem structure in Section 11.1) with a maximum value of 32767 (Section 11.7), whereas Posix semaphores are normally stored as integers with possibly larger allowed values (Section 10.13). The constant SEMVMX is defined by some implementations to be the System V maximum value, or we define it to be 32767 in Figure 10.51.

51–53   If the semaphore already exists and the caller does not specify O_EXCL, this is not an error. In this situation, the code falls through to open (not create) the existing semaphore.

Figure 10.53 shows the second half of our sem_open function.

my_pxsem_svsem/sem_open.c

```
55     /*
56      * (O_CREAT not secified) or
57      * (O_CREAT without O_EXCL and semaphore already exists).
58      * Must open semaphore and make certain it has been initialized.
59      */
60     if ( (key = ftok(pathname, 1)) == (key_t) - 1)
61         goto err;
62     if ( (semid = semget(key, 0, semflag)) == -1)
63         goto err;

64     arg.buf = &seminfo;
65     for (i = 0; i < MAX_TRIES; i++) {
66         if (semctl(semid, 0, IPC_STAT, arg) == -1)
67             goto err;
68         if (arg.buf->sem_otime != 0)
69             goto finish;
70         sleep(1);
71     }
72     errno = ETIMEDOUT;
73  err:
74     save_errno = errno;           /* don't let semctl() change errno */
75     if (semid != -1)
76         semctl(semid, 0, IPC_RMID);
77     errno = save_errno;
78     return (SEM_FAILED);

79  finish:
80     if ( (sem = malloc(sizeof(sem_t))) == NULL)
81         goto err;

82     sem->sem_semid = semid;
83     sem->sem_magic = SEM_MAGIC;
84     return (sem);
85 }
```

my_pxsem_svsem/sem_open.c

Figure 10.53 sem_open function: second half.

Open existing semaphore

55–63   For an existing semaphore (the O_CREAT flag is not specified or O_CREAT is specified by itself and the semaphore already exists), we open the System V semaphore with
semget. Notice that sem_open does not have a *mode* argument when O_CREAT is not
specified, but semget requires the equivalent of a *mode* argument even if an existing
semaphore is just being opened. Earlier in the function, we assigned a default value
(the SVSEM_MODE constant from our unpipc.h header) that we pass to semget when
O_CREAT is not specified.

Wait for semaphore to be initialized

64–72   We then verify that the semaphore has been initialized by calling semctl with a
command of IPC_STAT, waiting for sem_otime to be nonzero.

Error returns

73–78   When an error occurs, we are careful not to change errno.

Allocate `sem_t` datatype

79-84   We allocate space for a `sem_t` datatype and store the System V semaphore ID in the structure. A pointer to the `sem_t` datatype is the return value from the function.

`sem_close` Function

Figure 10.54 shows our `sem_close` function, which just calls `free` to return the dynamically allocated memory that was used for the `sem_t` datatype.

```
                                                        ─ my_pxsem_svsem/sem_close.c
 1 #include    "unpipc.h"
 2 #include    "semaphore.h"

 3 int
 4 sem_close(sem_t *sem)
 5 {
 6     if (sem->sem_magic != SEM_MAGIC) {
 7         errno = EINVAL;
 8         return (-1);
 9     }
10     sem->sem_magic = 0;          /* just in case */

11     free(sem);
12     return (0);
13 }
                                                        ─ my_pxsem_svsem/sem_close.c
```

Figure 10.54 `sem_close` function.

`sem_unlink` Function

Our `sem_unlink` function, shown in Figure 10.55, removes the ancillary file and the System V semaphore associated with our Posix semaphore.

Obtain System V key associated with pathname

8-16   `ftok` converts the pathname into a System V IPC key. The ancillary file is then removed by `unlink`. (We do so now, in case one of the remaining functions returns an error.) We open the System V semaphore with `semget` and then remove it with a command of `IPC_RMID` to `semctl`.

`sem_post` Function

Figure 10.56 shows our `sem_post` function, which increments the value of a semaphore.

11-16   We call `semop` with a single operation that increments the semaphore value by one.

`sem_wait` Function

The next function is shown in Figure 10.57; it is `sem_wait`, which waits for the value of the semaphore to exceed 0.

11-16   We call `semop` with a single operation that decrements the semaphore value by one.

—————————————————————————— my_pxsem_svsem/sem_unlink.c

```
 1 #include    "unpipc.h"
 2 #include    "semaphore.h"

 3 int
 4 sem_unlink(const char *pathname)
 5 {
 6     int    semid;
 7     key_t  key;

 8     if ( (key = ftok(pathname, 1)) == (key_t) - 1)
 9         return (-1);
10     if (unlink(pathname) == -1)
11         return (-1);
12     if ( (semid = semget(key, 1, SVSEM_MODE)) == -1)
13         return (-1);
14     if (semctl(semid, 0, IPC_RMID) == -1)
15         return (-1);
16     return (0);
17 }
```

—————————————————————————— my_pxsem_svsem/sem_unlink.c

Figure 10.55 sem_unlink function.

————————————————————————————— my_pxsem_svsem/sem_post.c

```
 1 #include    "unpipc.h"
 2 #include    "semaphore.h"

 3 int
 4 sem_post(sem_t *sem)
 5 {
 6     struct sembuf op;

 7     if (sem->sem_magic != SEM_MAGIC) {
 8         errno = EINVAL;
 9         return (-1);
10     }
11     op.sem_num = 0;
12     op.sem_op = 1;
13     op.sem_flg = 0;
14     if (semop(sem->sem_semid, &op, 1) < 0)
15         return (-1);
16     return (0);
17 }
```

————————————————————————————— my_pxsem_svsem/sem_post.c

Figure 10.56 sem_post function.

sem_trywait Function

Our sem_trywait function, the nonblocking version of sem_wait, is shown in Figure 10.58.

13   The only change from our sem_wait function in Figure 10.57 is specifying sem_flg as IPC_NOWAIT. If the operation cannot be completed without blocking the calling thread, the return value from semop is EAGAIN, which is what sem_trywait must return if the operation cannot be completed without blocking.

———————————————————————— my_pxsem_svsem/sem_wait.c

```
 1 #include     "unpipc.h"
 2 #include     "semaphore.h"

 3 int
 4 sem_wait(sem_t *sem)
 5 {
 6     struct sembuf op;

 7     if (sem->sem_magic != SEM_MAGIC) {
 8         errno = EINVAL;
 9         return (-1);
10     }
11     op.sem_num = 0;
12     op.sem_op = -1;
13     op.sem_flg = 0;
14     if (semop(sem->sem_semid, &op, 1) < 0)
15         return (-1);
16     return (0);
17 }
```

———————————————————————— my_pxsem_svsem/sem_wait.c

Figure 10.57 sem_wait function.

——————————————————————— my_pxsem_svsem/sem_trywait.c

```
 1 #include     "unpipc.h"
 2 #include     "semaphore.h"

 3 int
 4 sem_trywait(sem_t *sem)
 5 {
 6     struct sembuf op;

 7     if (sem->sem_magic != SEM_MAGIC) {
 8         errno = EINVAL;
 9         return (-1);
10     }
11     op.sem_num = 0;
12     op.sem_op = -1;
13     op.sem_flg = IPC_NOWAIT;
14     if (semop(sem->sem_semid, &op, 1) < 0)
15         return (-1);
16     return (0);
17 }
```

——————————————————————— my_pxsem_svsem/sem_trywait.c

Figure 10.58 sem_trywait function.

sem_getvalue Function

The final function is shown in Figure 10.59; it is sem_getvalue, which returns the current value of the semaphore.

11-14   The current value of the semaphore is obtained with a command of GETVAL to semctl.

```
                                                        —— my_pxsem_svsem/sem_getvalue.c
 1 #include     "unpipc.h"
 2 #include     "semaphore.h"

 3 int
 4 sem_getvalue(sem_t *sem, int *pvalue)
 5 {
 6     int     val;

 7     if (sem->sem_magic != SEM_MAGIC) {
 8         errno = EINVAL;
 9         return (-1);
10     }
11     if ( (val = semctl(sem->sem_semid, 0, GETVAL)) < 0)
12         return (-1);
13     *pvalue = val;
14     return (0);
15 }
                                                        —— my_pxsem_svsem/sem_getvalue.c
```

Figure 10.59 sem_getvalue function.

10.17 Summary

Posix semaphores are counting semaphores, and three basic operations are provided:

1. create a semaphore,

2. wait for a semaphore's value to be greater than 0 and then decrement the value, and

3. post to a semaphore by incrementing its value and waking up any threads waiting for the semaphore.

Posix semaphores can be named or memory-based. Named semaphores can always be shared between different processes, whereas memory-based semaphores must be designated as process-shared when created. The persistence of these two types of semaphores also differs: named semaphores have at least kernel persistence, whereas memory-based semaphores have process persistence.

The producer–consumer problem is the classic example for demonstrating semaphores. In this chapter, our first solution had one producer thread and one consumer thread, our next solution allowed multiple producer threads and one consumer thread, and our final solution allowed multiple consumer threads. We then showed that the classic problem of double buffering is just a special case of the producer–consumer problem, with one producer and one consumer.

Three sample implementations of Posix semaphores were provided. The first, using FIFOs, is the simplest because much of the synchronization is handled by the kernel's read and write functions. The next implementation used memory-mapped I/O, similar to our implementation of Posix message queues in Section 5.8, and used a mutex and condition variable for synchronization. Our final implementation used System V semaphores, providing a simpler interface to these semaphores.

Exercises

10.1   Modify the `produce` and `consume` functions in Section 10.6 as follows. First, swap the order of the two calls to `Sem_wait` in the consumer, to generate a deadlock (as we discussed in Section 10.6). Next, add a call to `printf` before each call to `Sem_wait`, indicating which thread (the producer or the consumer) is waiting for which semaphore. Add another call to `printf` after the call to `Sem_wait`, indicating that the thread got the semaphore. Reduce the number of buffers to 2, and then build and run this program to verify that it leads to a deadlock.

10.2   Assume that we start four copies of our program that calls our `my_lock` function from Figure 10.19:

> % **lockpxsem & lockpxsem & lockpxsem & lockpxsem &**

Each of the four processes starts with an `initflag` of 0, so each one calls `sem_open` specifying `O_CREAT`. Is this OK?

10.3   What happens in the previous exercise if one of the four programs terminates after calling `my_lock` but before calling `my_unlock`?

10.4   What could happen in Figure 10.37 if we did not initialize both descriptors to –1?

10.5   In Figure 10.37, why do we save the value of `errno` and then restore it, instead of coding the two calls to `close` as

```
if (sem->fd[0] >= 0)
    close(sem->fd[0]);
if (sem->fd[1] >= 0)
    close(sem->fd[1]);
```

10.6   What happens if two processes call our FIFO implementation of `sem_open` (Figure 10.37) at about the same time, both specifying `O_CREAT` with an initial value of 5? Can the FIFO ever be initialized (incorrectly) to 10?

10.7   With Figures 10.43 and 10.44, we described a possible race condition if two processes both try to create a semaphore at about the same time. Yet in the solution to the previous problem, we said that Figure 10.37 does not have a race condition. Explain.

10.8   Posix.1 makes it optional for `sem_wait` to detect that it has been interrupted by a caught signal and return `EINTR`. Write a test program to determine whether your implementation detects this or not.

Also run your test program using our implementations that use FIFOs (Section 10.14), memory-mapped I/O (Section 10.15), and System V semaphores (Section 10.16).

10.9   Which of our three implementations of `sem_post` are async-signal-safe (Figure 5.10)?

10.10   Modify the producer–consumer solution in Section 10.6 to use a `pthread_mutex_t` datatype for the `mutex` variable, instead of a semaphore. Does any measurable change in performance occur?

10.11   Compare the timing of named semaphores (Figures 10.17 and 10.18) with memory-based semaphores (Figure 10.20).

11

System V Semaphores

11.1 Introduction

When we described the concept of a semaphore in Chapter 10, we first described

- a *binary semaphore*: a semaphore whose value is 0 or 1. This was similar to a mutex lock (Chapter 7), in which the semaphore value is 0 if the resource is locked, or 1 if the resource is available.

The next level of detail expanded this into

- a *counting semaphore*: a semaphore whose value is between 0 and some limit (which must be at least 32767 for Posix semaphores). We used these to count resources in our producer–consumer problem, with the value of the semaphore being the number of resources available.

In both types of semaphores, the *wait* operation waits for the semaphore value to be greater than 0, and then decrements the value. The *post* operation just increments the semaphore value, waking up any threads awaiting the semaphore value to be greater than 0.

System V semaphores add another level of detail to semaphores by defining

- a *set of counting semaphores*: one or more semaphores (a set), each of which is a counting semaphore. There is a limit to the number of semaphores per set, typically on the order of 25 semaphores (Section 11.7). When we refer to a "System V semaphore," we are referring to a set of counting semaphores. when we refer to a "Posix semaphore," we are referring to a single counting semaphore.

For every set of semaphores in the system, the kernel maintains the following structure of information, defined by including `<sys/sem.h>`:

```
struct semid_ds {
  struct ipc_perm  sem_perm;  /* operation permission struct */
  struct sem       *sem_base;  /* ptr to array of semaphores in set */
  ushort           sem_nsems;  /* # of semaphores in set */
  time_t           sem_otime;  /* time of last semop() */
  time_t           sem_ctime;  /* time of creation or last IPC_SET */
};
```

The `ipc_perm` structure was described in Section 3.3 and contains the access permissions for this particular semaphore.

The `sem` structure is the internal data structure used by the kernel to maintain the set of values for a given semaphore. Every member of a semaphore set is described by the following structure:

```
struct sem {
  ushort_t  semval;   /* semaphore value, nonnegative */
  short     sempid;   /* PID of last successful semop(), SETVAL, SETALL */
  ushort_t  semncnt;  /* # awaiting semval > current value */
  ushort_t  semzcnt;  /* # awaiting semval = 0 */
};
```

Note that `sem_base` contains a pointer to an array of these `sem` structures: one array element for each semaphore in the set.

In addition to maintaining the actual values for each semaphore in the set, the kernel also maintains three other pieces of information for each semaphore in the set: the process ID of the process that performed the last operation on this value, a count of the number of processes waiting for the value to increase, and a count of the number of processes waiting for the value to become zero.

> Unix 98 says that the above structure is anonymous. The name that we show, sem, is from the historical System V implementation.

We can picture a particular semaphore in the kernel as being a `semid_ds` structure that points to an array of `sem` structures. If the semaphore has two members in its set, we would have the picture shown in Figure 11.1. In this figure, the variable `sem_nsems` has a value of two, and we have denoted each member of the set with the subscripts [0] and [1].

11.2 `semget` Function

The `semget` function creates a semaphore set or accesses an existing semaphore set.

```
#include  <sys/sem.h>

int semget(key_t key, int nsems, int oflag);
```

Returns: nonnegative identifier if OK, −1 on error

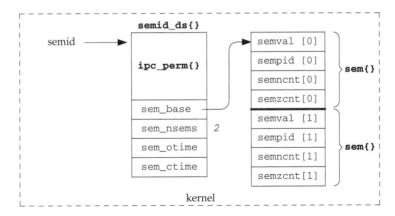

Figure 11.1 Kernel data structures for a semaphore set with two values in the set.

The return value is an integer called the *semaphore identifier* that is used with the `semop` and `semctl` functions.

The *nsems* argument specifies the number of semaphores in the set. If we are not creating a new semaphore set but just accessing an existing set, we can specify this argument as 0. We cannot change the number of semaphores in a set once it is created.

The *oflag* value is a combination of the SEM_R and SEM_A constants shown in Figure 3.6. R stands for "read" and A stands for "alter." This can be bitwise-ORed with either IPC_CREAT or IPC_CREAT | IPC_EXCL, as discussed with Figure 3.4.

When a new semaphore set is created, the following members of the `semid_ds` structure are initialized:

- The `uid` and `cuid` members of the `sem_perm` structure are set to the effective user ID of the process, and the `gid` and `cgid` members are set to the effective group ID of the process.
- The read–write permission bits in `oflag` are stored in `sem_perm.mode`.
- `sem_otime` is set to 0, and `sem_ctime` is set to the current time.
- `sem_nsems` is set to *nsems*.
- The `sem` structure associated with each semaphore in the set is *not* initialized. These structures are initialized when `semctl` is called with either the SETVAL or SETALL commands.

Initialization of Semaphore Value

Comments in the source code in the 1990 edition of this book incorrectly stated that the semaphore values in the set were initialized to 0 by `semget` when a new set was created. Although some systems do initialize the semaphore values to 0, this is not guaranteed. Indeed, older implementations of System V do not initialize the semaphore values at all, leaving their values as whatever they were the last time that piece of memory was used.

Most manual pages for semget say nothing at all about the initial values of the semaphores when a new set is created. The X/Open XPG3 portability guide (1989) and Unix 98 correct this omission and explicitly state that the semaphore values are not initialized by semget and are initialized only by calling semctl (which we describe shortly) with a command of either SETVAL (set one value in the set) or SETALL (set all the values in the set).

This requirement of two function calls to create a semaphore set (semget) and then initialize it (semctl) is a fatal flaw in the design of System V semaphores. A partial solution is to specify IPC_CREAT | IPC_EXCL when calling semget, so that only one process (the first one to call semget) creates the semaphore. This process then initializes the semaphore. The other processes receive an error of EEXIST from semget and they then call semget again, without specifying either IPC_CREAT or IPC_EXCL.

But a race condition still exists. Assume that two processes both try to create and initialize a one-member semaphore set at about the same time, both executing the following numbered lines of code:

```
1   oflag = IPC_CREAT | IPC_EXCL | SVSEM_MODE;
2   if ( (semid = semget(key, 1, oflag)) >= 0) {
            /* success, we are the first, so initialize */
3       arg.val = 1;
4       Semctl(semid, 0, SETVAL, arg);

5   } else if (errno == EEXIST) {
            /* already exists, just open */
6       semid = Semget(key, 1, SVSEM_MODE);

7   } else
8       err_sys("semget error");

9   Semop(semid, ...);    /* decrement the semaphore by 1 */
```

The following scenario could occur:

1. The first process executes lines 1–3 and is then stopped by the kernel.
2. The kernel starts the second process, which executes lines 1, 2, 5, 6, and 9.

Even though the first process to create the semaphore will be the only process to initialize the semaphore, since it takes two steps to do the creation and initialization, the kernel can switch to another process between these two steps. That other process can then use the semaphore (line 9 in the code fragment), but the semaphore value has not been initialized by the first process. The semaphore value, when the second process executes line 9, is indeterminate.

Fortunately, there is a way around this race condition. We are guaranteed that the sem_otime member of the semid_ds structure is set to 0 when a new semaphore set is created. (The System V manuals have stated this fact for a long time, as do the XPG3 and Unix 98 standards.) This member is set to the current time only by a successful call to semop. Therefore, the second process in the preceding example must call semctl with a command of IPC_STAT after its second call to semget succeeds (line 6 in the code fragment). It then waits for sem_otime to be nonzero, at which time it knows that the semaphore has been initialized and that the process that did the initialization has successfully called semop. This means the process that creates the semaphore must initialize its value *and* must call semop before any other process can use the semaphore. We show examples of this technique in Figures 10.52 and 11.7.

> Posix named semaphores avoid this problem by having one function (sem_open) create and initialize the semaphore. Furthermore, even if O_CREAT is specified, the semaphore is initialized only if it does not already exist.

> Whether this potential race condition is a problem also depends on the application. With some applications (e.g., our producer–consumer as in Figure 10.21), one process always creates and initializes the semaphore. No race condition would exist in this scenario. But in other applications (e.g., our file locking example in Figure 10.19), no single process creates and initializes the semaphore: the first process to open the semaphore must create it and initialize it, and the race condition must be avoided.

11.3 semop Function

Once a semaphore set is opened with semget, operations are performed on one or more of the semaphores in the set using the semop function.

```
#include   <sys/sem.h>

int semop(int semid, struct sembuf *opsptr, size_t nops);
```
Returns: 0 if OK, −1 on error

opsptr points to an array of the following structures:

```
struct sembuf {
    short    sem_num;   /* semaphore number: 0, 1, ..., nsems-1 */
    short    sem_op;    /* semaphore operation: <0, 0, >0 */
    short    sem_flg;   /* operation flags: 0, IPC_NOWAIT, SEM_UNDO */
};
```

The number of elements in the array of sembuf structures pointed to by *opsptr* is specified by the *nops* argument. Each element in this array specifies an operation for one particular semaphore value in the set. The particular semaphore value is specified by the sem_num value, which is 0 for the first element, one for the second, and so on, up to *nsems−1*, where *nsems* is the number of semaphore values in the set (the second argument in the call to semget when the semaphore set was created).

> We are guaranteed only that the structure contains the three members shown. It might contain other members, and we have no guarantee that the members are in the order that we show. This means that we must not statically initialize this structure, as in
>
> ```
> struct sembuf   ops[2] = {
>     0, 0, 0,            /* wait for [0] to be 0 */
>     0, 1, SEM_UNDO      /* then increment [0] by 1 */
> };
> ```

but must use run-time initialization, as in

```
struct sembuf  ops[2];

ops[0].sem_num = 0;          /* wait for [0] to be 0 */
ops[0].sem_op  = 0;
ops[0].sem_flg = 0;
ops[1].sem_num = 0;          /* then increment [0] by 1 */
ops[1].sem_op  = 1;
ops[1].sem_flg = SEM_UNDO;
```

The array of operations passed to the `semop` function are guaranteed to be performed *atomically* by the kernel. The kernel either does *all* the operations that are specified, or it does *none* of them. We show an example of this in Section 11.5.

Each particular operation is specified by a `sem_op` value, which can be negative, 0, or positive. In the discussion that follows shortly, we refer to the following items:

- `semval`: the current value of the semaphore (Figure 11.1).

- `semncnt`: the number of threads waiting for `semval` to be greater than its current value (Figure 11.1).

- `semzcnt`: the number of threads waiting for `semval` to be 0 (Figure 11.1).

- `semadj`: the adjustment value for the calling process for the specified semaphore. This value is updated only if the `SEM_UNDO` flag is specified in the `sem_flg` member of the `sembuf` structure for this operation. This is a conceptual variable that is maintained by the kernel for each process that specifies the `SEM_UNDO` flag in a semaphore operation; a structure member with the name of `semadj` need not exist.

- A given semaphore operation is made nonblocking by specifying the `IPC_NOWAIT` flag in the `sem_flg` member of the `sembuf` structure. When this flag is specified and the given operation cannot be completed without putting the calling thread to sleep, `semop` returns an error of `EAGAIN`.

- When a thread is put to sleep waiting for a semaphore operation to complete (we will see that the thread can be waiting either for the semaphore value to be 0 or for the value to be greater than 0), and the thread catches a signal, and the signal handler returns, the `semop` function is interrupted and returns an error of `EINTR`. In the terminology of p. 124 of UNPv1, `semop` is a *slow system call* that is interrupted by a caught signal.

- When a thread is put to sleep waiting for a semaphore operation to complete and that semaphore is removed from the system by some other thread or process, `semop` returns an error of `EIDRM` ("identifier removed").

We now describe the operation of `semop`, based on the three possible values of each specified `sem_op` operation: positive, 0, or negative.

1. If `sem_op` is positive, the value of `sem_op` is added to `semval`. This corresponds to the release of resources that a semaphore controls.

If the SEM_UNDO flag is specified, the value of sem_op is subtracted from the semaphore's semadj value.

2. If sem_op is 0, the caller wants to wait until semval is 0. If semval is already 0, return is made immediately.

    If semval is nonzero, the semaphore's semzcnt value is incremented and the calling thread is blocked until semval becomes 0 (at which time, the semaphore's semzcnt value is decremented). As mentioned earlier, the thread is not put to sleep if IPC_NOWAIT is specified. The sleep returns prematurely with an error if a caught signal interrupts the function or if the semaphore is removed.

3. If sem_op is negative, the caller wants to wait until the semaphore's value becomes greater than or equal to the absolute value of sem_op. This corresponds to the allocation of resources.

    If semval is greater than or equal to the absolute value of sem_op, the absolute value of sem_op is subtracted from semval. If the SEM_UNDO flag is specified, the absolute value of sem_op is added to the semaphore's semadj value.

    If semval is less than the absolute value of sem_op, the semaphore's semncnt value is incremented and the calling thread is blocked until semval becomes greater than or equal to the absolute value of sem_op. When this change occurs, the thread is unblocked, the absolute value of sem_op is subtracted from semval, and the semaphore's semncnt value is decremented. If the SEM_UNDO flag is specified, the absolute value of sem_op is added to the semaphore's semadj value. As mentioned earlier, the thread is not put to sleep if IPC_NOWAIT is specified. Also, the sleep returns prematurely with an error if a caught signal interrupts the function or if the semaphore is removed.

> If we compare these operations to the operations allowed on a Posix semaphore, the latter allows operations of only –1 (sem_wait) and +1 (sem_post). System V semaphores allow the value to go up or down by increments other than one, and also allow waiting for the semaphore value to be 0. These more general operations, along with the fact that System V semaphores can have a set of values, is what complicates System V semaphores, compared to the simpler Posix semaphores.

11.4 semctl Function

The semctl function performs various control operations on a semaphore.

```
#include   <sys/sem.h>

int semctl(int semid, int semnum, int cmd, ... /* union semun arg */ );
```
                                    Returns: nonnegative value if OK (see text), –1 on error

The first argument *semid* identifies the semaphore, and *semnum* identifies the member of the semaphore set (0, 1, and so on, up to *nsems−1*). The *semnum* value is used only for the GETVAL, SETVAL, GETNCNT, GETZCNT, and GETPID commands.

The fourth argument is optional, depending on the *cmd* (see the comments in the union below). When required, it is the following union:

```
union semun {
  int                val;    /* used for SETVAL only */
  struct semid_ds   *buf;    /* used for IPC_SET and IPC_STAT */
  ushort            *array;  /* used for GETALL and SETALL */
};
```

This union does not appear in any system header and must be declared by the application. (We define it in our unpipc.h header, Figure C.1.) It is passed by value, not by reference. That is, the actual value of the union is the argument, not a pointer to the union.

> Unfortunately, some systems (FreeBSD and Linux) define this union as a result of including the <sys/sem.h> header, making it hard to write portable code. Even though having the system header declare this union makes sense, Unix 98 states that it must be explicitly declared by the application.

The following values for the *cmd* are supported. Unless stated otherwise, a return value of 0 indicates success, and a return value of −1 indicates an error.

GETVAL   Return the current value of semval as the return value of the function. Since a semaphore value is never negative (semval is declared as an unsigned short), a successful return value is always nonnegative.

SETVAL   Set the value of semval to *arg.val*. If this is successful, the semaphore adjustment value for this semaphore is set to 0 in all processes.

GETPID   Return the current value of sempid as the return value of the function.

GETNCNT   Return the current value of semncnt as the return value of the function.

GETZCNT   Return the current value of semzcnt as the return value of the function.

GETALL   Return the values of semval for each member of the semaphore set. The values are returned through the *arg.array* pointer, and the return value of the function is 0. Notice that the caller must allocate an array of unsigned short integers large enough to hold all the values for the set, and then set *arg.array* to point to this array.

SETALL   Set the values of semval for each member of the semaphore set. The values are specified through the *arg.array* pointer.

IPC_RMID   Remove the semaphore set specified by *semid* from the system.

IPC_SET   Set the following three members of the semid_ds structure for the semaphore set from the corresponding members in the structure pointed to by the *arg.buf* argument: sem_perm.uid, sem_perm.gid, and `sem_perm.mode`. The `sem_ctime` member of the `semid_ds` structure is also set to the current time.

IPC_STAT   Return to the caller (through the *arg.buf* argument) the current `semid_ds` structure for the specified semaphore set. Notice that the caller must first allocate a `semid_ds` structure and set *arg.buf* to point to this structure.

11.5 Simple Programs

Since System V semaphores have kernel persistence, we can demonstrate their usage by writing a small set of programs to manipulate them and seeing what happens. The values of the semaphores will be maintained by the kernel from one of our programs to the next.

semcreate Program

Our first program shown in Figure 11.2 just creates a System V semaphore set. The `-e` command-line option specifies the `IPC_EXCL` flag, and the number of semaphores in the set must be specified by the final command-line argument.

——————————————————————— svsem/semcreate.c

```
 1 #include    "unpipc.h"

 2 int
 3 main(int argc, char **argv)
 4 {
 5     int     c, oflag, semid, nsems;

 6     oflag = SVSEM_MODE | IPC_CREAT;
 7     while ( (c = Getopt(argc, argv, "e")) != -1) {
 8         switch (c) {
 9         case 'e':
10             oflag |= IPC_EXCL;
11             break;
12         }
13     }
14     if (optind != argc - 2)
15         err_quit("usage: semcreate [ -e ] <pathname> <nsems>");
16     nsems = atoi(argv[optind + 1]);

17     semid = Semget(Ftok(argv[optind], 1), nsems, oflag);
18     exit(0);
19 }
```

——————————————————————— svsem/semcreate.c

Figure 11.2 `semcreate` program.

semrmid Program

The next program, shown in Figure 11.3, removes a semaphore set from the system. A command of `IPC_RMID` is executed through the `semctl` function to remove the set.

`semsetvalues` Program

Our `semsetvalues` program (Figure 11.4) sets all the values in a semaphore set.

Get number of semaphores in set

11–15   After obtaining the semaphore ID with `semget`, we issue an `IPC_STAT` command to `semctl` to fetch the `semid_ds` structure for the semaphore. The `sem_nsems` member is the number of semaphores in the set.

Set all the values

19–24   We allocate memory for an array of `unsigned shorts`, one per set member, and copy the values from the command-line into the array. A command of `SETALL` to `semctl` sets all the values in the semaphore set.

`semgetvalues` Program

Figure 11.5 shows our `semgetvalues` program, which fetches and prints all the values in a semaphore set.

Get number of semaphores in set

11–15   After obtaining the semaphore ID with `semget`, we issue an `IPC_STAT` command to `semctl` to fetch the `semid_ds` structure for the semaphore. The `sem_nsems` member is the number of semaphores in the set.

Get all the values

16–22   We allocate memory for an array of `unsigned shorts`, one per set member, and issue a command of `GETALL` to `semctl` to fetch all the values in the semaphore set. Each value is printed.

`semops` Program

Our `semops` program, shown in Figure 11.6, executes an array of operations on a semaphore set.

Command-line options

7–19   An option of `-n` specifies the `IPC_NOWAIT` flag for each operation, and an option of `-u` specifies the `SEM_UNDO` flag for each operation. Note that the `semop` function allows us to specify a different set of flags for each member of the `sembuf` structure (that is, for the operation on each member of the set), but for simplicity we have these command-line options specify that flag for all specified operations.

Allocate memory for the operations

20–29   After opening the semaphore set with `semget`, an array of `sembuf` structures is allocated, one element for each operation specified on the command line. Unlike the previous two programs, this program allows the user to specify fewer operations than members of the semaphore set.

Execute the operations

30   `semop` executes the array of operations on the semaphore set.

svsem/semrmid.c

```
 1 #include    "unpipc.h"

 2 int
 3 main(int argc, char **argv)
 4 {
 5     int     semid;

 6     if (argc != 2)
 7         err_quit("usage: semrmid <pathname>");

 8     semid = Semget(Ftok(argv[1], 1), 0, 0);
 9     Semctl(semid, 0, IPC_RMID);

10     exit(0);
11 }
```
svsem/semrmid.c

Figure 11.3 semrmid program.

svsem/semsetvalues.c

```
 1 #include    "unpipc.h"

 2 int
 3 main(int argc, char **argv)
 4 {
 5     int     semid, nsems, i;
 6     struct semid_ds seminfo;
 7     unsigned short *ptr;
 8     union semun arg;

 9     if (argc < 2)
10         err_quit("usage: semsetvalues <pathname> [ values ... ]");

11         /* first get the number of semaphores in the set */
12     semid = Semget(Ftok(argv[1], 1), 0, 0);
13     arg.buf = &seminfo;
14     Semctl(semid, 0, IPC_STAT, arg);
15     nsems = arg.buf->sem_nsems;

16         /* now get the values from the command line */
17     if (argc != nsems + 2)
18         err_quit("%d semaphores in set, %d values specified", nsems, argc - 2);

19         /* allocate memory to hold all the values in the set, and store */
20     ptr = Calloc(nsems, sizeof(unsigned short));
21     arg.array = ptr;
22     for (i = 0; i < nsems; i++)
23         ptr[i] = atoi(argv[i + 2]);
24     Semctl(semid, 0, SETALL, arg);

25     exit(0);
26 }
```
svsem/semsetvalues.c

Figure 11.4 semsetvalues program.

svsem/semgetvalues.c

```
 1 #include      "unpipc.h"

 2 int
 3 main(int argc, char **argv)
 4 {
 5     int     semid, nsems, i;
 6     struct semid_ds seminfo;
 7     unsigned short *ptr;
 8     union semun arg;

 9     if (argc != 2)
10         err_quit("usage: semgetvalues <pathname>");

11         /* first get the number of semaphores in the set */
12     semid = Semget(Ftok(argv[1], 1), 0, 0);
13     arg.buf = &seminfo;
14     Semctl(semid, 0, IPC_STAT, arg);
15     nsems = arg.buf->sem_nsems;

16         /* allocate memory to hold all the values in the set */
17     ptr = Calloc(nsems, sizeof(unsigned short));
18     arg.array = ptr;

19         /* fetch the values and print */
20     Semctl(semid, 0, GETALL, arg);
21     for (i = 0; i < nsems; i++)
22         printf("semval[%d] = %d\n", i, ptr[i]);

23     exit(0);
24 }
```
svsem/semgetvalues.c

Figure 11.5 semgetvalues program.

svsem/semops.c

```
 1 #include      "unpipc.h"

 2 int
 3 main(int argc, char **argv)
 4 {
 5     int     c, i, flag, semid, nops;
 6     struct sembuf *ptr;

 7     flag = 0;
 8     while ( (c = Getopt(argc, argv, "nu")) != -1) {
 9         switch (c) {
10         case 'n':
11             flag |= IPC_NOWAIT; /* for each operation */
12             break;

13         case 'u':
14             flag |= SEM_UNDO;   /* for each operation */
15             break;
16         }
17     }
18     if (argc - optind < 2)      /* argc - optind = #args remaining */
19         err_quit("usage: semops [ -n ] [ -u ] <pathname> operation ...");
```

```
20      semid = Semget(Ftok(argv[optind], 1), 0, 0);
21      optind++;
22      nops = argc - optind;

23          /* allocate memory to hold operations, store, and perform */
24      ptr = Calloc(nops, sizeof(struct sembuf));
25      for (i = 0; i < nops; i++) {
26          ptr[i].sem_num = i;
27          ptr[i].sem_op = atoi(argv[optind + i]);      /* <0, 0, or >0 */
28          ptr[i].sem_flg = flag;
29      }
30      Semop(semid, ptr, nops);

31      exit(0);
32  }
```
—— *svsem/semops.c*

Figure 11.6 semops program.

Examples

We now demonstrate the five programs that we have just shown, looking at some of the features of System V semaphores.

```
solaris % touch /tmp/rich
solaris % semcreate -e /tmp/rich 3
solaris % semsetvalues /tmp/rich 1 2 3
solaris % semgetvalues /tmp/rich
semval[0] = 1
semval[1] = 2
semval[2] = 3
```

We first create a file named /tmp/rich that will be used (by ftok) to identify the semaphore set. semcreate creates a set with three members. semsetvalues sets the values to 1, 2, and 3, and these values are then printed by semgetvalues.

We now demonstrate the atomicity of the set of operations when performed on a semaphore set.

```
solaris % semops -n /tmp/rich -1 -2 -4
semctl error: Resource temporarily unavailable
solaris % semgetvalues /tmp/rich
semval[0] = 1
semval[1] = 2
semval[2] = 3
```

We specify the nonblocking flag (-n) and three operations, each of which decrements a value in the set. The first operation is OK (we can subtract 1 from the first member of the set whose value is 1), the second operation is OK (we can subtract 2 from the second member of the set whose value is 2), but the third operation cannot be performed (we cannot subtract 4 from the third member of the set whose value is 3). Since the last operation cannot be performed, and since we specified nonblocking, an error of EAGAIN is returned. (Had we not specified the nonblocking flag, our program would have just blocked.) We then verify that none of the values in the set were changed. Even though the first two operations could be performed, since the final operation could not be performed, none of the three operations are performed. The atomicity of semop means that either *all* of the operations are performed or *none* of the operations are performed.

We now demonstrate the SEM_UNDO property of System V semaphores.

```
solaris % semsetvalues /tmp/rich 1 2 3    set to known values
solaris % semops -u /tmp/rich -1 -2 -3    specify SEM_UNDO for each operation
solaris % semgetvalues /tmp/rich
semval[0] = 1                              all the changes were undone when semops terminated
semval[1] = 2
semval[2] = 3
solaris % semops /tmp/rich -1 -2 -3        do not specify SEM_UNDO
solaris % semgetvalues /tmp/rich
semval[0] = 0                              the changes were not undone
semval[1] = 0
semval[2] = 0
```

We first reset the three values to 1, 2, and 3 with semsetvalues and then specify operations of −1, −2, and −3 with our semops program. This causes all three values to become 0, but since we specify the −u flag to our semops program, the SEM_UNDO flag is specified for each of the three operations. This causes the semadj value for the three members to be set to 1, 2, and 3, respectively. Then when our semops program terminates, these three semadj values are added back to the current values of each of the three members (which are all 0), causing their final values to be 1, 2, and 3, as we verify with our semgetvalues program. We then execute our semops program again, but without the −u flag, and this leaves the three values at 0 when our semops program terminates.

11.6 File Locking

We can provide a version of our my_lock and my_unlock functions from Figure 10.19, implemented using System V semaphores. We show this in Figure 11.7.

First try an exclusive create

13-17   We must guarantee that only one process initializes the semaphore, so we specify IPC_CREAT | IPC_EXCL. If this succeeds, that process calls semctl to initialize the semaphore value to 1. If we start multiple processes at about the same time, each of which calls our my_lock function, only one will create the semaphore (assuming it does not already exist), and then that process initializes the semaphore too.

Semaphore already exists; just open

18-20   The first call to semget will return an error of EEXIST to the other processes, which then call semget again, but without the IPC_CREAT | IPC_EXCL flags.

Wait for semaphore to be initialized

21-28   We encounter the same race condition that we talked about with the initialization of System V semaphores in Section 11.2. To avoid this, any process that finds that the semaphore already exists must call semctl with a command of IPC_STAT to look at

lock/locksvsem.c

```
 1 #include    "unpipc.h"

 2 #define LOCK_PATH   "/tmp/svsemlock"
 3 #define MAX_TRIES   10

 4 int     semid, initflag;
 5 struct sembuf postop, waitop;

 6 void
 7 my_lock(int fd)
 8 {
 9     int     oflag, i;
10     union semun arg;
11     struct semid_ds seminfo;

12     if (initflag == 0) {
13         oflag = IPC_CREAT | IPC_EXCL | SVSEM_MODE;
14         if ( (semid = semget(Ftok(LOCK_PATH, 1), 1, oflag)) >= 0) {
15                 /* success, we're the first so initialize */
16             arg.val = 1;
17             Semctl(semid, 0, SETVAL, arg);

18         } else if (errno == EEXIST) {
19                 /* someone else has created; make sure it's initialized */
20             semid = Semget(Ftok(LOCK_PATH, 1), 1, SVSEM_MODE);
21             arg.buf = &seminfo;
22             for (i = 0; i < MAX_TRIES; i++) {
23                 Semctl(semid, 0, IPC_STAT, arg);
24                 if (arg.buf->sem_otime != 0)
25                     goto init;
26                 sleep(1);
27             }
28             err_quit("semget OK, but semaphore not initialized");

29         } else
30             err_sys("semget error");
31     init:
32         initflag = 1;
33         postop.sem_num = 0;      /* and init the two semop() structures */
34         postop.sem_op = 1;
35         postop.sem_flg = SEM_UNDO;
36         waitop.sem_num = 0;
37         waitop.sem_op = -1;
38         waitop.sem_flg = SEM_UNDO;
39     }
40     Semop(semid, &waitop, 1);   /* down by 1 */
41 }

42 void
43 my_unlock(int fd)
44 {
45     Semop(semid, &postop, 1);   /* up by 1 */
46 }
```

lock/locksvsem.c

Figure 11.7 File locking using System V semaphores.

the `sem_otime` value for the semaphore. Once this value is nonzero, we know that the process that created the semaphore has initialized it, and has called `semop` (the call to `semop` is at the end of this function). If the value is still 0 (which should happen very infrequently), we `sleep` for 1 second and try again. We limit the number of times that we try this, to avoid sleeping forever.

Initialize `sembuf` structures

33–38   As we mentioned earlier, there is no guaranteed order of the members in the `sembuf` structure, so we cannot statically initialize them. Instead, we allocate two of these structures and fill them in at run time, when the process calls `my_lock` for the first time. We specify the `SEM_UNDO` flag, so that if a process terminates while holding the lock, the kernel will release the lock (see Exercise 10.3).

Creating a semaphore on its first use is easy (each process tries to create it but ignores an error if the semaphore already exists), but removing it after all the processes are done is much harder. In the case of a printer daemon that uses the sequence number file to assign job numbers, the semaphore would remain in existence all the time. But other applications might want to delete the semaphore when the file is deleted. In this case, a record lock might be better than a semaphore.

11.7 Semaphore Limits

As with System V message queues, there are certain system limits with System V semaphores, most of which arise from their original System V implementation (Section 3.8). These are shown in Figure 11.8. The first column is the traditional System V name for the kernel variable that contains this limit.

Name	Description	DUnix 4.0B	Solaris 2.6
`semmni`	max # unique semaphore sets, systemwide	16	10
`semmsl`	max # semaphores per semaphore set	25	25
`semmns`	max # semaphores, systemwide	400	60
`semopm`	max # operations per `semop` call	10	10
`semmnu`	max # of undo structures, systemwide		30
`semume`	max # of undo entries per undo structure	10	10
`semvmx`	max value of any semaphore	32767	32767
`semaem`	max adjust-on-exit value	16384	16384

Figure 11.8 Typical limits for System V semaphores.

Apparently no `semmnu` limit exists for Digital Unix.

Example

The program in Figure 11.9 determines the limits shown in Figure 11.8.

—————————————————————————— svsem/limits.c

```
 1 #include    "unpipc.h"

 2         /* following are upper limits of values to try */
 3 #define MAX_NIDS    4096        /* max # semaphore IDs */
 4 #define MAX_VALUE   1024*1024   /* max semaphore value */
 5 #define MAX_MEMBERS 4096        /* max # semaphores per semaphore set */
 6 #define MAX_NOPS    4096        /* max # operations per semop() */
 7 #define MAX_NPROC   Sysconf(_SC_CHILD_MAX)

 8 int
 9 main(int argc, char **argv)
10 {
11     int    i, j, semid, sid[MAX_NIDS], pipefd[2];
12     int    semmni, semvmx, semmsl, semmns, semopn, semaem, semume, semmnu;
13     pid_t *child;
14     union semun arg;
15     struct sembuf ops[MAX_NOPS];

16         /* see how many sets with one member we can create */
17     for (i = 0; i <= MAX_NIDS; i++) {
18         sid[i] = semget(IPC_PRIVATE, 1, SVSEM_MODE | IPC_CREAT);
19         if (sid[i] == -1) {
20             semmni = i;
21             printf("%d identifiers open at once\n", semmni);
22             break;
23         }
24     }
25         /* before deleting, find maximum value using sid[0] */
26     for (j = 7; j < MAX_VALUE; j += 8) {
27         arg.val = j;
28         if (semctl(sid[0], 0, SETVAL, arg) == -1) {
29             semvmx = j - 8;
30             printf("max semaphore value = %d\n", semvmx);
31             break;
32         }
33     }
34     for (j = 0; j < i; j++)
35         Semctl(sid[j], 0, IPC_RMID);

36         /* determine max # semaphores per semaphore set */
37     for (i = 1; i <= MAX_MEMBERS; i++) {
38         semid = semget(IPC_PRIVATE, i, SVSEM_MODE | IPC_CREAT);
39         if (semid == -1) {
40             semmsl = i - 1;
41             printf("max of %d members per set\n", semmsl);
42             break;
43         }
44         Semctl(semid, 0, IPC_RMID);
45     }

46         /* find max of total # of semaphores we can create */
47     semmns = 0;
48     for (i = 0; i < semmni; i++) {
49         sid[i] = semget(IPC_PRIVATE, semmsl, SVSEM_MODE | IPC_CREAT);
50         if (sid[i] == -1) {
```

```
51               /*
52                * Up to this point each set has been created with semmsl
53                * members.  But this just failed, so try recreating this
54                * final set with one fewer member per set, until it works.
55                */
56               for (j = semmsl - 1; j > 0; j--) {
57                   sid[i] = semget(IPC_PRIVATE, j, SVSEM_MODE | IPC_CREAT);
58                   if (sid[i] != -1) {
59                       semmns += j;
60                       printf("max of %d semaphores\n", semmns);
61                       Semctl(sid[i], 0, IPC_RMID);
62                       goto done;
63                   }
64               }
65               err_quit("j reached 0, semmns = %d", semmns);
66           }
67           semmns += semmsl;
68       }
69       printf("max of %d semaphores\n", semmns);
70   done:
71       for (j = 0; j < i; j++)
72           Semctl(sid[j], 0, IPC_RMID);

73           /* see how many operations per semop() */
74       semid = Semget(IPC_PRIVATE, semmsl, SVSEM_MODE | IPC_CREAT);
75       for (i = 1; i <= MAX_NOPS; i++) {
76           ops[i - 1].sem_num = i - 1;
77           ops[i - 1].sem_op = 1;
78           ops[i - 1].sem_flg = 0;
79           if (semop(semid, ops, i) == -1) {
80               if (errno != E2BIG)
81                   err_sys("expected E2BIG from semop");
82               semopn = i - 1;
83               printf("max of %d operations per semop()\n", semopn);
84               break;
85           }
86       }
87       Semctl(semid, 0, IPC_RMID);

88           /* determine the max value of semadj */
89           /* create one set with one semaphore */
90       semid = Semget(IPC_PRIVATE, 1, SVSEM_MODE | IPC_CREAT);
91       arg.val = semvmx;
92       Semctl(semid, 0, SETVAL, arg);   /* set value to max */
93       for (i = semvmx - 1; i > 0; i--) {
94           ops[0].sem_num = 0;
95           ops[0].sem_op = -i;
96           ops[0].sem_flg = SEM_UNDO;
97           if (semop(semid, ops, 1) != -1) {
98               semaem = i;
99               printf("max value of adjust-on-exit = %d\n", semaem);
100              break;
101          }
102      }
103      Semctl(semid, 0, IPC_RMID);
```

```
104              /* determine max # undo structures */
105              /* create one set with one semaphore; init to 0 */
106          semid = Semget(IPC_PRIVATE, 1, SVSEM_MODE | IPC_CREAT);
107          arg.val = 0;
108          Semctl(semid, 0, SETVAL, arg);   /* set semaphore value to 0 */
109          Pipe(pipefd);
110          child = Malloc(MAX_NPROC * sizeof(pid_t));
111          for (i = 0; i < MAX_NPROC; i++) {
112              if ( (child[i] = fork()) == -1) {
113                  semmnu = i - 1;
114                  printf("fork failed, semmnu at least %d\n", semmnu);
115                  break;
116              } else if (child[i] == 0) {
117                  ops[0].sem_num = 0; /* child does the semop() */
118                  ops[0].sem_op = 1;
119                  ops[0].sem_flg = SEM_UNDO;
120                  j = semop(semid, ops, 1);   /* 0 if OK, -1 if error */
121                  Write(pipefd[1], &j, sizeof(j));
122                  sleep(30);             /* wait to be killed by parent */
123                  exit(0);               /* just in case */
124              }
125              /* parent reads result of semop() */
126              Read(pipefd[0], &j, sizeof(j));
127              if (j == -1) {
128                  semmnu = i;
129                  printf("max # undo structures = %d\n", semmnu);
130                  break;
131              }
132          }
133          Semctl(semid, 0, IPC_RMID);
134          for (j = 0; j <= i && child[j] > 0; j++)
135              Kill(child[j], SIGINT);

136              /* determine max # adjust entries per process */
137              /* create one set with max # of semaphores */
138          semid = Semget(IPC_PRIVATE, semmsl, SVSEM_MODE | IPC_CREAT);
139          for (i = 0; i < semmsl; i++) {
140              arg.val = 0;
141              Semctl(semid, i, SETVAL, arg);  /* set semaphore value to 0 */
142              ops[i].sem_num = i;
143              ops[i].sem_op = 1;       /* add 1 to the value */
144              ops[i].sem_flg = SEM_UNDO;
145              if (semop(semid, ops, i + 1) == -1) {
146                  semume = i;
147                  printf("max # undo entries per process = %d\n", semume);
148                  break;
149              }
150          }
151          Semctl(semid, 0, IPC_RMID);
152      exit(0);
153  }
```
svsem/limits.c

Figure 11.9 Determine the system limits on System V semaphores.

11.8 Summary

The following changes occur when moving from Posix semaphores to System V semaphores:

1. System V semaphores consist of a set of values. When specifying a group of semaphore operations to apply to a set, either all of the operations are performed or none of the operations are performed.

2. Three operations may be applied to each member of a semaphore set: test for the value being 0, add an integer to the value, and subtract an integer from the value (assuming that the value remains nonnegative). The only operations allowed for a Posix semaphore are to increment by one and to decrement by one (assuming that the value remains nonnegative).

3. Creating a System V semaphore set is tricky because it requires two operations to create the set and then initialize the values, which can lead to race conditions.

4. System V semaphores provide an "undo" feature that reverses a semaphore operation upon process termination.

Exercises

11.1   Figure 6.8 was a modification to Figure 6.6 that accepted an identifier instead of a pathname to specify the queue. We showed that the identifier is all we need to know to access a System V message queue (assuming we have adequate permission). Make similar modifications to Figure 11.6 and show that the same feature applies to System V semaphores.

11.2   What happens in Figure 11.7 if the LOCK_PATH file does not exist?

Part 4

Shared Memory

12

Shared Memory Introduction

12.1 Introduction

Shared memory is the fastest form of IPC available. Once the memory is mapped into the address space of the processes that are sharing the memory region, no kernel involvement occurs in passing data between the processes. What is normally required, however, is some form of synchronization between the processes that are storing and fetching information to and from the shared memory region. In Part 3, we discussed various forms of synchronization: mutexes, condition variables, read–write locks, record locks, and semaphores.

> What we mean by "no kernel involvement" is that the processes do not execute any system calls into the kernel to pass the data. Obviously, the kernel must establish the memory mappings that allow the processes to share the memory, and then manage this memory over time (handle page faults, and the like).

Consider the normal steps involved in the client–server file copying program that we used as an example for the various types of message passing (Figure 4.1).

- The server reads from the input file. The file data is read by the kernel into its memory and then copied from the kernel to the process.

- The server writes this data in a message, using a pipe, FIFO, or message queue. These forms of IPC normally require the data to be copied from the process to the kernel.

> We use the qualifier *normally* because Posix message queues can be implemented using memory-mapped I/O (the mmap function that we describe in this chapter), as we showed in Section 5.8 and as we show in the solution to Exercise 12.2. In Figure 12.1, we assume

303

that Posix message queues are implemented within the kernel, which is another possibility. But pipes, FIFOs, and System V message queues all involve copying the data from the process to the kernel for a `write` or `msgsnd`, or copying the data from the kernel to the process for a `read` or `msgrcv`.

- The client reads the data from the IPC channel, normally requiring the data to be copied from the kernel to the process.

- Finally, the data is copied from the client's buffer, the second argument to the `write` function, to the output file.

A total of four copies of the data are normally required. Additionally, these four copies are done between the kernel and a process, often an expensive copy (more expensive than copying data within the kernel, or copying data within a single process). Figure 12.1 depicts this movement of the data between the client and server, through the kernel.

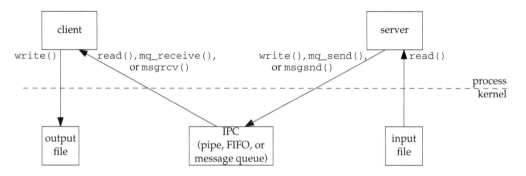

Figure 12.1 Flow of file data from server to client.

The problem with these forms of IPC—pipes, FIFOs, and message queues—is that for two processes to exchange information, the information has to go through the kernel.

Shared memory provides a way around this by letting two or more processes share a region of memory. The processes must, of course, coordinate or synchronize the use of the shared memory among themselves. (Sharing a common piece of memory is similar to sharing a disk file, such as the sequence number file used in all the file locking examples.) Any of the techniques described in Part 3 can be used for this synchronization.

The steps for the client–server example are now as follows:

- The server gets access to a shared memory object using (say) a semaphore.

- The server reads from the input file into the shared memory object. The second argument to the `read`, the address of the data buffer, points into the shared memory object.

- When the read is complete, the server notifies the client, using a semaphore.

- The client writes the data from the shared memory object to the output file.

This scenario is depicted in Figure 12.2.

Figure 12.2 Copying file data from server to client using shared memory.

In this figure the data is copied only twice—from the input file into shared memory and from shared memory to the output file. We draw one dashed box enclosing the client and the shared memory object, and another dashed box enclosing the server and the shared memory object, to reinforce that the shared memory object appears in the address space of both the client and the server.

The concepts involved in using shared memory are similar for both the Posix interface and the System V interface. We describe the former in Chapter 13 and the latter in Chapter 14.

In this chapter, we return to our sequence-number-increment example that we started in Chapter 9. But we now store the sequence number in memory instead of in a file.

We first reiterate that memory is *not* shared by default between a parent and child across a `fork`. The program in Figure 12.3 has a parent and child increment a global integer named `count`.

Create and initialize semaphore

12-14   We create and initialize a semaphore that protects what we think is a shared variable (the global `count`). Since this assumption is false, this semaphore is not really needed. Notice that we remove the semaphore name from the system by calling `sem_unlink`, but although this removes the pathname, it has no effect on the semaphore that is already open. We do this so that the pathname is removed from the filesystem even if the program aborts.

Set standard output unbuffered and `fork`

15   We set standard output unbuffered because both the parent and child will be writing to it. This prevents interleaving of the output from the two processes.

16-29   The parent and child each execute a loop that increments the counter the specified number of times, being careful to increment the variable only when the semaphore is held.

```
                                                                   ──── shm/incr1.c
 1 #include    "unpipc.h"

 2 #define SEM_NAME    "mysem"

 3 int    count = 0;

 4 int
 5 main(int argc, char **argv)
 6 {
 7     int    i, nloop;
 8     sem_t  *mutex;

 9     if (argc != 2)
10         err_quit("usage: incr1 <#loops>");
11     nloop = atoi(argv[1]);

12         /* create, initialize, and unlink semaphore */
13     mutex = Sem_open(Px_ipc_name(SEM_NAME), O_CREAT | O_EXCL, FILE_MODE, 1);
14     Sem_unlink(Px_ipc_name(SEM_NAME));

15     setbuf(stdout, NULL);       /* stdout is unbuffered */
16     if (Fork() == 0) {          /* child */
17         for (i = 0; i < nloop; i++) {
18             Sem_wait(mutex);
19             printf("child: %d\n", count++);
20             Sem_post(mutex);
21         }
22         exit(0);
23     }
24         /* parent */
25     for (i = 0; i < nloop; i++) {
26         Sem_wait(mutex);
27         printf("parent: %d\n", count++);
28         Sem_post(mutex);
29     }
30     exit(0);
31 }
                                                                   ──── shm/incr1.c
```

Figure 12.3 Parent and child both increment the same global.

If we run this program and look only at the output when the system switches between the parent and child, we have the following:

```
child: 0              child runs first, counter starts at 0
child: 1
. . .
child: 678
child: 679
parent: 0             child is stopped, parent runs, counter starts at 0
parent: 1
. . .
parent: 1220
parent: 1221
child: 680            parent is stopped, child runs
```

```
child: 681
 . . .
child: 2078
child: 2079
parent: 1222          child is stopped, parent runs
parent: 1223
```

                               and so on

As we can see, both processes have their own copy of the global `count`. Each starts with the value of this variable as 0, and each increments its own copy of this variable. Figure 12.4 shows the parent before calling `fork`.

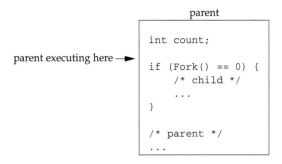

Figure 12.4 Parent before calling `fork`.

When `fork` is called, the child starts with its own copy of the parent's data space. Figure 12.5 shows the two processes after `fork` returns.

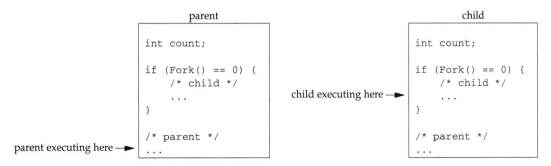

Figure 12.5 Parent and child after `fork` returns.

We see that the parent and child each have their own copy of the variable `count`.

12.2 mmap, munmap, and msync Functions

The `mmap` function maps either a file or a Posix shared memory object into the address space of a process. We use this function for three purposes:

1. with a regular file to provide memory-mapped I/O (Section 12.3),

2. with special files to provide anonymous memory mappings (Sections 12.4 and 12.5), and

3. with shm_open to provide Posix shared memory between unrelated processes (Chapter 13).

```
#include <sys/mman.h>

void *mmap(void *addr, size_t len, int prot, int flags, int fd, off_t offset);
```
                        Returns: starting address of mapped region if OK, MAP_FAILED on error

addr can specify the starting address within the process of where the descriptor *fd* should be mapped. Normally, this is specified as a null pointer, telling the kernel to choose the starting address. In any case, the return value of the function is the starting address of where the descriptor has been mapped.

len is the number of bytes to map into the address space of the process, starting at *offset* bytes from the beginning of the file. Normally, *offset* is 0. Figure 12.6 shows this mapping.

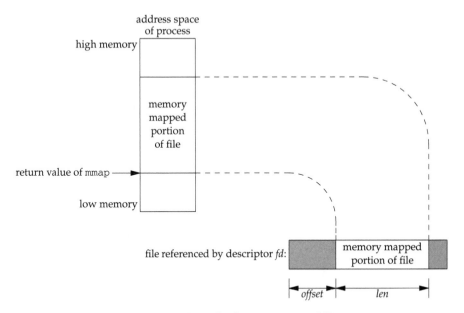

Figure 12.6 Example of memory-mapped file.

The protection of the memory-mapped region is specified by the *prot* argument using the constants in Figure 12.7. The common value for this argument is PROT_READ | PROT_WRITE for read–write access.

prot	Description
PROT_READ	data can be read
PROT_WRITE	data can be written
PROT_EXEC	data can be executed
PROT_NONE	data cannot be accessed

Figure 12.7 *prot* argument for mmap.h>.

flags	Description
MAP_SHARED	changes are shared
MAP_PRIVATE	changes are private
MAP_FIXED	interpret the *addr* argument exactly

Figure 12.8 *flags* argument for mmap.

The *flags* are specified by the constants in Figure 12.8. Either the MAP_SHARED or the MAP_PRIVATE flag must be specified, optionally ORed with MAP_FIXED. If MAP_PRIVATE is specified, then modifications to the mapped data by the calling process are visible only to that process and do not change the underlying object (either a file object or a shared memory object). If MAP_SHARED is specified, modifications to the mapped data by the calling process are visible to all processes that are sharing the object, and these changes do modify the underlying object.

For portability, MAP_FIXED should not be specified. If it is not specified, but *addr* is not a null pointer, then it is implementation dependent as to what the implementation does with *addr*. The nonnull value of *addr* is normally taken as a hint about where the memory should be located. Portable code should specify *addr* as a null pointer and should not specify MAP_FIXED.

One way to share memory between a parent and child is to call mmap with MAP_SHARED before calling fork. Posix.1 then guarantees that memory mappings in the parent are retained in the child. Furthermore, changes made by the parent are visible to the child and vice versa. We show an example of this shortly.

After mmap returns success, the *fd* argument can be closed. This has no effect on the mapping that was established by mmap.

To remove a mapping from the address space of the process, we call munmap.

```
#include <sys/mman.h>

int munmap(void *addr, size_t len);
```
                                                              Returns: 0 if OK, −1 on error

The *addr* argument is the address that was returned by mmap, and the *len* is the size of that mapped region. Further references to these addresses result in the generation of a SIGSEGV signal to the process (assuming, of course, that a later call to mmap does not reuse this portion of the address space).

If the mapped region was mapped using MAP_PRIVATE, the changes made are discarded.

In Figure 12.6, the kernel's virtual memory algorithm keeps the memory-mapped file (typically on disk) synchronized with the memory-mapped region in memory, assuming a MAP_SHARED segment. That is, if we modify a location in memory that is memory-mapped to a file, then at some time later the kernel will update the file accordingly. But sometimes, we want to make certain that the file on disk corresponds to what is in the memory-mapped region, and we call msync to perform this synchronization.

```
#include <sys/mman.h>

int msync(void *addr, size_t len, int flags);
```
                                                    Returns: 0 if OK, −1 on error

The *addr* and *len* arguments normally refer to the entire memory-mapped region of memory, although subsets of this region can also be specified. The *flags* argument is formed from the combination of constants shown in Figure 12.9.

Constant	Description
MS_ASYNC	perform asynchronous writes
MS_SYNC	perform synchronous writes
MS_INVALIDATE	invalidate cached data

Figure 12.9 *flags* for msync function.

One of the two constants MS_ASYNC and MS_SYNC must be specified, but not both. The difference in these two is that MS_ASYNC returns once the write operations are queued by the kernel, whereas MS_SYNC returns only after the write operations are complete. If MS_INVALIDATE is also specified, all in-memory copies of the file data that are inconsistent with the file data are invalidated. Subsequent references will obtain data from the file.

Why Use mmap?

Our description of mmap so far has implied a memory-mapped file: some file that we open and then map into our address space by calling mmap. The nice feature in using a memory-mapped file is that all the I/O is done under the covers by the kernel, and we just write code that fetches and stores values in the memory-mapped region. We never call read, write, or lseek. Often, this can simplify our code.

> Recall our implementation of Posix message queues using mmap and the storing of values into a msg_hdr structure in Figure 5.30 and the fetching of values from a msg_hdr structure in Figure 5.32.

Beware of some caveats, however, in that not all files can be memory mapped. Trying to map a descriptor that refers to a terminal or a socket, for example, generates an error return from mmap. These types of descriptors must be accessed using read and write (or variants thereof).

Another use of mmap is to provide shared memory between unrelated processes. In this case, the actual contents of the file become the initial contents of the memory that is shared, and any changes made by the processes to this shared memory are then copied back to the file (providing filesystem persistence). This assumes that MAP_SHARED is specified, which is required to share the memory between processes.

> Details on the implementation of mmap and its relationship to the kernel's virtual memory algorithms are provided in [McKusick et al. 1996] for 4.4BSD and in [Vahalia 1996] and [Goodheart and Cox 1994] for SVR4.

12.3 Increment Counter in a Memory-Mapped File

We now modify Figure 12.3 (which did not work) so that the parent and child share a piece of memory in which the counter is stored. To do so, we use a memory-mapped file: a file that we open and then mmap into our address space. Figure 12.10 shows the new program.

New command-line argument

11–14   We have a new command-line argument that is the name of a file that will be memory mapped. We open the file for reading and writing, creating the file if it does not exist, and then write an integer with a value of 0 to the file.

mmap then close descriptor

15–16   We call mmap to map the file that was just opened into the memory of this process. The first argument is a null pointer, telling the system to pick the starting address. The length is the size of an integer, and we specify read–write access. By specifying a fourth argument of MAP_SHARED, any changes made by the parent will be seen by the child, and vice versa. The return value is the starting address of the memory region that will be shared, and we store it in ptr.

fork

20–34   We set standard output unbuffered and call fork. The parent and child both increment the integer counter pointed to by ptr.

Memory-mapped files are handled specially by fork, in that memory mappings created by the parent before calling fork are shared by the child. Therefore, what we have done by opening the file and calling mmap with the MAP_SHARED flag is provide a piece of memory that is shared between the parent and child. Furthermore, since the shared memory is a memory-mapped file, any changes to the shared memory (the piece of memory pointed to by ptr of size sizeof(int)) are also reflected in the actual file (whose name was specified by the command-line argument).

——— *shm/incr2.c*

```
 1 #include     "unpipc.h"

 2 #define SEM_NAME    "mysem"

 3 int
 4 main(int argc, char **argv)
 5 {
 6     int     fd, i, nloop, zero = 0;
 7     int     *ptr;
 8     sem_t   *mutex;

 9     if (argc != 3)
10         err_quit("usage: incr2 <pathname> <#loops>");
11     nloop = atoi(argv[2]);

12         /* open file, initialize to 0, map into memory */
13     fd = Open(argv[1], O_RDWR | O_CREAT, FILE_MODE);
14     Write(fd, &zero, sizeof(int));
15     ptr = Mmap(NULL, sizeof(int), PROT_READ | PROT_WRITE, MAP_SHARED, fd, 0);
16     Close(fd);

17         /* create, initialize, and unlink semaphore */
18     mutex = Sem_open(Px_ipc_name(SEM_NAME), O_CREAT | O_EXCL, FILE_MODE, 1);
19     Sem_unlink(Px_ipc_name(SEM_NAME));

20     setbuf(stdout, NULL);           /* stdout is unbuffered */
21     if (Fork() == 0) {              /* child */
22         for (i = 0; i < nloop; i++) {
23             Sem_wait(mutex);
24             printf("child: %d\n", (*ptr)++);
25             Sem_post(mutex);
26         }
27         exit(0);
28     }
29         /* parent */
30     for (i = 0; i < nloop; i++) {
31         Sem_wait(mutex);
32         printf("parent: %d\n", (*ptr)++);
33         Sem_post(mutex);
34     }
35     exit(0);
36 }
```
——— *shm/incr2.c*

Figure 12.10 Parent and child incrementing a counter in shared memory.

If we execute this program, we see that the memory pointed to by `ptr` is indeed shared between the parent and child. We show only the values when the kernel switches between the two processes.

```
solaris % incr2 /tmp/temp.1 10000
child: 0                   child starts first
child: 1
 . . .
child: 128
child: 129
parent: 130                child is stopped, parent starts
```

```
parent: 131
.  .  .
parent: 636
parent: 637
child: 638              parent is stopped, child starts
child: 639

.  .  .
child: 1517
child: 1518
parent: 1519            child is stopped, parent starts
parent: 1520

.  .  .
parent: 19999          final line of output
solaris % od -D /tmp/temp.1
0000000 0000020000
0000004
```

Since the file was memory mapped, we can look at the file after the program terminates with the od program and see that the final value of the counter (20,000) is indeed stored in the file.

Figure 12.11 is a modification of Figure 12.5 showing the shared memory, and showing that the semaphore is also shared. We show the semaphore as being in the kernel, but as we mentioned with Posix semaphores, this is not a requirement. Whatever implementation is used, the semaphore must have at least kernel persistence. The semaphore could be stored as another memory-mapped file, as we demonstrated in Section 10.15.

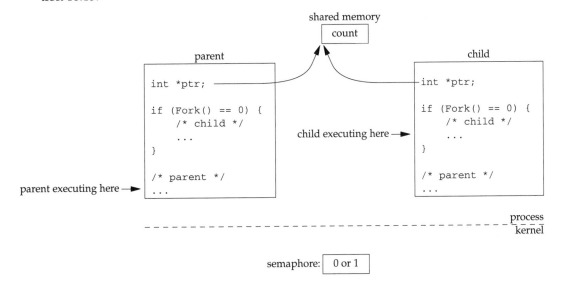

Figure 12.11 Parent and child sharing memory and a semaphore.

We show that the parent and child each have their own copy of the pointer ptr, but each copy points to the same integer in shared memory: the counter that both processes increment.

We now modify our program from Figure 12.10 to use a Posix memory-based semaphore instead of a Posix named semaphore, and store this semaphore in the shared memory. Figure 12.12 is the new program.

shm/incr3.c

```
 1 #include    "unpipc.h"

 2 struct shared {
 3     sem_t    mutex;           /* the mutex: a Posix memory-based semaphore */
 4     int      count;           /* and the counter */
 5 } shared;

 6 int
 7 main(int argc, char **argv)
 8 {
 9     int      fd, i, nloop;
10     struct shared *ptr;

11     if (argc != 3)
12         err_quit("usage: incr3 <pathname> <#loops>");
13     nloop = atoi(argv[2]);

14         /* open file, initialize to 0, map into memory */
15     fd = Open(argv[1], O_RDWR | O_CREAT, FILE_MODE);
16     Write(fd, &shared, sizeof(struct shared));
17     ptr = Mmap(NULL, sizeof(struct shared), PROT_READ | PROT_WRITE,
18             MAP_SHARED, fd, 0);
19     Close(fd);

20         /* initialize semaphore that is shared between processes */
21     Sem_init(&ptr->mutex, 1, 1);

22     setbuf(stdout, NULL);        /* stdout is unbuffered */
23     if (Fork() == 0) {           /* child */
24         for (i = 0; i < nloop; i++) {
25             Sem_wait(&ptr->mutex);
26             printf("child: %d\n", ptr->count++);
27             Sem_post(&ptr->mutex);
28         }
29         exit(0);
30     }
31         /* parent */
32     for (i = 0; i < nloop; i++) {
33         Sem_wait(&ptr->mutex);
34         printf("parent: %d\n", ptr->count++);
35         Sem_post(&ptr->mutex);
36     }
37     exit(0);
38 }
```

shm/incr3.c

Figure 12.12 Counter and semaphore are both in shared memory.

Define structure that will be in shared memory

2-5   We define a structure containing the integer counter and a semaphore to protect it. This structure will be stored in the shared memory object.

Map the memory

14-19   We create the file that will be mapped, and write a structure of 0 to the file. All we are doing is initializing the counter, because the value of the semaphore will be initialized by the call to `sem_init`. Nevertheless, writing an entire structure of 0 is simpler than to try to write only an integer of 0.

Initialize semaphore

20-21   We are now using a memory-based semaphore, instead of a named semaphore, so we call `sem_init` to initialize its value to 1. The second argument must be nonzero, to indicate that the semaphore is being shared between processes.

Figure 12.13 is a modification of Figure 12.11, noting the change that the semaphore has moved from the kernel into shared memory.

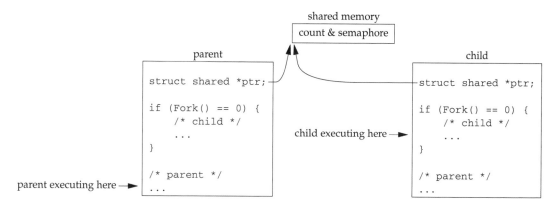

Figure 12.13   Counter and semaphore are now in shared memory.

12.4 4.4BSD Anonymous Memory Mapping

Our examples in Figures 12.10 and 12.12 work fine, but we have to create a file in the filesystem (the command-line argument), call `open`, and then `write` zeros to the file to initialize it. When the purpose of calling `mmap` is to provide a piece of mapped memory that will be shared across a `fork`, we can simplify this scenario, depending on the implementation.

1.   4.4BSD provides *anonymous memory mapping*, which completely avoids having to create or open a file. Instead, we specify the *flags* as `MAP_SHARED` | `MAP_ANON` and the *fd* as –1. The *offset* is ignored. The memory is initialized to 0. We show an example of this in Figure 12.14.

2.   SVR4 provides `/dev/zero`, which we `open`, and we use the resulting descriptor in the call to `mmap`. This device returns bytes of 0 when read, and anything written to the device is discarded. We show an example of this in Figure 12.15.

(Many Berkeley-derived implementations, such as SunOS 4.1.x and BSD/OS 3.1, also support /dev/zero.)

Figure 12.14 shows the only portion of Figure 12.10 that changes when we use 4.4BSD anonymous memory mapping.

shm/incr_map_anon.c
```
3 int
4 main(int argc, char **argv)
5 {
6     int     i, nloop;
7     int     *ptr;
8     sem_t   *mutex;

9     if (argc != 2)
10        err_quit("usage: incr_map_anon <#loops>");
11    nloop = atoi(argv[1]);

12        /* map into memory */
13    ptr = Mmap(NULL, sizeof(int), PROT_READ | PROT_WRITE,
14            MAP_SHARED | MAP_ANON, -1, 0);
```
shm/incr_map_anon.c

Figure 12.14 4.4BSD anonymous memory mapping.

6-11   The automatic variables fd and zero are gone, as is the command-line argument that specified the pathname that was created.

12-14   We no longer open a file. The MAP_ANON flag is specified in the call to mmap, and the fifth argument (the descriptor) is –1.

12.5 SVR4 /dev/zero Memory Mapping

Figure 12.15 shows the only portion of Figure 12.10 that changes when we map /dev/zero.

shm/incr_dev_zero.c
```
3 int
4 main(int argc, char **argv)
5 {
6     int     fd, i, nloop;
7     int     *ptr;
8     sem_t   *mutex;

9     if (argc != 2)
10        err_quit("usage: incr_dev_zero <#loops>");
11    nloop = atoi(argv[1]);

12        /* open /dev/zero, map into memory */
13    fd = Open("/dev/zero", O_RDWR);
14    ptr = Mmap(NULL, sizeof(int), PROT_READ | PROT_WRITE, MAP_SHARED, fd, 0);
15    Close(fd);
```
shm/incr_dev_zero.c

Figure 12.15 SVR4 memory mapping of /dev/zero.

6-11   The automatic variable zero is gone, as is the command-line argument that specified the pathname that was created.

12-15   We open /dev/zero, and the descriptor is then used in the call to mmap. We are guaranteed that the memory-mapped region is initialized to 0.

12.6 Referencing Memory-Mapped Objects

When a regular file is memory mapped, the size of the mapping in memory (the second argument to mmap) normally equals the size of the file. For example, in Figure 12.12 the file size is set to the size of our shared structure by write, and this value is also the size of the memory mapping. But these two sizes—the file size and the memory-mapped size—can differ.

We will use the program shown in Figure 12.16 to explore the mmap function in more detail.

———————————————————————————————— shm/test1.c

```
 1 #include      "unpipc.h"

 2 int
 3 main(int argc, char **argv)
 4 {
 5     int      fd, i;
 6     char     *ptr;
 7     size_t   filesize, mmapsize, pagesize;

 8     if (argc != 4)
 9         err_quit("usage: test1 <pathname> <filesize> <mmapsize>");
10     filesize = atoi(argv[2]);
11     mmapsize = atoi(argv[3]);

12         /* open file: create or truncate; set file size */
13     fd = Open(argv[1], O_RDWR | O_CREAT | O_TRUNC, FILE_MODE);
14     Lseek(fd, filesize - 1, SEEK_SET);
15     Write(fd, "", 1);

16     ptr = Mmap(NULL, mmapsize, PROT_READ | PROT_WRITE, MAP_SHARED, fd, 0);
17     Close(fd);

18     pagesize = Sysconf(_SC_PAGESIZE);
19     printf("PAGESIZE = %ld\n", (long) pagesize);

20     for (i = 0; i < max(filesize, mmapsize); i += pagesize) {
21         printf("ptr[%d] = %d\n", i, ptr[i]);
22         ptr[i] = 1;
23         printf("ptr[%d] = %d\n", i + pagesize - 1, ptr[i + pagesize - 1]);
24         ptr[i + pagesize - 1] = 1;
25     }
26     printf("ptr[%d] = %d\n", i, ptr[i]);

27     exit(0);
28 }
```

———————————————————————————————— shm/test1.c

Figure 12.16 Memory mapping when mmap equals file size.

Command-line arguments

8–11   The command-line arguments specify the pathname of the file that will be created and memory mapped, the size to which that file is set, and the size of the memory mapping.

Create, open, truncate file; set file size

12–15   The file being opened is created if it does not exist, or truncated to a size of 0 if it already exists. The size of the file is then set to the specified size by seeking to that size minus 1 byte and writing 1 byte.

Memory map file

16–17   The file is memory mapped, using the size specified as the final command-line argument. The descriptor is then closed.

Print page size

18–19   The page size of the implementation is obtained using `sysconf` and printed.

Read and store the memory-mapped region

20–26   The memory-mapped region is read (the first byte of each page and the last byte of each page), and the values printed. We expect the values to all be 0. We also set the first and last bytes of the page to 1. We expect one of the references to generate a signal eventually, which will terminate the program. When the `for` loop terminates, we print the first byte of the next page, expecting this to fail (assuming that the program has not already failed).

The first scenario that we show is when the file size equals the memory-mapped size, but this size is not a multiple of the page size.

```
solaris % ls -l foo
foo: No such file or directory
solaris % test1 foo 5000 5000
PAGESIZE = 4096
ptr[0] = 0
ptr[4095] = 0
ptr[4096] = 0
ptr[8191] = 0
Segmentation Fault(coredump)
solaris % ls -l foo
-rw-r--r--   1 rstevens other1      5000 Mar 20 17:18 foo
solaris % od -b -A d foo
0000000 001 000 000 000 000 000 000 000 000 000 000 000 000 000 000 000
0000016 000 000 000 000 000 000 000 000 000 000 000 000 000 000 000 000
*
0004080 000 000 000 000 000 000 000 000 000 000 000 000 000 000 000 001
0004096 001 000 000 000 000 000 000 000 000 000 000 000 000 000 000 000
0004112 000 000 000 000 000 000 000 000 000 000 000 000 000 000 000 000
*
0005000
```

The page size is 4096 bytes, and we are able to read the entire second page (indexes 4096 through 8191), but a reference to the third page (index 8192) generates SIGSEGV, which the shell prints as "Segmentation Fault." Even though we set ptr[8191] to 1, this value is not written to the file, and the file's size remains 5000. The kernel lets us read and write that portion of the final page beyond our mapping (since the kernel's memory protection works with pages), but anything that we write to this extension is not written to the file. The other 3 bytes that we set to 1, indexes 0, 4095, and 4096, are copied back to the file, which we verify with the od command. (The -b option says to print the bytes in octal, and the -A d option says to print the addresses in decimal.) Figure 12.17 depicts this example.

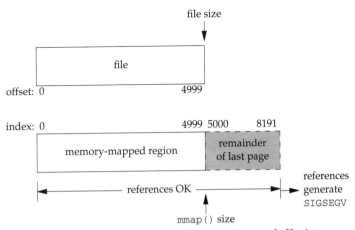

Figure 12.17 Memory mapping when mmap size equals file size.

If we run our example under Digital Unix, we see similar results, but the page size is now 8192.

```
alpha % ls -l foo
foo not found
alpha % test1 foo 5000 5000
PAGESIZE = 8192
ptr[0] = 0
ptr[8191] = 0
Memory fault(coredump)
alpha % ls -l foo
-rw-r--r--   1 rstevens operator     5000 Mar 21 08:40 foo
```

We are still able to reference beyond the end of our memory-mapped region but within that page of memory (indexes 5000 through 8191). Referencing ptr[8192] generates SIGSEGV, as we expect.

In our next example with Figure 12.16, we specify a memory mapping (15000 bytes) that is larger than the file size (5000 bytes).

```
solaris % rm foo
solaris % test1 foo 5000 15000
PAGESIZE = 4096
ptr[0] = 0
ptr[4095] = 0
ptr[4096] = 0
```

```
ptr[8191] = 0
Bus Error(coredump)
solaris % ls -l foo
-rw-r--r--   1 rstevens other1      5000 Mar 20 17:37 foo
```

The results are similar to our earlier example when the file size and the memory map size were the same (both 5000). This example generates SIGBUS (which the shell prints as "Bus Error"), whereas the previous example generated SIGSEGV. The difference is that SIGBUS means we have referenced within our memory-mapped region but beyond the size of the underlying object. The SIGSEGV in the previous example meant we had referenced beyond the end of our memory-mapped region. What we have shown here is that the kernel knows the size of the underlying object that is mapped (the file foo in this case), even though we have closed the descriptor for that object. The kernel allows us to specify a size to mmap that is larger than the size of this object, but we cannot reference beyond its end (except for the bytes within the final page that are beyond the end of the object, indexes 5000 through 8191). Figure 12.18 depicts this example.

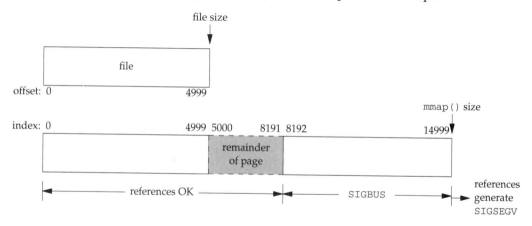

Figure 12.18 Memory mapping when mmap size exceeds file size.

Our next program is shown in Figure 12.19. It shows a common technique for handling a file that is growing: specify a memory-map size that is larger than the file, keep track of the file's current size (making certain not to reference beyond the current end-of-file), and then just let the file's size increase as more data is written to the file.

Open file

9-11   We open a file, creating it if it does not exist or truncating it if it already exists. The file is memory mapped with a size of 32768, even though the file's current size is 0.

Increase file size

12-16   We increase the size of the file, 4096 bytes at a time, by calling ftruncate (Section 13.3), and fetch the byte that is now the final byte of the file.

shm/test2.c

```
 1 #include    "unpipc.h"

 2 #define FILE    "test.data"
 3 #define SIZE    32768

 4 int
 5 main(int argc, char **argv)
 6 {
 7     int     fd, i;
 8     char    *ptr;

 9         /* open: create or truncate; then mmap file */
10     fd = Open(FILE, O_RDWR | O_CREAT | O_TRUNC, FILE_MODE);
11     ptr = Mmap(NULL, SIZE, PROT_READ | PROT_WRITE, MAP_SHARED, fd, 0);

12     for (i = 4096; i <= SIZE; i += 4096) {
13         printf("setting file size to %d\n", i);
14         Ftruncate(fd, i);
15         printf("ptr[%d] = %d\n", i - 1, ptr[i - 1]);
16     }

17     exit(0);
18 }
```

shm/test2.c

Figure 12.19 Memory map example that lets the file size grow.

When we run this program, we see that as we increase the size of the file, we are able to reference the new data through our established memory map.

```
alpha % ls -l test.data
test.data: No such file or directory
alpha % test2
setting file size to 4096
ptr[4095] = 0
setting file size to 8192
ptr[8191] = 0
setting file size to 12288
ptr[12287] = 0
setting file size to 16384
ptr[16383] = 0
setting file size to 20480
ptr[20479] = 0
setting file size to 24576
ptr[24575] = 0
setting file size to 28672
ptr[28671] = 0
setting file size to 32768
ptr[32767] = 0
alpha % ls -l test.data
-rw-r--r--   1 rstevens other1      32768 Mar 20 17:53 test.data
```

This example shows that the kernel keeps track of the size of the underlying object that is memory mapped (the file test.data in this example), and we are always able to reference bytes that are within the current file size that are also within our memory map. We obtain identical results under Solaris 2.6.

This section has dealt with memory-mapped files and mmap. In Exercise 13.1, we modify our two programs to work with Posix shared memory and see the same results.

12.7   Summary

Shared memory is the fastest form of IPC available, because one copy of the data in the shared memory is available to all the threads or processes that share the memory. Some form of synchronization is normally required, however, to coordinate the various threads or processes that are sharing the memory.

This chapter has focused on the mmap function and the mapping of regular files into memory, because this is one way to share memory between related or unrelated processes. Once we have memory mapped a file, we no longer use read, write, or lseek to access the file; instead, we just fetch or store the memory locations that have been mapped to the file by mmap. Changing explicit file I/O into fetches and stores of memory can often simplify our programs and sometimes increase performance.

When the memory is to be shared across a subsequent fork, this can be simplified by not creating a regular file to map, but using anonymous memory mapping instead. This involves either a new flag of MAP_ANON (for Berkeley-derived kernels) or mapping /dev/zero (for SVR4-derived kernels).

Our reason for covering mmap in such detail is both because memory mapping of files is a useful technique and because mmap is used for Posix shared memory, which is the topic of the next chapter.

Also available are four additional functions (that we do not cover) defined by Posix dealing with memory management:

- mlockall causes all of the memory of the process to be memory resident. munlockall undoes this locking.

- mlock causes a specified range of addresses of the process to be memory resident, where the function arguments are a starting address and a number of bytes from that address. munlock unlocks a specified region of memory.

Exercises

12.1   What would happen in Figure 12.19 if we executed the code within the for loop one more time?

12.2   Assume that we have two processes, a sender and a receiver, with the former just sending messages to the latter. Assume that System V message queues are used and draw a diagram of how the messages go from the sender to the receiver. Now assume that our implementation of Posix message queues from Section 5.8 is used, and draw a diagram of the transfer of messages.

12.3   With `mmap` and `MAP_SHARED`, we said that the kernel virtual memory algorithm updates the actual file with any modifications that are made to the memory image. Read the manual page for `/dev/zero` to determine what happens when the kernel writes the changes back to the file.

12.4   Modify Figure 12.10 to specify `MAP_PRIVATE` instead of `MAP_SHARED`, and verify that the results are similar to the results from Figure 12.3. What are the contents of the file that is memory mapped?

12.5   In Section 6.9, we mentioned that one way to `select` on a System V message queue is to create a piece of anonymous shared memory, create a child, and let the child block in its call to `msgrcv`, reading the message into shared memory. The parent also creates two pipes; one is used by the child to notify the parent that a message is ready in shared memory, and the other pipe is used by the parent to notify the child that the shared memory is now available. This allows the parent to `select` on the read end of the pipe, along with any other descriptors on which it wants to `select`. Code this solution. Call our `my_shm` function (Figure A.46) to allocate the anonymous shared memory object. Use our `msgcreate` and `msgsnd` programs from Section 6.6 to create the message queue, and then place records onto the queue. The parent should just print the size and type of each message that the child reads.

13

Posix Shared Memory

13.1 Introduction

The previous chapter described shared memory in general terms, along with the mmap function. Examples were shown that used mmap to provide shared memory between a parent and child:

- using a memory-mapped file (Figure 12.10),
- using 4.4BSD anonymous memory mapping (Figure 12.14), and
- using /dev/zero anonymous memory mapping (Figure 12.15).

We now extend the concept of shared memory to include memory that is shared between unrelated processes. Posix.1 provides two ways to share memory between unrelated processes.

1. *Memory-mapped files*: a file is opened by open, and the resulting descriptor is mapped into the address space of the process by mmap. We described this technique in Chapter 12 and showed its use when sharing memory between a parent and child. Memory-mapped files can also be shared between unrelated processes.

2. *Shared memory objects*: the function shm_open opens a Posix.1 IPC name (perhaps a pathname in the filesystem), returning a descriptor that is then mapped into the address space of the process by mmap. We describe this technique in this chapter.

Both techniques require the call to mmap. What differs is how the descriptor that is an argument to mmap is obtained: by open or by shm_open. We show this in Figure 13.1. Both are called *memory objects* by Posix.

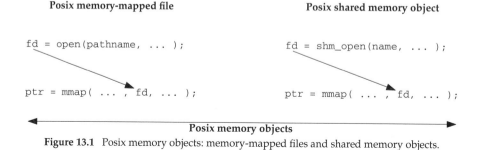

Figure 13.1   Posix memory objects: memory-mapped files and shared memory objects.

13.2   `shm_open` and `shm_unlink` Functions

The two-step process involved with Posix shared memory requires

1. calling shm_open, specifying a name argument, to either create a new shared memory object or to open an existing shared memory object, followed by

2. calling mmap to map the shared memory into the address space of the calling process.

The name argument used with shm_open is then used by any other processes that want to share this memory.

> The reason for this two-step process, instead of a single step that would take a name and return an address within the memory of the calling process, is that mmap already existed when Posix invented its form of shared memory. Clearly, a single function could do both steps. The reason that shm_open returns a descriptor (recall that mq_open returns an mqd_t value and sem_open returns a pointer to a sem_t value) is that an open descriptor is what mmap uses to map the memory object into the address space of the process.

```
#include <sys/mman.h>

int shm_open(const char *name, int oflag, mode_t mode);
```
                                                  Returns: nonnegative descriptor if OK, −1 on error
```
int shm_unlink(const char *name);
```
                                                                  Returns: 0 if OK, −1 on error

We described the rules about the *name* argument in Section 2.2.

The *oflag* argument must contain either O_RDONLY (read-only) or O_RDWR (read–write), and the following flags can also be specified: O_CREAT, O_EXCL, or O_TRUNC. The O_CREAT and O_EXCL flags were described in Section 2.3. If O_TRUNC is specified along with O_RDWR, then if the shared memory object already exists, it is truncated to 0-length.

mode specifies the permission bits (Figure 2.4) and is used when the O_CREAT flag is specified. Note that unlike the mq_open and sem_open functions, the *mode* argument to shm_open must always be specified. If the O_CREAT flag is not specified, then this argument can be specified as 0.

The return value from shm_open is an integer descriptor that is then used as the fifth argument to mmap.

The shm_unlink function removes the name of a shared memory object. As with all the other unlink functions (the unlink of a pathname in the filesystem, the mq_unlink of a Posix message queue, and the sem_unlink of a Posix named semaphore), unlinking a name has no effect on existing references to the underlying object, until all references to that object are closed. Unlinking a name just prevents any subsequent call to open, mq_open, or sem_open from succeeding.

13.3 ftruncate and fstat Functions

When dealing with mmap, the size of either a regular file or a shared memory object can be changed by calling ftruncate.

```
#include <unistd.h>

int ftruncate(int fd, off_t length);
```
                                                        Returns: 0 if OK, −1 on error

Posix defines the function slightly differently for regular files versus shared memory objects.

- For a regular file: If the size of the file was larger than *length*, the extra data is discarded. If the size of the file was smaller than *length*, whether the file is changed or its size is increased is unspecified. Indeed, for a regular file, the portable way to extend the size of the file to *length* bytes is to lseek to offset *length–1* and write 1 byte of data. Fortunately, almost all Unix implementations support extending a file with ftruncate.

- For a shared memory object: ftruncate sets the size of the object to *length*.

We call ftruncate to specify the size of a newly created shared memory object or to change the size of an existing object. When we open an existing shared memory object, we can call fstat to obtain information about the object.

```
#include <sys/types.h>
#include <sys/stat.h>

int fstat(int fd, struct stat *buf);
```

Returns: 0 if OK, −1 on error

A dozen or more members are in the `stat` structure (Chapter 4 of APUE talks about all the members in detail), but only four contain information when *fd* refers to a shared memory object.

```
struct stat {
    ...
    mode_t  st_mode;    /* mode: S_I{RW}{USR,GRP,OTH} */
    uid_t   st_uid;     /* user ID of owner */
    gid_t   st_gid;     /* group ID of owner */
    off_t   st_size;    /* size in bytes */
    ...
};
```

We show examples of these two function in the next section.

> Unfortunately, Posix.1 does not specify the initial contents of a newly created shared memory object. The description of the `shm_open` function states that "The shared memory object shall have a size of 0." The description of `ftruncate` specifies that for a regular file (not shared memory), "If the file is extended, the extended area shall appear as if it were zero-filled." But nothing is said in the description of `ftruncate` about the new contents of a shared memory object that is extended. The Posix.1 Rationale states that "If the memory object is extended, the contents of the extended areas are zeros" but this is the Rationale, not the official standard. When the author asked on the `comp.std.unix` newsgroup about this detail, the opinion was expressed that some vendors objected to an initialize-to-0 requirement, because of the overhead. If a newly extended piece of shared memory is not initialized to some value (i.e., if the contents are left as is), this could be a security hole.

13.4   Simple Programs

We now develop some simple programs that operate on Posix shared memory.

`shmcreate` Program

Our `shmcreate` program, shown in Figure 13.2, creates a shared memory object with a specified name and length.

19–22   `shm_open` creates the shared memory object. If the `-e` option is specified, it is an error if the object already exists. `ftruncate` sets the length, and `mmap` maps the object into the address space of the process. The program then terminates. Since Posix shared memory has at least kernel persistence, this does not remove the shared memory object.

pxshm/shmcreate.c

```
 1 #include    "unpipc.h"

 2 int
 3 main(int argc, char **argv)
 4 {
 5     int     c, fd, flags;
 6     char    *ptr;
 7     off_t   length;

 8     flags = O_RDWR | O_CREAT;
 9     while ( (c = Getopt(argc, argv, "e")) != -1) {
10         switch (c) {
11         case 'e':
12             flags |= O_EXCL;
13             break;
14         }
15     }
16     if (optind != argc - 2)
17         err_quit("usage: shmcreate [ -e ] <name> <length>");
18     length = atoi(argv[optind + 1]);

19     fd = Shm_open(argv[optind], flags, FILE_MODE);
20     Ftruncate(fd, length);

21     ptr = Mmap(NULL, length, PROT_READ | PROT_WRITE, MAP_SHARED, fd, 0);

22     exit(0);
23 }
```

pxshm/shmcreate.c

Figure 13.2 Create a Posix shared memory object of a specified size.

`shmunlink` Program

Figure 13.3 shows our trivial program that calls `shm_unlink` to remove the name of a shared memory object from the system.

pxshm/shmunlink.c

```
 1 #include    "unpipc.h"

 2 int
 3 main(int argc, char **argv)
 4 {
 5     if (argc != 2)
 6         err_quit("usage: shmunlink <name>");

 7     Shm_unlink(argv[1]);

 8     exit(0);
 9 }
```

pxshm/shmunlink.c

Figure 13.3 Unlink the name of a Posix shared memory object.

`shmwrite` Program

Figure 13.4 is our `shmwrite` program, which writes a pattern of 0, 1, 2, ..., 254, 255, 0, 1, and so on, to a shared memory object.

—— pxshm/shmwrite.c

```
 1 #include    "unpipc.h"

 2 int
 3 main(int argc, char **argv)
 4 {
 5     int    i, fd;
 6     struct stat stat;
 7     unsigned char *ptr;

 8     if (argc != 2)
 9         err_quit("usage: shmwrite <name>");

10         /* open, get size, map */
11     fd = Shm_open(argv[1], O_RDWR, FILE_MODE);
12     Fstat(fd, &stat);
13     ptr = Mmap(NULL, stat.st_size, PROT_READ | PROT_WRITE,
14             MAP_SHARED, fd, 0);
15     Close(fd);

16         /* set: ptr[0] = 0, ptr[1] = 1, etc. */
17     for (i = 0; i < stat.st_size; i++)
18         *ptr++ = i % 256;

19     exit(0);
20 }
```

—— pxshm/shmwrite.c

Figure 13.4 Open a shared memory object and fill it with a pattern.

10–15   The shared memory object is opened by `shm_open`, and we fetch its size with `fstat`. We then map it using `mmap` and `close` the descriptor.

16–18   The pattern is written to the shared memory.

`shmread` Program

Our `shmread` program, shown in Figure 13.5, verifies the pattern that was written by `shmwrite`.

—— pxshm/shmread.c

```
 1 #include    "unpipc.h"

 2 int
 3 main(int argc, char **argv)
 4 {
 5     int    i, fd;
 6     struct stat stat;
 7     unsigned char c, *ptr;

 8     if (argc != 2)
 9         err_quit("usage: shmread <name>");
```

```
10              /* open, get size, map */
11      fd = Shm_open(argv[1], O_RDONLY, FILE_MODE);
12      Fstat(fd, &stat);
13      ptr = Mmap(NULL, stat.st_size, PROT_READ,
14              MAP_SHARED, fd, 0);
15      Close(fd);

16              /* check that ptr[0] = 0, ptr[1] = 1, etc. */
17      for (i = 0; i < stat.st_size; i++)
18          if ( (c = *ptr++) != (i % 256))
19              err_ret("ptr[%d] = %d", i, c);

20      exit(0);
21 }
```
———————————————————————————————————— *pxshm/shmread.c*

Figure 13.5 Open a shared memory object and verify its data pattern.

10–15   The shared memory object is opened read-only, its size is obtained by `fstat`, it is mapped by `mmap` (for reading only), and the descriptor is closed.

16–19   The pattern written by `shmwrite` is verified.

Examples

We create a shared memory object whose length is 123,456 bytes under Digital Unix 4.0B named `/tmp/myshm`.

```
alpha % shmcreate /tmp/myshm 123456
alpha % ls -l /tmp/myshm
-rw-r--r--    1 rstevens system     123456 Dec 10 14:33 /tmp/myshm
alpha % od -c /tmp/myshm
0000000   \0  \0  \0  \0  \0  \0  \0  \0  \0  \0  \0  \0  \0  \0  \0  \0
*
0361100
```

We see that a file with the same name is created in the filesystem. Using the `od` program, we can verify that the object's initial contents are all 0. (Octal 0361100, the byte offset just beyond the final byte of the file, equals 123,456.)

Next, we run our `shmwrite` program and use `od` to verify that the initial contents are as expected.

```
alpha % shmwrite /tmp/myshm
alpha % od -x /tmp/myshm | head -4
0000000   0100 0302 0504 0706 0908 0b0a 0d0c 0f0e
0000020   1110 1312 1514 1716 1918 1b1a 1d1c 1f1e
0000040   2120 2322 2524 2726 2928 2b2a 2d2c 2f2e
0000060   3130 3332 3534 3736 3938 3b3a 3d3c 3f3e
alpha % shmread /tmp/myshm
alpha % shmunlink /tmp/myshm
```

We verify the shared memory object's contents with `shmread` and then unlink the name.

If we run our `shmcreate` program under Solaris 2.6, we see that a file is created in the `/tmp` directory with the specified size.

```
solaris % shmcreate -e /testshm 123
solaris % ls -l /tmp/.*testshm*
-rw-r--r--   1 rstevens other1   123 Dec 10 14:40 /tmp/.SHMtestshm
```

Example

We now provide a simple example in Figure 13.6 to demonstrate that a shared memory
object can be memory mapped starting at different addresses in different processes.

pxshm/test3.c
```
 1 #include    "unpipc.h"

 2 int
 3 main(int argc, char **argv)
 4 {
 5     int     fd1, fd2, *ptr1, *ptr2;
 6     pid_t   childpid;
 7     struct stat stat;

 8     if (argc != 2)
 9         err_quit("usage: test3 <name>");

10     shm_unlink(Px_ipc_name(argv[1]));
11     fd1 = Shm_open(Px_ipc_name(argv[1]), O_RDWR | O_CREAT | O_EXCL, FILE_MODE);
12     Ftruncate(fd1, sizeof(int));
13     fd2 = Open("/etc/motd", O_RDONLY);
14     Fstat(fd2, &stat);

15     if ( (childpid = Fork()) == 0) {
16         /* child */
17         ptr2 = Mmap(NULL, stat.st_size, PROT_READ, MAP_SHARED, fd2, 0);
18         ptr1 = Mmap(NULL, sizeof(int), PROT_READ | PROT_WRITE,
19                 MAP_SHARED, fd1, 0);
20         printf("child: shm ptr = %p, motd ptr = %p\n", ptr1, ptr2);

21         sleep(5);
22         printf("shared memory integer = %d\n", *ptr1);
23         exit(0);
24     }
25         /* parent: mmap in reverse order from child */
26     ptr1 = Mmap(NULL, sizeof(int), PROT_READ | PROT_WRITE, MAP_SHARED, fd1, 0);
27     ptr2 = Mmap(NULL, stat.st_size, PROT_READ, MAP_SHARED, fd2, 0);
28     printf("parent: shm ptr = %p, motd ptr = %p\n", ptr1, ptr2);
29     *ptr1 = 777;
30     Waitpid(childpid, NULL, 0);

31     exit(0);
32 }
```
pxshm/test3.c

Figure 13.6 Shared memory can appear at different addresses in different processes.

10-14   We create a shared memory segment whose name is the command-line argument,
set its size to the size of an integer, and then open the file /etc/motd.

15-30   We fork, and both the parent and child call mmap twice, but in a different order.
Each prints the starting address of each memory-mapped region. The child then sleeps

for 5 seconds, the parent stores the value 777 in the shared memory region, and then the child prints this value.

When we run this program, we see that the shared memory object is memory mapped at different starting addresses in the parent and child.

```
solaris % test3 test3.data
parent: shm ptr = eee30000, motd ptr = eee20000
child: shm ptr = eee20000, motd ptr = eee30000
shared memory integer = 777
```

Nevertheless, the parent stores 777 into 0xeee30000, and the child reads this value from 0xeee20000. The pointers ptr1 in the parent and child both point to the same shared memory segment, even though the value of each pointer is different in each process.

13.5 Incrementing a Shared Counter

We now develop an example similar to the one shown in Section 12.3, in which multiple processes increment a counter that is stored in shared memory. We store the counter in shared memory and use a named semaphore for synchronization, but we no longer need a parent–child relationship. Since Posix shared memory objects and Posix named semaphores are referenced by names, the various processes that are incrementing the counter can be unrelated, as long as each knows the IPC names and each has adequate permission for the IPC objects (shared memory and semaphore).

Figure 13.7 shows the server that creates the shared memory object, creates and initializes the semaphore, and then terminates.

Create shared memory object

13–19   We call shm_unlink in case the shared memory object still exists, followed by shm_open to create the object. The size of the object is set to the size of our shmstruct structure by ftruncate, and then mmap maps the object into our address space. The descriptor is closed.

Create and initialize semaphore

20–22   We call sem_unlink, in case the semaphore still exists, followed by sem_open to create the named semaphore and initialize it to 1. It will be used as a mutex by any process that increments the counter in the shared memory object. The semaphore is then closed.

Terminate

23   The process terminates. Since Posix shared memory has at least kernel persistence, the object remains in existence until all open references are closed (when this process terminates there are no open references) *and* explicitly unlinked.

Our program must use different names for the shared memory object and the semaphore. There is no guarantee that the implementation adds anything to the Posix IPC names to differentiate among message queues, semaphores, and shared memory. We have seen that Solaris prefixes these three types of names with .MQ, .SEM, and .SHM, but Digital Unix does not.

pxshm/server1.c

```
 1 #include    "unpipc.h"

 2 struct shmstruct {                /* struct stored in shared memory */
 3     int     count;
 4 };
 5 sem_t  *mutex;                    /* pointer to named semaphore */

 6 int
 7 main(int argc, char **argv)
 8 {
 9     int     fd;
10     struct shmstruct *ptr;

11     if (argc != 3)
12         err_quit("usage: server1 <shmname> <semname>");

13     shm_unlink(Px_ipc_name(argv[1]));   /* OK if this fails */
14         /* create shm, set its size, map it, close descriptor */
15     fd = Shm_open(Px_ipc_name(argv[1]), O_RDWR | O_CREAT | O_EXCL, FILE_MODE);
16     Ftruncate(fd, sizeof(struct shmstruct));
17     ptr = Mmap(NULL, sizeof(struct shmstruct), PROT_READ | PROT_WRITE,
18             MAP_SHARED, fd, 0);
19     Close(fd);

20     sem_unlink(Px_ipc_name(argv[2]));   /* OK if this fails */
21     mutex = Sem_open(Px_ipc_name(argv[2]), O_CREAT | O_EXCL, FILE_MODE, 1);
22     Sem_close(mutex);

23     exit(0);
24 }
```

pxshm/server1.c

Figure 13.7 Program that creates and initializes shared memory and semaphore.

Figure 13.8 shows our client program that increments the counter in shared memory some number of times, obtaining the semaphore each time it increments the counter.

Open shared memory

15-18   shm_open opens the shared memory object, which must already exist (since O_CREAT is not specified). The memory is mapped into the address space of the process by mmap, and the descriptor is then closed.

Open semaphore

19   The named semaphore is opened.

Obtain semaphore and increment counter

20-26   The counter is incremented the number of times specified by the command-line argument. We print the old value of the counter each time, along with the process ID, since we will run multiple copies of this program at the same time.

─── *pxshm/client1.c*

```
 1 #include    "unpipc.h"

 2 struct shmstruct {                    /* struct stored in shared memory */
 3     int     count;
 4 };
 5 sem_t  *mutex;                        /* pointer to named semaphore */

 6 int
 7 main(int argc, char **argv)
 8 {
 9     int     fd, i, nloop;
10     pid_t   pid;
11     struct shmstruct *ptr;

12     if (argc != 4)
13         err_quit("usage: client1 <shmname> <semname> <#loops>");
14     nloop = atoi(argv[3]);

15     fd = Shm_open(Px_ipc_name(argv[1]), O_RDWR, FILE_MODE);
16     ptr = Mmap(NULL, sizeof(struct shmstruct), PROT_READ | PROT_WRITE,
17               MAP_SHARED, fd, 0);
18     Close(fd);

19     mutex = Sem_open(Px_ipc_name(argv[2]), 0);

20     pid = getpid();
21     for (i = 0; i < nloop; i++) {
22         Sem_wait(mutex);
23         printf("pid %ld: %d\n", (long) pid, ptr->count++);
24         Sem_post(mutex);
25     }
26     exit(0);
27 }
```

─── *pxshm/client1.c*

Figure 13.8 Program that increments a counter in shared memory.

We first start the server and then run three copies of the client in the background.

```
solaris % server1 shm1 sem1      creates and initializes shared memory and semaphore

solaris % client1 shm1 sem1 10000 &   client1 shm1 sem1 10000 & \
client1 shm1 sem1 10000 &
[2] 17976                         process IDs output by shell
[3] 17977
[4] 17978
pid 17977: 0                      and this process runs first
pid 17977: 1
. . .                             process 17977 continues
pid 17977: 32
pid 17976: 33                     kernel switches processes
. . .                             process 17976 continues
pid 17976: 707
pid 17978: 708                    kernel switches processes
. . .                             process 17978 continues
```

```
pid 17978: 852
pid 17977: 853                          kernel switches processes
   . . .                                and so on
pid 17977: 29998
pid 17977: 29999                        final value output, which is correct
```

13.6 Sending Messages to a Server

We now modify our producer–consumer example as follows. A server is started that creates a shared memory object in which messages are placed by client processes. Our server just prints these messages, although this could be generalized to do things similarly to the syslog daemon, which is described in Chapter 13 of UNPv1. We call these other processes clients, because that is how they appear to our server, but they may well be servers of some form to other clients. For example, a Telnet server is a client of the syslog daemon when it sends log messages to the daemon.

Instead of using one of the message passing techniques that we described in Part 2, shared memory is used to contain the messages. This, of course, necessitates some form of synchronization between the clients that are storing messages and the server that is retrieving and printing the messages. Figure 13.9 shows the overall design.

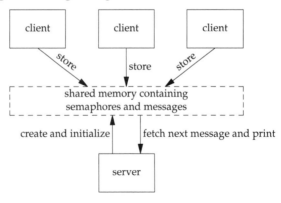

Figure 13.9 Multiple clients sending messages to a server through shared memory.

What we have here are multiple producers (the clients) and a single consumer (the server). The shared memory appears in the address space of the server and in the address space of each client.

Figure 13.10 is our cliserv2.h header, which defines a structure with the layout of the shared memory object.

Basic semaphores and variables

5–8   The three Posix memory-based semaphores, mutex, nempty, and nstored, serve the same purpose as the semaphores in our producer–consumer example in Section 10.6. The variable nput is the index (0, 1, ... NMESG-1) of the next location to store a message. Since we have multiple producers, this variable must be in the shared memory and can be referenced only while the mutex is held.

————————————————————————————————— pxshm/cliserv2.h

```
 1 #include    "unpipc.h"

 2 #define MESGSIZE    256         /* max #bytes per message, incl. null at end */
 3 #define NMESG        16         /* max #messages */

 4 struct shmstruct {             /* struct stored in shared memory */
 5     sem_t  mutex;              /* three Posix memory-based semaphores */
 6     sem_t  nempty;
 7     sem_t  nstored;
 8     int    nput;              /* index into msgoff[] for next put */
 9     long   noverflow;         /* #overflows by senders */
10     sem_t  noverflowmutex;    /* mutex for noverflow counter */
11     long   msgoff[NMESG];      /* offset in shared memory of each message */
12     char   msgdata[NMESG * MESGSIZE];  /* the actual messages */
13 };
```

————————————————————————————————— pxshm/cliserv2.h

Figure 13.10 Header that defines layout of shared memory.

Overflow counter

9–10   The possibility exists that a client wants to send a message but all the message slots are taken. But if the client is actually a server of some type (perhaps an FTP server or an HTTP server), the client does not want to wait for the server to free up a slot. Therefore, we will write our clients so that they do not block but increment the `noverflow` counter when this happens. Since this overflow counter is also shared among all the clients and the server, it too requires a mutex so that its value is not corrupted.

Message offsets and data

11–12   The array `msgoff` contains offsets into the `msgdata` array of where each message begins. That is, `msgoff[0]` is 0, `msgoff[1]` is 256 (the value of `MESGSIZE`), `msgoff[2]` is 512, and so on.

Be sure to understand that we must use *offsets* such as these when dealing with shared memory, because the shared memory object can get mapped into a different physical address in each process that maps the object. That is, the return value from `mmap` can be different for each process that calls `mmap` for the same shared memory object. For this reason, we cannot use *pointers* within the shared memory object that contain actual addresses of variables within the object.

Figure 13.11 is our server that waits for a message to be placed into shared memory by one of the clients, and then prints the message.

Create shared memory object

10–16   `shm_unlink` is called first to remove the shared memory object, if it still exists. The object is created by `shm_open` and then mapped into the address space by `mmap`. The descriptor is then closed.

Initialize array of offsets

17–19   The array of offsets is initialized to contain the offset of each message.

pxshm/server2.c

```
 1 #include    "cliserv2.h"

 2 int
 3 main(int argc, char **argv)
 4 {
 5     int     fd, index, lastnoverflow, temp;
 6     long    offset;
 7     struct shmstruct *ptr;

 8     if (argc != 2)
 9         err_quit("usage: server2 <name>");

10         /* create shm, set its size, map it, close descriptor */
11     shm_unlink(Px_ipc_name(argv[1]));    /* OK if this fails */
12     fd = Shm_open(Px_ipc_name(argv[1]), O_RDWR | O_CREAT | O_EXCL, FILE_MODE);
13     ptr = Mmap(NULL, sizeof(struct shmstruct), PROT_READ | PROT_WRITE,
14                MAP_SHARED, fd, 0);
15     Ftruncate(fd, sizeof(struct shmstruct));
16     Close(fd);

17         /* initialize the array of offsets */
18     for (index = 0; index < NMESG; index++)
19         ptr->msgoff[index] = index * MESGSIZE;

20         /* initialize the semaphores in shared memory */
21     Sem_init(&ptr->mutex, 1, 1);
22     Sem_init(&ptr->nempty, 1, NMESG);
23     Sem_init(&ptr->nstored, 1, 0);
24     Sem_init(&ptr->noverflowmutex, 1, 1);

25         /* this program is the consumer */
26     index = 0;
27     lastnoverflow = 0;
28     for ( ; ; ) {
29         Sem_wait(&ptr->nstored);
30         Sem_wait(&ptr->mutex);
31         offset = ptr->msgoff[index];
32         printf("index = %d: %s\n", index, &ptr->msgdata[offset]);
33         if (++index >= NMESG)
34             index = 0;          /* circular buffer */
35         Sem_post(&ptr->mutex);
36         Sem_post(&ptr->nempty);

37         Sem_wait(&ptr->noverflowmutex);
38         temp = ptr->noverflow;  /* don't printf while mutex held */
39         Sem_post(&ptr->noverflowmutex);
40         if (temp != lastnoverflow) {
41             printf("noverflow = %d\n", temp);
42             lastnoverflow = temp;
43         }
44     }

45     exit(0);
46 }
```

pxshm/server2.c

Figure 13.11 Our server that fetches and prints the messages from shared memory.

Initialize semaphores

20–24   The four memory-based semaphores in the shared memory object are initialized. The second argument to sem_init is nonzero for each call, since the semaphore is in shared memory and will be shared between processes.

Wait for message, and then print

25–36   The first half of the for loop is the standard consumer algorithm: wait for nstored to be greater than 0, wait for the mutex, process the data, release the mutex, and increment nempty.

Handle overflows

37–43   Each time around the loop, we also check for overflows. We test whether the counter noverflows has changed from its previous value, and if so, print and save the new value. Notice that we fetch the current value of the counter while the noverflowmutex is held, but then release it before comparing and possibly printing it. This demonstrates the general rule that we should always write our code to perform the minimum number of operations while a mutex is held.

Our client program is shown in Figure 13.12.

Command-line arguments

10–13   The first command-line argument is the name of the shared memory object, the next is the number of messages to store for the server, and the last one is the number of microseconds to pause between each message. By starting multiple copies of our client and specifying a small value for this pause, we can force an overflow to occur, and verify that the server handles it correctly.

Open and map shared memory

14–18   We open the shared memory object, assuming that it has already been created and initialized by the server, and then map it into our address space. The descriptor can then be closed.

Store messages

19–31   Our client follows the basic algorithm for the consumer but instead of calling sem_wait(nempty), which is where the consumer blocks if there is no room in the buffer for its message, we call sem_trywait, which will not block. If the value of the semaphore is 0, an error of EAGAIN is returned. We detect this error and increment the overflow counter.

> sleep_us is a function from Figures C.9 and C.10 of APUE. It sleeps for the specified number of microseconds, and is implemented by calling either select or poll.

32–37   While the mutex semaphore is held we obtain the value of offset and increment nput, but we then release the mutex before copying the message into the shared memory. We should do only those operations that must be protected while holding the semaphore.

—————————————————————————— pxshm/client2.c

```
1 #include    "cliserv2.h"

2 int
3 main(int argc, char **argv)
4 {
5     int     fd, i, nloop, nusec;
6     pid_t   pid;
7     char    mesg[MESGSIZE];
8     long    offset;
9     struct shmstruct *ptr;

10    if (argc != 4)
11        err_quit("usage: client2 <name> <#loops> <#usec>");
12    nloop = atoi(argv[2]);
13    nusec = atoi(argv[3]);

14        /* open and map shared memory that server must create */
15    fd = Shm_open(Px_ipc_name(argv[1]), O_RDWR, FILE_MODE);
16    ptr = Mmap(NULL, sizeof(struct shmstruct), PROT_READ | PROT_WRITE,
17              MAP_SHARED, fd, 0);
18    Close(fd);

19    pid = getpid();
20    for (i = 0; i < nloop; i++) {
21        Sleep_us(nusec);
22        snprintf(mesg, MESGSIZE, "pid %ld: message %d", (long) pid, i);

23        if (sem_trywait(&ptr->nempty) == -1) {
24            if (errno == EAGAIN) {
25                Sem_wait(&ptr->noverflowmutex);
26                ptr->noverflow++;
27                Sem_post(&ptr->noverflowmutex);
28                continue;
29            } else
30                err_sys("sem_trywait error");
31        }
32        Sem_wait(&ptr->mutex);
33        offset = ptr->msgoff[ptr->nput];
34        if (++(ptr->nput) >= NMESG)
35            ptr->nput = 0;       /* circular buffer */
36        Sem_post(&ptr->mutex);
37        strcpy(&ptr->msgdata[offset], mesg);
38        Sem_post(&ptr->nstored);
39    }
40    exit(0);
41 }
```

—————————————————————————— pxshm/client2.c

Figure 13.12 Client that stores messages in shared memory for server.

We first start our server in the background and then run our client, specifying 50 messages with no pause between each message.

```
solaris % server2 serv2 &
[2]     27223
solaris % client2 serv2 50 0
index = 0: pid 27224: message 0
index = 1: pid 27224: message 1
index = 2: pid 27224: message 2
. . .                                   continues like this
index = 15: pid 27224: message 47
index = 0: pid 27224: message 48
index = 1: pid 27224: message 49      no messages lost
```

But if we run our client again, we see some overflows.

```
solaris % client2 serv2 50 0
index = 2: pid 27228: message 0
index = 3: pid 27228: message 1
. . .                                   continues OK
index = 10: pid 27228: message 8
index = 11: pid 27228: message 9
noverflow = 25                          server detects 25 messages lost
index = 12: pid 27228: message 10
index = 13: pid 27228: message 11
. . .                                   continues OK for messages 12–22
index = 9: pid 27228: message 23
index = 10: pid 27228: message 24
```

This time, the client appears to have stored messages 0 through 9, which were then fetched and printed by the server. The client then ran again, storing messages 10 through 49, but there was room for only the first 15 of these, and the remaining 25 (messages 25 through 49) were not stored because of overflow.

Obviously, in this example, we caused the overflow by having the client generate the messages as fast as it can, with no pause between each message, which is not a typical real-world scenario. The purpose of this example, however, is to demonstrate how to handle situations in which no room is available for the client's message but the client does not want to block. This is not unique to shared memory—the same scenario can happen with message queues, pipes, and FIFOs.

> Overrunning a receiver with data is not unique to this example. Section 8.13 of UNPv1 talks about this with regard to UDP datagrams, and the UDP socket receive buffer. Section 18.2 of TCPv3 describes how Unix domain datagram sockets return an error of ENOBUFS to the sender when the receiver's buffer overflows, which differs from UDP. In Figure 13.12, our client (the sender) knows when the server's buffer has overflowed, so if this code were placed into a general-purpose function for other programs to call, the function could return an error to the caller when the server's buffer overflows.

13.7 Summary

Posix shared memory is built upon the mmap function from the previous chapter. We first call shm_open, specifying a Posix IPC name for the shared memory object, obtain a descriptor, and then memory map the descriptor with mmap. The result is similar to a memory-mapped file, but the shared memory object need not be implemented as a file.

Since shared memory objects are represented by descriptors, their size is set with ftruncate, and information about an existing object (protection bits, user ID, group ID, and size) is returned by fstat.

When we covered Posix message queues and Posix semaphores, we provided sample implementations based on memory-mapped I/O in Sections 5.8 and 10.15. We do not do this for Posix shared memory, because the implementation would be trivial. If we are willing to memory map a file (as is done by the Solaris and Digital Unix implementations), then shm_open is implemented by calling open, and shm_unlink is implemented by calling unlink.

Exercises

13.1 Modify Figures 12.16 and 12.19 to work with Posix shared memory instead of a memory-mapped file, and verify that the results are the same as shown for a memory-mapped file.

13.2 In the for loops in Figures 13.4 and 13.5, the C idiom *ptr++ is used to step through the array. Would it be preferable to use ptr[i] instead?

14

System V Shared Memory

14.1 Introduction

System V shared memory is similar in concept to Posix shared memory. Instead of calling shm_open followed by mmap, we call shmget followed by shmat.

For every shared memory segment, the kernel maintains the following structure of information, defined by including <sys/shm.h>:

```
struct shmid_ds {
  struct ipc_perm shm_perm;    /* operation permission struct */
  size_t          shm_segsz;   /* segment size */
  pid_t           shm_lpid;    /* pid of last operation */
  pid_t           shm_cpid;    /* creator pid */
  shmatt_t        shm_nattch;  /* current # attached */
  shmat_t         shm_cnattch; /* in-core # attached */
  time_t          shm_atime;   /* last attach time */
  time_t          shm_dtime;   /* last detach time */
  time_t          shm_ctime;   /* last change time of this structure */
};
```

We described the ipc_perm structure in Section 3.3, and it contains the access permissions for the shared memory segment.

14.2 shmget Function

A shared memory segment is created, or an existing one is accessed, by the shmget function.

343

```
#include   <sys/shm.h>

int shmget(key_t key, size_t size, int oflag);
```

Returns: shared memory identifier if OK, –1 on error

The return value is an integer called the *shared memory identifier* that is used with the three other shm*XXX* functions to refer to this segment.

key can be either a value returned by ftok or the constant IPC_PRIVATE, as discussed in Section 3.2.

size specifies the size of the segment, in bytes. When a new shared memory segment is created, a nonzero value for *size* must be specified. If an existing shared memory segment is being referenced, *size* should be 0.

oflag is a combination of the read–write permission values shown in Figure 3.6. This can be bitwise-ORed with either IPC_CREAT or IPC_CREAT | IPC_EXCL, as discussed with Figure 3.4.

When a new shared memory segment is created, it is initialized to *size* bytes of 0.

Note that shmget creates or opens a shared memory segment, but does not provide access to the segment for the calling process. That is the purpose of the shmat function, which we describe next.

14.3 `shmat` Function

After a shared memory segment has been created or opened by shmget, we attach it to our address space by calling shmat.

```
#include   <sys/shm.h>

void *shmat(int shmid, const void *shmaddr, int flag);
```

Returns: starting address of mapped region if OK, –1 on error

shmid is an identifier returned by shmget. The return value from shmat is the starting address of the shared memory segment within the calling process. The rules for determining this address are as follows:

- If *shmaddr* is a null pointer, the system selects the address for the caller. This is the recommended (and most portable) method.

- If *shmaddr* is a nonnull pointer, the returned address depends on whether the caller specifies the SHM_RND value for the *flag* argument:

  - If SHM_RND is not specified, the shared memory segment is attached at the address specified by the *shmaddr* argument.

  - If SHM_RND is specified, the shared memory segment is attached at the address specified by the *shmaddr* argument, rounded down by the constant SHMLBA. LBA stands for "lower boundary address."

By default, the shared memory segment is attached for both reading and writing by the calling process, if the process has read–write permissions for the segment. The SHM_RDONLY value can also be specified in the *flag* argument, specifying read-only access.

14.4 shmdt Function

When a process is finished with a shared memory segment, it detaches the segment by calling shmdt.

```
#include  <sys/shm.h>

int shmdt(const void *shmaddr);
```
Returns: 0 if OK, −1 on error

When a process terminates, all shared memory segments currently attached by the process are detached.

Note that this call does not delete the shared memory segment. Deletion is accomplished by calling shmctl with a command of IPC_RMID, which we describe in the next section.

14.5 shmctl Function

shmctl provides a variety of operations on a shared memory segment.

```
#include  <sys/shm.h>

int shmctl(int shmid, int cmd, struct shmid_ds *buff);
```
Returns: 0 if OK, −1 on error

Three commands are provided:

IPC_RMID   Remove the shared memory segment identified by *shmid* from the system and destroy the shared memory segment.

IPC_SET   Set the following three members of the shmid_ds structure for the shared memory segment from the corresponding members in the structure pointed to by the *buff* argument: shm_perm.uid, shm_perm.gid, and shm_perm.mode. The shm_ctime value is also replaced with the current time.

IPC_STAT   Return to the caller (through the *buff* argument) the current shmid_ds structure for the specified shared memory segment.

14.6 Simple Programs

We now develop some simple programs that operate on System V shared memory.

shmget Program

Our shmget program, shown in Figure 14.1, creates a shared memory segment using a specified pathname and length.

```
                                                          ───── svshm/shmget.c
 1 #include     "unpipc.h"

 2 int
 3 main(int argc, char **argv)
 4 {
 5     int     c, id, oflag;
 6     char    *ptr;
 7     size_t  length;

 8     oflag = SVSHM_MODE | IPC_CREAT;
 9     while ( (c = Getopt(argc, argv, "e")) != -1) {
10         switch (c) {
11         case 'e':
12             oflag |= IPC_EXCL;
13             break;
14         }
15     }
16     if (optind != argc - 2)
17         err_quit("usage: shmget [ -e ] <pathname> <length>");
18     length = atoi(argv[optind + 1]);

19     id = Shmget(Ftok(argv[optind], 1), length, oflag);
20     ptr = Shmat(id, NULL, 0);

21     exit(0);
22 }
                                                          ───── svshm/shmget.c
```

Figure 14.1 Create a System V shared memory segment of a specified size.

19   shmget creates the shared memory segment of the specified size. The pathname passed as a command-line argument is mapped into a System V IPC key by ftok. If the -e option is specified, it is an error if the segment already exists. If we know that the segment already exists, the length on the command line should be specified as 0.

20   shmat attaches the segment into the address space of the process. The program then terminates. Since System V shared memory has at least kernel persistence, this does not remove the shared memory segment.

shmrmid Program

Figure 14.2 shows our trivial program that calls shmctl with a command of IPC_RMID to remove a shared memory segment from the system.

—————————————————————————— svshm/shmrmid.c
```
 1 #include     "unpipc.h"

 2 int
 3 main(int argc, char **argv)
 4 {
 5     int     id;

 6     if (argc != 2)
 7         err_quit("usage: shmrmid <pathname>");

 8     id = Shmget(Ftok(argv[1], 1), 0, SVSHM_MODE);
 9     Shmctl(id, IPC_RMID, NULL);

10     exit(0);
11 }
```
—————————————————————————— svshm/shmrmid.c

Figure 14.2 Remove a System V shared memory segment.

shmwrite **Program**

Figure 14.3 is our shmwrite program, which writes a pattern of 0, 1, 2, ..., 254, 255, 0, 1, and so on, to a shared memory segment.

—————————————————————————— svshm/shmwrite.c
```
 1 #include     "unpipc.h"

 2 int
 3 main(int argc, char **argv)
 4 {
 5     int     i, id;
 6     struct shmid_ds buff;
 7     unsigned char *ptr;

 8     if (argc != 2)
 9         err_quit("usage: shmwrite <pathname>");

10     id = Shmget(Ftok(argv[1], 1), 0, SVSHM_MODE);
11     ptr = Shmat(id, NULL, 0);
12     Shmctl(id, IPC_STAT, &buff);

13         /* set: ptr[0] = 0, ptr[1] = 1, etc. */
14     for (i = 0; i < buff.shm_segsz; i++)
15         *ptr++ = i % 256;

16     exit(0);
17 }
```
—————————————————————————— svshm/shmwrite.c

Figure 14.3 Open a shared memory segment and fill it with a pattern.

10–12   The shared memory segment is opened by shmget and attached by shmat. We fetch its size by calling shmctl with a command of IPC_STAT.

13–15   The pattern is written to the shared memory.

shmread Program

Our shmread program, shown in Figure 14.4, verifies the pattern that was written by shmwrite.

─── *svshm/shmread.c*
```
 1 #include    "unpipc.h"

 2 int
 3 main(int argc, char **argv)
 4 {
 5     int     i, id;
 6     struct shmid_ds buff;
 7     unsigned char c, *ptr;

 8     if (argc != 2)
 9         err_quit("usage: shmread <pathname>");

10     id = Shmget(Ftok(argv[1], 1), 0, SVSHM_MODE);
11     ptr = Shmat(id, NULL, 0);
12     Shmctl(id, IPC_STAT, &buff);

13         /* check that ptr[0] = 0, ptr[1] = 1, etc. */
14     for (i = 0; i < buff.shm_segsz; i++)
15         if ( (c = *ptr++) != (i % 256))
16             err_ret("ptr[%d] = %d", i, c);

17     exit(0);
18 }
```
─── *svshm/shmread.c*

Figure 14.4 Open a shared memory segment and verify its data pattern.

10-12   The shared memory segment is opened and attached. Its size is obtained by calling shmctl with a command of IPC_STAT.

13-16   The pattern written by shmwrite is verified.

Examples

We create a shared memory segment whose length is 1234 bytes under Solaris 2.6. The pathname used to identify the segment (e.g., the pathname passed to ftok) is the pathname of our shmget executable. Using the pathname of a server's executable file often provides a unique identifier for a given application.

```
solaris % shmget shmget 1234
solaris % ipcs -bmo
IPC status from <running system> as of Thu Jan  8 13:17:06 1998
T        ID     KEY         MODE        OWNER    GROUP NATTCH       SEGSZ
Shared Memory:
m         1    0x0000f12a --rw-r--r-- rstevens  other1      0        1234
```

We run the ipcs program to verify that the segment has been created. We notice that the number of attaches (which is stored in the shm_nattch member of the shmid_ds structure) is 0, as we expect.

Next, we run our `shmwrite` program to set the contents of the shared memory segment to the pattern. We verify the shared memory segment's contents with `shmread` and then remove the identifier.

```
solaris % shmwrite shmget
solaris % shmread shmget
solaris % shmrmid shmget
solaris % ipcs -bmo
IPC status from <running system> as of Thu Jan  8 13:18:01 1998
T       ID     KEY       MODE        OWNER    GROUP NATTCH       SEGSZ
Shared Memory:
```

We run `ipcs` to verify that the shared memory segment has been removed.

> When the name of the server executable is used as an argument to `ftok` to identify some form of System V IPC, the absolute pathname would normally be specified, such as `/usr/bin/myserverd`, and not a relative pathname as we have used (`shmget`). We have been able to use a relative pathname for the examples in this section because all of the programs have been run from the directory containing the server executable. Realize that `ftok` uses the i-node of the file to form the IPC identifier (e.g., Figure 3.2), and whether a given file is referenced by an absolute pathname or by a relative pathname has no effect on the i-node.

14.7 Shared Memory Limits

As with System V message queues and System V semaphores, certain system limits exist on System V shared memory (Section 3.8). Figure 14.5 shows the values for some different implementations. The first column is the traditional System V name for the kernel variable that contains this limit.

Name	Description	DUnix 4.0B	Solaris 2.6
shmmax	max #bytes for a shared memory segment	4,194,304	1,048,576
shmmnb	min #bytes for a shared memory segment	1	1
shmmni	max #shared memory identifiers, systemwide	128	100
shmseg	max #shared memory segments attached per process	32	6

Figure 14.5 Typical system limits for System V shared memory.

Example

The program in Figure 14.6 determines the four limits shown in Figure 14.5.

—————————————————— svshm/limits.c

```
1 #include    "unpipc.h"

2 #define MAX_NIDS    4096

3 int
4 main(int argc, char **argv)
```

```
 5 {
 6     int     i, j, shmid[MAX_NIDS];
 7     void    *addr[MAX_NIDS];
 8     unsigned long size;

 9         /* see how many identifiers we can "open" */
10     for (i = 0; i <= MAX_NIDS; i++) {
11         shmid[i] = shmget(IPC_PRIVATE, 1024, SVSHM_MODE | IPC_CREAT);
12         if (shmid[i] == -1) {
13             printf("%d identifiers open at once\n", i);
14             break;
15         }
16     }
17     for (j = 0; j < i; j++)
18         Shmctl(shmid[j], IPC_RMID, NULL);

19         /* now see how many we can "attach" */
20     for (i = 0; i <= MAX_NIDS; i++) {
21         shmid[i] = Shmget(IPC_PRIVATE, 1024, SVSHM_MODE | IPC_CREAT);
22         addr[i] = shmat(shmid[i], NULL, 0);
23         if (addr[i] == (void *) -1) {
24             printf("%d shared memory segments attached at once\n", i);
25             Shmctl(shmid[i], IPC_RMID, NULL);    /* the one that failed */
26             break;
27         }
28     }
29     for (j = 0; j < i; j++) {
30         Shmdt(addr[j]);
31         Shmctl(shmid[j], IPC_RMID, NULL);
32     }

33         /* see how small a shared memory segment we can create */
34     for (size = 1;; size++) {
35         shmid[0] = shmget(IPC_PRIVATE, size, SVSHM_MODE | IPC_CREAT);
36         if (shmid[0] != -1) {    /* stop on first success */
37             printf("minimum size of shared memory segment = %lu\n", size);
38             Shmctl(shmid[0], IPC_RMID, NULL);
39             break;
40         }
41     }

42         /* see how large a shared memory segment we can create */
43     for (size = 65536;; size += 4096) {
44         shmid[0] = shmget(IPC_PRIVATE, size, SVSHM_MODE | IPC_CREAT);
45         if (shmid[0] == -1) {    /* stop on first failure */
46             printf("maximum size of shared memory segment = %lu\n", size - 4096);
47             break;
48         }
49         Shmctl(shmid[0], IPC_RMID, NULL);
50     }

51     exit(0);
52 }
```
svshm/limits.c

Figure 14.6 Determine the system limits on shared memory.

We run this program under Digital Unix 4.0B.

```
alpha % limits
127 identifiers open at once
32 shared memory segments attached at once
minimum size of shared memory segment = 1
maximum size of shared memory segment = 4194304
```

The reason that Figure 14.5 shows 128 identifiers but our program can create only 127 identifiers is that one shared memory segment has already been created by a system daemon.

14.8 Summary

System V shared memory is similar in concept to Posix shared memory. The most common function calls are

- shmget to obtain an identifier,
- shmat to attach the shared memory segment to the address space of the process,
- shmctl with a command of IPC_STAT to fetch the size of an existing shared memory segment, and
- shmctl with a command of IPC_RMID to remove a shared memory object.

One difference is that the size of a Posix shared memory object can be changed at any time by calling ftruncate (as we demonstrated in Exercise 13.1), whereas the size of a System V shared memory object is fixed by shmget.

Exercises

14.1   Figure 6.8 was a modification to Figure 6.6 that accepted an identifier instead of a pathname to specify the queue. We showed that the identifier is all we need to know to access a System V message queue (assuming we have adequate permission). Make similar modifications to Figure 14.4 and show that the same feature applies to System V shared memory.

Part 5

Remote Procedure Calls

15

Doors

15.1 Introduction

When discussing client–server scenarios and procedure calls, there are three different types of procedure calls, which we show in Figure 15.1.

1. A *local procedure call* is what we are familiar with from our everyday C programming: the procedure (function) being called and the calling procedure are both in the same process. Typically, some machine instruction is executed that transfers control to the new procedure, and the called procedure saves machine registers and allocates space on the stack for its local variables.

2. A *remote procedure call* (RPC) is when the procedure being called and the calling procedure are in different processes. We normally refer to the caller as the client and the procedure being called as the server. In the middle scenario in Figure 15.1, we show the client and server executing on the same host. This is a frequently occurring special case of the bottom scenario in this figure, and this is what *doors* provide us: the ability for a process to call a procedure (function) in another process on the same host. One process (a server) makes a procedure available within that process for other processes (clients) to call by creating a door for that procedure. We can also think of doors as a special type of IPC, since information, in the form function arguments and return values, is exchanged between the client and server.

3. RPC in general allows a client on one host to call a server procedure on another host, as long as the two hosts are connected by some form of network (the bottom scenario in Figure 15.1). This is what we describe in Chapter 16.

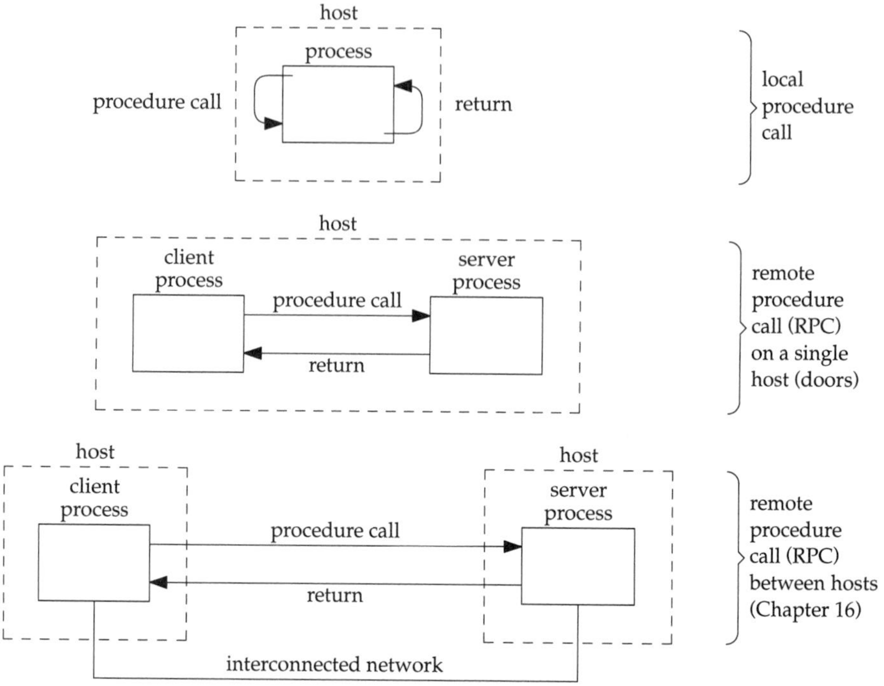

Figure 15.1 Three different types of procedure calls.

Historically, doors were developed for the Spring distributed operating system, details of which are available at http://www.sun.com/tech/projects/spring. A description of the doors IPC mechanism in this operating system is in [Hamilton and Kougiouris 1993].

Doors then appeared in Solaris 2.5, although the only manual page contained just a warning that doors were an experimental interface used only by some Sun applications. With Solaris 2.6, the interface was documented in eight manual pages, but these manual pages list the stability of the interface as "evolving." Expect that changes might occur to the API that we describe in this chapter with future releases of Solaris. A preliminary version of doors for Linux is being developed: http://www.cs.brown.edu/~tor/doors.

The implementation of doors in Solaris 2.6 involves a library (containing the door_XXX functions that we describe in this chapter), which is linked with the user's application (-ldoor), and a kernel filesystem (/kernel/sys/doorfs).

Even though doors are a Solaris-only feature, we describe them in detail because they provide a nice introduction to remote procedure calls, without having to deal with any networking details. We will also see in Appendix A that they are as fast, if not faster, than all other forms of message passing.

Local procedure calls are *synchronous*: the caller does not regain control until the called procedure returns. Threads can be thought of as providing a form of *asynchronous* procedure call: a function is called (the third argument to pthread_create), and both that function and the caller appear to execute at the same time. The caller can wait for the new thread to finish by calling `pthread_join`. Remote procedure calls can be either synchronous or asynchronous, but we will see that door calls are synchronous.

Within a process (client or server), doors are identified by descriptors. Externally, doors may be identified by pathnames in the filesystem. A server creates a door by calling `door_create`, whose argument is a pointer to the procedure that will be associated with this door, and whose return value is a descriptor for the newly created door. The server then associates a pathname with the door descriptor by calling `fattach`. A client opens a door by calling `open`, whose argument is the pathname that the server associated with the door, and whose return value is the client's descriptor for this door. The client then calls the server procedure by calling `door_call`. Naturally, a server for one door could be a client for another door.

We said that door calls are *synchronous*: when the client calls `door_call`, this function does not return until the server procedure returns (or some error occurs). The Solaris implementation of doors is also tied to threads. Each time a client calls a server procedure, a thread in the server process handles this client's call. Thread management is normally done automatically by the doors library, creating new threads as they are needed, but we will see how a server process can manage these threads itself, if desired. This also means that a given server can be servicing multiple client calls of the same server procedure at the same time, with one thread per client. This is a *concurrent* server. Since multiple instances of a given server procedure can be executing at the same time (each instance as one thread), the server procedures must be thread safe.

When a server procedure is called, both *data* and *descriptors* can be passed from the client to the server. Both data and descriptors can also be passed back from the server to the client. Descriptor passing is inherent to doors. Furthermore, since doors are identified by descriptors, this allows a process to pass a door to some other process. We say more about descriptor passing in Section 15.8.

Example

We begin our description of doors with a simple example: the client passes a long integer to the server, and the server returns the square of that value as the long integer result. Figure 15.2 shows the client. (We gloss over many details in this example, all of which we cover later in the chapter.)

Open the door

8–10   The door is specified by the pathname on the command line, and it is opened by calling `open`. The returned descriptor is called the *door descriptor*, but sometimes we just call it the *door*.

Set up arguments and pointer to result

11–18   The `arg` structure contains a pointer to the arguments and a pointer to the results. `data_ptr` points to the first byte of the arguments, and `data_size` specifies the number of argument bytes. The two members `desc_ptr` and `desc_num` deal with the passing of descriptors, which we describe in Section 15.8. `rbuf` points to the first byte of the result buffer, and `rsize` is its size.

```
                                                        ——————— doors/client1.c
 1 #include    "unpipc.h"

 2 int
 3 main(int argc, char **argv)
 4 {
 5     int     fd;
 6     long    ival, oval;
 7     door_arg_t arg;

 8     if (argc != 3)
 9         err_quit("usage: client1 <server-pathname> <integer-value>");

10     fd = Open(argv[1], O_RDWR); /* open the door */

11         /* set up the arguments and pointer to result */
12     ival = atol(argv[2]);
13     arg.data_ptr = (char *) &ival;   /* data arguments */
14     arg.data_size = sizeof(long);     /* size of data arguments */
15     arg.desc_ptr = NULL;
16     arg.desc_num = 0;
17     arg.rbuf = (char *) &oval;   /* data results */
18     arg.rsize = sizeof(long);    /* size of data results */

19         /* call server procedure and print result */
20     Door_call(fd, &arg);
21     printf("result: %ld\n", oval);

22     exit(0);
23 }
                                                        ——————— doors/client1.c
```

Figure 15.2 Client that sends a long integer to the server to be squared.

Call server procedure and print result

19-21   We call the server procedure by calling door_call, specifying as arguments the door descriptor and a pointer to the argument structure. Upon return, we print the result.

The server program is shown in Figure 15.3. It consists of a server procedure named servproc and a main function.

Server procedure

2-10   The server procedure is called with five arguments, but the only one we use is dataptr, which points to the first byte of the arguments. The long integer argument is fetched through this pointer and squared. Control is passed back to the client, along with the result, by door_return. The first argument points to the result, the second is the size of the result, and the remaining two deal with the returning of descriptors.

Create a door descriptor and attach to pathname

17-21   A door descriptor is created by door_create. The first argument is a pointer to the function that will be called for this door (servproc). After this descriptor is obtained, it must be associated with a pathname in the filesystem, because this path-name is how the client identifies the door. This association is done by creating a regular

—— doors/server1.c

```
 1 #include    "unpipc.h"

 2 void
 3 servproc(void *cookie, char *dataptr, size_t datasize,
 4          door_desc_t *descptr, size_t ndesc)
 5 {
 6     long    arg, result;

 7     arg = *((long *) dataptr);
 8     result = arg * arg;
 9     Door_return((char *) &result, sizeof(result), NULL, 0);
10 }

11 int
12 main(int argc, char **argv)
13 {
14     int    fd;

15     if (argc != 2)
16         err_quit("usage: server1 <server-pathname>");

17         /* create a door descriptor and attach to pathname */
18     fd = Door_create(servproc, NULL, 0);

19     unlink(argv[1]);
20     Close(Open(argv[1], O_CREAT | O_RDWR, FILE_MODE));
21     Fattach(fd, argv[1]);

22         /* servproc() handles all client requests */
23     for ( ; ; )
24         pause();
25 }
```

—— doors/server1.c

Figure 15.3 Server that returns the square of a long integer.

file in the filesystem (we call `unlink` first, in case the file already exists, ignoring any error return) and calling `fattach`, an SVR4 function that associates a descriptor with a pathname.

Main server thread does nothing

22-24   The main server thread then blocks in a call to `pause`. All the work is done by the `servproc` function, which will be executed as another thread in the server process each time a client request arrives.

To run this client and server, we first start the server in one window

```
solaris % server1 /tmp/server1
```

and then start the client in another window, specifying the same pathname argument that we passed to the server:

```
solaris % client1 /tmp/server1 9
result: 81
solaris % ls -l /tmp/server1
Drw-r--r--   1 rstevens other1              0 Apr  9 10:09 /tmp/server1
```

The result is what we expect, and when we execute `ls`, we see that it prints the character D as the first character to indicate that this pathname is a door.

Figure 15.4 shows a diagram of what appears to be happening with this example. It appears that `door_call` calls the server procedure, which then returns.

Figure 15.5 shows what is actually going on when we call a procedure in a different process on the same host.

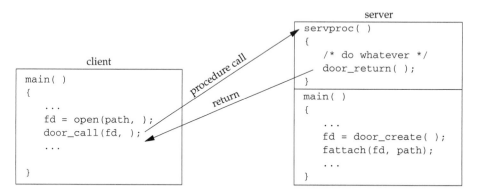

Figure 15.4 Apparent procedure call from one process to another.

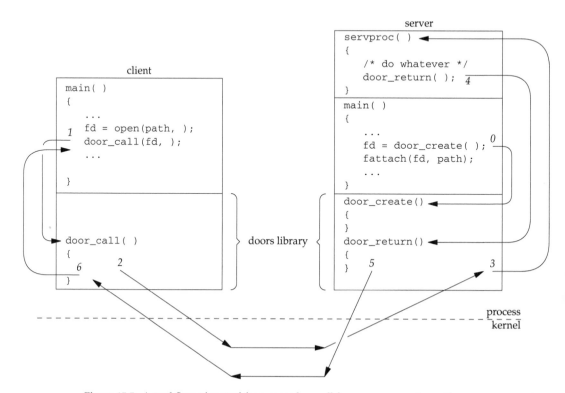

Figure 15.5 Actual flow of control for a procedure call from one process to another.

The following numbered steps in Figure 15.5 take place.

    0. The server process starts first, calls `door_create` to create a door descriptor referring to the function `servproc`, and then attaches this descriptor to a pathname in the filesystem.

    1. The client process starts and calls `door_call`. This is actually a function in the doors library.

    2. The `door_call` library function performs a system call into the kernel. The target procedure is identified and control is passed to some doors library function in the target process.

    3. The actual server procedure (named `servproc` in our example) is called.

    4. The server procedure does whatever it needs to do to handle the client request and calls `door_return` when it is done.

    5. `door_return` is actually a function in the doors library, and it performs a system call into the kernel.

    6. The client is identified and control is passed back to the client.

The remaining sections describe the doors API in more detail looking at many examples. In Appendix A, we will see that doors provide the fastest form of IPC, in terms of latency.

15.2 `door_call` Function

The `door_call` function is called by a client, and it calls a server procedure that is executing in the address space of the server process.

```
#include <door.h>

int door_call(int fd, door_arg_t *argp);
```
Returns: 0 if OK, −1 on error

The descriptor *fd* is normally returned by `open` (e.g., Figure 15.2). The pathname opened by the client identifies the server procedure that is called by `door_call` when this descriptor is the first argument.

    The second argument *argp* points to a structure describing the arguments and the buffer to be used to hold the return values:

```
typedef struct door_arg {
  char          *data_ptr;   /* call: ptr to data arguments;
                                 return: ptr to data results */
  size_t        data_size;   /* call: #bytes of data arguments;
                                 return: actual #bytes of data results */
  door_desc_t   *desc_ptr;   /* call: ptr to descriptor arguments;
                                 return: ptr to descriptor results */
  size_t        desc_num;    /* call: number of descriptor arguments;
                                 return: number of descriptor results */
  char          *rbuf;       /* ptr to result buffer */
  size_t        rsize;       /* #bytes of result buffer */
} door_arg_t;
```

Upon return, this structure describes the return values. All six members of this structure can change on return, as we now describe.

> The use of char * for the two pointers is strange and necessitates explicit casts in our code to avoid compiler warnings. We would expect void * pointers. We will see the same use of char * with the first argument to door_return. Solaris 2.7 will probably change the datatype of desc_num to be an unsigned int, and the final argument to door_return would change accordingly.

Two types of arguments and two types of results exist: data and descriptors.

- The *data arguments* are a sequence of data_size bytes pointed to by data_ptr. The client and server must somehow "know" the format of these arguments (and the results). For example, no special coding tells the server the datatypes of the arguments. In Figures 15.2 and 15.3, the client and server were written to know that the argument was one long integer and that the result was also one long integer. One way to encapsulate this information (for someone reading the code years later) is to put all the arguments into one structure, all the results into another structure, and define both structures in a header that the client and server include. We show an example of this with Figures 15.11 and 15.12. If there are no data arguments, we specify data_ptr as a null pointer and data_size as 0.

  > Since the client and server deal with binary arguments and results that are packed into an argument buffer and a result buffer, the implication is that the client and server must be compiled with the same compiler. Sometimes different compilers, on the same system, pack structures differently.

- The *descriptor arguments* are an array of door_desc_t structures, each one containing one descriptor that is passed from the client to the server procedure. The number of door_desc_t structures passed is desc_num. (We describe this structure and what it means to "pass a descriptor" in Section 15.8.) If there are no descriptor arguments, we specify desc_ptr as a null pointer and desc_num as 0.

- Upon return, data_ptr points to the *data results*, and data_size specifies the size of these results. If there are no data results, data_size will be 0, and we should ignore data_ptr.

- Upon return, there can also be *descriptor results*: desc_ptr points to an array of door_desc_t structures, each one containing one descriptor that was passed by the server procedure to the client. The number of door_desc_t structures returned is contained in desc_num. If there are no descriptor results, desc_num will be 0, and we should ignore desc_ptr.

Using the same buffer for the arguments and results is OK. That is, data_ptr and desc_ptr can point into the buffer specified by rbuf when door_call is called.

Before calling door_call, the client sets rbuf to point to a buffer where the results will be stored, and rsize is the buffer size. Normally upon return, data_ptr and desc_ptr both point into this result buffer. If this buffer is too small to hold the server's results, the doors library automatically allocates a new buffer in the caller's address space using mmap (Section 12.2) and updates rbuf and rsize accordingly. data_ptr and desc_ptr will then point into this newly allocated buffer. It is the caller's responsibility to notice that rbuf has changed and at some later time to return this buffer to the system by calling munmap with rbuf and rsize as the arguments to munmap. We show an example of this with Figure 15.7.

15.3 door_create Function

A server process establishes a server procedure by calling door_create.

```
#include <door.h>

typedef void Door_server_proc(void *cookie, char *dataptr, size_t datasize,
                              door_desc_t *descptr, size_t ndesc);

int door_create(Door_server_proc *proc, void *cookie, u_int attr);
```
Returns: nonnegative descriptor if OK, −1 on error

In this declaration, we have added our own typedef, which simplifies the function prototype. This typedef says that door server procedures (e.g., servproc in Figure 15.3) are called with five arguments and return nothing.

When door_create is called by a server, the first argument *proc* is the address of the server procedure that will be associated with the door descriptor that is the return value of this function. When this server procedure is called, its first argument *cookie* is the value that was passed as the second argument to door_create. This provides a way for the server to cause some pointer to be passed to this procedure every time that procedure is called by a client. The next four arguments to the server procedure, *dataptr*, *datasize*, *descptr*, and *ndesc*, describe the data arguments and the descriptor arguments from the client: the information described by the first four members of the door_arg_t structure that we described in the previous section.

The final argument to door_create, *attr*, describes special attributes of this server procedure, and is either 0 or the bitwise-OR of the following two constants:

DOOR_PRIVATE   The doors library automatically creates new threads in the server process as needed to call the server procedures as client requests arrive. By default, these threads are placed into a process-wide thread pool and can be used to service a client request for any door in the server process.

Specifying the DOOR_PRIVATE attribute tells the library that this door is to have its own pool of server threads, separate from the process-wide pool.

DOOR_UNREF   When the number of descriptors referring to this door goes from two to one, the server procedure is called with a second argument (*dataptr*) of DOOR_UNREF_DATA. The *descptr* argument is a null pointer, and both *datasize* and *ndesc* are 0. We show some examples of this attribute starting with Figure 15.16.

The return value from a server procedure is declared as void because a server procedure never returns by calling return or by falling off the end of the function. Instead, the server procedure calls door_return, which we describe in the next section.

We saw in Figure 15.3 that after obtaining a door descriptor from door_create, the server normally calls fattach to associate that descriptor with a pathname in the filesystem. The client opens that pathname to obtain its door descriptor for its call to door_call.

> fattach is not a Posix.1 function but it is required by Unix 98. Also, a function named fdetach undoes this association, and a command named fdetach just invokes this function.

Door descriptors created by door_create have the FD_CLOEXEC bit set in the descriptor's file descriptor flags. This means the descriptor will be closed by the kernel if this process calls any of the exec functions. With regard to fork, even though all descriptors open in the parent are then shared by the child, only the parent will receive door invocations from clients; none are delivered to the child, even though the descriptor returned by door_create is open in the child.

> If we consider that a door is identified by a process ID and the address of a server procedure to call (which we will see in the door_info_t structure in Section 15.6), then these two rules regarding fork and exec make sense. A child will never get any door invocations, because the process ID associated with the door is the process ID of the parent that called door_create. A door descriptor must be closed upon an exec, because even though the process ID does not change, the address of the server procedure associated with the door has no meaning in the newly invoked program that runs after exec.

15.4 door_return Function

When a server procedure is done it returns by calling door_return. This causes the associated door_call in the client to return.

```
#include <door.h>

int door_return(char *dataptr, size_t datasize, door_desc_t *descptr, size_t ndesc);
```
Returns: no return to caller if OK, –1 on error

The data results are specified by *dataptr* and *datasize,* and the descriptor results are specified by *descptr* and *ndesc.*

15.5 door_cred Function

One nice feature of doors is that the server procedure can obtain the client's credentials on every call. This is done with the door_cred function.

```
#include <door.h>

int door_cred(door_cred_t *cred);
```
Returns: 0 if OK, –1 on error

The door_cred_t structure that is pointed to by *cred* contains the client's credentials on return.

```
typedef struct door_cred {
  uid_t  dc_euid;  /* effective user ID of client */
  gid_t  dc_egid;  /* effective group ID of client */
  uid_t  dc_ruid;  /* real user ID of client */
  gid_t  dc_rgid;  /* real group ID of client */
  pid_t  dc_pid;   /* process ID of client */
} door_cred_t;
```

Section 4.4 of APUE talks about the difference between the effective and real IDs, and we show an example with Figure 15.8.

Notice that there is no descriptor argument to this function. It returns information about the client of the current door invocation, and must therefore be called by the server procedure or some function called by the server procedure.

15.6 door_info Function

The door_cred function that we just described provides information for the server about the client. The client can find information about the server by calling the door_info function.

```
#include <door.h>

int door_info(int fd, door_info_t *info);
```
Returns: 0 if OK, –1 on error

fd specifies an open door. The `door_info_t` structure that is pointed to by *info* contains information about the server on return.

```
typedef struct door_info {
    pid_t        di_target;      /* server process ID */
    door_ptr_t   di_proc;        /* server procedure */
    door_ptr_t   di_data;        /* cookie for server procedure */
    door_attr_t  di_attributes;  /* attributes associated with door */
    door_id_t    di_uniquifier;  /* unique number */
} door_info_t;
```

`di_target` is the process ID of the server, and `di_proc` is the address of the server procedure within the server process (which is probably of little use to the client). The cookie pointer that is passed as the first argument to the server procedure is returned as `di_data`.

The current attributes of the door are contained in `di_attributes`, and we described two of these in Section 15.3: `DOOR_PRIVATE` and `DOOR_UNREF`. Two new attributes are `DOOR_LOCAL` (the procedure is local to this process) and `DOOR_REVOKE` (the server has revoked the procedure associated with this door by calling the `door_revoke` function).

Each door is assigned a systemwide unique number when created, and this is returned as `di_uniquifier`.

This function is normally called by the client, to obtain information about the server. But it can also be issued by a server procedure with a first argument of `DOOR_QUERY`: this returns information about the calling thread. In this scenario, the address of the server procedure (`di_proc`) and the cookie (`di_data`) might be of interest.

15.7 Examples

We now show some examples of the five functions that we have described.

`door_info` Function

Figure 15.6 shows a program that opens a door, then calls `door_info`, and prints information about the door.

doors/doorinfo.c
```
 1 #include    "unpipc.h"

 2 int
 3 main(int argc, char **argv)
 4 {
 5     int       fd;
 6     struct stat stat;
 7     struct door_info info;

 8     if (argc != 2)
 9         err_quit("usage: doorinfo <pathname>");

10     fd = Open(argv[1], O_RDONLY);
11     Fstat(fd, &stat);
```

```
12      if (S_ISDOOR(stat.st_mode) == 0)
13          err_quit("pathname is not a door");

14      Door_info(fd, &info);
15      printf("server PID = %ld, uniquifier = %ld",
16              (long) info.di_target, (long) info.di_uniquifier);
17      if (info.di_attributes & DOOR_LOCAL)
18          printf(", DOOR_LOCAL");
19      if (info.di_attributes & DOOR_PRIVATE)
20          printf(", DOOR_PRIVATE");
21      if (info.di_attributes & DOOR_REVOKED)
22          printf(", DOOR_REVOKED");
23      if (info.di_attributes & DOOR_UNREF)
24          printf(", DOOR_UNREF");
25      printf("\n");

26      exit(0);
27  }
```
── *doors/doorinfo.c*

Figure 15.6 Print information about a door.

We open the specified pathname and first verify that it is a door. The st_mode member of the stat structure for a door will contain a value so that the S_ISDOOR macro is true. We then call door_info.

We first run the program specifying a pathname that is not a door, and then run it on the two doors that are used by Solaris 2.6.

```
solaris % doorinfo /etc/passwd
pathname is not a door

solaris % doorinfo /etc/.name_service_door
server PID = 308, uniquifier = 18, DOOR_UNREF
solaris % doorinfo /etc/.syslog_door
server PID = 282, uniquifier = 1635

solaris % ps -f -p 308
    root    308    1  0   Apr 01 ?          0:34 /usr/sbin/nscd
solaris % ps -f -p 282
    root    282    1  0   Apr 01 ?          0:10 /usr/sbin/syslogd -n -z 14
```

We use the ps command to see what program is running with the process ID returned by door_info.

Result Buffer Too Small

When describing the door_call function, we mentioned that if the result buffer is too small for the server's results, a new buffer is automatically allocated. We now show an example of this. Figure 15.7 shows the new client, a simple modification of Figure 15.2.

19–23   In this version of our program, we print the address of our oval variable, the contents of data_ptr, which points to the result on return from door_call, and the address and size of the result buffer (rbuf and rsize).

```
                                                                    ──────── doors/client2.c
 1 #include    "unpipc.h"

 2 int
 3 main(int argc, char **argv)
 4 {
 5     int     fd;
 6     long    ival, oval;
 7     door_arg_t arg;

 8     if (argc != 3)
 9         err_quit("usage: client2 <server-pathname> <integer-value>");

10     fd = Open(argv[1], O_RDWR); /* open the door */

11         /* set up the arguments and pointer to result */
12     ival = atol(argv[2]);
13     arg.data_ptr = (char *) &ival;  /* data arguments */
14     arg.data_size = sizeof(long);   /* size of data arguments */
15     arg.desc_ptr = NULL;
16     arg.desc_num = 0;
17     arg.rbuf = (char *) &oval;  /* data results */
18     arg.rsize = sizeof(long);   /* size of data results */

19         /* call server procedure and print result */
20     Door_call(fd, &arg);
21     printf("&oval = %p, data_ptr = %p, rbuf = %p, rsize  = %d\n",
22             &oval, arg.data_ptr, arg.rbuf, arg.rsize);
23     printf("result: %ld\n", *((long *) arg.data_ptr));

24     exit(0);
25 }
                                                                    ──────── doors/client2.c
```

Figure 15.7 Print address of result.

When we run this program, we have not changed the size of the result buffer from Figure 15.2, so we expect to find that `data_ptr` and `rbuf` both point to our `oval` variable, and that `rsize` is 4 bytes. Indeed, this is what we see:

```
solaris % client2 /tmp/server2 22
&oval = effff740, data_ptr = effff740, rbuf = effff740, rsize  = 4
result: 484
```

We now change only one line in Figure 15.7, decreasing the size of the client's result buffer by 1 byte. The new version of line 18 from Figure 15.7 is

```
        arg.rsize = sizeof(long) - 1;   /* size of data results */
```

When we execute this new client program, we see that a new result buffer has been allocated and `data_ptr` points to this new buffer.

```
solaris % client3 /tmp/server3 33
&oval = effff740, data_ptr = ef620000, rbuf = ef620000, rsize  = 4096
result: 1089
```

The allocated size of 4096 is the page size on this system, which we saw in Section 12.6. We can see from this example that we should always reference the server's result through the `data_ptr` pointer, and not through our variables whose addresses were passed in `rbuf`. That is, in our example, we should reference the long integer result as `*(long *) arg.data_ptr)` and not as `oval` (which we did in Figure 15.2).

This new buffer is allocated by `mmap` and can be returned to the system using `munmap`. The client can also just keep using this buffer for subsequent calls to `door_call`.

`door_cred` Function and Client Credentials

This time, we make one change to our `servproc` function from Figure 15.3: we call the `door_cred` function to obtain the client credentials. Figure 15.8 shows the new server procedure; the client and the server `main` function do not change from Figures 15.2 and 15.3.

————————————————————————————— doors/server4.c

```
 1 #include     "unpipc.h"

 2 void
 3 servproc(void *cookie, char *dataptr, size_t datasize,
 4          door_desc_t *descptr, size_t ndesc)
 5 {
 6     long    arg, result;
 7     door_cred_t info;

 8         /* obtain and print client credentials */
 9     Door_cred(&info);
10     printf("euid = %ld, ruid = %ld, pid = %ld\n",
11            (long) info.dc_euid, (long) info.dc_ruid, (long) info.dc_pid);

12     arg = *((long *) dataptr);
13     result = arg * arg;
14     Door_return((char *) &result, sizeof(result), NULL, 0);
15 }
```

————————————————————————————— doors/server4.c

Figure 15.8 Server procedure that obtains and prints client credentials.

We first run the client and will see that the effective user ID equals the real user ID, as we expect. We then become the superuser, change the owner of the executable file to `root`, enable the set-user-ID bit, and run the client again.

```
solaris % client4 /tmp/server4 77      first run of client
result: 5929

solaris % su                           become superuser
Password:
Sun Microsystems Inc.    SunOS 5.6       Generic August 1997
solaris # cd directory containing executable
solaris # ls -l client4
-rwxrwxr-x   1 rstevens other1      139328 Apr 13 06:02 client4
solaris # chown root client4           change owner to root
solaris # chmod u+s client4            and turn on the set-user-ID bit
solaris # ls -l client4                check file permissions and owner
-rwsrwxr-x   1 root     other1      139328 Apr 13 06:02 client4
solaris # exit
```

```
solaris % ls -l client4
-rwsrwxr-x    1 root        other1      139328 Apr 13 06:02 client4
solaris % client4 /tmp/server4 77      and run the client again
result: 5929
```

If we look at the server output, we can see the change in the effective user ID the second time we ran the client.

```
solaris % server4 /tmp/server4
euid = 224, ruid = 224, pid = 3168
euid = 0, ruid = 224, pid = 3176
```

The effective user ID of 0 means the superuser.

Automatic Thread Management by Server

To see the thread management performed by the server, we have the server procedure print its thread ID when the procedure starts executing, and then we have it sleep for 5 seconds, to simulate a long running server procedure. The sleep lets us start multiple clients while an existing client is being serviced. Figure 15.9 shows the new server procedure.

doors/server5.c

```
 1 #include     "unpipc.h"

 2 void
 3 servproc(void *cookie, char *dataptr, size_t datasize,
 4          door_desc_t *descptr, size_t ndesc)
 5 {
 6     long    arg, result;

 7     arg = *((long *) dataptr);
 8     printf("thread id %ld, arg = %ld\n", pr_thread_id(NULL), arg);
 9     sleep(5);

10     result = arg * arg;
11     Door_return((char *) &result, sizeof(result), NULL, 0);
12 }
```

doors/server5.c

Figure 15.9 Server procedure that prints thread ID and sleeps.

We introduce a new function from our library, `pr_thread_id`. It has one argument (a pointer to a thread ID or a null pointer to use the calling thread's ID) and returns a `long` integer identifier for this thread (often a small integer). A process can always be identified by an integer value, its process ID. Even though we do not know whether the process ID is an `int` or a `long`, we just cast the return value from `getpid` to a `long` and print the value (Figure 9.2). But the identifier for a thread is a `pthread_t` datatype (called a thread ID), and this need not be an integer. Indeed, Solaris 2.6 uses small integers as the thread ID, whereas Digital Unix uses pointers. Often, however, we want to print a small integer identifier for a thread (as in this example) for debugging purposes. Our library function, shown in Figure 15.10, handles this problem.

```
                                                             ———— lib/wrappthread.c
245 long
246 pr_thread_id(pthread_t * ptr)
247 {
248 #if defined(sun)
249     return ((ptr == NULL) ? pthread_self() : *ptr);      /* Solaris */

250 #elif defined(__osf__) && defined(__alpha)
251     pthread_t tid;

252     tid = (ptr == NULL) ? pthread_self() : *ptr;    /* Digital Unix */
253     return (pthread_getsequence_np(tid));
254 #else
255         /* everything else */
256     return ((ptr == NULL) ? pthread_self() : *ptr);
257 #endif
258 }
                                                             ———— lib/wrappthread.c
```

Figure 15.10 `pr_thread_id` function: return small integer identifier for calling thread.

If the implementation does not provide a small integer identifier for a thread, the function could be more sophisticated, mapping the `pthread_t` values to small integers and remembering this mapping (in an array or linked list) for future calls. This is done in the `thread_name` function in [Lewis and Berg 1998].

Returning to Figure 15.9, we run the client three times in a row. Since we wait for the shell prompt before starting the next client, we know that the 5-second wait is complete at the server each time.

```
solaris % client5 /tmp/server5 55
result: 3025
solaris % client5 /tmp/server5 66
result: 4356
solaris % client5 /tmp/server5 77
result: 5929
```

Looking at the server output, we see that the same server thread services each client:

```
solaris % server5 /tmp/server5
thread id 4, arg = 55
thread id 4, arg = 66
thread id 4, arg = 77
```

We now start three clients at the same time:

```
solaris % client5 /tmp/server5 11 & client5 /tmp/server5 22 & \
client5 /tmp/server5 33 &
[2]     3812
[3]     3813
[4]     3814
solaris % result: 484
result: 121
result: 1089
```

The server output shows that two new threads are created to handle the second and third invocations of the server procedure:

```
thread id 4, arg = 22
thread id 5, arg = 11
thread id 6, arg = 33
```

We then start two more clients at the same time:

```
solaris % client5 /tmp/server5 11 & client5 /tmp/server5 22 &
[2]     3830
[3]     3831
solaris % result: 484
result: 121
```

and see that the server uses the previously created threads:

```
thread id 6, arg = 22
thread id 5, arg = 11
```

What we can see with this example is that the server process (i.e., the doors library that is linked with our server code) automatically creates server threads as they are needed. If an application wants to handle the thread management itself, it can, using the functions that we describe in Section 15.9.

We have also verified that the server procedure is a *concurrent* server: multiple instances of the same server procedure can be running at the same time, as separate threads, servicing different clients. Another way we know that the server is concurrent is that when we run three clients at the same time, all three results are printed 5 seconds later. If the server were *iterative*, one result would be printed 5 seconds after all three clients were started, the next result 5 seconds later, and the last result 5 seconds later.

Automatic Thread Management by Server: Multiple Server Procedures

The previous example had only one server procedure in the server process. Our next question is whether multiple server procedures in the same process can use the same thread pool. To test this, we add another server procedure to the server process and also recode this example to show a better style for handling the arguments and results between different processes.

Our first file is a header named squareproc.h that defines one datatype for the input arguments to our square function and one datatype for the output arguments. It also defines the pathname for this procedure. We show this in Figure 15.11.

Our new procedure takes a long integer input value and returns a double containing the square root of the input. We define the pathname, input structure, and output structure in our sqrtproc.h header, which we show in Figure 15.12.

We show our client program in Figure 15.13. It just calls the two procedures, one after the other, and prints the result. This program is similar to the other client programs that we have shown in this chapter.

Our two server procedures are shown in Figure 15.14. Each prints its thread ID and argument, sleeps for 5 seconds, computes the result, and returns.

The main function, shown in Figure 15.15, opens two door descriptors and associates each one with one of the two server procedures.

———————————————————————————————— *doors/squareproc.h*
```
1 #define PATH_SQUARE_DOOR       "/tmp/squareproc_door"

2 typedef struct {                     /* input to squareproc() */
3     long    arg1;
4 } squareproc_in_t;

5 typedef struct {                     /* output from squareproc() */
6     long    res1;
7 } squareproc_out_t;
```
———————————————————————————————— *doors/squareproc.h*

Figure 15.11 squareproc.h header.

———————————————————————————————— *doors/sqrtproc.h*
```
1 #define PATH_SQRT_DOOR   "/tmp/sqrtproc_door"

2 typedef struct {                     /* input to sqrtproc() */
3     long    arg1;
4 } sqrtproc_in_t;

5 typedef struct {                     /* output from sqrtproc() */
6     double  res1;
7 } sqrtproc_out_t;
```
———————————————————————————————— *doors/sqrtproc.h*

Figure 15.12 sqrtproc.h header.

———————————————————————————————— *doors/client7.c*
```
1 #include     "unpipc.h"
2 #include     "squareproc.h"
3 #include     "sqrtproc.h"

4 int
5 main(int argc, char **argv)
6 {
7     int     fdsquare, fdsqrt;
8     door_arg_t arg;
9     squareproc_in_t square_in;
10    squareproc_out_t square_out;
11    sqrtproc_in_t sqrt_in;
12    sqrtproc_out_t sqrt_out;

13    if (argc != 2)
14        err_quit("usage: client7 <integer-value>");

15    fdsquare = Open(PATH_SQUARE_DOOR, O_RDWR);
16    fdsqrt = Open(PATH_SQRT_DOOR, O_RDWR);

17        /* set up the arguments and call squareproc() */
18    square_in.arg1 = atol(argv[1]);
19    arg.data_ptr = (char *) &square_in;
20    arg.data_size = sizeof(square_in);
21    arg.desc_ptr = NULL;
22    arg.desc_num = 0;
23    arg.rbuf = (char *) &square_out;
24    arg.rsize = sizeof(square_out);
25    Door_call(fdsquare, &arg);
```

```
26          /* set up the arguments and call sqrtproc() */
27      sqrt_in.arg1 = atol(argv[1]);
28      arg.data_ptr = (char *) &sqrt_in;
29      arg.data_size = sizeof(sqrt_in);
30      arg.desc_ptr = NULL;
31      arg.desc_num = 0;
32      arg.rbuf = (char *) &sqrt_out;
33      arg.rsize = sizeof(sqrt_out);
34      Door_call(fdsqrt, &arg);

35      printf("result: %ld %g\n", square_out.res1, sqrt_out.res1);

36      exit(0);
37  }
```
doors/client7.c

Figure 15.13 Client program that calls our square and square root procedures.

doors/server7.c

```
 1  #include    "unpipc.h"
 2  #include    <math.h>
 3  #include    "squareproc.h"
 4  #include    "sqrtproc.h"

 5  void
 6  squareproc(void *cookie, char *dataptr, size_t datasize,
 7             door_desc_t *descptr, size_t ndesc)
 8  {
 9      squareproc_in_t  in;
10      squareproc_out_t out;

11      memcpy(&in, dataptr, min(sizeof(in), datasize));
12      printf("squareproc: thread id %ld, arg = %ld\n",
13             pr_thread_id(NULL), in.arg1);
14      sleep(5);

15      out.res1 = in.arg1 * in.arg1;
16      Door_return((char *) &out, sizeof(out), NULL, 0);
17  }

18  void
19  sqrtproc(void *cookie, char *dataptr, size_t datasize,
20           door_desc_t *descptr, size_t ndesc)
21  {
22      sqrtproc_in_t  in;
23      sqrtproc_out_t out;

24      memcpy(&in, dataptr, min(sizeof(in), datasize));
25      printf("sqrtproc: thread id %ld, arg = %ld\n",
26             pr_thread_id(NULL), in.arg1);
27      sleep(5);

28      out.res1 = sqrt((double) in.arg1);
29      Door_return((char *) &out, sizeof(out), NULL, 0);
30  }
```
doors/server7.c

Figure 15.14 Two server procedures.

```
                                                              ─── doors/server7.c
31 int
32 main(int argc, char **argv)
33 {
34      int     fd;

35      if (argc != 1)
36          err_quit("usage: server7");

37      fd = Door_create(squareproc, NULL, 0);
38      unlink(PATH_SQUARE_DOOR);
39      Close(Open(PATH_SQUARE_DOOR, O_CREAT | O_RDWR, FILE_MODE));
40      Fattach(fd, PATH_SQUARE_DOOR);

41      fd = Door_create(sqrtproc, NULL, 0);
42      unlink(PATH_SQRT_DOOR);
43      Close(Open(PATH_SQRT_DOOR, O_CREAT | O_RDWR, FILE_MODE));
44      Fattach(fd, PATH_SQRT_DOOR);

45      for ( ; ; )
46          pause();
47 }
                                                              ─── doors/server7.c
```

Figure 15.15 main function.

If we run the client, it takes 10 seconds to print the results (as we expect).

```
solaris % client7 77
result: 5929 8.77496
```

If we look at the server output, we see that the same thread in the server process handles both client requests.

```
solaris % server7
squareproc: thread id 4, arg = 77
sqrtproc: thread id 4, arg = 77
```

This tells us that any thread in the pool of server threads for a given process can handle a client request for any server procedure.

DOOR_UNREF Attribute for Servers

We mentioned in Section 15.3 that the DOOR_UNREF attribute can be specified to door_create as an attribute of a newly created door. The manual page says that when the number of descriptors referring to the door drops to one (that is, the reference count goes from two to one), a special invocation is made of the door's server procedure. What is special is that the second argument to the server procedure (the pointer to the data arguments) is the constant DOOR_UNREF_DATA. We will demonstrate three ways in which the door is referenced.

1. The descriptor returned by door_create in the server counts as one reference. In fact, the reason that the trigger for an unreferenced procedure is the transition of the reference count from two to one, and not from one to 0, is that the server process normally keeps this descriptor open for the duration of the process.

2. The pathname attached to the door in the filesystem also counts as one reference. We can remove this reference by calling the `fdetach` function, running
the `fdetach` program, or unlinking the pathname from the filesystem (either
the `unlink` function or the `rm` command).

3. The descriptor returned by `open` in the client counts as an open reference until
the descriptor is closed, either explicitly by calling `close` or implicitly by the
termination of the client process. In all the client processes that we have shown
in this chapter, this close is implicit.

Our first example shows that if the server closes its door descriptor after calling
`fattach`, an unreferenced invocation of the server procedure occurs immediately. Figure 15.16 shows our server procedure and the server `main` function.

```
                                                                    doors/serverunref1.c
 1 #include    "unpipc.h"

 2 void
 3 servproc(void *cookie, char *dataptr, size_t datasize,
 4          door_desc_t *descptr, size_t ndesc)
 5 {
 6     long    arg, result;

 7     if (dataptr == DOOR_UNREF_DATA) {
 8         printf("door unreferenced\n");
 9         Door_return(NULL, 0, NULL, 0);
10     }
11     arg = *((long *) dataptr);
12     printf("thread id %ld, arg = %ld\n", pr_thread_id(NULL), arg);
13     sleep(6);

14     result = arg * arg;
15     Door_return((char *) &result, sizeof(result), NULL, 0);
16 }

17 int
18 main(int argc, char **argv)
19 {
20     int    fd;

21     if (argc != 2)
22         err_quit("usage: server1 <server-pathname>");

23         /* create a door descriptor and attach to pathname */
24     fd = Door_create(servproc, NULL, DOOR_UNREF);

25     unlink(argv[1]);
26     Close(Open(argv[1], O_CREAT | O_RDWR, FILE_MODE));
27     Fattach(fd, argv[1]);
28     Close(fd);

29         /* servproc() handles all client requests */
30     for ( ; ; )
31         pause();
32 }
                                                                    doors/serverunref1.c
```

Figure 15.16 Server procedure that handles an unreferenced invocation.

7-10   Our server procedure recognizes the special invocation and prints a message. The thread returns from this special call by calling `door_return` with two null pointers and two sizes of 0.

28   We now `close` the door descriptor after `fattach` returns. The only use that the server has for this descriptor after `fattach` is if it needs to call `door_bind`, `door_info`, or `door_revoke`.

When we start the server, we notice that the unreferenced invocation occurs immediately:

```
solaris % serverunref1 /tmp/door1
door unreferenced
```

If we follow the reference count for this door, it becomes one after `door_create` returns and then two after `fattach` returns. The server's call to `close` reduces the count from two to one, triggering the unreferenced invocation. The only reference left for this door is its pathname in the filesystem, and that is what the client needs to refer to this door. That is, the client continues to work fine:

```
solaris % clientunref1 /tmp/door1 11
result: 121
solaris % clientunref1 /tmp/door1 22
result: 484
```

Furthermore, no further unreferenced invocations of the server procedure occur. Indeed, only one unreferenced invocation is delivered for a given door.

We now change our server back to the common scenario in which it does not `close` its door descriptor. We show the server procedure and the server `main` function in Figure 15.17. We leave in the 6-second sleep and also print when the server procedure returns. We start the server in one window, and then from another window we verify that the door's pathname exists in the filesystem and then remove the pathname with `rm`:

```
solaris % ls -l /tmp/door2
Drw-r--r--   1 rstevens other1            0 Apr 16 08:58 /tmp/door2
solaris % rm /tmp/door2
```

As soon at the pathname is removed, the unreferenced invocation is made of the server procedure:

```
solaris % serverunref2 /tmp/door2
door unreferenced          as soon as pathname is removed from filesystem
```

If we follow the reference count for this door, it becomes one after `door_create` returns and then two after `fattach` returns. When we `rm` the pathname, this command reduces the count from two to one, triggering the unreferenced invocation.

In our final example of this attribute, we again remove the pathname from the filesystem, but only after starting three client invocations of the door. What we show is that each client invocation increases the reference count, and only when all three clients

doors/serverunref2.c

```
 1 #include    "unpipc.h"

 2 void
 3 servproc(void *cookie, char *dataptr, size_t datasize,
 4          door_desc_t *descptr, size_t ndesc)
 5 {
 6     long    arg, result;

 7     if (dataptr == DOOR_UNREF_DATA) {
 8         printf("door unreferenced\n");
 9         Door_return(NULL, 0, NULL, 0);
10     }
11     arg = *((long *) dataptr);
12     printf("thread id %ld, arg = %ld\n", pr_thread_id(NULL), arg);
13     sleep(6);

14     result = arg * arg;
15     printf("thread id %ld returning\n", pr_thread_id(NULL));
16     Door_return((char *) &result, sizeof(result), NULL, 0);
17 }

18 int
19 main(int argc, char **argv)
20 {
21     int    fd;

22     if (argc != 2)
23         err_quit("usage: server1 <server-pathname>");

24         /* create a door descriptor and attach to pathname */
25     fd = Door_create(servproc, NULL, DOOR_UNREF);

26     unlink(argv[1]);
27     Close(Open(argv[1], O_CREAT | O_RDWR, FILE_MODE));
28     Fattach(fd, argv[1]);

29         /* servproc() handles all client requests */
30     for ( ; ; )
31         pause();
32 }
```

doors/serverunref2.c

Figure 15.17 Server that does not close its door descriptor.

terminate does the unreferenced invocation take place. We use our previous server from Figure 15.17, and our client is unchanged from Figure 15.2.

```
solaris % clientunref2 /tmp/door2 44 & clientunref2 /tmp/door2 55 & \
clientunref2 /tmp/door2 55 &
[2]     13552
[3]     13553
[4]     13554
solaris % rm /tmp/door2                    while the three clients are running
solaris % result: 1936
result: 3025
result: 4356
```

Here is the server output:

```
solaris % serverunref2 /tmp/door2
thread id 4, arg = 44
thread id 5, arg = 55
thread id 6, arg = 66
thread id 4 returning
thread id 5 returning
thread id 6 returning
door unreferenced
```

If we follow the reference count for this door, it becomes one after `door_create` returns and then two after `fattach` returns. As each client calls `open`, the reference count is incremented, going from two to three, from three to four, and then from four to five. When we `rm` the pathname, the count reduces from five to four. Then as each client terminates, the count goes from four to three, then three to two, then two to one, and this final decrement triggers the unreferenced invocation.

What we have shown with these examples is that even though the description of the `DOOR_UNREF` attribute is simple ("the unreferenced invocation occurs when the reference count goes from two to one"), we must understand this reference count to use this feature.

15.8 Descriptor Passing

When we think of passing an open descriptor from one process to another, we normally think of either

- a child sharing all the open descriptors with the parent after a call to `fork`, or

- all descriptors normally remaining open when `exec` is called.

In the first example, the process opens a descriptor, calls `fork`, and then the parent closes the descriptor, letting the child handle the descriptor. This passes an open descriptor from the parent to the child.

Current Unix systems extend this notion of descriptor passing and provide the ability to pass any open descriptor from one process to any other process, related or unrelated. Doors provide one API for the passing of descriptors from the client to the server, and from the server to the client.

> We described descriptor passing using Unix domain sockets in Section 14.7 of UNPv1. Berkeley-derived kernels pass descriptors using these sockets, and all the details are provided in Chapter 18 of TCPv3. SVR4 kernels use a different technique to pass a descriptor, the `I_SENDFD` and `I_RECVFD` `ioctl` commands, described in Section 15.5.1 of APUE. But an SVR4 process can still access this kernel feature using a Unix domain socket.

Be sure to understand what we mean by *passing a descriptor*. In Figure 4.7, the server opens the file and then copies the entire file across the bottom pipe. If the file's size is 1 megabyte, then 1 megabyte of data goes across the bottom pipe from the server to the client. But if the server passes a descriptor back to the client, instead of the file itself, then only the descriptor is passed across the bottom pipe in Figure 4.7 (which we assume is some small amount of kernel-specific information). The client then takes this descriptor and reads the file, writing its contents to standard output. All the file reading takes place in the client, and the server only opens the file.

Realize that the server *cannot* just write the descriptor number across the bottom pipe in Figure 4.7, as in

```
int     fd;

fd = Open( ... );
Write(pipefd, &fd, sizeof(int));
```

This approach does not work. Descriptor numbers are a per-process attribute. Suppose the value of fd is 4 in the server. Even if this descriptor is open in the client, it almost certainly does not refer to the same file as descriptor 4 in the server process. (The only time descriptor numbers mean something from one process to another is across a fork or across an exec.) If the lowest unused descriptor in the server is 4, then a successful open in the server will return 4. If the server "passes" its descriptor 4 to the client and the lowest unused descriptor in the client is 7, then we want descriptor 7 in the client to refer to the same file as descriptor 4 in the server. Figures 15.4 of APUE and 18.4 of TCPv3 show what must happen from the kernel's perspective: the two descriptors (4 in the server and 7 in the client, in our example) must both point to the same file table entry within the kernel. Some kernel black magic is involved in descriptor passing, but APIs like doors and Unix domain sockets hide all these internal details, allowing processes to pass descriptors easily from one process to another.

Descriptors are passed across a door from the client to server by setting the desc_ptr member of the door_arg_t structure to point to an array of door_desc_t structures, and setting door_num to the number of these structures. Descriptors are passed from the server to the client by setting the third argument of door_return to point to an array of door_desc_t structures, and setting the fourth argument to the number of descriptors being passed.

```
typedef struct door_desc {
    door_attr_t d_attributes;     /* tag for union */
    union {
      struct {                    /* valid if tag = DOOR_DESCRIPTOR */
        int        d_descriptor;  /* descriptor number */
        door_id_t  d_id;          /* unique id */
      } d_desc;
    } d_data;
} door_desc_t;
```

This structure contains a union, and the first member of the structure is a tag that identifies what is contained in the union. But currently only one member of the union is defined (a d_desc structure that describes a descriptor), and the tag (d_attributes) must be set to DOOR_DESCRIPTOR.

Example

We modify our file server example (recall Figure 1.9) so that the server opens the file, passes the open descriptor to the client, and the client then copies the file to standard output. Figure 15.18 shows the arrangement.

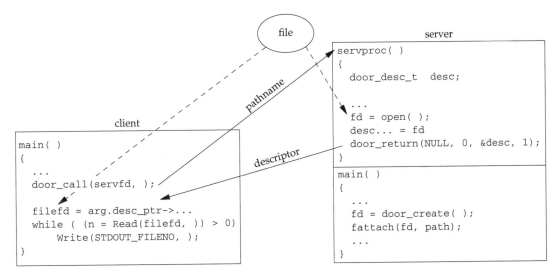

Figure 15.18 File server example with server passing back open descriptor.

Figure 15.19 shows the client program.

Open door, read pathname from standard input

9–15   The pathname associated with the door is a command-line argument and the door is opened. The filename that the client wants opened is read from standard input and the trailing newline is deleted.

Set up arguments and pointer to result

16–22   The `door_arg_t` structure is set up. We add one to the size of the pathname to allow the server to null terminate the pathname.

Call server procedure and check result

23–31   We call the server procedure and then check that the result is what we expect: no data and one descriptor. We will see shortly that the server returns data (containing an error message) only if it cannot open the file, in which case, our call to `err_quit` prints that error.

Fetch descriptor and copy file to standard output

32–34   The descriptor is fetched from the `door_desc_t` structure, and the file is copied to standard output.

```
                                                                              ———— doors/clientfd1.c
 1 #include     "unpipc.h"

 2 int
 3 main(int argc, char **argv)
 4 {
 5     int     door, fd;
 6     char    argbuf[BUFFSIZE], resbuf[BUFFSIZE], buff[BUFFSIZE];
 7     size_t  len, n;
 8     door_arg_t arg;

 9     if (argc != 2)
10         err_quit("usage: clientfd1 <server-pathname>");

11     door = Open(argv[1], O_RDWR);    /* open the door */

12     Fgets(argbuf, BUFFSIZE, stdin);      /* read pathname of file to open */
13     len = strlen(argbuf);
14     if (argbuf[len - 1] == '\n')
15         len--;                   /* delete newline from fgets() */

16         /* set up the arguments and pointer to result */
17     arg.data_ptr = argbuf;        /* data argument */
18     arg.data_size = len + 1;      /* size of data argument */
19     arg.desc_ptr = NULL;
20     arg.desc_num = 0;
21     arg.rbuf = resbuf;            /* data results */
22     arg.rsize = BUFFSIZE;         /* size of data results */

23     Door_call(door, &arg);        /* call server procedure */

24     if (arg.data_size != 0)
25         err_quit("%.*s", arg.data_size, arg.data_ptr);
26     else if (arg.desc_ptr == NULL)
27         err_quit("desc_ptr is NULL");
28     else if (arg.desc_num != 1)
29         err_quit("desc_num = %d", arg.desc_num);
30     else if (arg.desc_ptr->d_attributes != DOOR_DESCRIPTOR)
31         err_quit("d_attributes = %d", arg.desc_ptr->d_attributes);

32     fd = arg.desc_ptr->d_data.d_desc.d_descriptor;
33     while ( (n = Read(fd, buff, BUFFSIZE)) > 0)
34         Write(STDOUT_FILENO, buff, n);

35     exit(0);
36 }
                                                                              ———— doors/clientfd1.c
```

Figure 15.19 Client program for descriptor passing file server example.

Figure 15.20 shows the server procedure. The server `main` function has not changed from Figure 15.3.

Open file for client

9–14   We null terminate the client's pathname and try to open the file. If an error occurs, the data result is a string containing the error message.

————————————————————————————————————— doors/serverfd1.c

```
 1 #include    "unpipc.h"

 2 void
 3 servproc(void *cookie, char *dataptr, size_t datasize,
 4          door_desc_t *descptr, size_t ndesc)
 5 {
 6     int     fd;
 7     char    resbuf[BUFFSIZE];
 8     door_desc_t desc;
 9     dataptr[datasize - 1] = 0;   /* null terminate */
10     if ( (fd = open(dataptr, O_RDONLY)) == -1) {
11             /* error: must tell client */
12         snprintf(resbuf, BUFFSIZE, "%s: can't open, %s",
13                 dataptr, strerror(errno));
14         Door_return(resbuf, strlen(resbuf), NULL, 0);

15     } else {
16             /* open succeeded: return descriptor */
17         desc.d_data.d_desc.d_descriptor = fd;
18         desc.d_attributes = DOOR_DESCRIPTOR;
19         Door_return(NULL, 0, &desc, 1);
20     }
21 }
```

————————————————————————————————————— doors/serverfd1.c

Figure 15.20 Server procedure that opens a file and passes back its descriptor.

Success

15-20   If the open succeeds, only the descriptor is returned; there are no data results.

We start the server and specify its door pathname as /tmp/fd1 and then run the client:

```
solaris % clientfd1 /tmp/fd1
/etc/shadow
/etc/shadow: can't open, Permission denied
solaris % clientfd1 /tmp/fd1
/no/such/file
/no/such/file: can't open, No such file or directory
solaris % clientfd1 /tmp/fd1
/etc/ntp.conf                          a 2-line file
multicastclient 224.0.1.1
driftfile /etc/ntp.drift
```

The first two times, we specify a pathname that causes an error return, and the third time, the server returns the descriptor for a 2-line file.

> There is a problem with descriptor passing across a door. To see the problem in our example, just add a printf to the server procedure after a successful open. You will see that each descriptor value is one greater than the previous descriptor value. The problem is that the server is not closing the descriptors after it passes them to the client. But there is no easy way to do this. The logical place to perform the close would be after door_return returns, once the descriptor has been sent to the client, but door_return does not return! If we had been

using either `sendmsg` to pass the descriptor across a Unix domain socket, or `ioctl` to pass the descriptor across an SVR4 pipe, we could `close` the descriptor when `sendmsg` or `ioctl` returns. But the doors paradigm for passing descriptors is different from these two techniques, since no return occurs from the function that passes the descriptor. The only way around this problem is for the server procedure to somehow remember that it has a descriptor open and close it at some later time, which becomes very messy.

This problem should be fixed in Solaris 2.7 with the addition of a new `DOOR_RELEASE` attribute. The sender sets `d_attributes` to `DOOR_DESCRIPTOR | DOOR_RELEASE`, which tells the system to close the descriptor after passing it to the receiver.

15.9 `door_server_create` Function

We showed with Figure 15.9 that the doors library automatically creates new threads as needed to handle the client requests as they arrive. These are created by the library as detached threads, with the default thread stack size, with thread cancellation disabled, and with a signal mask and scheduling class that are initially inherited from the thread that called `door_create`. If we want to change any of these features or if we want to manage the pool of server threads ourselves, we call `door_server_create` and specify our own *server creation procedure*.

```
#include <door.h>

typedef void Door_create_proc(door_info_t *);

Door_create_proc *door_server_create(Door_create_proc *proc);
```
Returns: pointer to previous server creation procedure

As with our declaration of `door_create` in Section 15.3, we use C's `typedef` to simplify the function prototype for the library function. Our new datatype defines a server creation procedure as taking a single argument (a pointer to a `door_info_t` structure), and returning nothing (`void`). When we call `door_server_create`, the argument is a pointer to our server creation procedure, and the return value is a pointer to the previous server creation procedure.

Our server creation procedure is called whenever a new thread is needed to service a client request. Information on which server procedure needs the thread is in the `door_info_t` structure whose address is passed to the creation procedure. The `di_proc` member contains the address of the server procedure, and `di_data` contains the cookie pointer that is passed to the server procedure each time it is called.

An example is the easiest way to see what is happening. Our client does not change from Figure 15.2. In our server, we add two new functions in addition to our server procedure function and our server `main` function. Figure 15.21 shows an overview of the four functions in our server process, when some are registered, and when they are all called.

Figure 15.22 shows the server `main` function.

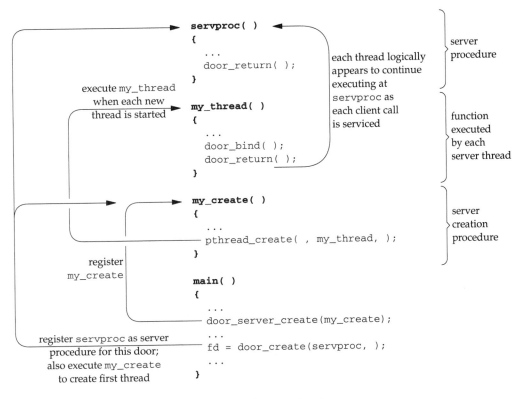

Figure 15.21 Overview of the four functions in our server process.

—— *doors/server6.c*
```
42 int
43 main(int argc, char **argv)
44 {
45     if (argc != 2)
46         err_quit("usage: server6 <server-pathname>");

47     Door_server_create(my_create);

48         /* create a door descriptor and attach to pathname */
49     Pthread_mutex_lock(&fdlock);
50     fd = Door_create(servproc, NULL, DOOR_PRIVATE);
51     Pthread_mutex_unlock(&fdlock);

52     unlink(argv[1]);
53     Close(Open(argv[1], O_CREAT | O_RDWR, FILE_MODE));
54     Fattach(fd, argv[1]);

55         /* servproc() handles all client requests */
56     for ( ; ; )
57         pause();
58 }
```
—— *doors/server6.c*

Figure 15.22 `main` function for example of thread pool management.

We have made four changes from Figure 15.3: (1) the declaration of the door descriptor `fd` is gone (it is now a global variable that we show and describe in Figure 15.23), (2) we protect the call to `door_create` with a mutex (which we also describe in Figure 15.23), (3) we call `door_server_create` before creating the door, specifying our server creation procedure (`my_thread`, which we show next), and (4) in the call to `door_create`, the final argument (the attributes) is now `DOOR_PRIVATE` instead of 0. This tells the library that this door will have its own pool of threads, called a *private server pool*.

Specifying a private server pool with `DOOR_PRIVATE` and specifying a server creation procedure with `door_server_create` are independent. Four scenarios are possible.

1. Default: *no* private server pools and *no* server creation procedure. The system creates threads as needed, and they all go into the process-wide thread pool.

2. `DOOR_PRIVATE` and *no* server creation procedure. The system creates threads as needed, and they go into the process-wide pool for doors created without `DOOR_PRIVATE` or into a door's private server pool for doors created with `DOOR_PRIVATE`.

3. *No* private server pools, but a server creation procedure is specified. The server creation procedure is called whenever a new thread is needed, and these threads all go into the process-wide thread pool.

4. `DOOR_PRIVATE` and a server creation procedure are both specified. The server creation procedure is called whenever a new thread is needed. When a thread is created, it should call `door_bind` to assign itself to the appropriate private server pool, or the thread will be assigned to the process-wide pool.

Figure 15.23 shows our two new functions: `my_create` is our server creation procedure, and it calls `my_thread` as the function that is executed by each thread that it creates.

Server creation procedure

30–41 Each time `my_create` is called, we create a new thread. But before calling `pthread_create`, we initialize its attributes, set the contention scope to `PTHREAD_SCOPE_SYSTEM`, and specify the thread as a detached thread. The thread is created and starts executing the `my_thread` function. The argument to this function is a pointer to the `door_info_t` structure. If we have a server with multiple doors and we specify a server creation procedure, this one server creation procedure is called when a new thread is needed for any of the doors. The only way for this server creation procedure and the thread start function that it specifies to `pthread_create` to differentiate between the different server procedures is to look at the `di_proc` pointer in the `door_info_t` structure.

> Setting the contention scope to `PTHREAD_SCOPE_SYSTEM` means this thread will compete for processor resources against threads in other processes. The alternative,

─── *doors/server6.c*
```
13 pthread_mutex_t fdlock = PTHREAD_MUTEX_INITIALIZER;
14 static int fd = -1;                 /* door descriptor */

15 void *
16 my_thread(void *arg)
17 {
18     int     oldstate;
19     door_info_t *iptr = arg;

20     if ((Door_server_proc *) iptr->di_proc == servproc) {
21         Pthread_mutex_lock(&fdlock);
22         Pthread_mutex_unlock(&fdlock);

23         Pthread_setcancelstate(PTHREAD_CANCEL_DISABLE, &oldstate);
24         Door_bind(fd);
25         Door_return(NULL, 0, NULL, 0);
26     } else
27         err_quit("my_thread: unknown function: %p", arg);
28     return (NULL);                    /* never executed */
29 }

30 void
31 my_create(door_info_t *iptr)
32 {
33     pthread_t tid;
34     pthread_attr_t attr;

35     Pthread_attr_init(&attr);
36     Pthread_attr_setscope(&attr, PTHREAD_SCOPE_SYSTEM);
37     Pthread_attr_setdetachstate(&attr, PTHREAD_CREATE_DETACHED);
38     Pthread_create(&tid, &attr, my_thread, (void *) iptr);
39     Pthread_attr_destroy(&attr);
40     printf("my_thread: created server thread %ld\n", pr_thread_id(&tid));
41 }
```
─── *doors/server6.c*

Figure 15.23 Our own thread management functions.

PTHREAD_SCOPE_PROCESS, means this thread will compete for processor resources only against other threads in this process. The latter will not work with doors, because the doors library requires that the kernel lightweight process performing the door_return be the same lightweight process that originated the invocation. An unbound thread (PTHREAD_SCOPE_PROCESS) could change lightweight processes during execution of the server procedure.

The reason for requiring that the thread be created as a detached thread is to prevent the system from saving any information about the thread when it terminates, because no one will be calling pthread_join.

Thread start function

15-20   my_thread is the thread start function specified by the call to pthread_create. The argument is the pointer to the door_info_t structure that was passed to my_create. The only server procedure that we have in this process is servproc, and we just verify that the argument references this procedure.

Wait for descriptor to be valid

21-22   The server creation procedure is called for the first time when `door_create` is called, to create an initial server thread. This call is issued from within the doors library before `door_create` returns. But the variable `fd` will not contain the door descriptor until `door_create` returns. (This is a chicken-and-egg problem.) Since we know that `my_thread` is running as a separate thread from the main thread that calls `door_create`, our solution to this timing problem is to use the mutex `fdlock` as follows: the main thread locks the mutex before calling `door_create` and unlocks the mutex when `door_create` returns and a value has been stored into `fd` (Figure 15.22). Our `my_thread` function just locks the mutex (probably blocking until the main thread has unlocked the mutex) and then unlocks it. We could have added a condition variable that the main thread signals, but we don't need it here, since we know the sequence of calls that will occur.

Disable thread cancellation

23   When a new Posix thread is created by `pthread_create`, thread cancellation is enabled by default. When cancellation is enabled, and a client aborts a `door_call` that is in progress (which we will demonstrate in Figure 15.31), the thread cancellation handlers (if any) are called, and the thread is then terminated. When cancellation is disabled (as we are doing here), and a client aborts a `door_call` that is in progress, the server procedure completes (the thread is not terminated), and the results from `door_return` are just discarded. Since the server thread is terminated when cancellation is enabled, and since the server procedure may be in the middle of an operation for the client (it may hold some locks or semaphores), the doors library disables thread cancellation for all the threads that it creates. If a server procedure wants to be canceled when a client terminates prematurely, that thread must enable cancellation and must be prepared to deal with it.

> Notice that the contention scope of `PTHREAD_SCOPE_SYSTEM` and the detached state are specified as attributes when the thread is created. But the cancellation mode can be set only by the thread itself once it is running. Indeed, even though we just disable cancellation, a thread can enable and disable cancellation whenever it wants.

Bind this thread to a door

24   We call `door_bind` to bind the calling thread to the private server pool associated with the door whose descriptor is the argument to `door_bind`. Since we need the door descriptor for this call, we made `fd` a global variable for this version of our server.

Make thread available for a client call

25   The thread makes itself available for incoming door invocations by calling `door_return` with two null pointers and two 0 lengths as the arguments.

We show the server procedure in Figure 15.24. This version is identical to the one in Figure 15.9.

To demonstrate what happens, we just start the server:

```
solaris % server6 /tmp/door6
my_thread: created server thread 4
```

doors/server6.c
```
 1 #include    "unpipc.h"

 2 void
 3 servproc(void *cookie, char *dataptr, size_t datasize,
 4          door_desc_t *descptr, size_t ndesc)
 5 {
 6     long    arg, result;

 7     arg = *((long *) dataptr);
 8     printf("thread id %ld, arg = %ld\n", pr_thread_id(NULL), arg);
 9     sleep(5);

10     result = arg * arg;
11     Door_return((char *) &result, sizeof(result), NULL, 0);
12 }
```
doors/server6.c

Figure 15.24 Server procedure.

As soon as the server starts and `door_create` is called, our server creation procedure is called the first time, even though we have not even started the client. This creates the first thread, which will wait for the first client call. We then run the client three times in a row:

```
solaris % client6 /tmp/door6 11
result: 121
solaris % client6 /tmp/door6 22
result: 484
solaris % client6 /tmp/door6 33
result: 1089
```

If we look at the corresponding server output, another thread is created when the first client call occurs (thread ID 5), and then thread number 4 services each of the client requests. The doors library appears to always keep one extra thread ready.

```
my_thread: created server thread 5
thread id 4, arg = 11
thread id 4, arg = 22
thread id 4, arg = 33
```

We then execute the client three times, all at about the same time in the background.

```
solaris % client6 /tmp/door6 44 & client6 /tmp/door6 55 & \
client6 /tmp/door6 66 &
[2]     4919
[3]     4920
[4]     4921
solaris % result: 1936
result: 4356
result: 3025
```

Looking at the corresponding server output, we see that two new threads are created (thread IDs 6 and 7), and threads 4, 5, and 6 service the three client requests:

```
thread id 4, arg = 44
my_thread: created server thread 6
thread id 5, arg = 66
my_thread: created server thread 7
thread id 6, arg = 55
```

15.10 `door_bind`, `door_unbind`, and `door_revoke` Functions

Three additional functions complete the doors API.

```
#include <door.h>

int door_bind(int fd);

int door_unbind(void);

int door_revoke(int fd);
```
All three return: 0 if OK, −1 on error

We introduced the `door_bind` function in Figure 15.23. It binds the calling thread to the private server pool associated with the door whose descriptor is *fd*. If the calling thread is already bound to some other door, an implicit unbind is performed.

`door_unbind` explicitly unbinds the calling thread from the door to which it has been bound.

`door_revoke` revokes access to the door identified by *fd*. A door descriptor can be revoked only by the process that created the descriptor. Any door invocation that is in progress when this function is called is allowed to complete normally.

15.11 Premature Termination of Client or Server

All our examples so far have assumed that nothing abnormal happens to either the client or server. We now consider what happens when errors occur at either the client or server. Realize that when the client and server are part of the same process (the local procedure call in Figure 15.1), the client does not need to worry about the server crashing and vice versa, because if either crashes the entire process crashes. But when the client and server are distributed to two processes, we must consider what happens if one of the two crashes and how the peer is notified of this failure. This is something we must worry about regardless of whether the client and server are on the same host or on different hosts.

Premature Termination of Server

While the client is blocked in a call to `door_call`, waiting for results, it needs to know if the server thread terminates for some reason. To see what happens, we have the server procedure thread terminate by calling `thread_exit`. This terminates just this thread, not the entire server process. Figure 15.25 shows the server procedure.

—— *doors/serverintr1.c*
```
 1 #include    "unpipc.h"

 2 void
 3 servproc(void *cookie, char *dataptr, size_t datasize,
 4          door_desc_t *descptr, size_t ndesc)
 5 {
 6     long    arg, result;

 7     pthread_exit(NULL);             /* and see what happens at client */
 8     arg = *((long *) dataptr);
 9     result = arg * arg;
10     Door_return((char *) &result, sizeof(result), NULL, 0);
11 }
```
—— *doors/serverintr1.c*

Figure 15.25 Server procedure that terminates itself after being invoked.

The remainder of the server does not change from Figure 15.3, and the client does not change from Figure 15.2.

When we run our client, we see that an error of EINTR is returned by `door_call` if the server procedure terminates before returning.

```
solaris % clientintr1 /tmp/door1 11
door_call error: Interrupted system call
```

Uninterruptability of `door_call` System Call

The `door_call` manual page warns that this function is not a restartable system call. (The `door_call` function in the doors library invokes a system call of the same name.) We can see this by changing our server so that the server procedure just sleeps for 6 seconds before returning, which we show in Figure 15.26.

—— *doors/serverintr2.c*
```
 1 #include    "unpipc.h"

 2 void
 3 servproc(void *cookie, char *dataptr, size_t datasize,
 4          door_desc_t *descptr, size_t ndesc)
 5 {
 6     long    arg, result;

 7     sleep(6);                       /* let client catch SIGCHLD */
 8     arg = *((long *) dataptr);
 9     result = arg * arg;
10     Door_return((char *) &result, sizeof(result), NULL, 0);
11 }
```
—— *doors/serverintr2.c*

Figure 15.26 Server procedure sleeps for 6 seconds.

We then modify our client from Figure 15.2 to establish a signal handler for SIGCHLD, `fork` a child process, and have the child sleep for 2 seconds and then terminate. Therefore, about 2 seconds after the client parent calls door_call, the parent catches SIGCHLD and the signal handler returns, interrupting the door_call system call. We show this client in Figure 15.27.

―― *doors/clientintr2.c*

```
 1 #include    "unpipc.h"

 2 void
 3 sig_chld(int signo)
 4 {
 5     return;                     /* just interrupt door_call() */
 6 }

 7 int
 8 main(int argc, char **argv)
 9 {
10     int     fd;
11     long    ival, oval;
12     door_arg_t arg;

13     if (argc != 3)
14         err_quit("usage: clientintr2 <server-pathname> <integer-value>");

15     fd = Open(argv[1], O_RDWR);  /* open the door */

16         /* set up the arguments and pointer to result */
17     ival = atol(argv[2]);
18     arg.data_ptr = (char *) &ival;  /* data arguments */
19     arg.data_size = sizeof(long);    /* size of data arguments */
20     arg.desc_ptr = NULL;
21     arg.desc_num = 0;
22     arg.rbuf = (char *) &oval;   /* data results */
23     arg.rsize = sizeof(long);    /* size of data results */

24     Signal(SIGCHLD, sig_chld);
25     if (Fork() == 0) {
26         sleep(2);               /* child */
27         exit(0);                /* generates SIGCHLD */
28     }
29         /* parent: call server procedure and print result */
30     Door_call(fd, &arg);
31     printf("result: %ld\n", oval);

32     exit(0);
33 }
```

―― *doors/clientintr2.c*

Figure 15.27 Client that catches SIGCHLD after 2 seconds.

The client sees the same error as if the server procedure terminated prematurely: EINTR.

```
solaris % clientintr2 /tmp/door2 22
door_call error: Interrupted system call
```

This means we must block any signals that might be generated during a call to door_call from being delivered to the process, because those signals will interrupt door_call.

Idempotent versus Nonidempotent Procedures

What if we know that we just caught a signal, detect the error of EINTR from door_call, and call the server procedure again, since we know that the error is from our caught signal and not from the server procedure terminating prematurely? This can lead to problems, as we will show.

First, we modify our server to (1) print its thread ID when it is called, (2) sleep for 6 seconds, and (3) print its thread ID when it returns. Figure 15.28 shows this version of our server procedure.

```
                                                         ———— doors/serverintr3.c
 1 #include    "unpipc.h"

 2 void
 3 servproc(void *cookie, char *dataptr, size_t datasize,
 4          door_desc_t *descptr, size_t ndesc)
 5 {
 6     long    arg, result;

 7     printf("thread id %ld called\n", pr_thread_id(NULL));
 8     sleep(6);                     /* let client catch SIGCHLD */
 9     arg = *((long *) dataptr);
10     result = arg * arg;
11     printf("thread id %ld returning\n", pr_thread_id(NULL));
12     Door_return((char *) &result, sizeof(result), NULL, 0);
13 }
                                                         ———— doors/serverintr3.c
```

Figure 15.28 Server procedure that prints its thread ID when called and when returning.

Figure 15.29 shows our client program.

2-8   We declare the global caught_sigchld and set this to one when the SIGCHLD signal is caught.

31-42   We now call door_call in a loop as long as the error is EINTR and this was caused by our signal handler.

If we look at just the client output, it appears OK:

```
solaris % clientintr3 /tmp/door3 33
calling door_call
calling door_call
result: 1089
```

door_call is called the first time, our signal handler is invoked about 2 seconds later and caught_sigchld is set to one, door_call returns EINTR, and we call door_call again. This second time, the server procedure proceeds to completion and the expected result is returned.

But looking at the server output, we see that the server procedure is called twice.

```
solaris % serverintr3 /tmp/door3
thread id 4 called
thread id 4 returning
thread id 5 called
thread id 5 returning
```

```
                                                                       ———— doors/clientintr3.c
 1 #include      "unpipc.h"

 2 volatile sig_atomic_t caught_sigchld;

 3 void
 4 sig_chld(int signo)
 5 {
 6     caught_sigchld = 1;
 7     return;                          /* just interrupt door_call() */
 8 }

 9 int
10 main(int argc, char **argv)
11 {
12     int     fd, rc;
13     long    ival, oval;
14     door_arg_t arg;

15     if (argc != 3)
16         err_quit("usage: clientintr3 <server-pathname> <integer-value>");

17     fd = Open(argv[1], O_RDWR); /* open the door */

18         /* set up the arguments and pointer to result */
19     ival = atol(argv[2]);
20     arg.data_ptr = (char *) &ival;  /* data arguments */
21     arg.data_size = sizeof(long);   /* size of data arguments */
22     arg.desc_ptr = NULL;
23     arg.desc_num = 0;
24     arg.rbuf = (char *) &oval;  /* data results */
25     arg.rsize = sizeof(long);   /* size of data results */

26     Signal(SIGCHLD, sig_chld);
27     if (Fork() == 0) {
28         sleep(2);                /* child */
29         exit(0);                 /* generates SIGCHLD */
30     }
31         /* parent: call server procedure and print result */
32     for ( ; ; ) {
33         printf("calling door_call\n");
34         if ( (rc = door_call(fd, &arg)) == 0)
35             break;               /* success */
36         if (errno == EINTR && caught_sigchld) {
37             caught_sigchld = 0;
38             continue;            /* call door_call() again */
39         }
40         err_sys("door_call error");
41     }
42     printf("result: %ld\n", oval);

43     exit(0);
44 }
                                                                       ———— doors/clientintr3.c
```

Figure 15.29 Client that calls door_call again after receiving EINTR.

When the client calls `door_call` the second time, after the first call is interrupted by the caught signal, this starts another thread that calls the server procedure a second time. If the server procedure is *idempotent*, this is OK. But if the server procedure is not idempotent, this is a problem.

The term *idempotent*, when describing a procedure, means the procedure can be called any number of times without harm. Our server procedure, which calculates the square of a number, is idempotent: we get the correct result whether we call it once or twice. Another example is a procedure that returns the current time and date. Even though this procedure may return different information each time (say it is called twice, 1 second apart, causing the returned times to differ by 1 second), it is still OK. The classic example of a nonidempotent procedure is one that subtracts some amount from a bank account: the end result is wrong unless this procedure is called only once.

Premature Termination of Client

We now see how a server procedure is notified if the client terminates after calling `door_call` but before the server returns. We show our client in Figure 15.30.

── doors/clientintr4.c

```
 1 #include     "unpipc.h"

 2 int
 3 main(int argc, char **argv)
 4 {
 5     int     fd;
 6     long    ival, oval;
 7     door_arg_t arg;

 8     if (argc != 3)
 9         err_quit("usage: clientintr4 <server-pathname> <integer-value>");

10     fd = Open(argv[1], O_RDWR); /* open the door */

11         /* set up the arguments and pointer to result */
12     ival = atol(argv[2]);
13     arg.data_ptr = (char *) &ival;  /* data arguments */
14     arg.data_size = sizeof(long);    /* size of data arguments */
15     arg.desc_ptr = NULL;
16     arg.desc_num = 0;
17     arg.rbuf = (char *) &oval;  /* data results */
18     arg.rsize = sizeof(long);    /* size of data results */

19         /* call server procedure and print result */
20     alarm(3);
21     Door_call(fd, &arg);
22     printf("result: %ld\n", oval);

23     exit(0);
24 }
```

── doors/clientintr4.c

Figure 15.30 Client that terminates prematurely after calling `door_call`.

20   The only change from Figure 15.2 is the call to alarm(3) right before the call to door_call. This function schedules a SIGALRM signal for 3 seconds in the future, but since we do not catch this signal, its default action terminates the process. This will cause the client to terminate before door_call returns, because we will put a 6-second sleep in the server procedure.

Figure 15.31 shows our server procedure and its thread cancellation handler.

doors/serverintr4.c

```
 1 #include     "unpipc.h"

 2 void
 3 servproc_cleanup(void *arg)
 4 {
 5     printf("servproc cancelled, thread id %ld\n", pr_thread_id(NULL));
 6 }

 7 void
 8 servproc(void *cookie, char *dataptr, size_t datasize,
 9          door_desc_t *descptr, size_t ndesc)
10 {
11     int     oldstate, junk;
12     long    arg, result;

13     Pthread_setcancelstate(PTHREAD_CANCEL_ENABLE, &oldstate);
14     pthread_cleanup_push(servproc_cleanup, NULL);
15     sleep(6);
16     arg = *((long *) dataptr);
17     result = arg * arg;
18     pthread_cleanup_pop(0);
19     Pthread_setcancelstate(oldstate, &junk);
20     Door_return((char *) &result, sizeof(result), NULL, 0);
21 }
```

doors/serverintr4.c

Figure 15.31 Server procedure that detects premature termination of client.

Recall our discussion of thread cancellation in Section 8.5 and our discussion of this with Figure 15.23. When the system detects that the client is terminating with a door_call in progress, the server thread handling that call is sent a cancellation request.

- If the server thread has cancellation disabled, nothing happens, the thread executes to completion (when it calls door_return), and the results are then discarded.

- If cancellation is enabled for the server thread, any cleanup handlers are called, and the thread is then terminated.

In our server procedure, we first call pthread_setcancelstate to enable cancellation, because when the doors library creates new threads, it disables thread cancellation. This function also saves the current cancellation state in the variable oldstate, and we restore this state at the end of the function. We then call pthread_cleanup_push to register our function `servproc_cleanup` as the cancellation handler. All our function does is print that the thread has been canceled, but this is where a server procedure can do whatever must be done to clean up after the terminated client: release mutexes, write a log file record, or whatever. When our cleanup handler returns, the thread is terminated.

We also put a 6-second sleep in our server procedure, to allow the client to abort while its `door_call` is in progress.

When we run our client twice, we see that the shell prints "Alarm clock" when our process is killed by a `SIGALRM` signal.

```
solaris % clientintr4 /tmp/door4 44
Alarm Clock
solaris % clientintr4 /tmp/door4 44
Alarm Clock
```

If we look at the corresponding server output, we see that each time the client terminates prematurely, the server thread is indeed canceled and our cleanup handler is called.

```
solaris % serverintr4 /tmp/door4
servproc canceled, thread id 4
servproc canceled, thread id 5
```

The reason we ran our client twice is to show that after the thread with an ID of 4 is canceled, a new thread is created by the doors library to handle the second client invocation.

15.12 Summary

Doors provide the ability to call a procedure in another process on the *same* host. In the next chapter we extend this concept of remote procedure calls by describing the calling of a procedure in another process on *another* host.

The basic functions are simple. A server calls `door_create` to create a door and associate it with a server procedure, and then calls `fattach` to attach the door to a pathname in the filesystem. The client calls `open` on this pathname and then `door_call` to call the server procedure in the server process. The server procedure returns by calling `door_return`.

Normally, the only permission testing performed for a door is that done by `open` when it creates the door, based on the client's user IDs and group IDs, along with the permission bits and owner IDs of the pathname. One nice feature of doors that we have not seen with the other forms of IPC in this text is the ability of the server to determine the client's credentials: the client's effective and real user IDs, and effective and real group IDs. These can be used by the server to determine whether it wants to service this client's request.

Doors allow the passing of descriptors from the client to the server and vice versa. This is a powerful technique, because so much in Unix is represented by a descriptor:

access to files for file or device I/O, access to sockets or XTI for network communication (UNPv1), and access to doors for RPC.

When calling procedures in another process, we must worry about premature termination of the peer, something we do not need to worry about with local procedure calls. A doors client is notified if the server thread terminates prematurely by an error return of EINTR from door_call. A doors server thread is notified if its client terminates while the client is blocked in a call to door_call by the receipt of a cancellation request for the server thread. The server thread must decide whether to handle this cancellation or not.

Exercises

15.1   How many bytes of information are passed as arguments by door_call from the client to the server?

15.2   In Figure 15.6, do we need to call fstat to first verify that the descriptor is a door? Remove this call and see what happens.

15.3   The Solaris 2.6 manual page for sleep(3C) states that "The current process is suspended from execution." In Figure 15.9, why is the doors library able to create the second and third threads (thread IDs 5 and 6) once the first thread (ID 4) starts running, since this statement would imply that the entire server process blocks as soon as one thread calls sleep?

15.4   In Section 15.3, we said that the FD_CLOEXEC bit is automatically set for descriptors created by door_create. But we can call fcntl after door_create returns and turn this bit off. What will happen if we do this, call exec, and then invoke the server procedure from a client?

15.5   In Figures 15.28 and 15.29, print the current time in the two calls to printf in the server and in the two calls to printf in the client. Run the client and server. Why does the first invocation of the server procedure return after 2 seconds?

15.6   Remove the mutex lock that protects fd in Figures 15.22 and 15.23 and verify that the program no longer works. What error do you see?

15.7   If the only characteristic of a server thread that we want to change is to enable cancellation, do we need to establish a server creation procedure?

15.8   Verify that door_revoke allows a client call that is in progress to complete, and determine what happens to door_call once the server procedure has been revoked.

15.9   In our solution to the previous exercise and in Figure 15.22, we said that the door descriptor needs to be a global when either the server procedure or the server creation procedure needs to use the descriptor. That statement is not true. Recode the solution to the previous exercise, keeping fd as an automatic variable in the main function.

15.10 In Figure 15.23, we call pthread_attr_init and pthread_attr_destroy every time a thread is created. Is this optimal?

16

Sun RPC

16.1 Introduction

When we build an application, our first choice is whether to

1. build one huge monolithic program that does everything, or
2. distribute the application among multiple processes that communicate with each other.

If we choose the second option, the next choice is whether to

2a. assume that all the processes run on the same host (allowing IPC to be used for communication between the processes), or
2b. assume that some of the processes will run on other hosts (necessitating some form of network communication between the processes).

If we look at Figure 15.1, the top scenario is case 1, the middle scenario is case 2a, and the bottom scenario is case 2b. Most of this text has focused on case (2a): IPC between processes on the same host, using message passing, shared memory, and possibly some form of synchronization. IPC between threads within the same process, or within threads in different processes, is just a special case of this scenario.

When we require network communications among the various pieces of the application, most applications are written using *explicit network programming*, that is, direct calls to either the sockets API or the XTI API, as described in UNPv1. Using the sockets API, clients call `socket`, `connect`, `read`, and `write`, whereas servers call `socket`, `bind`, `listen`, `accept`, `read`, and `write`. Most applications that we are familiar with (Web browsers, Web servers, Telnet clients, Telnet servers, etc.) are written this way.

An alternative way to write a distributed application is to use *implicit network programming*. Remote procedure calls, or RPC, provide such a tool. We code our application using the familiar procedure call, but the calling process (the client) and the process containing the procedure being called (the server) can be executing on different hosts. The fact that the client and server are running on different hosts, and that network I/O is involved in the procedure call, is for the most part transparent. Indeed, one metric by which to measure any RPC package is how transparent it makes the underlying networking.

Example

As an example of RPC, we recode Figures 15.2 and 15.3 to use Sun RPC instead of doors. The client calls the server's procedure with a long integer argument, and the return value is the square of that value. Figure 16.1 is our first file, square.x.

sunrpc/square1/square.x

```
1 struct square_in {                    /* input (argument) */
2     long    arg1;
3 };

4 struct square_out {                   /* output (result) */
5     long    res1;
6 };

7 program SQUARE_PROG {
8     version SQUARE_VERS {
9         square_out SQUAREPROC(square_in) = 1;    /* procedure number = 1 */
10    } =    1;                          /* version number */
11 } =    0x31230000;                    /* program number */
```

sunrpc/square1/square.x

Figure 16.1 RPC specification file.

These files whose name end in .x are called RPC specification files, and they define the server procedures along with their arguments and results.

Define argument and return value

1–6   We define two structures, one for the arguments (a single long), and one for the results (a single long).

Define program, version, and procedure

7–11   We define an RPC program named SQUARE_PROG that consists of one version (SQUARE_VERS), and in that version is a single procedure named SQUAREPROC. The argument to this procedure is a square_in structure, and its return value is a square_out structure. We also assign this procedure a number of 1, we assign the version a value of 1, and we assign the program number a 32-bit hexadecimal value. (We say more about these program numbers in Figure 16.9.)

We compile this specification file using a program supplied with the Sun RPC package, rpcgen.

The next program we write is the client main function that calls our remote procedure. We show this in Figure 16.2.

```
                                                               —— sunrpc/square1/client.c
 1 #include     "unpipc.h"           /* our header */
 2 #include     "square.h"           /* generated by rpcgen */

 3 int
 4 main(int argc, char **argv)
 5 {
 6     CLIENT *cl;
 7     square_in in;
 8     square_out *outp;

 9     if (argc != 3)
10         err_quit("usage: client <hostname> <integer-value>");

11     cl = Clnt_create(argv[1], SQUARE_PROG, SQUARE_VERS, "tcp");

12     in.arg1 = atol(argv[2]);
13     if ( (outp = squareproc_1(&in, cl)) == NULL)
14         err_quit("%s", clnt_sperror(cl, argv[1]));

15     printf("result: %ld\n", outp->res1);
16     exit(0);
17 }
                                                               —— sunrpc/square1/client.c
```

Figure 16.2 Client `main` function that calls remote procedure.

Include header generated by `rpcgen`

2   We #include the `square.h` header that is generated by `rpcgen`.

Declare client handle

6   We declare a *client handle* named `cl`. Client handles are intended to look like standard I/O `FILE` pointers (hence the uppercase name of `CLIENT`).

Obtain client handle

11   We call `clnt_create`, which returns a client handle upon success.

```
#include <rpc/rpc.h>

CLIENT *clnt_create(const char *host, unsigned long prognum,
                    unsigned long versnum, const char *protocol);

                            Returns: nonnull client handle if OK, NULL on error
```

As with standard I/O `FILE` pointers, we don't care what the client handle points to. It is probably some structure of information that is maintained by the RPC runtime system. `clnt_create` allocates one of these structures and returns its pointer to us, and we then pass this pointer to the RPC runtime each time we call a remote procedure.

The first argument to `clnt_create` is either the hostname or IP address of the host running our server. The second argument is the program name, and the third argument is the version number, both from our `square.x` file (Figure 16.1). The final argument is our choice of protocol, and we normally specify either TCP or UDP.

Call remote procedure and print result

12–15   We call our procedure, and the first argument is a pointer to the input structure (&in), and the second argument is the client handle. (In most standard I/O calls, the FILE handle is the final argument. Similarly, the CLIENT handle is normally the final argument to the RPC functions.) The return value is a pointer to the result structure. Notice that we allocate room for the input structure, but the RPC runtime allocates the result structure.

In our square.x specification file, we named our procedure SQUAREPROC, but from the client we call squareproc_1. The convention is that the name in the .x file is converted to lowercase and an underscore is appended, followed by the version number.

On the server side, all we write is our server procedure, which we show in Figure 16.3. The rpcgen program automatically generates the server main function.

————————————————————————— sunrpc/square1/server.c
```
1 #include    "unpipc.h"
2 #include    "square.h"

3 square_out *
4 squareproc_1_svc(square_in *inp, struct svc_req *rqstp)
5 {
6      static square_out out;

7      out.res1 = inp->arg1 * inp->arg1;
8      return (&out);
9 }
```
————————————————————————— sunrpc/square1/server.c

Figure 16.3 Server procedure that is called using Sun RPC.

Procedure arguments

3–4   We first notice that the name of our server procedure has _svc appended following the version number. This allows two ANSI C function prototypes in the square.h header, one for the function called by the client in Figure 16.2 (which had the client handle as an argument) and one for the actual server function (which has different arguments).

When our server procedure is called, the first argument is a pointer to the input structure, and the second argument is a pointer to a structure passed by the RPC runtime that contains information about this invocation (which we ignore in this simple procedure).

Execute and return

6–8   We fetch the input argument and calculate its square. The result is stored in a structure whose address is the return value from this function. Since we are returning the address of a variable from the function, that variable *cannot* be an automatic variable. We declare it as static.

> Astute readers will note that this prevents our server function from being thread safe. We discuss this in Section 16.2 and show a thread-safe version there.

We now compile our client under Solaris and our server under BSD/OS, start the server, and run the client.

```
solaris % client bsdi 11
result: 121
solaris % client 209.75.135.35 22
result: 484
```

The first time we specify the server's hostname, and the second time its IP address. This demonstrates that the `clnt_create` function and the RPC runtime functions that it calls allow either a hostname or an IP address.

We now demonstrate some error returns from `clnt_create` when either the host does not exist, or the host exists but is not running our server.

```
solaris % client nosuchhost 11
nosuchhost: RPC: Unknown host          from the RPC runtime
clnt_create error                      from our wrapper function
solaris % client localhost 11
localhost: RPC: Program not registered
clnt_create error
```

We have written a client and server and shown their use without any explicit network programming at all. Our client just calls two functions (`clnt_create` and `squareproc_1`), and on the server side, we have just written the function `squareproc_1_svc`. All the details involving XTI under Solaris, sockets under BSD/OS, and network I/O are handled by the RPC runtime. This is the purpose of RPC: to allow the programming of distributed applications without requiring explicit knowledge of network programming.

Another important point in this example is that the two systems, a Sparc running Solaris and an Intel x86 running BSD/OS, have different *byte orders*. That is, the Sparc is big endian and the Intel is little endian (which we show in Section 3.4 of UNPv1). These byte ordering differences are also handled automatically by the runtime library, using a standard called *XDR* (external data representation), which we discuss in Section 16.8.

More steps are involved in building this client and server than in the other programs in this text. Here are the steps involved in building the client executable:

```
solaris % rpcgen -C square.x
solaris % cc -c client.c -o client.o
solaris % cc -c square_clnt.c -o square_clnt.o
solaris % cc -c square_xdr.c -o square_xdr.o
solaris % cc -o client client.o square_clnt.o square_xdr.o libunpipc.a -lnsl
```

The `-C` option to rpcgen tells it to generate ANSI C prototypes in the `square.h` header. rpcgen also generates a *client stub* (`square_clnt.c`) and a file named `square_xdr.c` that handles the XDR data conversions. Our library (with functions used in this book) is `libunpipc.a`, and `-lnsl` specifies the system library with the networking functions under Solaris (which includes the RPC and XDR runtime).

We see similar commands when we build the server, although rpcgen does not need to be run again. The file `square_svc.c` contains the server `main` function, and `square_xdr.o`, the same file from earlier that contains the XDR functions, is also required by the server.

```
solaris % cc -c server.c -o server.o
solaris % cc -c square_svc.c -o square_svc.o
solaris % cc -o server server.o square_svc.o square_xdr.o libunpipc.a -lnsl
```

This generates a client and server that both run under Solaris.

When the client and server are being built for different systems (e.g., in our earlier example, we ran the client under Solaris and the server under BSD/OS), additional steps may be required. For example, some of the files must be either shared (e.g., NFS) or copied between the two systems, and files that are used by both the client and server (`square_xdr.o`) must be compiled on each system.

Figure 16.4 summarizes the files and steps required to build our client–server example. The three shaded boxes are the files that we must write. The dashed lines show the files that #include `square.h`.

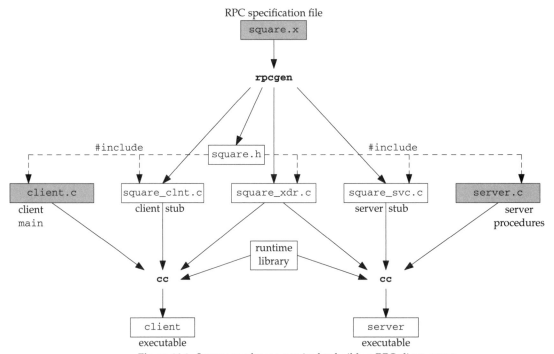

Figure 16.4 Summary of steps required to build an RPC client–server.

Figure 16.5 summarizes the steps that normally take place in a remote procedure call. The numbered steps are executed in order.

0. The sever is started and it registers itself with the port mapper on the server host. The client is then started, and it calls `clnt_create`, which contacts the port mapper on the server host to find the server's ephemeral port. The `clnt_create` function also establishes a TCP connection with the server (since we specified TCP

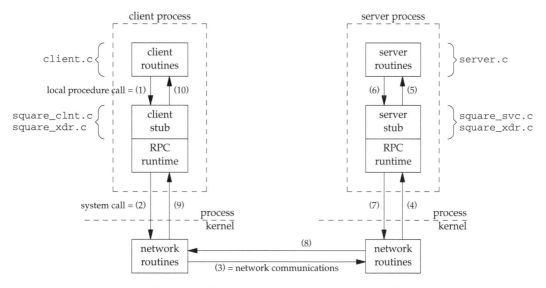

Figure 16.5 Steps involved in a remote procedure call.

as the protocol in Figure 16.2). We do not show these steps in the figure and save our detailed description for Section 16.3.

1. The client calls a local procedure, called the *client stub*. In Figure 16.2, this procedure was named `squareproc_1`, and the file containing the client stub was generated by `rpcgen` and called `square_clnt.c`. To the client, the client stub appears to be the actual server procedure that it wants to call. The purpose of the stub is to package up the arguments to the remote procedure, possibly put them into some standard format, and then build one or more network messages. The packaging of the client's arguments into a network message is termed *marshaling*. The client routines and the stub normally call functions in the RPC runtime library (e.g., `clnt_create` in our earlier example). When link editing under Solaris, these runtime functions are loaded from the `-lnsl` library, whereas under BSD/OS, they are in the standard C library.

2. These network messages are sent to the remote system by the client stub. This normally requires a system call into the local kernel (e.g., `write` or `sendto`).

3. The network messages are transferred to the remote system. The typical networking protocols used for this step are either TCP or UDP.

4. A *server stub* procedure is waiting on the remote system for the client's request. It unmarshals the arguments from the network messages.

5. The server stub executes a local procedure call to invoke the actual server function (our `squareproc_1_svc` procedure in Figure 16.3), passing it the arguments that it received in the network messages from the client.

6. When the server procedure is finished, it returns to the server stub, returning whatever its return values are.

7.   The server stub converts the return values, if necessary, and marshals them into one or more network messages to send back to the client.

8.   The messages are transferred back across the network to the client.

9.   The client stub reads the network messages from the local kernel (e.g., `read` or `recvfrom`).

10.   After possibly converting the return values, the client stub finally returns to the client function. This step appears to be a normal procedure return to the client.

History

Probably one of the earliest papers on RPC is [White 1975]. According to [Corbin 1991], White then moved to Xerox, and several RPC systems were developed there. One of these, Courier, was released as a product in 1981. The classic paper on RPC is [Birrell and Nelson 1984], which describes the RPC facility for the Cedar project running on single-user Dorado workstations at Xerox in the early 1980s. Xerox was implementing RPC on workstations before most people knew what workstations were! A Unix implementation of Courier was distributed for many years with the 4.x BSD releases, but today Courier is of historical interest only.

Sun released the first version of its RPC package in 1985. It was developed by Bob Lyon, who had left Xerox in 1983 to join Sun. Its official name is ONC/RPC: Open Network Computing Remote Procedure Call, but it is often called just "Sun RPC." Technically, it is similar to Courier. The original releases of Sun RPC were written using the sockets API and worked with either TCP or UDP. The publicly available source code release was called RPCSRC. In the early 1990s, this was rewritten to use TLI, the predecessor to XTI (described in Part 4 of UNPv1), and works with any networking protocol supported by the kernel. Publicly available source code implementations of both are available from `ftp://playground.sun.com/pub/rpc` with the sockets version named `rpcsrc` and the TLI version named `tirpcsrc` (called TI-RPC, where "TI" stands for "transport independent").

RFC 1831 [Srinivasan 1995a] provides an overview of Sun RPC and describes the format of the RPC messages that are sent across the network. RFC 1832 [Srinivasan 1995b] describes XDR, both the supported datatypes and their format "on the wire." RFC 1833 [Srinivasan 1995c] describes the binding protocols: RPCBIND and its predecessor, the port mapper.

Probably the most widespread application that uses Sun RPC is NFS, Sun's network filesystem. Normally, NFS is not built using the standard RPC tools, `rpcgen` and the RPC runtime library that we describe in this chapter. Instead, most of the library routines are hand-optimized and reside within the kernel for performance reasons. Nevertheless, most systems that support NFS also support Sun RPC.

In the mid-1980s, Apollo competed against Sun in the workstation market, and they designed their own RPC package to compete against Sun's, called NCA (Network Computing Architecture), and their implementation was called NCS (Network Computing System). NCA/RPC was the RPC protocol, NDR (Network Data Representation) was similar to Sun's XDR, and NIDL (Network Interface Definition Language) defined the interfaces between the clients and servers (e.g., similar to our `.x` file in Figure 16.1). The runtime library was called NCK (Network Computing Kernel).

Apollo was acquired by Hewlett Packard in 1989, and NCA was developed into the Open Software Foundation's Distributed Computing Environment (DCE), of which RPC is a fundamental element from which most pieces are built. More information on DCE is available from `http://www.camb.opengroup.org/tech/dce`. An implementation of the DCE RPC package has been made publicly available at `ftp://gatekeeper.dec.com/pub/DEC/DCE`. This directory also contains a 171-page document describing the internals of the DCE RPC package. DCE is available for many platforms.

> Sun RPC is more widespread than DCE RPC, probably because of its freely available implementation and its packaging as part of the basic system with most versions of Unix. DCE RPC is normally available as an add-on (i.e., separate cost) feature. Widespread porting of the publicly available implementation has not occurred, although a Linux port is underway. In this text, we cover only Sun RPC. All three RPC packages—Courier, Sun RPC, and DCE RPC—are amazingly similar, because the basic RPC concepts are the same.

> Most Unix vendors provide additional, detailed documentation on Sun RPC. For example, the Sun documentation is available at `http://docs.sun.com`, and in the Developer Collection, Volume 1, is a 280-page "ONC+ Developer's Guide." The Digital Unix documentation at `http://www.unix.digital.com/faqs/publications/pub_page/V40D_DOCS.HTM` includes a 116-page manual titled "Programming with ONC RPC."

> RPC itself is a controversial topic. Eight postings on this topic are contained in `http://www.kohala.com/~rstevens/papers.others/rpc.comments.txt`.

In this chapter, we assume TI-RPC (the transport independent version of RPC mentioned earlier) for most examples, and we talk about TCP and UDP as the supported protocols, even though TI-RPC supports any protocols that are supported by the host.

16.2 Multithreading

Recall Figure 15.9, in which we showed the automatic thread management performed by a doors server, providing a concurrent server by default. We now show that Sun RPC provides an *iterative server* by default. We start with the example from the previous section and modify only the server procedure. Figure 16.6 shows the new function, which prints its thread ID, sleeps for 5 seconds, prints its thread ID again, and returns.

We start the server and then run the client three times:

```
solaris % client localhost 22 & client localhost 33 & \
client localhost 44 &
[3]     25179
[4]     25180
[5]     25181
solaris % result: 484          about 5 seconds after the prompt is printed
result: 1936                   another 5 seconds later
result: 1089                   and another 5 seconds later
```

sunrpc/square2/server.c

```
 1 #include    "unpipc.h"
 2 #include    "square.h"

 3 square_out *
 4 squareproc_1_svc(square_in *inp, struct svc_req *rqstp)
 5 {
 6     static square_out out;

 7     printf("thread %ld started, arg = %ld\n",
 8             pr_thread_id(NULL), inp->arg1);
 9     sleep(5);
10     out.res1 = inp->arg1 * inp->arg1;
11     printf("thread %ld done\n", pr_thread_id(NULL));

12     return (&out);
13 }
```

sunrpc/square2/server.c

Figure 16.6 Server procedure that sleeps for 5 seconds.

Although we cannot tell from this output, a 5-second wait occurs between the printing of each result by the client. If we look at the server output, we see that the clients are handled iteratively: the first client's request is handled to completion, and then the second client's request is handled to completion, and finally the third client's request is handled to completion.

```
solaris % server
thread 1 started, arg = 22
thread 1 done
thread 1 started, arg = 44
thread 1 done
thread 1 started, arg = 33
thread 1 done
```

One thread handles all client requests: the server is not multithreaded by default.

> Our doors servers in Chapter 15 all ran in the foreground when started from the shell, as in
>
> ```
> solaris % server
> ```
>
> That allowed us to place debugging calls to printf in our server procedures. But Sun RPC servers, by default, run as daemons, performing the steps as outlined in Section 12.4 of UNPv1. This requires calling syslog from the server procedure to print any diagnostic information. What we have done, however, is specify the C compiler flag -DDEBUG when we compile our server, which is the equivalent of placing the line
>
> ```
> #define DEBUG
> ```
>
> in the server stub (the square_svc.c file that is generated by rpcgen). This stops the server main function from making itself a daemon, and leaves it connected to the terminal on which it was started. That is why we can call printf from our server procedure.

The provision for a multithreaded server appeared with Solaris 2.4 and is enabled by a -M command-line option to rpcgen. This makes the server code generated by rpcgen thread safe. Another option, -A, has the server automatically create threads as they are needed to process new client requests. We enable both options when we run rpcgen.

Both the client and server also require source code changes, which we should expect, given our use of static in Figure 16.3. The only change we make to our square.x file is to change the version from 1 to 2. Nothing changes in the declarations of the procedure's argument and result structures.

Figure 16.7 shows our new client program.

```
                                                    ──── sunrpc/square3/client.c
 1 #include      "unpipc.h"
 2 #include      "square.h"

 3 int
 4 main(int argc, char **argv)
 5 {
 6     CLIENT *cl;
 7     square_in in;
 8     square_out out;

 9     if (argc != 3)
10         err_quit("usage: client <hostname> <integer-value>");

11     cl = Clnt_create(argv[1], SQUARE_PROG, SQUARE_VERS, "tcp");

12     in.arg1 = atol(argv[2]);
13     if (squareproc_2(&in, &out, cl) != RPC_SUCCESS)
14         err_quit("%s", clnt_sperror(cl, argv[1]));

15     printf("result: %ld\n", out.res1);
16     exit(0);
17 }
                                                    ──── sunrpc/square3/client.c
```

Figure 16.7 Client main function for multithreaded server.

Declare variable to hold result

8   We declare a variable of type square_out, not a pointer to this type.

New argument for procedure call

12–14   A pointer to our out variable becomes the second argument to squareproc_2, and the client handle is the last argument. Instead of this function returning a pointer to the result (as in Figure 16.2), it now returns either RPC_SUCCESS or some other value if an error occurs. The clnt_stat enum in the <rpc/clnt_stat.h> header lists all the possible error returns.

Figure 16.8 shows our new server procedure. As with Figure 16.6, it prints its thread ID, sleeps for 5 seconds, prints another message, and returns.

New arguments and return value

3–12   The changes required for multithreading involve the function arguments and return value. Instead of returning a pointer to the result structure (as in Figure 16.3), a pointer to this structure is now the second argument to the function. The pointer to the svc_req structure moves to the third position. The return value is now TRUE upon success, or FALSE if an error is encountered.

```
                                                               sunrpc/square3/server.c
 1 #include    "unpipc.h"
 2 #include    "square.h"

 3 bool_t
 4 squareproc_2_svc(square_in *inp, square_out *outp, struct svc_req *rqstp)
 5 {
 6     printf("thread %ld started, arg = %ld\n",
 7             pr_thread_id(NULL), inp->arg1);
 8     sleep(5);
 9     outp->res1 = inp->arg1 * inp->arg1;
10     printf("thread %ld done\n", pr_thread_id(NULL));
11     return (TRUE);
12 }

13 int
14 square_prog_2_freeresult(SVCXPRT *transp, xdrproc_t xdr_result,
15                                 caddr_t result)
16 {
17     xdr_free(xdr_result, result);
18     return (1);
19 }
                                                               sunrpc/square3/server.c
```

Figure 16.8 Multithreaded server procedure.

New function to free XDR memory

13–19   Another source code change we must make is to provide a function that frees any
storage automatically allocated. This function is called from the server stub after the
server procedure returns and after the result has been sent to the client. In our example,
we just call the generic xdr_free routine. (We talk more about this function with Figure 16.19 and Exercise 16.10.) If our server procedure had allocated any storage necessary to hold the result (say a linked list), it would free that memory from this new
function.

We build our client and server and again run three copies of the client at the same
time:

```
solaris % client localhost 55 & client localhost 66 & \
client localhost 77 &
[3]     25427
[4]     25428
[5]     25429
solaris % result: 4356
result: 3025
result: 5929
```

This time we can tell that the three results are printed one right after the other. Looking
at the server output, we see that three threads are used, and all run simultaneously.

```
solaris % server
thread 1 started, arg = 55
thread 4 started, arg = 77
```

```
thread 6 started, arg = 66
thread 6 done
thread 1 done
thread 4 done
```

One unfortunate side effect of the source code changes required for multithreading is that not all systems support this feature. For example, Digital Unix 4.0B and BSD/OS 3.1 both provide the older RPC system that does not support multithreading. That means if we want to compile and run a program on both types of systems, we need #ifdefs to handle the differences in the calling sequences at the client and server ends. Of course, a nonthreaded client on BSD/OS, say, can still call a multithreaded server procedure running on Solaris, but if we have an RPC client (or server) that we want to compile on both types of systems, we need to modify the source code to handle the differences.

16.3 Server Binding

In the description of Figure 16.5, we glossed over step 0: how the server registers itself with its local port mapper and how the client discovers the value of this port. We first note that any host running an RPC server must be running the *port mapper*. The port mapper is assigned TCP port 111 and UDP port 111, and these are the only fixed Internet port assignments for Sun RPC. RPC servers always bind an ephemeral port and then register their ephemeral port with the local port mapper. When a client starts, it must first contact the port mapper on the server's host, ask for the server's ephemeral port number, and then contact the server on that ephemeral port. The port mapper is providing a name service whose scope is confined to that system.

> Some readers will claim that NFS also has a fixed port number assignment of 2049. Although many implementations use this port by default, and some older implementations still have this port number hardcoded into the client and server, most current implementations allow other ports to be used. Most NFS clients also contact the port mapper on the server host to obtain the port number.

> With Solaris 2.x, Sun renamed the port mapper RPCBIND. The reason for this change is that the term "port" implied Internet ports, whereas the TI-RPC package can work with any networking protocol, not just TCP and UDP. We will use the traditional name of port mapper. Also, in our discussion that follows, we assume that TCP and UDP are the only protocols supported on the server host.

The steps performed by the server and client are as follows:

1. When the system goes into multiuser mode, the port mapper is started. The executable name is typically `portmap` or `rpcbind`.

2. When our server starts, its `main` function (which is part of the server stub that is generated by `rpcgen`) calls the library function `svc_create`. This function determines the networking protocols supported by the host and creates a transport endpoint (e.g., socket) for each protocol, binding an ephemeral port to the TCP and UDP endpoints. It then contacts the local port mapper to register the TCP and UDP ephemeral port numbers with the RPC program number and version number.

The port mapper is itself an RPC program and the server registers itself with the port mapper using RPC calls (albeit to a known port, 111). A description of the procedures supported by the port mapper is given in RFC 1833 [Srinivasan 1995c]. Three versions of this RPC program exist: version 2 is the historical port mapper that handles just TCP and UDP ports, and versions 3 and 4 are the newer RPCBIND protocols.

We can see all the RPC programs that are registered with the port mapper by executing the rpcinfo program. We can execute this program to verify that port number 111 is used by the port mapper itself:

```
solaris % rpcinfo -p
  program vers proto   port  service
  100000    4   tcp    111   rpcbind
  100000    3   tcp    111   rpcbind
  100000    2   tcp    111   rpcbind
  100000    4   udp    111   rpcbind
  100000    3   udp    111   rpcbind
  100000    2   udp    111   rpcbind
```

(We have omitted many additional lines of output.) We see that Solaris 2.6 supports all three versions of the protocol, all at port 111, using either TCP or UDP. The mapping from the RPC program number to the service name is normally found in the file /etc/rpc. Executing the same command under BSD/OS 3.1 shows that it supports only version 2 of this program.

```
bsdi % rpcinfo -p
  program vers proto   port
  100000    2   tcp    111   portmapper
  100000    2   udp    111   portmapper
```

Digital Unix 4.0B also supports just version 2:

```
alpha % rpcinfo -p
  program vers proto   port
  100000    2   tcp    111   portmapper
  100000    2   udp    111   portmapper
```

Our server process then goes to sleep, waiting for a client request to arrive. This could be a new TCP connection on its TCP port, or the arrival of a UDP datagram on its UDP port. If we execute rpcinfo after starting our server from Figure 16.3, we see

```
solaris % rpcinfo -p
  program  vers proto   port  service
  824377344   1   udp   47972
  824377344   1   tcp   40849
```

where 824377344 equals 0x31230000, the program number that we assigned in Figure 16.1. We also assigned a version number of 1 in that figure. Notice that a server is ready to accept clients using either TCP or UDP, and the client chooses which of these two protocols to use when it creates the client handle (the final argument to clnt_create in Figure 16.2).

3. The client starts and calls `clnt_create`. The arguments (Figure 16.2) are the server's hostname or IP address, the program number, version number, and a string specifying the protocol. An RPC request is sent to the server host's port mapper (normally using UDP as the protocol for this RPC message), asking for the information on the specified program, version, and protocol. Assuming success, the port number is saved in the client handle for all future RPC calls using this handle.

In Figure 16.1, we assigned a program number of `0x31230000` to our program. The 32-bit program numbers are divided into groups, as shown in Figure 16.9.

Program number	Description
`0x00000000 - 0x1fffffff`	defined by Sun
`0x20000000 - 0x3fffffff`	defined by user
`0x40000000 - 0x5fffffff`	transient (for customer-written applications)
`0x60000000 - 0xffffffff`	reserved

Figure 16.9 Program number ranges for Sun RPC.

The `rpcinfo` program shows the programs currently registered on your system. Another source of information on the RPC programs supported on a given system is normally the `.x` files in the directory `/usr/include/rpcsvc`.

`inetd` and RPC Servers

By default, servers created by `rpcgen` can be invoked by the `inetd` superserver. (Section 12.5 of UNPv1 covers `inetd` in detail.) Examining the server stub generated by `rpcgen` shows that when the server `main` starts, it checks whether standard input is a XTI endpoint and, if so, assumes it was started by `inetd`.

Backing up, after creating an RPC server that will be invoked by `inetd`, the `/etc/inetd.conf` configuration file needs to be updated with the server information: the RPC program name, the program numbers that are supported, which protocols to support, and the pathname of the server executable. As an example, here is one line (wrapped to fit on this page) from the Solaris configuration file:

```
rstatd/2-4  tli  rpc/datagram_v  wait  root
        /usr/lib/netsvc/rstat/rpc.rstatd rpc.rstatd
```

The first field is the program name (which will be mapped to its corresponding program number using the `/etc/rpc` file), and the supported versions are 2, 3, and 4. The next field specifies a XTI endpoint (as opposed to a socket endpoint), and the third field specifies that all visible datagram protocols are supported. Looking at the file `/etc/netconfig`, there are two of these protocols: UDP and `/dev/clts`. (Chapter 29 of UNPv1 describes this file and XTI addresses.) The fourth field, `wait`, tells `inetd` to wait for this server to terminate before monitoring the XTI endpoint for another client request. All RPC servers in `/etc/inetd.conf` specify the `wait` attribute.

The next field, `root`, specifies the user ID under which the program will run, and the last two fields are the pathname of the executable and the program name with any arguments to be passed to the program (there are no command-line arguments for this program).

inetd will create the XTI endpoints and register them with the port mapper for the specified program and versions. We can verify this with rpcinfo:

```
solaris % rpcinfo | grep statd
100001    2    udp       0.0.0.0.128.11       rstatd      superuser
100001    3    udp       0.0.0.0.128.11       rstatd      superuser
100001    4    udp       0.0.0.0.128.11       rstatd      superuser
100001    2    ticlts    \000\000\020,        rstatd      superuser
100001    3    ticlts    \000\000\020,        rstatd      superuser
100001    4    ticlts    \000\000\020,        rstatd      superuser
```

The fourth field is the printable format for XTI addresses (which prints the individual bytes) and $128 \times 256 + 11$ equals 32779, which is the UDP ephemeral port number assigned to this XTI endpoint.

When a UDP datagram arrives for port 32779, inetd will detect that a datagram is ready to be read and it will fork and then exec the program /usr/lib/netsvc/rstat/rpc.rstatd. Between the fork and exec, the XTI endpoint for this server will be duplicated onto descriptors 0, 1, and 2, and all other inetd descriptors are closed (Figure 12.7 of UNPv1). inetd will also stop monitoring this XTI endpoint for additional client requests until this server (which will be a child of inetd) terminates—the wait attribute in the configuration file for this server.

Assuming this program was generated by rpcgen, it will detect that standard input is a XTI endpoint and initialize it accordingly as an RPC server endpoint. This is done by calling the RPC functions svc_tli_create and svc_reg, two functions that we do not cover. The second function does not register this server with the port mapper—that is done only once by inetd when it starts. The RPC server loop, a function named svc_run, will read the pending datagram and call the appropriate server procedure to handle the client's request.

Normally, servers invoked by inetd handle one client's request and terminate, allowing inetd to wait for the next client request. As an optimization, RPC servers generated by rpcgen wait around for a small amount of time (2 minutes is the default) in case another client request arrives. If so, this existing server that is already running will read the datagram and process the request. This avoids the overhead of a fork and an exec for multiple client requests that arrive in quick succession. After the small wait period, the server will terminate. This will generate SIGCHLD for inetd, causing it to start looking for arriving datagrams on the XTI endpoint again.

16.4 Authentication

By default, there is no information in an RPC request to identify the client. The server replies to the client's request without worrying about who the client is. This is called *null authentication* or AUTH_NONE.

The next level is called *Unix authentication* or AUTH_SYS. The client must tell the RPC runtime to include its identification (hostname, effective user ID, effective group ID, and supplementary group IDs) with each request. We modify our client–server from Section 16.2 to include Unix authentication. Figure 16.10 shows the client.

―――――――――――――――――――――――――――――――――――――― *sunrpc/square4/client.c*

```
 1 #include      "unpipc.h"
 2 #include      "square.h"

 3 int
 4 main(int argc, char **argv)
 5 {
 6     CLIENT *cl;
 7     square_in in;
 8     square_out out;

 9     if (argc != 3)
10         err_quit("usage: client <hostname> <integer-value>");

11     cl = Clnt_create(argv[1], SQUARE_PROG, SQUARE_VERS, "tcp");

12     auth_destroy(cl->cl_auth);
13     cl->cl_auth = authsys_create_default();

14     in.arg1 = atol(argv[2]);
15     if (squareproc_2(&in, &out, cl) != RPC_SUCCESS)
16         err_quit("%s", clnt_sperror(cl, argv[1]));

17     printf("result: %ld\n", out.res1);
18     exit(0);
19 }
```
―――――――――――――――――――――――――――――――――――――― *sunrpc/square4/client.c*

Figure 16.10 Client that provides Unix authentication.

12–13   These two lines are new. We first call `auth_destroy` to destroy the previous authentication associated with this client handle, the null authentication that is created by default. The function `authsys_create_default` creates the appropriate Unix authentication structure, and we store that in the `cl_auth` member of the `CLIENT` structure. The remainder of the client has not changed from Figure 16.7.

Figure 16.11 shows our new server procedure, modified from Figure 16.8. We do not show the `square_prog_2_freeresult` function, which does not change.

6–8   We now use the pointer to the `svc_req` structure that is always passed as an argument to the server procedure.

```
struct svc_req {
    u_long              rq_prog;      /* program number */
    u_long              rq_vers;      /* version number */
    u_long              rq_proc;      /* procedure number */
    struct opaque_auth  rq_cred;      /* raw credentials */
    caddr_t             rq_clntcred;  /* cooked credentials (read-only) */
    SVCXPRT            *rq_xprt;      /* transport handle */
};

struct opaque_auth {
    enum_t  oa_flavor;    /* flavor: AUTH_xxx constant */
    caddr_t oa_base;      /* address of more auth stuff */
    u_int   oa_length;    /* not to exceed MAX_AUTH_BYTES */
};
```

sunrpc/square4/server.c

```
 1 #include    "unpipc.h"
 2 #include    "square.h"

 3 bool_t
 4 squareproc_2_svc(square_in *inp, square_out *outp, struct svc_req *rqstp)
 5 {
 6     printf("thread %ld started, arg = %ld, auth = %d\n",
 7             pr_thread_id(NULL), inp->arg1, rqstp->rq_cred.oa_flavor);
 8     if (rqstp->rq_cred.oa_flavor == AUTH_SYS) {
 9         struct authsys_parms *au;

10         au = (struct authsys_parms *) rqstp->rq_clntcred;
11         printf("AUTH_SYS: host %s, uid %ld, gid %ld\n",
12                 au->aup_machname, (long) au->aup_uid, (long) au->aup_gid);
13     }
14     sleep(5);
15     outp->res1 = inp->arg1 * inp->arg1;
16     printf("thread %ld done\n", pr_thread_id(NULL));
17     return (TRUE);
18 }
```

sunrpc/square4/server.c

Figure 16.11 Server procedure that looks for Unix authentication.

The `rq_cred` member contains the raw authentication information, and its `oa_flavor` member is an integer that identifies the type of authentication. The term "raw" means that the RPC runtime has not processed the information pointed to by `oa_base`. But if the authentication type is one supported by the runtime, then the cooked credentials pointed to by `rq_clntcred` have been processed by the runtime into some structure appropriate for that type of authentication. We print the type of authentication and then check whether it equals `AUTH_SYS`.

9–12   For Unix authentication, the pointer to the cooked credentials (`rq_clntcred`) points to an `authsys_parms` structure containing the client's identity:

```
struct authsys_parms {
  u_long  aup_time;      /* credentials creation time */
  char    *aup_machname; /* hostname where client is located */
  uid_t   aup_uid;       /* effective user ID */
  gid_t   aup_gid;       /* effective group ID */
  u_int   aup_len;       /* #elements in aup_gids[] */
  gid_t   *aup_gids;     /* supplementary group IDs */
};
```

We obtain the pointer to this structure and print the client's hostname, effective user ID, and effective group ID.

If we start our server and run the client once, we get the following output from the server:

```
solaris % server
thread 1 started, arg = 44, auth = 1
AUTH_SYS: host solaris.kohala.com, uid 765, gid 870
thread 1 done
```

Unix authentication is rarely used, because it is simple to defeat. We can easily build our own RPC packets containing Unix authentication information, setting the user ID and group IDs to any values we want, and send it to the server. The server has no way to *verify* that we are who we claim to be.

> Actually, NFS uses Unix authentication by default, but the requests are normally sent by the NFS client's kernel and usually with a reserved port (Section 2.7 of UNPv1). Some NFS servers are configured to respond to a client's request only if it arrives from a reserved port. If you are trusting the client host to mount your filesystems, you are trusting that client's kernel to identify its users correctly. If a reserved port is not required by the server, then hackers can write their own programs that send NFS requests to an NFS server, setting the Unix authentication IDs to any values desired. Even if a reserved port is required by the server, if you have your own system on which you have superuser privileges, and you can plug your system into the network, you can still send your own NFS requests to the server.

An RPC packet, either a request or a reply, actually contains two fields related to authentication: the *credentials* and the *verifier* (Figures 16.30 and 16.32). A common analogy is a picture ID (passport, driver's license, or whatever). The credentials are the printed information (name, address, date of birth, etc.), and the verifier is the picture. There are also different forms of credentials: a picture is better than just listing the height, weight, and sex, for example. If we had an ID card without any form of identifying information (library cards are often examples of this), then we would have credentials without any verifier, and anyone could use the card and claim to be the owner.

In the case of null authentication, both the credentials and the verifier are empty. With Unix authentication, the credentials contain the hostname and the user and group IDs, but the verifier is empty. Other forms of authentication are supported, and the credentials and verifiers contain other information:

AUTH_SHORT   An alternate form of Unix authentication that is sent in the verifier field from the server back to the client in the RPC reply. It is a smaller amount of information than full Unix authentication, and the client can send this back to the server as the credentials in subsequent requests. The intent of this type of credential is to save network bandwidth and server CPU cycles.

AUTH_DES   DES is an acronym for the *Data Encryption Standard*, and this form of authentication is based on secret key and public key cryptography. This scheme is also called *secure RPC*, and when used as the basis for NFS, this is called *secure NFS*.

AUTH_KERB   This scheme is based on MIT's Kerberos system for authentication.

Chapter 19 of [Garfinkel and Spafford 1996] says more about the latter two forms of authentication, including their setup and use.

16.5 Timeout and Retransmission

We now look at the timeout and retransmission strategy used by Sun RPC. Two timeout values are used:

1. The *total timeout* is the total amount of time that a client waits for the server's reply. This value is used by both TCP and UDP.

2. The *retry timeout* is used only by UDP and is the amount of time between retransmissions of the client's request, waiting for the server's reply.

First, no need exists for a retry timeout with TCP because TCP is a reliable protocol. If the server host never receives the client's request, the client's TCP will time out and retransmit the request. When the server host receives the client's request, the server's TCP will acknowledge its receipt to the client's TCP. If the server's acknowledgment is lost, causing the client's TCP to retransmit the request, when the server TCP receives this duplicate data, it will be discarded and another acknowledgment sent by the server TCP. With a reliable protocol, the reliability (timeout, retransmission, handling of duplicate data or duplicate ACKs) is provided by the transport layer, and is not a concern of the RPC runtime. One request sent by the client RPC layer will be received as one request by the server RPC layer (or the client RPC layer will get an error indication if the request never gets acknowledged), regardless of what happens at the network and transport layers.

After we have created a client handle, we can call `clnt_control` to both query and set options that affect the handle. This is similar to calling `fcntl` for a descriptor, or calling `getsockopt` and `setsockopt` for a socket.

```
#include <rpc/rpc.h>

bool_t clnt_control(CLIENT *cl, unsigned int request, char *ptr);
```
Returns: TRUE if OK, FALSE on error

cl is the client handle, and what is pointed to by *ptr* depends on the *request*.

We modify our client from Figure 16.2 to call this function and print the two timeouts. Figure 16.12 shows our new client.

Protocol is a command-line argument

10–12 We now specify the protocol as another command-line argument and use this as the final argument to `clnt_create`.

Get total timeout

13–14 The first argument to `clnt_control` is the client handle, the second is the request, and the third is normally a pointer to a buffer. Our first request is CLGET_TIMEOUT, which returns the total timeout in the `timeval` structure whose address is the third argument. This request is valid for all protocols.

Try to get retry timeout

15–16 Our next request is CLGET_RETRY_TIMEOUT for the retry timeout, but this is valid only for UDP. Therefore, if the return value is FALSE, we print nothing.

We also modify our server from Figure 16.6 to sleep for 1000 seconds instead of 5 seconds, to guarantee that the client's request times out. We start the server on our host

sunrpc/square5/client.c

```
 1 #include    "unpipc.h"
 2 #include    "square.h"

 3 int
 4 main(int argc, char **argv)
 5 {
 6      CLIENT *cl;
 7      square_in in;
 8      square_out *outp;
 9      struct timeval tv;

10      if (argc != 4)
11          err_quit("usage: client <hostname> <integer-value> <protocol>");

12      cl = Clnt_create(argv[1], SQUARE_PROG, SQUARE_VERS, argv[3]);

13      Clnt_control(cl, CLGET_TIMEOUT, (char *) &tv);
14      printf("timeout = %ld sec, %ld usec\n", tv.tv_sec, tv.tv_usec);
15      if (clnt_control(cl, CLGET_RETRY_TIMEOUT, (char *) &tv) == TRUE)
16          printf("retry timeout = %ld sec, %ld usec\n", tv.tv_sec, tv.tv_usec);

17      in.arg1 = atol(argv[2]);
18      if ( (outp = squareproc_1(&in, cl)) == NULL)
19          err_quit("%s", clnt_sperror(cl, argv[1]));

20      printf("result: %ld\n", outp->res1);
21      exit(0);
22 }
```

sunrpc/square5/client.c

Figure 16.12 Client that queries and prints the two RPC timeout values.

bsdi and run the client twice, once specifying TCP and once specifying UDP, but the results are not what we expect:

```
solaris % date ; client bsdi 44 tcp ; date
Wed Apr 22 14:46:57 MST 1998
timeout = 30 sec, 0 usec          this says 30 seconds
bsdi: RPC: Timed out
Wed Apr 22 14:47:22 MST 1998      but this is 25 seconds later

solaris % date ; client bsdi 55 udp ; date
Wed Apr 22 14:48:05 MST 1998
timeout = -1 sec, -1 usec         bizarre
retry timeout = 15 sec, 0 usec    this turns out to be correct
bsdi: RPC: Timed out
Wed Apr 22 14:48:31 MST 1998      about 25 seconds later
```

In the TCP case, the total timeout is returned by clnt_control as 30 seconds, but our measurement shows a timeout of 25 seconds. With UDP, the total timeout is returned as −1.

To see what is happening here, look at the client stub, the function squareproc_1 in the file square_clnt.c that is generated by rpcgen. This function calls a library function named clnt_call, and the final argument is a timeval structure named

TIMEOUT that is declared in this file and is initialized to 25 seconds. This argument to clnt_call overrides the default of 30 seconds for TCP and the −1 values for UDP. This argument is used until the client explicitly sets the total timeout by calling clnt_control with a request of CLSET_TIMEOUT. If we want to change the total timeout, we should call clnt_control and should not modify the structure in the client stub.

> The only way to verify the UDP retry timeout is to watch the packets using tcpdump. This shows that the first datagram is sent as soon as the client starts, and the next datagram is about 15 seconds later.

TCP Connection Management

If we watch the TCP client–server that we just described using tcpdump, we see TCP's three-way handshake, followed by the client sending its request, and the server acknowledging this request. About 25 seconds later, the client sends a FIN, which is caused by the client process terminating, and the remaining three segments of the TCP connection termination sequence follow. Section 2.5 of UNPv1 describes these segments in more detail.

We want to show the following characteristics of Sun RPC's usage of TCP connections: a new TCP connection is established by the client's call to clnt_create, and this connection is used by all procedure calls associated with the specified program and version. A client's TCP connection is terminated either explicitly by calling clnt_destroy or implicitly by the termination of the client process.

```
#include <rpc/rpc.h>

void clnt_destroy(CLIENT *cl);
```

We start with our client from Figure 16.2 and modify it to call the server procedure twice, then call clnt_destroy, and then pause. Figure 16.13 shows the new client. Running this program yields the expected output:

```
solaris % client kalae 5
result: 25
result: 100
```
program just waits until we kill it

But the verification of our earlier statements is shown only by the tcpdump output. This shows that one TCP connection is created (by the call to clnt_create) and is used for both client requests. The connection is then terminated by the call to clnt_destroy, even though our client process does not terminate.

Transaction ID

Another part of the timeout and retransmission strategy is the use of a *transaction ID* or *XID* to identify the client requests and server replies. When a client issues an RPC call, the RPC runtime assigns a 32-bit integer XID to the call, and this value is sent in the

```
                                                          ─────────── sunrpc/square9/client.c
 1 #include      "unpipc.h"          /* our header */
 2 #include      "square.h"          /* generated by rpcgen */

 3 int
 4 main(int argc, char **argv)
 5 {
 6     CLIENT *cl;
 7     square_in in;
 8     square_out *outp;

 9     if (argc != 3)
10         err_quit("usage: client <hostname> <integer-value>");

11     cl = Clnt_create(argv[1], SQUARE_PROG, SQUARE_VERS, "tcp");

12     in.arg1 = atol(argv[2]);
13     if ( (outp = squareproc_1(&in, cl)) == NULL)
14         err_quit("%s", clnt_sperror(cl, argv[1]));
15     printf("result: %ld\n", outp->res1);

16     in.arg1 *= 2;
17     if ( (outp = squareproc_1(&in, cl)) == NULL)
18         err_quit("%s", clnt_sperror(cl, argv[1]));
19     printf("result: %ld\n", outp->res1);

20     clnt_destroy(cl);

21     pause();

22     exit(0);
23 }
                                                          ─────────── sunrpc/square9/client.c
```

Figure 16.13 Client program to examine TCP connection usage.

RPC message. The server must return this XID with its reply. The XID does not change when the RPC runtime retransmits a request. The XID serves two purposes:

1. The client verifies that the XID of the reply equals the XID that was sent with the request; otherwise the client ignores this reply. If TCP is being used, the client should rarely receive a reply with the incorrect XID, but with UDP, and the possibility of retransmitted requests and a lossy network, the receipt of a reply with the incorrect XID is a definite possibility.

2. The server is allowed to maintain a *cache* of the replies that it sends, and one of the items that it uses to determine whether a request is a duplicate is the XID. We describe this shortly.

The TI-RPC package uses the following algorithm for choosing an XID for a new request, where the ^ operator is C's bitwise exclusive OR:

```
struct timeval  now;

gettimeofday(&now, NULL);
xid = getpid() ^ now.tv_sec ^ now.tv_usec;
```

Server Duplicate Request Cache

To enable the RPC runtime to maintain a duplicate request cache, the server must call `svc_dg_enablecache`. Once this cache is enabled, there is no way to turn it off (other than termination of the server process).

```
#include <rpc/rpc.h>

int svc_dg_enablecache(SVCXPRT *xprt, unsigned long size);
```
                                                            Returns: 1 if OK, 0 on error

xprt is the transport handle, and this pointer is member of the `svc_req` structure (Section 16.4). The address of this structure is an argument to the server procedure. *size* is the number of cache entries for which memory should be allocated.

When this cache is enabled, the server maintains a FIFO (first-in, first-out) cache of all the replies that it sends. Each reply is uniquely identified by the following:

- program number,
- version number,
- procedure number,
- XID, and
- client address (IP address and UDP port).

Each time the RPC runtime in the server receives a client request, it first searches the cache to see whether it already has a reply for this request. If so, the cached reply is returned to the client instead of calling the server procedure again.

The purpose of the duplicate request cache is to avoid calling a server procedure multiple times when duplicate requests are received, probably because the server procedure is not *idempotent*. A duplicate request can be received because the reply was lost or because the client retransmission passes the reply in the network. Notice that this duplicate request cache applies only to datagram protocols such as UDP, because if TCP is being used, a duplicate request never makes it to the application; it is handled completely by TCP (see Exercise 16.6).

16.6   Call Semantics

In Figure 15.29, we showed a doors client that retransmitted its request to the server when the client's call to `door_call` was interrupted by a caught signal. But we then showed that this caused the server procedure to be called twice, not once. We then categorized server procedures into those that are *idempotent* (can be called any number of times without harm), and those that are not idempotent (such as subtracting money from a bank account).

Procedure calls can be placed into one of three categories:

1. *Exactly once* means the procedure was executed once, period. This type of operation is hard to achieve, owing to the possibility of server crashes.

2. *At most once* means the procedure was not executed at all or it was executed once. If a normal return is made to the caller, we know the procedure was executed once. But if an error return is made, we're not certain whether the procedure was executed once or not at all.

3. *At least once* means the procedure was executed at least once, but perhaps more. This is OK for idempotent procedures—the client keeps transmitting its request until it receives a valid response. But if the client has to send its request more than once to receive a valid response, a possibility exists that the procedure was executed more than once.

With a local procedure call, if the procedure returns, we know that it was executed exactly once, but if the process crashes after the procedure has been called, we don't know whether it was executed once or not at all. We must consider various scenarios with remote procedure calls:

- If TCP is being used and a reply is received, we know that the remote procedure was called exactly once. But if a reply is not received (say the server crashes), we don't know whether the server procedure executed to completion before the host crashed, or whether the server procedure had not yet been called (at-most-once semantics). Providing exactly-once semantics in the face of server crashes and extended network outages requires a transaction processing system, something that is beyond the capability of an RPC package.

- If UDP is being used without a server cache and a reply is received, we know that the server procedure was called at least once, but possibly more than once (at-least-once semantics).

- If UDP is being used with a server cache and a reply is received, we know that the server procedure was called exactly once. But if a reply is not received, we have at-most-once semantics, similar to the TCP scenario.

Given these three choices:

1. TCP,
2. UDP with a server cache, or
3. UDP without a server cache,

our recommendations are:

- Always use TCP unless the overhead of the TCP connections is excessive for the application.

- Use a transaction processing system for nonidempotent procedures that are important to do correctly (i.e., bank accounts, airline reservations, and the like).

- For a nonidempotent procedure, using TCP is preferable to UDP with a server cache. TCP was designed to be reliable from the beginning, and adding this to a UDP application is rarely the same as just using TCP (e.g., Section 20.5 of UNPv1).

- Using UDP without a server cache for an idempotent procedure is OK.

- Using UDP without a server cache for a nonidempotent procedure is dangerous.

We cover additional advantages of TCP in the next section.

16.7 Premature Termination of Client or Server

We now consider what happens when either the client or the server terminates prematurely and TCP is being used as the transport protocol. Since UDP is connectionless, when a process with an open UDP endpoint terminates, nothing is sent to the peer. All that will happen in the UDP scenario when one end crashes is that the peer will time out, possibly retransmit, and eventually give up, as discussed in the previous section. But when a process with an open TCP connection terminates, that connection is terminated, sending a FIN to the peer (pp. 36–37 of UNPv1), and we want to see what the RPC runtime does when it receives this unexpected FIN from its peer.

Premature Termination of Server

We first terminate the server prematurely while it is processing a client's request. The only change we make to our client is to remove the `"tcp"` argument from the call to `clnt_call` in Figure 16.2 and require the transport protocol to be a command-line argument, as in Figure 16.12. In our server procedure, we add a call to the `abort` function. This terminates the server process, causing the server's TCP to send a FIN to the client, which we can verify with `tcpdump`.

We first run our Solaris client to our BSD/OS server:

```
solaris % client bsdi 22 tcp
bsdi: RPC: Unable to receive; An event requires attention
```

When the server's FIN is received by the client, the RPC runtime is waiting for the server's reply. It detects the unexpected reply and returns an error from our call to `squareproc_1`. The error (`RPC_CANTRECV`) is saved by the runtime in the client handle, and the call to `clnt_sperror` (from our `Clnt_create` wrapper function) prints this as "Unable to receive." The remainder of the error message, "An event requires attention," corresponds to the XTI error saved by the runtime, and is also printed by `clnt_sperror`. About 30 different RPC_*xxx* errors can be returned by a client's call of a remote procedure, and they are listed in the `<rpc/clnt_stat.h>` header.

If we swap the hosts for the client and server, we see the same scenario, with the same error returned by the RPC runtime (`RPC_CANTRECV`), but a different message at the end.

```
bsdi % client solaris 11 tcp
solaris: RPC: Unable to receive; errno = Connection reset by peer
```

The Solaris server that we aborted above was not compiled as a multithreaded server, and when we called `abort`, the entire process was terminated. Things change if we are running a multithreaded server and only the thread servicing the client's call terminates. To force this scenario, we replace the call to `abort` with a call to `pthread_exit`, as we did with our doors example in Figure 15.25. We run our client under BSD/OS and our multithreaded server under Solaris.

```
bsdi % client solaris 33 tcp
solaris: RPC: Timed out
```

When the server thread terminates, the TCP connection to the client is *not* closed; it remains open in the server process. Therefore, no FIN is sent to the client, so the client just times out. We would see the same error if the server host crashed after the client's request was sent to the server and acknowledged by the server's TCP.

Premature Termination of Client

When an RPC client terminates while it has an RPC procedure call in progress using TCP, the client's TCP will send a FIN to the server when the client process terminates. Our question is whether the server's RPC runtime detects this condition and possibly notifies the server procedure. (Recall from Section 15.11 that a doors server thread is canceled when the client prematurely terminates.)

To generate this condition, our client calls `alarm(3)` right before calling the server procedure, and our server procedure calls `sleep(6)`. (This is what we did with our doors example in Figures 15.30 and 15.31. Since the client does not catch SIGALRM, the process is terminated by the kernel about 3 seconds before the server's reply is sent.) We run our client under BSD/OS and our server under Solaris.

```
bsdi % client solaris 44 tcp
Alarm call
```

This is what we expect at the client, but nothing different happens at the server. The server procedure completes its 6-second sleep and returns. If we watch what happens with `tcpdump` we see the following:

- When the client terminates (about 3 seconds after starting), the client TCP sends a FIN to the server, which the server TCP acknowledges. The TCP term for this is a *half-close* (Section 18.5 of TCPv1).

- About 6 seconds after the client and server started, the server sends its reply, which its TCP sends to the client. (Sending data across a TCP connection after receiving a FIN is OK, as we describe on pp. 130–132 of UNPv1, because TCP connections are full-duplex.) The client TCP responds with an RST (reset), because the client process has terminated. This will be recognized by the server on its next read or write on the connection, but nothing happens at this time.

We summarize the points made in this section.

- RPC clients and servers using UDP never know whether the other end terminates prematurely. They may time out when no response is received, but they cannot tell the type of error: premature process termination, crashing of the peer host, network unreachability, and so on.

- An RPC client or server using TCP has a better chance of detecting problems at the peer, because premature termination of the peer process automatically causes the peer TCP to close its end of the connection. But this does not help if the peer is a threaded RPC server, because termination of the peer thread does not close the connection. Also this does not help detect a crashing of the peer host, because when that happens, the peer TCP does not close its open connections. A timeout is still required to handle all these scenarios.

16.8 XDR: External Data Representation

When we used doors in the previous chapter to call a procedure in one process from another process, both processes were on the same host, so we had no data conversion problems. But with RPC between different hosts, the various hosts can use different data formats. First, the sizes of the fundamental C datatypes can be different (e.g., a long on some systems occupies 32 bits, whereas on others it occupies 64 bits), and second, the actual bit ordering can differ (e.g., big-endian versus little-endian byte ordering, which we talked about on pp. 66–69 and pp. 137–140 of UNPv1). We have already encountered this with Figure 16.3 when we ran our server on a little-endian x86 and our client on a big-endian Sparc, yet we were able to exchange a long integer correctly between the two hosts.

Sun RPC uses XDR, the *External Data Representation* standard, to describe and encode the data (RFC 1832 [Srinivasan 1995b]). XDR is both a language for *describing* the data and a set of rules for *encoding* the data. XDR uses *implicit typing*, which means the sender and receiver must both know the types and ordering of the data: for example, two 32-bit integer values followed by one single precision floating point value, followed by a character string.

> As a comparison, in the OSI world, ASN.1 (Abstract Syntax Notation one) is the normal way to describe the data, and BER (Basic Encoding Rules) is a common way to encode the data. This scheme also uses *explicit typing*, which means each data value is preceded by some value (a "specifier") describing the datatype that follows. In our example, the stream of bytes would contain the following fields, in order: a specifier that the next value is an integer, the integer value, a specifier that the next value is an integer, the integer value, a specifier that the next value is a floating point value, the floating point value, a specifier that the next value is a character string, the character string.

The XDR representation of all datatypes requires a multiple of 4 bytes, and these bytes are always transmitted in the big-endian byte order. Signed integer values are stored using two's complement notation, and floating point values are stored using the IEEE format. Variable-length fields always contain up to 3 bytes of padding at the end, so that the next item is on a 4-byte boundary. For example, a 5-character ASCII string would be transmitted as 12 bytes:

- a 4-byte integer count containing the value 5,
- the 5-byte string, and
- 3 bytes of 0 for padding.

When describing XDR and the datatypes that it supports, we have three items to consider:

1. How do we declare a variable of each type in our RPC specification file (our .x file) for rpcgen? Our only example so far (Figure 16.1) uses only a long integer.

2. Which C datatype does rpcgen convert this to in the .h header that it generates?

3. What is the actual format of the data that is transmitted?

Figure 16.14 answers the first two questions. To generate this table, an RPC specification file was created using all the supported XDR datatypes. The file was run through rpcgen and the resulting C header examined.

We now describe the table entries in more detail, referencing each by the number in the first column (1–15).

1. A const declaration is turned into a C #define.

2. A typedef declaration is turned into a C typedef.

3. These are the five signed integer datatypes. The first four are transmitted as 32-bit values by XDR, and the last one is transmitted as a 64-bit value by XDR.

> 64-bit integers are known to many C compilers as type long long int or just long long. Not all compilers and operating systems support these. Since the generated .h file declares the C variable of type longlong_t, some header needs to define
>
>   typedef long long longlong_t;
>
> An XDR long occupies 32 bits, but a C long on a 64-bit Unix system holds 64 bits (e.g., the LP64 model described on p. 27 of UNPv1). Indeed, these decade-old XDR names are unfortunate in today's world. Better names would have been something like int8_t, int16_t, int32_t, int64_t, and so on.

4. These are the five unsigned integer datatypes. The first four are transmitted as 32-bit values by XDR, and the last one is transmitted as a 64-bit value by XDR.

5. These are the three floating point datatypes. The first is transmitted as a 32-bit value, the second as a 64-bit value, and the third as a 128-bit value.

> Quadruple-precision floating point numbers are known in C as type long double. Not all compilers and operating systems support these. (Your compiler may allow long double, but treat it as a double.) Since the generated .h file declares the C variable of type quadruple, some header needs to define
>
>   typedef long double quadruple;
>
> Under Solaris 2.6, for example, we must include the line
>
>   %#include <floatingpoint.h>
>
> at the beginning of the .x file, because this header includes the required definition. The percent sign at the beginning of the line tells rpcgen to place the remainder of the line in the .h file.

	RPC specification file (.x)	C header file (.h)
1	`const name = value;`	`#define name value`
2	`typedef declaration;`	`typedef declaration;`

3	`char var;`
	`short var;`
	`int var;`
	`long var;`
	`hyper var;`
		`char var;`
		`short var;`
		`int var;`
		`long var;`
		`longlong_t var;`

4	`unsigned char var;`
	`unsigned short var;`
	`unsigned int var;`
	`unsigned long var;`
	`unsigned hyper var;`
		`u_char var;`
		`u_short var;`
		`u_int var;`
		`u_long var;`
		`u_longlong_t var;`

5	`float var;`
	`double var;`
	`quadruple var;`
		`float var;`
		`double var;`
		`quadruple var;`

6	`bool var;`	`bool_t var;`
7	`enum var { name = const, ... };`	`enum var { name = const, ... };` `typedef enum var var;`
8	`opaque var[n];`	`char var[n];`

9	`opaque var<m>;`	`struct {`
		`    u_int   var_len;`
		`    char   *var_val;`
		`} var;`

10	`string var<m>;`	`char *var;`
11	`datatype var[n];`	`datatype var[n];`

12	`datatype var<m>;`	`struct {`
		`    u_int   var_len;`
		`    datatype   *var_val;`
		`} var;`

13	`struct var { members ... };`	`struct var { members ... };` `typedef struct var var;`

14	`union var switch (int disc) {`
	`    case discvalueA:   armdeclA;`
	`    case discvalueB:   armdeclB;`
	`    ...`
	`    default:   defaultdecl;`
	`};`
		`struct var {`
		`    int disc;`
		`    union {`
		`        armdeclA;`
		`        armdeclB;`
		`        ...`
		`        defaultdecl;`
		`    } var_u;`
		`};`
		`typedef struct var var;`

15	`datatype *name;`	`datatype *name;`

Figure 16.14 Summary of datatypes supported by XDR and rpcgen.

6. The *boolean* datatype is equivalent to a signed integer. The RPC headers also #define the constant TRUE to be 1 and the constant FALSE to be 0.

7. An *enumeration* is equivalent to a signed integer and is the same as C's enum datatype. rpcgen also generates a typedef for the specified variable name.

8. *Fixed-length opaque data* is a specified number of bytes (n) that are transmitted as 8-bit values, uninterpreted by the runtime library.

9. *Variable-length opaque data* is also a sequence of uninterpreted bytes that are transmitted as 8-bit values, but the actual number of bytes is transmitted as an unsigned integer and precedes the data. When sending this type of data (e.g., when filling in the arguments prior to an RPC call), set the length before making the call. When this type of data is received, the length must be examined to determine how much data follows.

    The maximum length m can be omitted in the declaration. But if the length is specified at compile time, the runtime library will check that the actual length (what we show as the *var_len* member of the structure) does not exceed the value of m.

10. A *string* is a sequence of ASCII characters. In memory, a string is stored as a normal null-terminated C character string, but when a string is transmitted, it is preceded by an unsigned integer that specifies the actual number of characters that follows (not including the terminating null). When sending this type of data, the runtime determines the number of characters by calling strlen. When this type of data is received, it is stored as a null-terminated C character string.

    The maximum length m can be omitted in the declaration. But if the length is specified at compile time, the runtime library will check that the actual length does not exceed the value of m.

11. A *fixed-length array* of any datatype is transmitted as a sequence of n elements of that datatype.

12. A *variable-length array* of any datatype is transmitted as an unsigned integer that specifies the actual number of elements in the array, followed by the array elements.

    The maximum number of elements m can be omitted in the declaration. But if this maximum is specified at compile time, the runtime library will check that the actual length does not exceed the value of m.

13. A *structure* is transmitted by transmitting each member in turn. rpcgen also generates a typedef for the specified variable name.

14. A *discriminated union* is composed of an integer discriminant followed by a set of datatypes (called *arms*) based on the value of the discriminant. In Figure 16.14, we show that the discriminant must be an int, but it can also be an unsigned int, an enum, or a bool (all of which are transmitted as a 32-bit integer value). When a discriminated union is transmitted, the 32-bit value of

the discriminant is transmitted first, followed only by the arm value corresponding to the value of the discriminant. The default declaration is often void, which means that nothing is transmitted following the 32-bit value of the discriminant. We show an example of this shortly.

15. *Optional data* is a special type of union that we describe with an example in Figure 16.24. The XDR declaration looks like a C pointer declaration, and that is what the generated .h file contains.

Figure 16.16 summarizes the encoding used by XDR for its various datatypes.

Example: Using XDR without RPC

We now show an example of XDR but without RPC. That is, we will use XDR to encode a structure of binary data into a machine-independent representation that can be processed on other systems. This technique can be used to write files in a machine-independent format or to send data to another computer across a network in a machine-independent format. Figure 16.15 shows our RPC specification file, data.x, which is really just an XDR specification file, since we do not declare any RPC procedures.

> The filename suffix of .x comes from the term "XDR specification file." The RPC specification (RFC 1831) says that the RPC language, sometimes called RPCL, is identical to the XDR language (which is defined in RFC 1832), except for the addition of a program definition (which describes the program, versions, and procedures).

sunrpc/xdr1/data.x

```
 1 enum result_t {
 2     RESULT_INT = 1, RESULT_DOUBLE = 2
 3 };

 4 union union_arg switch (result_t result) {
 5 case RESULT_INT:
 6     int     intval;
 7 case RESULT_DOUBLE:
 8     double  doubleval;
 9 default:
10     void;
11 };

12 struct data {
13     short   short_arg;
14     long    long_arg;

15     string  vstring_arg < 128 >;    /* variable-length string */
16     opaque  fopaque_arg[3];     /* fixed-length opaque */
17     opaque  vopaque_arg <>;     /* variable-length opaque */
18     short   fshort_arg[4];      /* fixed-length array */
19     long    vlong_arg <>;       /* variable-length array */
20     union_arg uarg;
21 };
```

sunrpc/xdr1/data.x

Figure 16.15 XDR specification file.

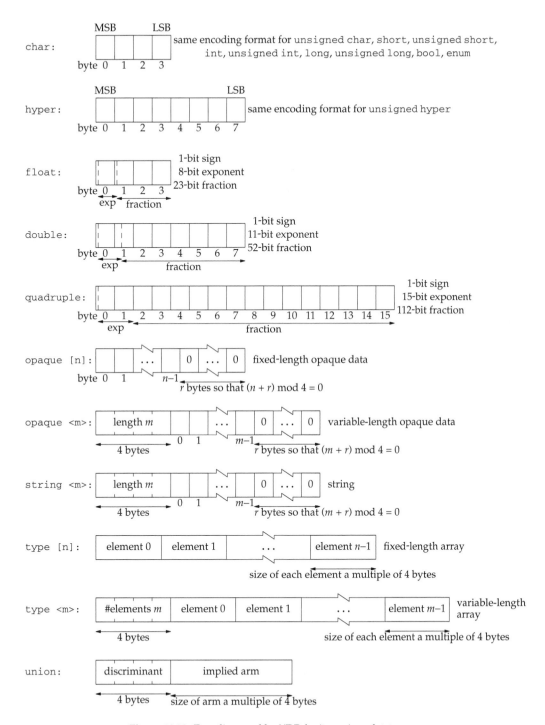

Figure 16.16 Encoding used by XDR for its various datatypes.

Declare enumeration and discriminated union

1-11   We declare an enumeration with two values, followed by a discriminated union that uses this enumeration as the discriminant. If the discriminant value is RESULT_INT, then an integer value is transmitted after the discriminant value. If the discriminant value is RESULT_DOUBLE, then a double precision floating point value is transmitted after the discriminant value; otherwise, nothing is transmitted after the discriminant value.

Declare structure

12-21   We declare a structure containing numerous XDR datatypes.

Since we do not declare any RPC procedures, if we look at all the files generated by rpcgen in Figure 16.4, we see that the client stub and server stub are not generated by rpcgen. But it still generates the data.h header and the data_xdr.c file containing the XDR functions to encode or decode the data items that we declared in our data.x file.

Figure 16.17 shows the data.h header that is generated. The contents of this header are what we expect, given the conversions shown in Figure 16.14.

In the file data_xdr.c, a function is defined named xdr_data that we can call to encode or decode the contents of the data structure that we define. (The function name suffix of _data comes from the name of our structure in Figure 16.15.) The first program that we write is called write.c, and it sets the values of all the variables in the data structure, calls the xdr_data function to encode all the fields into XDR format, and then writes the result to standard output.

Figure 16.18 shows this program.

Set structure members to some nonzero value

12-32   We first set all the members of the data structure to some nonzero value. In the case of variable-length fields, we must set the count and that number of values. For the discriminated union, we set the discriminant to RESULT_INT and the integer value to 123.

Allocate suitably aligned buffer

33   We call malloc to allocate room for the buffer that the XDR routines will store into, since it must be aligned on a 4-byte boundary, and just allocating a char array does not guarantee this alignment.

Create XDR memory stream

34   The runtime function xdrmem_create initializes the buffer pointed to by buff for XDR to use as a memory stream. We allocate a variable of type XDR named xhandle and pass the address of this variable as the first argument. The XDR runtime maintains the information in this variable (buffer pointer, current position in the buffer, and so on). The final argument is XDR_ENCODE, which tells XDR that we will be going from host format (our out structure) into XDR format.

── *sunrpc/xdr1/data.h*

```
 1 /*
 2  * Please do not edit this file.  It was generated using rpcgen.
 3  */

 4 #ifndef _DATA_H_RPCGEN
 5 #define _DATA_H_RPCGEN

 6 enum result_t {
 7     RESULT_INT = 1,
 8     RESULT_DOUBLE = 2
 9 };
10 typedef enum result_t result_t;

11 struct union_arg {
12     result_t result;
13     union {
14         int     intval;
15         double  doubleval;
16     } union_arg_u;
17 };
18 typedef struct union_arg union_arg;

19 struct data {
20     short   short_arg;
21     long    long_arg;
22     char    *vstring_arg;
23     char    fopaque_arg[3];
24     struct {
25         u_int   vopaque_arg_len;
26         char    *vopaque_arg_val;
27     } vopaque_arg;
28     short   fshort_arg[4];
29     struct {
30         u_int   vlong_arg_len;
31         long    *vlong_arg_val;
32     } vlong_arg;
33     union_arg uarg;
34 };
35 typedef struct data data;

36         /* the xdr functions */
37 extern bool_t xdr_result_t(XDR *, result_t *);
38 extern bool_t xdr_union_arg(XDR *, union_arg *);
39 extern bool_t xdr_data(XDR *, data *);

40 #endif  /* !_DATA_H_RPCGEN */
```
── *sunrpc/xdr1/data.h*

Figure 16.17 Header generated by rpcgen from Figure 16.15.

—————————————————————————————————— sunrpc/xdr1/write.c

```
 1 #include    "unpipc.h"
 2 #include    "data.h"

 3 int
 4 main(int argc, char **argv)
 5 {
 6     XDR     xhandle;
 7     data    out;                 /* the structure whose values we store */
 8     char    *buff;               /* the result of the XDR encoding */
 9     char    vop[2];
10     long    vlong[3];
11     u_int   size;

12     out.short_arg = 1;
13     out.long_arg = 2;
14     out.vstring_arg = "hello, world";   /* pointer assignment */

15     out.fopaque_arg[0] = 99;     /* fixed-length opaque */
16     out.fopaque_arg[1] = 88;
17     out.fopaque_arg[2] = 77;

18     vop[0] = 33;                 /* variable-length opaque */
19     vop[1] = 44;
20     out.vopaque_arg.vopaque_arg_len = 2;
21     out.vopaque_arg.vopaque_arg_val = vop;

22     out.fshort_arg[0] = 9999;    /* fixed-length array */
23     out.fshort_arg[1] = 8888;
24     out.fshort_arg[2] = 7777;
25     out.fshort_arg[3] = 6666;

26     vlong[0] = 123456;           /* variable-length array */
27     vlong[1] = 234567;
28     vlong[2] = 345678;
29     out.vlong_arg.vlong_arg_len = 3;
30     out.vlong_arg.vlong_arg_val = vlong;

31     out.uarg.result = RESULT_INT;   /* discriminated union */
32     out.uarg.union_arg_u.intval = 123;

33     buff = Malloc(BUFFSIZE);     /* must be aligned on 4-byte boundary */
34     xdrmem_create(&xhandle, buff, BUFFSIZE, XDR_ENCODE);

35     if (xdr_data(&xhandle, &out) != TRUE)
36         err_quit("xdr_data error");
37     size = xdr_getpos(&xhandle);
38     Write(STDOUT_FILENO, buff, size);

39     exit(0);
40 }
```

—————————————————————————————————— sunrpc/xdr1/write.c

Figure 16.18 Initialize the data structure and write it in XDR format.

Encode the structure

35-36   We call the `xdr_data` function, which was generated by `rpcgen` in the file `data_xdr.c`, and it encodes the `out` structure into XDR format. A return value of TRUE indicates success.

Obtain size of encoded data and `write`

37-38   The function `xdr_getpos` returns the current position of the XDR runtime in the output buffer (i.e., the byte offset of the next byte to store into), and we use this as the size of our `write`.

Figure 16.19 shows our `read` program, which reads the file that was written by the previous program, printing the values of all the members of the `data` structure.

Allocate suitably aligned buffer

11-13   We call `malloc` to allocate a buffer that is suitably aligned and read the file that was generated by the previous program into the buffer.

Create XDR memory stream, initialize buffer, and decode

14-17   We initialize an XDR memory stream, this time specifying XDR_DECODE to indicate that we want to convert from XDR format into host format. We initialize our `in` structure to 0 and call `xdr_data` to decode the buffer `buff` into our structure `in`. We must initialize the XDR destination to 0 (the `in` structure), because some of the XDR routines (notably `xdr_string`) require this. `xdr_data` is the same function that we called from Figure 16.18; what has changed is the final argument to `xdrmem_create`: in the previous program, we specified XDR_ENCODE, but in this program, we specify XDR_DECODE. This value is saved in the XDR handle (`xhandle`) by `xdrmem_create` and then used by the XDR runtime to determine whether to encode or decode the data.

Print structure values

18-42   We print all the members of our `data` structure.

Free any XDR-allocated memory

43   We call `xdr_free` to free the dynamic memory that the XDR runtime might have allocated (see also Exercise 16.10).

We now run our `write` program on a Sparc, redirecting standard output to a file named `data`:

```
solaris % write > data
solaris % ls -l data
-rw-rw-r--   1 rstevens other1       76 Apr 23 12:32 data
```

We see that the file size is 76 bytes, and that corresponds to Figure 16.20, which details the storage of the data (nineteen 4-byte values).

sunrpc/xdr1/read.c

```
 1 #include    "unpipc.h"
 2 #include    "data.h"

 3 int
 4 main(int argc, char **argv)
 5 {
 6     XDR     xhandle;
 7     int     i;
 8     char    *buff;
 9     data    in;
10     ssize_t n;

11     buff = Malloc(BUFFSIZE);    /* must be aligned on 4-byte boundary */
12     n = Read(STDIN_FILENO, buff, BUFFSIZE);
13     printf("read %ld bytes\n", (long) n);

14     xdrmem_create(&xhandle, buff, n, XDR_DECODE);
15     memset(&in, 0, sizeof(in));
16     if (xdr_data(&xhandle, &in) != TRUE)
17         err_quit("xdr_data error");

18     printf("short_arg = %d, long_arg = %ld, vstring_arg = '%s'\n",
19             in.short_arg, in.long_arg, in.vstring_arg);

20     printf("fopaque[] = %d, %d, %d\n",
21             in.fopaque_arg[0], in.fopaque_arg[1], in.fopaque_arg[2]);

22     printf("vopaque<> =");
23     for (i = 0; i < in.vopaque_arg.vopaque_arg_len; i++)
24         printf(" %d", in.vopaque_arg.vopaque_arg_val[i]);
25     printf("\n");

26     printf("fshort_arg[] = %d, %d, %d, %d\n", in.fshort_arg[0],
27             in.fshort_arg[1], in.fshort_arg[2], in.fshort_arg[3]);

28     printf("vlong<> =");
29     for (i = 0; i < in.vlong_arg.vlong_arg_len; i++)
30         printf(" %ld", in.vlong_arg.vlong_arg_val[i]);
31     printf("\n");

32     switch (in.uarg.result) {
33     case RESULT_INT:
34         printf("uarg (int) = %d\n", in.uarg.union_arg_u.intval);
35         break;
36     case RESULT_DOUBLE:
37         printf("uarg (double) = %g\n", in.uarg.union_arg_u.doubleval);
38         break;
39     default:
40         printf("uarg (void)\n");
41         break;
42     }

43     xdr_free(xdr_data, (char *) &in);

44     exit(0);
45 }
```

sunrpc/xdr1/read.c

Figure 16.19 Read the `data` structure in XDR format and print the values.

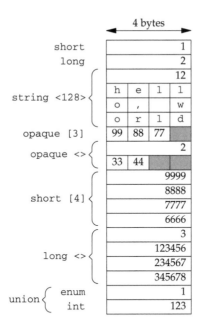

Figure 16.20 Format of the XDR stream written by Figure 16.18.

If we read this binary data file under BSD/OS or under Digital Unix, the results are what we expect:

```
bsdi % read < data
read 76 bytes
short_arg = 1, long_arg = 2, vstring_arg = 'hello, world'
fopaque[] = 99, 88, 77
vopaque<> = 33 44
fshort_arg[] = 9999, 8888, 7777, 6666
vlong<> = 123456 234567 345678
uarg (int) = 123

alpha % read < data
read 76 bytes
short_arg = 1, long_arg = 2, vstring_arg = 'hello, world'
fopaque[] = 99, 88, 77
vopaque<> = 33 44
fshort_arg[] = 9999, 8888, 7777, 6666
vlong<> = 123456 234567 345678
uarg (int) = 123
```

Example: Calculating the Buffer Size

In our previous example, we allocated a buffer of length BUFFSIZE (which is defined to be 8192 in our unpipc.h header, Figure C.1), and that was adequate. Unfortunately, no simple way exists to calculate the total size required by the XDR encoding of a given structure. Just calculating the `sizeof` the structure is wrong, because each member is encoded separately by XDR. What we must do is go through the structure, member by member, adding the size that will be used by the XDR encoding of each member. For example, Figure 16.21 shows a simple structure with three members.

—— sunrpc/xdr1/example.x
```
1 const    MAXC = 4;

2 struct example {
3     short    a;
4     double   b;
5     short    c[MAXC];
6 };
```
—— sunrpc/xdr1/example.x

Figure 16.21 XDR specification of a simple structure.

The program shown in Figure 16.22 calculates the number of bytes that XDR requires to encode this structure to be 28 bytes.

—— sunrpc/xdr1/example.c
```
1 #include    "unpipc.h"
2 #include    "example.h"

3 int
4 main(int argc, char **argv)
5 {
6     int      size;
7     example foo;

8     size = RNDUP(sizeof(foo.a)) + RNDUP(sizeof(foo.b)) +
9         RNDUP(sizeof(foo.c[0])) * MAXC;
10    printf("size = %d\n", size);
11    exit(0);
12 }
```
—— sunrpc/xdr1/example.c

Figure 16.22 Program to calculate the number of bytes that XDR encoding requires.

8–9   The macro RNDUP is defined in the `<rpc/xdr.h>` header and rounds its argument up to the next multiple of BYTES_PER_XDR_UNIT (4). For a fixed-length array, we calculate the size of each element and multiply this by the number of elements.

The problem with this technique is variable-length datatypes. If we declare `string d<10>`, then the maximum number of bytes required is RNDUP(sizeof(int) (for the length) plus RNDUP(sizeof(char)*10) (for the characters). But we cannot calculate a size for a variable-length declaration without a maximum, such as `float e<>`. The easiest solution is to allocate a buffer that should be larger than needed, and check for failure of the XDR routines (Exercise 16.5).

Example: Optional Data

There are three ways to specify optional data in an XDR specification file, all of which we show in Figure 16.23.

```
                                                          ─────── sunrpc/xdr1/opt1.x
 1 union optlong switch (bool flag) {
 2 case TRUE:
 3     long    val;
 4 case FALSE:
 5     void;
 6 };

 7 struct args {
 8     optlong arg1;                    /* union with boolean discriminant */
 9     long    arg2 < 1 >;              /* variable-length array with one element */
10     long    *arg3;                   /* pointer */
11 };
                                                          ─────── sunrpc/xdr1/opt1.x
```

Figure 16.23 XDR specification file showing three ways to specify optional data.

Declare union with boolean discriminant

1–8   We define a union with TRUE and FALSE arms and a structure member of this type. When the discriminant flag is TRUE, a long value follows; otherwise, nothing follows. When encoded by the XDR runtime, this will be encoded as either

- a 4-byte flag of 1 (TRUE) followed by a 4-byte value, or
- a 4-byte flag of 0 (FALSE).

Declare variable-length array

9   When we specify a variable-length array with a maximum of one element, it will be coded as either

- a 4-byte length of 1 followed by a 4-byte value, or
- a 4-byte length of 0.

Declare XDR pointer

10   A new way to specify optional data is shown for arg3 (which corresponds to the last line in Figure 16.14). This argument will be coded as either

- a 4-byte value of 1 followed by a 4-byte value, or
- a 4-byte value of 0

depending on the value of the corresponding C pointer when the data is encoded. If the pointer is nonnull, the first encoding is used (8 bytes), else the second encoding is used (4 bytes of 0). This is a handy way of encoding optional data when the data is referenced in our code by a pointer.

One implementation detail that makes the first two declarations generate identical encodings is that the value of TRUE is 1, which is also the length of the variable-length array when one element is present.

Figure 16.24 shows the .h file that is generated by rpcgen for this specification file.

14–21   Even though all three arguments will be encoded the same by the XDR runtime, the way we set and fetch their values in C is different for each one.

sunrpc/xdr1/opt1.h

```
 7 struct optlong {
 8     int     flag;
 9     union {
10         long    val;
11     } optlong_u;
12 };
13 typedef struct optlong optlong;

14 struct args {
15     optlong arg1;
16     struct {
17         u_int   arg2_len;
18         long    *arg2_val;
19     } arg2;
20     long    *arg3;
21 };
22 typedef struct args args;
```

sunrpc/xdr1/opt1.h

Figure 16.24 C header generated by rpcgen for Figure 16.23.

sunrpc/xdr1/opt1z.c

```
 1 #include    "unpipc.h"
 2 #include    "opt1.h"

 3 int
 4 main(int argc, char **argv)
 5 {
 6     int     i;
 7     XDR     xhandle;
 8     char    *buff;
 9     long    *lptr;
10     args    out;
11     size_t  size;

12     out.arg1.flag = FALSE;
13     out.arg2.arg2_len = 0;
14     out.arg3 = NULL;

15     buff = Malloc(BUFFSIZE);    /* must be aligned on 4-byte boundary */
16     xdrmem_create(&xhandle, buff, BUFFSIZE, XDR_ENCODE);

17     if (xdr_args(&xhandle, &out) != TRUE)
18         err_quit("xdr_args error");
19     size = xdr_getpos(&xhandle);

20     lptr = (long *) buff;
21     for (i = 0; i < size; i += 4)
22         printf("%ld\n", (long) ntohl(*lptr++));

23     exit(0);
24 }
```

sunrpc/xdr1/opt1z.c

Figure 16.25 None of the three arguments will be encoded.

Figure 16.25 is a simple program that sets the values of the three arguments so that none of the `long` values are encoded.

Set values

12–14   We set the discriminant of the `union` for the first argument to FALSE, the length of the variable-length array to 0, and the pointer corresponding to the third argument to NULL.

Allocate suitably aligned buffer and encode

15–19   We allocate a buffer and encode our `out` structure into an XDR memory stream.

Print XDR buffer

20–22   We print the buffer, one 4-byte value at a time, using the `ntohl` function (host-to-network long integer) to convert from the XDR big-endian byte order to the host's byte order. This shows exactly what has been encoded into the buffer by the XDR runtime:

```
solaris % opt1z
0
0
0
```

As we expect, each argument is encoded as 4 bytes of 0 indicating that no value follows.

Figure 16.26 is a modification of the previous program that assigns values to all three arguments, encodes them into an XDR memory stream, and prints the stream.

Set values

12–18   To assign a value to the `union`, we set the discriminant to TRUE and set the value. To assign a value to the variable-length array, we set the array length to 1, and its associated pointer points to the value. To assign a value to the third argument, we set the pointer to the address of the value.

When we run this program, it prints the expected six 4-byte values:

```
solaris % opt1
1                    discriminant value of TRUE
5
1                    variable-length array length
9876
1                    flag for nonnull pointer variable
123
```

Example: Linked List Processing

Given the capability to encode optional data from the previous example, we can extend XDR's pointer notation and use it to encode and decode linked lists containing a variable number of elements. Our example is a linked list of name–value pairs, and Figure 16.27 shows the XDR specification file.

1–5   Our `mylist` structure contains one name–value pair and a pointer to the next structure. The last structure in the list will have a null `next` pointer.

sunrpc/xdr1/opt1.c

```
 1 #include    "unpipc.h"
 2 #include    "opt1.h"

 3 int
 4 main(int argc, char **argv)
 5 {
 6     int    i;
 7     XDR    xhandle;
 8     char   *buff;
 9     long   lval2, lval3, *lptr;
10     args   out;
11     size_t size;

12     out.arg1.flag = TRUE;
13     out.arg1.optlong_u.val = 5;

14     lval2 = 9876;
15     out.arg2.arg2_len = 1;
16     out.arg2.arg2_val = &lval2;

17     lval3 = 123;
18     out.arg3 = &lval3;

19     buff = Malloc(BUFFSIZE);    /* must be aligned on 4-byte boundary */
20     xdrmem_create(&xhandle, buff, BUFFSIZE, XDR_ENCODE);

21     if (xdr_args(&xhandle, &out) != TRUE)
22         err_quit("xdr_args error");
23     size = xdr_getpos(&xhandle);

24     lptr = (long *) buff;
25     for (i = 0; i < size; i += 4)
26         printf("%ld\n", (long) ntohl(*lptr++));

27     exit(0);
28 }
```

sunrpc/xdr1/opt1.c

Figure 16.26 Assign values to all three arguments from Figure 16.23.

sunrpc/xdr1/opt2.x

```
 1 struct mylist {
 2     string  name <>;
 3     long    value;
 4     mylist *next;
 5 };

 6 struct args {
 7     mylist *list;
 8 };
```

sunrpc/xdr1/opt2.x

Figure 16.27 XDR specification for linked list of name–value pairs.

Figure 16.28 shows the .h file generated by rpcgen from Figure 16.27.

Figure 16.29 is our program that initializes a linked list containing three name–value pairs and then calls the XDR runtime to encode it.

——————————————————————————— sunrpc/xdr1/opt2.h

```
 7 struct mylist {
 8     char   *name;
 9     long    value;
10     struct mylist *next;
11 };
12 typedef struct mylist mylist;

13 struct args {
14     mylist *list;
15 };
16 typedef struct args args;
```

——————————————————————————— sunrpc/xdr1/opt2.h

Figure 16.28 C declarations corresponding to Figure 16.27.

——————————————————————————— sunrpc/xdr1/opt2.c

```
 1 #include    "unpipc.h"
 2 #include    "opt2.h"

 3 int
 4 main(int argc, char **argv)
 5 {
 6     int     i;
 7     XDR     xhandle;
 8     long    *lptr;
 9     args    out;            /* the structure that we fill */
10     char    *buff;          /* the XDR encoded result */
11     mylist  nameval[4];     /* up to 4 list entries */
12     size_t  size;

13     out.list = &nameval[2];   /* [2] -> [1] -> [0] */
14     nameval[2].name = "name1";
15     nameval[2].value = 0x1111;
16     nameval[2].next = &nameval[1];
17     nameval[1].name = "namee2";
18     nameval[1].value = 0x2222;
19     nameval[1].next = &nameval[0];
20     nameval[0].name = "nameee3";
21     nameval[0].value = 0x3333;
22     nameval[0].next = NULL;

23     buff = Malloc(BUFFSIZE);    /* must be aligned on 4-byte boundary */
24     xdrmem_create(&xhandle, buff, BUFFSIZE, XDR_ENCODE);

25     if (xdr_args(&xhandle, &out) != TRUE)
26         err_quit("xdr_args error");
27     size = xdr_getpos(&xhandle);

28     lptr = (long *) buff;
29     for (i = 0; i < size; i += 4)
30         printf("%8lx\n", (long) ntohl(*lptr++));

31     exit(0);
32 }
```

——————————————————————————— sunrpc/xdr1/opt2.c

Figure 16.29 Initialize linked list, encode it, and print result.

Initialize linked list

11-22   We allocate room for four list entries but initialize only three. The first entry is
nameval[2], then nameval[1], and then nameval[0]. The head of the linked list
(out.list) is set to &nameval[2]. Our reason for initializing the list in this order is
just to show that the XDR runtime follows the pointers, and the order of the linked list
entries that are encoded has nothing to do with which array entries are being used. We
have also initialized the values to hexadecimal values, because we will print the long
integer values in hex, because this makes it easier to see the ASCII values in each byte.

The output shows that each list entry is preceded by a 4-byte value of 1 (which we
can consider as either a length of 1 for a variable-length array, or as the boolean value
TRUE), and the fourth entry consists of just a 4-byte value of 0, indicating the end of the
list.

```
solaris % opt2
        1                      one element follows
        5                      string length
6e616d65                       n  a  m  e
31000000                       1, 3 bytes of pad
     1111                      corresponding value
        1                      one element follows
        6                      string length
6e616d65                       n  a  m  e
65320000                       e  2, 2 bytes of pad
     2222                      corresponding value
        1                      one element follows
        7                      string length
6e616d65                       n  a  m  e
65653300                       e  e  3, 1 byte of pad
     3333                      corresponding value
        0                      no element follows: end-of-list
```

If XDR decodes a linked list of this form, it will dynamically allocate memory for
the list entries and pointers, and link the pointers together, allowing us to traverse the
list easily in C.

16.9 RPC Packet Formats

Figure 16.30 shows the format of an RPC request when encapsulated in a TCP segment.
Since TCP is a byte stream and provides no message boundaries, some method of
delineating the messages must be provided by the application. Sun RPC defines a *record*
as either a request or reply, and each record is composed of one or more *fragments*. Each
fragment starts with a 4-byte value: the high-order bit is the final-fragment flag, and the
low-order 31 bits is the count. If the final-fragment bit is 0, then additional fragments
make up the record.

> This 4-byte value is transmitted in the big-endian byte order, the same as all 4-byte XDR inte-
> gers, but this field is not in standard XDR format because XDR does not transmit bit fields.

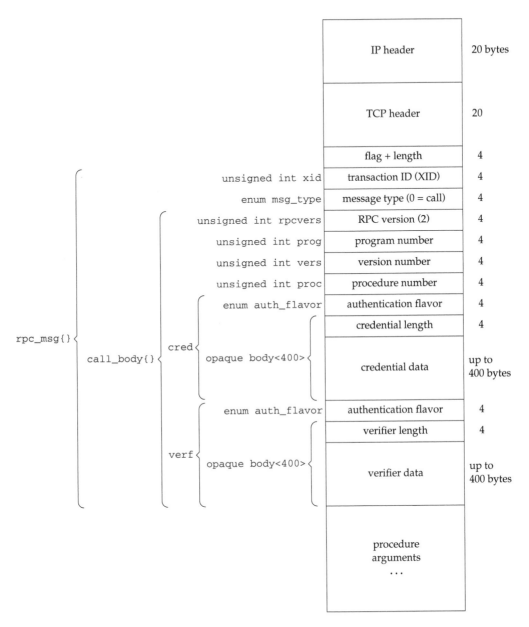

Figure 16.30 RPC request encapsulated in a TCP segment.

If UDP is being used instead of TCP, the first field following the UDP header is the XID, as we show in Figure 16.32.

With TCP, virtually no limit exists to the size of the RPC request and reply, because any number of fragments can be used and each fragment has a 31-bit length field. But with UDP, the request and reply must each fit in a single UDP datagram, and the maximum amount of data in this datagram is 65507 bytes (assuming IPv4). Many implementations prior to the TI-RPC package further limit the size of either the request or reply to around 8192 bytes, so if more than about 8000 bytes is needed for either the request or reply, TCP should be used.

We now show the actual XDR specification of an RPC request, taken from RFC 1831. The names that we show in Figure 16.30 were taken from this specification.

```
enum auth_flavor {
  AUTH_NONE  = 0,
  AUTH_SYS   = 1,
  AUTH_SHORT = 2
    /* and more to be defined */
};

struct opaque_auth {
  auth_flavor   flavor;
  opaque        body<400>;
};

enum msg_type {
  CALL  = 0,
  REPLY = 1
};

struct call_body {
  unsigned int  rpcvers;    /* RPC version: must be 2 */
  unsigned int  prog;       /* program number */
  unsigned int  vers;       /* version number */
  unsigned int  proc;       /* procedure number */
  opaque_auth   cred;       /* caller's credentials */
  opaque_auth   verf;       /* caller's verifier */
    /* procedure-specific parameters start here */
};

struct rpc_msg {
  unsigned int  xid;
  union switch (msg_type  mtype) {
  case CALL:
    call_body   cbody;
  case REPLY:
    reply_body  rbody;
  } body;
};
```

The contents of the variable-length opaque data containing the credentials and verifier depend on the flavor of authentication. For null authentication (the default), the length of the opaque data should be 0. For Unix authentication, the opaque data contains the following information:

```
struct authsys_parms {
  unsigned int  stamp;
  string        machinename<255>;
  unsigned int  uid;
  unsigned int  gid;
  unsigned int  gids<16>;
};
```

When the credential flavor is AUTH_SYS, the verifier flavor should be AUTH_NONE.

The format of an RPC reply is more complicated than that of a request, because errors can occur in the request. Figure 16.31 shows the possibilities.

Figure 16.32 shows the format of a successful RPC reply, this time showing the UDP encapsulation.

We now show the actual XDR specification of an RPC reply, taken from RFC 1831.

```
enum reply_stat {
  MSG_ACCEPTED = 0,
  MSG_DENIED   = 1
};

enum accept_stat {
  SUCCESS       = 0, /* RPC executed successfully */
  PROG_UNAVAIL  = 1, /* program # unavailable */
  PROG_MISMATCH = 2, /* version # unavailable */
  PROC_UNAVAIL  = 3, /* procedure # unavailable */
  GARBAGE_ARGS  = 4, /* cannot decode arguments */
  SYSTEM_ERR    = 5  /* memory allocation failure, etc. */
};

struct accepted_reply {
  opaque_auth  verf;
  union switch (accept_stat  stat) {
  case SUCCESS:
    opaque  results[0];    /* procedure-specific results start here */
  case PROG_MISMATCH:
    struct {
      unsigned int  low;  /* lowest version # supported */
      unsigned int  high; /* highest version # supported */
    } mismatch_info;
  default:  /* PROG_UNAVAIL, PROC_UNAVAIL, GARBAGE_ARGS, SYSTEM_ERR */
    void;
  } reply_data;
};

union reply_body switch (reply_stat  stat) {
  case MSG_ACCEPTED:
    accepted_reply  areply;
  case MSG_DENIED:
    rejected_reply  rreply;
} reply;
```

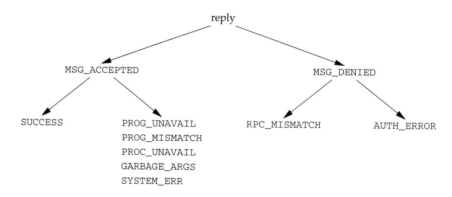

Figure 16.31 Possible RPC replies.

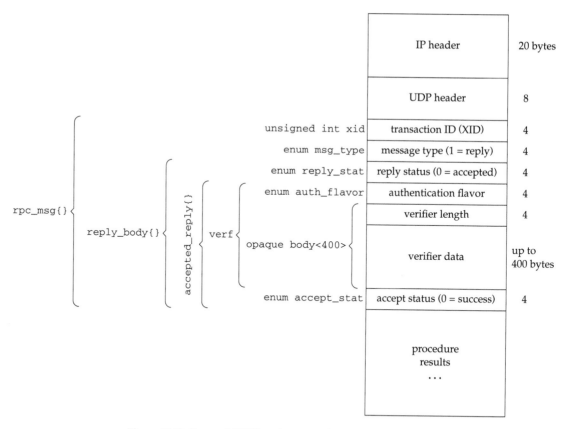

Figure 16.32 Successful RPC reply encapsulated as a UDP datagram.

The call can be rejected by the server if the RPC version number is wrong or if an authentication error occurs.

```
enum reject_stat {
    RPC_MISMATCH = 0, /* RPC version number not 2 */
    AUTH_ERROR   = 1  /* authentication error */
};

enum auth_stat {
    AUTH_OK             = 0,  /* success */
       /* following are failures at server end */
    AUTH_BADCRED        = 1,  /* bad credential (seal broken) */
    AUTH_REJECTEDCRED   = 2,  /* client must begin new session */
    AUTH_BADVERF        = 3,  /* bad verifier (seal broken) */
    AUTH_REJECTEDVERF   = 4,  /* verifier expired or replayed */
    AUTH_TOOWEAK        = 5,  /* rejected for security reasons */
       /* following are failures at client end */
    AUTH_INVALIDRESP    = 6,  /* bogus response verifier */
    AUTH_FAILED         = 7   /* reason unknown */
};

union rejected_reply switch (reject_stat  stat) {
  case RPC_MISMATCH:
    struct {
      unsigned int  low;  /* lowest RPC version # supported */
      unsigned int  high; /* highest RPC version # supported */
    } mismatch_info;
  case AUTH_ERROR:
    auth_stat  stat;
};
```

16.10 Summary

Sun RPC allows us to code distributed applications with the client running on one host and the server on another host. We first define the server procedures that the client can call and then write an RPC specification file that describes the arguments and return values for each of these procedures. We then write the client main function that calls the server procedures, and the server procedures themselves. The client code appears to just call the server procedures, but underneath the covers, network communication is taking place, hidden by the various RPC runtime routines.

The rpcgen program is a fundamental part of building applications using RPC. It reads our specification file, and generates the client stub and the server stub, as well as generating functions that call the required XDR runtime routines that will handle all the data conversions. The XDR runtime is also a fundamental part of this process. XDR defines a standard way of exchanging various data formats between different systems that may have different-sized integers, different byte orders, different floating point formats, and the like. As we showed, we can use XDR by itself, independent of the RPC package, just for exchanging data in a standard format using any form of communications to actually transfer the data (programs written using sockets or XTI, floppy disks, CD-ROMs, or whatever).

Sun RPC provides its own form of naming, using 32-bit program numbers, 32-bit version numbers, and 32-bit procedure numbers. Each host that runs an RPC server must run a program named the port mapper (now called RPCBIND). RPC servers bind ephemeral TCP and UDP ports and then register with the port mapper to associate these ephemeral ports with the programs and versions provided by the server. When an RPC client starts, it contacts the port mapper on the server's host to obtain the desired port number, and then contacts the server itself, normally using either TCP or UDP.

By default, no authentication is provided by RPC clients, and RPC servers handle any client request that they receive. This is the same as if we were to write our own client–server using either sockets or XTI. Sun RPC provides three additional forms of authentication: Unix authentication (providing the client's hostname, user ID, and group IDs), DES authentication (based on secret key and public key cryptography), and Kerberos authentication.

Understanding the timeout and retransmission strategy of the underlying RPC package is essential to using RPC (or any form of network programming). When a reliable transport layer such as TCP is used, only a total timeout is needed by the RPC client, as any lost or duplicated packets are handled completely by the transport layer. When an unreliable transport such as UDP is used, however, the RPC package has a retry timeout in addition to a total timeout. A transaction ID is used by the RPC client to verify that a received reply is the one desired.

Any procedure call can be classified as having exactly-once semantics, at-most-once semantics, or at-least-once semantics. With local procedure calls, we normally ignore this issue, but with RPC, we must be aware of the differences, as well as understanding the difference between an idempotent procedure (one that can be called any number of times without harm) and one that is not idempotent (and must be called only once).

Sun RPC is a large package, and we have just scratched the surface. Nevertheless, given the basics that have been covered in this chapter, complete applications can be written. Using rpcgen hides many of the details and simplifies the coding. The Sun manuals refer to various levels of RPC coding—the simplified interface, top level, intermediate level, expert level, and bottom level—but these categorizations are meaningless. The number of functions provided by the RPC runtime is 164, with the division as follows:

- 11 auth_ functions (authentication),
- 26 clnt_ functions (client side),
- 5 pmap_ functions (port mapper access),
- 24 rpc_ functions (general),
- 44 svc_ functions (server side), and
- 54 xdr functions (XDR conversions).

This compares to around 25 functions each for the sockets and XTI APIs, and less than 10 functions each for the doors API and the Posix and System V message queue APIs, semaphore APIs, and shared memory APIs. Fifteen functions deal with Posix threads, 10 functions with Posix condition variables, 11 functions with Posix read–write locks, and one function with fcntl record locking.

Exercises

16.1 When we start one of our servers, it registers itself with the port mapper. But if we terminate it, say with our terminal interrupt key, what happens to this registration? What happens if a client request arrives at some time later for this server?

16.2 We have a client–server using RPC with UDP, and it has no server reply cache. The client sends a request to the server but the server takes 20 seconds before sending its reply. The client times out after 15 seconds, causing the server procedure to be called a second time. What happens to the server's second reply?

16.3 The XDR `string` datatype is always encoded as a length followed by the characters. What changes if we want a fixed-length string and write, say, `char c[10]` instead of `string s<10>`?

16.4 Change the maximum size of the `string` in Figure 16.15 from 128 and 10, and run the `write` program. What happens? Now remove the maximum length specifier from the `string` declaration, that is, write `string vstring_arg<>` and compare the `data_xdr.c` file to one that is generated with a maximum length. What changes?

16.5 Change the third argument to `xdrmem_create` in Figure 16.18 (the buffer size) to 50 and see what happens.

16.6 In Section 16.5, we described the duplicate request cache that can be enabled when UDP is being used. We could say that TCP maintains its own duplicate request cache. What are we referring to, and how big is this TCP duplicate request cache? (*Hint*: How does TCP detect the receipt of duplicate data?)

16.7 Given the five elements that uniquely identify each entry in the server's duplicate request cache, in what order should these five values be compared, to require the fewest number of comparisons, when comparing a new request to a cache entry?

16.8 When watching the actual packets for our client–server from Section 16.5 using TCP, the size of the request segment is 48 bytes and the size of the reply segment is 32 bytes (ignoring the IPv4 and TCP headers). Account for these sizes (e.g., Figures 16.30 and 16.32). What will the sizes be if we use UDP instead of TCP?

16.9 Can an RPC client on a system that does not support threads call a server procedure that has been compiled to support threads? What about the differences in the arguments that we described in Section 16.2?

16.10 In our `read` program in Figure 16.19, we allocate room for the buffer into which the file is read, and that buffer contains the pointer `vstring_arg`. But where is the string stored that is pointed to by `vstring_arg`? Modify the program to verify your assumption.

16.11 Sun RPC defines the *null procedure* as the one with a procedure number of 0 (which is why we always started our procedure numbering with 1, as in Figure 16.1). Furthermore, every server stub generated by `rpcgen` automatically defines this procedure (which you can easily verify by looking at any of the server stubs generated by the examples in this chapter). The null procedure takes no arguments and returns nothing, and is often used for verifying that a given server is running, or to measure the round-trip time to the server. But if we look at the client stub, no stub is generated for this procedure. Look up the manual page for the `clnt_call` function and use it to call the null procedure for any of the servers shown in this chapter.

16.12 Why does no entry exist for a message size of 65536 for Sun RPC using UDP in Figure A.2? Why do no entries exist for message sizes of 16384 and 32768 for Sun RPC using UDP in Figure A.4?

16.13 Verify that omitting the call to `xdr_free` in Figure 16.19 introduces a *memory leak*. Add the statement

```
for ( ; ; ) {
```

immediately before calling `xdrmem_create`, and put the ending brace immediately before the call to `xdr_free`. Run the program and watch its memory size using `ps`. Then move the ending brace to follow the call to `xdr_free` and run the program again, watching its memory size.

Epilogue

This text has described in detail four different techniques for interprocess communication (IPC):

1. message passing (pipes, FIFOs, Posix and System V message queues),
2. synchronization (mutexes, condition variables, read–write locks, file and record locks, Posix and System V semaphores),
3. shared memory (anonymous, named Posix, named System V), and
4. procedure calls (Solaris doors, Sun RPC).

Message passing and procedure calls are often used by themselves, that is, they normally provide their own synchronization. Shared memory, on the other hand, usually requires some form of application-provided synchronization to work correctly. The synchronization techniques are sometimes used by themselves; that is, without the other forms of IPC.

After covering 16 chapters of details, the obvious question is: which form of IPC should be used to solve some particular problem? Unfortunately, there is no silver bullet regarding IPC. The vast number of different types of IPC provided by Unix indicates that no one solution solves all (or even most) problems. All that you can do is become familiar with the facilities provided by each form of IPC and then compare the features with the needs of your specific application.

We first list four items that must be considered, in case they are important for your application.

1. *Networked* versus *nonnetworked*. We assume that this decision has already been made and that IPC is being used between processes or threads on a single host.

If the application might be distributed across multiple hosts, consider using sockets instead of IPC, to simplify the later move to a networked application.

2. *Portability* (recall Figure 1.5). Almost all Unix systems support Posix pipes, Posix FIFOs, and Posix record locking. As of 1998, most Unix systems support System V IPC (messages, semaphores, and shared memory), whereas only a few support Posix IPC (messages, semaphores, and shared memory). More implementations of Posix IPC should appear, but it is (unfortunately) an option with Unix 98. Many Unix systems support Posix threads (which include mutexes and condition variables) or should support them in the near future. Some systems that support Posix threads do not support the process-shared attributes of mutexes and condition variables. The read–write locks required by Unix 98 should be adopted by Posix, and many versions of Unix already support some type of read–write lock. Memory-mapped I/O is widespread, and most Unix systems also provide anonymous memory mapping (either /dev/zero or MAP_ANON). Sun RPC should be available on almost all Unix systems, whereas doors are a Solaris-only feature (for now).

3. *Performance*. If this is a critical item in your design, run the programs developed in Appendix A on your own systems. Better yet, modify these programs to simulate the environment of your particular application and measure their performance in this environment.

4. *Realtime scheduling*. If you need this feature and your system supports the Posix realtime scheduling option, consider the Posix functions for message passing and synchronization (message queues, semaphores, mutexes, and condition variables). For example, when someone posts to a Posix semaphore on which multiple threads are blocked, the thread that is unblocked is chosen in a manner appropriate to the scheduling policies and parameters of the blocked threads. System V semaphores, on the other hand, make no such guarantee.

To help understand some of the features and limitations of the various types of IPC, we summarize some of the major differences:

- Pipes and FIFOs are byte streams with no message boundaries. Posix messages and System V messages have record boundaries that are maintained from the sender to the receiver. (With regard to the Internet protocols described in UNPv1, TCP is a byte stream, but UDP provides messages with record boundaries.)

- Posix message queues can send a signal to a process or initiate a new thread when a message is placed onto an empty queue. No similar form of notification is provided for System V message queues. Neither type of message queue can be used directly with either select or poll (Chapter 6 of UNPv1), although we provided workarounds in Figure 5.14 and Section 6.9.

- The bytes of data in a pipe or FIFO are first-in, first-out. Posix messages and System V messages have a priority that is assigned by the sender. When reading a Posix message queue, the highest priority message is always returned first.

When reading a System V message queue, the reader can ask for any priority message that it wants.

- When a message is placed onto a Posix or System V message queue, or written to a pipe or FIFO, one copy is delivered to exactly one thread. No peeking capability exists (similar to the sockets MSG_PEEK flag; Section 13.7 of UNPv1), and these messages cannot be broadcast or multicast to multiple recipients (as is possible with sockets and XTI using the UDP protocol; Chapters 18 and 19 of UNPv1).

- Mutexes, condition variables, and read–write locks are all unnamed: they are memory-based. They can be shared easily between the different threads within a single process. They can be shared between different processes only if they are stored in memory that is shared between the different processes. Posix semaphores, on the other hand, come in two flavors: named and memory-based. Named semaphores can always be shared between different processes (since they are identified by Posix IPC names), and memory-based semaphores can be shared between different processes if the semaphore is stored in memory that is shared between the different processes. System V semaphores are also named, using the key_t datatype, which is often obtained from the pathname of a file. These semaphores can be shared easily between different processes.

- fcntl record locks are automatically released by the kernel if the process holding the lock terminates without releasing the lock. System V semaphores have this feature as an option. Mutexes, condition variables, read–write locks, and Posix semaphores do not have this feature.

- Each fcntl lock is associated with some range of bytes (what we called a "record") in the file referenced by the descriptor. Read–write locks are not associated with any type of record.

- Posix shared memory and System V shared memory both have kernel persistence. They remain in existence until explicitly deleted, even if they are not currently being used by some process.

- The size of a Posix shared memory object can be extended while the object is being used. The size of a System V shared memory segment is fixed when it is created.

- The kernel limits for the three types of System V IPC often require tuning by the system administrator, because their default values are usually inadequate for real-world applications (Section 3.8). The kernel limits for the three types of Posix IPC usually require no tuning at all.

- Information about System V IPC objects (current size, owner ID, last-modification time, etc.) is available with a command of IPC_STAT with the three XXXctl functions, and with the ipcs command. No standard way exists to obtain this information about Posix IPC objects. If the implementation uses files in the filesystem for these objects, then the information is available with the stat function or with the ls command, if we know the mapping from the Posix

IPC name to the pathname. But if the implementation does not use files, this information may not be available.

- Of the various synchronization techniques—mutexes, condition variables, read–write locks, record locks, and Posix and System V semaphores—the only functions that can be called from a signal handler (Figure 5.10) are sem_post and fcntl.

- Of the various message passing techniques—pipes, FIFOs, and Posix and System V message queues—the only functions that can be called from a signal handler are read and write (for pipes and FIFOs).

- Of all the message passing techniques, only doors accurately provide the client's identity to the server (Section 15.5). In Section 5.4, we mentioned two other types of message passing that also identify the client: BSD/OS provides this identity when a Unix domain socket is used (Section 14.8 of UNPv1), and SVR4 passes the sender's identity across a pipe when a descriptor is passed across the pipe (Section 15.3.1 of APUE).

Appendix A

Performance Measurements

A.1 Introduction

In the text, we have covered six types of message passing:

- pipes,
- FIFOs,
- Posix message queues,
- System V message queues,
- doors, and
- Sun RPC,

and five types of synchronization:

- mutexes and condition variables,
- read–write locks,
- `fcntl` record locking,
- Posix semaphores, and
- System V semaphores.

We now develop some simple programs to measure the performance of these types of IPC, so we can make intelligent decisions about when to use a particular form of IPC.

When comparing the different forms of message passing, we are interested in two measurements.

1. The *bandwidth* is the speed at which we can move data through the IPC channel. To measure this, we send lots of data (millions of bytes) from one process to another. We also measure this for different sizes of the I/O operation (`writes` and `reads` for pipes and FIFOs, for example), expecting to find that the bandwidth increases as the amount of data per I/O operation increases.

457

2. The *latency* is how long a small IPC message takes to go from one process to another and back. We measure this as the time for a 1-byte message to go from one process to another, and back (the round-trip time).

In the real world, the bandwidth tells us how long bulk data takes to be sent across an IPC channel, but IPC is also used for small control messages, and the time required by the system to handle these small messages is provided by latency. Both numbers are important.

To measure the various forms of synchronization, we modify our program that increments a counter in shared memory, with either multiple threads or multiple processes incrementing the counter. Since the increment is a simple operation, the time required is dominated by the time of the synchronization primitives.

> The simple programs used in this Appendix to measure the various forms of IPC are loosely based on the lmbench suite of benchmarks that is described in [McVoy and Staelin 1996]. This is a sophisticated set of benchmarks that measure many characteristics of a Unix system (context switch time, I/O throughput, etc.) and not just IPC. The source code is publicly available: http://www.bitmover.com/lmbench.

> The numbers shown in this Appendix are provided to let us compare the techniques described in this book. An ulterior motive is to show how simple measuring these values is. Before making choices among the various techniques, you should measure these performance numbers on your own systems. Unfortunately, as easy as the numbers are to measure, when anomalies are detected, explaining these is often very hard, without access to the source code for the kernel or libraries in question.

A.2   Results

We now summarize all the results from this Appendix, for easy reference when going through the various programs that we show.

The two systems used for all the measurements are a SparcStation 4/110 running Solaris 2.6 and a Digital Alpha (DEC 3000 model 300, Pelican) running Digital Unix 4.0B. The following lines were added to the Solaris /etc/system file:

```
set msgsys:msginfo_msgmax = 16384
set msgsys:msginfo_msgmnb = 32768
set msgsys:msginfo_msgseg = 4096
```

This allows 16384-byte messages on a System V message queue (Figure A.2). The same changes were accomplished with Digital Unix by specifying the following lines as input to the Digital Unix sysconfig program:

```
ipc:
        msg-max = 16384
        msg-mnb = 32768
```

Message Passing Bandwidth Results

Figure A.2 lists the bandwidth results measured on a Sparc running Solaris 2.6, and Figure A.3 graphs these values. Figure A.4 lists the bandwidth results measured on an Alpha running Digital Unix 4.0B, and Figure A.5 graphs these values.

As we might expect, the bandwidth normally increases as the size of the message increases. Since many implementations of System V message queues have small kernel limits (Section 3.8), the largest message is 16384 bytes, and even for messages of this size, kernel defaults had to be increased. The decrease in bandwidth above 4096 bytes for Solaris is probably caused by the configuration of the internal message queue limits. For comparison with UNPv1, we also show the values for a TCP socket and a Unix domain socket. These two values were measured using programs in the lmbench package using only 65536-byte messages. For the TCP socket, the two processes were both on the same host.

Message Passing Latency Results

Figure A.1 lists the latency results measured under Solaris 2.6 and Digital Unix 4.0B.

	Latency (microseconds)								
	Pipe	Posix message queue	System V message queue	Doors	Sun RPC TCP	Sun RPC UDP	TCP socket	UDP socket	Unix domain socket
Solaris 2.6	324	584	260	121	1891	1677	798	755	465
DUnix 4.0B	574	995	625		1648	1373	848	639	289

Figure A.1 Latency to exchange a 1-byte message using various forms of IPC.

In Section A.4, we show the programs that measured the first six values, and the remaining three are from the lmbench suite. For the TCP and UDP measurements, the two processes were on the same host.

Message size	Bandwidth (MBytes/sec)							
	Pipe	Posix message queue	System V message queue	Doors	Sun RPC TCP	Sun RPC UDP	TCP socket	Unix domain socket
1024	6.3	3.7	4.9	6.3	0.5	0.5		
2048	8.7	5.3	6.3	10.0	0.9	1.0		
4096	9.8	8.4	6.6	12.6	1.6	2.8		
8192	12.7	10.2	5.8	14.4	2.4	2.8		
16384	13.1	11.6	6.1	16.8	3.2	3.4		
32768	13.2	13.4		11.4	3.5	4.3		
65536	13.7	14.4		12.2	3.7		13.2	11.3

Figure A.2 Bandwidth for various types of message passing (Solaris 2.6).

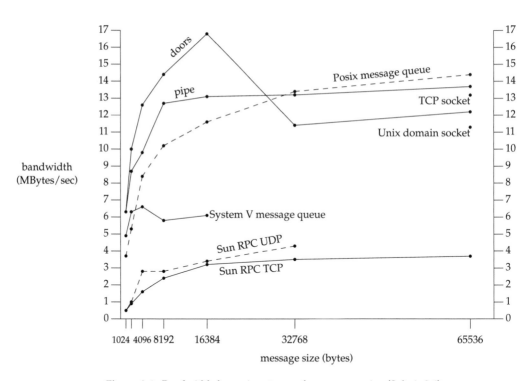

Figure A.3 Bandwidth for various types of message passing (Solaris 2.6).

Message size	Bandwidth (MBytes/sec)						
	Pipe	Posix message queue	System V message queue	Sun RPC TCP	Sun RPC UDP	TCP socket	Unix domain socket
1024	9.9	1.8	12.7	0.6	0.6		
2048	15.2	3.5	15.0	0.8	1.0		
4096	17.1	5.9	21.1	1.3	1.8		
8192	16.5	8.6	17.1	1.8	2.5		
16384	17.3	11.7	17.3	2.3			
32768	15.9	14.0		2.6			
65536	14.2	9.4		2.8		4.6	18.0

Figure A.4 Bandwidth for various types of message passing (Digital Unix 4.0B).

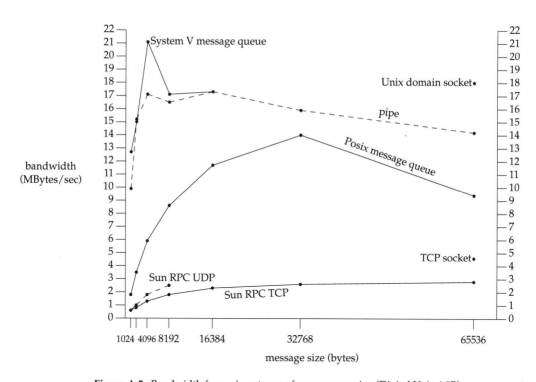

Figure A.5 Bandwidth for various types of message passing (Digital Unix 4.0B).

Thread Synchronization Results

Figure A.6 lists the time required by one or more threads to increment a counter that is in shared memory using various forms of synchronization under Solaris 2.6, and Figure A.7 graphs these values. Each thread increments the counter 1,000,000 times, and the number of threads incrementing the counter varied from one to five. Figure A.8 lists these values under Digital Unix 4.0B, and Figure A.9 graphs these values.

The reason for increasing the number of threads is to verify that the code using the synchronization technique is correct and to see whether the time starts increasing nonlinearly as the number of threads increases. We can measure `fcntl` record locking only for a single thread, because this form of synchronization works between processes and not between multiple threads within a single process.

Under Digital Unix, the times become very large for the two types of Posix semaphores with more than one thread, indicating some type of anomaly. We do not graph these values.

> One possible reason for these larger-than-expected numbers is that this program is a pathological synchronization test. That is, the threads do nothing but synchronization, and the lock is held essentially all the time. Since the threads are created with process contention scope, by default, each time a thread loses its timeslice, it probably holds the lock, so the new thread that is switched to probably blocks immediately.

Process Synchronization Results

Figures A.6 and A.7 and Figures A.8 and A.9 showed the measurements of the various synchronization techniques when used to synchronize the *threads* within a single process. Figures A.10 and A.11 show the performance of these techniques under Solaris 2.6 when the counter is shared between different *processes*. Figures A.12 and A.13 show the process synchronization results under Digital Unix 4.0B. The results are similar to the threaded numbers, although the two forms of Posix semaphores are now similar for Solaris. We plot only the first value for `fcntl` record locking, since the remaining values are so large. As we noted in Section 7.2, Digital Unix 4.0B does not support the `PTHREAD_PROCESS_SHARED` feature, so we cannot measure the mutex values between different processes. We again see some type of anomaly for Posix semaphores under Digital Unix when multiple processes are involved.

# threads	Time required to increment a counter in shared memory (seconds)						
	Posix mutex	Read–write lock	Posix memory semaphore	Posix named semaphore	System V semaphore	System V semaphore with UNDO	`fcntl` record locking
1	0.7	2.0	4.5	15.4	16.3	21.1	89.4
2	1.5	5.4	9.0	31.1	31.5	37.5	
3	2.2	7.5	14.4	46.5	48.3	57.7	
4	2.9	13.7	18.2	62.5	65.8	75.8	
5	3.7	19.7	22.8	76.8	81.8	90.0	

Figure A.6 Time required to increment a counter in shared memory (Solaris 2.6).

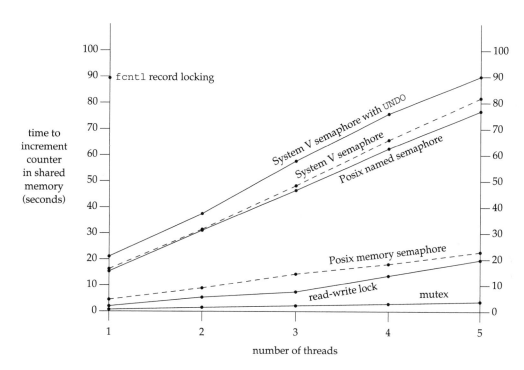

Figure A.7 Time required to increment a counter in shared memory (Solaris 2.6).

# threads	Time required to increment a counter in shared memory (seconds)						
	Posix mutex	Read–write lock	Posix memory semaphore	Posix named semaphore	System V semaphore	System V semaphore with UNDO	fcntl record locking
1	2.9	12.9	13.2	14.2	26.6	46.6	96.4
2	11.4	40.8	742.5	771.6	54.9	93.9	
3	28.4	73.2	1080.5	1074.7	84.5	141.9	
4	49.3	95.0	1534.1	1502.2	109.9	188.4	
5	67.3	126.3	1923.3	1764.1	137.3	233.6	

Figure A.8 Time required to increment a counter in shared memory (Digital Unix 4.0B).

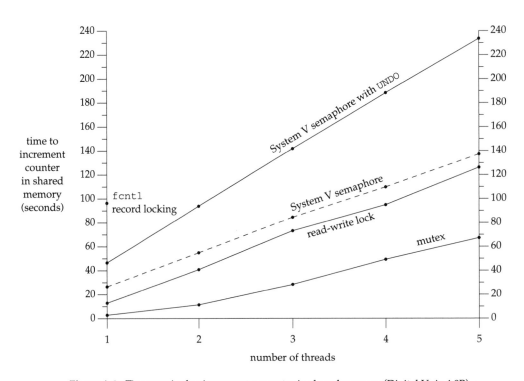

Figure A.9 Time required to increment a counter in shared memory (Digital Unix 4.0B).

# processes	Time required to increment a counter in shared memory (seconds)						
	Posix mutex	Read–write lock	Posix memory semaphore	Posix named semaphore	System V semaphore	System V semaphore with UNDO	fcntl record locking
1	0.8	1.9	13.6	14.3	17.3	22.1	90.7
2	1.6	3.9	29.2	29.2	34.9	41.6	244.5
3	2.3	6.4	41.6	42.9	54.0	60.1	376.4
4	3.1	12.2	57.3	58.8	72.4	81.9	558.0
5	4.0	20.4	70.4	73.5	87.8	102.6	764.0

Figure A.10 Time required to increment a counter in shared memory (Solaris 2.6).

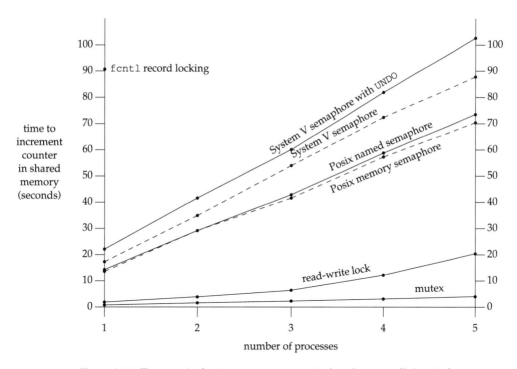

Figure A.11 Time required to increment a counter in shared memory (Solaris 2.6).

# processes	Time required to increment a counter in shared memory (seconds)				
	Posix memory semaphore	Posix named semaphore	System V semaphore	System V semaphore with UNDO	`fcntl` record locking
1	12.8	12.5	30.1	49.0	98.1
2	664.8	659.2	58.6	95.7	477.1
3	1236.1	1269.8	96.4	146.2	1785.2
4	1772.9	1804.1	120.3	197.0	2582.8
5	2179.9	2196.8	147.7	250.9	3419.2

Figure A.12   Time required to increment a counter in shared memory (Digital Unix 4.0B).

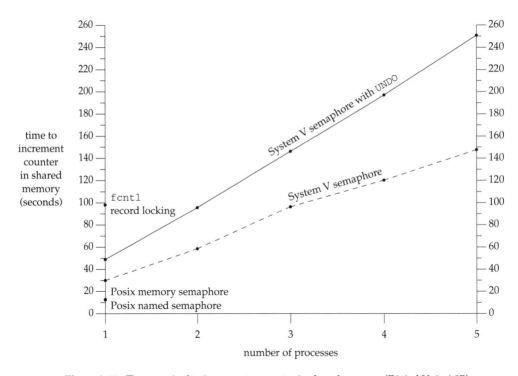

Figure A.13   Time required to increment a counter in shared memory (Digital Unix 4.0B).

A.3 Message Passing Bandwidth Programs

This section shows the three programs that measure the bandwidth of pipes, Posix message queues, and System V message queues. We showed the results of these programs in Figures A.2 and A.3.

Pipe Bandwidth Program

Figure A.14 shows an overview of the program that we are about to describe.

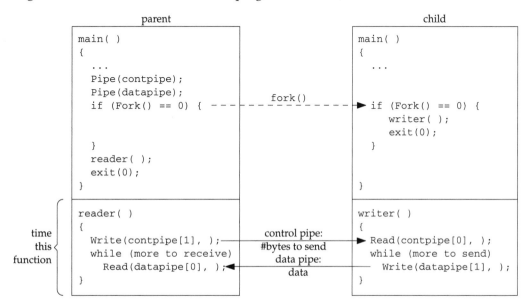

Figure A.14 Overview of program to measure the bandwidth of a pipe.

Figure A.15 shows the first half of our `bw_pipe` program, which measures the bandwidth of a pipe.

Command-line arguments

11-15   The command-line arguments specify the number of loops to perform (typically five in the measurements that follow), the number of megabytes to transfer (an argument of 10 causes $10 \times 1024 \times 1024$ bytes to be transferred), and the number of bytes for each `write` and `read` (which varies between 1024 and 65536 in the measurements that we showed).

Allocate buffer and touch it

16-17   `valloc` is a version of `malloc` that allocates the requested amount of memory starting on a page boundary. Our function `touch` (Figure A.17) stores 1 byte of data in each page of the buffer, forcing the kernel to page-in each page comprising the buffer. We do so before any timing is done.

——————————————————————————————————————— *bench/bw_pipe.c*

```
 1 #include    "unpipc.h"

 2 void    reader(int, int, int);
 3 void    writer(int, int);

 4 void    *buf;
 5 int     totalnbytes, xfersize;

 6 int
 7 main(int argc, char **argv)
 8 {
 9     int     i, nloop, contpipe[2], datapipe[2];
10     pid_t   childpid;

11     if (argc != 4)
12         err_quit("usage: bw_pipe <#loops> <#mbytes> <#bytes/write>");
13     nloop = atoi(argv[1]);
14     totalnbytes = atoi(argv[2]) * 1024 * 1024;
15     xfersize = atoi(argv[3]);

16     buf = Valloc(xfersize);
17     Touch(buf, xfersize);

18     Pipe(contpipe);
19     Pipe(datapipe);

20     if ( (childpid = Fork()) == 0) {
21         writer(contpipe[0], datapipe[1]);    /* child */
22         exit(0);
23     }
24         /* parent */
25     Start_time();
26     for (i = 0; i < nloop; i++)
27         reader(contpipe[1], datapipe[0], totalnbytes);
28     printf("bandwidth: %.3f MB/sec\n",
29             totalnbytes / Stop_time() * nloop);
30     kill(childpid, SIGTERM);
31     exit(0);
32 }
```

——————————————————————————————————————— *bench/bw_pipe.c*

Figure A.15 main function to measure the bandwidth of a pipe.

valloc is not part of Posix.1 and is listed as a "legacy" interface by Unix 98: it was required by an earlier version of the X/Open specification but is now optional. Our Valloc wrapper function calls malloc if valloc is not supported.

Create two pipes

18-19   Two pipes are created: contpipe[0] and contpipe[1] are used to synchronize the two processes at the beginning of each transfer, and datapipe[0] and datapipe[1] are used for the actual data transfer.

fork to create child

20-31   A child process is created, and the child (a return value of 0) calls the writer function while the parent calls the reader function. The reader function in the parent is called `nloop` times. Our `start_time` function is called immediately before the loop begins, and our `stop_time` function is called as soon as the loop terminates. These two functions are shown in Figure A.17. The bandwidth that is printed is the total number of bytes transferred each time around the loop, divided by the time needed to transfer the data (`stop_time` returns this as the number of microseconds since `start_time` was called), times the number of loops. The child is then killed with the `SIGTERM` signal, and the program terminates.

The second half of the program is shown in Figure A.16, and contains the two functions `writer` and `reader`.

—————————————————————————————— *bench/bw_pipe.c*
```
33 void
34 writer(int contfd, int datafd)
35 {
36     int      ntowrite;

37     for ( ; ; ) {
38         Read(contfd, &ntowrite, sizeof(ntowrite));

39         while (ntowrite > 0) {
40             Write(datafd, buf, xfersize);
41             ntowrite -= xfersize;
42         }
43     }
44 }

45 void
46 reader(int contfd, int datafd, int nbytes)
47 {
48     ssize_t n;

49     Write(contfd, &nbytes, sizeof(nbytes));

50     while ((nbytes > 0) &&
51            ((n = Read(datafd, buf, xfersize)) > 0)) {
52         nbytes -= n;
53     }
54 }
```
—————————————————————————————— *bench/bw_pipe.c*

Figure A.16 `writer` and `reader` functions to measure bandwidth of a pipe.

writer function

33–44   This function is an infinite loop that is called by the child. It waits for the parent to say that it is ready to receive the data, by reading an integer on the control pipe that specifies the number of bytes to write to the data pipe. When this notification is received, the child writes the data across the pipe to the parent, `xfersize` bytes per write.

reader function

45–54   This function is called by the parent in a loop. Each time the function is called, it writes an integer to the control pipe telling the child how many bytes to write to the pipe. The function then calls `read` in a loop, until all the data has been received.

Our `start_time`, `stop_time`, and `touch` functions are shown in Figure A.17.

—— *lib/timing.c*

```
 1 #include    "unpipc.h"

 2 static struct timeval tv_start, tv_stop;

 3 int
 4 start_time(void)
 5 {
 6     return (gettimeofday(&tv_start, NULL));
 7 }

 8 double
 9 stop_time(void)
10 {
11     double  clockus;

12     if (gettimeofday(&tv_stop, NULL) == -1)
13         return (0.0);
14     tv_sub(&tv_stop, &tv_start);
15     clockus = tv_stop.tv_sec * 1000000.0 + tv_stop.tv_usec;
16     return (clockus);
17 }

18 int
19 touch(void *vptr, int nbytes)
20 {
21     char    *cptr;
22     static int pagesize = 0;

23     if (pagesize == 0) {
24         errno = 0;
25 #ifdef  _SC_PAGESIZE
26         if ( (pagesize = sysconf(_SC_PAGESIZE)) == -1)
27             return (-1);
28 #else
29         pagesize = getpagesize();    /* BSD */
30 #endif
31     }
32     cptr = vptr;
33     while (nbytes > 0) {
34         *cptr = 1;
35         cptr += pagesize;
36         nbytes -= pagesize;
37     }
38     return (0);
39 }
```

—— *lib/timing.c*

Figure A.17 Timing functions: `start_time`, `stop_time`, and `touch`.

The `tv_sub` function is shown in Figure A.18; it subtracts two `timeval` structures, storing the result in the first structure.

――― *lib/tv_sub.c*
```
 1 #include     "unpipc.h"

 2 void
 3 tv_sub(struct timeval *out, struct timeval *in)
 4 {
 5     if ((out->tv_usec -= in->tv_usec) < 0) {     /* out -= in */
 6         --out->tv_sec;
 7         out->tv_usec += 1000000;
 8     }
 9     out->tv_sec -= in->tv_sec;
10 }
```
――― *lib/tv_sub.c*

Figure A.18 `tv_sub` function: subtract two `timeval` structures.

On a Sparc running Solaris 2.6, if we run our program five times in a row, we get

```
solaris % bw_pipe 5 10 65536
bandwidth: 13.722 MB/sec
solaris % bw_pipe 5 10 65536
bandwidth: 13.781 MB/sec
solaris % bw_pipe 5 10 65536
bandwidth: 13.685 MB/sec
solaris % bw_pipe 5 10 65536
bandwidth: 13.665 MB/sec
solaris % bw_pipe 5 10 65536
bandwidth: 13.584 MB/sec
```

Each time we specify five loops, 10,485,760 bytes per loop, and 65536 bytes per `write` and `read`. The average of these five runs is the 13.7 MBytes/sec value shown in Figure A.2.

Posix Message Queue Bandwidth Program

Figure A.19 is our `main` program that measures the bandwidth of a Posix message queue. Figure A.20 shows the `writer` and `reader` functions. This program is similar to our previous program that measures the bandwidth of a pipe.

> Note that our program must specify the maximum number of messages that can exist on the queue, when we create the queue, and we specify this as four. The capacity of the IPC channel can affect the performance, because the writing process can send this many messages before its call to `mq_send` blocks, forcing a context switch to the reading process. Therefore, the performance of this program depends on this magic number. Changing this number from four to eight under Solaris 2.6 had no effect on the numbers in Figure A.2, but this same change under Digital Unix 4.0B decreased the performance by 12%. We would have guessed the performance would increase with a larger number of messages, because this could halve the number of context switches. But if a memory-mapped file is used, this doubles the size of that file and the amount of memory that is `mmap`ed.

bench/bw_pxmsg.c

```
 1 #include    "unpipc.h"
 2 #define NAME    "bw_pxmsg"

 3 void    reader(int, mqd_t, int);
 4 void    writer(int, mqd_t);

 5 void    *buf;
 6 int     totalnbytes, xfersize;

 7 int
 8 main(int argc, char **argv)
 9 {
10     int     i, nloop, contpipe[2];
11     mqd_t   mq;
12     pid_t   childpid;
13     struct mq_attr attr;

14     if (argc != 4)
15         err_quit("usage: bw_pxmsg <#loops> <#mbytes> <#bytes/write>");
16     nloop = atoi(argv[1]);
17     totalnbytes = atoi(argv[2]) * 1024 * 1024;
18     xfersize = atoi(argv[3]);

19     buf = Valloc(xfersize);
20     Touch(buf, xfersize);

21     Pipe(contpipe);
22     mq_unlink(Px_ipc_name(NAME));   /* error OK */
23     attr.mq_maxmsg = 4;
24     attr.mq_msgsize = xfersize;
25     mq = Mq_open(Px_ipc_name(NAME), O_RDWR | O_CREAT, FILE_MODE, &attr);

26     if ( (childpid = Fork()) == 0) {
27         writer(contpipe[0], mq);    /* child */
28         exit(0);
29     }
30         /* parent */
31     Start_time();
32     for (i = 0; i < nloop; i++)
33         reader(contpipe[1], mq, totalnbytes);
34     printf("bandwidth: %.3f MB/sec\n",
35             totalnbytes / Stop_time() * nloop);

36     kill(childpid, SIGTERM);
37     Mq_close(mq);
38     Mq_unlink(Px_ipc_name(NAME));
39     exit(0);
40 }
```

bench/bw_pxmsg.c

Figure A.19 main function to measure bandwidth of a Posix message queue.

———————————————————————————— bench/bw_pxmsg.c
```
41 void
42 writer(int contfd, mqd_t mqsend)
43 {
44     int     ntowrite;

45     for ( ; ; ) {
46         Read(contfd, &ntowrite, sizeof(ntowrite));

47         while (ntowrite > 0) {
48             Mq_send(mqsend, buf, xfersize, 0);
49             ntowrite -= xfersize;
50         }
51     }
52 }

53 void
54 reader(int contfd, mqd_t mqrecv, int nbytes)
55 {
56     ssize_t n;

57     Write(contfd, &nbytes, sizeof(nbytes));

58     while ((nbytes > 0) &&
59            ((n = Mq_receive(mqrecv, buf, xfersize, NULL)) > 0)) {
60         nbytes -= n;
61     }
62 }
```
———————————————————————————— bench/bw_pxmsg.c

Figure A.20 `writer` and `reader` functions to measure bandwidth of a Posix message queue.

System V Message Queue Bandwidth Program

Figure A.21 is our `main` program that measures the bandwidth of a System V message queue, and Figure A.22 shows the `writer` and `reader` functions.

———————————————————————————— bench/bw_svmsg.c
```
 1 #include    "unpipc.h"

 2 void    reader(int, int, int);
 3 void    writer(int, int);

 4 struct msgbuf *buf;
 5 int     totalnbytes, xfersize;

 6 int
 7 main(int argc, char **argv)
 8 {
 9     int     i, nloop, contpipe[2], msqid;
10     pid_t   childpid;

11     if (argc != 4)
12         err_quit("usage: bw_svmsg <#loops> <#mbytes> <#bytes/write>");
13     nloop = atoi(argv[1]);
14     totalnbytes = atoi(argv[2]) * 1024 * 1024;
15     xfersize = atoi(argv[3]);
```

```
16      buf = Valloc(xfersize);
17      Touch(buf, xfersize);
18      buf->mtype = 1;

19      Pipe(contpipe);
20      msqid = Msgget(IPC_PRIVATE, IPC_CREAT | SVMSG_MODE);

21      if ( (childpid = Fork()) == 0) {
22          writer(contpipe[0], msqid);      /* child */
23          exit(0);
24      }
25      Start_time();
26      for (i = 0; i < nloop; i++)
27          reader(contpipe[1], msqid, totalnbytes);
28      printf("bandwidth: %.3f MB/sec\n",
29              totalnbytes / Stop_time() * nloop);

30      kill(childpid, SIGTERM);
31      Msgctl(msqid, IPC_RMID, NULL);
32      exit(0);
33  }
```

bench/bw_svmsg.c

Figure A.21 main function to measure bandwidth of a System V message queue.

bench/bw_svmsg.c

```
34 void
35 writer(int contfd, int msqid)
36 {
37      int     ntowrite;

38      for ( ; ; ) {
39          Read(contfd, &ntowrite, sizeof(ntowrite));

40          while (ntowrite > 0) {
41              Msgsnd(msqid, buf, xfersize - sizeof(long), 0);
42              ntowrite -= xfersize;
43          }
44      }
45  }

46 void
47 reader(int contfd, int msqid, int nbytes)
48 {
49      ssize_t n;

50      Write(contfd, &nbytes, sizeof(nbytes));

51      while ((nbytes > 0) &&
52              ((n = Msgrcv(msqid, buf, xfersize - sizeof(long), 0, 0)) > 0)) {
53          nbytes -= n + sizeof(long);
54      }
55  }
```

bench/bw_svmsg.c

Figure A.22 writer and reader functions to measure bandwidth of a System V message queue.

Doors Bandwidth Program

Our program to measure the bandwidth of the doors API is more complicated than the previous ones in this section, because we must `fork` before creating the door. Our parent creates the door and then notifies the child that the door can be opened by writing to a pipe.

Another change is that unlike Figure A.14, the `reader` function is not receiving the data. Instead, the data is being received by a function named `server` that is the server procedure for the door. Figure A.23 shows an overview of the program.

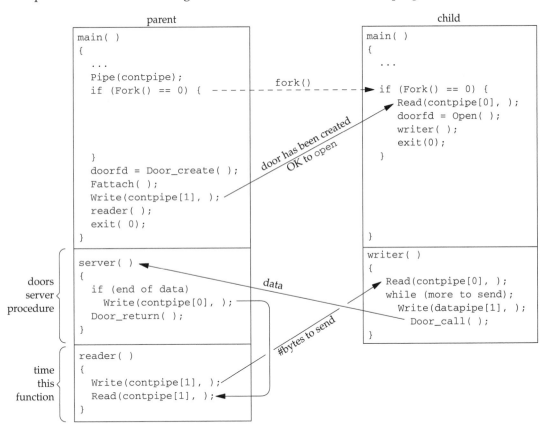

Figure A.23 Overview of program to measure the bandwidth of the doors API.

Since doors are supported only under Solaris, we simplify the program by assuming a full-duplex pipe (Section 4.4).

Another change from the previous programs is the fundamental difference between message passing, and procedure calling. In our Posix message queue program, for example, the writer just writes messages to a queue in a loop, and this is asynchronous. At some point, the queue will fill, or the writing process will lose its time slice of the processor, and the reader runs and reads the messages. If, for example, the queue held eight messages and the writer wrote eight messages each time it ran, and the reader read all eight messages each time it ran, to send N messages would involve N/4 context switches (N/8 from the writer to the reader, and another N/8 from the reader to the writer). But the doors API is synchronous: the caller blocks each time it calls `door_call` and cannot resume until the server procedure returns. To exchange N messages now involves N×2 context switches. We will encounter the same problem when we measure the bandwidth of RPC calls. Despite the increased number of context switches, note from Figure A.3 that doors provide the fastest IPC bandwidth up through a message size of around 25000 bytes.

Figure A.24 shows the `main` function of our program. The `writer`, `server`, and `reader` functions are shown in Figure A.25.

Sun RPC Bandwidth Program

Since procedure calls in Sun RPC are synchronous, we have the same limitation that we mentioned with our doors program. It is also easier with RPC to generate two programs, a client and a server, because that is what `rpcgen` generates. Figure A.26 shows the RPC specification file. We declare a single procedure that takes a variable-length of opaque data as input and returns nothing.

Figure A.27 shows our client program, and Figure A.28 shows our server procedure. We specify the protocol (TCP or UDP) as a command-line argument for the client, allowing us to measure both protocols.

bench/bw_door.c

```
 1 #include     "unpipc.h"

 2 void     reader(int, int);
 3 void     writer(int);
 4 void     server(void *, char *, size_t, door_desc_t *, size_t);

 5 void    *buf;
 6 int      totalnbytes, xfersize, contpipe[2];

 7 int
 8 main(int argc, char **argv)
 9 {
10     int     i, nloop, doorfd;
11     char    c;
12     pid_t   childpid;
13     ssize_t n;

14     if (argc != 5)
15         err_quit("usage: bw_door <pathname> <#loops> <#mbytes> <#bytes/write>");
16     nloop = atoi(argv[2]);
17     totalnbytes = atoi(argv[3]) * 1024 * 1024;
18     xfersize = atoi(argv[4]);

19     buf = Valloc(xfersize);
20     Touch(buf, xfersize);

21     unlink(argv[1]);
22     Close(Open(argv[1], O_CREAT | O_EXCL | O_RDWR, FILE_MODE));
23     Pipe(contpipe);              /* assumes full-duplex SVR4 pipe */

24     if ( (childpid = Fork()) == 0) {
25             /* child = client = writer */
26         if ( (n = Read(contpipe[0], &c, 1)) != 1)
27             err_quit("child: pipe read returned %d", n);
28         doorfd = Open(argv[1], O_RDWR);

29         writer(doorfd);
30         exit(0);
31     }
32         /* parent = server = reader */
33     doorfd = Door_create(server, NULL, 0);
34     Fattach(doorfd, argv[1]);
35     Write(contpipe[1], &c, 1);  /* tell child door is ready */

36     Start_time();
37     for (i = 0; i < nloop; i++)
38         reader(doorfd, totalnbytes);
39     printf("bandwidth: %.3f MB/sec\n",
40             totalnbytes / Stop_time() * nloop);
41     kill(childpid, SIGTERM);
42     unlink(argv[1]);
43     exit(0);
44 }
```

bench/bw_door.c

Figure A.24 main function to measure the bandwidth of the doors API.

```
                                                                  ── bench/bw_door.c
45 void
46 writer(int doorfd)
47 {
48     int     ntowrite;
49     door_arg_t arg;

50     arg.desc_ptr = NULL;          /* no descriptors to pass */
51     arg.desc_num = 0;
52     arg.rbuf = NULL;              /* no return values expected */
53     arg.rsize = 0;

54     for ( ; ; ) {
55         Read(contpipe[0], &ntowrite, sizeof(ntowrite));

56         while (ntowrite > 0) {
57             arg.data_ptr = buf;
58             arg.data_size = xfersize;
59             Door_call(doorfd, &arg);
60             ntowrite -= xfersize;
61         }
62     }
63 }

64 static int ntoread, nread;

65 void
66 server(void *cookie, char *argp, size_t arg_size,
67         door_desc_t *dp, size_t n_descriptors)
68 {
69     char    c;

70     nread += arg_size;
71     if (nread >= ntoread)
72         Write(contpipe[0], &c, 1);  /* tell reader() we are all done */

73     Door_return(NULL, 0, NULL, 0);
74 }

75 void
76 reader(int doorfd, int nbytes)
77 {
78     char    c;
79     ssize_t n;

80     ntoread = nbytes;              /* globals for server() procedure */
81     nread = 0;

82     Write(contpipe[1], &nbytes, sizeof(nbytes));

83     if ( (n = Read(contpipe[1], &c, 1)) != 1)
84         err_quit("reader: pipe read returned %d", n);
85 }
                                                                  ── bench/bw_door.c
```

Figure A.25 writer, server, and reader functions for doors API bandwidth measurement.

———————————————————————————————— bench/bw_sunrpc.x

```
 1 %#define      DEBUG          /* so server runs in foreground */

 2 struct data_in {
 3   opaque    data<>;       /* variable-length opaque data */
 4 };

 5 program BW_SUNRPC_PROG {
 6     version BW_SUNRPC_VERS {
 7         void    BW_SUNRPC(data_in) = 1;
 8     } = 1;
 9 } = 0x31230001;
```

———————————————————————————————— bench/bw_sunrpc.x

Figure A.26 RPC specification file for our bandwidth measurements of Sun RPC.

——————————————————————————————— bench/bw_sunrpc_client.c

```
 1 #include    "unpipc.h"
 2 #include    "bw_sunrpc.h"

 3 void   *buf;
 4 int     totalnbytes, xfersize;

 5 int
 6 main(int argc, char **argv)
 7 {
 8     int     i, nloop, ntowrite;
 9     CLIENT *cl;
10     data_in in;

11     if (argc != 6)
12         err_quit("usage: bw_sunrpc_client <hostname> <#loops>"
13                  " <#mbytes> <#bytes/write> <protocol>");
14     nloop = atoi(argv[2]);
15     totalnbytes = atoi(argv[3]) * 1024 * 1024;
16     xfersize = atoi(argv[4]);

17     buf = Valloc(xfersize);
18     Touch(buf, xfersize);

19     cl = Clnt_create(argv[1], BW_SUNRPC_PROG, BW_SUNRPC_VERS, argv[5]);

20     Start_time();
21     for (i = 0; i < nloop; i++) {
22         ntowrite = totalnbytes;
23         while (ntowrite > 0) {
24             in.data.data_len = xfersize;
25             in.data.data_val = buf;
26             if (bw_sunrpc_1(&in, cl) == NULL)
27                 err_quit("%s", clnt_sperror(cl, argv[1]));
28             ntowrite -= xfersize;
29         }
30     }
31     printf("bandwidth: %.3f MB/sec\n",
32            totalnbytes / Stop_time() * nloop);
33     exit(0);
34 }
```

——————————————————————————————— bench/bw_sunrpc_client.c

Figure A.27 RPC client program for bandwidth measurement.

```
                                                               ──── bench/bw_sunrpc_server.c
 1 #include     "unpipc.h"
 2 #include     "bw_sunrpc.h"

 3 #ifndef RPCGEN_ANSIC
 4 #define bw_sunrpc_1_svc bw_sunrpc_1
 5 #endif

 6 void *
 7 bw_sunrpc_1_svc(data_in * inp, struct svc_req *rqstp)
 8 {
 9     static int nbytes;

10     nbytes = inp->data.data_len;
11     return (&nbytes);                /* must be nonnull, but xdr_void() will ignore */
12 }
                                                               ──── bench/bw_sunrpc_server.c
```

Figure A.28 RPC server procedure for bandwidth measurement.

A.4   Message Passing Latency Programs

We now show the three programs that measure the latency of pipes, Posix message queues, and System V message queues. The performance numbers were shown in Figure A.1.

Pipe Latency Program

The program to measure the latency of a pipe is shown in Figure A.29.

doit function

2-9   This function runs in the parent and its clock time is measured. It writes 1 byte to a pipe (that is read by the child) and reads 1 byte from another pipe (that is written to by the child). This is what we described as the latency: how long it takes to send a small message and receive a small message in reply.

Create pipes

19-20   Two pipes are created and `fork` creates a child, leading to the arrangement shown in Figure 4.6 (but without the unused ends of each pipe closed, which is OK). Two pipes are needed for this test, since pipes are half-duplex, and we want two-way communication between the parent and child.

Child echoes 1-byte message

22-27   The child is an infinite loop that reads a 1-byte message and sends it back.

Measure parent

29-34   The parent first calls the `doit` function to send a 1-byte message to the child and read its 1-byte reply. This makes certain that both processes are running. The `doit` function is then called in a loop and the clock time is measured.

bench/lat_pipe.c

```
 1 #include      "unpipc.h"

 2 void
 3 doit(int readfd, int writefd)
 4 {
 5     char    c;

 6     Write(writefd, &c, 1);
 7     if (Read(readfd, &c, 1) != 1)
 8         err_quit("read error");
 9 }

10 int
11 main(int argc, char **argv)
12 {
13     int     i, nloop, pipe1[2], pipe2[2];
14     char    c;
15     pid_t   childpid;

16     if (argc != 2)
17         err_quit("usage: lat_pipe <#loops>");
18     nloop = atoi(argv[1]);

19     Pipe(pipe1);
20     Pipe(pipe2);

21     if ( (childpid = Fork()) == 0) {
22         for ( ; ; ) {                   /* child */
23             if (Read(pipe1[0], &c, 1) != 1)
24                 err_quit("read error");
25             Write(pipe2[1], &c, 1);
26         }
27         exit(0);
28     }
29         /* parent */
30     doit(pipe2[0], pipe1[1]);

31     Start_time();
32     for (i = 0; i < nloop; i++)
33         doit(pipe2[0], pipe1[1]);
34     printf("latency: %.3f usec\n", Stop_time() / nloop);

35     Kill(childpid, SIGTERM);
36     exit(0);
37 }
```

bench/lat_pipe.c

Figure A.29 Program to measure the latency of a pipe.

On a Sparc running Solaris 2.6, if we run the program five times in a row, we get

```
solaris % lat_pipe 10000
latency: 278.633 usec
solaris % lat_pipe 10000
latency: 397.810 usec
solaris % lat_pipe 10000
latency: 392.567 usec
solaris % lat_pipe 10000
latency: 266.572 usec
solaris % lat_pipe 10000
latency: 284.559 usec
```

The average of these five runs is 324 microseconds, which we show in Figure A.1. These times include two context switches (parent-to-child, then child-to-parent), four system calls (write by parent, read by child, write by child, and read by parent), and the pipe overhead for 1 byte of data in each direction.

Posix Message Queue Latency Program

Our program to measure the latency of a Posix message queue is shown in Figure A.30.

25-28 Two message queues are created: one is used from the parent to the child, and the other from the child to the parent. Although Posix messages have a priority, allowing us to assign different priorities for the messages in the two different directions, mq_receive always returns the next message on the queue. Therefore, we cannot use just one queue for this test.

System V Message Queue Latency Program

Figure A.31 shows our program that measures the latency of a System V message queue.

Only one message queue is created, and it contains messages in both directions: parent-to-child and child-to-parent. The former have a type field of 1, and the latter have a type field of 2. The fourth argument to msgrcv in doit is 2, to read only messages of this type, and the fourth argument to msgrcv in the child is 1, to read only messages of this type.

> In Sections 9.3 and 11.3, we mentioned that many kernel-defined structures cannot be statically initialized because Posix.1 and Unix 98 guarantee only that certain members are present in the structure. These standards do not guarantee the order of these members, and the structures might contain other, nonstandard, members too. But in this program, we statically initialize the msgbuf structures, because System V message queues guarantee that this structure contains a long message type field followed by the actual data.

—— *bench/lat_pxmsg.c*
```
1 #include    "unpipc.h"
2 #define NAME1    "lat_pxmsg1"
3 #define NAME2    "lat_pxmsg2"
4 #define MAXMSG    4          /* room for 4096 bytes on queue */
5 #define MSGSIZE 1024
```

```
 6 void
 7 doit(mqd_t mqsend, mqd_t mqrecv)
 8 {
 9     char    buff[MSGSIZE];

10     Mq_send(mqsend, buff, 1, 0);
11     if (Mq_receive(mqrecv, buff, MSGSIZE, NULL) != 1)
12         err_quit("mq_receive error");
13 }

14 int
15 main(int argc, char **argv)
16 {
17     int     i, nloop;
18     mqd_t   mq1, mq2;
19     char    buff[MSGSIZE];
20     pid_t   childpid;
21     struct mq_attr attr;

22     if (argc != 2)
23         err_quit("usage: lat_pxmsg <#loops>");
24     nloop = atoi(argv[1]);

25     attr.mq_maxmsg = MAXMSG;
26     attr.mq_msgsize = MSGSIZE;
27     mq1 = Mq_open(Px_ipc_name(NAME1), O_RDWR | O_CREAT, FILE_MODE, &attr);
28     mq2 = Mq_open(Px_ipc_name(NAME2), O_RDWR | O_CREAT, FILE_MODE, &attr);

29     if ( (childpid = Fork()) == 0) {
30         for ( ; ; ) {              /* child */
31             if (Mq_receive(mq1, buff, MSGSIZE, NULL) != 1)
32                 err_quit("mq_receive error");
33             Mq_send(mq2, buff, 1, 0);
34         }
35         exit(0);
36     }
37         /* parent */
38     doit(mq1, mq2);

39     Start_time();
40     for (i = 0; i < nloop; i++)
41         doit(mq1, mq2);
42     printf("latency: %.3f usec\n", Stop_time() / nloop);

43     Kill(childpid, SIGTERM);
44     Mq_close(mq1);
45     Mq_close(mq2);
46     Mq_unlink(Px_ipc_name(NAME1));
47     Mq_unlink(Px_ipc_name(NAME2));
48     exit(0);
49 }
```

—— *bench/lat_pxmsg.c*

Figure A.30 Program to measure the latency of a Posix message queue.

```
                                                                ———— bench/lat_svmsg.c
 1 #include     "unpipc.h"
 2 struct msgbuf    p2child = { 1, { 0 } };      /* type = 1 */
 3 struct msgbuf    child2p = { 2, { 0 } };      /* type = 2 */
 4 struct msgbuf    inbuf;

 5 void
 6 doit(int msgid)
 7 {
 8     Msgsnd(msgid, &p2child, 0, 0);
 9     if (Msgrcv(msgid, &inbuf, sizeof(inbuf.mtext), 2, 0) != 0)
10         err_quit("msgrcv error");
11 }

12 int
13 main(int argc, char **argv)
14 {
15     int     i, nloop, msgid;
16     pid_t   childpid;

17     if (argc != 2)
18         err_quit("usage: lat_svmsg <#loops>");
19     nloop = atoi(argv[1]);

20     msgid = Msgget(IPC_PRIVATE, IPC_CREAT | SVMSG_MODE);

21     if ( (childpid = Fork()) == 0) {
22         for ( ; ; ) {                      /* child */
23             if (Msgrcv(msgid, &inbuf, sizeof(inbuf.mtext), 1, 0) != 0)
24                 err_quit("msgrcv error");
25             Msgsnd(msgid, &child2p, 0, 0);
26         }
27         exit(0);
28     }
29         /* parent */
30     doit(msgid);

31     Start_time();
32     for (i = 0; i < nloop; i++)
33         doit(msgid);
34     printf("latency: %.3f usec\n", Stop_time() / nloop);

35     Kill(childpid, SIGTERM);
36     Msgctl(msgid, IPC_RMID, NULL);
37     exit(0);
38 }
                                                                ———— bench/lat_svmsg.c
```

Figure A.31 Program to measure the latency of a System V message queue.

Doors Latency Program

Our program to measure the latency of the doors API is shown in Figure A.32. The child creates the door and associates the function `server` with the door. The parent then opens the door and invokes `door_call` in a loop. One byte of data is passed as an argument, and nothing is returned.

—————————————————————————————— bench/lat_door.c

```
 1 #include    "unpipc.h"

 2 void
 3 server(void *cookie, char *argp, size_t arg_size,
 4         door_desc_t *dp, size_t n_descriptors)
 5 {
 6     char    c;

 7     Door_return(&c, sizeof(char), NULL, 0);
 8 }

 9 int
10 main(int argc, char **argv)
11 {
12     int     i, nloop, doorfd, contpipe[2];
13     char    c;
14     pid_t   childpid;
15     door_arg_t arg;

16     if (argc != 3)
17         err_quit("usage: lat_door <pathname> <#loops>");
18     nloop = atoi(argv[2]);

19     unlink(argv[1]);
20     Close(Open(argv[1], O_CREAT | O_EXCL | O_RDWR, FILE_MODE));
21     Pipe(contpipe);

22     if ( (childpid = Fork()) == 0) {
23         doorfd = Door_create(server, NULL, 0);
24         Fattach(doorfd, argv[1]);
25         Write(contpipe[1], &c, 1);

26         for ( ; ; )                     /* child = server */
27             pause();
28         exit(0);
29     }
30     arg.data_ptr = &c;              /* parent = client */
31     arg.data_size = sizeof(char);
32     arg.desc_ptr = NULL;
33     arg.desc_num = 0;
34     arg.rbuf = &c;
35     arg.rsize = sizeof(char);

36     if (Read(contpipe[0], &c, 1) != 1)  /* wait for child to create */
37         err_quit("pipe read error");
38     doorfd = Open(argv[1], O_RDWR);
39     Door_call(doorfd, &arg);    /* once to start everything */

40     Start_time();
41     for (i = 0; i < nloop; i++)
42         Door_call(doorfd, &arg);
43     printf("latency: %.3f usec\n", Stop_time() / nloop);

44     Kill(childpid, SIGTERM);
45     unlink(argv[1]);
46     exit(0);
47 }
```

—————————————————————————————— bench/lat_door.c

Figure A.32 Program to measure the latency of the doors API.

Sun RPC Latency Program

To measure the latency of the Sun RPC API, we write two programs, a client and a server (similar to what we did when we measured the bandwidth). We use the same RPC specification file (Figure A.26), but our client calls the null procedure this time. Recall from Exercise 16.11 that this procedure takes no arguments and returns nothing, which is what we want to measure the latency. Figure A.33 shows the client. As in the solution to Exercise 16.11, we must call `clnt_call` directly to call the null procedure; a stub function is not provided in the client stub.

—————————————— bench/lat_sunrpc_client.c
```
 1 #include     "unpipc.h"
 2 #include     "lat_sunrpc.h"

 3 int
 4 main(int argc, char **argv)
 5 {
 6     int     i, nloop;
 7     CLIENT *cl;
 8     struct timeval tv;

 9     if (argc != 4)
10         err_quit("usage: lat_sunrpc_client <hostname> <#loops> <protocol>");
11     nloop = atoi(argv[2]);

12     cl = Clnt_create(argv[1], BW_SUNRPC_PROG, BW_SUNRPC_VERS, argv[3]);

13     tv.tv_sec = 10;
14     tv.tv_usec = 0;
15     Start_time();
16     for (i = 0; i < nloop; i++) {
17         if (clnt_call(cl, NULLPROC, xdr_void, NULL,
18                       xdr_void, NULL, tv) != RPC_SUCCESS)
19             err_quit("%s", clnt_sperror(cl, argv[1]));
20     }
21     printf("latency: %.3f usec\n", Stop_time() / nloop);
22     exit(0);
23 }
```
—————————————— bench/lat_sunrpc_client.c

Figure A.33 Sun RPC client for latency measurement.

We compile our server with the server function from Figure A.28, but that function is never called. Since we used `rpcgen` to build the client and server, we need to define at least one server procedure, but we never call it. The reason we used `rpcgen` is that it automatically generates the server `main` with the null procedure, which we need.

A.5 Thread Synchronization Programs

To measure the time required by the various synchronization techniques, we create some number of threads (one to five for the measurements shown in Figures A.6 and A.8) and each thread increments a counter in shared memory a large number of times, using the different forms of synchronization to coordinate access to the shared counter.

Posix Mutex Program

Figure A.34 shows the global variables and the `main` function for our program to measure Posix mutexes.

────────────────────────── bench/incr_pxmutex1.c

```
 1 #include     "unpipc.h"

 2 #define MAXNTHREADS 100

 3 int      nloop;

 4 struct {
 5     pthread_mutex_t mutex;
 6     long     counter;
 7 } shared = {
 8     PTHREAD_MUTEX_INITIALIZER
 9 };

10 void     *incr(void *);

11 int
12 main(int argc, char **argv)
13 {
14     int     i, nthreads;
15     pthread_t tid[MAXNTHREADS];

16     if (argc != 3)
17         err_quit("usage: incr_pxmutex1 <#loops> <#threads>");
18     nloop = atoi(argv[1]);
19     nthreads = min(atoi(argv[2]), MAXNTHREADS);

20         /* lock the mutex */
21     Pthread_mutex_lock(&shared.mutex);

22         /* create all the threads */
23     Set_concurrency(nthreads);
24     for (i = 0; i < nthreads; i++) {
25         Pthread_create(&tid[i], NULL, incr, NULL);
26     }
27         /* start the timer and unlock the mutex */
28     Start_time();
29     Pthread_mutex_unlock(&shared.mutex);

30         /* wait for all the threads */
31     for (i = 0; i < nthreads; i++) {
32         Pthread_join(tid[i], NULL);
33     }
34     printf("microseconds: %.0f usec\n", Stop_time());
35     if (shared.counter != nloop * nthreads)
36         printf("error: counter = %ld\n", shared.counter);

37     exit(0);
38 }
```

────────────────────────── bench/incr_pxmutex1.c

Figure A.34 Global variables and `main` function to measure Posix mutex synchronization.

Shared data

4-9   The shared data between the threads consists of the mutex itself and the counter. The mutex is statically initialized.

Lock mutex and create threads

20-26   The main thread locks the mutex before the threads are created, so that no thread can obtain the mutex until all the threads have been created and the mutex is released by the main thread. Our set_concurrency function is called and the threads are created. Each thread executes the incr function, which we show next.

Start timer and release the mutex

27-36   Once all the threads are created, the timer is started and the mutex is released. The main thread then waits for all the threads to finish, at which time the timer is stopped and the total number of microseconds is printed.

Figure A.35 shows the incr function that is executed by each thread.

—————————————————————————————— bench/incr_pxmutex1.c
```
39 void *
40 incr(void *arg)
41 {
42     int     i;

43     for (i = 0; i < nloop; i++) {
44         Pthread_mutex_lock(&shared.mutex);
45         shared.counter++;
46         Pthread_mutex_unlock(&shared.mutex);
47     }
48     return (NULL);
49 }
```
—————————————————————————————— bench/incr_pxmutex1.c

Figure A.35   Increment a shared counter using a Posix mutex.

Increment counter in critical region

44-46   The counter is incremented after obtaining the mutex. The mutex is released.

Read–Write Lock Program

Our program that uses read–write locks is a slight modification to our program that uses Posix mutexes. Each thread must obtain a write lock on the read–write lock before incrementing the shared counter.

> Few systems implement the Posix read–write locks that we described in Chapter 8, which are part of Unix 98 and are being considered by the Posix.1j working group. The read–write lock measurements described in this Appendix were made under Solaris 2.6 using the Solaris read–write locks described in the rwlock(3T) manual page. This implementation provides the same functionality as the proposed read–write locks, and the wrapper functions required to use these functions from the functions we described in Chapter 8 are trivial.

Under Digital Unix 4.0B, our measurements were made using the Digital thread-independent services read–write locks, described on the `tis_rwlock` manual pages. We do not show the simple modifications to Figures A.36 and A.37 for these read–write locks.

Figure A.36 shows the `main` function, and Figure A.37 shows the `incr` function.

———————————————————————— bench/incr_rwlock1.c

```
 1 #include    "unpipc.h"
 2 #include    <synch.h>            /* Solaris header */

 3 void    Rw_wrlock(rwlock_t *rwptr);
 4 void    Rw_unlock(rwlock_t *rwptr);

 5 #define MAXNTHREADS 100

 6 int     nloop;

 7 struct {
 8     rwlock_t rwlock;            /* the Solaris datatype */
 9     long    counter;
10 } shared;                       /* init to 0 -> USYNC_THREAD */

11 void    *incr(void *);

12 int
13 main(int argc, char **argv)
14 {
15     int     i, nthreads;
16     pthread_t tid[MAXNTHREADS];

17     if (argc != 3)
18         err_quit("usage: incr_rwlock1 <#loops> <#threads>");
19     nloop = atoi(argv[1]);
20     nthreads = min(atoi(argv[2]), MAXNTHREADS);

21         /* obtain write lock */
22     Rw_wrlock(&shared.rwlock);

23         /* create all the threads */
24     Set_concurrency(nthreads);
25     for (i = 0; i < nthreads; i++) {
26         Pthread_create(&tid[i], NULL, incr, NULL);
27     }
28         /* start the timer and release the write lock */
29     Start_time();
30     Rw_unlock(&shared.rwlock);

31         /* wait for all the threads */
32     for (i = 0; i < nthreads; i++) {
33         Pthread_join(tid[i], NULL);
34     }
35     printf("microseconds: %.0f usec\n", Stop_time());
36     if (shared.counter != nloop * nthreads)
37         printf("error: counter = %ld\n", shared.counter);

38     exit(0);
39 }
```

———————————————————————— bench/incr_rwlock1.c

Figure A.36 `main` function to measure read–write lock synchronization.

—————————————————————————————— bench/incr_rwlock1.c

```
40 void *
41 incr(void *arg)
42 {
43     int     i;

44     for (i = 0; i < nloop; i++) {
45         Rw_wrlock(&shared.rwlock);
46         shared.counter++;
47         Rw_unlock(&shared.rwlock);
48     }
49     return (NULL);
50 }
```

—————————————————————————————— bench/incr_rwlock1.c

Figure A.37 Increment a shared counter using a read–write lock.

Posix Memory-Based Semaphore Program

We measure both Posix memory-based semaphores and Posix named semaphores. Figure A.39 shows the `main` function for the memory-based semaphore program, and Figure A.38 shows its `incr` function.

18-19   A semaphore is created with a value of 0, and the second argument of 0 to `sem_init` says that the semaphore is shared between the threads of the calling process.

20-27   After all the threads are created, the timer is started and `sem_post` is called once by the main thread.

—————————————————————————————— bench/incr_pxsem1.c

```
37 void *
38 incr(void *arg)
39 {
40     int     i;

41     for (i = 0; i < nloop; i++) {
42         Sem_wait(&shared.mutex);
43         shared.counter++;
44         Sem_post(&shared.mutex);
45     }
46     return (NULL);
47 }
```

—————————————————————————————— bench/incr_pxsem1.c

Figure A.38 Increment a shared counter using a Posix memory-based semaphore.

——————————————————————————————————— *bench/incr_pxsem1.c*

```
 1 #include    "unpipc.h"

 2 #define MAXNTHREADS 100

 3 int     nloop;

 4 struct {
 5     sem_t   mutex;                    /* the memory-based semaphore */
 6     long    counter;
 7 } shared;

 8 void   *incr(void *);

 9 int
10 main(int argc, char **argv)
11 {
12     int     i, nthreads;
13     pthread_t tid[MAXNTHREADS];

14     if (argc != 3)
15         err_quit("usage: incr_pxsem1 <#loops> <#threads>");
16     nloop = atoi(argv[1]);
17     nthreads = min(atoi(argv[2]), MAXNTHREADS);

18         /* initialize memory-based semaphore to 0 */
19     Sem_init(&shared.mutex, 0, 0);

20         /* create all the threads */
21     Set_concurrency(nthreads);
22     for (i = 0; i < nthreads; i++) {
23         Pthread_create(&tid[i], NULL, incr, NULL);
24     }
25         /* start the timer and release the semaphore */
26     Start_time();
27     Sem_post(&shared.mutex);

28         /* wait for all the threads */
29     for (i = 0; i < nthreads; i++) {
30         Pthread_join(tid[i], NULL);
31     }
32     printf("microseconds: %.0f usec\n", Stop_time());
33     if (shared.counter != nloop * nthreads)
34         printf("error: counter = %ld\n", shared.counter);

35     exit(0);
36 }
```

——————————————————————————————————— *bench/incr_pxsem1.c*

Figure A.39 main function to measure Posix memory-based semaphore synchronization.

Posix Named Semaphore Program

Figure A.41 shows the `main` function that measures Posix named semaphores, and Figure A.40 shows its `incr` function.

```
                                                  ─────── bench/incr_pxsem2.c
40 void *
41 incr(void *arg)
42 {
43     int     i;

44     for (i = 0; i < nloop; i++) {
45         Sem_wait(shared.mutex);
46         shared.counter++;
47         Sem_post(shared.mutex);
48     }
49     return (NULL);
50 }
                                                  ─────── bench/incr_pxsem2.c
```

Figure A.40 Increment a shared counter using a Posix named semaphore.

System V Semaphore Program

The `main` function of our program that measures System V semaphores is shown in Figure A.42, and Figure A.43 shows its `incr` function.

20–23   A semaphore is created consisting of one member, and its value is initialized to 0.

24–29   Two `semop` structures are initialized: one to post-to the semaphore and one to wait-for the semaphore. Notice that the `sem_flg` member of both structures is 0: the SEM_UNDO flag is not specified.

System V Semaphore with SEM_UNDO Program

The only difference in our program that measures System V semaphores with the SEM_UNDO feature from Figure A.42 is setting the `sem_flg` member of the two `semop` structures to SEM_UNDO instead of 0. We do not show this simple modification.

——————————————————————————— bench/incr_pxsem2.c

```
 1 #include    "unpipc.h"

 2 #define MAXNTHREADS 100
 3 #define NAME    "incr_pxsem2"

 4 int     nloop;

 5 struct {
 6     sem_t  *mutex;              /* pointer to the named semaphore */
 7     long    counter;
 8 } shared;

 9 void   *incr(void *);

10 int
11 main(int argc, char **argv)
12 {
13     int     i, nthreads;
14     pthread_t tid[MAXNTHREADS];

15     if (argc != 3)
16         err_quit("usage: incr_pxsem2 <#loops> <#threads>");
17     nloop = atoi(argv[1]);
18     nthreads = min(atoi(argv[2]), MAXNTHREADS);

19         /* initialize named semaphore to 0 */
20     sem_unlink(Px_ipc_name(NAME));  /* error OK */
21     shared.mutex = Sem_open(Px_ipc_name(NAME), O_CREAT | O_EXCL, FILE_MODE, 0);

22         /* create all the threads */
23     Set_concurrency(nthreads);
24     for (i = 0; i < nthreads; i++) {
25         Pthread_create(&tid[i], NULL, incr, NULL);
26     }
27         /* start the timer and release the semaphore */
28     Start_time();
29     Sem_post(shared.mutex);

30         /* wait for all the threads */
31     for (i = 0; i < nthreads; i++) {
32         Pthread_join(tid[i], NULL);
33     }
34     printf("microseconds: %.0f usec\n", Stop_time());
35     if (shared.counter != nloop * nthreads)
36         printf("error: counter = %ld\n", shared.counter);
37     Sem_unlink(Px_ipc_name(NAME));

38     exit(0);
39 }
```

——————————————————————————— bench/incr_pxsem2.c

Figure A.41 main function to measure Posix named semaphore synchronization.

bench/incr_svsem1.c

```
 1 #include    "unpipc.h"

 2 #define MAXNTHREADS 100

 3 int     nloop;

 4 struct {
 5     int     semid;
 6     long    counter;
 7 } shared;

 8 struct sembuf postop, waitop;

 9 void    *incr(void *);

10 int
11 main(int argc, char **argv)
12 {
13     int     i, nthreads;
14     pthread_t tid[MAXNTHREADS];
15     union semun arg;

16     if (argc != 3)
17         err_quit("usage: incr_svsem1 <#loops> <#threads>");
18     nloop = atoi(argv[1]);
19     nthreads = min(atoi(argv[2]), MAXNTHREADS);

20         /* create semaphore and initialize to 0 */
21     shared.semid = Semget(IPC_PRIVATE, 1, IPC_CREAT | SVSEM_MODE);
22     arg.val = 0;
23     Semctl(shared.semid, 0, SETVAL, arg);
24     postop.sem_num = 0;           /* and init the two semop() structures */
25     postop.sem_op = 1;
26     postop.sem_flg = 0;
27     waitop.sem_num = 0;
28     waitop.sem_op = -1;
29     waitop.sem_flg = 0;

30         /* create all the threads */
31     Set_concurrency(nthreads);
32     for (i = 0; i < nthreads; i++) {
33         Pthread_create(&tid[i], NULL, incr, NULL);
34     }
35         /* start the timer and release the semaphore */
36     Start_time();
37     Semop(shared.semid, &postop, 1);    /* up by 1 */

38         /* wait for all the threads */
39     for (i = 0; i < nthreads; i++) {
40         Pthread_join(tid[i], NULL);
41     }
42     printf("microseconds: %.0f usec\n", Stop_time());
43     if (shared.counter != nloop * nthreads)
44         printf("error: counter = %ld\n", shared.counter);
45     Semctl(shared.semid, 0, IPC_RMID);

46     exit(0);
47 }
```

bench/incr_svsem1.c

Figure A.42 main function to measure System V semaphore synchronization.

bench/incr_svsem1.c
```
48 void *
49 incr(void *arg)
50 {
51     int     i;

52     for (i = 0; i < nloop; i++) {
53         Semop(shared.semid, &waitop, 1);
54         shared.counter++;
55         Semop(shared.semid, &postop, 1);
56     }
57     return (NULL);
58 }
```
bench/incr_svsem1.c

Figure A.43 Increment a shared counter using a System V semaphore.

fcntl Record Locking Program

Our final program uses `fcntl` record locking to provide synchronization. The `main` function is shown in Figure A.45. This program will run successfully when only one thread is specified, because `fcntl` locks are between different processes, not between the different threads of a single process. When multiple threads are specified, each thread can always obtain the requested lock (that is, the calls to `writew_lock` never block, since the calling process already owns the lock), and the final value of the counter is wrong.

18–22   The pathname of the file to create and then use for locking is a command-line argument. This allows us to measure this program when this file resides on different filesystems. We expect this program to run slower when this file is on an NFS mounted filesystem, which requires that both systems (the NFS client and NFS server) support NFS record locking.

The `incr` function using record locking is shown in Figure A.44.

bench/incr_fcntl1.c
```
44 void *
45 incr(void *arg)
46 {
47     int     i;

48     for (i = 0; i < nloop; i++) {
49         Writew_lock(shared.fd, 0, SEEK_SET, 0);
50         shared.counter++;
51         Un_lock(shared.fd, 0, SEEK_SET, 0);
52     }
53     return (NULL);
54 }
```
bench/incr_fcntl1.c

Figure A.44 Increment a shared counter using `fcntl` record locking.

bench/incr_fcntl1.c

```
 4 #include    "unpipc.h"

 5 #define MAXNTHREADS 100

 6 int     nloop;

 7 struct {
 8     int     fd;
 9     long    counter;
10 } shared;

11 void   *incr(void *);

12 int
13 main(int argc, char **argv)
14 {
15     int     i, nthreads;
16     char    *pathname;
17     pthread_t tid[MAXNTHREADS];

18     if (argc != 4)
19         err_quit("usage: incr_fcntl1 <pathname> <#loops> <#threads>");
20     pathname = argv[1];
21     nloop = atoi(argv[2]);
22     nthreads = min(atoi(argv[3]), MAXNTHREADS);

23         /* create the file and obtain write lock */
24     shared.fd = Open(pathname, O_RDWR | O_CREAT | O_TRUNC, FILE_MODE);
25     Writew_lock(shared.fd, 0, SEEK_SET, 0);

26         /* create all the threads */
27     Set_concurrency(nthreads);
28     for (i = 0; i < nthreads; i++) {
29         Pthread_create(&tid[i], NULL, incr, NULL);
30     }
31         /* start the timer and release the write lock */
32     Start_time();
33     Un_lock(shared.fd, 0, SEEK_SET, 0);

34         /* wait for all the threads */
35     for (i = 0; i < nthreads; i++) {
36         Pthread_join(tid[i], NULL);
37     }
38     printf("microseconds: %.0f usec\n", Stop_time());
39     if (shared.counter != nloop * nthreads)
40         printf("error: counter = %ld\n", shared.counter);
41     Unlink(pathname);

42     exit(0);
43 }
```

bench/incr_fcntl1.c

Figure A.45 main function to measure fcntl record locking.

A.6 Process Synchronization Programs

In the programs in the previous section, sharing a counter between multiple threads was simple: we just stored the counter as a global variable. We now modify these programs to provide synchronization between different processes.

To share the counter between a parent and its children, we store the counter in shared memory that is allocated by our my_shm function, shown in Figure A.46.

—————————————————————————————— lib/my_shm.c
```
 1 #include    "unpipc.h"

 2 void *
 3 my_shm(size_t nbytes)
 4 {
 5     void    *shared;

 6 #if    defined(MAP_ANON)
 7     shared = mmap(NULL, nbytes, PROT_READ | PROT_WRITE,
 8                   MAP_ANON | MAP_SHARED, -1, 0);

 9 #elif   defined(HAVE_DEV_ZERO)
10     int    fd;

11         /* memory map /dev/zero */
12     if ( (fd = open("/dev/zero", O_RDWR)) == -1)
13         return (MAP_FAILED);
14     shared = mmap(NULL, nbytes, PROT_READ | PROT_WRITE, MAP_SHARED, fd, 0);
15     close(fd);

16 #else
17 #error cannot determine what type of anonymous shared memory to use
18 #endif
19     return (shared);            /* MAP_FAILED on error */
20 }
```
—————————————————————————————— lib/my_shm.c

Figure A.46 Create some shared memory for a parent and its children.

If the system supports the MAP_ANON flag (Section 12.4), we use it; otherwise, we memory map /dev/zero (Section 12.5).

Further modifications depend on the type of synchronization and what happens to the underlying datatype when fork is called. We described some of these details in Section 10.12.

- Posix mutex: the mutex must be stored in shared memory (with the shared counter), and the PTHREAD_PROCESS_SHARED attribute must be set when the mutex is initialized. We show the code for this program shortly.

- Posix read–write lock: the read–write lock must be stored in shared memory (with the shared counter), and the PTHREAD_PROCESS_SHARED attribute must be set when the read–write is initialized.

- Posix memory-based semaphores: the semaphore must be stored in shared memory (with the shared counter), and the second argument to `sem_init` must be 1, to specify that the semaphore is shared between processes.

- Posix named semaphores: either we can have the parent and each child call `sem_open` or we can have the parent call `sem_open`, knowing that the semaphore will be shared by the child across the `fork`.

- System V semaphores: nothing special need be coded, since these semaphores can always be shared between processes. The children just need to know the semaphore's identifier.

- `fcntl` record locking: nothing special need be coded, since descriptors are shared by the child across a `fork`.

We show only the code for the Posix mutex program.

Posix Mutex Program

The `main` function for our first program uses a Posix mutex to provide synchronization and is shown in Figure A.48. Its `incr` function is shown in Figure A.47.

19-20   Since we are using multiple processes (the children of a parent), we must place our `shared` structure into shared memory. We call our `my_shm` function (Figure A.46).

21-26   Since the mutex is in shared memory, we cannot statically initialize it, so we call `pthread_mutex_init` after setting the `PTHREAD_PROCESS_SHARED` attribute. The mutex is locked.

27-36   All the children are created, the timer is started, and the mutex is unlocked.

37-43   The parent waits for all the children and then stops the timer.

―― *bench/incr_pxmutex5.c*
```
46 void *
47 incr(void *arg)
48 {
49     int     i;

50     for (i = 0; i < nloop; i++) {
51         Pthread_mutex_lock(&shared->mutex);
52         shared->counter++;
53         Pthread_mutex_unlock(&shared->mutex);
54     }
55     return (NULL);
56 }
```
―― *bench/incr_pxmutex5.c*

Figure A.47 `incr` function to measure Posix mutex locking between processes.

―――――――――――――――――――――――― bench/incr_pxmutex5.c

```
 1 #include    "unpipc.h"

 2 #define MAXNPROC    100

 3 int    nloop;

 4 struct shared {
 5     pthread_mutex_t mutex;
 6     long    counter;
 7 } *shared;                  /* pointer; actual structure in shared memory */

 8 void   *incr(void *);

 9 int
10 main(int argc, char **argv)
11 {
12     int    i, nprocs;
13     pid_t    childpid[MAXNPROC];
14     pthread_mutexattr_t mattr;

15     if (argc != 3)
16         err_quit("usage: incr_pxmutex5 <#loops> <#processes>");
17     nloop = atoi(argv[1]);
18     nprocs = min(atoi(argv[2]), MAXNPROC);

19         /* get shared memory for parent and children */
20     shared = My_shm(sizeof(struct shared));

21         /* initialize the mutex and lock it */
22     Pthread_mutexattr_init(&mattr);
23     Pthread_mutexattr_setpshared(&mattr, PTHREAD_PROCESS_SHARED);
24     Pthread_mutex_init(&shared->mutex, &mattr);
25     Pthread_mutexattr_destroy(&mattr);
26     Pthread_mutex_lock(&shared->mutex);

27         /* create all the children */
28     for (i = 0; i < nprocs; i++) {
29         if ( (childpid[i] = Fork()) == 0) {
30             incr(NULL);
31             exit(0);
32         }
33     }
34         /* parent: start the timer and unlock the mutex */
35     Start_time();
36     Pthread_mutex_unlock(&shared->mutex);

37         /* wait for all the children */
38     for (i = 0; i < nprocs; i++) {
39         Waitpid(childpid[i], NULL, 0);
40     }
41     printf("microseconds: %.0f usec\n", Stop_time());
42     if (shared->counter != nloop * nprocs)
43         printf("error: counter = %ld\n", shared->counter);

44     exit(0);
45 }
```

―――――――――――――――――――――――― bench/incr_pxmutex5.c

Figure A.48 main function to measure Posix mutex locking between processes.

Appendix B

A Threads Primer

B.1 Introduction

This appendix summarizes the basic Posix thread functions. In the traditional Unix model, when a process needs something performed by another entity, it forks a child process and lets the child perform the processing. Most network servers under Unix, for example, are written this way.

Although this paradigm has served well for many years, there are problems with fork:

- fork is expensive. Memory is copied from the parent to the child, all descriptors are duplicated in the child, and so on. Current implementations use a technique called *copy-on-write*, which avoids a copy of the parent's data space to the child until the child needs its own copy; but regardless of this optimization, fork is expensive.

- Interprocess communication (IPC) is required to pass information between the parent and child *after* the fork. Information from the parent to the child *before* the fork is easy, since the child starts with a copy of the parent's data space and with a copy of all the parent's descriptors. But returning information from the child to the parent takes more work.

Threads help with both problems. Threads are sometimes called *lightweight processes*, since a thread is "lighter weight" than a process. That is, thread creation can be 10–100 times faster than process creation.

All threads within a process share the same global memory. This makes the sharing of information easy between the threads, but along with this simplicity comes the problem of *synchronization*. But more than just the global variables are shared. All threads within a process share:

- process instructions,
- most data,
- open files (e.g., descriptors),
- signal handlers and signal dispositions,
- current working directory, and
- user and group IDs.

But each thread has its own:

- thread ID,
- set of registers, including program counter and stack pointer,
- stack (for local variables and return addresses),
- errno,
- signal mask, and
- priority.

B.2   Basic Thread Functions: Creation and Termination

In this section, we cover five basic thread functions.

pthread_create Function

When a program is started by exec, a single thread is created, called the *initial thread* or *main thread*. Additional threads are created by pthread_create.

```
#include <pthread.h>

int pthread_create(pthread_t *tid, const pthread_attr_t *attr,
                   void *(*func)(void *), void *arg);
```

Returns: 0 if OK, positive E*xxx* value on error

Each thread within a process is identified by a *thread ID*, whose datatype is pthread_t. On successful creation of a new thread, its ID is returned through the pointer *tid*.

Each thread has numerous *attributes*: its priority, its initial stack size, whether it should be a daemon thread or not, and so on. When a thread is created, we can specify these attributes by initializing a pthread_attr_t variable that overrides the default. We normally take the default, in which case, we specify the *attr* argument as a null pointer.

Finally, when we create a thread, we specify a function for it to execute, called its *thread start function*. The thread starts by calling this function and then terminates either explicitly (by calling pthread_exit) or implicitly (by letting this function return). The address of the function is specified as the *func* argument, and this function is called with a single pointer argument, *arg*. If we need multiple arguments to the function, we must package them into a structure and then pass the address of this structure as the single argument to the start function.

Notice the declarations of *func* and *arg*. The function takes one argument, a generic pointer (void *), and returns a generic pointer (void *). This lets us pass one pointer (to anything we want) to the thread, and lets the thread return one pointer (again, to anything we want).

The return value from the Pthread functions is normally 0 if OK or nonzero on an error. But unlike most system functions, which return −1 on an error and set errno to a positive value, the Pthread functions return the positive error indication as the function's return value. For example, if pthread_create cannot create a new thread because we have exceeded some system limit on the number of threads, the function return value is EAGAIN. The Pthread functions do not set errno. The convention of 0 for OK or nonzero for an error is fine, since all the E*xxx* values in <sys/errno.h> are positive. A value of 0 is never assigned to one of the E*xxx* names.

pthread_join Function

We can wait for a given thread to terminate by calling pthread_join. Comparing threads to Unix processes, pthread_create is similar to fork, and pthread_join is similar to waitpid.

```
#include <pthread.h>

int pthread_join(pthread_t tid, void **status);
```
                                  Returns: 0 if OK, positive E*xxx* value on error

We must specify the *tid* of the thread for which we wish to wait. Unfortunately, we have no way to wait for any of our threads (similar to waitpid with a process ID argument of −1).

If the *status* pointer is nonnull, the return value from the thread (a pointer to some object) is stored in the location pointed to by *status*.

pthread_self Function

Each thread has an ID that identifies it within a given process. The thread ID is returned by pthread_create, and we saw that it was used by pthread_join. A thread fetches this value for itself using pthread_self.

```
#include <pthread.h>

pthread_t pthread_self(void);
```
                                           Returns: thread ID of calling thread

Comparing threads to Unix processes, pthread_self is similar to getpid.

`pthread_detach` Function

A thread is either *joinable* (the default) or *detached*. When a joinable thread terminates, its thread ID and exit status are retained until another thread in the process calls `pthread_join`. But a detached thread is like a daemon process: when it terminates, all its resources are released, and we cannot wait for it to terminate. If one thread needs to know when another thread terminates, it is best to leave the thread as joinable.

The `pthread_detach` function changes the specified thread so that it is detached.

```
#include <pthread.h>

int pthread_detach(pthread_t tid);
```
Returns: 0 if OK, positive Exxx value on error

This function is commonly called by the thread that wants to detach itself, as in

```
pthread_detach(pthread_self());
```

`pthread_exit` Function

One way for a thread to terminate is to call `pthread_exit`.

```
#include <pthread.h>

void pthread_exit(void *status);
```
Does not return to caller

If the thread is not detached, its thread ID and exit status are retained for a later `pthread_join` by some other thread in the calling process.

The pointer *status* must not point to an object that is local to the calling thread (e.g., an automatic variable in the thread start function), since that object disappears when the thread terminates.

A thread can terminate in two other ways:

- The function that started the thread (the third argument to `pthread_create`) can `return`. Since this function must be declared as returning a `void` pointer, that return value is the exit status of the thread.

- If the `main` function of the process returns or if any thread calls `exit` or `_exit`, the process terminates immediately, including any threads that are still running.

Appendix C

Miscellaneous Source Code

C.1 `unpipc.h` Header

Almost every program in the text includes our `unpipc.h` header, shown in Figure C.1. This header includes all the standard system headers that most network programs need, along with some general system headers. It also defines constants such as MAXLINE and ANSI C function prototypes for the functions that we define in the text (e.g., px_ipc_name) and all the wrapper functions that we use. We do not show these prototypes.

lib/unpipc.h

```
 1 /* Our own header.  Tabs are set for 4 spaces, not 8 */

 2 #ifndef __unpipc_h
 3 #define __unpipc_h

 4 #include    "../config.h"       /* configuration options for current OS */
 5                                 /* "../config.h" is generated by configure */

 6 /* If anything changes in the following list of #includes, must change
 7    ../aclocal.m4 and ../configure.in also, for configure's tests. */

 8 #include    <sys/types.h>       /* basic system data types */
 9 #include    <sys/time.h>        /* timeval{} for select() */
10 #include    <time.h>            /* timespec{} for pselect() */
11 #include    <errno.h>
12 #include    <fcntl.h>           /* for nonblocking */
13 #include    <limits.h>          /* PIPE_BUF */
14 #include    <signal.h>
15 #include    <stdio.h>
16 #include    <stdlib.h>
17 #include    <string.h>
18 #include    <sys/stat.h>        /* for S_xxx file mode constants */
```

```
19 #include    <unistd.h>
20 #include    <sys/wait.h>

21 #ifdef  HAVE_MQUEUE_H
22 #include    <mqueue.h>          /* Posix message queues */
23 #endif

24 #ifdef  HAVE_SEMAPHORE_H
25 #include    <semaphore.h>       /* Posix semaphores */
26 #ifndef SEM_FAILED
27 #define SEM_FAILED  ((sem_t *)(-1))
28 #endif

29 #endif

30 #ifdef  HAVE_SYS_MMAN_H
31 #include    <sys/mman.h>        /* Posix shared memory */
32 #endif

33 #ifndef MAP_FAILED
34 #define MAP_FAILED  ((void *)(-1))
35 #endif

36 #ifdef  HAVE_SYS_IPC_H
37 #include    <sys/ipc.h>         /* System V IPC */
38 #endif

39 #ifdef  HAVE_SYS_MSG_H
40 #include    <sys/msg.h>         /* System V message queues */
41 #endif

42 #ifdef  HAVE_SYS_SEM_H
43 #ifdef  __bsdi__
44 #undef  HAVE_SYS_SEM_H          /* hack: BSDI's semctl() prototype is wrong */
45 #else
46 #include    <sys/sem.h>         /* System V semaphores */
47 #endif

48 #ifndef HAVE_SEMUN_UNION
49 union semun {                   /* define union for semctl() */
50     int     val;
51     struct semid_ds *buf;
52     unsigned short *array;
53 };
54 #endif
55 #endif  /* HAVE_SYS_SEM_H */

56 #ifdef  HAVE_SYS_SHM_H
57 #include    <sys/shm.h>         /* System V shared memory */
58 #endif

59 #ifdef  HAVE_SYS_SELECT_H
60 #include    <sys/select.h>      /* for convenience */
61 #endif

62 #ifdef  HAVE_POLL_H
63 #include    <poll.h>            /* for convenience */
64 #endif
```

```
65 #ifdef   HAVE_STROPTS_H
66 #include    <stropts.h>           /* for convenience */
67 #endif

68 #ifdef   HAVE_STRINGS_H
69 #include    <strings.h>           /* for convenience */
70 #endif

71 /* Next two headers are normally needed for socket/file ioctl's:
72  * <sys/ioctl.h> and <sys/filio.h>.
73  */
74 #ifdef   HAVE_SYS_IOCTL_H
75 #include    <sys/ioctl.h>
76 #endif
77 #ifdef   HAVE_SYS_FILIO_H
78 #include    <sys/filio.h>
79 #endif

80 #ifdef   HAVE_PTHREAD_H
81 #include    <pthread.h>
82 #endif

83 #ifdef   HAVE_DOOR_H
84 #include    <door.h>              /* Solaris doors API */
85 #endif

86 #ifdef   HAVE_RPC_RPC_H
87 #ifdef _PSX4_NSPACE_H_TS          /* Digital Unix 4.0b hack, hack, hack */
88 #undef   SUCCESS
89 #endif
90 #include    <rpc/rpc.h>           /* Sun RPC */
91 #endif

92 /* Define bzero() as a macro if it's not in standard C library. */
93 #ifndef HAVE_BZERO
94 #define bzero(ptr,n)         memset(ptr, 0, n)
95 #endif

96 /* Posix.1g requires that an #include of <poll.h> define INFTIM, but many
97    systems still define it in <sys/stropts.h>.  We don't want to include
98    all the streams stuff if it's not needed, so we just define INFTIM here.
99    This is the standard value, but there's no guarantee it is -1. */
100 #ifndef INFTIM
101 #define INFTIM           (-1)    /* infinite poll timeout */
102 #ifdef   HAVE_POLL_H
103 #define INFTIM_UNPH              /* tell unpxti.h we defined it */
104 #endif
105 #endif

106 /* Miscellaneous constants */
107 #ifndef PATH_MAX                 /* should be in <limits.h> */
108 #define PATH_MAX    1024         /* max # of characters in a pathname */
109 #endif

110 #define MAX_PATH    1024
111 #define MAXLINE     4096         /* max text line length */
112 #define BUFFSIZE    8192         /* buffer size for reads and writes */
```

```
113 #define FILE_MODE     (S_IRUSR | S_IWUSR | S_IRGRP | S_IROTH)
114                        /* default permissions for new files */
115 #define DIR_MODE      (FILE_MODE | S_IXUSR | S_IXGRP | S_IXOTH)
116                        /* default permissions for new directories */

117 #define SVMSG_MODE    (MSG_R | MSG_W | MSG_R>>3 | MSG_R>>6)
118                        /* default permissions for new SV message queues */
119 #define SVSEM_MODE    (SEM_R | SEM_A | SEM_R>>3 | SEM_R>>6)
120                        /* default permissions for new SV semaphores */
121 #define SVSHM_MODE    (SHM_R | SHM_W | SHM_R>>3 | SHM_R>>6)
122                        /* default permissions for new SV shared memory */

123 typedef void Sigfunc (int);     /* for signal handlers */

124 #ifdef  HAVE_SIGINFO_T_STRUCT
125 typedef void Sigfunc_rt (int, siginfo_t *, void *);
126 #endif

127 #define min(a,b)      ((a) < (b) ? (a) : (b))
128 #define max(a,b)      ((a) > (b) ? (a) : (b))

129 #ifndef HAVE_TIMESPEC_STRUCT
130 struct timespec {
131     time_t  tv_sec;                 /* seconds */
132     long    tv_nsec;                /* and nanoseconds */
133 };
134 #endif

135 /*
136  * In our wrappers for open(), mq_open(), and sem_open() we handle the
137  * optional arguments using the va_XXX() macros.  But one of the optional
138  * arguments is of type "mode_t" and this breaks under BSD/OS because it
139  * uses a 16-bit integer for this datatype.  But when our wrapper function
140  * is called, the compiler expands the 16-bit short integer to a 32-bit
141  * integer.  This breaks our call to va_arg().  All we can do is the
142  * following hack.  Other systems in addition to BSD/OS might have this
143  * problem too ...
144  */

145 #ifdef  __bsdi__
146 #define va_mode_t    int
147 #else
148 #define va_mode_t    mode_t
149 #endif

150        /* our record locking macros */
151 #define read_lock(fd, offset, whence, len) \
152             lock_reg(fd, F_SETLK, F_RDLCK, offset, whence, len)
153 #define readw_lock(fd, offset, whence, len) \
154             lock_reg(fd, F_SETLKW, F_RDLCK, offset, whence, len)
155 #define write_lock(fd, offset, whence, len) \
156             lock_reg(fd, F_SETLK, F_WRLCK, offset, whence, len)
157 #define writew_lock(fd, offset, whence, len) \
158             lock_reg(fd, F_SETLKW, F_WRLCK, offset, whence, len)
159 #define un_lock(fd, offset, whence, len) \
160             lock_reg(fd, F_SETLK, F_UNLCK, offset, whence, len)
161 #define is_read_lockable(fd, offset, whence, len) \
```

```
162                    lock_test(fd, F_RDLCK, offset, whence, len)
163 #define is_write_lockable(fd, offset, whence, len) \
164                    lock_test(fd, F_WRLCK, offset, whence, len)
```
                                                                    ——— *lib/unpipc.h*

Figure C.1 Our header unpipc.h.

C.2 config.h **Header**

The GNU autoconf tool was used to aid in the portability of all the source code in this text. It is available from ftp://prep.ai.mit.edu/pub/gnu/. This tool generates a shell script named configure that you must run after downloading the software onto your system. This script determines the features provided by your Unix system: are System V message queues supported? is the uint8_t datatype defined? is the gethostname function provided? and so on, generating a header named config.h. This header is the first header included by our unpipc.h header in the previous section. Figure C.2 shows the config.h header for Solaris 2.6 when used with the gcc compiler.

The lines beginning with #define in column 1 are for features that the system provides. The lines that are commented out and contain #undef are features that the system does not provide.

                                                          ——— *sparc-sun-solaris2.6/config.h*
```
 1 /* config.h.  Generated automatically by configure.   */
 2 /* Define the following if you have the corresponding header */
 3 #define CPU_VENDOR_OS "sparc-sun-solaris2.6"
 4 #define HAVE_DOOR_H 1                    /* <door.h> */
 5 #define HAVE_MQUEUE_H 1                  /* <mqueue.h> */
 6 #define HAVE_POLL_H 1                    /* <poll.h> */
 7 #define HAVE_PTHREAD_H 1                 /* <pthread.h> */
 8 #define HAVE_RPC_RPC_H 1                 /* <rpc/rpc.h> */
 9 #define HAVE_SEMAPHORE_H 1               /* <semaphore.h> */
10 #define HAVE_STRINGS_H 1                 /* <strings.h> */
11 #define HAVE_SYS_FILIO_H 1               /* <sys/filio.h> */
12 #define HAVE_SYS_IOCTL_H 1               /* <sys/ioctl.h> */
13 #define HAVE_SYS_IPC_H 1                 /* <sys/ipc.h> */
14 #define HAVE_SYS_MMAN_H 1                /* <sys/mman.h> */
15 #define HAVE_SYS_MSG_H 1                 /* <sys/msg.h> */
16 #define HAVE_SYS_SEM_H 1                 /* <sys/sem.h> */
17 #define HAVE_SYS_SHM_H 1                 /* <sys/shm.h> */
18 #define HAVE_SYS_SELECT_H 1              /* <sys/select.h> */
19 /* #undef   HAVE_SYS_SYSCTL_H */         /* <sys/sysctl.h> */
20 #define HAVE_SYS_TIME_H 1                /* <sys/time.h> */

21 /* Define if we can include <time.h> with <sys/time.h> */
22 #define TIME_WITH_SYS_TIME 1

23 /* Define the following if the function is provided */
24 #define HAVE_BZERO 1
25 #define HAVE_FATTACH 1
26 #define HAVE_POLL 1
```

```
27 /* #undef   HAVE_PSELECT */
28 #define HAVE_SIGWAIT 1
29 #define HAVE_VALLOC 1
30 #define HAVE_VSNPRINTF 1

31 /* Define the following if the function prototype is in a header */
32 #define HAVE_GETHOSTNAME_PROTO 1     /* <unistd.h> */
33 #define HAVE_GETRUSAGE_PROTO 1       /* <sys/resource.h> */
34 /* #undef   HAVE_PSELECT_PROTO */    /* <sys/select.h> */
35 #define HAVE_SHM_OPEN_PROTO 1        /* <sys/mman.h> */
36 #define HAVE_SNPRINTF_PROTO 1        /* <stdio.h> */
37 #define HAVE_THR_SETCONCURRENCY_PROTO 1      /* <thread.h> */

38 /* Define the following if the structure is defined. */
39 #define HAVE_SIGINFO_T_STRUCT 1      /* <signal.h> */
40 #define HAVE_TIMESPEC_STRUCT 1       /* <time.h> */
41 /* #undef   HAVE_SEMUN_UNION */      /* <sys/sem.h> */

42 /* Devices */
43 #define HAVE_DEV_ZERO 1

44 /* Define the following to the appropriate datatype, if necessary */
45 /* #undef   int8_t */                /* <sys/types.h> */
46 /* #undef   int16_t */               /* <sys/types.h> */
47 /* #undef   int32_t */               /* <sys/types.h> */
48 /* #undef   uint8_t */               /* <sys/types.h> */
49 /* #undef   uint16_t */              /* <sys/types.h> */
50 /* #undef   uint32_t */              /* <sys/types.h> */
51 /* #undef   size_t */                /* <sys/types.h> */
52 /* #undef   ssize_t */               /* <sys/types.h> */

53 #define POSIX_IPC_PREFIX "/"
54 #define RPCGEN_ANSIC 1               /* defined if rpcgen groks -C option */
```
————————————————————————————————— *sparc-sun-solaris2.6/config.h*

Figure C.2 Our `config.h` header for Solaris 2.6.

C.3   Standard Error Functions

We define our own set of error functions that are used throughout the text to handle error conditions. The reason for our own error functions is to let us write our error handling with a single line of C code, as in

```
if (error condition)
        err_sys (printf format with any number of arguments);
```

instead of

```
if (error condition) {
    char buff[200];
    snprintf(buff, sizeof(buff), printf format with any number of arguments);
    perror(buff);
    exit(1);
}
```

Our error functions use the variable-length argument list facility from ANSI C. See Section 7.3 of [Kernighan and Ritchie 1988] for additional details.

Figure C.3 lists the differences between the various error functions. If the global integer daemon_proc is nonzero, the message is passed to syslog with the indicated level (see Chapter 12 of UNPv1 for details on syslog); otherwise, the error is output to standard error.

Function	strerror (errno) ?	Terminate ?	syslog level
err_dump	yes	abort();	LOG_ERR
err_msg	no	return;	LOG_INFO
err_quit	no	exit(1);	LOG_ERR
err_ret	yes	return;	LOG_INFO
err_sys	yes	exit(1);	LOG_ERR

Figure C.3 Summary of our standard error functions.

Figure C.4 shows the five functions from Figure C.3.

—————————————————————————— lib/error.c

```
 1 #include    "unpipc.h"

 2 #include    <stdarg.h>        /* ANSI C header file */
 3 #include    <syslog.h>        /* for syslog() */

 4 int     daemon_proc;          /* set nonzero by daemon_init() */

 5 static void err_doit(int, int, const char *, va_list);

 6 /* Nonfatal error related to a system call.
 7  * Print a message and return. */

 8 void
 9 err_ret(const char *fmt,...)
10 {
11     va_list ap;

12     va_start(ap, fmt);
13     err_doit(1, LOG_INFO, fmt, ap);
14     va_end(ap);
15     return;
16 }

17 /* Fatal error related to a system call.
18  * Print a message and terminate. */

19 void
20 err_sys(const char *fmt,...)
21 {
22     va_list ap;

23     va_start(ap, fmt);
24     err_doit(1, LOG_ERR, fmt, ap);
25     va_end(ap);
26     exit(1);
27 }
```

```
28 /* Fatal error related to a system call.
29  * Print a message, dump core, and terminate. */

30 void
31 err_dump(const char *fmt, ...)
32 {
33     va_list ap;

34     va_start(ap, fmt);
35     err_doit(1, LOG_ERR, fmt, ap);
36     va_end(ap);
37     abort();                     /* dump core and terminate */
38     exit(1);                     /* shouldn't get here */
39 }

40 /* Nonfatal error unrelated to a system call.
41  * Print a message and return. */

42 void
43 err_msg(const char *fmt, ...)
44 {
45     va_list ap;

46     va_start(ap, fmt);
47     err_doit(0, LOG_INFO, fmt, ap);
48     va_end(ap);
49     return;
50 }

51 /* Fatal error unrelated to a system call.
52  * Print a message and terminate. */

53 void
54 err_quit(const char *fmt, ...)
55 {
56     va_list ap;

57     va_start(ap, fmt);
58     err_doit(0, LOG_ERR, fmt, ap);
59     va_end(ap);
60     exit(1);
61 }

62 /* Print a message and return to caller.
63  * Caller specifies "errnoflag" and "level". */

64 static void
65 err_doit(int errnoflag, int level, const char *fmt, va_list ap)
66 {
67     int     errno_save, n;
68     char    buf[MAXLINE + 1];

69     errno_save = errno;          /* value caller might want printed */
70 #ifdef  HAVE_VSNPRINTF
71     vsnprintf(buf, MAXLINE, fmt, ap);   /* this is safe */
72 #else
73     vsprintf(buf, fmt, ap);      /* this is not safe */
74 #endif
75     n = strlen(buf);
```

```
76      if (errnoflag)
77          snprintf(buf + n, MAXLINE - n, ": %s", strerror(errno_save));
78      strcat(buf, "\n");

79      if (daemon_proc) {
80          syslog(level, buf);
81      } else {
82          fflush(stdout);              /* in case stdout and stderr are the same */
83          fputs(buf, stderr);
84          fflush(stderr);
85      }
86      return;
87  }
```
—— *lib/error.c*

Figure C.4 Our standard error functions.

Appendix D

Solutions to Selected Exercises

Chapter 1

1.1 Both processes only need to specify the O_APPEND flag to the open function, or the append mode to the fopen function. The kernel then ensures that each write is appended to the file. This is the easiest form of file synchronization to specify. (Pages 60–61 of APUE talk about this in more detail.) The synchronization issues become more complex when existing data in the file is updated, as in a database system.

1.2 Something like the following is typical:

```
#ifdef  _REENTRANT
#define errno   (*_errno())
#else
extern int  errno;
#endif
```

If _REENTRANT is defined, references to errno call a function named _errno that returns the address of the calling thread's errno variable. This variable is possibly stored as thread-specific data (Section 23.5 of UNPv1). If _REENTRANT is not defined, then errno is a global int.

Chapter 2

2.1 These two bits can change the effective user ID and/or the effective group ID of the program that is running. These two effective IDs are used in Section 2.4.

2.2   First specify both O_CREAT and O_EXCL, and if this returns success, a new object has been created. But if this fails with an error of EEXIST, then the object already exists and the program must call the open function again, without specifying either O_CREAT or O_EXCL. This second call should succeed, but a chance exists (albeit small) that it fails with an error of ENOENT, which indicates that some other thread or process has removed the object between the two calls.

Chapter 3

3.1   Our program is shown in Figure D.1.

svmsg/slotseq.c

```
1 #include    "unpipc.h"

2 int
3 main(int argc, char **argv)
4 {
5      int     i, msqid;
6      struct msqid_ds info;

7      for (i = 0; i < 10; i++) {
8          msqid = Msgget(IPC_PRIVATE, SVMSG_MODE | IPC_CREAT);
9          Msgctl(msqid, IPC_STAT, &info);
10         printf("msqid = %d, seq = %lu\n", msqid, info.msg_perm.seq);

11         Msgctl(msqid, IPC_RMID, NULL);
12     }
13     exit(0);
14 }
```

svmsg/slotseq.c

Figure D.1   Print identifier and slot usage sequence number.

3.2   The first call to msgget uses the first available message queue, whose slot usage sequence number is 20 after running the program in Figure 3.7 two times, returning an identifier of 1000. Assuming the next available message queue has never been used, its slot usage sequence number will be 0, returning an identifier of 1.

3.3   Our simple program is shown in Figure D.2.

svmsg/testumask.c

```
1 #include    "unpipc.h"

2 int
3 main(int argc, char **argv)
4 {
5      Msgget(IPC_PRIVATE, 0666 | IPC_CREAT | IPC_EXCL);
6      unlink("/tmp/fifo.1");
7      Mkfifo("/tmp/fifo.1", 0666);

8      exit(0);
9 }
```

svmsg/testumask.c

Figure D.2   Test whether the file mode creation mask is used by msgget.

When we run this program we see that our file mode creation mask is 2 (turn off the other-write bit) and this bit is turned off in the FIFO, but this bit is not turned off in the message queue.

```
solaris % umask
02
solaris % testumask
solaris % ls -l /tmp/fifo.1
prw-rw-r--  1 rstevens other1      0 Mar 25 16:05 /tmp/fifo.1
solaris % ipcs -q
IPC status from <running system> as of Wed Mar 25 16:06:03 1998
T        ID     KEY        MODE       OWNER     GROUP
Message Queues:
q        200    00000000 --rw-rw-rw- rstevens   other1
```

3.4 With `ftok`, the possibility always exists that some other pathname on the system can lead to the same key as the one being used by our server. With `IPC_PRIVATE`, the server knows that it is creating a new message queue, but the server must then write the resulting identifier into some file for the clients to read.

3.5 Here is one way to detect the collisions:

```
solaris % find / -links 1 -not -type 1 -print |
xargs -n1 ftok1 > temp.1
solaris % wc -l temp.1
  109351 temp.1

solaris % sort +0 -1 temp.1 |
nawk '{ if (lastkey == $1)
          print lastline, $0
       lastline = $0
       lastkey = $1
}' > temp.2
solaris % wc -l temp.2
   82188 temp.2
```

In the `find` program, we ignore files with more than one link (since each link will have the same i-node), and we ignore symbolic links (since the `stat` function follows the link). The extremely high percentage of collisions (75.2%) is due to Solaris 2.x using only 12 bits of the i-node number. This means lots of collisions can occur on any filesystem with more than 4096 files. For example, the four files with i-node numbers 4096, 8192, 12288, and 16384 all have the same IPC key (assuming they are on the same filesystem).

This example was run on the same filesystems but using the `ftok` function from BSD/OS, which adds the entire i-node number into the key, and the number of collisions was only 849 (less than 1%).

Chapter 4

4.1 If `fd[1]` were left open in the child when the parent terminated, the child's `read` of `fd[1]` would not return an end-of-file, because this descriptor is still open in the child. By closing `fd[1]` in the child, this guarantees that as soon as the parent terminates, all its descriptors are closed, causing the child's `read` of `fd[1]` to return 0.

4.2   If the order of the calls is swapped, some other process can create the FIFO between the calls to `open` and `mkfifo`, causing the latter to fail.

4.3   If we execute

```
solaris % mainpopen 2>temp.stderr
/etc/ntp.conf > /myfile
solaris % cat temp.stderr
sh: /myfile: cannot create
```

we see that `popen` returns success, but we read just an end-of-file with `fgets`. The shell error message is written to standard error.

4.5   Change the first call to `open` to specify the nonblocking flag:

```
readfifo = Open(SERV_FIFO, O_RDONLY | O_NONBLOCK, 0);
```

This call then returns immediately, and the next call to `open` (for write-only) also returns immediately, since the FIFO is already open for reading. But to avoid an error from `readline`, the O_NONBLOCK flag must be turned off for the descriptor `readfifo` before calling `readline`.

4.6   If the client were to `open` its client-specific FIFO (read-only) before opening the server's well-known FIFO (write-only), a deadlock would occur. The only way to avoid the deadlock is to `open` the two FIFOs in the order shown in Figure 4.24 or to use the nonblocking flag.

4.7   The disappearance of the writer is signaled by an end-of-file for the reader.

4.8   Figure D.3 shows our program.

pipe/test1.c

```
 1 #include    "unpipc.h"

 2 int
 3 main(int argc, char **argv)
 4 {
 5     int     fd[2];
 6     char    buff[7];
 7     struct stat info;

 8     if (argc != 2)
 9         err_quit("usage: test1 <pathname>");

10     Mkfifo(argv[1], FILE_MODE);
11     fd[0] = Open(argv[1], O_RDONLY | O_NONBLOCK);
12     fd[1] = Open(argv[1], O_WRONLY | O_NONBLOCK);

13         /* check sizes when FIFO is empty */
14     Fstat(fd[0], &info);
15     printf("fd[0]: st_size = %ld\n", (long) info.st_size);
16     Fstat(fd[1], &info);
17     printf("fd[1]: st_size = %ld\n", (long) info.st_size);
```

```
18        Write(fd[1], buff, sizeof(buff));
19            /* check sizes when FIFO contains 7 bytes */
20        Fstat(fd[0], &info);
21        printf("fd[0]: st_size = %ld\n", (long) info.st_size);
22        Fstat(fd[1], &info);
23        printf("fd[1]: st_size = %ld\n", (long) info.st_size);

24        exit(0);
25 }
```
—— *pipe/test1.c*

Figure D.3 Determine whether `fstat` returns the number of bytes in a FIFO.

4.9 `select` returns that the descriptor is writable, but the call to `write` then elicits
`SIGPIPE`. This concept is described on pages 153–155 of UNPv1; when a read (or
write) error occurs, `select` returns that the descriptor is readable (or writable),
and the actual error is returned by read (or `write`). Figure D.4 shows our program.

—— *pipe/test2.c*
```
 1 #include     "unpipc.h"

 2 int
 3 main(int argc, char **argv)
 4 {
 5     int     fd[2], n;
 6     pid_t   childpid;
 7     fd_set  wset;

 8     Pipe(fd);
 9     if ( (childpid = Fork()) == 0) {       /* child */
10         printf("child closing pipe read descriptor\n");
11         Close(fd[0]);
12         sleep(6);
13         exit(0);
14     }
15         /* parent */
16     Close(fd[0]);                     /* in case of a full-duplex pipe */
17     sleep(3);
18     FD_ZERO(&wset);
19     FD_SET(fd[1], &wset);
20     n = select(fd[1] + 1, NULL, &wset, NULL, NULL);
21     printf("select returned %d\n", n);

22     if (FD_ISSET(fd[1], &wset)) {
23         printf("fd[1] writable\n");
24         Write(fd[1], "hello", 5);
25     }
26     exit(0);
27 }
```
—— *pipe/test2.c*

Figure D.4 Determine what `select` returns for writability when the read end of a pipe is closed.

Chapter 5

5.1   First create the queue without specifying any attributes, followed by a call to mq_getattr to obtain the default attributes. Then remove the queue and create it again, using the default value of either attribute that is not specified.

5.2   The signal is not generated for the second message, because the registration is removed every time the notification occurs.

5.3   The signal is not generated for the second message, because the queue was not empty when the message was received.

5.4   The GNU C compiler under Solaris 2.6 (which defines both constants as calls to sysconf) generates the errors

```
test1.c:13: warning: int format, long int arg (arg 2)
test1.c:13: warning: int format, long int arg (arg 3)
```

5.5   Under Solaris 2.6, we specify 1,000,000 messages of 10 bytes each. This leads to a file size of 20,000,536 bytes, which corresponds with our results from running Figure 5.5: 10 bytes of data per message, 8 bytes of overhead per message (perhaps for pointers), another 2 bytes of overhead per message (perhaps for 4-byte alignment), and 536 bytes of overhead per file. Before mq_open is called, the size of the program reported by ps is 1052 Kbytes, but after the message queue is created, the size is 20 Mbytes. This makes us think that Posix message queues are implemented using memory-mapped files, and that mq_open maps the file into the address space of the calling process. We obtain similar results under Digital Unix 4.0B.

5.6   A size argument of 0 is OK for the ANSI C memXXX functions. The original 1989 ANSI C standard X3.159–1989, also known as ISO/IEC 9899:1990, did not say this (and none of the manual pages that the author could find mentioned this), but *Technical Corrigendum Number 1* explicitly states that a size of 0 is OK (but the pointer arguments must still be valid). http://www.lysator.liu.se/c/ is a wonderful reference point for information on the C language.

5.7   For two-way communication between two processes, two message queues are needed (see for example, Figure A.30). Indeed, if we were to modify Figure 4.14 to use Posix message queues instead of pipes, we would see the parent read back what it wrote to the queue.

5.8   The mutex and condition variable are contained in the memory-mapped file, which is shared by all processes that have the queue open. Other processes may have the queue open, so a process that is closing its handle to the queue cannot destroy the mutex and condition variable.

5.9   An array cannot be assigned across an equals sign in C, whereas a structure can.

5.10   The main function spends almost all of its time blocked in a call to select, waiting for the pipe to be readable. Every time the signal is delivered, the return from the signal handler interrupts this call to select, causing it to return an error of

EINTR. To handle this, our `Select` wrapper function checks for this error, and calls `select` again, as shown in Figure D.5.

—— *lib/wrapunix.c*
```
313  int
314  Select(int nfds, fd_set *readfds, fd_set *writefds, fd_set *exceptfds,
315         struct timeval *timeout)
316  {
317      int     n;

318  again:
319      if ( (n = select(nfds, readfds, writefds, exceptfds, timeout)) < 0) {
320          if (errno == EINTR)
321              goto again;
322          else
323              err_sys("select error");
324      } else if (n == 0 && timeout == NULL)
325          err_quit("select returned 0 with no timeout");
326      return (n);                      /* can return 0 on timeout */
327  }
```
—— *lib/wrapunix.c*

Figure D.5 Our `Select` wrapper function that handles EINTR.

Page 124 of UNPv1 talks more about interrupted system calls.

Chapter 6

6.1   The remaining programs must then accept a numeric message queue identifier instead of a pathname (recall the output of Figure 6.3). This change could be made with a new command-line option in these other programs, or the assumption could be made that a pathname argument that is entirely numeric is an identifier and not a pathname. Since most pathnames that are passed to `ftok` are absolute pathnames, and not relative (i.e., they contain at least one slash character), this assumption is probably OK.

6.2   Messages with a type of 0 are not allowed, and a client can never have a process ID of 1, since this is normally the `init` process.

6.3   When only one queue is used in Figure 6.14, this malicious client affects all other clients. When we have one return queue per client (Figure 6.19), this client affects only its own queue.

Chapter 7

7.2   The process will terminate, probably before the consumer thread has finished, because calling `exit` terminates any threads still running.

7.3   Under Solaris 2.6, omitting the call to the `destroy` functions causes a memory leak, implying that the `init` functions are performing dynamic memory allocation. We do not see this under Digital Unix 4.0B, which just implies an implementation difference. The calls to the matching `destroy` functions are still required.

From an implementation perspective, Digital Unix appears to use the `attr_t` variable as the attributes object itself, whereas Solaris uses this variable as a pointer to a dynamically allocated object. Either implementation is fine.

Chapter 9

9.1   Depending on your system, you may need to increase the loop counter from 20, to see the errors.

9.2   To make the standard I/O stream unbuffered, we add the line

```
setvbuf(stdout, NULL, _IONBF, 0);
```

to the `main` function, before the `for` loop. This should have no effect, because there is only one call to `printf` and the string is terminated with a newline. Normally, standard output is line buffered, so in either case (line buffered or unbuffered), the single call to `printf` ends up in a single `write` call to the kernel.

9.3   We change the call to `printf` to be

```
snprintf(line, sizeof(line), "%s: pid = %ld, seq# = %d\n",
         argv[0], (long) pid, seqno);
for (ptr = line; (c = *ptr++) != 0; )
    putchar(c);
```

and declare `c` as an integer and `ptr` as a `char*`. If we leave in the call to `setvbuf`, making standard output unbuffered, this causes the standard I/O library to call `write` once per character that is output, instead of once per line. This involves more CPU time, and provides more opportunities for the kernel to switch between the two processes. We should see more errors with this program.

9.4   Since multiple processes are allowed to have read locks for the same region of a file, this is the same as having no locks at all for our example.

9.5   Nothing changes, because the nonblocking flag for a descriptor has no effect on `fcntl` advisory locking. What determines whether a call to `fcntl` blocks or not is whether the command is `F_SETLKW` (which always blocks) or `F_SETLK` (which never blocks).

9.6   The `loopfcntlnonb` program operates as expected, because, as we showed in the previous exercise, the nonblocking flag has no effect on a program that performs `fcntl` locking. But the nonblocking flag does affect the `loopnonenonb` program, which performs no locking. As we said in Section 9.5, a nonblocking call to `read` or `write` for a file for which mandatory locking is enabled, returns an error of `EAGAIN` if the `read` or `write` conflicts with an existing lock. We see this error as either

```
read error: Resource temporarily unavailable
```

or

```
write error: Resource temporarily unavailable
```

and we can verify that the error is `EAGAIN` by executing

```
solaris % grep Resource /usr/include/sys/errno.h
#define EAGAIN  11      /* Resource temporarily unavailable */
```

9.7   Under Solaris 2.6, mandatory locking increases the clock time by about 16% and it increases the system CPU time by about 20%. The user CPU time remains the same, as we expect, because the extra time is within the kernel checking every read and write, not within our process.

9.8   Locks are granted on a per-process basis, not on a per-thread basis. To see contention for lock requests, we must have different processes trying to obtain the locks.

9.9   If another copy of the daemon were running and we open with the O_TRUNC flag, this would wipe out the process ID stored by the first copy of the daemon. We cannot truncate the file until we know we are the only copy running.

9.10 SEEK_SET is always preferable. The problem with SEEK_CUR is that it depends on the current offset in the file, which is specified by lseek. But if we call lseek and then fcntl, we are using two function calls to perform what is a single operation, and a chance exists that another thread can change the current offset by calling lseek between our two function calls. (Recall that all threads share the same descriptors. Also recall that fcntl record locks are for locking between different processes and not for locking between the different threads within one process.) Similarly, if we specify SEEK_END, a chance exists that another thread can append data to the file before we obtain a lock based on what we think is the end of the file.

Chapter 10

10.1   Here is the output under Solaris 2.6:

```
solaris % deadlock 100
prod: calling sem_wait(nempty)                i=0 loop for producer
prod: got sem_wait(nempty)
prod: calling sem_wait(mutex)
prod: got sem_wait(mutex), storing 0

prod: calling sem_wait(nempty)                i=1 loop for producer
prod: got sem_wait(nempty)
prod: calling sem_wait(mutex)
prod: got sem_wait(mutex), storing 1

prod: calling sem_wait(nempty)                start next loop, but no empty slots
                                              context switch from producer to consumer
cons: calling sem_wait(mutex)                 i=0 loop for consumer
cons: got sem_wait(mutex)
cons: calling sem_wait(nstored)
cons: got sem_wait(nstored)
cons: fetched 0

cons: calling sem_wait(mutex)                 i=0 loop for consumer
cons: got sem_wait(mutex)
cons: calling sem_wait(nstored)
```

```
cons: got sem_wait(nstored)
cons: fetched 1

cons: calling sem_wait(mutex)
cons: got sem_wait(mutex)
cons: calling sem_wait(nstored)        consumer blocks here forever
                                       context switch from consumer to producer

prod: got sem_wait(nempty)
prod: calling sem_wait(mutex)          producer blocks here forever
```

10.2   This is OK given the rules for semaphore initialization that we specified when we described sem_open: if the semaphore already exists, it is not initialized. So only the first of the four programs that calls sem_open actually initializes the semaphore value to 1. When the remaining three call sem_open with the O_CREAT flag, the semaphore will already exist, so its value is not initialized again.

10.3   This is a problem. The semaphore is automatically closed when the process terminates, but the value of the semaphore is not changed. This will prevent any of the other three programs from obtaining the lock, causing another type of deadlock.

10.4   If we did not initialize the descriptors to –1, their initial value is unknown, since malloc does not initialize the memory that it allocates. So if one of the calls to open fails, the calls to close at the label error could close some descriptor that the process is using. By initializing the descriptors to –1, we know that the calls to close will have no effect (other than returning an error that we ignore) if that descriptor has not been opened yet.

10.5   A chance exists, albeit slight, that close could be called for a valid descriptor and could return some error, thereby changing errno from the value that we want to return. Since we want to save the value of errno to return to the caller, to do so explicitly is better than counting on some side effect (that close will not return an error when a valid descriptor is closed).

10.6   No race condition exists in this function, because the mkfifo function returns an error if the FIFO already exists. If two processes call this function at about the same time, the FIFO is created only once. The second process to call mkfifo will receive an error of EEXIST, causing the O_CREAT flag to be turned off, preventing another initialization of the FIFO.

10.7   Figure 10.37 does not have the race condition that we described with Figure 10.43 because the initialization of the semaphore is performed by writing data to the FIFO. If the process that creates the FIFO is suspended by the kernel after it calls mkfifo but before it writes the data bytes to the FIFO, the second process will just open the FIFO and block the first time it calls sem_wait, because the newly created FIFO will be empty until the first process (which created the FIFO) writes the data bytes to the FIFO.

10.8   Figure D.6 shows the test program. Both the Solaris 2.6 and Digital Unix 4.0B implementations detect being interrupted by a caught signal and return EINTR.

——————————————————————————————— pxsem/testeintr.c

```
 1 #include     "unpipc.h"

 2 #define NAME     "testeintr"

 3 static void sig_alrm(int);

 4 int
 5 main(int argc, char **argv)
 6 {
 7     sem_t  *sem1, sem2;

 8         /* first test a named semaphore */
 9     sem_unlink(Px_ipc_name(NAME));
10     sem1 = Sem_open(Px_ipc_name(NAME), O_RDWR | O_CREAT | O_EXCL,
11                     FILE_MODE, 0);
12     Signal(SIGALRM, sig_alrm);
13     alarm(2);
14     if (sem_wait(sem1) == 0)
15         printf("sem_wait returned 0?\n");
16     else
17         err_ret("sem_wait error");
18     Sem_close(sem1);

19         /* now a memory-based semaphore with process scope */
20     Sem_init(&sem2, 1, 0);
21     alarm(2);
22     if (sem_wait(&sem2) == 0)
23         printf("sem_wait returned 0?\n");
24     else
25         err_ret("sem_wait error");
26     Sem_destroy(&sem2);

27     exit(0);
28 }

29 static void
30 sig_alrm(int signo)
31 {
32     printf("SIGALRM caught\n");
33     return;
34 }
```

——————————————————————————————— pxsem/testeintr.c

Figure D.6 Test whether `sem_wait` detects `EINTR`.

Our implementation using FIFOs returns `EINTR`, because `sem_wait` blocks in a call to `read` on a FIFO, which must return the error. Our implementation using memory-mapped I/O does not return any error, because `sem_wait` blocks in a call to `pthread_cond_wait` and this function does not return `EINTR` when interrupted by a caught signal. (We saw another example of this with Figure 5.29.) Our implementation using System V semaphores returns `EINTR`, because `sem_wait` blocks in a call to `semop`, which returns the error.

10.9 The implementation using FIFOs (Figure 10.40) is async-signal-safe because `write` is async-signal-safe. The implementation using a memory-mapped file

(Figure 10.47) is not, because none of the `pthread_XXX` functions are async-signal-safe. The implementation using System V semaphores (Figure 10.56) is not, because `semop` is not listed as async-signal-safe by Unix 98.

Chapter 11

11.1   Only one line needs to change:

```
<           semid = Semget(Ftok(argv[optind], 0), 0, 0);
---
>           semid = atol(argv[optind]);
```

11.2   The call to `ftok` will fail, causing our `Ftok` wrapper to terminate. The `my_lock` function could call `ftok` before calling `semget`, check for an error of `ENOENT`, and create the file if it does not exist.

Chapter 12

12.1   The file size would be increased by another 4096 bytes (to 36864), but our reference to the new end-of-file (index 36863) might generate a `SIGSEGV` signal, since the size of the memory-mapped region is 32768. The reason we say "might" and not "will" is that it depends on the page size.

12.2   Figure D.7 shows the scenario assuming a System V message queue, and Figure D.8 shows the Posix message queue scenario. The calls to `memcpy` in the sender occur when `mq_send` is called (Figure 5.30), and the calls to `memcpy` in the receiver occur when `mq_receive` is called (Figure 5.32).

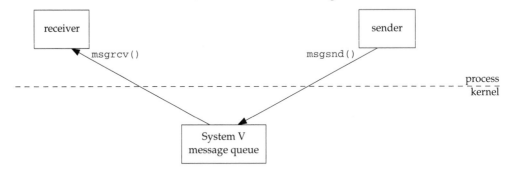

Figure D.7 Sending messages using a System V message queue.

12.3   Any `read` from `/dev/zero` returns the requested number of bytes, all containing 0. Any data written to this device is simply discarded, just like `writes` to `/dev/null`.

12.4   The final contents of the file are 4 bytes of 0 (assuming a 32-bit `int`).

12.5   Figure D.9 shows our program.

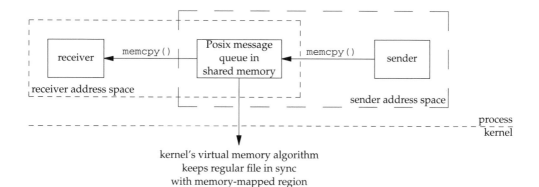

Figure D.8 Sending messages using a Posix message queue implemented using mmap.

```
                                                                  shm/svmsgread.c
 1 #include      "unpipc.h"

 2 #define MAXMSG  (8192 + sizeof(long))

 3 int
 4 main(int argc, char **argv)
 5 {
 6     int     pipe1[2], pipe2[2], mqid;
 7     char    c;
 8     pid_t   childpid;
 9     fd_set  rset;
10     ssize_t n, nread;
11     struct msgbuf *buff;

12     if (argc != 2)
13         err_quit("usage: svmsgread <pathname>");

14     Pipe(pipe1);                    /* 2-way communication with child */
15     Pipe(pipe2);

16     buff = My_shm(MAXMSG);        /* anonymous shared memory with child */

17     if ( (childpid = Fork()) == 0) {
18         Close(pipe1[1]);            /* child */
19         Close(pipe2[0]);

20         mqid = Msgget(Ftok(argv[1], 1), MSG_R);
21         for ( ; ; ) {
22                 /* block, waiting for message, then tell parent */
23             nread = Msgrcv(mqid, buff, MAXMSG, 0, 0);
24             Write(pipe2[1], &nread, sizeof(ssize_t));

25                 /* wait for parent to say shm is available */
26             if ( (n = Read(pipe1[0], &c, 1)) != 1)
27                 err_quit("child: read on pipe returned %d", n);
28         }
29         exit(0);
30     }
```

```
31              /* parent */
32      Close(pipe1[0]);
33      Close(pipe2[1]);

34      FD_ZERO(&rset);
35      FD_SET(pipe2[0], &rset);
36      for ( ; ; ) {
37          if ( (n = select(pipe2[0] + 1, &rset, NULL, NULL, NULL)) != 1)
38              err_sys("select returned %d", n);
39          if (FD_ISSET(pipe2[0], &rset)) {
40              n = Read(pipe2[0], &nread, sizeof(ssize_t));
41              if (n != sizeof(ssize_t))
42                  err_quit("parent: read on pipe returned %d", n);

43              printf("read %d bytes, type = %ld\n", nread, buff->mtype);
44              Write(pipe1[1], &c, 1);

45          } else
46              err_quit("pipe2[0] not ready");
47      }

48      Kill(childpid, SIGTERM);
49      exit(0);
50 }
```
—— *shm/svmsgread.c*

Figure D.9 Example of parent and child setup to use `select` with System V messages.

Chapter 13

13.1   Figure D.10 shows our modified version of Figure 12.16, and Figure D.11 shows our modified version of Figure 12.19. Notice in the first program that we must set the size of the shared memory object using `ftruncate`; we cannot use `lseek` and `write`.

—— *pxshm/test1.c*
```
 1 #include    "unpipc.h"

 2 int
 3 main(int argc, char **argv)
 4 {
 5     int     fd, i;
 6     char    *ptr;
 7     size_t  shmsize, mmapsize, pagesize;

 8     if (argc != 4)
 9         err_quit("usage: test1 <name> <shmsize> <mmapsize>");
10     shmsize = atoi(argv[2]);
11     mmapsize = atoi(argv[3]);

12     /* open shm: create or truncate; set shm size */
13     fd = Shm_open(Px_ipc_name(argv[1]), O_RDWR | O_CREAT | O_TRUNC,
14                 FILE_MODE);
15     Ftruncate(fd, shmsize);
```

```
16        ptr = Mmap(NULL, mmapsize, PROT_READ | PROT_WRITE, MAP_SHARED, fd, 0);
17        Close(fd);

18        pagesize = Sysconf(_SC_PAGESIZE);
19        printf("PAGESIZE = %ld\n", (long) pagesize);

20        for (i = 0; i < max(shmsize, mmapsize); i += pagesize) {
21            printf("ptr[%d] = %d\n", i, ptr[i]);
22            ptr[i] = 1;
23            printf("ptr[%d] = %d\n", i + pagesize - 1, ptr[i + pagesize - 1]);
24            ptr[i + pagesize - 1] = 1;
25        }
26        printf("ptr[%d] = %d\n", i, ptr[i]);

27        exit(0);
28 }
```
pxshm/test1.c

Figure D.10 Memory mapping when mmap equals shared memory size.

pxshm/test1.c
```
 1 #include    "unpipc.h"

 2 #define FILE      "test.data"
 3 #define SIZE      32768

 4 int
 5 main(int argc, char **argv)
 6 {
 7     int     fd, i;
 8     char    *ptr;

 9         /* open shm: create or truncate; then mmap shm */
10     fd = Shm_open(Px_ipc_name(FILE), O_RDWR | O_CREAT | O_TRUNC, FILE_MODE);
11     ptr = Mmap(NULL, SIZE, PROT_READ | PROT_WRITE, MAP_SHARED, fd, 0);

12     for (i = 4096; i <= SIZE; i += 4096) {
13         printf("setting shm size to %d\n", i);
14         Ftruncate(fd, i);
15         printf("ptr[%d] = %d\n", i - 1, ptr[i - 1]);
16     }

17     exit(0);
18 }
```
pxshm/test1.c

Figure D.11 Memory-map example that lets the shared memory size grow.

13.2   One possible problem with *ptr++ is that the pointer returned by mmap is modified, preventing a later call to munmap. If the pointer is needed at a later time, it
must be either saved, or not modified.

Chapter 14

14.1   Only one line needs to change:

```
13c13
<       id = Shmget(Ftok(argv[1], 0), 0, SVSHM_MODE);
---
>       id = atol(argv[1]);
```

Chapter 15

15.1   There are `data_size + (desc_num × sizeof(door_desc_t))` bytes of arguments.

15.2   No, we do not need to call `fstat`. If the descriptor does not refer to a door, `door_info` returns an error of `EBADF`:

```
solaris % doorinfo /etc/passwd
door_info error: Bad file number
```

15.3   The manual page is wrong. Posix.1 states correctly that "The *sleep()* function shall cause the current thread to be suspended from execution."

15.4   The results are unpredictable (although a core dump is a pretty safe bet), because the address of the server procedure associated with the door will cause some random code in the newly `execed` program to be called as a function.

15.5   When the client's `door_call` is terminated by the caught signal, the server process must be notified because the server thread handling this client (thread ID 4 in our output) is then sent a cancellation request. But we said with Figure 15.23 that for all the server threads automatically created by the doors library, cancellation is disabled, and hence this thread is not terminated. Instead, the call to `sleep(6)`, in which the server procedure is blocked, appears to return prematurely when the client's `door_call` is terminated, about 2 seconds after the server procedure was called. But the server thread still proceeds to completion.

15.6   The error that we see is

```
solaris % server6 /tmp/door6
my_thread: created server thread 4
door_bind error: Bad file number
```

When starting the server 20 times in a row, the error occurred five times. This error is nondeterministic.

15.7   No. All that is required is to enable cancellation each time the server procedure is called, as we do in Figure 15.31. Although this technique calls the function `pthread_setcancelstate` every time the server procedure is invoked, instead of just once when the thread starts, this overhead is probably trivial.

15.8   To test this, we modify one of our servers (say Figure 15.9) to call `door_revoke` from the server procedure. Since the door descriptor is the argument to door_revoke, we must also make `fd` a global. We then execute our client (say Figure 15.2) twice:

```
solaris % client8 /tmp/door8 88
result: 7744
solaris % client8 /tmp/door8 99
door_call error: Bad file number
```

The first invocation returns successfully, verifying our statement that door_revoke does not affect a call that is in progress. The second invocation tells us that the error from door_call is EBADF.

15.9   To avoid making `fd` a global, we use the cookie pointer that we can pass to door_create and that is then passed to the server procedure every time it is called. Figure D.12 shows the server process.

doors/server9.c
```
 1 #include     "unpipc.h"

 2 void
 3 servproc(void *cookie, char *dataptr, size_t datasize,
 4          door_desc_t *descptr, size_t ndesc)
 5 {
 6     long    arg, result;

 7     Door_revoke(*((int *) cookie));
 8     arg = *((long *) dataptr);
 9     printf("thread id %ld, arg = %ld\n", pr_thread_id(NULL), arg);

10     result = arg * arg;
11     Door_return((char *) &result, sizeof(result), NULL, 0);
12 }

13 int
14 main(int argc, char **argv)
15 {
16     int     fd;

17     if (argc != 2)
18         err_quit("usage: server9 <server-pathname>");

19         /* create a door descriptor and attach to pathname */
20     fd = Door_create(servproc, &fd, 0);

21     unlink(argv[1]);
22     Close(Open(argv[1], O_CREAT | O_RDWR, FILE_MODE));
23     Fattach(fd, argv[1]);

24         /* servproc() handles all client requests */
25     for ( ; ; )
26         pause();
27 }
```
doors/server9.c

Figure D.12   Using the cookie pointer to avoid making `fd` a global.

We could easily make the same change to Figures 15.22 and 15.23, since the cookie pointer is available to our my_thread function (in the door_info_t structure), which passes a pointer to this structure to the newly created thread (which needs the descriptor for the call to `door_bind`).

15.10 In this example, the thread attributes never change, so we could initialize the attributes once (in the `main` function).

Chapter 16

16.1 The port mapper does not monitor the servers that register with it, to try and detect if they crash. After we terminate our client, the port mapper mappings remain in place, as we can verify with the `rpcinfo` program. So a client who contacts the port mapper after our server terminates will get an OK return from the port mapper with the port numbers in use before the server terminated. But when a client tries to contact the TCP server, the RPC runtime will receive an RST (reset) in response to its SYN (assuming that no other process has since been assigned that same port on the server host), causing an error return from `clnt_create`. A UDP client's call to `clnt_create` will succeed (since there is no connection to establish), but when the client sends a UDP datagram to the old server port, nothing will be returned (assuming again that no other process has since been assigned that same port on the server host) and the client's procedure call will eventually time out.

16.2 The RPC runtime returns the server's first reply to the client when it is received, about 20 seconds after the client's call. The next reply for the server will just be held in the client's network buffer for this endpoint until either the endpoint is closed, or until the next read of this buffer by the RPC runtime. Assume that the client issues a second call to this server immediately after receiving the first reply. Assuming no network loss, the next datagram that will arrive on this endpoint will be the server's reply to the client's retransmission. But the RPC runtime will ignore this reply, since the XID will correspond to the client's first procedure call, which cannot equal the XID used for this second procedure call.

16.3 The C structure member is `char c[10]`, but this will be encoded by XDR as ten 4-byte integers. If you really want a fixed-length string, use the fixed-length opaque datatype.

16.4 The call to `xdr_data` returns `FALSE`, because its call to `xdr_string` (look at the `data_xdr.c` file) returns `FALSE`.

When a maximum length is specified, it is coded as the final argument to `xdr_string`. When this maximum length is omitted, the final argument is the one's complement of 0, (which is $2^{32} - 1$, assuming 32-bit integers).

16.5 The XDR routines all check that adequate room is available in the buffer for the data that is being encoded into the buffer, and they return an error of `FALSE` when the buffer is full. Unfortunately, there is no way to distinguish among the different possible errors from the XDR functions.

16.6 We could say that TCP's use of sequence numbers to detect duplicate data is, in effect, a duplicate request cache, because these sequence numbers identify any old segment that arrives as containing duplicate data that TCP has already acknowledged. For a given connection (e.g., for a given client's IP address and port), the size of this cache would be one-half of TCP's 32-bit sequence number space, or 2^{31}, about 2 gigabytes.

16.7 Since all five values for a given request must be equal to all five values in the cache entry, the first value compared should be the one most likely to be unequal, and the last value compared should be the one least likely to be unequal. The actual order of the comparisons in the TI-RPC package is (1) XID, (2) procedure number, (3) version number, (4) program number, and (5) client's address. Given that the XID changes for every request, to compare it first makes sense.

16.8 In Figure 16.30, starting with the flag/length field and including 4 bytes for the long integer argument, there are 12 4-byte fields, for a total of 48 bytes. With the default of null authentication, the credential data and verifier data will both be empty. That is, the credentials and verifier will both take 8 bytes: 4 bytes for the authentication flavor (AUTH_NONE) and 4 bytes for the authentication length (which has a value of 0).

In the reply (look at Figure 16.32 but realize that since TCP is being used, a 4-byte flag/length field will precede the XID), there are eight 4-byte fields, starting with the flag/length field and ending with 4 bytes of long integer result. They total 32 bytes.

When UDP is used, the only change in the request and reply is the absence of the 4-byte flag/length field. This gives a request size of 44 bytes and a reply size of 28 bytes, which we can verify with tcpdump.

16.9 Yes. The difference in argument handling, both at the client end and at the server end, is local to that host and independent of the packets that traverse the network. The client main calls a function in the client stub to generate a network record, and the server main calls a function in the server stub to process this network record. The RPC record that is transmitted across the network is defined by the RPC protocol, and this does not change, regardless of whether either end supports threads or not.

16.10 The XDR runtime dynamically allocates space for these strings. We verify this fact by adding the following line to our read program:

```
printf("sbrk() = %p, buff = %p, in.vstring_arg = %p\n",
        sbrk(NULL), buff, in.vstring_arg);
```

The sbrk function returns the current address at the top of the program's data segment, and the memory just below this is normally the region from which malloc takes its memory. Running this program yields

```
sbrk() = 29638, buff = 25e48, in.vstring_arg = 27e58
```

which shows that the pointer vstring_arg points into the region used by malloc. Our 8192-byte buff goes from 0x25e48 to 0x27e47, and the string is stored just beyond this buffer.

16.11 Figure D.13 shows the client program. Note that the final argument to
`clnt_call` is an actual `timeval` structure and not a pointer to one of these
structures. Also note that the third and fifth arguments to `clnt_call` must be
nonnull function pointers to XDR routines, so we specify `xdr_void`, the XDR
function that does nothing. (You can verify that this is the way to call a function
with no arguments or no return values, by writing a trivial RPC specification file
that defines a function with no arguments and no return values, running
`rpcgen`, and examining the client stub that is generated.)

sunrpc/square10/client.c

```
1 #include      "unpipc.h"        /* our header */
2 #include      "square.h"        /* generated by rpcgen */

3 int
4 main(int argc, char **argv)
5 {
6     CLIENT *cl;
7     struct timeval tv;

8     if (argc != 3)
9         err_quit("usage: client <hostname> <protocol>");

10     cl = Clnt_create(argv[1], SQUARE_PROG, SQUARE_VERS, argv[2]);

11     tv.tv_sec = 10;
12     tv.tv_usec = 0;
13     if (clnt_call(cl, NULLPROC, xdr_void, NULL,
14                   xdr_void, NULL, tv) != RPC_SUCCESS)
15         err_quit("%s", clnt_sperror(cl, argv[1]));

16     exit(0);
17 }
```

sunrpc/square10/client.c

Figure D.13 Client program that calls the server's null procedure.

16.12 The resulting UDP datagram size (65536 + 20 + RPC overhead) exceeds 65535, the
maximum size of an IPv4 datagram. In Figure A.4, there are no values for Sun
RPC using UDP for message sizes of 16384 and 32768, because this is an older
RPCSRC 4.0 implementation that limits the size of the UDP datagrams to around
9000 bytes.

Bibliography

Whenever an electronic copy was found of a paper or report referenced in this bibliography, its URL is included. Be aware that these URLs can change over time, and readers are encouraged to check the Errata for this text on the author's home page for any changes: `http://www.kohala.com/~rstevens`.

Bach, M. J. 1986. *The Design of the UNIX Operating System.* Prentice Hall, Englewood Cliffs, N.J.

Birrell, A. D., and Nelson, B. J. 1984. "Implementing Remote Procedure Calls," *ACM Transactions on Computer Systems*, vol. 2, no. 1, pp. 39–59 (Feb.).

Butenhof, D. R. 1997. *Programming with POSIX Threads.* Addison-Wesley, Reading, Mass.

Corbin, J. R. 1991. *The Art of Distributed Applications: Programming Techniques for Remote Procedure Calls.* Springer-Verlag, New York.

Garfinkel, S. L., and Spafford, E. H. 1996. *Practical UNIX and Internet Security, Second Edition.* O'Reilly & Associates, Sebastopol, Calif.

Goodheart, B., and Cox, J. 1994. *The Magic Garden Explained: The Internals of UNIX System V Release 4, An Open Systems Design.* Prentice Hall, Englewood Cliffs, N.J.

Hamilton, G., and Kougiouris, P. 1993. "The Spring Nucleus: A Microkernel for Objects," *Proceedings of the 1993 Summer USENIX Conference*, pp. 147–159, Cincinnati, Oh.

    `http://www.kohala.com/~rstevens/papers.others/springnucleus.1993.ps`

IEEE. 1996. "Information Technology—Portable Operating System Interface (POSIX)—Part 1: System Application Program Interface (API) [C Language]," IEEE Std 1003.1, 1996 Edition, Institute of Electrical and Electronics Engineers, Piscataway, N. J. (July).

> This version of Posix.1 contains the 1990 base API, the 1003.1b realtime extensions (1993), the 1003.1c Pthreads (1995), and the 1003.1i technical corrections (1995). This is also International Standard ISO/IEC 9945-1: 1996 (E). Ordering information on IEEE standards and draft standards is available at http://www.ieee.org. Unfortunately, the IEEE standards are not freely available on the Internet.

Josey, A., ed. 1997. *Go Solo 2: The Authorized Guide to Version 2 of the Single UNIX Specification.* Prentice Hall, Upper Saddle River, N.J.

> Also note that many of the Unix 98 specifications (e.g., all of the manual pages) are available online at http://www.UNIX-systems.org/online.html.

Kernighan, B. W., and Pike, R. 1984. *The UNIX Programming Environment.* Prentice Hall, Englewood Cliffs, N.J.

Kernighan, B. W., and Ritchie, D. M. 1988. *The C Programming Language, Second Edition.* Prentice Hall, Englewood Cliffs, N.J.

Kleiman, S., Shah, D., and Smaalders, B. 1996. *Programming with Threads.* Prentice Hall, Upper Saddle River, N.J.

Lewis, B., and Berg, D. J. 1998. *Multithreaded Programming with Pthreads.* Prentice Hall, Upper Saddle River, N.J.

McKusick, M. K., Bostic, K., Karels, M. J., and Quarterman, J. S. 1996. *The Design and Implementation of the 4.4BSD Operating System.* Addison-Wesley, Reading, Mass.

McVoy, L., and Staelin, C. 1996. "lmbench: Portable Tools for Performance Analysis," *Proceedings of the 1996 Winter Technical Conference*, pp. 279–294, San Diego, Calif.

> This suite of benchmark tools, along with this paper, are available from http://www.bitmover.com/lmbench.

Rochkind, M. J. 1985. *Advanced UNIX Programming.* Prentice Hall, Englewood Cliffs, N.J.

Salus, P. H. 1994. *A Quarter Century of Unix.* Addison-Wesley, Reading, Mass.

Srinivasan, R. 1995a. "RPC: Remote Procedure Call Protocol Specification Version 2," RFC 1831, 18 pages (Aug.).

Srinivasan, R. 1995b. "XDR: External Data Representation Standard," RFC 1832, 24 pages (Aug.).

Srinivasan, R. 1995c. "Binding Protocols for ONC RPC Version 2," RFC 1833, 14 pages (Aug.).

Stevens, W. R. 1992. *Advanced Programming in the UNIX Environment.* Addison-Wesley, Reading, Mass.

> All the details of Unix programming. Referred to throughout this text as APUE.

Stevens, W. R. 1994. *TCP/IP Illustrated, Volume 1: The Protocols.* Addison-Wesley, Reading, Mass.

> A complete introduction to the Internet protocols. Referred to throughout this text as TCPv1.

Stevens, W. R. 1996. *TCP/IP Illustrated, Volume 3: TCP for Transactions, HTTP, NNTP, and the UNIX Domain Protocols.* Addison-Wesley, Reading, Mass.

> Referred to throughout this text as TCPv3.

Stevens, W. R. 1998. *UNIX Network Programming, Volume 1, Second Edition, Networking APIs: Sockets and XTI.* Prentice Hall, Upper Saddle River, N.J.

> Referred to throughout this text as UNPv1.

Vahalia, U. 1996. *UNIX Internals: The New Frontiers.* Prentice Hall, Upper Saddle River, N.J.

White, J. E. 1975. "A High-Level Framework for Network-Based Resource Sharing," RFC 707, 27 pages (Dec.).

> `http://www.kohala.com/~rstevens/papers.others/rfc707.txt`

Wright, G. R., and Stevens, W. R. 1995. *TCP/IP Illustrated, Volume 2: The Implementation.* Addison-Wesley, Reading, Mass.

> The implementation of the Internet protocols in the 4.4BSD-Lite operating system. Referred to throughout this text as TCPv2.

Index

Rather than provide a separate glossary (with most of the entries being acronyms), this index also serves as a glossary for all the acronyms used in this book. The primary entry for the acronym appears under the acronym name. For example, all references to Remote Procedure Call appear under RPC. The entry under the compound term "Remote Procedure Call" refers back to the main entry under RPC.

The notation "definition of" appearing with a C function refers to the boxed function prototype for that function, its primary description. The "definition of" notation for a structure refers to its primary definition. Some functions also contain the notation "source code" if a source code implementation for that function appears in the text.

Function prototype	page
`long pr_thread_id(pthread_t *ptr);`	371
`char *px_ipc_name(const char *name);`	21
`int sem_close(sem_t *sem);`	226
`int sem_destroy(sem_t *sem);`	239
`int sem_getvalue(sem_t *sem, int *valp);`	227
`int sem_init(sem_t *sem, int shared, unsigned int value);`	239
`sem_t *sem_open(const char *name, int oflag, ...` `/* mode_t mode, unsigned int value */ );`	225
`int sem_post(sem_t *sem);`	227
`int sem_trywait(sem_t *sem);`	226
`int sem_unlink(const char *name);`	226
`int sem_wait(sem_t *sem);`	226
`int semctl(int semid, int semnum, int cmd, ... /* union semun arg */ );`	287
`int semget(key_t key, int nsems, int oflag);`	282
`int semop(int semid, struct sembuf *opsptr, size_t nops);`	285
`int shm_open(const char *name, int oflag, mode_t mode);`	326
`int shm_unlink(const char *name);`	326
`void *shmat(int shmid, const void *shmaddr, int flag);`	344
`int shmctl(int shmid, int cmd, struct shmid_ds *buff);`	345
`int shmdt(const void *shmaddr);`	345
`int shmget(key_t key, size_t size, int oflag);`	344
`Sigfunc_rt *signal_rt(int signo, Sigfunc_rt *func);`	105
`int sigwait(const sigset_t *set, int *sig);`	95
`int start_time(void);`	470
`double stop_time(void);`	470
`int svc_dg_enablecache(SVCXPRT *xprt, unsigned long size);`	422
`int touch(void *vptr, int nbytes);`	470
`void tv_sub(struct timeval *out, struct timeval *in);`	471